INSIDERS' GUIDE® TO

VIRGINIA'S BLUE RIDGE

NINTH EDITION

MARY ALICE BLACKWELL AND
ANNE PATTERSON CAUSEY

INSIDERS' GUIDE®

GUILFORD, CONNECTICUT
AN IMPRINT OF THE GLOBE PEQUOT PRESS

The prices and rates in this guidebook were confirmed at press time. We recommend, however, that you call establishments before traveling to obtain current information.

INSIDERS' GUIDE®

Copyright © 2003, 2005 by The Globe Pequot Press
A previous edition of this guide was published by Falcon Publishing, Inc. in 1999.

Text design by LeAnna Weller Smith
Maps by XNR Productions, Inc. © The Globe Pequot Press

ISSN: 1092-4906
ISBN: 0-7627-3460-4

Manufactured in the United States of America
Ninth Edition/First Printing

View of the Blue Ridge. BRAND X

[Top] *Blue Ridge Express, the mid-Atlantic's first high-speed lift.* WINTERGREEN RESORT
[Bottom] *Wintergreen offers skiing for all skill levels.* WINTERGREEN RESORT

[Top] *View of the Plunge Trail.* WINTERGREEN RESORT
[Bottom] *Children can explore the outdoors at Wintergreen.* WINTERGREEN RESORT

The Blue Ridge area offers a variety of activities for families. WINTERGREEN RESORT

Many visitors find their dream home in the Blue Ridge. MARY ALICE BLACKWELL

[Top] *The historic Lafayette Hotel in Stanardsville.* MARY ALICE BLACKWELL
[Bottom] *The Silver Thatch Inn in Charlottesville dates back to 1780.* MARY ALICE BLACKWELL

[Top] *The Inn at Kelly's Ford is a serene yet historic site.* MARY ALICE BLACKWELL
[Bottom] *Graves Mountain Lodge is tucked in the hills of Madison County.* MARY ALICE BLACKWELL

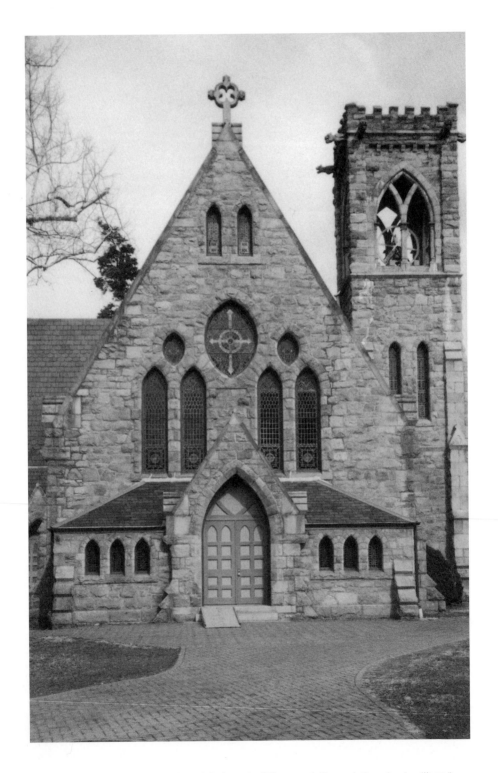

The Chapel at the University of Virginia is part of Thomas Jefferson's "academic village."
ANNE P. CAUSEY

Charlottesville's Downtown Mall is the place to shop or dine. MARY ALICE BLACKWELL

[Top] *Gary Simmers at Landwirt Vineyard in Rockingham County.* ANNE P. CAUSEY
[Bottom] *The Charlottesville Fun Park's miniature golf course.* MARY ALICE BLACKWELL

[Top] *Golf year-round at nationally ranked Stoney Creek Golf Course.* WINTERGREEN RESORT
[Bottom] *At 4,000 feet, Devils Knob is Virginia's highest course.* WINTERGREEN RESORT

[Top] *Leesburg's Market Station offers shopping in a historic setting.* ANNE P. CAUSEY
[Bottom] *Riders in Albemarle County in the heart of horse country.* JANET A. ROSS

Yoder's Country Market in Madison County. MARY ALICE BLACKWELL

Lucketts Bridge crosses over the Potomac River. RACHEL K. BLACKWELL

CONTENTS

Preface xxvi

Acknowledgments xxviii

How to Use This Book 1

Area Overview 3

Getting Around 44

Hotels and Motels 54

Bed-and-Breakfasts and Country Inns 77

Resorts 123

Restaurants 138

Nightlife 179

Shopping 190

Attractions 232

Kidstuff 279

The Arts 303

Annual Events and Festivals 329

The Blue Ridge Parkway and Skyline Drive 359

The Civil War 374

Wineries 387

Horse Country 408

Recreation 418

Skiing 452

Relocation 459

Education 487

Index 503

About the Authors 526

CONTENTS

Directory of Maps

Virginia's Blue Ridge xix

Shenandoah Valley Region xx

Roanoke Valley Region xxi

East of the Blue Ridge Region xxii

New River Valley Region xxiii

Alleghany Highlands Region xxiv

Virginia's Wine Country xxv

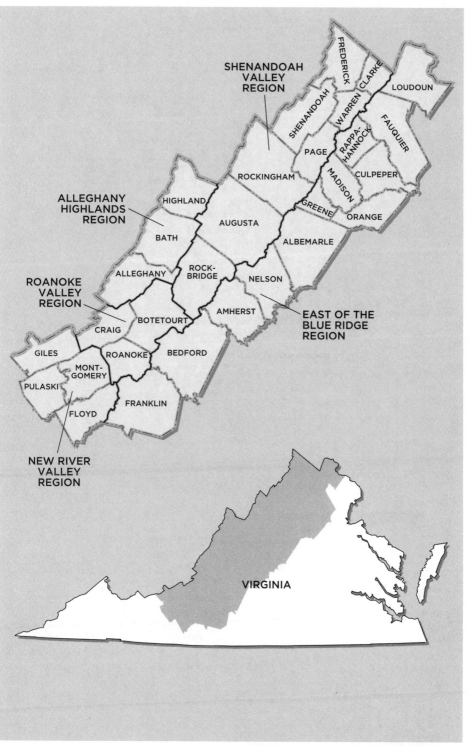

Virginia's Blue Ridge

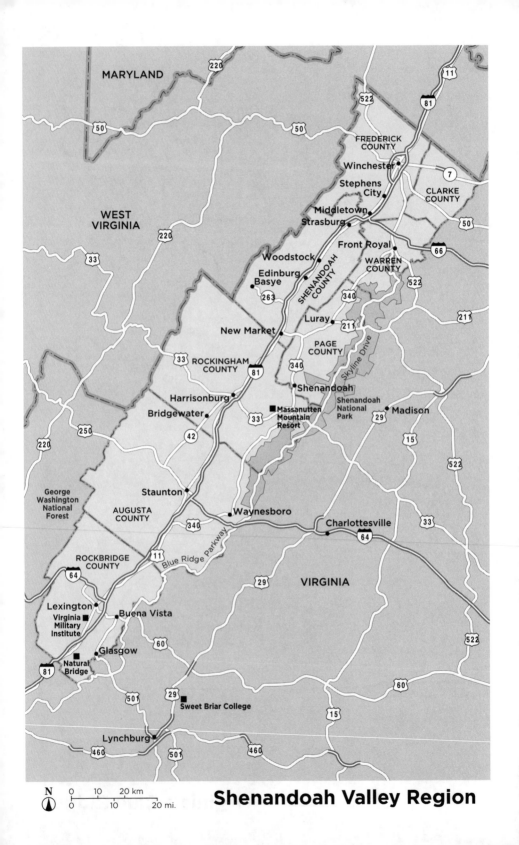

Shenandoah Valley Region

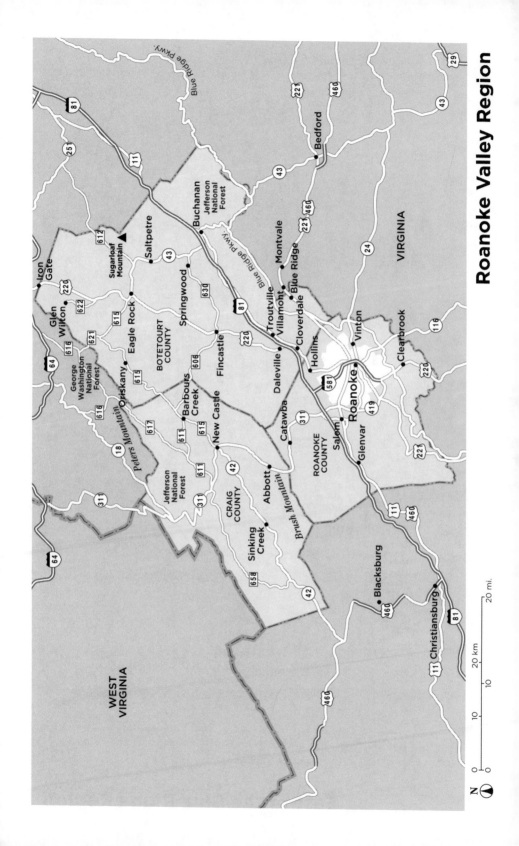

Roanoke Valley Region

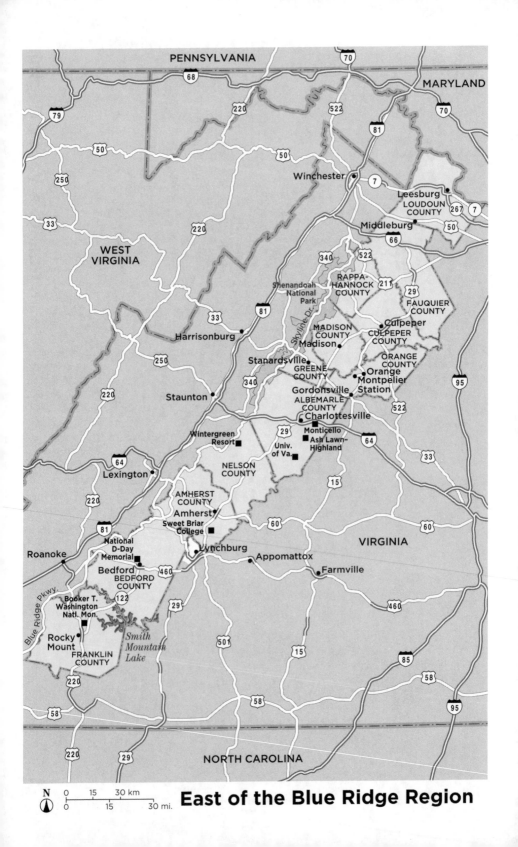

East of the Blue Ridge Region

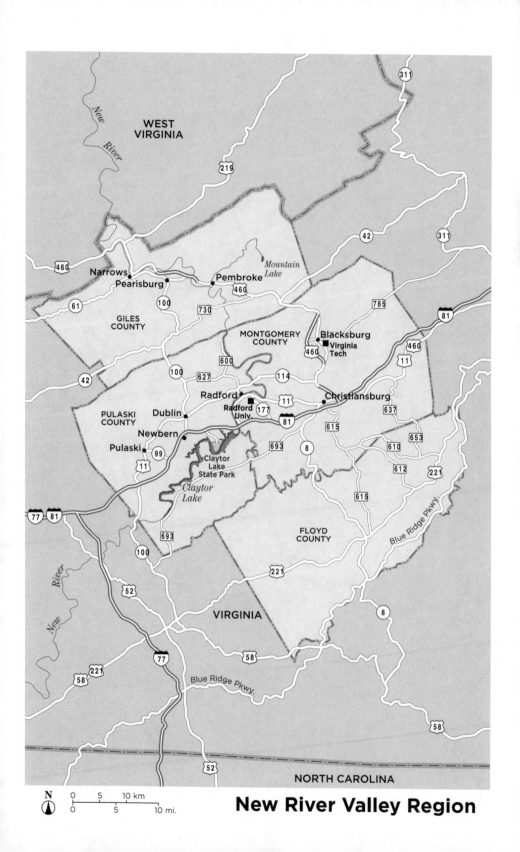

New River Valley Region

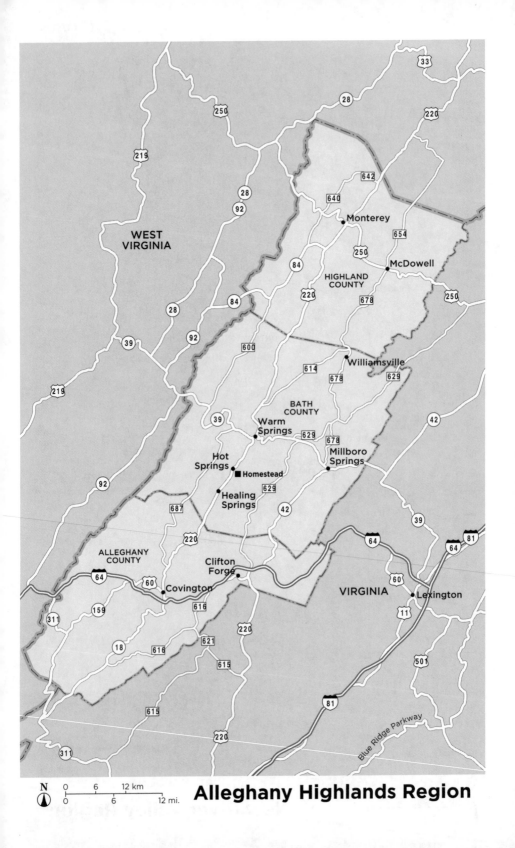

Alleghany Highlands Region

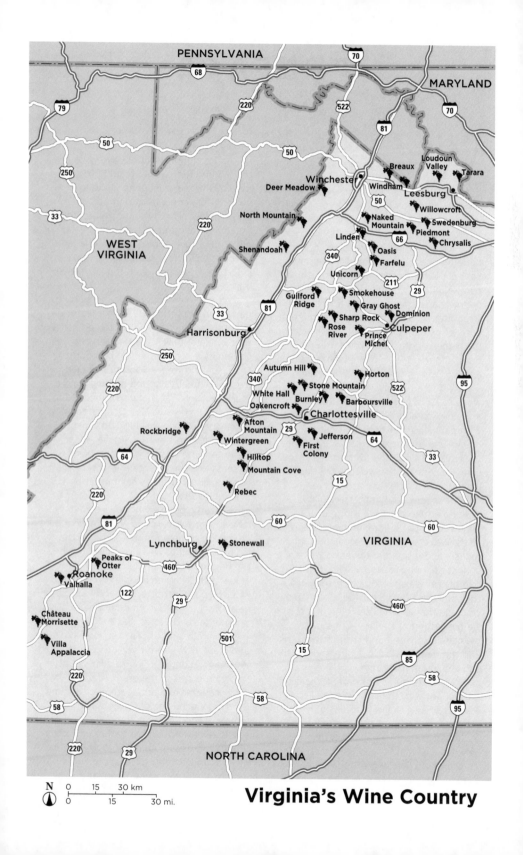

Virginia's Wine Country

PENNSYLVANIA

MARYLAND

WEST VIRGINIA

VIRGINIA

NORTH CAROLINA

Breaux
Loudoun Valley
Tarara
Windham
Leesburg
Winchester
Deer Meadow
Willowcroft
North Mountain
Naked Mountain
Swedenburg
Piedmont
Chrysalis
Linden
Shenandoah
Oasis
Farfelu
Unicorn
Guilford Ridge
Smokehouse
Gray Ghost
Dominion
Sharp Rock
Rose River
Prince Michel
Culpeper
Harrisonburg
Autumn Hill
Horton
Stone Mountain
White Hall
Burnley
Barboursville
Oakencroft
Charlottesville
Afton Mountain
Jefferson
Wintergreen
First Colony
Hilltop
Mountain Cove
Rockbridge
Rebec
Lynchburg
Stonewall
Peaks of Otter
Roanoke
Valhalla
Château Morrisette
Villa Appalaccia

N
0   15   30 km
0   15   30 mi.

PREFACE

Welcome to our favorite place, where every day is a feast for the senses.

This is the nostalgic land of Earl Hamner Jr.'s John Boy and the Walton family. You can still find a lot of general stores like Ike Godsey's. You can still find clucking, blue-haired ladies preparing banana pudding and fried chicken for Sunday School picnics in the country and small congregations worshiping in white, clapboard chapels. You can still find the strong family values that compel generations of extended families to all live down the same country lane. You'll find neighbors who mind their own business but are ever willing to lend a helping hand.

Welcome to a place where people still wave to strangers on backcountry roads, and children and the family dog still swim with patched inner tubes in pristine creeks under covered bridges. Welcome to life in the slow lane, with many of the same benefits but few of the hassles of life in the fast lane.

For sheer beauty and tranquility, nothing equals the Blue Ridge of Virginia's mountains, flora, fauna, rivers, and lakes. We're a rhapsody of riotous yellow fuchsia and redbud in the spring. We're a sonnet of sunny meadows with hovering hummingbirds and singing songbirds in the summer. We're a painter's palette of colors in the autumn. We're an aria to the simple setting of the first Christmas as we celebrate with handwrought wreaths and the trees we just cut out back on the snow-covered mountain.

We revere our environment, realizing a covenant with the land. We're filled with a sense of awe that a pinpoint of light bursting through a cloud can make a mountain appear to be wrapped in red velvet.

Ours also is a land of great dynamics. We are inventors, like Cyrus McCormick, whose Shenandoah Valley mechanical reaper revolutionized the world. We are the land of Thomas Jefferson, the quintessential Renaissance man who invented not only the concept of democracy in America but also the dumbwaiter, the original mimeograph, and the brave art of eating the "love apple." We are the land of robots and fiber optics in Roanoke and smart road technology in the New River Valley.

We are a land of great leaders and the birthplace of presidents. On our Natural Bridge, George Washington carved his initials and later bailed Washington and Lee University out of impending bankruptcy. Ours is a land where Robert E. Lee led troops to great valor and honor during a four-year Civil War that was supposed to last just a few weeks. Our Shenandoah Valley is where Stonewall Jackson exasperated his students at the Virginia Military Institute with his toughness and humorlessness and then went on to create a legend in military strategy still taught by U.S. military leaders.

We are a people who revere our history and honor our dead. We preserve our crumbling cemeteries and battlefields as hallowed ground. We build museums in the tiniest of communities as we welcome at least a half million people a year to Monticello in Charlottesville and Montpelier near Orange. We build monuments to Civil War battles and World War II victories.

We are a land of great scholarship and creativity, where the slave Booker T. Washington grew up in Franklin County to become one of the great African-American thinkers and leaders of all time. Born in Winchester, groundbreaking female author Willa Cather cultivated her sensitive descriptions of nature and immigrants and became a great journalist and novelist. In Lynchburg the great Harlem Renaissance poet Anne Spencer entertained Martin Luther King, Congressman Adam Clayton Powell, Justice Thurgood Marshall, and singers Paul Robeson and Marion Anderson at her garden home.

This is also a land of enormous, diverse culture. We flatfoot on Friday nights in the Alleghany Highlands. We go to drive-in movies and eat buttered popcorn in Rockbridge County while celebrities fly in from around the world to see our Virginia Film Festival in nearby Charlottesville. In Amherst County we provide one of the largest residential colonies in the world for international artists and writers to stir their creative juices. At our colleges and cities, we display works of art and crafts equal to that of any metropolitan area in the country.

We're a big playground. In Virginia's state parks, voted the best in America, you can camp, hike, bike, canoe, golf, boat, swim, horseback ride, hunt, fish, hang glide, and soar until you drop!

We're a land of festivity looking for excuses to celebrate. We stage festivals to honor everything from apples, strawberries, garlic, dogwoods, wine, and maple sugar to folklife and railroads.

This is also a land of superlatives. No matter which region of the Blue Ridge you visit, you'll find "the biggest," "the oldest," "the most important," or "nationally known" and "internationally acclaimed." Every region is a gem of multifaceted culture, like precious stones on a necklace, the common thread being the beauty of the Blue Ridge and our vast quality of life.

We are Charlottesville, land of Jeffersonian mystique and international chic. We are Staunton, heart of the Blue Ridge with our famous Fourth of July picnics in Gypsy Hill Park, begun by the world-famous Statler Brothers. We are Roanoke, "Capital of the Blue Ridge," the largest metropolitan area off the Blue Ridge Parkway, voted by travel writers as the most beautiful road in the world. We are the intellectually stimulating New River Valley, home to gigantic Virginia Tech as well as a tie-dyed counterculture that came to Floyd County and never left the '60s. We're the staid German Baptists at Smith Mountain Lake, the playground of western Virginia, and we still hunt for the cryptic, elusive Beale Treasure in nearby Bedford County. We're Jerry Falwell and the Moral Majority in Lynchburg, the home of one of the largest churches in America. We're the residents of the pastoral Alleghany Highlands, where the sheep outnumber the human population and life is as slow and sweet as the maple sugar trickling down the trees in the spring.

Welcome to our favorite place. Everywhere you travel you'll find beauty that stops you in your tracks, people who are courteous, trusting, and kind, and the opportunity to be transformed by the goodness of your environment.

The dream of the good life is all around you in the Blue Ridge. Welcome—whether you decide to stay for a day or a lifetime.

ACKNOWLEDGMENTS

A book like this one is really the project of many, either those who write it, those who gather the information, those who provide tips, encouragement, and insight, or those who simply allow you to vent when you get close to the edge. That being said, I'd like to acknowledge Heather, Regina, Margaret, and others at my workplace who granted me days off to work on this project. We share the staffing of a busy public service desk, and I appreciate all the extra time I could find during the weekdays. Thanks, too, goes to my family, Patrick and Edith Causey, Mary, John, Margaret, Rick, Patricia, Dan, Lewis, Abby, Karen, Emily, Caroline, Michael, and Ginger, as well as Elise, Johnny, Jinah, Tommy, Samantha, Gabby, Michael Jr., Joey, and Aidan. The support of Mary Alice's family is always a blessing: Rachel, Seth, Linet, Nicolette, and Eric. And of course, her mother, Janet Ross, who comes in like a lifesaver, keeping our spirits up and taking on the last-minute, difficult tasks. Janet, we owe you so much! Then there are the friends who listen to my whining and that's not easy: Linda, Maryanne, Elizabeth, and Jen. I'd also like to thank all the folks in the Blue Ridge who sit at desks at the visitor centers, the chambers, the schools, and the museums or run around in the attractions and the shops and the restaurants. Your warmth and enthusiasm continues to remind people about the joys of visiting this great region.

Lastly, I'd like to thank my coauthor, Mary Alice. She's truly a workhorse and a best friend. Without you I could never complete a project like this one. Thanks for your intelligence, energy, and dedication. We truly make an excellent team.

—Anne Causey

I can't open an *Insiders' Guide* without thinking about the late Lin Chaff. One of the original authors of this guide, her presence will always be felt within these pages.

I never would have agreed to take on a project so large without the help of my coauthor Anne Causey. Her knowledge of the area combined with her talents as a writer, editor, and researcher are evident throughout this book. Her strength, support, and unending supply of Hershey Kisses are what kept me going into the wee hours. She's also my best friend.

But this book still would be nothing but piles of paper on my kitchen table if it weren't for the support and help of Janet A. Ross. I call her Mom. She's my rock. Two years after helping me through breast cancer, she's now battling the same demon—a disease that claimed my grandmother, her mother. But she's made it seem like a cakewalk, competing in a 4-mile race while doing research for our Restaurants, Kidstuff, Attractions, and Resorts chapters. Thank you for your skill, your love, and your inspiration.

All of my family has been there through thick and thin, especially Rachel Blackwell, Seth Blackwell, Linet Blackwell, Nicolette Blackwell, Eric Blackwell, Rachell Deane, and Seda Khoranian. I've had to say goodbye to some: Lloyd Blackwell, my dad, and Richard Botkin, my grandfather. But there are others who have helped fill the void, including Glenda Blackwell; Jennifer, Scott and Brandon Newbold; and Chris, Jane, Madeline, and Waverly Blackwell.

There are those who have helped shoulder the load in other places. Jane Dunlap Norris (and her wonderful husband, Walt), Jennifer McManamay, David A. Maurer, and Ben Wood held down the fort at my day job at *The Daily Progress*. Connie Forsyth, Vicki Keyser, and all the wonderful women with the Charlottesville Women's Four Miler training program helped me maintain my sanity and my somewhat awkward running form. For the team of doctors, nurses, and specialists who kept all my parts in working order—thank you, thank you, thank you.

And, of course, there are the patient folks at The Globe Pequot Press—especially Elizabeth M. Taylor, Mike Urban, and Joshua Rosenberg—who allowed us the opportunity and time to write about our favorite neighborhoods.

Speaking of neighbors, I can't give enough kudos to Catherine Fox at the Roanoke Valley Convention and Visitor Center. She is a wonderful spokesperson for the Roanoke Valley and beyond. She went out of her way to help, and her efforts are greatly appreciated. Indeed, this book wouldn't have been possible without all the wonderful people at all the wonderful places along our Blue Ridge. There are Penny Lloyd at Virginia's Explore Park, Frankee Love at Wintergreen Resort, Gary Michael at James Madison University, Linda Staley at Mountain Lake, and Eileen Judah at The Homestead. There are just too many to name. So turn the pages and see for yourself. Better yet, drop in and visit. They're good folks.

—Mary Alice Blackwell

HOW TO USE THIS BOOK

If you haven't been here before, or even if you have, bring along your book and let us guide you to the best of the region—the best restaurants, accommodations, museums, shops, kids' activities, and more. We live here, so we know about this area. We recommend places we like to visit or that we recommend to our friends. In keeping with the area's southern hospitality, we consider you a friend, too.

Of course, with a region as large as the Blue Ridge, we are bound to have left something out. If your favorite isn't included here, drop us a note. We are always interested in feedback.

The region covered in this book includes 30 counties from historic Frederick to rural Franklin, with scores of towns and cities in between.

With more than a third of the state to cover, we put a lot of thought into how to organize this book and present the material in a sensible and accessible way. Nearly every chapter is presented geographically, in regional segments, from north to south and east to west. We've defined five regions: the Shenandoah Valley, the Roanoke Valley, East of the Blue Ridge (also sometimes called the foothills), the New River Valley, and the Alleghany Highlands.

Most chapters start with a regional header to orient you, followed by information about counties and cities in that region, with the overall geographic traffic pattern flowing south from the top of the Blue Ridge area, zigzagging back and forth from east to west.

We begin the book by introducing, in a general way, the five main regions of the Blue Ridge and their cities and towns. This is not meant to be the kind of guide that you must read from beginning to end to reap the benefit of buying it, but we do recommend that you start out by reading these overviews. They will give you an indication of what the areas have to offer, what makes our cities, towns, and villages unique and worth visiting.

After the overviews comes the bulk of the book: sections on such topics as Civil War sites, restaurants, and accommodations, each using the same geographical framework. In other words, if you're interested in visiting a winery in the Shenandoah Valley, look under that region's heading in the Wineries chapter. The same rule applies with nightspots, shopping, bed-and-breakfast inns, and almost all the other topics we cover.

We alter our organization a bit in the Recreation chapter, which is arranged by type of activity, and in the Annual Events and Festivals chapter, which is chronological by months of the year. However, the geographic flow continues under those headings.

Another exception to this organization is the chapter on the Skyline Drive and the Blue Ridge Parkway. Here, we let you know where you can eat and spend the night without departing from the two connecting mountaintop highways.

Throughout the chapters we've provided Insiders' Tips (indicated by [i]) for quick insights. We've included maps to help you understand visually how the regions are divided and what towns and cities belong in each one. You may also want to keep a more detailed road map handy to pinpoint some of the smaller highways and byways.

We hope you have a good time exploring both this guide and the beautiful Blue Ridge area. Let us know what you think of the book, its organization, and helpfulness. Write us at: Insiders' Guides, The Globe Pequot Press, P.O. Box 480, Guilford, CT 06437. Or visit our Web site at www.InsidersGuide.com and make your comments there.

AREA OVERVIEW

For many travelers, a vacation wouldn't be complete without an understanding of the history and flavor of each destination. This state is overflowing with interesting places and people linked to our nation's past.

Presidents Thomas Jefferson, James Madison, and James Monroe—whose homes are popular attractions in Albemarle and Orange Counties—were part of what historians have called the Virginia Dynasty. In fact, the Commonwealth has earned the nickname Mother of Presidents with four other native-born presidents: William Henry Harrison, John Tyler, Zachary Taylor, and Staunton's own Woodrow Wilson.

What we hope to do is give you a brief understanding of the people and events that shaped our communities. In this chapter we've tried to highlight important historical facts about each area in the Blue Ridge and to provide descriptions of local attractions. These regional overviews are a great place to begin any Insider's vacation. So read on and then turn to related chapters for more details. We hope our research will enrich your travels.

SHENANDOAH VALLEY

Shenandoah. The name conjures up images of rolling green farmland, beautiful old barns, and the legendary Shenandoah River that winds north to Harpers Ferry, West Virginia. The American Indians called the river Shenandoah, meaning "daughter of the stars," for the sparkling points of light on its broad surface. The 200-mile-long valley that shares its path and its name stretches from Frederick and Clarke Counties in the north almost to Roanoke in the south.

White explorers traveled through the valley as early as the mid-1600s, but it wasn't until the early 1700s that the first German and Scots-Irish families began to put down roots here. They had migrated south from Maryland and Pennsylvania seeking fertile, cheap land and greater freedom for themselves and their children. Original barns and homesteads dot the landscape of the valley, and many museums along Interstate 81, including the Shenandoah Valley Folk Art Museum and Heritage Center in Dayton, the Frontier Culture Museum in Staunton, and Explore Park near Roanoke, give visitors a closer look at the daily lives of these rugged pioneers.

Some of the heaviest fighting of the Civil War took place in the valley, and many of the war's hardiest soldiers hailed from here. According to Lt. Col. C. F. R. Henderson, author of the two-volume *Stonewall Jackson and the Civil War,* "No better material for soldiers ever existed than the men of the valley. . . . All classes mingle in the ranks, and all ages. . . . They were a mountain people, nurtured in a wholesome climate, bred to manly sports, and hardened by the free life of the field and forest. To social distinctions they gave little heed. They were united for a common purpose."

The valley is also the burial place of many heroes of that terrible war. Robert E. Lee and Stonewall Jackson were laid to rest in Lexington. Lee was president of the city's Washington College (now Washington and Lee) after the war, and Jackson had taught natural philosophy at Virginia Military Institute for years. Jackson's horse, Little Sorrel, also is buried close to his master in Lexington.

The Shenandoah Valley was home to other great American leaders. Woodrow Wilson was born in Staunton, and a museum next to his birthplace tells all about his life and his vision for world peace. Also in Lexington is a museum hon-

Virginia's Blue Ridge Vital Statistics

State capital: Richmond

State nicknames: Old Dominion, and Mother of Presidents

State bird: Cardinal

State tree: Dogwood

State dog: American foxhound

State motto: *Sic Semper Tyrannis* (Thus ever to tyrants)

Population: 7,078,515 for Virginia; 1,543,235 for Blue Ridge

Cities in the Blue Ridge: Bedford, Buena Vista, Charlottesville, Clifton Forge, Covington, Culpeper, Harrisonburg, Lexington, Lynchburg, Radford, Roanoke, Salem, Staunton, Waynesboro, Winchester

Major universities: James Madison University, Radford University, University of Virginia, Virginia Tech

Average temperature: 80°F in summer, 40°F in winter

Area in square miles: 42,774.20 for Virginia; 14,064.85 for Blue Ridge

Governor: Mark R. Warner (D)

Famous sons and daughters of the Blue Ridge: Russell Baker, columnist; Richard E. Byrd, North Pole explorer; Roy Clark, country singer; George Washington Carver, educator and orator; Willa Cather, author; Patsy Cline, country singer; Jerry Falwell, minister; Earl Hamner, creator of *The Waltons* and *Falcon Crest;* Patrick Henry, patriot; Sam Houston, politician; Thomas "Stonewall" Jackson, Confederate general; Thomas Jefferson, president; Robert E. Lee, Confederate general; Meriwether Lewis, explorer; James Madison, president; George C. Marshall, general and secretary of state; Dave Matthews Band, rock band; Cyrus McCormick, inventor; James Monroe, president; Ralph Sampson, NBA player; Kate Smith, singer; Sam Snead, golfer; Statler Brothers, country singers; Jeb Stuart, Confederate officer; Zachary Taylor, president; Booker T. Washington, educator; Woodrow Wilson, president

oring George C. Marshall, a VMI graduate who went on to lead the U.S. Army during World War II and later devised a plan to rebuild Europe after the war.

Visitors to the valley need not have a strong interest in history to enjoy the area's attractions. Majestic caverns filled with ancient and colorful calcite formations await the curious. The magnificence of Natural Bridge, once owned by Thomas Jefferson, is another destination. Rivers invite you to take a lazy canoe trip or an action-packed whitewater run.

Antiques lovers will delight in shops set in charming small towns. The northern stretch of U.S. Highway 11, between Winchester and Staunton, is known as Antiques Alley, with dozens of shops and antiques centers interspersed between the two cities.

If you time your visit right, you'll catch some of the East's finest fairs and festivals,

Some of the famous sons and daughters who call the Blue Ridge home: Rita Mae Brown, best-selling author; Rita Dove, poet laurete of United States and Pulitzer Prize winner; Robert Duvall, Academy Award–winning actor; Lawerence Eagleburger, secretary of state; Schuyler Fisk, actress; John Grisham, best-selling author; Tami Hoag, best-selling author; Howie Long, NFL star; Daphne Reid, actress; Tim Reid, actor; Sissy Spacek, Academy Award–winning actress; Henry Taylor, Pulitzer Prize–winning poet; Paul Wagner, Academy Award–winning documentary filmmaker

Major roads in the Blue Ridge: Interstate 64, Interstate 66, I-81, U.S. Highway 29, US 11, the Blue Ridge Parkway, and the Skyline Drive

Major airport: Washington Dulles International Airport

Driving laws: Motorists may be charged with a misdemeanor for aggressive driving. It is illegal to drive with an open container of alcohol in the vehicle. Right turn on red is permitted unless stated otherwise. Seat belts must be worn at all times in moving vehicles. Headlights must be turned on when wipers are in use. Speed limit on most state highways is 55 mph, and speed limit on most interstates is 65 mph.

State parks in the Blue Ridge: Claytor Lake State Park, Douthat State Park, Fairy Stone State Park, Raymond "Andy" Guest Jr. Shenandoah River State Park, New River Trail State Park, Sky Meadows State Park, Smith Mountain Lake State Park

Important dates: Jamestown, the first English settlement in America, was founded in 1607; Virginia became 10th state on June 25, 1788; Thomas Jefferson asked Congress to fund the Lewis and Clark expedition in 1803; Cyrus McCormick invented the reaper in 1831; Civil War ended when Lee surrendered to Grant at Appomattox on April 9, 1865; L. Douglas Wilder became the first African-American governor in the United States in 1990; U.S. Supreme Court rules Virginia Military Institute's all-male admissions policy unconstitutional in 1996.

including Virginia's No. 1 agricultural fair at Harrisonburg, the Maple Festival in Highland County, and the popular Apple Blossom Festival in Winchester.

Downtown districts beg for exploration on foot, offering a concentration of beautiful architecture, fine restaurants, boutiques, and galleries. You can spend hours exploring Roanoke's city market area or historic downtown Lexington, Winchester, or Staunton.

Modern accommodations are plentiful in the valley, and you'll discover quaint inns and bed-and-breakfasts in beautifully restored old homes. The Virginia Tourism Corp, (800) 847–4882, has information on many accommodations. For other services see our Bed-and-Breakfasts and Country Inns chapter.

The Shenandoah Valley has many more villages and towns than we can highlight, but the following introductions will give you a taste of what each area has to offer. A good way to get a flavor of the valley is to take a drive down US 11 from Winchester to Staunton. There's less traffic so you can take your time enjoying the rolling hills and small towns filled with quaint shops and beautiful old homes.

Frederick County

WINCHESTER

Once called Frederick Town after Frederick, father of King George III, Winchester and the surrounding area was settled by Pennsylvania Quakers in 1732. Soon after, Germans, Scots, Irish, English, Welsh, and French Huguenots also followed the Great Wagon Road from Pennsylvania and put down roots here. Winchester was a thriving center of commerce during the settlement of our nation; pioneers obtained their wagons and provisions here for trips farther west and south.

Frederick County (population 59,200) and Winchester saw much action during the Civil War. The armies of the North and South engaged in five battles and many skirmishes within or near Winchester, which changed hands more than 100 times. Stonewall Jackson used a home on Braddock Street for his headquarters during the war, and today his office remains much the way it was during his stay.

When he was 16, George Washington started his career in Winchester as a surveyor. Later, the father of our country saw to the protection of Virginia's frontier, overseeing the construction of Fort Loudoun in Winchester. He also was elected to his first political office, as a member of the House of Burgesses, in Winchester.

Country-music fans know Winchester as the birthplace of Patsy Cline, that spunky, honey-voiced singer of the early '60s. In 1963 the 30-year-old Cline was killed in an airplane crash. She is buried in a simply marked grave at the Shenandoah Memorial Cemetery on U.S. Highway 522, also known as the Patsy Cline Memorial Highway.

On a literary note, the Winchester area was also the birthplace of another pioneering woman, novelist Willa Cather. Cather's family moved from Frederick County to Nebraska when she was 10. Other projects to preserve Winchester's history include the construction of a history museum of Shenandoah Valley at Glen Burnie, and Historic House, a project of several million dollars. Kernstown Battlefield was recently purchased and opened to visitors, and plans are under way to turn Fort Collier into a historic site.

Winchester, population 23,585, is probably best known for its annual Shenandoah Apple Blossom Festival. For four days every May, the town plays host to more than 250,000 visitors who gather to enjoy a parade, arts and crafts festivals, races, dances, and a circus.

For more information about the Winchester area, call the Winchester-Frederick County Convention and Visitor Center at (800) 662-1360 or (540) 662-4135. You can also write to them at 1360 South Pleasant Valley Road, Winchester 22601, or go to their Web site at www.visitwinchesterva.com. You can contact the chamber of commerce at 2 North Cameron Street, Winchester, or call (540) 662-4118.

STEPHENS CITY

Chartered in 1758, Stephens City is second only to Winchester as the oldest town in the Shenandoah Valley. It was originally called Stephensburg after its founder, Lewis Stephens, who owned all of the town's 900 acres. As it expanded north, the town was called Newton and eventually was renamed Stephens City in the late 1900s. Rumor has it that Stephens City was almost picked as the county seat, but a bit of toddy swayed voters in favor of nearby Winchester.

Located just 8 miles south of Winchester, Stephens City became a transportation hub thanks to its location along Highway 277 and US 11. In fact, more than a dozen wagon makers and an equal number of blacksmiths set up shop on the busy corridor to Alexandria. The advent of the railroad nearly wiped out the need for these horse-drawn industries, but wagon rides are still a big part of the annual Newtown Heritage Festival in late May.

Although Stephens City (population 1,146) has grown along with the times, part of Main Street (along US 11) is much the way it was back in the early days when homes were built close to the road so that families would have room for gardens out back. A walking tour of the city will take you past the home of wagon maker John Cryder and John Lemley's blacksmith shop. Dr. John Watkins Walls's house is still there. His son, William, assisted Dr. Hunter McGuire in amputating Stonewall Jackson's arm. While many places were vandalized during the Civil War, you can still see the site of the Lutheran and Reform Church that dates back to 1786. Old Town Cemetery, too, still stands guard over many members of the founding Stephens family.

Today, Stephens City has seen tremendous commercial and residential growth. The area is also home to many of the county's finest orchards, including Rinker Orchard on Marlboro Road. For more information about Stephens City, contact the Winchester-Frederick Convention and Visitor Center at 1360 South Pleasant Valley Road, Winchester 22601, or go to www.visitwinchesterva.com. Call (800) 662-1360 or (540) 662-4135.

MIDDLETOWN

This quaint town in southern Frederick County, population 1,015, celebrated its bicentennial in 1996. Many of the old homes in town are said to have weathered bullets and cannonballs from the raging Civil War and, thanks to the vision of Peter Senseney, the blade of 20th-century bulldozers. When the town was chartered in 1896, Senseney required that all homes be built well back from the road. (When the Valley Pike was widened in the 1930s, none of the homes had to be torn down or moved.)

Middletown lies along US 11, once the Great Wagon Road, the most important frontier highway in Colonial America. It has always been a favorite stopping place for valley travelers and has settled into an unhurried pace since I-81 siphoned off the faster traffic. A tavern built on the roadside in 1797 later became a stagecoach relay station and an inn; it's still in operation as the Wayside Inn and Restaurant, a beautifully restored watering hole in the center of town. The inn is a paradise for antiques lovers with its Colonial furnishings, rare antiques, and historic paintings. It's also noted for its hearty regional American cuisine.

Middletown is home to Belle Grove plantation house, a large gray stone mansion built between 1794 and 1797 by Isaac Hite, who married James Madison's sister. In October the lush green fields of the plantation attract crowds for a major Civil War reenactment hosted by the Cedar Creek Battlefield Foundation Inc. It's notable as one of the few reenactments to take place on an original Civil War battlefield.

Wayside Theatre in downtown Middletown is the second-oldest theater in the state and hosts dramas, comedies, and mysteries from March through December. Some famous faces got their start here, including Susan Sarandon, Jill Eikenberry, and Peter Boyle.

For more information about Middletown attractions, contact the Winchester-Frederick Convention and Visitor Center at 1360 South Pleasant Valley Road, Winchester 22601, or go to www.visitwinchester va.com. You also can call (800) 662-1360 or (540) 662-4135.

Warren County

FRONT ROYAL

This northern Blue Ridge town in Warren County (population 31,500) was once known as Helltown for all the shootings, brawls, and hard drinking that went on here in the mid-1700s. Today Front Royal and surrounding Warren County, only 57 miles from the Beltway, are fast becoming a bedroom community of Washington, D.C. But Front Royal is also the northern gateway to the wilderness of the Shenandoah National Park. The north and south forks of the majestic Shenandoah River come together here, and campgrounds and canoe outfitters abound.

Front Royal, population 13,589, has a revitalized downtown business district full

Although there are no historical sites in her honor, Grandma Moses used to call the Shenandoah Valley home. Long before she began her painting career at the age of 70 in New York, she lived on her "Mount Airy" farm near Staunton with her husband and children.

of interesting boutiques and antiques shops. An old-fashioned town clock sits in the village common, where a gazebo and picnic tables welcome tourists and downtown workers to sit for a spell.

The town has a Confederate museum that documents how this important rail and river junction withstood numerous clashes during the Civil War. History buffs can spend hours retracing the exploits of Mosby's Raiders or tracking Stonewall Jackson's famous Valley Campaign. Other attractions in the Front Royal area include Skyline Caverns, the Skyline Drive, and a couple of wineries, Oasis Vineyard and Linden Vineyards, offering tours and tastings.

For more information, write to the Front Royal and Warren County Visitor Center at 414 East Main Street, Front Royal 22630. You can call them at (540) 635-5788 or (800) 338-2576. Visit their Web site at www.ci.front-royal.va.us. Call the chamber of commerce at (540) 635-3185.

Shenandoah County

STRASBURG

Staufferstadt is the original name of Strasburg, a busy little town just south of Middletown in Shenandoah County (population 35,000). German Mennonites and Dunkards from York County, Pennsylvania, settled the village, which was renamed Strasburg in 1761.

Later the town was nicknamed Pottown for the high-quality pottery produced here during the antebellum period. The first potter came in 1761, and since then at least 17 potters have produced earthen and stoneware in Strasburg. You can see some of this pottery in the Strasburg Museum, which also displays Civil War relics, Native American artifacts, and blacksmith collections.

History buffs will also enjoy the Museum of the American Presidents with its displays of presidential artifacts (a lock of George Washington's hair, for example) and biographical sketches of each of our 42 presidents. Those interested in the Civil War will want to stop by Hupp's Hill Battlefield Park.

Lovers of antiques will have a heyday in Strasburg. More than 100 dealers of high-quality antiques are housed under one roof in the downtown Strasburg Emporium. You'll find not only furniture representing every American era but also chandeliers, rugs, quilts, lace, pottery, baskets, iron beds, and estate jewelry.

A great place to stay overnight in this town of 4,017 is the Hotel Strasburg, a renovated Victorian hotel decorated with antiques that also are for sale. The hotel's restaurant has a popular following among folks from nearby valley towns and is by far one of the best places to dine for miles around.

For more information on Strasburg, Woodstock, New Market, Edinburg, Mount Jackson, Basye, and Orkney Springs, contact Shenandoah County Tourism at 600 North Main Street, Suite 101, Woodstock 22664, (540) 459-6227, or go online to www.shenandoahtravel.org.

WOODSTOCK

This charming valley settlement was chartered in 1761 by an act of the Virginia Assembly, sponsored by George Washington, a representative from Frederick County. The Woodstock Museum on West Court Street has artifacts such as portraits, quilts, and a moonshine still recalling the valley's early settlement. You can take a walking tour through town, where you can see examples of Federal, Greek Revival, and Classic Revival architecture.

By Any Other Name

Botetourt: bot-a-tot
Buena Vista: byou-na vista
Fauquier: fau-keer
Goshen: go-shun
Grottoes: grot-toes
McGaheysville: ma-gack-ees-ville
Michie: mick-ey
Monticello: mont-a-chello

Montpelier: mont-peel-yer
Schuyler: sky-ler
Stanardsville: stan-dards-ville
Staunton: stan-ton
Taliaferro: tol-a-ver
Rio Road (in Charlottesville): rye-o road
Weyers Cave: we-yers cave
Wytheville: with-ville

Woodstock, with a population of 3,592, is the county seat of Shenandoah and home to the oldest courthouse still in use west of the Blue Ridge. Another impressive structure in town is the massive Massanutten Military Academy, a coeducational school dating back to 1899.

Nearby Orkney Springs hosts the Shenandoah Valley Music Festival every spring and summer. Concerts are held in a covered, open-air pavilion and on the grounds of the historic Orkney Springs Hotel. This former hotel used to be 19th-century mineral springs spa and resort.

EDINBURG

If you can, try to stop by Edinburg, population 813, about the third full weekend in September, when the whole town turns out for the annual Edinburg Ole' Time Festival. It's like stepping back in time, especially when you are surrounded by the large white homes with wraparound porches dating back to the 1800s. You also won't want to miss the Edinburg Mill. Built in 1848, it survived a fiery threat from the Union soldiers during the Civil War.

Edinburg is also home to many wonderful shops along Main Street and the scenic Shenandoah Vineyards. The vineyard is open for tours and tastings.

MOUNT JACKSON

Dating back to 1812, Mount Jackson was originally called Mount Pleasant, but the name was changed in honor of a frequent visitor, President Andrew Jackson. The small town of 1,164 is rich in history. Several of its buildings served as hospitals for both the Confederate and Union armies. Right on US 11 is Soldiers Cemetery, the only cemetery in Virginia in which only Confederate soldiers are buried.

Just south of Mount Jackson on Highway 720 is Meem's Bottom Bridge, the longest covered bridge of the nine remaining in Virginia. The 200-foot single-span bridge was built by Franklin Hiser in 1892 so that he could have easy access to his apple orchard. It is the last remaining covered bridge in the Shenandoah.

NEW MARKET

Here you will find caverns, museums, Shenvalee Golf Resort, a battlefield historical park, and an excellent tourist information center for the whole Shenandoah Valley.

New Market was settled later than other valley towns. English settlers from the North and East named their village after a horse-racing town in England, and in the early days a racetrack actually operated near New Market. New Market is famous for the 1864 battle that involved 247 cadets fresh from the classrooms of Virginia Military Institute (see our Civil War chapter). You can view a stirring account of the battle on film at the Hall of Valor Museum at the New Market Battlefield Historical State Park. The museum also presents a nonpartisan view of major Civil War events with its murals and life-size models. Each May the 220-acre battlefield hosts the state's longest running re-enactment: the Reenactment of the Battle of New Market.

New Market, now a town of 1,637, is also at the epicenter of valley caverns: Shenandoah, Endless, Luray, and Grand are accessible here.

While it sounds like a "sleeper" of an attraction, you shouldn't miss the Bedrooms of America Museum on Congress Street (US 11). Eleven rooms of authentic furniture show every period of America's bedrooms from 1650 through 1930.

Page County

LURAY

Luray is a central gateway to the 105-mile-long Skyline Drive. Page County (population 23,100) is bordered by the Shenandoah National Park on the east and the George Washington National Forest on the west.

Luray, with a population of 4,871, is the county seat of Page and the home of the internationally famed Luray Caverns, which can be explored in an hour-long guided tour. Housed in the same complex is the Historic Car and Carriage Caravan, an exhibit of antique cars, carriages, coaches, and costumes.

Shenandoah River Outfitters in Luray and the Down River Canoe Company in nearby Bentonville offer canoe trips on the south fork of the Shenandoah River, which travels the entire length of Page County. Guilford Ridge Vineyard is just a few miles out of town and offers tours and tastings of its wines by appointment (see our Wineries

chapter). And would you believe one of the state's largest reptile collections is in Luray? The Luray Zoo on U.S. Highway 211 will keep your kids squealing for hours. Tame deer and llamas inhabit the petting zoo.

A good time to visit the area is Columbus Day weekend in October, when Page County throws its annual Heritage Festival. First held in 1969, it is one of the oldest arts and crafts shows in Virginia.

The town is interested in preserving its history and highlighting its natural resources. The railroad station in Luray is being renovated with plans to use the building for visitor information purposes. The Greenway, adjacent to Main Street, is a quarter-mile-long paved walking path where you can enjoy the ducks and the trout pond.

For more information on Page County, contact the Luray-Page County Chamber of Commerce at 46 East Main Street, Luray 22835, (540) 743-3915. See the Web site at www.luraypage.com.

Harrisonburg and Rockingham County

In the geographic center of the Shenandoah Valley sit Harrisonburg and Rockingham County. This area is known for panoramic vistas, abundant recreational opportunities, and rich history. Harrisonburg, the home of 40,468 people, serves as the financial and retail center for eight counties, including three in neighboring West Virginia. For travelers, it's a great place to settle in for a while and explore other attractions in the valley.

A thriving city, Harrisonburg is noted for its high quality of life. The downtown is undergoing a revitalization and was recently designated a Main Street Community, one of only three in the state. A transportation museum is in the works in the Hardesty–Higgins House on South Main Street, the second oldest building in Harrisonburg. The Virginia Quilt Museum is another downtown attraction that opened recently (see our Attractions chapter). A big addition to the city in 1998 was the Court Square Theater downtown, converted from the old Rockingham Motor Company building. The theater features diverse entertainment such as live dramas, movies, and musical performances. Some great restaurants are in Harrisonburg, too, including one of the state's best, the Joshua Wilton House on Main Street.

Opportunities for higher education abound in the area. Bridgewater College, Eastern Mennonite University, and James Madison University are all here, so students and professors comprise a large part of the population. These schools also bring an abundance of educational and cultural opportunities to the community.

With hundreds of acres of farms and 67,700 residents, Rockingham County is the state's leading producer of dairy, poultry, and beef products. In fact, the county ranks second in the nation for the number of turkeys produced, according to a recent agricultural census. So valuable is poultry to the county's economy that a proud statue of a turkey stands alongside US 11.

In nearby Dayton, visitors will enjoy a wonderful indoor farmers' market with more than 20 shops that sell fresh cheeses, baked goods, antiques, bulk grains, and spices. The market and many of the businesses are owned by Mennonites, and it's not unusual to see a black carriage or two with horses parked out front—about 1,000 Old Order Mennonites, easily identified by their simple style of dress, live in the area. Also in Dayton is Silver Lake Mill, a restored 1822 mill complete with changing gears, located on Silver Lake Road. You can stop in for tours and shopping.

More than 139,000 acres of George Washington and Jefferson National Forests lie in western Rockingham County. On the east, the county is bordered by the Shenandoah National Park. With so much forested land, it's no wonder that this county has such wonderful hunting and fishing opportunities (see our Recreation chapter). The Massanutten mountain range

is just east of town and is home to Massanutten Resort, a year-round residential community known for its ski slopes, golf courses, and impressive indoor sports complex.

Another recreational attraction just south of Harrisonburg (in Augusta County) is Natural Chimneys, a place where huge rocks tower to heights of 120 feet. From one perspective, these rocks resemble a foreboding medieval-style castle with turrets and towers, and this may have inspired the creation of the Natural Chimneys Jousting Tournament more than 180 years ago. The tournament is the oldest continuously held sporting event in America, having begun in 1821. Modern-day knights still match their skills in the ancient art of jousting here on the third Saturday in August every year. The Natural Chimneys Regional Park has 120 campsites, a swimming pool, picnic area, camp store, nature and bike trails, and more.

For more about attractions in the Harrisonburg and Rockingham County area, contact the Chamber of Commerce at (540) 434-3862, www.hrchamber.org, or the Harrisonburg–Rockingham Convention and Visitors Bureau at 10 East Gay Street, Harrisonburg 22802, (540) 434-2319, or visit the Web site at www.hrcvb.org.

Augusta County

STAUNTON

Called the Queen City on the Great Wagon Road, Staunton celebrated its 250th anniversary in 1997. A great city to explore on foot—if you don't mind a few hills—Staunton is full of Victorian, Greek Revival, and Italianate architecture; unique shops; one-of-a-kind eateries; and important historical sites. The city is the birthplace of President Woodrow Wilson, who was born in 1856 to a Presbyterian minister and his wife in a Greek Revival manse on Coalter Street. Today the manse is open for tours and sits next to a museum where you can learn all about Wilson's life, his political views, and his vision for world peace. The Woodrow Wilson Museum also houses the president's 1919 Pierce Arrow limousine.

Staunton is home to the Blackfriars Playhouse, the only exact replica of William Shakespeare's famed English stage. Another major attraction in Staunton is the Frontier Culture Museum, an indoor-outdoor living museum that features four authentic working farms and all kinds of domesticated critters. Staunton is an appropriate place for a museum that documents life in frontier America. It is the seat of Augusta County (population 65,600), which once stretched all the way to Mississippi. Most early settlers in the area were Scotch Irish, including John Lewis, the first white man to build a homestead here in 1732. In 1749 Lewis's son, Thomas, laid out lots and streets for the new town of Staunton, named in honor of Lady Rebecca Staunton, Gov. William Gooch's wife.

Nineteenth-century Staunton grew by leaps and bounds following incorporation as a town in 1801. Education became a priority, with the establishment of the Virginia Institute for the Deaf and the Blind in 1839, Augusta Female Seminary in 1842 (now Mary Baldwin College), Virginia Female Institute in 1844 (now Stuart Hall School), and Staunton Military Academy in 1884.

The railroad came to Staunton in 1854, stimulating the city's growth as a center of commerce for the region. Today Amtrak serves this city of 23,800, and the old C & O train station is a showcase of meticulous restoration work.

The wharf area has undergone restoration work; the old mill buildings and warehouses contain antiques shops, a pottery workshop and studio, and a marvelous antique-car dealership. The Historic Staunton Foundation has a detailed brochure to guide visitors on a walking tour of the city.

Other attractions in Staunton include the beautiful Gypsy Hill Park and the Statler Brothers gift shop. Yes, these famous, down-home country music stars still live in their hometown.

For additional information about Staunton, contact the Staunton Visitor Center at 35 South New Street any day of the week, (540) 332-3971, or visit the other visitor center at the Frontier Culture Museum. You can also check out their Web site at www.staunton.va.us.

WAYNESBORO, STUARTS DRAFT, AND FISHERSVILLE

Waynesboro, too, passed a milestone in 1997 with a weeklong bicentennial celebration. Named in honor of Revolutionary War hero Gen. Anthony Wayne, Waynesboro thrived as an industrial community during the late 1800s, a trend that continues today. Thanks in part to its convenient location just 8 miles east of I-81 and right off I-64, companies such as Invista Inc. and Hershey have plants near here.

Waynesboro, a city of 19,520 residents, extends to Afton Mountain, from which you can see all the way to Charlottesville and beyond. The Shenandoah National Park's southern tip ends on that mountain, and the Blue Ridge Parkway begins its southern trek there. One note of caution: Beware crossing Afton Mountain during foggy weather; many fatal accidents have occurred here during thick fog, so stay put if such conditions exist.

In Waynesboro the P. Buckley Moss Museum is in a tall brick house surrounded by trees, a scene reminiscent of one of her famous watercolors. The museum is within easy walking distance of the Waynesboro Village Factory Outlet Mall, where you can find bargains in designer clothing, leather goods, imported china, and more.

While in Waynesboro, you can also watch age-old techniques of brass molding at the Virginia Metalcrafters factory showroom. The Shenandoah Valley Art Center in downtown Waynesboro offers residents and visitors a place to enjoy the arts through exhibits, workshops, classes, and performances.

Mennonites who live near Stuarts Draft

have established some businesses such as the Cheese Shop that provide a refreshing alternative to standard grocery stores. And Milmont Greenhouses, on U.S. Highway 340, has grown from a Mennonite housewife's hobby nearly 20 years ago to a bustling business today. Speaking of green things, one of the leading perennial nurseries in the nation, Andre Viette Farm and Nursery, is based in Fishersville and is definitely worth visiting.

Recreational opportunities abound in the area. The Sherando Lake State Park is just outside Waynesboro, and Shenandoah Acres Resort, a fun family stop, is in Stuarts Draft.

For more information about attractions in the East Augusta County area, contact the Greater Augusta Regional Chamber of Commerce at 30 Ladd Road, P.O. Box 1107, Fishersville 22939. You can call them at (540) 324-1133, or reach them online at www.augustachamber.org or www.waynesboro.va.us

Lexington and Rockbridge County

Perhaps more than any other place in the valley, downtown Lexington has retained the graceful beauty and genteel character of its prosperous past. And no other city or town in the Blue Ridge has a history that is so well preserved and honored by its citizens. The town's heritage includes four of America's greatest generals. It seems that everywhere you go, you are walking on historic, hallowed ground.

Throughout Lexington's history, the presence of great military leaders has inspired its preservation efforts—George Washington, the great Confederate generals Robert E. Lee and Thomas J. "Stonewall" Jackson, and World War II hero Gen. George C. Marshall, the Nobel Peace Prize-winning creator of the Marshall Plan that rebuilt war-torn Europe—all contribute to Lexington's history.

Lexington, with 6,800 residents, is the historic and cultural heart of Rockbridge

> *October is the "peak" season to visit the Blue Ridge. It's a great time to catch the brilliant fall foliage while you tour a winery, take in a festival, or watch a Civil War reenactment.*

County (population 20,800), where most prosperous residents enjoy a genteel country-estate way of life. Many are early retirees who devote their considerable knowledge and energy to the community as volunteers and activists. Others are college professors at nearby Virginia Military Institute (VMI) and Washington and Lee (W&L) University.

The county boasts the breathtaking 3-mile-long Goshen Pass, a journey along the Maury River lined with rhododendron, laurel, ferns, mosses, magnificent pines, hemlocks, maples, dogwood, and mountain ash. Goshen Pass, a popular place for swimming, tubing, canoeing, and picnicking, is so beautiful that one prominent Lexington citizen, Matthew Fontaine Maury, asked that after he died, his body be carried through the pass when the rhododendron were in bloom. Complying with his request in 1873, Virginia Military Institute cadets formed an honor guard and gave their professor his last wish.

The roles that Lexington's world-famous universities, VMI and Washington and Lee, have played in the area's historic culture cannot be underestimated. In 1796 George Washington saved W&L from bankruptcy with a gift of $50,000, which still receives dividends. For their role in the Civil War, VMI cadets are immortalized forever both on campus, with the statue *Virginia Mourning Her Dead,* and at the New Market Battlefield Museum and Hall of Valor (an hour north of the city). The Civil War Battle of New Market in 1864 was the first and only time in American history that an entire student body was recruited to fight a battle. When the smoke cleared, 10 cadets lay dead.

As a city that has had more than its share of encounters with famous presidents, it has had one rather unlikely encounter. Visitors can see the National Historic Landmark cadet barracks where actor Ronald Reagan's movie *Brother Rat* was filmed. The movie's premiere was held at Lexington's State Theatre.

VMI in 1997 lost one of its toughest battles ever—deciding whether to admit women, as ordered by the Supreme Court in 1996, or go private. Its board decided the costs of going private were not realistic, so women were admitted in the fall of 1997.

Many of Lexington's attractions focus on its famous former citizens. There's the Stonewall Jackson House, where the tough general lived while teaching natural philosophy at VMI. In 2004 the Stonewall Jackson House reopened after extensive renovations that re-created the appearance of the original museum. There's the Stonewall Jackson Cemetery, his final resting place after he was mistakenly killed by his own soldiers. You can see his bullet-pierced raincoat at the VMI Museum. In a ceremony attended by hundreds and covered by the *Wall Street Journal* in 1997, the curious taxidermy display of his favorite war horse, Little Sorrel, was finally laid to rest after being on display for a century.

Lee Chapel, still in use by W&L students, is another famous site. The striking white statue of the recumbent Lee by sculptor Edward Valentine is alone worth a visit to Lexington. The chapel also is the site of the famous Peale portrait of George Washington. You can see Lee's office as he left it in 1870 after assuming the presidency of W&L following his Civil War defeat. Lee's favorite mount, Traveler, also is buried on campus.

The third famous military landmark to see is the George C. Marshall Museum, where Marshall, VMI class of 1901, began a remarkable military career that led to his position as U.S. Army Chief of Staff and later recipient of the Nobel Prize in 1953. An electric map detailing the military march of World War II shows the breadth of what this military genius accomplished and why the United States earned a repu-

tation worldwide as a country with a heart in the aftermath of the war.

Lexington's historic sites are well documented by its history-loving populace. You can even see the troughs where its famous equine residents, Little Sorrel and Traveler, refreshed themselves. A walking tour map will keep you exploring enough bridges and locks, churches, cemeteries, houses, mills, baths, and springs to quench even the most avid history buff's thirst for knowledge, including a nearby museum dedicated to Cyrus McCormick, inventor of the mechanized reaper. The pamphlet is available at the Lexington Visitor Center.

Every summer day, the Lexington Carriage Company leaves its hitching post at the visitor center and carries passengers along the same streets Jackson and Lee rode on their famous horses.

Since the memory of two famous horses are awarded such places of honor in Lexington, it stands to reason the Commonwealth of Virginia saw fit to award Lexington its $12 million Horse Center, situated on 400 rolling acres. It is one of the top equine facilities in the United States with 4,000 spectator seats, 750 permanent stalls, and a gigantic show arena. Its schedule of events includes everything from the Bonnie Blue Nationals to the Northeast Peruvian Horse Club Show.

Also bringing fame and visitors to the area is Lime Kiln Theatre, named by *Theatre Journal* as "the most unusual theater setting in the United States" because of its location in an abandoned kiln beside a craggy, wildflower-strewn hillside. Lime Kiln puts on an array of plays and musicals every summer that highlights the history and culture of the southern mountains. In 2004 the Theatre at the Lime Kiln expanded by buying the Troubador Theatre, enabling plays to be shown year-round.

Going out into the countryside, there's the beautiful Chessie Nature Trail along the Maury River and numerous hiking paths in nearby mountains, among them the Appalachian Trail. Opportunities for horseback riding abound. There also are compa-

Span of Time

There are eight covered bridges known to exist in Virginia, and five have been preserved as landmarks. Three others are on private property.

Humpback Bridge, 1857
Highway 60, near Covington in Alleghany County
Over the Dunlap Creek

Meem's Bottom Bridge, 1894
Highway 706, 2 miles south of Mount Jackson in Shenandoah County
Over the north fork of the Shenandoah River

Jack's Creek Bridge, 1914
Highway 615, south of Woolwine in Patrick County
Over the Smith River

Sinking Creek Bridge, 1916
Highway 601, north of Newport in Giles County
Over Sinking Creek

Bob White Bridge, 1921
Highway 869, near Woolwine in Patrick County
Over the Smith River

On private property: Biedler Farm Bridge in Rockingham County, C.K. Reynolds Covered Bridge in Giles County, and Links Farm Bridge in Giles County.

nies eager to outfit you with gear and shuttle you to your canoeing adventure down the mighty James and the rushing Maury Rivers (see our Recreation chapter).

The great outdoors should also include a visit to Hull's Drive-In, one of the premier mom-and-pop operations anywhere and one of the few surviving drive-in theaters in Virginia. It's open weekends April through October.

In Buena Vista, 6 miles east of Lexington and the only other city in the county, you will find much of the county's manufacturing industry. Every Labor Day, Buena Vista attracts huge crowds and state political leaders to a popular festival in Glen Maury Park.

Do not leave Rockbridge County without visiting Natural Bridge, one of the seven natural wonders of the world. The awesome limestone bridge is 215 feet high and 90 feet long (see our Attractions chapter).

Whether visiting the Lexington area for its history, beauty, or attractions, you'll be impressed with its sense of historical importance, its gracious old homes, and its vibrant downtown district with fine restaurants and one-of-a-kind shops.

For more information on Rockbridge County or Lexington, contact the Lexington Visitor Center, 106 East Washington Street, Lexington 24450. You can call them at (540) 463-3777 or (877) 453-9822, or visit them online at www.lexingtonvirginia.com.

ROANOKE VALLEY

The Roanoke Valley of Virginia, including Roanoke, Botetourt, and Craig Counties, the Town of Vinton, and City of Salem, is home to about a quarter-million people who work and play in a cultured, historical place of incredible beauty.

Even I-81, which connects the Roanoke Valley, is beautiful. One of the first things visitors usually say is they can't get over the absence of potholes and rough pavement. Then they marvel at all the wildflowers, redbud, yellow forsythia, and flowering orchards along western Virginia's main thoroughfare.

People usually don't set out to move to the Roanoke Valley. Instead, they are converted into relocating here. When you talk to people about how they came to live here, so many times the story starts out, "We were driving down the Blue Ridge Parkway, when we were so smitten that we moved here without even having jobs." Or else they discovered the Roanoke Valley while hiking on the Appalachian Trail, taking the Bikecentennial path coast to coast, or vacationing at nearby Smith Mountain Lake. Inevitably, the conversation ends with, ". . . and we'd never go back home. We'll never leave this place."

Consider this: The Roanoke Valley of Virginia was the first in the state to have curbside recycling, mandatory comprehensive recycling, and a downtown recycling program that also was a first on the North American continent. This should tell you something about Valley citizens' overwhelming sensitivity to their environment.

In 2002 *Money* magazine listed Roanoke as one of the best places for retirement. *Parenting* magazine has called the Roanoke Valley one of the 10 best places to raise a family in the United States. The U.S. Department of Education has recognized Roanoke Valley schools for being among the nation's best. *Inc.* magazine named the Roanoke Valley one of the country's top 100 hot spots for business development. The region is blessed with many community-minded businesses and industries.

Botetourt County

If Virginia can be referred to as the "Mother of States," then Botetourt could be called the "Mother of Counties." With a population of 32,000, the county is home to an independent, history-loving people who are smug in the fact that their county,

a land grant to Lord Botetourt, once stretched the whole way to the Mississippi River. Historic Fincastle has been the county seat since 1770. This vast tract of land once included the entire present state of Kentucky and much of what is now West Virginia, Ohio, Indiana, and Illinois.

George Washington, Patrick Henry, and Thomas Jefferson either appeared in Fincastle or sent their agents to lay claim to tracts of wilderness lands. Jefferson designed a county courthouse. After the Lewis and Clark expedition west, William Clark returned to Fincastle to marry resident Judith Hancock. Thousands of English, German, and Scots-Irish pioneers passed through on their way down the great Valley Road that traversed the famed Shenandoah Valley to settle the western frontier country.

Combining the talents of German craftsmen and Scots-Irish merchants and lawyers, Fincastle's founding fathers built a town of well-proportioned houses and public buildings, a substantial number of which still survive. These include the Old Jail Building, the Court House Complex, the Presbyterian Church, and the Botetourt County Historical Museum and Courthouse complex.

Tour Fincastle and see beautiful wrought-iron fences, balconies and gates, flagstone walks from the early 19th century, horse-mounting stones in front of the Presbyterian Church, and early gravestones in church cemeteries, with the oldest dating to 1795. Steeples contain bells, the focal point of a much publicized and honored tradition of ringing out the old and ringing in the New Year.

Agriculture is still a big industry, but farmland is at a premium. There are bounties on Botetourt County real estate, with people desperate to buy the scenic farmland, which has often been in the same family for generations.

Two scenic landmarks tourists especially enjoy are the unusual huge, jutting Eagle Rock boulders off U.S. Highway 220—they appear to be on the verge of falling at any moment into the gorge.

Beyond on US 220 is Eagle Rock's Roaring Run Furnace, part of the George Washington and Jefferson National Forests and typical of the scores of iron furnaces that were scattered throughout the hills and mountains of western Virginia. The single-stack, hot-blast charcoal furnace, built of large, squared stones, was constructed in 1832, rebuilt in 1845, and rebuilt again early in the Civil War. Most of the pig iron produced was shipped to Richmond for the war effort.

A third landmark here on the National Register of Historic Places is Wilson Warehouse, built in 1839 at Washington and Lowe Streets and now Buchanan's Community House. It is a relic of western Virginia's antebellum prosperity.

It stands to reason that Botetourt County's largest and most popular festival is Fincastle Festival in September. Attending the festival, sponsored by Historic Fincastle Inc., and held in the charming, historic downtown, is serendipity to lovers of fine art and crafts, since Fincastle is home to several well-known Virginia artists.

Recreational opportunities abound, including hiking the Appalachian and Bikecentennial trails that pass by Blue Ridge Road in Troutville. Other major activities are canoeing or floating the James River and Craig's Creek and hunting, camping, and fishing.

Although Botetourt County is a county with a past, it is definitely one with a bright future while it tries to hang on to its pastoral environment. For more information, contact the Botetourt County Chamber of Commerce at P.O. Box 81, Fincastle 24090, (540) 473–8280, or reach them on the Web at www.bot-co-chamber.com.

Craig County

Just as Botetourt residents are trying to protect their pristine environment, the rural residents of pastoral Craig (population 5,000) fiercely guard their stake in God's Country. Tourism is a major industry in this county, which is more than half covered by the George Washington and Jefferson National Forests.

The county got its name from Robert Craig, delegate to the General Assembly from Roanoke County who was instrumental in legislation that formed Craig County in 1851. New Castle was designated the county seat, and the historic courthouse was erected the same year by slave labor. Its bell was cast at the same foundry as the Liberty Bell.

The county seat contains several charming old buildings that have been designated historical landmarks, including the courthouse (which was miraculously spared during the Civil War), a jail, Central Hotel and Star Saloon (now official headquarters of the Craig County Historical Society), First National Bank, and the G.W. Layman office building. You'll see several lovely old homes in the area, including the Layman house (c. 1901), on the corner of Highways 311 and 42, and the big, brick castlelike Todd house at the top of the hill going out of town on Highway 42. In 1997 the town received a $16,000 state grant for more historic renovation. Buildings that have been restored include the old general store, the old train depot, the old hotel, and the mill in the town of Paint Bank, as well as the old Paint Bank School.

Also worth a visit is Tingler's Mill at Paint Bank. While this particular mill was built in 1873, grinding had been going on at the site since 1783. Henry Tingler was excused from military service in the Confederate Army because grinding meal was a higher war need. After 182 years of daily operation, the mill closed in 1965 but has been restored and is open for tours. Here's an interesting, little-known fact: Because of Civil War geographical boundary changes, the mill has been in two different states and five different counties without ever having been moved. In 1783 the land was part of Botetourt County, remaining so until 1792, when Monroe County, Virginia, was created. In 1851 Craig County was carved from parts of Botetourt, Monroe, Roanoke, and Giles Counties. In 1863 that portion of the county joined Monroe

> *When considering trips to the Blue Ridge, think about a hub-and-spoke concept: Stay in a metropolitan area and take side trips to smaller towns and attractions. After your first day, you'll get a feel for how long it takes to get places.*

County when West Virginia was formed during the Civil War, but it was returned to Craig County after the war.

The route of Gen. David Hunter's retreat in the summer of 1864 still has natives talking. The Union soldiers burned marriage records and Deed Book 1 and spilled ink on all the others. Then they chopped up parts of the courthouse for kindling. However, an order to burn the courthouse was somehow overlooked.

This gentle beauty of a county, rich in history, is noted as one of the most popular playgrounds in western Virginia. The scenery is spectacular. If you want to see the epitome of a quaint country road, travel Highway 42 from New Castle to Giles County. This delightful road, which crosses the eastern Continental Divide, passes old farms with rail fences, graveyards of Civil War veterans, and late 19th-century houses.

Highway 658 in the John's Creek area takes you to the sites of two now-defunct summer resorts where people would come to "take the cure," as they called it, of the orange sulphur mineral waters. The 1987 movie *In a Shallow Grave* used the site of Blue Healing Springs resort's crumbling dance hall.

Another site to see is Hebron Church, built in 1830, which has a slave balcony. It's locked during the week, but arrangements may be made to visit through the Craig County Historical Society (see our Attractions chapter).

The Appalachian Trail is one of the county's major attractions. Thirty miles of the Maine-to-Georgia footpath pass through this area, and several shelters and camping facilities are scattered along the way.

For mountain-bike enthusiasts, hikers, and horseback riders, Craig County is peppered with trails that range from the easy to challenging, and all have scenic value. Some local favorites include Highway 179, the road over Bald Mountain, and Highway 177 over Potts Mountain. Highway 188, the road across the top of Brush Mountain, will take you past the monument where World War II hero Audie Murphy's plane crashed.

If you're looking for adventure, wildlife, blessed isolation, and meditation, Craig County is the place to live or visit. For more information, contact the County of Craig, Corner of Court and Main Streets, New Castle 24127, (540) 864-5010, or go to the Web site at www.co.craig.va.us.

Roanoke County

Roanoke County (population 85,937) is a mostly affluent suburban area surrounding the City of Roanoke. It includes the placid, comfortable town of Vinton. The county is noted for its superior school system, network of top-notch recreational centers, and willingness to finance a superior quality of life for its citizens.

In 1838 mountainous Roanoke County was carved out of the huge county of Botetourt. Many of its communities are named for its peaks; one of the most unusual may be Twelve O'Clock Knob, so named because slaves west of Salem could look at the mountain and tell it was time for lunch when the sun was at a point just over the 2,707-foot peak. Underground springs, another of the area's natural resources, inspired other names, such as Virginia Etna Springs, site of a former water-bottling plant, and Big Cook Spring in Bonsack, an area heavily touched by the Civil War because of several blanket factories there. Legend has it that one factory was burned to the ground by the Yankees, but the other was spared because its owner, with fingers crossed, promised not to sell blankets to the Confederate merchants down the road in Roanoke City.

Another spring, Botetourt Springs, became the site of Hollins University, one of the most prestigious undergraduate women's colleges in America (graduate programs are coeducational).

Bonsack, east of Vinton, was the home of Jim Bonsack, who quit Roanoke College to work on a competition to invent the first cigarette-rolling machine. Young Bonsack won the $75,000 competition, patented his machine in 1880 at the age of 22, made a fortune, and spawned a national industry.

Roanoke County's pioneering spirit has extended to modern times. It has been nationally recognized for governmental cooperation in a joint industrial park and library built with Botetourt County. In 1989 Roanoke was named an All-America City for its governmental cooperation, quality of life, and support of the Explore Project.

Virginia's popular Explore Park is located near Roanoke at milepost 115 on the Blue Ridge Parkway. There, historic interpreters represent 1671 Totero Indians living in a woodlands village, a newly constructed 1750s frontier fort, and demonstrations of life in the Roanoke Valley in 1850, including a blacksmith, a schoolmaster, a batteauman, and a miller.

Recreation and historical preservation have been a longtime focus for Roanoke Countians. Green Hill Park is the site of the annual autumn Roanoke Symphony Polo Cup, benefiting the Roanoke Youth Symphony. It is one of 44 parks and recreational facilities in the Roanoke Valley.

Roanoke County is known for its family-oriented neighborhoods with styles ranging from urban town houses to bucolic farmhouses and suburban subdivisions. Families also like the county for its superior school system, which offers remedial education and classes for the gifted.

Major employers include ITT, manufacturer of night-vision goggles, and Allstate Insurance. Tanglewood Mall is the county's busy shopping destination, and numerous family restaurants in the same area make this a magnet for the whole valley.

Most of all, however, Roanoke County is known as a desirable place to live because of the high quality and variety of suburban services it offers residents. For more information, contact the Salem-Roanoke County Chamber of Commerce, 611 East Main Street, Salem 24153, (540) 387–0267, or visit www.s-rcchamber.org.

ROANOKE

Capital of the Blue Ridge, Roanoke (population 95,600) has it all: history, culture, close-knit neighborhoods, and a heady sense of environment. Its downtown was the first in North America to offer recycling, thanks to Downtown Roanoke Inc.

These happy environmental facts are the products of a cutting-edge grassroots environmental group, Clean Valley Council, gutsy government officials willing to take a stand, and Cycle Systems, an 80-year-old, fourth-generation recycling firm that has led Virginia in the recycling effort. Just like at Disneyland, you can count the moments before a piece of dropped litter is whisked out of sight . . . that is, if anybody has the gall to drop a piece in this earth-conscious area.

You'll probably do a double-take the first time you see the Roanoke Star, visible for a radius of 60 miles. The 100-foot-high star, which turned 50 in 1999, is a popular landmark for airplane pilots who frequently feel compelled to explain to passengers that what they think they're seeing below really is a gigantic, artificial star. The star has lured many people, including Elvis Presley, who donned a disguise to see it after a concert when his curiosity got the best of him. Beside the star are scores of unique animals at Mill Mountain Zoological Park.

And, just in case you think Roanokers are the only ones who brag about their community, let's talk about awards. A University of Kentucky study called Roanoke one of the nation's top 20 cities for quality of life. The *Zero Population Growth* newsletter said Roanoke is one of the 10 least stressful cities for quality of life. Downtown Roanoke's revitalization has been touted as one of America's 10 best by the National

Trust for Historic Preservation. Its cultural center, Center in the Square, was named one of the best 25 attractions in the world in 1996 and received the prestigious Bruner Award for urban excellence in 1997. Roanoke's historic city market was named one of the nation's top destinations to visit in 1996. And five times in the past decade, Roanoke has received the All-America City designation. In 2004 the book *Cities Ranked and Rated* by Peter Sander and Bert Sperling rated Roanoke as the 11th best city in the United States to live in.

Always a crossroads for commerce, Roanoke's story began in the early 17th century. Native resistance to settlers was fierce. The city, formerly called Big Lick for its salt marshes, was later named Roanoke. "Rawrenock," meaning white beads, actually shells with holes worn on strings around the neck and arms and passed as currency among Native Americans, was described early on by Capt. John White, who attempted to settle Roanoke Island in North Carolina.

Little towns were the foundation for what is now the city of Roanoke. New Antwerp appeared in 1802 followed by Gainesborough in 1825 and Old Lick in 1834. Big Lick, chartered in 1874 with 500 citizens, became a railroad crossroads. After Norfolk and Western Railroad came to town in 1882, Roanoke grew quickly. Its historic city market still functions and is the anchor of the revitalized City Market square downtown.

Roanoke is the largest metropolitan city in Virginia west of Richmond and off the widely traveled Blue Ridge Parkway. It is the major center for transportation, served by the Norfolk Southern Railway, the Valley Metro bus system, and a modern airport with a $25 million airport terminal built in 1990. The city is also the medical center of western Virginia, with more than 2,400 hospital beds and a gigantic medical center, Carilion Roanoke Memorial Hospital.

The Roanoke Valley has a culture all its own. The Roanoke Symphony has been featured on *Today* and in the *New York Times* and the *Wall Street Journal.* Cultural complements include Opera Roanoke and Center in the Square.

A national exhibition, "To the Rescue," puts Roanoke on the map as the birthplace of the volunteer rescue squad movement.

A lighted fountain of recycled metal, which you can see off Interstate 581, is a monument of sorts to Roanoke's devotion to recycling. It was a gift of Cycle Systems. In 2004 the Museum of Transportation added a new pavilion to protect the historic railside collection and added a new interactive playground for children.

There's family entertainment aplenty in Roanoke. Striving to live up to its nickname as Festival City, Roanoke hosts the blockbuster, two-weekend-long Roanoke Festival in the Park each May. Nearly 400,000 people attend this celebration of art, music, and the human spirit that signals the start of summer in Roanoke. Other festivals include the Chili Cook-off and Community School Strawberry Festival the first May weekend, when palates burning from flaming chili can get cooling ice cream and berries just down the block.

Roanoke is a great jumping-off point for side trips. The number of attractions within an hour's radius is unbelievable, and you'd need a good week's stay just to have time to see and do even half of what's available. Be sure to stop by the beautiful new headquarters of the Roanoke Valley Convention & Visitors Bureau at 101 Shenandoah Avenue NE, Roanoke, 24016; (800) 635–5535 or (540) 345–6025. You can check them out on the Web at www.visitroanokeva.com. The visitor center is in the newly renovated Norfolk and Western passenger station, which was built in 1905. It shares the complex with the new O. Winston Link Museum.

SALEM

An old story has made its rounds in the *Roanoke Times* newspaper office about a cub reporter who, having just moved to Salem and feeling a sense of isolation, asked a veteran reporter just how long it would take to get accepted by her neighbors.

"Oh, about three," the old Salem native replied.

"Three years?" responded the incredulous cub.

"No, three generations, my dear!" was the reply.

To say the city of Salem (population 24,836) has a sense of its own history and self-sufficiency is an understatement. Salem, its name derived from *shalom,* meaning peace, is the oldest and southernmost community in the Roanoke Valley. That historical fact pervades Salem's quaint, charming culture. Many of its historic downtown Victorian homes, with stained-glass windows, tin roofs, and pointed towers, are on the National Historic Register. The city celebrated its 200th birthday in June 2002.

Gen. Andrew Lewis started the settlement in 1768 when he acquired his estate, Richfield. In 1806 a charter to James Simpson created the town of Salem out of the Lewis estate, bounded by Union Street, Church Alley, and Clay and Calhoun Streets. Salem was chartered as a city in 1968. The Salem Museum and Historical Society is housed in a National Historic Register building, the Williams–Brown House, which is typical of buildings in the mid-19th century that catered to travelers.

Salem also has an excellent sense of community, especially when it comes to sports. The Salem Civic Center is the site of the fabulous Salem Fair and Exposition, the second-largest fair in Virginia.

You can do everything there from bungee jump to watch pigs race. The Civic Center seats 7,500 and offers a wide and varied program of community events.

For example, it's home to the Roanoke Valley Horse Show, one of the 10 largest in the country. Salemites' love for athletics borders on the fanatic, and considerable emphasis is placed on recreation, with more opportunities available than in most other areas of similar size. Facilities include an 8,000-seat football stadium for the beloved Salem High Spartans. Salem also provides exciting Class A professional baseball through the Salem Avalanche, a farm team that plays at Salem Memorial Baseball Stadium.

Salemites also have a collective heart that never stops beating for their own. When high school football star Chance Crawford was paralyzed by a spinal injury during a football game in the early '80s, the townspeople rallied to pay his medical expenses. Beyond that, an annual ball tournament was arranged to assure the Crawfords would have no financial worries. As a final tribute, Crawford was overwhelmingly elected to public office.

Festivals are especially popular. Olde Salem Days in September features one of the largest antique car shows on the East Coast as well as fine Salem art. One of the Roanoke Valley's best-known artists, Walter Biggs, lived here, and his legacy is carried on by Salem artists.

Vigorous industries, such as General Electric and the regional Veterans Administration Hospital, are here. Salem is home to Roanoke College, a Lutheran-affiliated private liberal-arts school that lends enormous culture to the area's charm. Salem's downtown shopping district has numerous antique stores and mom-and-pop operations. Roanoke College students enjoy the local hangouts Mac & Bob's, Macados, and Mill Mountain Coffee & Tea.

Many of Salem's citizens work, live, and play within its boundaries and never feel the need to leave their beloved city, regardless of how long it really takes to become an Insider. For more information, contact the Salem Visitor Center, 1001 Roanoke Boulevard, Salem 24153 (888) VA–SALEM or (540) 375–3004, or visit www.visitsalemva.com.

VINTON

Vinton, a small, unpretentious town (population 7,782) east of Roanoke, must be doing something right. Over the past several decades, in the midst of its homespun lifestyle, it has spawned and nurtured some of Virginia's most important modern leaders.

Vinton also is an important leader in its own right. In 1990 it put other Virginia municipalities on notice when its forward-looking town council began the first mandatory comprehensive recycling program in the state, effectively reducing landfilled solid waste by 25 percent..Vinton is also proud of a school system that has ranked among the state's top 10, and its populace comes out in droves for the William Byrd High Terriors. Its school system has the highest average achievement scores in the Valley, and teachers' salaries rank ninth in the state.

Gish's Mill, built prior to 1838, provided a start for the town. David Gish sold his mill to Isaac White Vineyard in 1867, and by that time enough people had settled around the mill to form the basis of the town of Vinton. Although the mill burned, some of the brick walls still stand. The town was chartered in 1884 and relied on the railroad for employment. Moving into the future, the N & W Railway continued to be Vinton's most important industry. Today, Precision Weaving is Vinton's largest employer.

Vinton residents play as hard as they work, having easy access to recreation by the town's proximity to the Blue Ridge Parkway. Vinton's Old-Time Bluegrass Festival in August and the Farmer's Market are annual excuses to have a good time. And Vinton hosts the oldest festival in the Roanoke Valley, the Dogwood Festival, always a pageantry of queens, bands, floats, and politicians that has attracted a number of celebrities over the past three decades. The first-class, all-American parade always ends at the Vinton War Memorial, Vinton's landmark building and cultural center.

Vinton serves its citizens well with plentiful recreational and spectator sports activities. Its municipal pool is beautiful, and its recreation department program and special events are second to none. Vinton's untapped tourism potential is enormous as the center of the politically designated Blue Ridge Region of Virginia. In addition to being next to the well-traveled Parkway (nine million visitors a year travel the Virginia section), Vinton is the last commercial center before Smith Mountain Lake, Virginia's largest lake. It also is the gateway to Virginia's Explore Park.

In the meantime, it's the epitome of small-town living, and the best is yet to come. For more information, contact the Town of Vinton at 311 South Pollard Street, Vinton 24179, (540) 983-0613, or on the Web at www.town.vinton.va.us.

EAST OF THE BLUE RIDGE

This gorgeous stretch of land begins in Loudoun County, with its famous hunt country and landed gentry, and sweeps southward along the mountains all the way through Charlottesville and Lynchburg to Franklin County south of Roanoke.

For the most part we are talking about rural territory with few glaring billboards, convenience stores, and shopping malls. It's an area rich in history that has little in common with the Shenandoah Valley across the mountains. In fact, the mountains had blocked early attempts at expansion from the east. Whereas the valley was settled primarily by Scotch-Irish and Germans who migrated south from Pennsylvania and Maryland, the foothills east of the Blue Ridge, especially Charlottesville and lands to the north, became home to families moving west from Richmond and the Tidewater area.

Though I-66 cuts across the region, there is no north-south interstate paralleling the Shenandoah Valley's I-81. US 29 is the major artery from Culpeper to Lynchburg, along which you will find wineries, splendid antiques shops, and quaint country stores. The secondary roads winding through the region will also carry you through hunt country on your way to gorgeous bed-and-breakfasts and country inns, vineyards, pick-your-own apple orchards, and historic mansions open for tours.

It takes a little more effort to tour this region and to do it right, but it's worth it.

Middleburg and Loudoun County

Middleburg, right on the line between Loudoun and Fauquier Counties, is the acknowledged hunt country capital and is surrounded by the estates of some of the country's wealthiest and most powerful people. Yet you'd be hard-pressed to identify some of them as they run errands in Middleburg dressed in jeans and gum boots. Until her death, Jackie Kennedy Onassis was a regular in Middleburg, fox-hunting with the locals and browsing the town's elegant shops. Philanthropist Paul Mellon and the late ambassador Pamela Harriman had estates in the area, as does actor Robert Duvall. Before her divorce from Sen. John Warner (who owned a farm nearby), Elizabeth Taylor shopped in the local grocery stores. Paul Newman has been known to pop in for lunch at Red Fox Tavern when he has been racing cars at Summit Point in nearby West Virginia.

Middleburg is a delightful anachronism because life follows a centuries-old rhythm as unchanged as its stone walls and pre–Civil War mansions. Horses are a part of daily life and a great equalizer. Your status in the real world matters a lot less than your horsemanship. You can rub elbows with celebrities and the horsey crowd during races and horse shows at Glenwood Park or at the Red Fox Tavern.

Most people are surprised Middleburg's town proper is so small (population 641) and so uniformly historic. This is, of course, by design. If area property owners have anything to do with it, Middleburg will never see a 7-Eleven or McDonald's, nor will it give way to the wave of development working its way west from Washington, D.C. Very seldom does anything smaller than a 100-acre estate come on the market here. The locals opposed the Walt Disney Company when the entertainment giant planned to build a theme park in Haymarket, just east of Middleburg. Despite having the governor in its corner, Disney finally yielded to the powerful local forces and gave up the project.

There is plenty to see and do in Loudoun, a county of 211,146 people, especially in Leesburg (population 34,073) and the postcard-perfect villages of Waterford and Hillsboro. Historical sites abound. Morven Park, built in 1780, was the home of two Virginia governors. There is also Oak Hill, the last home of President James Monroe, historic Oatlands Plantations, which schedules special events for the entire family throughout the year, and the Goose Creek Rural Historic District, about 10,000 acres that were once home to Quaker settlers. The village of Lincoln offers a wide variety of 18th-, 19th-, and 20th-century rural architecture.

Also in Loudoun are the towns of Hamilton, Lovettsville, Purcellville (population 4,787), and Round Hill.

For more information on Loudoun County, contact the Loudoun Convention and Visitor Association, 222 Catoctin Circle, Suite 100, Leesburg 20175–3730. You can call (800) 752–6118 or (703) 771–2617. The office is open daily. Check them out online at www.visitloudoun.org. The county has a handy bunch of information on its government Web site as well, www .loudoun.gov/business.

Warrenton and Fauquier County

Fauquier (population 55,100), named in honor of Lieutenant Governor Francis Fauquier, claims some of the most productive pastures in America, places where thoroughbreds thrive and the economy is still largely driven by a multimillion-dollar equine industry. Paris and Upperville afford some of the most scenic and historic real estate in the Old Dominion. The historic district in Upperville includes many 19th-century buildings made of brick, wood, and logs. This small community that formed in 1797 on the turnpike from Alexandria to Winchester got its name from its residential section, or "upper," end of the town.

Warrenton, the county seat with 6,670 residents, was originally known as Fauquier Court House. The moniker was changed to match an academy named in honor of Gen. Joseph Warren, a Revolutionary War hero. When Warrenton was occupied by Union troops during the Civil War, the town was the site of several raids by Col. John Mosby, also known as the Gray Ghost. He later made his home here after the war. In fact, he is buried in the Warrenton Cemetery, and a monument in his honor stands beside the courthouse.

A popular statue of Chief Justice John Marshall was erected in 1959 during the county's bicentennial celebration. His family home, Oak Hill, was built in 1773. Other favorite attractions in Fauquier County include Warrenton's Old Jail Museum, built in 1779, the Flying Circus Airshow in Bealeton, and the Warrenton Hunt, which started in 1883.

For more information on Fauquier County, contact the Warrenton-Fauquier County Visitor Center, 33 North Calhoun Street, Warrenton 20186, (540) 341-0988, or check them out at www.fauquier county.gov.

Rappahannock County

Rappahannock County (population 6,900) to the south is home to one of the most charming, even Utopian, towns in America, "Little" Washington. It is the oldest of the 28 towns in the United States named for the Father of Our Country, who surveyed and laid out the town around 1749. Washington has its own internationally known five-star restaurant and inn, a performing arts center, an artists' cooperative, and several classy galleries, boutiques, and antiques shops.

Rappahannock's county seat, historic

Sperryville, sits below the entrance to the Skyline Drive. It's a great little town to explore on foot, with antiques stores, galleries, arts and crafts studios, and a shop where you can buy American Indian weavings, jewelry, quilts, and crafts. Rappahannock, by the way, is one of the few counties along the Blue Ridge that derived its name from its earliest settlers. The county took its name from the river, which was named for the Rappahannock Indians, one of the five Powhatan tribes.

Among the northern foothills are two entries into Shenandoah National Park: Thornton Gap at US 211 near Sperryville and Swift Run Gap at U.S. Highway 33, which passes through Greene County.

For more information, contact the Rappahannock County Administrator's Office at P.O. Box 519, Washington 22747. The phone number is (540) 675-5330.

Madison County

Madison County, at 12,500 residents, has no road into Shenandoah National Park, a source of long-standing frustration among many residents. The county lost more land to the national park than any other and was reportedly promised a gateway, but for some reason national leaders reneged. This history explains in large part the level of local outrage when park officials proposed expanding the national park's boundaries into the county. The officials eventually dropped the idea, realizing how ugly a battle it would be.

Ironically, Madison County has received national acclaim for one of its scenic roads, but not the Skyline Drive. The Highway 231 Scenic Byway, which runs through 50 miles of the Piedmont from Sperryville south to Shadwell, near Charlottesville, was named one of America's 10 Most Outstanding Scenic Byways. The recognition came from Scenic America of Washington, D.C., an organization that seeks to call attention to outstanding routes and preserve endangered ones.

Graves Mountain Lodge, an inn in Madison County nestled quietly against the mountains, continues to offer respite, fun, and good food to visitors and locals alike. In 2004 the Lodge in Syria bought 145 adjoining acres that included an old gristmill, hiking trails, a conference center, and rental accommodations. Madison County's earliest settlers were German ironworkers. When they had completed the terms of their indentured servitude at Lord Spotswood's Germanna mines in Orange County, the Germans set out to build new lives for themselves as craftsmen and farmers. That tradition continues in Madison County. Many craftspeople, such as furniture makers, potters, wood carvers, quilters, and jewelry artisans, make this area their home.

For more information on Madison County, call the Madison County Chamber of Commerce at (540) 948-4455. The address is P.O. Box 373, Madison 22727, and the Web address is www.madison-va .com.

Greene County

Greene County (population 16,779) is a bedroom community for Charlottesville and as such has been doing some major growing over the last few years. Not only have several new housing developments sprung up around Ruckersville, but US 33 widened into a four-lane bypass around Stanardsville, and a handful of fast-food restaurants have come to town. There are even plans under way for several new gated communities in the Ruckersville area.

Greene County has one of three major access roads to the Skyline Drive on US 33, which twists up over the mountain and connects with the scenic drive at Swift Run Gap. Adding to Greene's status as a natural area, in the summer of 2004, the Nature Conservancy bought 830 acres on Hightop Mountain. The land, considered one of the best examples of Piedmont hardwood forests in Virginia, will be preserved as an

> *Virginia is represented by two Republicans, Sen. George Allen and Sen. John W. Warner. You can make your voice heard by contacting: Sen. John Warner, 225 Russell Senate Office Building, Washington, D.C., 20510, (202) 224-2023; Sen. George Allen, 204 Russell Senate Office Building, Washington, D.C., 20510, (202) 224-4024.*

intact forest. It is home to black bears and rare flora. Some hiking and other appropriate uses are planned for the newly designated natural area. Drop by the Blue Ridge Pottery on US 33 leading to the Skyline Drive and chat with local potter Alan Ward as he works at his wheel. The store, which occupies the former Golden Horseshoe Inn built in 1827, is a kind of headquarters for arts and crafts made especially in Greene County (see our Shopping chapter).

For more details on Greene County, contact the Greene County Visitor Center, housed in the new Virginia Company building, 9661 Spottswood Trail, Stanardsville 22973, or call (434) 985-9756.

Orange County

The beautiful, rolling hills of Orange County hold many historical attractions, including Montpelier, the 2,700-acre estate that was the lifelong home of James Madison and his equally famous and more popular wife, Dolley.

Orange County, which 26,000 people call home, contains many reminders of the terrible war that nearly split our country in two. The Wilderness Battlefields in the eastern end of the county were the scene of the first clash between the troops of Robert E. Lee and Ulysses S. Grant in May 1864 in which 26,000 soldiers died. The battlefields are open for self-guided tours.

Nearby Gordonsville is home to the Exchange Hotel, a restored railroad hotel that served as a military hospital during the war. It served more than 23,000 soldiers within a year's time. It now houses an excellent Civil War museum.

Closer to Charlottesville are the Barboursville Ruins, what's left of a mansion designed by Thomas Jefferson for James Barbour, governor of Virginia, U.S. senator, secretary of war, and minister to England.

Montpelier, settled by Madison's grandparents and now owned by the National Trust for Historic Preservation, is open for tours. In 2004 a major renovation began to downsize the huge salmon-colored mansion to its original presidential roots. The historic home is still open during the construction, and you can even stop in and watch the work in progress. The major transformation was something Marion duPont Scott had decreed when she donated the property to the state. The estate hosts a wine festival every May, featuring live music, crafts, food, and local wines. Montpelier is also the scene of steeplechase races on the first Saturday of every November. Since 1928 this hallowed tradition has drawn huge crowds of horse lovers.

The James Madison Museum is in nearby Orange, where you can visit the only surviving example of Thomas Jefferson's design for church architecture, St. Thomas Episcopal Church.

Orange County also boasts a thriving vineyard industry, harvesting a sizable amount of grapes each year. Along with the Barboursville Winery, which has been praised by *Wine Spectator* magazine, the county is home to the smaller Burnley Vineyards, one of the oldest vineyards in the region, and the newer Horton Cellars Winery (see our Wineries chapter).

For more information about these and other attractions and fine bed-and-breakfasts in Orange County, contact the Visitor Bureau, P.O. Box 133, Orange 22960, (540) 672-1653. Visit in person at 122 East Main Street or go online at www.visitoc va.com.

Charlottesville and Albemarle County

In 2004 Bert Sperling and Peter Sander in their book, *Cities Ranked and Rated,* listed Charlottesville as the number-one city in the nation in which to live. Residents of Charlottesville already know that it is a crown jewel of a city, with so much beauty, history, culture, and lively commerce that it's no wonder it is growing by leaps and bounds. If he were alive, Thomas Jefferson, a native of the territory, would probably roll his eyes and sigh at the traffic congestion that now clogs such major arteries as U.S. Highway 250 and US 29. Such is the cost of the city's allure, though area residents are working hard to establish a plan for controlled growth for its 40,000 residents.

Fortunately, Albemarle County (population 84,000), which surrounds Charlottesville on all sides, remains largely rural, with rolling pastures, elegant horse farms, and lush forests that lead up to the wilderness of the Shenandoah National Park. And the city itself contains many enclaves of natural beauty, from the lovely gardens along the colonnade at the University of Virginia to fine old homes surrounded by mounds of azaleas, rhododendrons, and camellias.

Monticello, the architectural wonder Jefferson designed and never stopped tinkering with, remains the area's leading attraction. The mountaintop estate opens its doors to visitors seven days a week, inviting all to glimpse Jefferson's genius through his architecture, gardens, and innovations. Another fascinating exhibit about Jefferson's domestic life at Monticello lies down the hill and next to I-64 at the Monticello Visitor Center (see our Attractions chapter).

Thanks to Jefferson's architectural abilities, the campus of the University of Virginia is considered one of the most beautiful in the nation. Jefferson designed the Rotunda of his academic village after the Roman Pantheon. The graceful

Rotunda, the pavilions and their gardens, and the whitewashed colonnade comprise the original university buildings. In 1976 the American Institute of Architects voted the original campus the most outstanding achievement in American architecture.

Not far from Monticello, on another mountain slope, is the home of James Monroe, Jefferson's friend and America's fifth president. Strutting, showy peacocks grace the lawn at Ash Lawn–Highland, where visitors can witness Monroe's cultured lifestyle and learn about a working farm of the 19th century. The boxwood-covered grounds come to life in the summer, when opera performances entertain guests under the stars (see our Arts chapter).

You'll find reminders of this rich history in the streets of downtown Charlottesville, especially around Court Square, where Jefferson and Monroe spent much of their leisure time. Here many buildings bear plaques dating to the early days of the city, making it easy to imagine what the city must have looked like when Jefferson practiced law here.

The Albemarle County Courthouse, built in 1762, served as the meeting place of the Virginia Legislature as the leaders fled Cornwallis's approaching army in 1781. State legislator Daniel Boone was one of the seven men captured in a surprise raid on Charlottesville led by British Cavalry General Banastre Tarleton during that campaign. Tarleton failed at capturing then-governor Jefferson but nabbed Boone at the corner of Jefferson and Park Streets.

History buffs are not the only ones interested in the downtown historic district. Folks of all ages enjoy strolling along the pedestrian Downtown Mall, lined on both sides with boutiques, restaurants, bookstores, movie theaters, art galleries, and an ice-skating rink. On Fridays, April through September, the Mall hosts a free concert series at its outdoor amphitheater. The series features wonderful local bands from this music-rich town (the Dave Matthews Band got its start in Charlottesville and has even played at this concert series). The culinary scene in

Charlottesville has become rather lively and diverse as well. You'll be tempted by the Indian, Vietnamese, French, German, Italian, Brazilian, and American nouvelle cuisine in the area.

Many famous figures of the film and literary world make their home in the Charlottesville area. Charlottesvillians are reportedly known for their ability to fake nonchalance at the sight of such individuals as Sissy Spacek, John Grisham, John Gardner, Rita Dove, and Rita Mae Brown. It is considered gauche to gawk or ask for an autograph, and this must be one reason these famous folks seem to have found such a comfortable life here.

Of course, Charlottesville's association with the rich and famous is nothing new. The area was the setting for part of *Giant*, the Western film starring Elizabeth Taylor, Rock Hudson, and James Dean. Randolph Scott, a leading star in *Ride the High Country,* one of the greatest Westerns ever made, lived at Montpelier for a couple of years when he was married to Marion duPont.

The affluence of Charlottesville has had a positive effect with the backing of such cultural resources as the Virginia Film Festival and the Virginia Festival of the Book. Patricia Kluge, ex-wife of one of the richest men in America, provided the primary means to establish the film festival, held at UVA every October. Illustrious special guests have included Jason Robards, Jimmy Stewart, Gregory Peck, Ann-Margret, Charlton Heston, and a host of screenwriters, critics, and academics.

A trip to Charlottesville isn't complete without at least one stop at a local winery for a sample, a bottle, or a tour to learn how wine is made. At least a dozen wineries sit within easy driving distance of Charlottesville.

For more information, contact the Charlottesville/Albemarle Convention & Visitor Bureau, 600 College Drive, Charlottesville 22902, (434) 977-1783; (877) 386-1102, or check them out at www .soveryva.com. The University of Virginia also runs an information center at its police department at 2304 Ivy Road, Charlottesville 22903, (434) 924-7166. Look up UVA at www.virginia.edu.

Nelson County

Roughly a quarter of this rural, agricultural county lies in the George Washington and Jefferson National Forests. Wintergreen Resort, a four-season vacation paradise with a year-round residential community, hugs the mountains in the western part of the county. Crabtree Falls, a spectacular series of cascades, is one of the highlights of the forest along Highway 56, the scenic road that crosses the mountains and enters the Shenandoah Valley at Vesuvius. Apples are a mainstay of the local economy, and beef cattle is the second-leading industry.

In 2004 the first 2 miles of the 7-mile Blue Ridge Rail Trail was installed. When finished, the trail will stretch from the train depot in Nelson County to the Tye River in Amherst County. The trail is open to hiking, biking, horseback riding, and bird-watching. Earl Hamner Jr., who wrote the hit family television show of the '70s *The Waltons,* grew up in the tiny town of Schuyler (pronounced SKY-ler). For years fans have come to Schuyler searching for the old homeplace and other landmarks of the show. In 1992 the Waltons' Mountain Museum opened in the very school attended by Hamner and his siblings. Actual sets from the show are set up in former classrooms, and all sorts of interesting memorabilia is displayed.

Another attraction in Nelson County is Oak Ridge, a 4,800-acre estate that belonged to Thomas Fortune Ryan, a leading financier at the turn of the 20th century. A restored 50-room mansion, with its formal Italian gardens, greenhouse, and 80 outbuildings, serves as a backdrop for a variety of festivals and cultural events, including the Nelson County Summer Festival in June.

Nelson County (population 14,400) has six vineyards offering tours and wine tastings, enjoyable outings any time of year but especially in the autumn.

For more information on Nelson County, contact the Nelson County Division of Tourism at 8519 Thomas Nelson Highway, Lovingston 22949, (434) 263-7015 or (800) 282-8223, or visit www.nelsoncounty.com.

Lynchburg and Amherst County

I consider it one of the most interesting spots in the state. —Thomas Jefferson

Democracy's founding father, who scandalized Lynchburg society by eating a "love apple" (tomatoes were thought to be poisonous), summed up best how Lynchburg's citizens feel about their city and its vast array of cultural, educational, and recreational opportunities. In 2004 Sperling and Sander, of *Money Magazine,* published their book, *Cities Ranked and Rated,* which listed Lynchburg as the nation's number 15 city in which to live.

For the past 25 years, the national spotlight has shone on the politically active pastor of Lynchburg's internationally known Thomas Roads Baptist Church, the Rev. Jerry Falwell. Known as the City of Churches, Lynchburg (population 65,200) has more than 100 other houses of worship in addition to the church that launched the Moral Majority. Although the Quakers were the first religious group to settle here and strongly influenced Lynchburg's history, their opposition to slavery caused them to migrate to Ohio and Indiana.

Long before Falwell built his national church from a small Lynchburg congregation, Lynchburg's central location and role in transporting goods by river and railroad had already made it famous. Lynchburg's founder and namesake, John Lynch, was from hardworking Irish stock. His father, Irish runaway Charles Lynch, decided to learn a trade and at the age of 15 apprenticed himself to a wealthy Quaker tobacco planter. The relationship worked out so well, the Roman Catholic Lynch married the planter's daughter. Their equally enterprising son, reared as a Quaker, started a ferry service across the James River in 1757—at the tender age of 17. In 1786 the Virginia General Assembly granted John Lynch a charter for a town, 45 acres of his own land. Lynchburg was incorporated as a town in 1805 and a city in 1852. Lynch also built the city's first bridge, replacing his ferry in 1812.

Historically known as the Hill City, Lynchburg attracted industrial magnates who dealt in tobacco and iron, the chief products of early Lynchburg. Their ornate, luxurious homes, bordered by enormous decorative wrought-iron fences, are alone worth a visit. The oldest public cemetery in Virginia still in use, Old City Cemetery, in 2004 opened a Victorian mourning museum, which depicts 19th- and 20th-century American mourning customs.

In the decade before the Civil War, Lynchburg was one of the two wealthiest cities per capita in the United States. As you would expect, its moneyed citizenry spawned a rich culture. Sarah Bernhardt and Anna Pavlova appeared at the Academy of Music, which opened in 1905. The old music hall was purchased by Liberty University with plans to restore it. Jones Memorial Library was completed in 1908 and is one of America's foremost genealogical research libraries. Lynchburg's Fine Arts Center, the city's cultural nucleus, houses two art galleries, a theater, two dance studios, and the oldest continuous theater group in the country. Each year, thousands of people take classes, hear concerts, and see plays, ballet, and art exhibits at the center.

Scores of famous authors sprang from Lynchburg's culture. Two of its most famous gained their fame for their books on the opposite sides of democratic and racial issues. Historian Dr. Douglas Southall Freeman, born in Lynchburg in 1886, received 24 honorary degrees and two Pulitzer Prizes, one in 1936 for his four-volume work, *The Life of Robert E. Lee*. The other, in 1948, was for a series on

George Washington. Anne Spencer, an African-American poet born in 1882, is the only Virginian whose works are included in the *Norton Anthology of Modern American and British Poetry*. She helped establish Lynchburg's first lending library for African Americans and started Lynchburg's first NAACP chapter. Frequent visitors to Spencer's restored home, garden, and studio, Edan Kraal (open by appointment to visitors at 1313 Pierce Street), included Dr. Martin Luther King Jr., Dr. George Washington Carver, Jackie Robinson, and Marion Anderson, the African-American singing star who was denied entrance to perform in Washington's Daughters of the American Revolution (DAR) concert hall because of her race.

Interestingly enough, one of the founders of the DAR, Ellet Cabell, was born at Point of Honor, a beautifully restored Lynchburg mansion, now a museum, in the same area as Spencer's house. Point of Honor, so named for the gun duels fought there, was built by Dr. George Cabell Sr., whose most famous patient was Patrick Henry. Point of Honor is part of Lynchburg's city museum system.

Any discussion of Lynchburg's history must also include the influence of Carter Glass, born in Lynchburg in 1858 and secretary of the treasury under President Woodrow Wilson. Glass served as a Virginia state senator from 1899 to 1902, in the U.S. House of Representatives from 1902 to 1918, and represented Virginia in the U.S. Senate from 1920 to 1946. He was the first living person to appear alone on a regular U.S. coin.

Lynchburg's quality of life is also greatly enhanced by its bustling community market at Bateau Landing, where shoppers can choose fresh produce and homemade goods. The annual Bateau Festival held in June celebrates the historic James River's contributions with entertainment, historic crafts exhibits, and the start of the bateau race to Richmond. Kaleidoscope is an annual fall festival celebrating life in Central Virginia with an arts festival, bands, riverfront jamboree, craft show, pops picnic (dining on the lawn to some great music), and the Lynchburg Symphony.

Lynchburg has long been a leading industrial city. It has one of the highest per capita manufacturing employment in Virginia. Today it is also home to thousands of businesses, and it has led the way in developing one of the state's first small business incubators.

In 1889 the young pharmacist Charles Brown began selling his Chap Stick lip balm. Since, his C.B. Fleet Company's product line has expanded to other national items, including the first disposable enema and Summer's Eve douche.

As a major manufacturing center, Lynchburg played an important role in the Civil War. Perhaps none was more urgent than the advance of medicine for Civil War soldiers brought to the Pest House by Dr. John Jay Terrell. At the Pest House, in the historic Lynchburg Confederate Cemetery, you can view displays of Dr. Terrell's pace-setting work in establishing sanitary standards, including his 19th-century medical kit.

Lynchburg is home to eight diverse colleges. Randolph-Macon Woman's College was the first woman's college in the South to be accredited and the first to receive a Phi Beta Kappa chapter. Sweet Briar is another well-known woman's college and is affiliated with the Virginia Center for the Creative Arts, an internationally recognized Amherst County working retreat for writers, artists, and composers. Also here are Jerry Falwell's Liberty University, Lynchburg College, a liberal arts school, a community college, seminary, and two business colleges.

Lynchburg's public schools also are outstanding. Both of its high schools and one of its middle schools have been designated as model schools by the Commonwealth of Virginia. The city also has 10 private schools, including the Virginia School of the Arts, a private boarding school of dance for high school students.

A hub for day trips, Lynchburg offers many nearby opportunities for sightseeing.

Twenty miles east is Appomattox, the site where our nation reunited after the Civil War. Monument Terrace, in the center of Lynchburg's downtown, honors the heroes of all wars.

For more information, contact the Lynchburg Visitor Center at 216 12th Street, Lynchburg 24504, (434) 847-1811, or go to www.DiscoverLynchburg.org. You can also contact the Greater Lynchburg Chamber of Commerce at P.O. Box 2027, 2015 Memorial Avenue, Lynchburg 24501, (434) 845-5966, or visit them online at www.lynchburgchamber.org.

North of Lynchburg, Amherst County (population 31,800) was first inhabited by the Monacan Indians. It is named for Sir Jeffrey Amherst, the British commander of all forces in America from 1758 to 1763. Amherst led the British armies that successfully drove France from Canada and was the British hero of the Revolutionary War Battle of Ticonderoga against the upstart Colonists.

Amherst County was created in 1761 from a section of Albemarle County. In 1807 it was divided, and the northern part became Nelson County. Tobacco and apples were early cash crops.

Three-fourths of the county's rolling terrain is forests. The Blue Ridge Parkway offers dramatic views while providing the perfect spot for an afternoon picnic. The county is a popular recreation area boasting magnificent mountain views, clean air, and thousands of acres of unspoiled forests, rivers, and lakes. Numerous leisure and recreational activities can be found in the George Washington and Jefferson National Forests. The Appalachian Trail bisects Amherst County and affords the serious hiker the ultimate challenge. Winton Country Club, the 18th-century manor that was once the home of Patrick Henry's sister, opens its 18-hole championship golf course to the public here.

The Amherst County Museum, in the German Revival–style Kearfott-Wood House, built in 1907 by Dr. Kearfott, was expanded to include four exhibit rooms and a gift shop. A reference library here is available to the public. You can reach the Amherst County Chamber of Commerce at (434) 946-0990, or write to P.O. Box 560, Amherst 24521. The Web address is www.amherstvachamber.com. If in town, stop by their office in the back of the Amherst County Museum at 154 South Main Street.

SMITH MOUNTAIN LAKE

How do you spell relief?

L-A-K-E. Smith Mountain, that is, western Virginia's biggest playground and Virginia's largest lake. Smith Mountain Lake is 20,000 acres of placid waters, 40 miles long, and surrounded by 500 miles of shoreline.

It touches Franklin, Bedford, and Pittsylvania Counties (combined population 170,145). The lake is a colorful place where people love to go and hate to leave. Purple sunsets, stunning blue water, and a lot of wildlife, such as glossy green-headed mallard ducks and chubby, gray-striped bass, add to the local color.

As lakes go, Smith Mountain is relatively new. Like its older sister, Claytor Lake, south in Pulaski, Smith Mountain was formed when the Roanoke River was dammed to generate electrical power for Appalachian Power Company. It took six years and a crew of 200 to move 300,000 cubic yards of earth to make way for the 175,000 cubic feet of concrete used to build the Smith Mountain Dam. Full pond is 613 feet above sea level. The river started filling Smith Mountain Lake on September 24, 1963, and reached capacity on March 7, 1966. Archaeologists examining the excavation necessary to build the dam determined that Algonquins fished and hunted here long before anybody else did.

While Smith Mountain was a popular spot from day one, a real breakthrough for the lake was when developer Dave Wilson started Bernard's Landing Resort in the early '80s. Wilson is widely credited with being the moving force behind opening the lake to everyone and making it a major western Virginia tourist attraction. Since then, Bernard's Landing Resort and its gourmet restaurant, the Landing, have become important tourist attractions at the lake, bringing in people from around the country as condominium owners, many of whom offer public rentals.

A second important addition to the lake's culture was the building of Bridgewater Plaza at Hales Ford Bridge on Highway 122. The center of Smith Mountain's social life and nightlife, the Plaza has restaurants, a marina, small shops, and Harbortown Miniature Golf Course, which is built out over the water. Bands play here on weekends during the summer.

The year-round lake community, who live in the three counties that surround the lake, include the staid German Baptist population, which rarely mingles socially with outsiders. They dress similarly to Mennonites and can be identified by the women's mesh bonnets and the men's long beards. Widely known for their agricultural prowess, they live on some of the most beautiful farms you'll ever see and make or grow virtually everything they need.

The lake offers plenty of things to do on weekdays and weekends. A major attraction is Booker T. Washington National Monument, the former home of the famous African-American statesman, 6 miles south of Hales Ford Bridge on Highway 122. Also stop by American Electric's visitor center at the Dam off Highway 40 on Highway 908. It's full of hands-on exhibits for the kids and interesting audiovisuals about how the lake was formed. Smith Mountain Lake State Park has a full calendar of summertime activities including swimming, fishing, and canoeing (see our Recreation chapter).

Golf is a major attraction for residents. However, unless you're a member of the Waterfront or Water's Edge residential community, your game will be at Westlake's 18 beautiful holes or Mariner's Landing. Westlake's restaurant is also open to the public. As with the other planned communities, it sells villa homesites for those who want to live and play by a golf course.

Other pastimes are parasailing and riding Jet Skis. For the serious boater, there is the Smith Mountain Yacht Club and at least several dozen marinas offering services ranging from houseboats to restaurants to dry dock. A word of caution: If you are interested in a quiet day on the water, Saturday probably is not the day to be out and about because of weekender traffic.

Now, let's talk about fishing, the original reason many people came to the lake. Smith Mountain has a well-deserved reputation as an angler's paradise, especially for striped bass. Some coves literally churn with stripers, especially in the autumn. Getting them to bite your bait is another matter. (See our Recreation chapter's "Fishing" section.)

Now that you've hooked your fish and are also hooked on the lake, let's turn our attention to buying your own vacation home here. Many a millionaire was made from lake real estate. People all over western Virginia are kicking themselves that they didn't buy when land was cheap. There are many tales of people recouping their original investment 10 times over within a decade. Those days, however, are long gone.

Regardless of whether you're just visiting or planning to buy real estate and stay, Smith Mountain will win your heart while you're here. There's nothing more spectacular than a Smith Mountain sunset or more beautiful than the early morning mist blanketing the lake. You'll return many times to enjoy the view and have some fun. And that's no fish tale! For more information, contact the Smith Mountain Lake Chamber of Commerce and Visitor Center, located at Bridgewater Plaza, 16430 Booker T. Washington Highway 2, Moneta 24121. Here, you can pick up brochures about marinas, Jet Ski and boat rentals, lake homes for rent, campgrounds, and fishing guides. Call the Chamber at (800) 676-8203 or (540) 721-1203, or check out its Web site at www.smlchamber.com.

Bedford City and County

It's here Thomas Jefferson came to get away from it all at his summer home, Poplar Forest. That alone should tell you something about the quality of life in Bedford County. And some things never change. Even if nobody ever finds the famous Beale Treasure here, you can easily make a case that Bedford County and its charming county seat are a real "find" in themselves. Let's talk history.

The fastest-growing county outside the Urban Crescent of Northern Virginia, Bedford County (population 60,300) borders Smith Mountain Lake and is home to Smith Mountain Lake State Park. Bedford also is off the Blue Ridge Parkway, close to one of the Parkway's main attractions, the Peaks of Otter Lodge and Restaurant at milepost 86, on a spectacular twin-peaked mountain that can be seen for miles.

Bedford, home to 6,300 residents, is a Main Street Downtown Revitalization City with organizations devoted to its historic past. A wonderful museum and the Bedford County Public Library are downtown.

Bedford County was named for John Russell, fourth duke of Bedford, who, as secretary of state for the southern department of Great Britain, had supervision of Colonial affairs. The county was formed in 1754 from Lunenburg County and part of Albemarle County. The city was chartered in 1968; in the early '80s it renovated its historic downtown, where interesting shops and restaurants contribute to the ambience.

Recreation abounds in Bedford County, with the Jefferson section of the National Forest on the north offering the many diversions of the Blue Ridge, including hunting, fishing, camping, picnicking, and trails for both horseback riding and biking. Part of the Appalachian Trail passes through the area, with this section especially full of wildflowers and wildlife. The James River flows through in the northeast. City residents enjoy the 59-acre Liberty Lake Park, the heart of recreation. Bedford Lake and Park, 35 acres with a white-sand beach off Highway 639, offers swimming, boating, fishing, and camping.

The county is largely rural, with half of its land devoted to farming, dairy and beef cattle, and orchards. One of the oldest trees on record, definitely the oldest in Virginia, stands at Poplar Park in Bedford. This tree is the largest yellow poplar tree in the world and the largest tree in Virginia. Bedford also is a manufacturing base for industries that make everything from pottery, clocks, and golf carts to food flavoring and stew.

Bedford citizens have a rich small-town culture. The county's Sedalia Center offers classes in everything from classical music to back-to-the-land survival skills and is a tremendous asset to the community. Every Christmas, an estimated 100,000 visitors come to see the lighting display erected by the 200 retired Benevolent and Protective Order of Elks at that fraternal organization's national home.

Poplar Forest, just outside of Lynchburg, is one of the area's most popular destinations as history lovers flock to see the ongoing excavation and renovation of Thomas Jefferson's beloved octagonal retreat home (see our Attractions chapter).

The devout Christian with an imagination will enjoy seeing Holy Land USA, a 400-acre nature sanctuary whose aim is to be a replica of the Holy Land in Israel. Its owners invite study groups and individuals for a free walking tour. Primitive camping is allowed.

But what puts Bedford on the map nationally is the new D-Day Memorial. This striking outdoor memorial commemorating the U.S. soldiers who died in the WWII storming of Normandy opened in June 2001 after receiving sanction and major funding from Congress in 1996. Bedford was chosen because it lost a greater percentage of its men in that battle than any other town in the United States. A dedicated group of D-Day veterans fought for years to make the monument happen, and 57 years after the historic battle that

changed the face of the war, they finally see a well-deserved dream come true.

For more information, contact the Bedford Area Chamber of Commerce at 305 East Main Street, Bedford 24523, (540) 586–9401. Check them out on the Web at www.bedfordchamber.va-web.com. You can also contact the Bedford Visitor Center at 816 Burks Hill Road, Bedford 24523, (540) 587–5681, and go online to www.visitbedford.com.

Franklin County

Franklin County calls itself the Land Between the Lakes, Smith Mountain, and Philpott. More miles of shoreline touch Franklin County than either of the other two border counties, Bedford or Pittsylvania. Excluding part-time residents who own lake vacation homes, Franklin County's population is 48,100.

For a small, rural area, Franklin County has several national claims to fame. It has one of the proudest African-American cultures of any place in the Blue Ridge, evidenced by the Booker T. Washington National Monument. The famous former slave who became one of America's most important scholars and educators lived on a farm that is now the focus of the park near Hales Ford Bridge (see our Attractions chapter).

Franklin County's other national claim to fame is a Blue Ridge researcher's dream, the acclaimed Blue Ridge Institute at Ferrum College, where the annual October Blue Ridge Folklife Festival pays tribute to the treasured yet nearly forgotten skills of its Blue Ridge culture (see our Annual Events and Festivals chapter). The Institute is a national treasure that promotes a culture. It greatly transcends what many Franklin Countians take for granted as everyday life. The Institute offers a museum, archives, and records division and a re-created 1800s German-American farmstead to preserve the best of Blue Ridge culture. One of its finest creations, produced for Franklin County's Bicentennial in 1986, is a pictorial record of Franklin County life and culture.

The Blue Ridge Institute's Folklife Festival brings many skilled, working craftspeople in for the delight of visitors. You will see demonstrations of spinning, quilt making, shingle chopping, and other home-spun crafts. The Festival also offers unique spectator sports, such as Coon Dog Trials.

Ferrum College greatly enriches the quality of life for Franklin County residents. In 1997 it sponsored an environmental symposium that attracted nationally known speakers. Its fine arts program supports the Jack Tale Players, whose song and drama touring company brings to life the legends of the Upland South. Both students and residents enjoy participating in the Blue Ridge Summer Dinner Theatre.

The culture of Franklin County is vastly different, from the early settlers in the county seat of Rocky Mount to the transplanted northerners at Smith Mountain Lake. Yet a third culture, the German Baptist population, mostly keeps to itself. One exception is Boone's Country Store in Burnt Chimney. The best sticky buns on earth and other tempting edibles are prepared daily at this German Baptist store.

Franklin County's history is as rich and varied as its people. Its first residents were German, French, English, and Scotch-Irish settlers who moved from Pennsylvania in 1750. The county was formed in 1786 by the General Assembly. Munitions for Revolutionary War patriots were made from locally mined iron ore at an ironworks on Furnace Creek, which is the county's oldest landmark.

One of the Civil War's most respected Confederate leaders, Lt. Gen. Jubal Early, second in command only to Gen. Stonewall Jackson, was born here. A foundation is restoring his birth home. Rocky Mount is full of many interesting historical buildings. One, the Claiborne House Bed and Breakfast, is open to the public.

Franklin County is also an outdoor paradise for hunting and fishing. Smith Mountain and Philpott Lakes offer wonderful fishing if you have the patience and the

right bait. Philpott, a 3,000-acre lake built by the U.S. Army Corps of Engineers, is more rustic than Smith Mountain and also offers boating, a beach, and camping. For hunting, wild turkey proves to be the most popular game in the area.

A different kind of recreation is found at the popular Franklin County Speedway in Calloway. You can find out about individual races by going to the Web site at www.callowayusa.com.

Of all the counties surrounding the lake, Franklin's housing costs and taxes are generally the lowest, excluding its lakefront property. Farmland, scarce in so many areas of the Blue Ridge, is plentiful here. You're within easy commuting distance of either the Roanoke Valley or Martinsville, known for its furniture outlets.

When you're between stops, visit the land between the lakes. Whether you play, shop, or visit one of its national attractions, you'll find plenty to fill up your time. For more information, contact the Franklin County Chamber of Commerce at 261 Franklin Street, Rocky Mount 24151, or P.O. Box 158, Rocky Mount 24151, (540) 483-9542, or go online to www.franklin countyva.org.

NEW RIVER VALLEY

The academically stimulating, scenic, and mountainous New River Valley of Virginia is one of the most steadily growing areas of the Blue Ridge. It includes Montgomery County and the towns of Blacksburg and Christiansburg, the city of Radford, and Floyd, Giles, and Pulaski Counties. Although all are in the same area, you couldn't find a more diverse cultural group. The common thread again is the sheer beauty of the environment.

From the 1970s to 1990, the New River Valley's population grew by nearly a fourth to 152,720. People just keep on coming, and few ever leave. That's due to the presence of Virginia Tech, Virginia's largest university, with more than 25,000 students, as well as Radford University's 9,200 students. Every year, scores of mountain-struck students are smitten by the New River Valley Flu, a curious mental illness that causes them to turn down lucrative jobs in the big city and vow to flip hamburgers or do whatever they have to in order to stay in the area.

Blacksburg was named by Rand McNally as one of the top 20 places to live in the United States. A publication for mature adults names it as one of the best retirement spots in the country. The reasons are diverse but mostly involve the winning combination of a scenic mountain vacation land and extraordinary cultural enrichment from its multinational university population.

An interesting historical fact is that the New River is actually old—really old! According to legend it's the second-oldest river in the world; only Egypt's historic Nile is older. The 300-million-year-old river is an anomaly because it flows from south to north and cuts through the Alleghenies from east to west. The New River is 320 miles long from its headwaters near Blowing Rock, North Carolina, to the point in West Virginia where it tumultuously joins the Gauley River to form some of the best white-water rafting in the East. Outfitters at the Gauley River Gorge regularly host celebrities and nearby Washington politicians, such as Ted Kennedy, who are looking for a refreshing crash of water instead of a staggering crush of paper.

Unlike the populous Nile River area, the New River Valley was a vast, empty land with no permanent inhabitants when the first white explorers saw the area in 1654. Drapers Meadow near Blacksburg is regarded as the first New River settlement. Germans in Prices Fork and Dunkards in Radford established themselves about the same time. Native Americans ventured in only to hunt. For the first settlers, the natives were a threat greater than cold or starvation. Bands of Shawnees periodically would sweep in to kill settlers and destroy their homes. One such episode—a 1755 massacre of many Drapers Meadow residents—became the inspiration for a play. In

the attack, Mary Draper Ingles and Betty Robinson Draper were taken hostage; Mary escaped and found her way home by following the New River.

The New River Valley has an exciting textbook history that's matched by its history of research and development. Virginia Tech's IBM 3090 supercomputer was the first in the nation to be fully integrated with a university's computing network and made generally available to faculty and students. The *National Enquirer* once described Blacksburg as a village that had gone computer berserk. Blacksburg was featured as the lead story, "The Electronic Village," in *Reader's Digest* in 1996.

Montgomery County

BLACKSBURG

The largest town in Virginia in both population and land, Blacksburg (population 39,573) sits majestically on a mountain plateau between two of nature's masterpieces, the Blue Ridge Mountains of Virginia and the great Alleghenies.

The growing town has a national recognition as an ideal community, charming but with a constant flow of professors and students who lend to it most of its culture. Newcomers, students, and others are easily and quickly assimilated into the town's uniquely wonderful, abundant social life.

Touring Broadway shows, well-known speakers, and popular musicians appear regularly on campus. Several university performing arts groups and the Theatre Arts Program are recognized nationally. Tech's NCAA Division I basketball and football teams often appear in postseason contests, and tailgating is the event every autumn. You've never seen anything until you see the enthusiasm when the Tech Hokies meet the University of Virginia Cavaliers.

These glowing quality-of-life reports can be attributed to the sprawling presence of Virginia Tech and its innumerable cultural offerings, many of which are free to the Blacksburg community. It would be difficult to find another community in Virginia with as many professionals of every type, from educators to seafood industry experts. One of its most famous, Prof. James Robertson (see our Civil War chapter), was named the foremost Civil War historian in America by the United Daughters of the Confederacy.

Tech's outreach into the community through its Extension Service and other programs affects the quality of life across Virginia. While businesses are sending their problems to researchers, local veterinarians, for example, routinely send their toughest cases to Tech's Veterinary School.

However, Tech wasn't always the town's main focal point. Blacksburg's name comes from the William Black family, who contributed acreage after Blacksburg was granted a town charter in 1798. For 75 years the town was known as a quiet and pleasant place to live. Then, in 1872, Dr. Henry Black petitioned the General Assembly to establish a land-grant university in his town. The university opened with one building and 43 students.

Since then the town and college relationship has created a community that combines a small-town atmosphere with big-city sophistication. Shopping malls and Blacksburg's active downtown offer many things you usually see only in places like Washington, D.C. Yet the pace of life is relaxed. You won't see any smog to speak of, smell many fumes, or be bothered by excessive noise. Blacksburg takes its quality of life seriously. Its town council is mostly made up, traditionally, of Tech educators who put their theories into practice.

Amid all this heady academia, there's a universal love for recreation. You can immerse yourself in all kinds of outdoor fun within minutes. Floating down the New River with an inner tube and cooler is a popular pastime.

Transportation is efficient, with a terrific bicycle path reminiscent of big-city parks. The National Association of Public Transit has ranked Blacksburg's municipal bus system as the best in the nation for its size. The heavily used Virginia Tech Montgomery Executive Airport sees many corporate jets.

As one of the fastest-growing, progressive communities in Virginia, many more people come to Blacksburg than leave. And, with all the area has to offer, that's liable to remain the trend for a long, long time. For details, visit the Montgomery County Chamber of Commerce and Visitor Center at 612 New River Road, New River Valley Mall, Christiansburg 24073, or call (540) 382–4010. You can also go online to www.montgomery.org.

CHRISTIANSBURG

Christiansburg (population 16,947), Montgomery County's seat and the fourth-largest town population in Virginia, is a charming, historic place anchoring a county population of 84,000. The county's rural villages of Shawsville and Riner are equally quaint. Highway 8 W. connects the county to the 469-mile-long Blue Ridge Parkway. A quiet river that flows under Main Street (the Wilderness Trail) marks the Continental Divide, where flowing groundwater changes its course toward the Ohio-Mississippi river system.

The last legal gun duel in this country, the Lewis-McHenry, was fought in Christiansburg's renovated Cambria historic district in 1808. Depot Street, location of the Christiansburg Depot Museum, was the site of the depot burned in 1864 by the Union army. The Cambria Emporium, built in 1908, is now the site of a fabulous antiques mall with its own antique General Store.

The town's skyline is dotted with history, including the steeples of Old Methodist Church, built in the early 19th century; Christiansburg Presbyterian, c. 1853; and Schaeffer Memorial Baptist, erected in 1884.

Christiansburg's founder was Col. William Christian, an Irish Colonial settler. The town served as an outpost on the Wilderness Trail, opened by Daniel Boone as the gateway to the West for settlers such as Davy Crockett. In 1866 the legendary Booker T. Washington of nearby Franklin County supervised the Christiansburg Industrial School for black children.

The northern portion of Montgomery County contains nearly 20,000 acres of the Jefferson National Forest. The Bikecentennial and Appalachian Trails pass through the county. Between Blacksburg and Christiansburg, on U.S. Highway 460, is the 90-acre Montgomery County Park, one of the area's many recreation spots. Facilities here include a swimming pool, bathhouse, fitness trail, and picnic area. In all, the county has four 18-hole golf courses, and a wealth of swimming pools, ballfields, playgrounds, and tennis courts.

An added plus for Montgomery County is that real estate, both land and houses, costs significantly less than it does in Blacksburg. For the same money you can get so much more, with a fantastic quality of life as well.

For more information, contact the Montgomery County Chamber of Commerce and Visitor Center at 612 New River Road, New River Valley Mall, Christiansburg 24073, or call (540) 382–4010, or go online to www.montgomery.org.

Giles County

If you love dramatic mountain scenery, don't miss Giles County, especially the autumn vista from US 460 traveling south from Blacksburg. Giles County (population 16,600) is a mountain haven of forests, cliffs, cascading waterfalls, fast-flowing creeks and streams, and, of course, the scenic New River. Its county seat, Pearisburg, is one of only two towns on the Maine-to-Georgia Appalachian Trail. Of the four covered bridges left in the Blue Ridge, three are in Giles County at Sinking Creek (see our Attractions chapter).

Giles County is a paradise for outdoors lovers. Whether your preference is for golfing a challenging emerald-green course, fly-casting in an ice-cold mountain stream

for trout, canoeing the New River's white water, or hiking, Giles has it. Giles's most scenic attraction and one of the most-photographed in the Blue Ridge is the Cascades waterfall, which awaits you at the end of a rigorous 3-mile hiking trail in Pembroke (see our Recreation chapter); the trek is not recommended for small children. After your uphill pull, which seems to last forever, your excellent reward for this adventure is bathing at the foot of the tumbling, 60-foot-high waterfall.

A tamer destination, and just as much fun for kids, is Castle Rock Recreation Area, for golf, tennis, and swimming. Or rent a canoe and kayak at New River Canoe Livery (see our Recreation chapter). Giles County's most famous attraction is the fabulous Mountain Lake Hotel and Resort, set atop the second-highest mountain, Salt Pond Mountain, in Virginia and overlooking the town of Blacksburg, miles away (see our Resorts chapter). For years, it has been known for the beauty of its stone lodge and its gourmet cuisine. It is also known for the movie *Dirty Dancing*, filmed here as the epitome of early '60s-era great resorts.

Another popular scenic destination is the attractive village of Newport, with its country store and steepled church. The quaint hamlet nestles at the foot of Gap Mountain at Sinking Creek.

Formed in 1806, the county was named for Gov. William Giles. In addition to tourism, Giles County's biggest employer is the Celanese Plant in Narrows. A bedroom community to many professionals, the county has a school system with one of Virginia's lowest student-to-teacher ratios—16 to 1—emphasizing a personal approach to instruction.

In addition to far-flung outdoor recreation, Giles also offers the culture of its historic Andrew Johnston House and great antiques shopping. A lot of Virginia Tech educators and professionals have discovered Giles, so you may have trouble finding available farmland. However, mountaintop chalets and homes come on the market at any given time. Contact the New River Valley Association of Realtors, (540)

953-0040. For more information on Giles County, contact the chamber of commerce at 101 South Main Street, Pearisburg 24134, (540) 921-5000 or visit them at http://i-plus.net/gec/main2.htm.

RADFORD

For quality of life, Radford (population 15,800) has the whole country beat—that is, if you want to stake it on longevity. The late Margaret Skeete, who died there in 1993 at the age of 114, was considered the oldest person in the United States and was listed in *The Guinness Book of Records.* Maybe living beside one of the oldest rivers in the world, the New River, had something to do with Skeete's remarkably long life. The river, which flows through this university city, adds something special to its quality of life.

Radford, the region's only independent city, was incorporated in 1892 and grew to be an important rail division point. It also became the home of Radford University, enrollment 9,100, and was the site of Mary Draper Ingles's long, harrowing escape from the Shawnees.

Another of Radford's major attractions is 58-acre Bisset Park, with a walking trail beside nearly a mile of the tree-lined New River. This perfect park is capped off with a gazebo, swimming pool, several playgrounds, and a tennis court. If you were to design the recreational area of your dreams, this would probably be it!

Radford's energetic downtown is a Main Street community and has seen numerous unique small businesses start up, many serving the student population.

The impact of Radford University on the city is comparable to that of neighboring Virginia Tech's on the town of Blacksburg. The Dedmon Center, a $13 million athletic facility, is an unbelievable community gem featuring an air-supported fabric roof atop a gymnasium and natatorium. The adjacent grounds have several softball, soccer, field hockey, and flag football fields. Radford is also fanatic about its high school Bobcats' sports teams.

Other noted Radford facilities include the 2,000-square-foot Flossie Martin Art Gallery, one of the Blue Ridge region's finest. A guest professor program has brought in entertainer Steve Allen, civil rights activist Jesse Jackson, Nobel Prize winner Elie Wiesel, Egypt's widowed Jihan Sadat (who displayed her own personal Egyptian art collection), and columnist Jack Anderson.

The city also has an outstanding academic tradition with its primary and secondary schools. Its school system, heavily influenced by college-educated parents, has been nominated by the Commonwealth of Virginia as one of the nation's best.

Radford's environment beside the sometimes placid, sometimes raging New River is symbolic of Radford's dynamic quality of life. For more information, contact the Radford Chamber of Commerce and Visitor Center at 27 West Main Street, Radford 24141, (540) 639-2202, or visit www.radfordchamber.com.

Pulaski City and County

The town of Pulaski (population 9,566) and Pulaski County (population 34,700), named for Count Pulaski of Poland, a Revolutionary War hero, has attractions ranging from historic sites to water recreation and sports, including a speedway and a farm baseball team.

Old Newbern, Pulaski's first county seat and the only Virginia town totally encompassed in a historic district, is recognized by both the National Historic Register and the Virginia Landmarks Commission. You can tour the Wilderness Road Museum. Pulaski's renovated historic Main Street is also a fun stroll past several charming shops and quaint restaurants, mostly examples of Victorian architecture. Pulaski's downtown also is blessed with the New River Valley's cultural gem, its Fine Arts Center, which is housed in an

1898 Victorian commercial building (see our Arts chapter).

Outdoors enthusiasts will feel right at home at Claytor Lake. Like its younger counterpart, Smith Mountain Lake, Claytor was formed in 1939 to generate electricity for Appalachian Power Company (now American Electric Power). It is the centerpiece of a 472-acre state park that's a haven for boaters, anglers, horseback riders, campers, and swimmers (its white-sand beach will make you think you're at the ocean). Nearby is a spectacular condominium development, Mallard Point. The county has another nice outdoor area, Gatewood Reservoir Park, in the Jefferson National Forest, 15 minutes west of the town of Pulaski.

Sports fans will appreciate the Motormile Speedway, on US 11. Open early April through late September, it is a NASCAR–Nextel racing series track seating thousands of fans. Pulaski County also is home to the highly respected New River Community College in Dublin.

Pulaski County workers also have an impressive mix of job opportunities. Volvo Trucks North America is one of the largest employers along with the Pulaski Furniture Company and Pfizer.

For more information, contact the Pulaski County Chamber of Commerce at 4440 Cleburn Boulevard, Dublin 24084, or call (540) 674-1991. You also can go online at www.pulaskichamber.info.

Floyd County

Follow Highway 8 south from Christiansburg and you'll find yourself in Floyd County (population 13,874). Just as movie stars are attracted to Charlottesville, '60s-era holdouts have been migrating to Floyd for the past 40 years. Their tie-dyed counterculture communes nestle quietly along with small farms in a county that promotes a small employer such as Chateau Morrisette Winery as one of its major industries. Many residents live quietly off the land. Someone has described Floyd

County as "going to a 4-H camp and taking a turn to the Age of Aquarius."

A planned counterculture community has established several self-sufficient eco-villages in Floyd County. These international communities focus on sustainable agriculture, spiritual development, and art.

Just don't go to Floyd actively looking for the counterculture. They have ingratiated themselves to the local farmers with their true sense of community spirit and are safely tucked away in the hills of Floyd, bothering no one and expecting the same treatment. The followers of this alternative lifestyle are most visible elsewhere, actually, at regional arts and crafts shows, where they sell their wares ranging from twisted grapevine baskets to tie-dyed and batik clothing and pottery. However, you don't have to leave Floyd to buy their wares.

One of the most prolific and amazing arts and crafts stores in the Blue Ridge, New Mountain Mercantile, 6 miles off the Blue Ridge Parkway on Locust Street, is the central location for area craftspeople to display and sell their wares. You can spend hours investigating the building, art gallery, and upstairs Byrd's Walden Pond Products, which offers self-help tapes and herbal body care, among other back-to-the-earth products.

Locals also can be found hanging out at the Blue Ridge Restaurant, in an early 1900s bank building.

The most famous regional landmark for both locals and tourists is the inimitable Floyd Country Store, where every Friday and Saturday is a hoedown! The Jamborees offer pure mountain music and dancing and a fun, friendly family atmosphere. Next door is the largest distributor of bluegrass and old-time music in the world. Other places that endear Floyd County to shoppers seeking the wild and wonderful are Schoolhouse Fabrics, housed in what was once an 1846 school, and Chateau Morrisette Winery in Meadows of Dan (see our Shopping and Wineries chapters for the whole scoop). In 2000 Floyd saw another winery open, Boundary Rock Farm and Vineyard, a family-run farm, which also grows grapes and blueberries to sell at the markets.

The most famous national landmark here is the picturesque Mabry Mill Blue Ridge Parkway Visitor Center, campground, and recreation area. The restaurant here is quite good. The real feast, however, is one for the senses at the old-time, water-powered gristmill and interpretive historical buildings. This is usually the first place western Virginians take internationals for a true taste of American history and beauty.

The history of Floyd is actually rather sketchy, according to its chamber of commerce. Early land surveys showed an attempt to settle the area in 1740. The county was officially formed from Montgomery County in 1831. Floyd's original name was Jacksonville, named for Andrew Jackson, our nation's seventh president. Incorporated in 1858, the town changed its name to Floyd in 1896, although no one knows the official reason why.

When you visit the New River Valley, take a day to check out Floyd County, mingle with the locals, see some terrific arts and crafts, and listen to some of the best bluegrass and gospel you'll ever hear. Floyd County truly is a sightseer's delight and photographer's paradise with the Blue Ridge Parkway's misty mountain views and miles of split-log fences. A map is smart when traveling Floyd's miles of rural, obscure back roads. You can receive this map and other information from the Floyd County Chamber of Commerce, P.O. Box 510, Floyd 24091, (540) 745-4407. The chamber is located on 108 South Locust Street. Check out the Web site at www .visitfloyd.org.

ALLEGHANY HIGHLANDS
Alleghany County

Lovers of the outdoors, sports, antiques, railroads, history, and good food can find their favorite things in Alleghany County (population 12,926). The county, situated on the Allegheny mountain range and half covered by the George Washington and Jefferson National Forests, is the western gateway to Virginia. This vacation playground filled with gorgeous scenery is next door to wild, wonderful West Virginia's Greenbrier County, home of the world-famous Greenbrier Resort.

Before the formation of Alleghany County, property records were provided from Fincastle in Botetourt County, a two-day trip. So, in 1822, the County of Alleghany was formed, named after the mountains in which it lies, although the county name was spelled differently than that of the mountains.

Its county seat, Covington, was named in honor of Gen. Leonard Covington, hero of the War of 1812 and confidant to James Madison and Thomas Jefferson. Clifton Forge, the county's other populous area, was named for its iron production; it contributed cannons and cannonballs to the Civil War effort. During the Civil War, Alleghany County furnished more soldiers to the Confederacy than it had voters and suffered greatly in the war, since it was located next to West Virginia, which joined the Union.

After the war, Clifton Forge was selected by the Chesapeake and Ohio (C & O) Railway as the site of its new depot. The coming of the railroad triggered economic growth, and in 1906 Clifton Forge received its city charter. Natural resources have always been Alleghany County's main industry; hemp, used in rope production, was an early product. The biggest boost to industrial progress came in 1899, when the West Virginia Pulp and Paper Co. decided to put a mill in Covington. The railroad and Mead–Westvaco Paper Mill continue to play important roles in the county's culture and economy.

Many of the county's attractions are tied to its history. In the charming historic city of Clifton Forge, the C & O Historical Society preserves the railroad's artifacts and equipment. Also worth a visit is the Alleghany Highlands Arts and Crafts Center, displaying fine regional arts and crafts (see our Arts chapter).

Lucy Selina Furnace stacks, more than 100 feet tall, are reminders of the area's 19th-century iron industry. A stunning Victorian mansion built by the owner of the rich iron mines has been turned into the charming Fernstone Manor. Local lore says a staff of eight was required just to maintain its gardens.

Nearby is the Longdale Recreation Area, which features miles of mountain trails, camping, and sand-beach swimming. All are off I-64's exit 10 on Highway 269 in Longdale. Roaring Run Recreation Area, the site of the ruins of an 1838 iron furnace, is another wonderful place to hike and picnic. It's off US 220 S.

Other historic points of interest are Fort Young, a reconstruction of the original French and Indian War fort off I-64, exit 4, near Covington. Lovers of architecture will enjoy seeing Oakland Grove Presbyterian Church, which served as a hospital during the Civil War. It can be seen in Selma off I-64, exit 7.

Outdoorsy fun awaits at several other Alleghany County sites. Twelve miles of water entice visitors to Lake Moomaw, a relatively new lake formed for power generation 19 miles from Covington. (See our Recreation chapter.) Residents and visitors have taken advantage of waterskiing, boating, fishing, and swimming. Douthat State Park's 50-acre lake also offers a beach, boating, excellent trout fishing, restaurant, and lodge, as well as cabins, campgrounds, and miles of hiking trails.

Rock lovers will want to visit Rainbow Gap or Iron Gate Gorge, which create a geologist's paradise a mile south of Clifton Forge on US 220. For 12 million years, the Jackson River has been working on this masterpiece.

The people are friendly and downright glad to see you in Alleghany County. Brochures of all the area's attractions can be picked up at the Jerry's Run Virginia Welcome Center on I-64 in Covington. Or contact the Alleghany Highlands Chamber of Commerce at 241 West Main Street, Covington 24426, (540) 962-2178. The Web address is www.ahchamber.com.

Bath County

Nestled between Alleghany and Highland Counties and bordering West Virginia, Bath County (population 4,900) doesn't even have a stoplight. What it does have attracts visitors, whether they're on a budget or staying at the world-famous Homestead Resort.

The bubbly mineral springs, or baths, that gave the county its name are a source of pleasure for visitors. Bath County was founded in 1745 by pioneers of mostly Scotch-Irish descent, most notably John Lewis, who settled at Fort Lewis. One son, Charles, died in the historic Battle of Point Pleasant in 1774. The other son, John, built the first hotel on the site of the present Homestead Resort in 1766. His structure was destroyed by fire in 1901. In the meantime, M.E. Ingalls, president of the Chesapeake and Ohio Railroad, bought the site, and the modern era of the resort was launched.

Some historic sites in the county are the Hidden Valley Bed-and-Breakfast (formerly called Warwickton Mansion), site of the movie *Sommersby;* Three Hills Inn, home of early-1900s Civil War novel writer Mary Johnston; and Windy Cove Presbyterian Church at Millboro.

The real history of the county, however, lies in its springs, which have been drawing people for more than 200 years. Wrote one visitor in 1750, "The spring water is very clear and warmer than new milk." Thermal springs are found at Warm Springs, Hot Springs, and Bolar Springs, at temperatures ranging from 77 to 106 degrees F. They flow at rates ranging from 2,500 to 5,000 gallons a minute. The water has a soft fizz of tickling bubbles, and taking the baths is like lowering yourself into a warm vat of Quibell.

Public pools have been open at Warm Springs since 1761 and look today much as they did then. The covered pools were the cultural center of the rich and famous. Thomas Jefferson "took the waters" here for his health, as did the frail Mrs. Robert E. Lee (she had crippling arthritis), whose chair, used to lower her into the pool, is still on display at the ladies' pool.

Thus, the stage was set for the aristocracy to visit this scenic land, which is nearly 90 percent forest. That's how the internationally known Homestead resort, detailed in the Resorts chapter, came into being. As Bath County celebrated its bicentennial in 1991, the Ingalls family celebrated its 100th year of running the famous Homestead. It was purchased in 1993 by Resorts International of Dallas, Texas, and was extensively renovated. The Homestead offers the superlatives of everything—recreation, dining, shopping—in a setting of style and grandeur equaled only by its neighbor, the Greenbrier, in nearby White Sulphur Springs, West Virginia.

The same crowd that goes to the Homestead are regulars at an absolutely serendipitous place, Garth Newel Music Center. The sound of critically acclaimed chamber music wafts through the mountains throughout the year, attracting cultured people from around the world. You never know which celebrity you'll see there taking in a concert while staying at the Homestead or visiting friends at a country estate. Locals leave them alone, though.

You don't need to be wealthy, however, to really enjoy your stay in Bath County. The county has a number of nice bed-and-breakfast inns and an outstanding one, Fort Lewis Lodge. At Fort Lewis, spring and summer offer lazy tubing down the placid Cowpasture River, hiking, and camping. It's a wholesome, airy retreat the whole family will enjoy (see our Bed-and-Breakfasts and Country Inns chapter).

Dining is a pleasure here as well. The Waterwheel Restaurant at the Inn at Gristmill Square, restored by the Hirsh family, is the center of Warm Springs, with its dining, shops, and lodging.

Spelunkers will find adventures in Burnsville's large caverns and sunken caves, while the forests and mountains beckon those who hike, hunt, fish, or ride. The George Washington and Jefferson National Forests and Gathright Game Management Area are in the county.

The Bath County Chamber of Commerce has a visitors brochure that will tell you everything you need to know about this natural, genteel land. Contact them at P.O. Box 718, Hot Springs 24445, (800) 628-8092, or (540) 839-5409. Check them out online at www.bathcountyva.org.

Highland County

Nicknamed the Switzerland of Virginia, scenic Highland County (population 2,500) has more sheep than people, on land with a higher mean elevation than any county east of the Mississippi River.

Few places have preserved their surroundings and privacy so well. Even Highland County's official brochure invites businesses to locate here providing their "environment won't be endangered." One of the most influential conservation groups in America, the Ruffled Grouse Society, was founded here in 1961.

Highland County was established in 1847 from the counties of Bath and Pendleton, in what is now West Virginia. Its county seat, Monterey (population 158), sits 3,000 feet above sea level, while its western border in the Allegheny Mountains reaches elevations of 4,500 feet.

Once the hunting grounds for the Shawnee, Highland was first entered by European settlers in the 1700s, when it was still a part of Augusta County, of which it remained until 1787. In the 10-year-long Indian War of 1754, the county was on the frontier. Highland men also made up the company that fought the Battle of Point Pleasant under the command of Col. Andrew Lewis.

An interesting note: German Gen. Erwin Rommel, the Desert Fox, visited Highland County prior to World War I so he could study Stonewall Jackson's military tactics at McDowell. Talk about biting the hand that feeds you! Later, Rommel used the same tactics against the United States and its allies.

To the visitor, Highland County is both beautiful and severe. Every March, this small population rallies to put on one of the top 20 festivals in America, the Highland County Maple Festival, which draws 70,000 over a two-weekend span. The festival takes you back to the time when tree sugar and tree 'lasses were found on every table, and when "opening" the trees and boiling down the sugar water were highland spring rituals. Pancake (with maple syrup, of course) and trout suppers centered around the county seat of Monterey are unforgettable.

A sugar tour winds through some of the loveliest spots in Virginia on Highways 637 and 640. Maple sugar camps throughout the county welcome visitors to view the actual process of syrup making, from tapping the trees to collecting the colorless, almost tasteless sugar water. Gathered in plastic buckets or by plastic tubing, the water is then boiled in kettles, pans, or evaporators until a barrel is finally reduced to a gallon of pure maple syrup. Tour maps of numerous camps are provided at the festival. One of the best things about the festival is tasting and shopping for all the pure maple syrup goodies—sugar candy, donuts glazed with maple syrup, and funnel cakes—available at a cost vastly below retail. Highland's downtown antiques stores also open for the occasion.

Summers are as cool here as any in the East. One word of warning: If you're driving in from another part of the Blue Ridge, expect to find snow on the ground as late as April, since Highland County gets about 65 inches of the white stuff a year. Bring jackets; the temperature will probably be at least 10 degrees colder than where you came from.

Outside of the maple culture, there are other interesting places to visit. If you want to see where many of those mouth-watering trout come from—and part of the reason behind this area's distinction as Trout Capital of the Eastern United States—visit the Virginia Trout Company on US 220 north of Monterey. In business for 40 years, the facility hatches rainbow trout from eggs and raises them to adulthood. You can fish for your own, buy them frozen, or just watch them swim in the cold mountain water. The hatchery is open six days a week.

While you're in Highland County, you also can see the Confederate Breastworks (breast-high trenches) built in 1862 by 4,000 Confederate troops as a defense against Union soldiers. They are at the top of Shenandoah Mountain on US 250 at the Highland-Augusta County line.

Also on US 250 east of McDowell is the McDowell Battlefield, where 4,500 Confederate troops under Gen. Stonewall Jackson defeated 2,268 Union soldiers in a bloody conflict in 1862. This engagement was the first victory in Jackson's famous Valley Campaign. Nearby McDowell Presbyterian Church was used as a hospital, and soldiers are buried there.

People enjoy Highland as much for what is missing—traffic, pollution, noise, and crowds—as for what is there. The pace is slow and the scenery beautiful. It's considered the best place in Virginia to bird-watch, and fans say species that have flown the coop from other parts of the state can still be found here.

If you feel like flying the coop yourself, come to Highland and slow down. Contact the Highland County Chamber of Commerce at P.O. Box 223, Monterey 24465, (540) 468-2550. You can stop by the Highland Center on Spruce Street or go online to www.highlandcounty.org to order brochures or a relocation packet.

GETTING AROUND

We've long been reminded by the travel industry that "getting there is half the fun." In Virginia's Blue Ridge, drive on the scenic roads, fly into mountain-ringed airports, or take efficient metro bus systems to your favorite destinations. You'll find that the old axiom is true: Getting here is a pleasure unto itself.

With its beautiful scenic mountains and interesting historical sites, Virginia is one of the most popular destinations in the Southeast. The Blue Ridge of Virginia is second only to Williamsburg among tourism destinations in the Old Dominion.

Travel experiences to the Blue Ridge are often among the most memorable and relaxing of times for visitors. But it helps to be armed with the right maps and travel information.

HIGHWAYS AND BYWAYS

The Blue Ridge of Virginia is laced with world-renowned tourism routes such as the Skyline Drive and the Blue Ridge Parkway, as well as scenic byways. All lead to their own wonderlands of hiking trails and magic mountain moments. (See our chapter on the Blue Ridge Parkway and Skyline Drive.) An interesting route is the "Smart Highway," a 6-mile connector road from Blacksburg to Interstate 81.

i *To avoid getting an expensive ticket, be sure to obey the High Occupancy Vehicles laws when traveling in Northern Virginia on Interstate 66, Interstate 95, Interstate 395, or the Dulles Toll Road. Read the signs. HOV2 means two travelers must be in the car to drive on the marked lanes. HOV3 means three passengers in a car.*

Before you begin your trip, be sure to write the Commonwealth for two essential maps: the Virginia State Transportation Map and the Map of Scenic Roads in Virginia. You can order both from the Virginia Department of Transportation, 1401 East Broad Street, Richmond 23219, (804) 786-2801 or visit www.virginiadot.org.

Major Highways

For modern highway efficiency, the Blue Ridge offers I-81 and Interstate 64, which intersect in the Shenandoah Valley. These are two of the busiest interstate roads in the Southeast. The Blue Ridge Parkway and the Skyline Drive run parallel to I-81, which passes through the Shenandoah Valley's major cities of Harrisonburg, Staunton, Lexington, Winchester, and Roanoke.

Intersecting I-81 is I-64, which runs from Charlottesville west to West Virginia and east to Richmond.

East of the Blue Ridge, U.S. Highway 29 running north and south connects smaller towns to the more metropolitan Lynchburg, while U.S. Highway 460 runs east and west, intersecting Bedford and Lynchburg before proceeding westward through the New River Valley. If you want rest stops with bathroom facilities, stick to I-81. Otherwise, you'll find the going mountainous and slow.

Byways

For beauty and adventure, the Blue Ridge byways have it all: more than 2,000 miles of special roads that offer something for everyone. A journey along the Blue Ridge

of Virginia's scenic roads is one that is measured in memories instead of miles.

As an example, one of the most beautiful of these is Highway 39 to Goshen Pass, outside of Lexington. Point yourself west and head out of town. Before long, you'll come upon the Virginia Horse Center, a modern facility that operates year-round and hosts horse show auctions, festivals, and educational clinics (see our Horse Country chapter).

From this point on, the elevation increases to Goshen Pass. Here, you'll find easy access to roadside pulloffs from which you might see someone fishing or kayaking. These are perfect spots for a picnic, followed by some relaxation, as you daydream to the soothing sounds of the Maury River's rippling waters.

Continuing, you'll enter George Washington and Jefferson National Forests, surrounded by natural beauty and a world at peace with itself. Next will come Warm Springs, which got its name from the natural mineral springs that make places such as the Homestead resort famous.

As you continue your journey toward the West Virginia border, you'll pass Hidden Valley Recreation Area and Blowing Springs Recreation Area, providing opportunities for camping, hiking, and fishing.

At the end of Highway 39, we guarantee a refreshment of mind, spirit, and body. Such are the miracles of the Blue Ridge byways. Many more are outlined on the special map provided by the commonwealth, (804) 786-2838.

Far southwestern Virginia is notorious for its rugged mountain roads that wind through coalfields, tunnels, and mountain passes. These routes confounded even adventurous Daniel Boone, who steered clear of certain areas while leading settlers down the Wilderness Trail through the Cumberland Gap in 1775.

The Blue Ridge has come a long way since then. Daniel Boone and his entourage could never have imagined the well-placed private and major public airports that provide access to tourism and industry.

AIRPORTS

Both public and private airports, some convenient to major resorts, are an important means for out-of-state tourists to visit the area. More than 300 airports serve travelers in Virginia. These range from grass landing strips to large international facilities. Commercial airports generate 35 percent of the air industry's economic impact in Virginia, while general aviation airports account for only 7 percent. Yet the importance of general aviation in the Blue Ridge is recognized by a constant upgrading of the existing air transportation system.

Of the existing system in the Blue Ridge, three large airports—Charlottesville, Roanoke, and Lynchburg—receive varied commercial passenger service. They also provide a wide range of general aviation services for corporate and private aircraft. Others, such as the renovated Shenandoah Valley Regional at Weyers Cave and Ingalls Field, next to the Homestead resort in Bath County, have limited scheduled flights. The majority of Blue Ridge airports are designed to accommodate single-engine and light twin-engine aircraft, which represent more than 90 percent of Virginia's aircraft.

In this chapter, we list the commercial airports, north to south, then the remaining scheduled service and general aviation airports.

Commercial Airports

Washington Dulles International Airport
45020 Aviation Drive, Sterling
(703) 572-2700
www.mwaa.com
Located at the northern tip of the Blue Ridge, Dulles Airport in Loudoun and Fairfax Counties is the perfect place for out-of-state travelers to begin their journey to the beautiful Blue Ridge Mountains of Virginia.

Consider renting a car from one of the nine rental agencies at the airport. Take

If you will be driving in Virginia's busier localities for an extended time, you might consider purchasing a Smart Tag. These tags allow you to prepay your tolls so you won't have to wait at toll-booths. This automated toll collection system is used on the Dulles Toll Road, a 14-mile highway from the Capital Beltway west to Washington Dulles International Airport. The tags also work for toll roads in Richmond, Chesapeake, and heading to the Outer Banks of North Carolina. Visit www.smart-tag.com or call (888) 327-8655.

Route 28 to I–66 to I–81 and take the scenic Skyline Drive across the Blue Ridge Mountains as a starter. Alternatively, take Route 28 to Route 7 to historic Leesburg. Continue through the renowned Virginia horse country in Middleburg in Loudoun County and Fauquier County. Refer to the Horse Country chapter to maximize your experience.

Dulles Airport is home to 40 airlines flying to 72 U.S. cities and 37 foreign destinations. There are an average of 1,500 flights in and out of the airport daily. This fluctuates with the international flight schedule. Dulles, which carries 20 million passengers a year, is served by 15 major domestic airlines, 8 regional airlines, and 20 major international airlines.

Besides the car rental agencies, there are limousines and taxis available. The Washington Flyer bus travels between Ronald Reagan Washington National Airport, West Falls Church Metro station, and Washington Dulles International Airport. There are 20,000 parking spaces, and a five-story 4,600-space daily parking garage opened in 2003.

Charlottesville–Albemarle Airport
100 Bowen Loop, Charlottesville
(434) 973-8341
www.gocho.com
Charlottesville–Albemarle Airport is 8 miles

north of Charlottesville in Albemarle County. It is accessible via US 29 and Highway 649. The airport is served by three airlines that provide 60 daily flights to and from major hubs in Atlanta, Charlotte, Pittsburgh, Philadelphia, LaGuardia, Cincinnati, and Washington Dulles. From these points, connections are available to more than 2,000 cities worldwide.

The terminal consists of a 60,000-square-foot building with three airline ticket counters and five airline gate areas, baggage claim space, a 500-space daily parking area and 61-space hourly parking lot. The gift shop carries magazines, books, and novelties.

Car rental and on-call taxi services are available. Many of the local hotels provide courtesy shuttle service to and from the airport.

The Charlottesville–Albemarle Airport's market includes Charlottesville and the counties of Albemarle, Greene, Madison, Culpeper, Orange, Louisa, Fluvanna, Nelson, Augusta, and Rockingham.

General aviation services are provided by Piedmont Hawthorne, (434) 978-1474, and include aircraft fueling, hangaring, and maneuvering. Auto rental service is provided at the general aviation terminal, and courtesy vehicles are also available.

Airlines: U.S. Airway Express, (800) 428–4322; United Express, (800) 241–6522; Delta Connection, (800) 221-1212

Car Rentals: Avis, (434) 973-6000; Hertz, (434) 297-4288; National, (434) 974-4664

Taxis: Taxi companies are available on a first-in, first-out basis and are typically waiting in front of the terminal.

Lynchburg Regional Airport
4308 Wards Road, Lynchburg
(434) 455–6090
www.lynchburgva.gov/airport
The Lynchburg Regional Airport is 6 miles south of Lynchburg in Campbell County and is accessible via US 29. The airport is served by two airlines that provide 22 departures per day to three major hub airports, including Charlotte, Atlanta, and

Pittsburgh international airports. From these points, connections are available to more than 200 domestic and international destinations.

The Lynchburg Airport's west central Virginia market area includes the cities of Bedford and Lynchburg and the counties of Amherst, Appomattox, Bedford, and Campbell.

Airport facilities consist of a 35,000-square-foot terminal building, with numerous counters, six airline gate areas, second-level boarding capabilities, and a 400-space daily parking area. A new addition that opened in May 2004 is a kiosk that sells fresh, hot foods including burgers and sandwiches as well as salads, bagels, fresh fruits, and specialty coffee beverages. The prices are reasonable, and you can enjoy your meal at one of the tables overlooking the runway.

Car rental and on-call taxi service also serve the airport. A number of hotels provide courtesy shuttle van service to and from their properties.

General aviation services are provided by Virginia Aviation, (800) 543-6845, for aircraft fueling, hangaring, maneuvering, and flight instruction. This company also provides aircraft repair services, aircraft rentals and charter services, parking, and tie-down.

In the spring of 2003, the Lynchburg airport, through Delta Connection carrier Atlanta Southeast Airlines, offered customers the first regional jet service. The new flights replaces the 30-passenger Embraer Brasilia turboprop aircraft. This increased the number of seats available to customers each day by 33 percent.

Airlines: Delta Connection/Atlantic Southeast Airlines, (800) 221-1212; and U.S. Airways Express, (800) 428-4322

Car Rentals: Avis, (434) 239-3622, (800) 831-2847; Budget, (434) 237-6284, (800) 763-2999; Hertz, (800) 654-3131

Taxi/Limousine: Airport Limo, (434) 239-1777; K&J Limousine, (866) 557-3326

Parking: Republic Parking Systems, (434) 239-7574

Roanoke Regional Airport
**5202 Aviation Drive NW, Roanoke
(540) 362-1999
www.roanokeairport.com**

Roanoke Regional Airport is 3 miles northwest of Roanoke via Interstate 581. It is served by four major airlines or their regional affiliates, which make 38 departures per day to 8 major hub airports, including New York, Atlanta, Chicago, and Detroit. From these points, connections are available to any location all over the world. The Roanoke Regional Airport's market includes the cities of Roanoke and Radford and the counties of Alleghany, Bedford, Botetourt, Craig, Franklin, Floyd, Giles, Montgomery, Roanoke, Pulaski, and Wythe.

The airport's dramatic glass-front, 96,000-square-foot building features four Jetway loading bridges, a modern baggage handling system, and a panoramic view of the Blue Ridge Mountains. Parking is ample, with 1,038 daily and 227 hourly parking spaces. Other features are an on-site travel agency, a First Union Bank ATM, a snack bar, a restaurant and gift shop, a lounge, a telephone hotel reservation system, and free wireless access in the entire terminal.

Ground transportation is available from car rental companies and two on-call limousine services. A number of hotels provide courtesy shuttle van service to and from their properties. There are also taxis available.

Piedmont Hawthorne Aviation, (540) 563-4401, provides general aviation services including aircraft fueling, hangaring, and maneuvering. Piedmont Hawthorne also offers aircraft maintenance, as does

---

The Washington Flyer, a connector bus service, travels between West Falls Church Metro (Washington, D.C., subway station), and Washington Dulles International Airport.

Roanoke Aero Services, (540) 563-5212. Air charters are offered by Piedmont Hawthorne, Executive Air Inc., (540) 362-9728, and a host of other companies.

Airlines: U.S. Airways Express, (800) 428-4322; United Express, (800) 864-8331; Northwest Airlink, (800) 225-2525; Comair, the Delta Connection, (800) 354-9822; ASA, Delta Connection, (800) 282-3424

Car Rentals: Avis, (540) 366-2436; Budget, (540) 265-7328; Enterprise, (540) 563-8055; Hertz, (540) 366-3421; National/Alamo, (540) 563-5050

Ground Transportation: Cartier Limousine, (540) 982-5466; Roanoke Airport Limo, (540) 345-7710; Yellow Cab, (540) 345-7711; Liberty Cab, (540) 344-1776

Parking: (540) 362-0630

General Aviation Airports

Winchester Regional Airport
491 Airport Road, Winchester
(540) 662-5786

This airport at the northern end of the Shenandoah Valley is 2 miles south of Winchester and 42 miles northwest of Washington Dulles International. Operated from 7:00 A.M. to 7:00 P.M. weekdays and 7:00 A.M. to 5:00 P.M. weekends, the airport has 24-hour U.S. Customs service, but you need to make arrangements ahead of time. After-hours service is available to pilots along with an all-weather access Localizer NDB approach, automated weather observation system, Pan Am WeatherMation, and a 5,500-foot runway with pilot-activated lighting. An executive meeting room with audiovisual equipment, fax, and computer modem access makes business travel easier.

Available on field is flight instruction, two flight schools, and aircraft maintenance facilities. Car rentals are also available through prearranged reservations. Nightly tie-down fee is $5.00.

Front Royal–Warren County Airport
229 Stokes Airport Road, Front Royal
(540) 635-3570

The airport is nestled in the beautiful Civil War Historic Shenandoah Valley, at the base of the Skyline Drive and Massanutten mountains. From dusk to dawn, accessible activities include bicycle trails, camping, bed-and-breakfasts, and a variety of restaurants. A new facility includes a terminal building; 3,000-by-100-foot lighted runway with fuel, hangars, and ramp space; and overnight parking for $5.00. Also available are scenic flights for $45.00 for 20 minutes, flight training, on-demand charter, and maintenance.

Sky Bryce Airport
County Road 836, off Highway 263, Basye
(540) 856-2121
www.bryceresort.com

This unattended private airport with a 2,240-foot asphalt runway is within walking distance of Bryce Resort, a large recreational family resort offering year-round activities. No fuel or maintenance is available. The airport is open for daylight VFR operations only. The landing fee is $5.00.

Luray Caverns Airport
1504 Airport Road
(540) 743-6070

Luray Caverns Airport has a 3,125-foot paved, lighted runway, sells fuel, has overnight tie-downs, and charges no fees for incoming craft. Between the world-famous Luray Caverns and the Caverns Country Club Resort, this facility offers free transportation from the airport to all Luray Caverns facilities. Luray also offers sightseeing flights and area tours of the Blue Ridge Mountains, ranging from $60 to $120.

New Market Airport
59 River Road, New Market
(540) 740-3949
www.risingphoenixaviation.com

This airport 2 miles west of historic New

Market and the Shenandoah Valley Travel Association Visitor Center has a flight training school, sightseeing rides, hot-air ballooning, aircraft rental, and radio-operated lights. Also available are maintenance, inspection, a pilot and novelty shop, and 24-hour self-service fueling. Hours of operation are 9:00 A.M. to 5:00 P.M. Monday through Friday, and 9:00 A.M. to 3:00 P.M. Saturday. Tie-down is $5.00 nightly. Enterprise Car Rental will deliver from Harrisonburg.

Bridgewater Air Park
1402 Airport Road, Bridgewater
(540) 828-6070
www.dynamicaviation.com
Operated by Dynamic Aviation Group and close to Bridgewater College, this airport sells fuel and has limited overnight tie-down sites at no fee. Hours of operation are 9:00 A.M. to 1:00 P.M. weekdays. Taxi service is available from Harrisonburg.

Orange County Airport
19103 Constitution Highway, Orange
(540) 672-2158
This small airport off Route 20 has a 3,200-foot runway and a small terminal. It also offers 100 low-lead fuel and Jet A Fuel. There are tie-downs for $15 a month, but tie-downs for the day are free. This is an interesting airport to visit, as the Sky-dive Orange parachute club does most of their dives here, daily in the summer and Wednesday, Friday, and weekends in the winter. You can find out more by calling (540) 672-5054 or checking out their Web site at www.skydiveorange.com.

Shenandoah Valley Regional Airport
77 Aviation Circle, Weyers Cave
(540) 234-8304
www.flyshd.com
Shenandoah Valley Regional Airport is centrally located to serve the cities of Harrisonburg, Staunton, and Waynesboro and the counties of Augusta and Rockingham. The 10,000-square-foot General Aviation Terminal Building offers fixed base services, including fuel. Two terminals offer

To help you navigate busy I-81, Virginia has a helpful number, 511. Just call to find out road, weather, and traffic conditions. You can even find out about nearby attractions, restaurants, hotels, gas stations, locksmiths, tow trucks, and veterinarians. If you are outside the I-81 region, call (800) 578-4111.

free use of PanAm WeatherMation and Automated Weather Observation System. An executive meeting room with audiovisual equipment and computer modem access make business travel easier.

Services available include air-charter service, corporate management services, aircraft rental, flight instruction, a restaurant, a testing facility, and aircraft maintenance facilities. Airline service is provided by U.S. Airways, (540) 234-9257, with daily departures to Pittsburgh. Ground transportation is provided by local taxi services, which include Waynesboro City Taxi, (540) 949-8245; Yellow Cab, (540) 434-2515; and Staunton City Taxi, (540) 886-3471. Also available is limo service from AB Luxury Suburban Airport and Limousine Service, (540) 248-0597; and Rodney's Limousine Service, (540) 448-4688. Rental cars are available from Avis, (540) 234-9961; Hertz, (540) 234-9411; and Enterprise, (800) 736-8222.

Eagles Nest
249 Aero Drive, Waynesboro
(540) 943-4447
www.eaglesnest.aero
Close to Wintergreen Resort, Eagles Nest offers fuel and mechanical service, with one mechanic on the field. The tie-down fee is $5.00 nightly, but if you buy fuel, the fee will be waived. Aircraft rental and instruction are available.

Virginia Tech Montgomery Executive Airport
1600 Ramble Road, Blacksburg
(540) 231-4444
Adjacent to the Virginia Tech Corporate

Research Center and a mile from the main 24,000-student campus, this busy airport is situated on the Eastern Continental Divide at 2,134 feet above sea level. Since 2004, the airport has been run by an airport authority. A terminal features a large lounge, pilot lounge, and unique architecture sporting the old beams of the original hangar. The runway is lighted and complemented by full-instrument approach capabilities. Hard-surface tie-downs cost $5.00 nightly. The $8.00 twin-engine first-night fee is waived with the purchase of fuel. Nearby car rental services include Enterprise Car Rental, (540) 552-0455. Taxi service can be arranged.

New River Valley Airport
5391 CV Jackson Road, Dublin
(540) 674-4141

Two miles north of Dublin, New River offers fuel, tie-down, and hangar space, when available. Flight training and aircraft rental is available. The runway is 6,200 feet long with ILS. Rental cars are available from Enterprise in town. The airport is within a short drive of Radford University and Virginia Tech and close to New River Community College.

Culpeper Regional Airport
12517 Beverly Ford Road (Route 676)
(540) 825-8280

The 5,000-by-100-foot runway and enlarged parking apron accommodates all types of corporate and private aircraft. Capital improvements include lighting, the expansion of the runway, and taxiways. Services include flight and ground school, ramp services, mechanical repair and parts, and tie-down for $5.00 for single engine and $10.00 for twin engine per night.

Falwell Aviation Inc.
4332 Richmond Highway, Lynchburg
(434) 845-8769

Falwell, within the city limits of Lynchburg, offers fuel, maintenance, hangar space, flight instruction, aircraft rental, and turbojet, turboprop, and piston aircraft for charter. No landing or parking fees are

charged, but it costs $2.50 for overnight tie-down.

New London Airport
114 Wheel Drive, Forest
(434) 525-2988

Between Lynchburg and Smith Mountain Lake, this airport offers fuel and minor maintenance. There is no tie-down fee. Skydiving is available. Auto drag races are held at the airport 11 times a year.

Smith Mountain Lake Airport
1090 Cutless Road, Moneta
(540) 297-4500

Adjacent to Virginia's largest lake, Smith Mountain Lake Airport offers fuel and sightseeing flights to see the lake or Peaks of Otter. Tie-down is $5.00 a day and $10.00 overnight.

Ingalls Field
Highway 703, Hot Springs
(540) 839-5326

Gateway to the world-famous Homestead Resort, Ingalls Field might have no planes one day and look like O'Hare the next, depending on which conventions are meeting in the area. Because of the nature of its largest client, the Homestead resort, catering is available. It is the highest public airport in elevation east of the Mississippi River that can service jets.

Rental cars and limo service are available to Hot Springs, Warm Springs, and other Bath County points of interest. Overnight tie-down, parking fees, and landing fees depend on the size of incoming aircraft. Fuel prices are reasonable.

METRO BUS LINES

Due to increased concern over energy consumption, ozone pollution, and other critical issues facing the planet, public transportation is no longer just an alternative but an environmentally responsible way to travel. Major cities in the Blue Ridge offer bus transportation that is clean, accessible, and inexpensive.

For a guide to public transportation in Virginia, call the Virginia Division of Tourism at (804) 786–4484 or (800) 824–3866. You'll receive a state highway map prepared by the Virginia Department of Transportation.

Greater Roanoke Valley Metro Transit Company
1108 Campbell Avenue SE, Roanoke
(540) 982-0305
www.valleymetro.com
Greater Roanoke Valley Metro Transit Company is Roanoke's regional transportation system, serving more than 5,500 passengers daily with its fleet of 42 buses. It has an extensive outreach program and tries hard to accommodate everyone from eager tourists to the disabled, who are given special consideration with STAR service.

The modern main terminal, Campbell Court, is in the heart of the thriving shopping district, across from First Union Bank on Campbell Avenue. Efficient and modern, the service is highly regarded by locals.

Riders may send for a bus guide in advance. Exact fare or your ticket should be ready, since bus drivers do not carry change. Weekly passes are available.

Started in August 2004, the Smartway Bus links Roanoke, Salem, Christiansburg, and Blacksburg. Call (800) 388-7005. No smoking, eating, or drinking is permitted on the vehicles. Signal the bus operator a block before you want to get off. Service is provided to Bedford and there is limited service to Roanoke County.

Loudoun Transit Service
109 North Bailey Lane, Purcellville
(540) 338-1610
www. transitservices.org
Loudoun County offers three main routes to help combat the traffic congestion in bustling Northern Virginia. The Leesburg Fix Route operates 8:30 A.M. to 5:30 P.M. Monday through Friday. The Sterling Service is a cross-county route that links Loudoun Hospital Center at Landsdowne

to Sterling. Senior citizens can ride this route for free on Thursday. The Western Loudoun Service is a first-come, first-serve, curb-to-curb route that travels from Leesburg to Sterling. Loudoun Transit also offers JAM. This service gives you transportation to your workplace, but you need to call in advance to set up a standing reservation.

Also in Loudoun County there is another transit, the Loudoun County Commuter Bus Service that links riders from commuter parking lots at Great Falls to Washington, D.C. and the Pentagon. This weekday service includes a fleet of 19 55-seat buses, each equipped with its own bathroom. Call (877) 465-2287.

Charlottesville Transit Service (CTS)
315 Fourth Street NW, Charlottesville
(434) 434–RIDE, (434) 296-7433
www.charlottesville.org/transit
The City of Charlottesville's Transit Service and University Transit work together to provide dependable, efficient, convenient, and safe transportation. Riders may send for a bus guide in advance. When riding, you should have exact fare or a ticket. Tickets may be purchased at City Hall, Piedmont Virginia Community College, Fourth Street, or at the University Transit office on Millmont Street, (434) 924-7711. Most routes operate from 6:20 A.M. to

For those traveling I-64 over Afton Mountain, there is now a way to see weather conditions before you even take to the road. Call 511 or go to www.travel shenandoah.com and click on "Travel Conditions." A map appears along with a Web cam icon. When you point to the icon, a video shot of I-64 and Route 250 at Afton Mountain appears, as well as a summary of weather conditions. I-64 at Afton Mountain's higher elevations is known for its fog because of the colliding warm and cold air masses, and for its icy conditions in the winter.

midnight. For a great way to get around central Charlottesville and the university, and avoid some of the parking and traffic hassles, hop on the free trolley that travels from downtown Charlottesville to the University of Virginia central grounds, and "the Corner" from 6:30 A.M. to midnight, Monday through Saturday. The guide clearly marks designated transfer points and routes in various colors. Eating, drinking, and smoking are not permitted. Two front seats may be reserved for senior citizens or those with disabilities.

Blacksburg Transit
2800 Commerce Street, Blacksburg
(540) 961-1185
www.btransit.org
This bus service can really come in handy when it comes to combating the traffic of this sprawling university town. It serves Blacksburg and the large campus of Virginia Tech. Catch a ride 6:30 A.M. to 12:45 A.M. Monday through Wednesday, 6:30 A.M. to 2:45 A.M. Thursday and Friday, 8:00 A.M. to 2:45 A.M. Saturday, and 10:00 A.M. to 11:30 P.M. on Sunday. You must have correct change or a monthly pass.

Greater Lynchburg Transit Company
825 Kemper Street, Lynchburg
(434) 847-7771
www.gltconline.com
The Kemper Street Station has served Lynchburg continuously since 1912, first as a busy train station for Southern Railway. As commercia6l air travel increased during the 1960s, use of Kemper Street station waned. By the 1990s, the building was in shambles. The late 1990s brought renewed interest in the station and money for renovation, including the addition of bus services. After Amtrak moved to the track level in 2001, Greyhound Bus Lines and the Greater Lynchburg Transit Company's customer service center opened offices on the street level of the station in January 2002.

Housed with the Greyhound Terminal, Greater Lynchburg Transit Company operates 11 routes serving the City of Lynchburg and parts of Amherst County. Its fleet of more than two dozen buses radiates from a main terminal at Plaza Shopping Center, the only transfer point between Memorial Avenue and Lakeside Drive. It arrives at Plaza Shopping Center every half hour. You can write for a bus guide or pick one up on any bus or at the transit office. Exact fare or a pass is required. The Greater Lynchburg Transit Company Trolley is a replica of streetcars of old. It can be rented for special events such as weddings and store openings (in the Lynchburg area only).

Harrisonburg Public Transportation
475 East Washington Street
Harrisonburg
(540) 432-0492
www.ci.harrisonburg.va.us
While you visit Harrisonburg, hop on this bus to get around town and to visit the campus of James Madison University. Because the bus serves both JMU students and citizens, the hours of operation are longer than in many localities in the Shenandoah Valley. It operates 7:00 A.M. to midnight Monday through Thursday, 7:00 A.M. to 3:00 A.M. Friday, 9:00 A.M. to 3:00 A.M. Saturday, and 11:00 A.M. to midnight on Sunday.

Virginia Regional Transit Association
Davis Street, Culpeper
(540) 829-0505
An 18-passenger bus serves the city, beginning at the train depot, heading to the hospital, doctors' offices, shopping centers, and grocery stores. The hours of operation are 7:00 A.M. to 5:00 P.M., Monday through Friday, and 9:30 A.M. to 2:30 P.M. Saturday. An on-demand bus was added to the county in October 2004.

TRANS-CITY BUS LINES

Greyhound cross-country buses serve major Blue Ridge cities, including Charlottesville, Lynchburg, Winchester, and Roanoke. A Greyhound bus leaves from

Charlottesville to Roanoke four times a day, and from Charlottesville to Washington, D.C., three times a day. Call (800) 231-2222 for more information, schedules, and prices. Or log on to www.greyhound.com.

RAILROADS

Many of the communities along the Blue Ridge sprang up along the railroad routes that crisscross the state. But with the advent of the automobile, trains began to fall out of favor. Today only a handful of cities have stops for passenger traffic. Amtrak runs two main routes through the Blue Ridge area, stopping for passengers on request at depots such as Culpeper.

The Cardinal route, from Union Station in D.C. to Chicago, has stops in Alexandria, Manassas, Culpeper, Charlottesville, Staunton, and Clifton Forge. This route operates on Sunday, Wednesday, and Friday.

The Crescent run, from Penn Station in New York to New Orleans, takes a more north-south route with in-state stops at Alexandria, Manassas, Culpeper, Charlottesville, Lynchburg, and Danville. This route operates daily. Since the Crescent line travels through Culpeper on its way to Washington, D.C., and New York each morning and returns again in the evening, residents can take it for day trips or commuting.

Options range from sleeper cars and coach seating to services for travelers with disabilities. For schedules and reservations, call Amtrak at (800) 872-7245, or find them online at www.amtrak.com.

HOTELS AND MOTELS

A key part to any vacation is finding a nice place to relax after a long day of sightseeing. The Blue Ridge has a wide selection of comfortable accommodations to fit any budget.

In this chapter, we provide a cross section of the motel and hotel options in our area. Remember, this is a guide, not a directory. The region is so big, we can't include every option available to travelers. But we can point you toward some of our favorites. See our Resorts and Bed-and-Breakfasts and Country Inns chapters for additional lodging choices. For those looking for something a little closer to the mountains, the Blue Ridge Parkway and Skyline Drive chapter also includes several cabins, lodges, and campgrounds.

PRICE CODE

Room rates vary according to location and degree of luxury, so we've categorized each property by using dollar signs based on the nightly rate for two people for a standard room.

$	less than $40
$$	$40 to $60
$$$	$61 to $85
$$$$	$86 and more

Unless we specify otherwise, major credit cards are accepted. Most hotels and motels do not allow pets, but we'll let you know the ones that do.

SHENANDOAH VALLEY
Frederick County

Hampton Inn $$$
1655 Apple Blossom Drive, Winchester
(540) 667-8011, (800) 426-7866
One of Winchester's newest facilities, this 100-room inn is just across the street from Shenandoah University. Amenities include a swimming pool, deluxe continental breakfast, free local phone calls, and free in-room movies. For the business-minded, ask about computer modem jacks and high-speed Internet access, or the business center with local Internet access and meeting room for small business meetings or private parties. More than 85 percent of the inn is nonsmoking. The newly remodeled inn is near several restaurants, historic sites, and a shopping mall. Children 18 and younger stay for free when accompanied by a parent.

Holiday Inn $$$
1017 Millwood Pike, Winchester
(540) 667-3300
www.holiday-inn.com
This 173-room motel is a convenient base of operations for exploring historic Winchester and is close to shopping malls and movie theaters. Amenities include nonsmoking rooms, free and pay movies, convenient parking, a swimming pool, a fitness center and exercise room, a restaurant, and a lounge. No matter which direction you're traveling, it's easy to find—right at the intersection of Interstate 81, U.S. Highway 50, U.S. Highway 17, and U.S. Highway 522.

Holiday Inn Express $$$
165 Town Run Lane, Stephens City
(540) 869-0909, (800) 785-7555
The newest hotel in Frederick County, the Express is within driving range of Olde Town, Belle Grove Plantation, and Wayside Theater. The 69-room inn offers an outdoor swimming pool, exercise room, an on-premise laundry and valet service, remote-control TV, a free breakfast bar, 24-hour coffee service, and free local calls.

There are nine king whirlpool suites, and refrigerators and microwaves are available in some rooms. The inn also features fax and copying services and meeting rooms that seat up to 30. Ask about discounts.

Shoney's Inn $$$
1347 Berryville Avenue, Winchester
(540) 665-1700, (800) 552-4667

George Washington didn't sleep here, but this hotel is within miles of the first president's office. Other nearby historical attractions include Stonewall Jackson's headquarters, Belle Grove Plantation, and Patsy Cline's birthplace. The inn features 98 rooms, including 13 king whirlpool rooms with microwaves and refrigerators. Amenities include an indoor pool, fitness room, sauna, free local calls, and cable TV. Continental breakfast and newspapers are available in the lobby. Fax service and meeting rooms are available. Shoney's Restaurant is adjacent to the inn. Children 18 and younger stay free in a parent's room. Discounts are available.

Wingate Inn $$$$
150 Wingate Drive, Winchester
(540) 678-4283, (877) 946-3585
www.winchesterwingate.com

Enjoy your stay in one of the 84 rooms at this pretty new hotel in Winchester, where you'll find high-quality amenities and comfort. Business folks will like the two-line desk phone with speaker, dataport voice mail, conference call capabilities, free high-speed Internet access, and cordless phone. There are also meeting facilities for up to 50 guests, an executive boardroom, and a 24-hour business center that is free to guests. For those who want to kick back a bit, the rooms feature a 25-inch color TV with a free movie channel, microwave, and refrigerator. The remodeled rooms also come with a coffeemaker, hair dryer, iron, ironing board, and safe. Guests can also enjoy an indoor pool, fitness center and whirlpool, and a full, hot breakfast.

Warren County

Quality Inn Skyline Drive $$$
10 Commerce Avenue, Front Royal
(540) 635-3161

The three-floor 108-room Quality Inn, near the northern entrance to the Skyline Drive, is a good overnight stop before going on the scenic highway. It's also convenient for exploring Front Royal or taking part in one of the town's excellent festivals. The motel rooms are comfortable and have irons and cable TV; some have microwaves and refrigerators. Mary B's Family Restaurant is open for breakfast, lunch, and dinner; several other restaurants also are nearby.

Shenandoah County

Hotel Strasburg $$$
213 South Holliday Street, Strasburg
(540) 465-9191
www.hotelstrasburg.com

This white clapboard structure was built as a hospital after the Civil War. Decorated in antique Victorian furniture and folk and fine art (all of which is for sale), the hotel is decidedly charming, from the comfortable public rooms to the second-story balcony porch. The 29 cozy guest rooms have private baths, nine with Jacuzzis, and are individually decorated with period furniture, quilts, Victorian wall and floor coverings, and classic window treatments. A banquet room was added in 1997. Other special touches are toiletries, fresh flowers, baskets of greenery, and big, fluffy towels. Suites and staterooms also include a sitting area. Three beautifully appointed dining rooms and a lounge serve excellent continental meals with a country touch. On weekdays continental breakfast is included in the price of a room. This grand old hotel is within walking distance of the massive Strasburg Emporium (see our Shopping chapter), Stonewall Jackson Museum at Hupp's Hill, Wayside Theater, and Half Moon Beach. Golf packages with nearby courses are available.

New Market Battlefield Days Inn $$$
9360 George Collins Parkway
New Market
(540) 740-4100, (800) 329-7466
www.daysinn.com
On May 15, 1864, Union troops occupied Manor's Hill while the Confederates grouped to the south on Shirley's Ridge. The Confederate troops enlisted the help of young cadets from Virginia Military Institute and pushed the Yankees north. Ninety percent of the battle and casualties occurred on Manor's Hill, where the New Market Battlefield Days Inn now stands. The New Market Battlefield Park Hall of Valor and Military Museum, dedicated to the cadets of VMI, is adjacent to the hotel. Other attractions in the area include Shenandoah and Endless caverns and the New Market historic district. The 85 guest rooms feature king-size or double beds, complimentary continental breakfast, and cable TV. The motel has an outdoor pool.

Quality Inn Shenandoah Valley $$$$
162 West Old Crossroads Street
New Market
(540) 740-3141, (800) 367-5151
www.qualityinn-shenandoahvalley.com
The Johnny Appleseed Restaurant and Apple Core Village Gift Shop are special attractions at this motel. Extra touches include in-room complimentary sunrise coffee and sunset cider. The 100 spacious rooms have free in-room movies, and the outdoor pool is a good spot for relaxing

afternoons. The inn also has a fitness room and miniature golf course and is near historic New Market, Luray Caverns, and the New Market Battlefield.

Ramada Inn $$$$
1130 Motel Drive, Woodstock
(540) 459-5000
Rooms in this 126-unit motel have all the creature comforts, including free satellite TV and an outdoor lounge. The Post Cards Restaurant serves three meals a day. Woodstock is a historic town, containing the oldest county courthouse (1792) in use west of the Blue Ridge Mountains. The town's lookout tower provides a spectacular view of the Seven Bends of the Shenandoah River. Wheelchair-accessible rooms are available.

The Shenvalee Golf Resort $$$
9660 Fairway Drive, New Market
(540) 740-3181
www.shenvalee.com
This 42-room lodge has rooms overlooking the fairway or at poolside. The 27-hole PGA golf course has a practice driving range and a fully equipped pro shop. The resort also has regulation tennis courts, a large swimming pool, and a fishing pond. You can take your meals in the dining room or visit the Sand Trap Tavern for a casual evening. To find the resort, take exit 264 off I-81 and go 1 mile on U.S. Highway 11 S.

Page County

Brookside Cabins $$$$
2978 U.S. Highway 211 E, Luray
(540) 743-5698, (800) 299-2655
www.brooksidecabins.com
Your hosts, Bob and CeCe Castle, oversee a rare sort of accommodation—luxury cabins, with resident peacocks adding a royal touch. These charming cabins have modern baths, queen-size beds, refrigerators, coffeemakers, elegant country decor, and air-conditioning and heat year-round. Front porches and private decks overlook a

If you are planning a spring break, don't forget about college graduations. Hundreds of parents and relatives will be looking for hotels in and around Charlottesville, Blacksburg, and Harrisonburg, so make your reservations well in advance.

brook. Some cabins have fireplaces and indoor hot tubs. The cabins are adjacent to the Brookside Restaurant, where home-style cooking is served in a family-style setting (see our Restaurants chapter). An art gallery and gift shop feature limited-edition prints, unique items from local artists and artisans, and other mementos of the Valley. The cabins are minutes from the Luray Caverns, Shenandoah National Park, the Skyline Drive, and New Market Battlefield.

Budget Inn $$$
320 West Main Street, Luray
(540) 743-5176, (800) 858-9800
Affordable, quiet, and clean—that's what travelers will find at this small, no-frills motel. Cable TV, microwaves, fridges, and phones are in each of the 33 rooms. King-size and double beds and nonsmoking rooms are available. A continental breakfast is offered, and several restaurants are 2 blocks away in downtown Luray.

Days Inn Luray $$$
138 Whispering Hill Road, Luray
(540) 743-4521
www.daysinn-luray.com
Of the 101 guest rooms, 15 are furnished with antiques, and eight rooms have Jacuzzis. Other amenities include cable TV, miniature golf, an outdoor pool, and a full-service restaurant. The Skyline Drive is minutes away.

Rockingham County

Comfort Inn $$$$
1440 East Market Street, Harrisonburg
(540) 433-6066, (800) 228-5150
This chain hotel has won awards for hospitality. Nonsmoking and wheelchair-accessible rooms are available, and the hotel serves a complimentary continental breakfast every morning. The facility has an outdoor pool. Harrisonburg is in the heart of the valley, bordered by Shenandoah National Park on the east and George Washington and Jefferson National Forests on the west. Do as the

locals do: Head for the woods for fishing, hiking, biking, and horseback riding. The Comfort Inn won the Three Diamond AAA Gold Hospitality Award in 2001. Discounts are available for military, AAA, and AARP.

Courtyard by Marriott $$$$
1890 Evelyn Byrd Avenue, Harrisonburg
(540) 432-3031, (800) 321-2211
www.courtyard.com
A luxurious lobby with a lounge and fireplace sets the tempo for spacious rooms in this 125-room hotel, which opened in 2000, just off the intersection of busy U.S. Highway 33 and I-81. Choose among four room types, including king suites—some with their own Jacuzzis and wet bars. The hotel sits high on a hill, so ask for a room with a balcony if you want to admire the night lights of Harrisonburg. Other in-room amenities include coffeemakers, hair dryers, irons and ironing boards, and cable television with HBO. Courtyard offers an indoor pool, hot tub and exercise room, guest laundry, high-speed Internet access, and a work desk with phone and voice mail. An on-site restaurant serves a full breakfast buffet. There is also a meeting room and executive boardroom, wheelchair-accessible facilities, and rooms that cater to smokers or nonsmokers.

Four Points by Sheraton $$$$
1400 East Market Street, Harrisonburg
(540) 433-2521
The Sheraton's 140 rooms are a bit pricier than other area motels, but amenities include nonsmoking rooms, wheelchair-accessible rooms, indoor heated pool, meeting rooms, a Jacuzzi, a sauna, a restaurant, and a lounge with entertainment most nights of the week. Four Points renovated its lobby, rooms, and pool in 2001. AAA and AARP discounts are available.

Hampton Inn $$$
85 University Boulevard, Harrisonburg
(540) 432-1111, (800) HAMPTON
Here's another hotel with a prime location on busy US 33. Welcoming visitors since

1984, the hotel experienced a major renovation in 2003. You have 163 rooms to choose from; some have larger living areas, and two have king beds with pull-out couch, microwaves, fridge, desk, and fax machine. There are also an outdoor pool and a conference room, while the rooms come equipped with blow dryers, iron and ironing board, coffeemakers, cable television, and HBO. There are non-smoking rooms and wheelchair-accessible facilities. Don't forget to enjoy the complimentary continental breakfast. Hampton Inn discounts for AAA, AARP, and for government and military employees.

Quite a number of hotels, especially smaller or older accommodations, allow four-legged guests. Call ahead to see if Fido can accompany you. There often is a small deposit required.

Holiday Inn Express $$$$
3325 South Main Street, Harrisonburg
(540) 433-9999
This cheery blue-and-white hotel sits right off I-81 on Route 11. The 72 rooms offer cable television, high-speed Internet access, refrigerators and microwaves, iron and ironing board, hair dryers, coffee machines, and indoor pool and spa as well as a small fitness center. Check out the continental breakfast and the business center, which has a computer for guest use. There are four Jacuzzi suites, two presidential suites, wheelchair-accessible rooms, and even one with a roll-in shower. The hotel provides discounts for AAA, AARP, and government employees.

Jameson Inn $$$
1881 Evelyn Byrd Avenue, Harrisonburg
(540) 442-1515, (800) JAMESON
www.jamesoninns.com
This new hotel (built in 2002) has an impressive Colonial look with its stately black-and-white façade. The inside is a little more modest (as is the cost), and one

has a choice of 67 rooms and the use of a conference room. The hotel has an outdoor pool, fitness center, cable television and HBO, high-speed Internet access, an extended continental breakfast, wheelchair-accessible rooms, nonsmoking rooms, and even pet-friendly rooms (up to 25 pounds). There are also some two-room suites with microwave and refrigerator. The Jameson offers coffee, tea, and hot chocolate 24 hours and provides discounts for AAA, AARP, and government employees.

The Village Inn $$$
4979 South Valley Pike, Harrisonburg
(540) 434-7355, (800) 736-7355
www.shenandoah.org/villageinn
Folks return again and again to this inn, where comfortable rooms and a variety of amenities, including a large outdoor pool, whirlpool baths, and full-service restaurant, keep guests happy. Single, double, or queen-size beds are available, and some rooms even have decks overlooking the rolling hills of the Shenandoah Valley. All 37 rooms have cable TV with remotes, direct-dial telephones, and individually controlled heat and air-conditioning. A suite, kitchenette, wheelchair-accessible rooms, pet-friendly, and nonsmoking rooms also are available. AAA discounts are available.

Augusta County

Best Western Staunton Inn $$$
92 Rowe Road, Staunton
(540) 885-1112
www.bestwestern.com
A popular place for business and vacation travelers in Staunton, Best Western Staunton Inn has the advantage of being beside one of Staunton's better restaurants, Rowe's Family Restaurant, at exit 222 off I-81. It's just a few minutes driving time to downtown Staunton, Mary Baldwin College, and the Museum of American Frontier Culture. The inn, with 80 guest rooms in a four-story building, serves a

continental breakfast. An indoor heated swimming pool and protected corridors keep the weather from being a problem. Two double or king-size beds are available, along with nonsmoking rooms on request. Pets are allowed.

Comfort Inn Staunton $$$$
1302 Richmond Avenue, Staunton
(540) 886-5000, (800) 228-5150
This 98-room hotel is centrally located in the Shenandoah Valley just off I-81 on U.S. Highway 250, making it an ideal home base from which to explore the area's attractions. It's also a convenient stop for travelers. Amenities include an outdoor pool, in-room coffeemakers, microwaves, fridges, clock radios, and remote-control cable TV with free HBO. For a treat, stay in one of the hotel's whirlpool rooms. Rates include a complimentary continental breakfast and newspaper. Board games also are furnished at the front desk. Corporate and group discounts are available.

Hampton Inn $$$$
40 Payne Lane, Staunton
(540) 886-7000, (800) HAMPTON
If you like to shop, this inn is right across the street from Staunton's Colonial mall, plus it's just 2 miles from Historic Downtown and the Woodrow Wilson Birthplace. This three-story hotel features a free continental breakfast, HBO, an outdoor pool, exercise room, and free passes to the YMCA or nearby spa. The inn also will provide alarm clocks for the hearing impaired or high-speed Internet access for those who bring along work from the office. Sixty-five of the 75 rooms are nonsmoking. Ask about discounts for seniors and AAA.

Holiday Inn Staunton $$$$
152 Fairway Lane, Staunton
(540) 248-6020, (800) 932-9061
Historic Downtown Staunton is less than five minutes from this 114-room hotel. Also nearby are the Woodrow Wilson Birthplace and the Museum of American Frontier Culture. Three suites are available, as are non-

smoking and wheelchair-accessible rooms. Other amenities include an indoor/outdoor heated pool and golf and tennis privileges at the adjacent Country Club of Staunton. Golf/lodging packages also are available. A full-service restaurant in the hotel serves international cuisine, and the lounge features weekend entertainment.

The Inn at Afton $$$
185 Afton Circle, Waynesboro
(540) 942-5201, (800) 860-8559
www.theinnatafton.com
Enjoy fabulous views from atop Afton Mountain at this 118-room hotel. The Inn is convenient to Interstate 64 and about 25 minutes west of Charlottesville. King-size beds and nonsmoking rooms are available, and all rooms come with free local calling and DirectTV. Be sure to request a view room; you won't be disappointed by the breathtaking scenery. A heated pool is on-site, as is the hotel's restaurant, Dulaney's Steak and Seafood Restaurant, which offers room service to the hotel during breakfast, lunch, and dinner.

Quality Inn Waynesboro $$$
640 West Broad Street, Waynesboro
(540) 942-1171, (800) 228-5151
Complimentary continental breakfast and USA Today newspapers are included in the price of rooms at this comfortable spot. You can also make free local calls, and all 75 rooms have remote-control cable TV with HBO. You can request room

Even though some of our hotels are located in rural America, more and more are revamping their amenities with the vacationer/businessperson in mind. Many hotels come equipped with data-port telephones and offer free high-speed Internet service. If you find yourself in a hotel without, visit a nearby college or public library, where many locals first learn to search the Web and use e-mail.

microwaves and refrigerators, and all rooms have coffeemakers. During the warm months, guests can unwind in the spacious outdoor pool. The Quality Inn is close to Wintergreen Resort, Waynesboro Factory Outlet Village, the Blue Ridge Parkway, the Skyline Drive, and the Museum of American Frontier Culture.

Lexington

Best Western Inn at Hunt Ridge $$$$
I-81 and Highway 39, Lexington
(540) 464-1500, (800) 464-1501
To match the beautiful Lexington country-side, this country-themed inn offers 100 guest rooms with a view of the Blue Ridge like no other in the area. You can relax in Hobbies lounge or take a dip in the indoor/outdoor pool. You'll be close to the Virginia Horse Center and Historic Down-town Lexington, and you can take advan-tage of G. Willaker's restaurant, which serves all three meals and provides room service. Other extras include in-room cof-feemakers, electronic door locks, interior corridors, and a guest laundry room. There is a $25 fee if you want to bring your pet.

Comfort Inn $$$$
Off I-81 exit 191 and I-64, exit 55
Lexington
(540) 463-7311, (800) 628-1958
Near the Virginia Horse Center and His-toric Downtown Lexington, Comfort Inn is the perfect central location for day trips. It offers a complimentary continental break-fast, in-room coffeemakers, electronic door locks, interior corridors, a glass ele-vator, guest laundry, an indoor pool, and free local calls. Children younger than 18 stay free. Several restaurants are next to the hotel. Pets are welcome for a $25 fee.

Hampton Inn $$$
401 East Nelson Street, Lexington
(540) 463-2223, (800) 426-7866
How can a hotel that opened in 1997 be listed on the National Register of Historic Places? When Hampton Inn unveiled its

new 86-room hotel, it managed to com-bine the old with the new. Just 1 block from Historic Downtown Lexington, the main hotel is attached to a 19th-century manor house. Ten of the rooms are located in the 1827 structure and are dec-orated with a bed-and-breakfast flair. Each room is named for historical people or places from Lexington—the Washington and Lee Room, the Stonewall Jackson Room—and some feature fireplaces and period furniture. The rates for the manor house rooms run from $200 to $350. The remaining rooms on the hotel side start in the low $80s and include balconies, microwaves, minifridges, and coffeemak-ers. A continental breakfast is provided, along with free local calls, HBO, and Dis-ney channels. In the warmer months, you can use the outdoor pool and Jacuzzi, while a weight room offers year-round exercise opportunities.

Holiday Inn Express $$$$
I-64 and US 11 N, Lexington
(540) 463-7351, (800) 480-3043
This beautifully renovated hotel offers Lex-ington's best complimentary deluxe conti-nental breakfast. Each of the 72 rooms offers in-room coffeemakers, electronic door locks, cable TV, and free HBO. Holiday Inn Express is close to Historic Downtown Lexington, Virginia Military Institute, Wash-ington and Lee University, and the Virginia Horse Center. It is a perfect location to start several day trips. Senior citizen and AAA discounts are available.

Howard Johnson Inn and
Restaurant $$$
I-64 and I-81, exit 195, Lexington
(540) 463-9181, (800) 456-4656
This mountain view inn is directly off I-81 at exit 195. Nearby you will find Historic Downtown Lexington, Natural Bridge, Vir-ginia Horse Center, and many other points of interest for all ages. The inn features 100 rooms with 50 mountain-view rooms and wheelchair-accessible rooms. The facility also has an on-site restaurant that offers banquet and meeting facilities, an

outdoor pool, cable TV with free HBO, and guest laundry. AARP, AAA, and group discounts are available. Pets can stay for $5.00 per night per pet.

Sheridan Livery Inn   **$$$**
35 North Main Street, Lexington
(540) 464-1887
www.sheridanliveryinn.com
This quaint little 12-room inn has a fascinating history as a stagecoach service and livery stable, as well as a perfect location in historic downtown Lexington. In 1887 Irish immigrant John Sheridan opened the Sheridan Livery Stable to provide horse trading and boarding as well as stagecoach and mail delivery service. In 1919 Sheridan sold the building, and it passed through several owners until Ugo and Gina Benincasa bought it in 1994. In 1997 they opened it as the inn, restaurant, lounge, and outdoor cafe. The inn has three two-room suites (two with king-size bed) with queen sleeper sofa, wet bar, and color television. Rooms have refrigerators, and a continental breakfast is included with the stay. A balcony overlooks Main Street. The building is a historic-looking brick and has a quaint back patio with a green awning. The restaurant is pretty with a fountain in the center and large picture windows and attracts a dressy clientele. Dinner entrees are around $20 and include steak, duck, shrimp, lamb, and numerous fish specials.

Wingate Inn   **$$$$**
1108 North Lee Highway, Lexington
(540) 464-8100
www.wingateinns.com
Especially for those going to an event at the popular Virginia Horse Center, this is a great choice. The hotel, built in 2001, has a wide and handsome lobby. The 84 rooms and two suites have cable and free HBO, coffeemaker, iron, ironing board, microfridge, and in-room safe. There is also free high-speed Internet access, two-line desk phone with speaker, data port, voice mail and conference call capabilities, and a cordless phone. The hotel has a

heated indoor pool, fitness center and whirlpool, a complimentary breakfast, a 24-hour business center, and meeting facilities for up to 50 people. AAA and AARP discounts are provided.

Natural Bridge

Relax Inn   **$$**
4852 South Lee Highway, Natural Bridge
(540) 291-2143
In the heart of the Shenandoah Valley near Natural Bridge, the Blue Ridge Parkway, and Historic Lexington, this 15-room motel offers amenities for the traveler in a country setting. Travelers return time and again for its excellent rates, friendly staff, and adjacent restaurant with wholesome home cooking. The rooms are extra clean, and smoking and nonsmoking rooms are available. Discounts are available for AAA and AARP.

ROANOKE VALLEY

Roanoke, Troutville, and Salem

AmeriSuites Roanoke/
Valley View Mall   **$$$$**
5040 Valley View Boulevard, off
Interstate 581, Roanoke
(540) 366-4700, (800) 833-1516
www.amerisuites.com
AmeriSuites makes the extra space, convenience, and luxury of 128 all-suite accommodations affordable. The hotel is close to attractions, shopping, and restaurants. Features include an indoor heated pool, a fitness center, and complimentary continental breakfast. All suites include a wet bar, microwave, iron and ironing board, refrigerator, and coffeemaker. Each suite also has a 26-inch TV and voice mail. Business travelers will appreciate the phone dataports in each suite. Weekend and midweek specials may be available.

Best Western Inn at Valley View $$$$
5050 Valley View Boulevard, Roanoke
(540) 362-2400, (800) 362-2410
One mile from Roanoke Regional Airport, this three-story inn at Roanoke's largest shopping mall, Valley View, has 85 rooms with indoor corridors. The decor follows a country theme with Shaker-style furniture. Nonsmoking rooms and rooms with king-size beds are available. Amenities include cable TV, an indoor pool, in-room coffeemakers, and complimentary continental breakfast. Numerous nationally known restaurants are nearby. This hotel is the perfect location from which to take a day trip. To get here, take exit 3E off Hershberger Road. AARP and AAA discounts are available.

Clarion Hotel Roanoke Airport $$$$
3315 Ordway Drive, Roanoke
(540) 362-4500, (800) 252-7466
Indoor/outdoor pools, tennis courts, volleyball, and golf are available at this outstanding hotel. Each of the 154 guest rooms is equipped with satellite TV, two phones, individual climate control, radio, and two double beds or a king-size bed. Pets are allowed. Clarion Hotel has more than 11,500 square feet in meeting and conference facilities. The main ballroom can accommodate events from a small dinner of 20 to a banquet of 400 people. A conference center and luxurious hospitality suites are ideal for business meeting and social functions. AARP discounts are available. Pets weighing less than 40 pounds can stay with a $35 fee.

Colony House Motor Lodge $$$
3560 Franklin Road, Roanoke
(540) 345-0411, (866) 203-5850
Colony House is 2 miles north of the Roanoke entrance to the spectacular Blue Ridge Parkway. This small, quiet inn specializes in personal service. The 67 rooms are air-conditioned and carpeted and have direct-dial phones, cable TV, and king-, queen- or double-size beds. A few suites are available, and the Lodge has an outdoor pool. You're close to great restaurants, terrific shopping, the interstate highway, and downtown. Colony House is an ideal base for business travelers and tourists. Special AAA and AARP discounts also apply.

Comfort Inn-Roanoke/Troutville $$$
Lee Highway, Troutville
(540) 992-5600, (800) 628-1957
Seventy-two guest rooms are available at this hotel, each equipped with cable TV. Other amenities include nonsmoking rooms, an outdoor pool, enclosed corridors, and in-room coffeemakers. Several restaurants are nearby. This a perfect location for day-trippers. Senior citizen and AAA discounts are offered. Pets are allowed with a $20 deposit.

Comfort Suites at Ridgewood Farm $$$$
2898 Keagy Road, Salem
(540) 375-4800, (800) 628-1922
The Comfort Suites at Ridgewood Farm is nestled on a hilltop overlooking the beautiful Roanoke Valley with a spectacular mountain view. Conveniently located, the hotel offers interior corridors, electronic door locks, an elevator, an outdoor pool and whirlpool, complimentary breakfast, and breakfast area with an outdoor balcony overlooking the mountains. Each double- and king-bed suite features a guest living area with desks with a two-line telephone, special lighting, 25-inch TV with remote, in-room coffeemaker, wet bar, refrigerator, microwave, large wardrobe closets, and nightlights. Because of its convenient location, it is the perfect place for day trips.

Econo Lodge $$
301 Wildwood Road, Salem
(540) 389-0280
This hotel, 3.5 miles west of downtown Salem off I-81, is close to shopping, dining, attractions, and major corporations. This clean, efficient accommodation has 60 all-ground-floor rooms with refrigerators, microwaves, cable TV, kitchenettes, non-smoking rooms, complimentary coffee

service, and free local calls. Senior and AAA discounts are available. Small pets can stay for a $5.00 one-time fee.

Hampton Inn Airport $$$
6621 Thirlane Road, Roanoke
(540) 265-2600, (800) 426-7866
Conveniently located a half mile from I-81 and 2 miles from Roanoke Regional Airport, this Hampton Inn offers 79 spacious guest rooms, including two extended-stay king suites with a beautiful view of the Blue Ridge Mountains. Amenities include a free deluxe continental breakfast, *USA Today* newspaper, guest laundry, free shuttle service, microfridges, VCRs, and dataport phones in all rooms. Coffeemakers are in all rooms. Activities available for guests are an outdoor pool and exercise room.

Hampton Inn Salem $$$
1886 Electric Road, Salem
(540) 776-6500, (800) HAMPTON
This conveniently located Hampton Inn opened in September 1997. It provides many amenities to its guests, including a free deluxe continental breakfast, free local phone calls, an exercise and fitness room, guest laundry, and an outdoor pool. Each room is complete with wireless connections, a microfridge, and TV with VCR. Also available are nonsmoking rooms and luxurious suites with whirlpools. Special extras for business executives are the business center, which is complete with FAX, computer, and dataport, and six hospitality suite/meeting rooms.

Hampton Inn Tanglewood $$$
3816 Franklin Road SW, Roanoke
(540) 989-4000, (800) 426-7866
Just 3 miles from downtown, close to Roanoke Memorial Hospital and across from Tanglewood Mall, the 58-room Hampton Inn on Franklin Road offers an expanded continental breakfast, cable TV, in-house movies, coffeemakers, direct-dial phones, irons and ironing boards, copier and fax service, king deluxe rooms, continental breakfast, hair dryers, refrigerator/freezer and microwave, and nonsmoking

rooms. Hospital and commercial rates are offered.

Holiday Inn Airport $$$
6626 Thirlane Road NW, Roanoke
(540) 366-8861, (800) HOLIDAY
Only minutes from Valley View Mall and Roanoke Regional Airport, the Holiday Inn Airport offers complimentary transportation for busy travelers and executives. The hotel offers amenities to help you relax, including Sir Pete's Pub with several TVs, international beer, and arcade games. Sir Pete's Grille serves exciting menu items. Sunday noon buffet is one of the longest-running in Roanoke, and this is also a popular place for business lunches. There are coffeemakers in all rooms and fridges upon request. King leisure rooms, double rooms, parlor suites, and executive suites are available. Pets can stay for $25.

Holiday Inn Express $$$$
3139 Lee Highway, I-81 S exit 150-A
Troutville
(540) 966-4444, (800) HOLIDAY
The Roanoke Valley's newest Holiday Inn sports all the amenities guests have been asking for at Holiday Inns. All 82 rooms have wireless hookups, microwaves, refrigerators, remote-control TVs, movie rental, and complimentary continental breakfast. Local calls are free. Kids stay for free. Guests can use the outdoor pool, exercise room, and sauna. Options are nonsmoking rooms, wheelchair-accessible rooms, and Jacuzzi suites. Business guests can use the fax and copy service and meeting rooms. Golf and tennis are nearby, as are Hollins University, Natural Bridge and the Blue Ridge Parkway.

Holiday Inn Express Roanoke $$$
815 Gainesboro Road, Roanoke
(540) 982-0100, (800) HOLIDAY
The owners of the Holiday Inn Express know that it's the little touches that make a stay more pleasant. Guests are treated to a complimentary deluxe breakfast, coffee, newspaper, and ice. The 98 rooms feature firm, extra-length beds, and each room has

a clock radio, coffeemakers, irons, ironing boards, hair dryers, and a remote-control 25-inch TV with cable—including HBO, ESPN, and Disney—and complimentary passes to the YMCA and fitness center across the street. Many rooms have sofas and desks, and some are equipped with whirlpool baths, microwaves, and refrigerators. Nonsmoking rooms and facilities for the disabled are available, and guests may use the outdoor pool.

Holiday Inn Hotel Tanglewood $$$$
4468 Starkey Road, Roanoke
(540) 774-4400, (800) HOLIDAY
Close to Tanglewood Mall and just minutes from downtown Roanoke, this hotel's 196 guest rooms are traditionally furnished. Each comes with climate control, cable TV, a radio, and two vanity dressing areas. EJ's Landing, in the hotel, serves buffet breakfast or regional cuisine and also serves up a breathtaking view of the Blue Ridge Mountains. For some excitement, try the EJ's Lounge. The hotel offers outdoor swimming. Complimentary shuttle service to the airport is available. A concierge level makes this an especially popular place with business travelers who like personal touches such as a complimentary newspaper and breakfast, hors d'oeuvres, and nightly turndown service. AARP and AAA rates are available.

Hotel Roanoke &
Conference Center $$$
110 Shenandoah Avenue, Roanoke
(540) 985-5900, (800) 222-TREE
The renovated landmark Hotel Roanoke & Conference Center has thrived in its several years of operation after being closed for five years. Built in 1882, this sleeping Tudor-style giant has been revitalized as a Doubletree hotel in partnership with Virginia Tech, an arrangement brought about when the hotel's previous owner, Norfolk Southern Railway, gave the grand dame of luxury hotels to the university in 1989. The reopening of the hotel, cherished by generations for its service, style, and sophistication, has been embraced nationwide by those who

remember Miss Virginia pageants and peanut soup. Visitors to any of the 332 rooms will be pleased to see the best was saved and the rest was modernized.

More than 105 years old, this hotel has been completely restored, from its Florentine marble floors to frescoes and vaulted ceilings. Renovations were completed in 2001 to update the guest rooms. Visitors can stay in the same rooms where John D. Rockefeller, Amelia Earhart, Gen. Dwight Eisenhower, and Elvis Presley stayed and looked out upon Mill Mountain. Both the hotel and conference center have been equipped with 21st-century technology, including dual-line telephones, voice mail, and high-speed computer hookups in every room. Hair dryers, coffeemakers, irons, and ironing boards are in all rooms, and you can relax in the hot tub by the outdoor pool. The conference center can accommodate more than 4,500 people, with 20 meeting rooms. A fitness facility and guest services are available. Visitors can have a drink in the Pine Room or dine in style in the Regency Room.

Howard Johnsons $$
437 Roanoke Road, Daleville
(540) 992-1234
Just off I-81, a beautiful hilltop location with panoramic mountain views beckons travelers to this 98-room facility, each equipped with microwave, coffeepots, and refrigerators. Seven miles from Roanoke, Best Western has the advantage of being in beautiful Botetourt County, known for its flowering orchards with bountiful fruit and country scenery. In addition to being clean and offering a variety of accommodation options, the inn has one of the area's largest outdoor pools. Senior and AAA discounts are available. Pets are allowed for a one-time $15 fee.

The Jefferson Lodge $$
616 South Jefferson Street, Roanoke
(540) 342-2951, (800) 950-2580
The Jefferson Lodge is in the heart of downtown Roanoke, just a few blocks from the main public library, city and fed-

eral government buildings, hospitals, and shopping. It is only 3 blocks to the City Market and Center in the Square. One hundred rooms await guests. Free parking, coin-operated laundry, and color TV are all provided for your comfort. An outdoor swimming pool and a Chinese restaurant are on the property. Special group rates are available. Pets are welcome with a $150 deposit.

Motel 6 $$
3695 Thirlane Road, Roanoke
(540) 563-0229

Close to the airport, Valley View Mall, and many major restaurants, Motel 6, with 127 rooms on five floors, is a good choice for travelers who want cleanliness and ample amenities. Attractive rooms feature king-size or double beds and cable TV. Non-smoking rooms are available. Free local calls and fax capabilities are available. Everyone can enjoy an outdoor pool in summer. Pets are allowed.

Quality Inn-Roanoke/Salem $$$
179 Sheraton Drive, Salem
(540) 562-1912, (800) 459-4949

The Quality Inn was completely renovated in 2002, offering some of the best facilities in the lodging industry. New furniture and fixtures, sliding glass doors, and a balcony are some of the features you will find here. The hotel has interior corridors. Each room comes with a microwave, refrigerator, coffeemaker, hair dryer, iron and ironing board, dataports, and a 25-inch television. There's a complimentary continental breakfast, and if you overdo it, you can work it off in the fitness room. This is a great place to stay with the kids because of the large outdoor swimming pool, kiddie pool, playground, volleyball court, and picnic areas. Business folks are not left out, as there is a business center and private meeting and banquet rooms available. For $15 pets can stay, too.

The Patrick Henry Hotel $$$
617 South Jefferson Street, Roanoke
(540) 345-8811, (800) 303-0988

If you're staying in downtown Roanoke, this historic property is a fine choice. It's within walking distance to all the downtown attractions. When the Patrick Henry Hotel opened its doors for the first time in 1925, its 11-story exterior was already a wonder, but visitors and guests were astounded by the beauty of the interior. Today, the hotel, with its ornate decor, has been restored to its previous splendor, and it is one of two operating Virginia Historic Landmark hotels in Roanoke. To say the guest rooms are spacious is an understatement. Each has been modernized, but in a way that reflects the hotel's historic heritage. Rooms have kitchenettes with refrigerators and microwaves. Complimentary health club facilities are nearby. Some rooms are outfitted with amenities such as hair dryers, irons, and toiletries. Suites are available.

Ramada Inn and Conference Center
Salem $$$
1671 Skyview Road, Salem
(540) 389-7061
www.ramada.com

Conveniently located off I-81 at exit 137, Ramada Inn Salem offers a spectacular view of the Blue Ridge Mountains, accommodations, complimentary continental breakfast, and a free daily paper. All guest rooms offer coffeemaker, hair dryer, iron and ironing board, dataport, large screen TV with cable, and individual voice mail systems. Guests may choose executive king rooms or double bedrooms for families. There are wheelchair-accessible rooms available, and pets are allowed with a $15 one-time fee. Guests are encouraged to cool off in the beautiful outdoor pool/kiddie pool or relax in the Skyview Restaurant, where kids eat free. At Ramada Inn Salem, expect excellent service, lovely surroundings, and comfortable accommodations. Discounts are offered for AARP and AAA.

Rodeway Inn $$
526 Orange Avenue, Roanoke
(540) 981-9341, (800) 228-2000

Access to the Roanoke Civic Center is

about as simple as it gets from this hotel, since the center is just across the street. The Rodeway Inn is also less than a mile away from Center in the Square, the historic farmers' market, and the Virginia Transportation Museum. A continental breakfast is offered each morning. The guest rooms have cable TV. Fax service, Internet hookups, and a guest laundry are available. Ask about group, discount, and seasonal rates. Discounts available for AAA and AARP members.

Sleep Inn Tanglewood $$$$
4045 Electric Road, Roanoke
(540) 772-1500, (800) 628-1929
The Sleep Inn, in the Tanglewood Mall area off I-581 at the Highway 419 exit, is the area's new high-tech lodging for business and vacation travelers. The inn has 82 nicely decorated rooms with state-of-the-art security systems. Extras include a large desk in each room with wireless service. The extra-large showers feature massaging shower heads. A complimentary *USA Today* newspaper and in-room coffee service are included with a complimentary breakfast. Nonsmoking rooms are available. Each room has a satellite TV. A business center is equipped with a computer and wireless service. Business associates may charge meals to nearby restaurants including Texas Steak House, Ragazzi's, and Mac & Maggie's. Pets stay for $20.

Travelodge-Roanoke North $$
2619 Lee Highway S, Troutville
(540) 992-6700, (800) 578-7878
Travelodge wants you to feel at home, so it provides a free continental breakfast, an outdoor pool, and free local calls. All 108 rooms offer attractive furniture, cable TV, executive work areas, coffeemakers, dataports, and direct-dial telephones. Children stay free when sharing a room with their parents. Efficiency rooms are available for relocating personnel or long-term visitors. Pets are welcome. Several restaurants are adjacent.

Wyndham Roanoke Airport Hotel $$$
2801 Hershberger Road NW, Roanoke
(540) 563-9300, (800) WYNDHAM
Situated on 12 landscaped acres, the hotel welcomes its guests in an elegant lobby. Nearby is the hotel restaurant, Lily's. The hotel has 320 guest rooms and suites with numerous amenities, such as individual climate control, a radio, irons, ironing boards, shower massages, remote-control cable TV, two direct-dial telephones with message lights, video messages, and complimentary personal-care products. Room service, airport transportation, and free parking are other services here.

The Wyndham has indoor and outdoor pools, a fitness center, a sauna and whirlpool, and two lighted tennis courts. For evening entertainment, guests can go to the hotel's lounge, Charades. The grand ballroom, Shenandoah Ballroom, and six meeting rooms can accommodate groups of 20 to 900. Seventeen conference rooms are available, with more than 12,800 square feet of flexible space. Special rates include Two for Breakfast Weekends, Honeymoon Packages, and long-term rates.

EAST OF THE BLUE RIDGE
Loudoun County

Best Western Leesburg Hotel and Conference Center $$$$
726 East Market Street, Leesburg
(703) 777-9400, (800) 528-1234
If your trip includes a flight to or from the area, this hotel is an excellent choice. It offers a complimentary airport shuttle to Dulles Airport with 24-hour notice. There are 99 rooms to choose from with either a king-size or two queen-size beds; there are smoking and nonsmoking options as well as wheelchair-accessible rooms. Make yourself comfortable with a complimentary deluxe continental breakfast buffet while enjoying *USA Today* (on weekdays). Rooms have coffeemakers, microwaves and refrigerators, hair dryers, irons and

full-size ironing boards, cable TV, guest laundry, free local calls, dataport telephones, and voice mail. There is also wireless service in the lobby and breakfast room. If you're in the mood to relax or stay fit, the hotel has a fitness center, an outdoor pool, and a picnic area with grills. They also have a business center with Internet access and meeting and banquet facilities. Need a snack after all that relaxation? The hotel serves fresh-popped popcorn every afternoon!

Days Inn $$$
721 East Market Street, Leesburg
(703) 777-6622, (800) 329-7466
In the heart of downtown, you will be within a 1-mile radius of several shopping centers and restaurants. Days Inn offers a free continental breakfast, cable TV and free HBO. The enclosed two-story building has 81 rooms—several are connecting rooms—plus four wheelchair-accessible rooms. Guests may choose king or double beds. Nonsmoking rooms are available. Children younger than 17 may stay for free in a parent's room. Ask about other discounts. Pets can stay for $6.00 per night.

Holiday Inn $$$$
1500 East Market Street, Leesburg
(703) 771-9200, (888) 850-8545
The former Carradoc Hall was grand as a historic mansion and is even grander as a full-service hotel. The 122 guest rooms and four mansion suites are elegantly decorated, as is the Lighthouse Tavern and Mansion House Restaurant, which serves breakfast, lunch, and dinner. The hotel has an outdoor pool, exercise room, and free airport shuttle. Many sporting and historic attractions are nearby.

Fauquier County

Comfort Inn $$$$
7379 Comfort Inn Drive, Warrenton
(540) 349-8900
Of the 97 rooms in this upscale motel, 49

are king suites and four are Jacuzzi suites. Several units offer a kitchen, living area, and bedroom. All rooms have a refrigerator and coffeemaker, microwaves, irons, ironing boards, and hair dryers. Nonsmoking rooms also are available. A deluxe continental breakfast, newspaper, and local calls are complimentary. Other amenities include a laundry, fitness room, basketball court, picnic tables, barbecue grill, and an outdoor pool. Comfort Inn is pet friendly.

Howard Johnson Inn $$$
6 Broadview Avenue, Warrenton
(540) 347-4141, (800) I-GO-HOJO
This newly remodeled 80-room facility has complimentary morning coffee and newspaper, cable TV, and an outdoor pool. Nonsmoking rooms are available. Discounts include AARP and AAA.

Culpeper County

Comfort Inn $$$$
890 Willis Lane, Culpeper
(540) 825-4900, (800) 228-5150
In downtown Culpeper, this 49-room motel features an outdoor swimming pool, in-room coffeemakers, free continental breakfast, cable TV, irons, ironing boards, and hair dryers. King-size beds and nonsmoking rooms are available. Although no room service is offered, several restaurants are nearby. There are discounts for AARP and AAA, and pets may stay for $15 per night.

Holiday Inn Culpeper $$$$
791 Madison Road, Culpeper
(540) 825-1253, (800) HOLIDAY
Easy access off U.S. Highway 29 makes this a convenient and affordable stop for travelers. The 158-room two-story motel has a restaurant and lounge, adult and children's outdoor pools, and laundry services. Rooms are equipped with fridges, microwaves, irons, ironing boards, and hair dryers. Banquet facilities can accommodate up to 375.

Super 8 Motel   **$$$**
889 Willis Lane, Culpeper
(540) 825-8088, (800) 800-8000
Affordably priced, this 61-room motel provides free extended cable TV, free local calls, and complimentary coffee and toast bar. Nonsmoking rooms, microwave/refrigerator units, and fax service also are available. Your pet can stay, too, for an additional $10.

Albemarle County

Best Western Cavalier Inn $$$$
105 North Emmet Street, Charlottesville
(434) 296-8111
The 118-room Cavalier is next to the University of Virginia in the center of Charlottesville. Suites, wheelchair-accessible rooms, and nonsmoking rooms are available. Rooms have coffeemakers, hair dryers, and free local calls, plus you can get a microwave and a refrigerator on request. The Inn has an outdoor swimming pool and serves a free continental breakfast to guests. Special packages are available for families, senior citizens, sporting events, and business meetings. There is also a President's Package, which includes tickets to Monticello, Ash Lawn–Highland, and Michie Tavern.

Comfort Inn Charlottesville $$$$
1807 Emmet Street, Charlottesville
(434) 293-6188, (800) 228-5150
The Comfort Inn in Charlottesville offers double and king rooms. Easy access to the US 250 bypass puts the University of Virginia and historic sites such as Monticello within minutes of the hotel. Amenities include free continental breakfast, cable TV, morning newspapers, in-room coffeemakers, and an outdoor pool. Nearly three-fourths of the 64 rooms are nonsmoking rooms. Be sure to book early during college football season and graduation, when the town fills up. Pets are allowed.

Courtyard by Marriott–North $$$$
638 Hillsdale Drive, Charlottesville
(434) 973-7100, (800) 321-2211
Shopping, historic sites, and the University of Virginia are all close to Courtyard by Marriott. Of the 150 rooms, 120 are nonsmoking. All have cable TV, high-speed Internet access, and free in-room coffeemakers. Six wheelchair-accessible rooms and 12 suites are available. Guests may use the indoor pool, whirlpool, and exercise room. The inn has a restaurant. Discounts are available for AAA and senior citizens older than 62.

Courtyard by Marriott–UVA/Medical Center $$$$
1201 West Main Street, Charlottesville
(434) 977-1700, (800) 321-2211
www.courtyard.com/chodt
This new hotel, conveniently located near the lovely campus of the University of Virginia and the bustling UVA hospital, has 137 rooms and seven suites. Rooms are equipped with a large work desk, voice mail, two phone lines, speakerphone, dataports, coffeemaker, iron and ironing board, and hair dryer. It's not all work, as there is cable TV, HBO, pay-per-view movies, and an indoor pool, hot tub, and fitness room. You can stop for a nice breakfast daily in the hotel's restaurant, Cafe 1201. Dinner is served Monday through Saturday.

Days Inn Charlottesville–University $$$$
1600 Emmet Street, Charlottesville
(434) 293-9111
www.daysinn.com
All 129 rooms and two suites at this hotel are handsomely decorated and equipped with cable TV. The exercise room has a treadmill, Universal gym, and recumbent bikes; outside is a large pool and a landscaped courtyard. The hotel has its own restaurant, Red Lobster. Ask about discounted rates.

Doubletree $$$$
990 Hilton Heights Road, Charlottesville
(434) 973-2121, (800) 494-9467
www.charlottesville.doubletree.com
Surrounded by 20 acres in the northern-most portion of Charlottesville, this 234-room hotel offers all the creature comforts in a palatial setting. Amenities include two restaurants, heated indoor and heated outdoor pools, whirlpools, an exercise room, tennis courts, and jogging trails. The comfortable rooms have TVs with in-room movies and games, hair dryers, irons, iron-ing boards, and high-speed Internet access. Charlottesville's largest conference facility, Doubletree has a banquet room that can accommodate large receptions and groups from 2 to 600. Discounts are available for AAA and AARP.

The English Inn $$$
2000 Morton Drive, Charlottesville
(434) 971-9900, (800) 786-5400
www.wytestone.com
Following the centuries-old British tradition, your breakfast is complimentary at this well-appointed chain hotel. Guests are served a continental morning meal in the Windsor Room, amid comfortable furnish-ings, a fireplace, and fine art. Other ameni-ties include an indoor pool, a sauna, and an exercise room with a Universal weight sys-tem. Guests also receive free passes to a nearby health club. The inn has 21 king suites, designed with a Queen Anne flair with a sitting room and wet bar. The king suites also include microwaves, refrigera-tors, and two televisions, one in the sitting area with a sofa that pulls out into a bed. The other 67 rooms are contemporary in style and have two double beds. All rooms have cable TV, AM/FM clock radio, shower massage, coffeemaker, hair dryer, iron, iron-ing boards, and automatic wake-up service. Banquet and meeting facilities are available. A courtesy shuttle serves airport travelers.

Hampton Inn $$$
2035 India Road, Charlottesville
(434) 978-7888, (800) HAMPTON
www.hamptoninn.com
This Hampton Inn, within walking distance of one of Charlottesville's movie theaters, has been listed in the top 10 percent of Hampton Inns for the past 16 years. Guests in the Hampton's 123 rooms enjoy free airport shuttles, free local calls, a same-day dry cleaning service, laundry service, and a breakfast bar with hot items. The spacious and comfortable air-conditioned rooms have 27-inch remote-control cable TV with HBO, hair dryers, and free high-speed wireless Internet access. Nonsmoking rooms are available. The Inn has an outdoor pool, and nine restaurants are nearby. Charlottesville's major attractions, such as UVA, Monticello, Ash Lawn–Highland, and Michie Tavern, are within easy reach of the inn, which is on US 29 north of the city at the Seminole Square Shopping Center.

Hampton Inn and Suites $$$$
900 West Main Street, Charlottesville
(804) 923-8600, (800) HAMPTON
www.hamptonsuites.com
Opened in the summer of 1997, this new hotel with 152 suites is designed with the business traveler in mind. There is a boardroom that seats 12 and a conference room that can seat up to 35. Of the 100 rooms, 25 are suites and 8 are equipped with fireplaces. The executive suites also offer microwaves and mini-refrigerators. Amenities include deluxe continental breakfast and a complimentary shuttle, plus free local calls and HBO. Several nearby restaurants are within walking dis-tance. The Inn is 1 block from the Univer-sity of Virginia.

Holiday Inn University Area Conference Center $$$$
1901 Emmet Street, Charlottesville
(434) 977-7700, (800) 242-5973
www.holidayinn.com
This pleasant hotel is on US 29 just north of Charlottesville, with easy access to the University of Virginia, Michie Tavern, Ash Lawn–Highland, and Monticello. The 171 rooms and one suite are modern and comfortably decorated; each offers cable

TV. The indoor heated pool has a patio area for relaxing or sunning outdoors in season. A free airport shuttle is available to guests. Damon's is open for breakfast, lunch, and dinner and provides room service for the hotel.

Holiday Inn–Monticello $$$$
1200 Fifth Street, Charlottesville
(434) 977-5100, (800) HOLIDAY
www.holidayinn.com
You'll be close to downtown Charlottesville and just 4 miles from historic attractions at this 130-room high-rise hotel. Amenities include in-room coffeemakers, free local calls, and extended cable TV packages. Meeting and banquet facilities are available for up to 150 people. The hotel's restaurant, Charlotte's, is open for breakfast and dinner.

Omni Charlottesville Hotel $$$$
235 West Main Street, Charlottesville
(434) 971-5500, (800) THE-OMNI
www.omnihotels.com
You can't beat this spectacular hotel's convenient Downtown Mall location, which puts guests within easy walking distance of many good restaurants, shops, and galleries. The hotel's facilities can accommodate all sorts of events, from a cocktail party for 30 to a conference for 600. Indoor/outdoor pools, a whirlpool, sauna, health club, and restaurant are on site. The 208 rooms and six suites are elegantly decorated; three are wheelchair accessible, and 99 percent of the rooms are designated nonsmoking.

Quality Inn–University $$$$
1600 Emmet Street, Charlottesville
(434) 971-3746, (800) 4CHOICE
All 69 rooms at this conveniently located hotel are handsomely decorated and equipped with cable TV. A deluxe continental breakfast is included in the price of the rooms. The exercise room has a treadmill and Universal gym; outside is a large pool and a landscaped courtyard. Ask about discounted rates for AAA and AARP.

Ramada Limited–Monticello $$$
2097 Inn Drive, Charlottesville
(434) 977-3300, (800) 272-6232
www.ramada.com
Newly renovated, this inn has 99 comfortable rooms with nice features and options such as whirlpools, king- and queen-size beds, nonsmoking units, and free cable TV. Guests are treated to a free deluxe continental breakfast, while a business center will provide you with a space to catch up on your work. The meeting and banquet space can accommodate up to 100. An exercise room, outdoor pool, and laundry are available to guests. The Ramada offers senior citizen and AAA discounts.

Red Carpet Inn $$$
405 Premier Circle, Charlottesville
(434) 973-8133, (800) 251-1962
www.redcarpetcville.com
Just off US 29 near shopping malls, restaurants, and shops and within a five-minute drive of the University of Virginia, this member of the clean and comfortable national motel chain has 115 rooms, all on one floor. The motel caters to a largely tourist crowd, along with UVA alums who flock to Charlottesville in the fall for football games and special events at the university. It's an affordable option, but book early for weekends any time of the year. The Inn features an outdoor pool, free cable, and coffee. Ten rooms come with a kitchenette.

Red Roof Inn $$$
1309 West Main Street, Charlottesville
(434) 295-4333, (800) RED-ROOF
www.redroofinn.com
Within walking distance of the University of Virginia, this renovated hotel is a perfect location for sightseeing or for families who are visiting relatives in the nearby UVa Hospital. In fact, Red Roof Inn offers hospital discounts. The eight-story hotel serves coffee in the lobby, and each room has cable TV with access to movies and video games. Of the 135 rooms, more than 90 are nonsmoking, with several larger

wheelchair-accessible rooms. The Inn offers a discount for Sam's Club members.

Residence Inn by Marriott $$$$
1111 Millmont Street, Charlottesville
(434) 923-0300, (800) 331-3131
www.marriott.com
They call this the next best thing to being at home. For business travelers or those who want more of the comforts of home, this new 108-room all-suite hotel is one of the only places in town that offers fully equipped kitchens in every room. You can choose one bedroom, two bedrooms, or even a studio that comes with more space than a traditional hotel room. Each suite has a work space; many feature multiple phone jacks for those who want to bring along their computers. If recreation is more your interest, there is an outdoor swimming pool and Sport Court for tennis, basketball, or volleyball. If you want a break from preparing your own meals, stop by the lobby for a complimentary continental breakfast. The staff also hosts a weekly social hour and barbecue. To make your stay easier, Marriott will provide daily housekeeping, a valet, a guest laundry, and they will even do your grocery shopping for you. Pets can stay, too, for a nonrefundable fee of $200.

Lynchburg

Best Value Inn $$
5016 South Amherst Highway
Lynchburg
(434) 845-7041, (888) 316-2378
You can absorb the beautiful view of the Blue Ridge Mountains from your patio or balcony at this 66-room hotel. Choose from single, double, and king-size beds; the latter includes a sleeper sofa and home office room. A microwave, refrigerator, coffeemaker, and hair dryer are in every room. Other amenities include a 25-inch color TV with three HBO channels. Enjoy a free continental breakfast and relax in the outdoor pool. Local phone calls are free. Smoking and nonsmoking

rooms are available. There's also a small meeting room.

Comfort Inn $$$$
3125 Albert Lankford Drive, Lynchburg
(434) 847-9041, (800) 228-5150
Comfort Inn Lynchburg offers guests a clean, comfortable, and affordable room in the heart of the city. All guests receive a free deluxe continental breakfast, the use of the exercise room, and a large outdoor pool. The meeting rooms are available for business meetings, family reunions, or wedding receptions. AAA or AARP discounts are welcome. Pets may stay for a $15 fee.

Days Inn Lynchburg $$$$
3320 Candler's Mountain Road
Lynchburg
(434) 847-8655, (800) 787-DAYS
Days Inn Lynchburg is an award-winner among the Days Inn chain. It is centrally located in Lynchburg and is easily accessible from Routes 29, 501, and 460. The hotel is directly across the street from the mall and within a mile of more than 20 restaurants. Electronic-card locks give an added feature of security. More than 75 percent of the 131 guest rooms are non-smoking, and half are equipped with microwaves, refrigerators, coffeemakers, digital satellite TVs, iron and ironing boards, hair dryers, alarm clocks, and snack packs. The hotel has a large pool and play area. Business travelers will appreciate the hotel's complimentary airport shuttle service. The hotel's DayBreak Family Restaurant serves breakfast and lunch. Small pets may stay with a deposit and fee.

Holiday Inn Express Lynchburg $$$
5600 Seminole Avenue, Lynchburg
(434) 237-7771, (800) 822-9899
www.hiexpress.com
The Express offers a free continental breakfast and comfortable, clean accommodations. The 102 guest rooms have king or double beds, remote-control cable TV, desks, sofas, and direct-dial touch-

tone phones. Nonsmoking rooms and facilities for the disabled are available, as are whirlpool baths or shower massages and swimming pools. Children younger than 16 stay free, and roll-away beds are complimentary. Corporate, senior citizen, and tour/group rates are available.

Radisson–Lynchburg　$$$$
2900 Candler's Mountain Road
Lynchburg
(434) 237-6333, (800) 333-3333
www.radisson.com
Families with children should consider the Lynchburg Radisson. In addition to adequate amenities and prompt service, children of any age stay for free when they occupy the same room as their parents. The 167 attractive guest rooms and suites are furnished with large, comfortable beds, cable TV, and direct-dial telephones. Suites also feature wet bars, refrigerators, and double, full-length, bifold mirrored doors. Wake-up service, a gift shop, a newsstand, and a courtesy van are other conveniences. The Radisson has an exercise room, a heated indoor pool, spa, and sauna. Johnny Bull's Restaurant serves some of the finest cuisine in Lynchburg, focusing on American, continental, and regional dishes. The Imbibery is the hotel's bar.

Ramada Inn & Conference Center　$$$
3436 Odd Fellows Road, Lynchburg
(434) 847-4424, (800) 2-RAMADA
www.lynchburg-ramada.com
Ramada Inn & Conference Center is the newest full-service hotel in the Greater Lynchburg area. The property, located just off US 29 Expressway at exit 7, features 216 guest rooms, a restaurant, lounge, and meeting/banquet rooms. When staying at the Inn, you'll enjoy great services in a convenient central location. Wake up to a free hot breakfast buffet (with corporate-rate rooms or higher) and complimentary coffee. Guest rooms have 20-inch remote-control cable TV and free HBO and data-port phones. There's also an outdoor pool. The Ramada Inn also has the Seasons Restaurant and Lounge as well as conven-

ient access to River Ridge Mall, Cattle Annie's, and other area attractions. AAA, AARP, corporate, government, and group discounts are available.

Smith Mountain Lake

Lake Inn at Westlake Corner　$$$
45 Enterprise Lane, Hardy
(540) 721-3383, (888) 466-LAKE
www.lakeinnmotel.com
The Lake Inn, popular with bass anglers, opened in 1996 with its new extension now totaling 60 rooms. It offers a variety of accommodations, including rechargeable outlets for boats, king- and queen-size beds, two wheelchair-accessible rooms, air-conditioning, cable TV and a recliner and coffeemaker in each room, and a continental breakfast. The location makes it convenient to the heartbeat of the lake. Pets are welcome in designated rooms.

Bedford County

Peaks of Otter Lodge　$$$$
Mile 86, Blue Ridge Parkway, Bedford
(540) 586-1081
www.peaksofotter.com
This popular lodge is like no hotel you've ever seen and is an autumn tradition for fall foliage fans around the world. Peaks of Otter is surrounded by the beauty of the Blue Ridge Mountains and lush green countryside, with a gorgeous lake nearly at its doorstep. The lodge's interior reflects the natural setting, with wood and subtly blended textures, tones, and colors.

The 63 rooms offer double beds and private baths. Each room opens onto a private balcony or patio. The lodge has no telephones and no TV, so you can truly unwind and relax away from the rat race. The lodge has a cocktail lounge and dining room. Call ahead for seasonal rates. (Also see our Blue Ridge Parkway and Skyline Drive chapter.)

Rocky Mount

Comfort Inn $$$
1730 North Main Street, Rocky Mount
(540) 489-4000, (800) 228-5150
Beautiful Smith Mountain Lake is just 20 miles away from this hotel. Ferrum College also is nearby. The 60 rooms have cable TV and AM/FM radios. A continental breakfast and sunrise coffee are complimentary to all guests. An outdoor pool is on the property. New to the Inn is Ippy's Restaurant, which offers lunch and full dinner menu plus a lounge. Also adjacent to the Inn is a new batting cage and miniature golf course.

NEW RIVER VALLEY
Montgomery County

AmeriSuites $$$$
1020 Plantation Road, Blacksburg
(540) 552-5636
www.amerisuites.com
This bright and shiny hotel opened in September 2000, just in time for the hot Virginia Tech football games, starring (now Atlanta Falcons quarterback) Michael Vick. Of course, hotels were still booked months in advance, but it was good to have additional lodging choices in the area. And this is a good one, since all 94 rooms are suites. Seventy-four feature either king-size beds or two doubles and a pullout sleeper sofa, while the remaining 20 have an easy chair and a large, L-shaped desk. Enjoy a complimentary continental breakfast, take a dip year-round in the indoor pool, or work out in the fitness center. Rooms also come with dataports, hair dryers, irons and ironing boards, and VCRs.

Best Western Red Lion $$$
900 Plantation Road, Blacksburg
(540) 552-7770, (800) 528-1234
www.bestwestern.com
This hotel on 13 wooded acres is an ideal site for a meeting or banquet, since the facilities can accommodate as many as 400. The 104 guest rooms include two suites and one wheelchair-accessible room. Breakfast is served in the dining room, and the hotel has a lounge that's open on Friday and Saturday nights. Reasonable-size pets are allowed.

Christiansburg Microtel Inn & Suites $$
135 Ponderosa Drive, Christiansburg
(540) 381-0500, (888) 771-7171
www.microtelinn.com
This economically priced hotel offers a lot for its price. The 86 rooms, including 31 suites, all have queen-size beds. There is a guest laundry, exercise room, and a complimentary continental breakfast. The suites also have refrigerators, microwaves, coffeemakers, one queen bedroom, and a sleeper sofa, as well as a dinette table and chairs.

Comfort Inn $$$
3705 South Main Street, Blacksburg
(540) 951-1500, (800) 228-5150
www.choicehotels.com
"People still refer to us as the new hotel—that's a good sign," reports one staff member. And indeed it still feels new, especially with the numerous renovations: new carpet, tile floors, wallpaper, and new vanities in the bathrooms. This Comfort Inn has 80 rooms, with your choice of two doubles or a king-size bed. Rooms come with high-speed Internet access, in-room safes, irons, ironing boards, hair dryers, coffeemakers, and HBO. Take time to relax in the seasonal outdoor heated pool and work out in the exercise facility. You can also sit down to a deluxe continental breakfast. Comfort Inn offers a courtesy shuttle.

Hampton Inn New River Valley $$$
380 Arbor Drive, Christiansburg
(540) 381-5874, (800) HAMPTON
This Hampton Inn opened in 2000. It has 119 rooms and the chain's customary complimentary full breakfast bar. You can also get your local calls free, HBO, and you may make use of the high-speed Internet

access in the rooms. Other amenities include the iron, ironing board, and hair dryer, as well as an outdoor pool and a fitness center that is open 24 hours. The hotel is convenient to many restaurants and the New River Valley Mall.

Holiday Inn $$$$
900 Prices Fork Road, Blacksburg
(540) 552-7001, (800) HOLIDAY
www.holiday-inn.com
If you're planning to visit Virginia Tech, this hotel is by far the most convenient, as it is located right across the street from the university. There are 148 rooms, including one suite and six larger rooms on the executive level that have a king-size bed and two doubles, as well as a refrigerator and comfy bathrobes. The remaining rooms offer a choice of a king-size bed or two doubles. You can swim year-round in the indoor pool, or enjoy the sun in the outdoor pool, tennis court, and volleyball court. You'll like this. Attitudes is the lounge where you can stop in for a drink, and Lattitudes is the restaurant where you can enjoy breakfast and dinner. Other room amenities include a coffeemaker, iron and ironing board, hair dryers, high-speed Internet access, on-command movie system, PlayStation, and ability to access the Web from the TV.

Quality Inn at Christianburg $$$
50 Hampton Boulevard, Christiansburg
(540) 382-2055, (800) 426-7866
This 124-room hotel is right off I-81 at exit 118C, making it a convenient stop for travelers who want to visit downtown Christiansburg or nearby Virginia Tech. Be prepared: Since the hotel is so close to Blacksburg, it is difficult to get reservations on those weekends when the Hokies have a home football game. Rates also may run a little higher for weekends and special events. There are rooms for all sizes, including queens, doubles, and kings. All the rooms are equipped with coffeemakers and irons and ironing boards and offer HBO and free local calls.

While all the rooms are equipped with high-speed Internet access, Quality Inn went one step further: There is wireless Internet access by the pool. Quality Inn also offers a fitness center and hot tub by the outdoor pool. A continental breakfast is provided each morning, but several restaurants are nearby, including local favorites the Huckleberry and the Farmhouse. Children younger than 18 stay free.

Ramada Limited $$$$
3503 Holiday Lane, Blacksburg
(540) 951-1330
www.ramadablacksburg.com
The hotel's 98 nicely decorated rooms have numerous conveniences. Each room is equipped with a refrigerator, coffeemaker, hair dryer, and AM/FM radios. Some rooms also have microwaves, Jacuzzis, and sauna baths. There is Internet access in the lobby and dataports in each room. Guests also are treated to a continental breakfast and a free newspaper. Banquet and meeting rooms are also available. A lounge, coin-operated laundry, and Showtime TV are available for guests.

Radford

Best Western Radford Inn $$$$
1501 Tyler Avenue, Radford
(540) 539-3000, (800) 528-1234
(800) 628-1955
Nestled in the heart of the New River Valley, the hotel offers 104 Colonial-style deluxe rooms, featuring cable TV, coffeemakers, hair dryers, and phones. A two-room Jacuzzi suite is available, as are rooms with king-size or double beds. You can choose between smoking and non-smoking. This is a good place for relaxing: The gazebo-style indoor swimming area has a whirlpool, sauna, and exercise facilities that are available year-round. Read a complimentary *USA Today* newspaper while sitting down for your continental breakfast at Spinnakers, the hotel's full-service restaurant. This popular restaurant

also serves lunch and dinner. Planning a big party? Banquet rooms and meeting facilities can meet your needs by accommodating up to 250 people. Pets are allowed with a fee.

Executive Motel $
7498 Lee Highway, Radford
(540) 639-1664
This small motel is clean and comfortable—and very affordable. Its location near St. Alban's Hospital and Radford Shopping Plaza provides added convenience. Each of the 26 rooms has two double beds, microwaves, a refrigerator, air-conditioning, direct-dial telephones, and cable TV with HBO. Many restaurants, including fast food, are nearby.

Super 8 Motel $$
1600 Tyler Avenue, Radford
(540) 731-9355, (800) 800-8000
Super 8 provides 58 rooms with a lot of amenities, including cable TV, waterbeds upon request, a 24-hour desk, wake-up calls, and free coffee each morning. And the rates are famously affordable. Non-smoking rooms and business singles are available upon request. Pets may stay for a $15 fee.

Pulaski County

Comfort Inn $$$
4424 Cleburne Boulevard, Dublin
(540) 674-1100, (800) 221-2222
Each of the 99 rooms has individual temperature control, cable TV, AM/FM clock radio, and direct-dial touch-tone phones. Some rooms have Jacuzzis. The conference room has a wet bar, and a private banquet room is also available. AARP and other discounts are offered. Pets are permitted for $10 a night.

ALLEGHANY HIGHLANDS
Alleghany County

Best Western Mountain View $$$
820 Madison Avenue, Covington
(540) 962-4951, (800) WESTERN
Guests at this hotel receive a full hot breakfast in the Brass Lantern, the hotel's restaurant that specializes in family dining and business lunches. All 77 rooms are equipped with cable TV, coffeemakers, dataports, hair dryers, and direct-dial phones. The hotel also has an outdoor pool and offers a laundry service. Banquet and meeting rooms are available and can serve up to 175 people. You can pop into the Bleachers Lounge for a cold beverage and watch a game on TV. There are non-smoking and king-size-bed options. Small pets are allowed.

Comfort Inn $$$
203 Interstate Drive, Covington
(540) 962-2141, (800) 221-2222
Here you will find 99 rooms with options of nonsmoking, king-size beds, and two-room suites. The rooms have coffeemakers, cable TV, and direct-dial phones with free local calls. Guests receive a free hot breakfast, and laundry service is available. If you are looking for a little exercise, Comfort Inn has an outdoor pool and an indoor whirlpool. For dinner, Harvey's is adjacent to the hotel, and shopping can be found within a 2-block radius of the hotel.

Bath County

Wilderness Ranch in
Bluegrass Hollow $$$$
Highway 683, Millboro
(540) 997-9225
Privacy, peace, and tranquillity are yours in these furnished log homes located on approximately 100 acres fully surrounded by the George Washington and Jefferson

i *If you're looking for accommodations in Highland County in mid-March, be sure to make reservations as soon as possible. The rural community of 2,500 gets an estimated 75,000 visitors for its annual Maple Festival.*

National Forests. If you want to get away from it all, this is the place. There are no telephones, no televisions. Just sit out on the swing on your very large porch and commune with nature. While trails from here lead directly into the forest, inside you have all the modern conveniences of home. There are a modern bathroom and fully equipped kitchen with a double stainless-steel sink, full-size refrigerators, four-burner stove, and microwave. You can enjoy the hiking trails or drive to the nearby historical sites or recreation areas. Doubles run $210 year-round for two people for two nights. Add on $15 per person per night if you would like to bring a group.

Highland County

Highland Inn   **$$**
Main Street, Monterey
(540) 468-2143, (888) 466-4682
Gregg and Deborah Morse are the innkeepers of this cozy spot in Monterey, fondly referred to as "Virginia's Switzer-land." This Victorian home was built in 1904 to serve the lodging needs of tourists escaping from the summer heat of nearby cities. Eastlake porches with gingerbread trim and rocking chairs are so inviting you will want to stay indefinitely. Each of the 18 guest rooms has a private bath and is individually decorated with antiques and collectibles. Choose a traditional room (double bed) or the premium room (king-size bed). Suites also come in two choices. The traditional suite features a full bed, parlor, and sleeper sofa. The premium suite has a canopied king-size bed with a parlor and pullout sofa bed. All rooms are non-smoking and offer cable TV and coffeemakers. There are no phones, however. If you want to make a call or hook up to a modem, you can use the ones in the library parlor. A complimentary continental breakfast is provided each morning in the Black Sheep Tavern. Highland Inn is listed on the National Register of Historic Places and is a Virginia Historic Landmark. Well-behaved pets can stay for $10.

BED-AND-BREAKFASTS
AND COUNTRY INNS

If the attractions aren't enough to draw you to the Blue Ridge, there's enough history and mystery at our inns to make it difficult for you to leave these cozy retreats. Slip into the tranquility of country life at an old stagecoach inn on the Valley Turnpike in Woodstock, or take a llama trek into the mountains at Applewood Inn. No matter what your interests, you can find the perfect place to relax.

Each of these grand old bed-and-breakfast inns and country inns has its own distinct charm, with histories as varied as the decor. You can stay on the former site of an ancient American Indian village at Silver Thatch Inn in Charlottesville. Or you may be swept away by the beauty of bubbling springs at Meadow Lane in Warm Springs.

A significant number of the inns are in restored, historic properties. Historic and other attractions of exceptional interest plus skiing, fishing, boating, swimming, and horseback riding are all within reasonable reach of a bed-and-breakfast inn. Many can accommodate special dinners, weddings, receptions, and other social and meeting functions.

Virginia is internationally known for Southern hospitality, and these antique country manors can convey to you a sense of tranquility that's hard to find anywhere else.

Many inns do not allow children and pets. We have indicated those that do accept them. Be sure to verify this before making a reservation.

PRICE CODE

As in our Hotels and Motels chapter, we provide a dollar key to assist you in determining the cost of a one-night stay for two at the inns we've listed in this chapter.

Note the rate indicated is for the standard accommodation; rates may vary according to additional amenities and special requests. Most inns require a deposit of one night's price to confirm reservations. Several of the lodgings list prices under the Modified American Plan, meaning prices reflect a night's stay as well as two meals (breakfast and dinner). The rates indicated here are for the high season, April through October; some inns reduce rates in the off-season, except those in ski areas.

$	$65 to $85
$$	$86 to $105
$$$	$106 to $120
$$$$	$121 and higher

Note that if an inn has rooms that fall within two price categories, it will be listed in the lower range. For example, if the rooms cost between $80 and $95, we will feature it in the $ category because you can find accommodations within the lower price bracket.

RESERVATION SERVICES

The following services are available to assist you in selecting a bed-and-breakfast or country inn.

Every January the **Bed & Breakfast Association of Virginia,** P.O. Box 1077, Stanardsville 20973, (888) 660–BBAV, www.innvirginia.com, puts out a descriptive booklet of unique lodging across the state called *Virginia's Inns and Bed & Breakfasts.*

The **Virginia Department of Tourism,** 901 East Byrd Street, Richmond 23219, (800) 847–4882, www.virginia.org, also includes bed-and-breakfasts in its catalog of lodgings, events, and attractions from across the state.

Blue Ridge Bed & Breakfast also publishes an online guide featuring more than 50 inns, farms, and historic houses in three states. Contact them at 2458 Castleman Road, Berryville 22611, (540) 955-1246, (800) 296-1246, or visit www.blueridge .bb.com.

SHENANDOAH VALLEY

Frederick County

Brownstone Cottage $$
161 McCarty Lane, Winchester
(540) 662-1962
www.brownstonecottage.com
If you are looking for a little pampering, start your visit at Brownstone Cottage. It's small: There are only two suites, but that's what owners Chuck and Sheila Brown say makes this inn special. "We get a lot of people from Washington who just want to get away from the rat race," Chuck Brown said. "We're not very big, so we kind of spoil them. They love the special attention."

The Browns will put you up in their home, a French-Armenian cottage that is more reminiscent of an English Tudor bed-and-breakfast. You can take in the scenic countryside from the deck or cozy up amid Victorian antiques in the sitting room. The Victorian Room has its own private whirlpool, sitting room, and a hand-carved cherry queen-size bed. The Emerald Suite includes a king-size bed, a daybed that converts into another king, a sitting area, and private bath. Children older than 12 are welcome.

Many inns and bed-and-breakfasts offer greatly reduced rates in the off-season (November through March, except in ski areas). You'll save money, and you can fully enjoy amenities such as fireplaces, hot cider, and snow-covered meadows.

Every morning, freshly brewed coffee will be waiting to start off a full country breakfast with Chuck's homemade pancakes or bread. The candlelit breakfast is served in the formal dining room on fine china.

The Inn at Vaucluse Spring $$$$
231 Vaucluse Spring Lane, Stephens City
(540) 869-0200, (800) 869-0525
www.vauclusespring.com
This classic Virginia inn offers 10 rooms, two suites, and three guest houses on the 100-acre estate of Shenandoah Valley artist John Chumley.

Owners Neil and Barry Myers call their renovated Manor House their crown jewel. Built by Capt. Strother Jones in 1785, the Manor House sits atop a hill with a commanding view of grazing Holstein cattle and the Blue Ridge Mountains beyond. Inside it's an antiques lover's dream. Each of the three upstairs bedrooms includes fireplaces with the original mantels, ancient heart-pine floors, and private baths with Jacuzzis. The stone-walled lower level features three more bedrooms and a common room filled with overstuffed chairs and the original cooking fireplace. The downstairs rooms all feature queen-size beds, private baths, and fireplaces.

Four accommodations are in the Chumley Homeplace, including the Chumley Suite and the Hite Suite. The two rooms in the new Cottage on the Hill have private outside entrances, two-person Jacuzzis, and private patios. The three guest houses, the Gallery, Mill House Studio, and Cabin on the Pond, feature king-size beds and two-person Jacuzzi tubs. The Mill House Studio, a two-level suite that overlooks Vaucluse Pond, used to serve as the artist's studio. The latest addition, the Cabin by the Pond, is a reconstructed log tobacco barn with a porch that overlooks the entire Spring Valley.

A three-course, made-from-scratch country breakfast is served daily in the Manor House dining rooms. For an additional charge (by reservation only), a three-course "Southern Comfort" Supper is available on Friday nights, and a four-course gourmet dinner is available on Saturday nights. Before the Saturday night dinner, guests gather at the Manor House for sangria or mulled wine, according to season, and socializing.

Civil War battlefields and the Skyline Drive are minutes away. Vaucluse is a non-smoking inn, but guests may smoke on the grounds. Children older than 10 are welcome.

Wayside Inn $$
7783 Main Street, Middletown
(540) 869-1797, (877) 869-1797
www.alongthewayside.com

Since 1797 this old stagecoach stop has been coddling travelers along U.S. Highway 11, once a major north-south thoroughfare. Two hundred years ago it served as the Wilkinson Tavern, later changing its name to Larrick's Hotel after the Civil War. A third floor was added in the 1900s, along with a new name, Wayside Inn.

This restored 18th-century country inn has maintained its flair for Southern hospitality. Each of its 24 guest rooms is furnished in period antiques, including four-poster beds with canopies, cannon-ball and acorn-carved details, plus French, Provincial, and Greek Revival period pieces. Allow yourself a couple of hours to examine the inn's artwork and curios.

For an additional charge you can savor a hearty breakfast, lunch, or dinner, or brunch on Sunday. The restaurant serves excellent Southern-style meals in seven private dining rooms and a large main dining area. The Wayside Theater (see our chapter on the Arts) is just down the street, and many historical attractions are nearby.

Clarke County

L'Auberge Provencal $$$$
U.S. Highway 340, White Post
(540) 837-1375, (800) 638-1702
www. laubergeprovencale.com

Many know L'Auberge Provencal as one of the finest restaurants in Virginia, but this French country inn also has been named one of the Twelve Most Romantic Hideaways in the East by *Discerning Traveler.*

Alain Borel, a fourth-generation chef from Avignon, France, and his wife, Celeste, moved to Virginia's Hunt Country and opened a restaurant in 1981 (see our Restaurants chapter). Guest rooms were soon added, and the 1753 fieldstone farmhouse is now a French masterpiece with 11 guest rooms and three dining rooms.

Rooms range from a country Victorian bedroom with two antique double beds and sitting area to La Suite Romantique. Ideal for honeymooners, this suite has a large bedroom with a king-size Alcove bed, a separate sitting room with a working fireplace, and a large private bathroom with a whirlpool tub and hand-painted Italian tiles. Six of the rooms have wood-burning fireplaces, and one is situated above the lovely rose patio with its own private deck.

The Villa La Campagnette—which translates to "small house in the country"—is the Borels' newest addition. Surrounded by old-growth trees and beautiful gardens, it is nestled on 18 private acres just 3 miles from L'Auberge Provencale. You would swear you just walked into a Mediterranean villa in the South of France. Formerly known as Roselawn, this 1890s home has been restored with the finest European flair—textured walls covered in French fabric, hand-painted tiles from Spain, and luxurious antique beds from Italy. If you look above the mantle in the sitting room, you'll find a marble plaque from Alain's grandfather's house in Avignon, the model for the new Villa La Campagnette. Here are one master bedroom and two suites, each individually decorated and all with private baths featuring spa-style showers for two.

The large master bedroom is Provencale in style, with a queen-size Italian brass and iron bed, a sitting area with Avignon wicker, and a private bath with Italian tiles and antique claw-foot slipper tub. The suites are even grander, with comfortable sitting rooms and four-poster beds. Villa guests also can enjoy the outdoor pool and Jacuzzi on the bricked terrace. A full gourmet breakfast is served each morning, featuring fresh homemade croissants, café au lait, and fresh juice. And that's just the beginning. The first course may feature orange blossom waffles with berries and crème fraiche or apple crepes with maple syrup. But there's more. The first course is followed by the entrees, such as eggs on sautéed tomato with herbs, wilted spinach, wild mushrooms, cottage fries, lobster cakes, and quail.

The Borels also have equipped all their rooms with complimentary fruit baskets, in-room coffee and tea, and comfy terry robes.

Nearby attractions include Long Branch Plantation, Shenandoah National Park, the Skyline Drive, and a host of wineries and antiques shops. Sports lovers also have ample opportunities to explore their skills, ranging from canoeing, hiking, and horseback riding to golfing, tennis, and balloon riding.

Children older than 10 are welcome, but, sorry, the pets must stay home.

Warren County

Chester House $$$
43 Chester Street, Front Royal
(540) 635-3937, (800) 621-0441
www.chesterhouse.com

Attorney Charles Samuels built Chester House in 1905 and spared no expense in creating his estate. Local artisans designed the intricate woodwork and dentil molding, and handsome marble mantels, fountains, and statuary were imported from Europe. Today, Chester House is a two-acre Italian Renaissance estate located in the heart of Front Royal's historic district.

The grounds are beautiful, with terraced gardens, wisteria arbors, a fountain fish pond, and almost an acre of formal and informal boxwoods. Owners Phillip Inge, Allen Hamblin, and Barbara Hamblin like to say they blend the old with the new. This is certainly apparent in Chester House's accommodations.

The Garden Cottage has a living and dining room, fireplace, TV, kitchen, loft with king-size bed, and a full bath with a whirlpool for two. The Royal Oak Suite is decorated with a four-poster queen-size bed, working fireplace, sitting room, private bath, and views of the gardens. The Blue Ridge Room has Shaker furniture, king-size bed, and a private bath. The Appalachian Room and Skyline Room have queen-size beds and private baths. The Shenandoah Suite has a king-size bed, sitting room, and original private bath with a claw-foot soaking tub with shower. Treats in your room include terry robes, toiletries, wine, beer, soft drinks, bottled water, mints, and homemade cookies. There is also free wireless high-speed Internet access.

Breakfast is served in the dining room with china, crystal, and silver and includes juices, home-baked breads and pastries, assorted cereals and fruits, select teas, and Allen's special "Chester House Coffee." Entrees may include Phillip's mile-high popovers or cinnamon brown sugar pancakes.

Front Royal is an excellent center from which to explore the area. Chester House is 1 mile from the Skyline Drive and only 70 miles from Washington, D.C. Within minutes of the house are caverns, battlefields, wineries, horseback riding, golf, tennis, fishing, and canoeing on the Shenandoah River. Downtown Front Royal offers the Confederate Museum, an old-time general store, new and used bookstores, and several antiques shops. Children older than 12 are welcome, and the hosts can recommend an excellent kennel in the area where you can board your pets.

Killahevlin $$$$
1401 North Royal Avenue, Front Royal
(540) 636-7335, (800) 847-6132
www.vairish.com

Irish immigrant and limestone baron William Carson built his home on the highest spot in Front Royal, calling it "Killyhevlin" for the place in Northern Ireland he cherished as a child. The house was designed by the architectural firm that created Washington's grand Old Executive Office Building. It is said that during the Civil War two of maverick Confederate Colonel John Singleton Mosby's men were hanged here, and Union troops often camped in this strategic spot.

Owner Susan O'Kelly has Irish roots and was captivated by the brick Edwardian mansion and Gaelic influences at the forefront of the house's decor. Each of the six accommodations has a queen-size bed, working fireplace, private bath with whirlpool tub and shower, and a wonderful view. Four of the six rooms have porches.

Breakfast, a sumptuous repast of Kona coffee, fresh fruits, breads, and a variety of entrees, is elegantly served. On-site is an Irish pub with complimentary Irish ale, wine, sodas, and snacks for guests. Sherry, cider, and champagne are available on request. Killahevlin is listed in both the National Register of Historic Places and the Virginia Landmarks Register.

Shenandoah County

The Inn at Narrow Passage $$$
US 11 at Chapman Landing Road
Woodstock
(540) 459-8000, (800) 458-8002
www.narrowpassage.com
This log inn overlooking the Shenandoah River has been welcoming and protecting travelers since the 1740s. Back then, it was a haven for settlers seeking refuge from Indian attacks along the "narrow passage," where only one wagon could pass one at a time, and travel was dangerous. It also served as Stonewall Jackson's headquarters during the Valley Campaign of 1862.

Ed and Ellen Markel have taken great care in restoring this landmark to its 18th-century look and maintaining the warm ambience of the original inn. It is furnished in antiques and Colonial reproductions. Each bedroom has comfortable amenities; many have working fireplaces. The inn is centrally heated and air-conditioned. Breakfast is served in the Colonial dining

room, often before a cheery fire. Guests can relax by the massive limestone fireplace in the living room or enjoy the views of the sloping lawns and river from the porch.

Hiking and fishing are recreational options at the inn. Nearby you'll find historic battlefields, wineries, caverns, and skiing at Bryce Resort. The inn is 2 miles from Interstate 81; take exit 283 just south of Woodstock. A conference room is available for executive retreats.

River'd Inn $$$$
1972 Artz Road, Woodstock
(540) 459-5369, (800) 637-4561
www.riverdinn.com
Cross over a low-water bridge on the north fork of the Shenandoah River, and if the river rises, the locals say you are "rivered in." This Victorian inn, at the base of Massanutten Mountain off US 11, sits on one of the famous seven bends of the Shenandoah. Host Diana Lurey oversees the 25 acres of secluded natural areas offering picnicking, hiking, and relaxing. A wraparound veranda and swimming pool are other leisure options.

The inn is centrally heated and air-conditioned, and the eight guest rooms are furnished with fine antiques. All rooms have queen-size beds, fireplaces, and private baths with whirlpool tubs.

The inn offers quiet dining in three elegant dining rooms, each with a distinctive fireplace and intimate seating. Meals are elegant, candlelight affairs with fresh-cut flowers, linen, china, and gourmet cuisine. A recent brunch featured assorted salads, mini muffins, omelets and eggs made to order, grilled salmon, warm bread pudding, apple-glazed pork, fresh-cut fruit, assorted cookies, and brownies. Dinners feature such gourmet mainstays as filet mignon, crawfish cake, swordfish, apple-bourbon duck, and rack of lamb. However, the menus change seasonally.

Country auctions, antiques and craft shops, horseback riding, fishing, and other river-oriented activities beckon. Nearby attractions include the New Market Battlefields and Civil War Museum, Massanutten and Bryce ski resorts, the Skyline Drive, caverns, Wayside Theater, and numerous other historic and cultural sites.

Page County

Bluemont Bed & Breakfast $$$
1852 US 340 Business, Luray
(540) 743-1268, (888) 465-8729
www.bluemontbb.com

Nestled among the rolling hills of the Shenandoah Valley, the Bluemont Bed & Breakfast welcomes visitors who just want to relax in between their rounds of hiking, touring historic sites, and visiting wineries. Hosts Eleanor and Alfred Ames have guaranteed that every room has a view, and that every guest's wish can be granted.

The three rooms are sunny and bright. The Mountain View Room does indeed have a wonderful view. During the day the sight of the Skyline Drive awaits you, and at night the twinkling lights of the Skyland Lodge can be seen. There is a cherry four-poster bed, fireplace, and sitting area. The Garden Room is decorated in pink with a rose border, and the Meadow Room is done in taupe with rust, green, and burgundy accents and has an excellent view of the Massanutten Mountains. All rooms have a TV and VCR, and plush robes await the guests. Other amenities include data-ports and a lounge with a microwave and a fridge stocked with complimentary snacks and drinks. Also in the lounge is a VHS tape library for your enjoyment.

Every morning guests enjoy a view along with their three-course country breakfast in the dining room. Early risers have coffee and tea already waiting for them. The Ameses can also pack a picnic for you to take along on your hikes or antiques shopping. Every evening there's a home-baked dessert waiting to top off your day. To make you feel more at home, the family cats, Callie and Fluffy, make their rounds, but they are not permitted in the guest area.

There is no smoking allowed at Bluemont, and children and pets cannot be accommodated. Special packages are available.

Jordan Hollow Farm Inn $$$$
326 Hawksbill Park Road, Stanley
(540) 778-2285, (888) 418-7000
www.jordanhollow.com

This 145-acre horse farm is nestled in a secluded hollow surrounded by the Shenandoah National Park and the George Washington and Jefferson National Forests. Though activities abound here, Jordan Hollow is about taking it easy. Innkeeper Gail Kyle invites guests to relax on the enormous wrap-around porch and walk through the lush meadows and fragrant woods. It's a farm environment with a steady, quiet pace.

Guests can bring and board their own horses if they choose. There also are plenty of walking paths and trails for those who prefer to rely on two legs.

The inn is quite large, with 15 guest rooms, all with private baths and some with fireplaces and Jacuzzis. The buildings, except for Arbor View Lodge and Mare Meadow Lodge, are the original farm buildings. The decor is eclectic with horse and garden themes.

The Farmhouse Restaurant serves a full breakfast and dinner in four dining rooms. The American regional cuisine takes advantage of seasonal ingredients, so menus change every few months.

For indoor entertainment, the Carriage House offers a large common area with games, books, and cable television. Other nearby activities include swimming, hiking, canoeing, fishing, skiing, museums, antiques, and craft shops. The farm is a short drive from Lake Arrowhead, Luray Caverns, Shenandoah National Park, and George Washington and Jefferson National Forests. Children are allowed in the family room, but be sure to notify the reservationist when you book your stay.

Milton House Bed & Breakfast $$
113 West Main Street, Stanley
(540) 778-2495, (800) 816-3731
www.miltonhouse-inn.com

This 1915 home was delivered to its original owners by U.S. mail. Ordered from the Sears catalog, the Milton was the name of one of the many Sears designs sold at the turn of the 20th century. Step through the door of this very American house and you step into a little piece of the United Kingdom.

Owners Ronnie and Yvonne Rowzie have decorated the Milton with a variety of English knickknacks and antiques. Yvonne is from the UK, and her collection of china teacups, eggcups, and teapots are on display for guests.

The inn is rich in detail—long, sweeping porches cooled by stately fir trees, leaded-glass windows that create a prism of sunbeams in the morning, detailed stenciling, and other period architectural attractions. Ronnie is proud of his gardens and works diligently to keep Milton House surrounded by well-landscaped plants and flowers.

All rooms have private baths, and a suite with a double shower is available. Several rooms have fireplaces. The property also includes a log cabin, built in 1991, with two deluxe accommodations, featuring hot tubs in both. One unit also has a kitchen.

Rates include a full buffet breakfast, and the adjacent Paisley Teapot tearoom is open to the public and for $12 serves a traditional English afternoon tea on china, complete with finger sandwiches, scones, cakes, and biscuits.

Milton House is 7 miles from Luray and is close to Shenandoah National Park, George Washington and Jefferson National Forests, New Market Battlefield, Massanutten Ski Resort, antiques shops, wineries, hiking trails, and great fishing and paddling spots.

The Ruffner House Inn $$$$
440 Ruffner House Road, Luray
(540) 743-7855
www.ruffnerhouse.com
This inn is actually two houses with six guest rooms with private baths that can accommodate as many as 16 people for reunions and retreats. But couples, too,

will enjoy the inn's 20-acre estate just outside Luray.

The ca. 1840 brick manor house has grandly scaled rooms with antique Victorian decor and fine art. Built in the early 1900s, the farmhouse boasts a marble and glass solarium. Purchased in 1999 by a Ruffner descendant, it's on the National Register of Historic Places and a stop on Virginia's Civil War Trails. Breakfast is served between 9:00 and 10:00 A.M., though you may request early coffee.

South Court Inn $$
160 South Court Street, Luray
(540) 843-0980, (888) 749-8055
www.southcourtinn.com
Years ago, Anita Potts was rooting around in an antiques shop and fell in love with a dust-covered turkey-shaped candy dish. She and her husband, Tom, never dreamed that purchase would lead to a huge collection of all things turkey, including tureens, cookie jars, and 30 different ironstone plate patterns. Neither did they think a large part of the collection would be on display in their then-undreamed-of bed-and-breakfast.

Located on two acres in the historic downtown of Luray, South Court Inn is a wonderful example of a late Victorian mansion, with a stone-floored veranda, sunroom, and brick veneer added in the 1930s. The Pottses spent three years restoring both the interior and exterior to its former Victorian elegance, and the effort shows. The inn's common areas are full of paneling, gleaming wood floors, and authentic colors and furniture of the era. There's even a cozy reading nook with hundreds of books tucked away on the second floor.

Also on the second floor are the three guest rooms, all named after the Pottses' grandmothers. The Edith Hayes and Emma Glen rooms are hung with brocade with carved queen-size canopy beds, claw-foot tubs, and feather pillows. The Mary Kenard, a sunny room done in blue and white, was upgraded in 2003 to feature a king-size half tester canopy bed with a wicker love seat and a shower for two. All rooms have fireplaces, chandeliers, period antiques, Oriental carpets, and private baths.

Just like their grandmothers, the owners serve up a full breakfast, complete with cereals, fruit, and a hot entree such as lemon cloud pancakes or cheese soufflé. The meal is served with coffee, tea, and juice. Meals are served on turkey-motif china from August through Thanksgiving, to give Anita a chance to showcase some of her collection. Afternoon tea can be served on request.

Children older than 12 are invited, but pets are not. However, arrangements can be made at a local kennel for your four-legged family member. Special packages are available.

White Fence Bed & Breakfast $$$$
275 Chapel Road, Stanley
(540) 778-4680, (800) 211-9885
www.whitefencebb.com

Tom and Gwen Paton bought this beautiful 1890 Victorian home, set on three acres, in 1998. The property features luxury cottages and suites, all with fireplaces and whirlpools.

The English Ivy Cottage is a historic building built in 1900 and was first used as a doctor's office. It has been redone into a private three-room suite, complete with a white picket fence headboard on the queen-size bed. There's a wood-burning fireplace and TV and VCR, and the breakfast room features an antique ice cream table and chairs in front of a bay window. A small refrigerator and coffeemaker are included. The bathroom includes a two-person Jacuzzi and separate shower. The Blue Ridge Carriage House is a private three-room suite done in tones of plum and teal. It features a log bed, love seat, fireplace, and TV and VCR. The adjacent breakfast room has a pub table and chairs that look out onto a wooded setting. There's also a Jacuzzi, small refrigerator, and coffeemaker. The Shenandoah Suite is a three-room suite in the 1890 main house and is decorated in plum, ivory, and sage. The bedroom has a queen-size sleigh bed,

fireplace, and sitting room with fireplace. All rooms have the original wood floors.

Guests have a choice of two breakfasts: a full breakfast served in the dining room, or a hearty continental breakfast brought to your room in a basket. The basket might include giant blueberry muffins, cereal, fruit, juice, and coffee. After breakfast, visit Luray Caverns, Shenandoah National Park, art galleries, or a battlefield. Lexington, Charlottesville, and Washington, D.C., are all a short drive away. Children are welcome.

Woodruff House Inns $$$
138 East Main Street, Luray
(540) 743-1494
www.woodruffinns.com

These highly rated Inns are described by innkeepers Debra and Lucas Woodruff as "fantasy Victorian," "fairy-tale Victorian," and "French country Victorian," and they deliver on that promise with antiques, Oriental rugs, and hallmark silver catching the firelight in cozy Victorian parlors. Expanded to include three neighboring Victorian houses, one cabin, and one cottage on the river, the Inns offer four suites and six guest rooms. All of the suites and most of the rooms come with Jacuzzis, and all have fireplaces. All meals are served in the elegant Victorian inn.

An elegant afternoon tea, morning gourmet coffee service in your room, and a fireside candlelight breakfast are included in the room price. A separate package includes a four-course dinner. Lucas Woodruff is a chef, so fantastic food is de rigueur. Private label wines from Virginia's Barboursville Vineyard are available, as well as an extensive collection from around the globe.

Three gardens (romantically lit after dusk) include gazebos and two hot tubs that set the tone for a romantic, relaxing evening. By day, visitors can take advantage of nearby attractions such as Luray Caverns, New Market Battlefields, or the Skyline Drive.

Rockingham County

Hearth N' Holly Inn   **$$**
46 Songbird Lane, Penn Laird
(540) 434-6766, (800) 209-1379
www.hearthnholly.com
Doris and Dennis Brown's pleasant bed-and-breakfast inn is 5 miles from I-81 and 10 minutes from Massanutten Resort and James Madison University. Situated on 15 acres, the Colonial and Victorian inn has three guest rooms with queen-size brass beds, private baths, TVs, and fireplaces.

A full country breakfast is served from 8:00 to 11:00 A.M. The innkeepers love pulling out all the stops to host weddings and other special events.

Diversions within easy reach include the theater, arts, and sports events at the university; skiing at Massanutten Resort; the Skyline Drive and the Blue Ridge Parkway; Civil War battlefields; and Endless, Grand, and Luray Caverns. Be warned: It will be hard to leave this inn, with its sunroom, picnic pavilion, hot tub, queen-size hammock, and wooded walking trails. In late 1997 the Browns added a full wraparound porch for those who would like to sit outside and enjoy the swings.

Joshua Wilton House, Inn,
and Restaurant   **$$$**
412 South Main Street, Harrisonburg
(540) 434-4464, (888) 2-WILTON
www.joshuawilton.com
Roberta and Craig Moore welcome guests to their elegantly restored Victorian home, which lies in the heart of the Shenandoah Valley. Restoration efforts have preserved much of the original architecture.

The Moores will spoil you with a complimentary glass of wine or beer in the evening, and their gourmet breakfast, including homemade pastries, fresh fruits, and a delicious pot of coffee, is enough to summon anyone out of bed. On-site is one of the state's most acclaimed restaurants with both cafe dining and fine dining available. The innovative menus feature a variety of locally grown foods (see our Restaurants chapter).

The Inn's bedrooms are furnished with period antiques to give them the charm of the 1880s. All five bedrooms have private baths, reading areas, and telephones. The Wilton House also has facilities for private parties, complete with an in-house wedding planner and catering director. The Inn also frequently hosts wine tastings, beer tastings, art shows, and other festivities throughout the year.

The Wilton House is within walking distance of James Madison University and downtown Harrisonburg. A variety of athletic activities, such as golfing, biking, hiking, swimming, and skiing, are accessible from the Inn. This old mansion is an oasis of quiet charm and gracious living surrounded by the Blue Ridge Mountains.

Augusta County

Belle Grae Inn   **$$$**
515 West Frederick Street, Staunton
(540) 886-5151, (888) 541-5151
www.bellegrae.com
The Belle Grae Inn is on the walking tour of architecturally rich historic Staunton and just a trolley ride or short walk to the Blackfriars Playhouse. This authentically restored inn, built in 1870, will please you with its 17 luxurious guest rooms and appetizing menu. It is named for two of the surrounding mountains, Betsy Belle and Mary Grae. The Scots-Irish settlers in the area, reminded of their homeland, named the mountains for Scottish land-

marks. Belle Grae sits atop a hill in historic Staunton. Wicker rockers invite relaxation on the veranda, and white gingerbread stylings decorate the porch of the main, original building.

One of the first things a guest sees is the double-entrance door with four stained-glass panels and a crystal oval in which the inn's name is engraved. Period reproductions and antiques, which are for sale, are found throughout the dining rooms, garden room, and other lovely rooms. The bedrooms each are furnished a little differently, but all are appropriate to the period. You can sit in front of your cozy fireplace (most rooms have them). Most rooms also have telephones, and all have private baths and such amenities as English herb soaps and bath oils. Joined by pathways and walks are four restored 1870s to 1890s vintage houses. These are available to families or for executive retreats.

Breakfast festivities begin at 7:00 A.M. in the garden room, where early risers may enjoy coffee, juice, poppy-seed bread (a house specialty), and complimentary newspapers. A full hot breakfast is also served from 8:00 A.M. to 9:00 A.M. Dining is a must at Belle Grae. Creative appetizers, a healthful soup, fresh salads, homemade breads, and beef, pork, chicken, pasta, and seafood entrees are offered Wednesday through Sunday evenings from 5:30 to 9:00 P.M. Be sure to save room for dessert. They're decadent.

Activities in the area include walking tours through gorgeous historic Staunton, shopping at a gigantic antique warehouse, or chess and backgammon in the quiet of the inn's sitting room.

Frederick House $$$
28 North New Street, Staunton
(540) 885-4220, (800) 334-5575
www.frederickhouse.com

Five stately houses were rescued from demolition and transformed into Frederick House. These Greek Revival buildings have been restored and the rooms inside graciously appointed with antiques and

paintings by Virginia artists. The oversize beds add an extra touch of comfort. Each of the 23 rooms has its own private bath, cable TV, telephone, and air-conditioning. A full, delicious, home-cooked breakfast is served each morning.

One activity we recommend is a relaxing stroll through the town to photograph Staunton's gorgeous architecture and to visit the town's antiques and specialty shops. The Blackfriars Playhouse and Woodrow Wilson's birthplace are only 2 blocks away (see our Attractions chapter), and Mary Baldwin College is next door. Cycling, hiking, and touring are perfect activities in the surrounding Blue Ridge and Allegheny Mountains. Hosts Joe and Evy Harman will point out places of interest and provide a bit of history as well.

The Inn at Keezletown Road $$
1224 Keezletown Road, Weyers Cave
(540) 234-0644, (800) 465-0100
www.keezlinn.com

This elegant, 100-year-old Victorian in the quaint village of Weyers Cave has spectacular views of the Blue Ridge Mountains. The four large guest rooms are furnished with antiques, comfortable beds, and Oriental rugs. Each has a private bath, sitting area, air-conditioning, and cable TV. All have queen-size beds, except for one, which affords either two twins or a king.

The innkeepers, Sandy and Alan Inabinet, provide a full country breakfast that includes fresh eggs from the inn's own chickens, pumpkin pancakes, and cheese grits. The grounds have wonderful gardens including a formal herb garden and a goldfish pond, and guests may walk on the adjacent trail through the town's park or sit and rock on the inn's porch.

The inn, just 10 minutes from Harrisonburg, is near historic sites. Other attractions are within easy driving distance, as are the Shenandoah Valley Regional Airport in Weyers Cave and several colleges. Children ages 14 and older are welcome. Smoking is limited to the garden and porch. Pets are not permitted.

The Iris Inn $$

191 Chinquapin Drive, Waynesboro
(540) 943-1991
www.irisinn.com

The charm and grace of Southern living in a totally modern facility surrounded by woods—that's the Iris Inn. The brick-and-cedar inn was built on 20 acres in 1991 and is ideal as a weekend retreat, business accommodation, or tranquil spot for the tourist. Its focus is on comfort, with nine spacious guest rooms decorated in nature and wildlife motifs, each with private bath and refrigerators; eight have modem access. The inn also has two suites in a separate building.

The main building has six guest rooms, each furnished with modern furniture, and each has a specific theme—the Deer Room, Wildflower Room, Pine Room, Bird Room, Woodland Room, and Duck Pond. The bright, airy rooms all have king- or queen-size beds (some have a daybed for a third person). One room is wheelchair accessible. The Hawk's Nest is an efficiency unit, complete with kitchenette and sitting area; it's ideal for longer stays and a favorite of honeymooners.

The Great Room, in addition to being the breakfast room, provides a gathering place around the high, stone fireplace where guests may relax and enjoy the woodland views. Beverages are available in the rooms, and a bottomless cookie jar is on the sideboard. A balcony library overlooks this beautiful room, providing panoramic views of the Shenandoah Valley. Wraparound porches on both floors and a three-story lookout tower—a hot tub is on its first floor!—are popular with guests.

In 1996 a new building was added to include two luxury suites, one of which converts to a meeting room. About 50 yards from the main house, this traditional, contemporary building has gas log fireplaces, spiral staircases, TVs, VCRs, and private balconies.

The full two-course breakfast includes home-baked breads, juice and fruit, fresh-brewed coffee, and an entree that changes daily. Nearby attractions are Waynesboro's Virginia Metalcrafters and P. Buckley Moss Museum, historic Monticello and Ash Lawn–Highland near Charlottesville, the Skyline Drive, the Blue Ridge Parkway, and the Appalachian Trail.

The Sampson Eagon Inn $$$

238 East Beverley Street, Staunton
(540) 886-8200, (800) 597-9722
www.eagoninn.com

This elegant inn, which has won preservation awards, is in the historic Gospel Hill section of Staunton, adjacent to the Woodrow Wilson Birthplace and Mary Baldwin College. The property's original owner, Sampson Eagon, was a Methodist preacher who held services on the grounds here during the 1790s.

Don't expect any preaching today, however: The inn is tailor-made for privacy, with three distinctive guest rooms and two suites, each furnished with beautiful period pieces, a queen-size canopied bed, cozy sitting area, and modern bath. Telephones, air-conditioning, and private TVs with VCRs are standard in the rooms. The inn even has a fax machine, in case you can't get away from the office completely.

The day begins with a full gourmet breakfast in the formal dining room (although the accent is on casual). Entrees include such dishes as pecan Belgian waffles, blueberry buttermilk soufflé pancakes, and an array of egg choices. Refreshments are available throughout the day, with beverages and gourmet chocolates brought right to your room. The menu changes daily and takes advantage of seasonal offerings.

Gourmet magazine writes that proprietors Frank and Laura Mattingly "take the second 'B' in B&B seriously." This antebellum home also has been included in *Southern Living* and *Travel and Leisure* magazines. This is indeed the place for a memorable retreat. The inn is only 1 block from Shenandoah Shakespeare's Blackfriars Playhouse, where you can round out the day with an evening with the Bard. The inn is not appropriate for children younger than 12 and does not accept pets. No smoking is allowed at the inn.

Thornrose House at Gypsy Hill $
531 Thornrose Avenue, Staunton
(540) 885-7026, (800) 861-4338
www.thornrosehouse.com

Otis and Suzanne Huston are the innkeepers at this beautiful bed-and-breakfast inn in Staunton's Gypsy Hill area. The moment you step into the grand entranceway, you begin to discover the charm of this Georgian Revival brick home and its five comfortable guest rooms. Named for English localities, each air-conditioned room is decorated in a rose motif and includes a private bath.

There is a sitting room on the second floor with a TV, while each room—one king, one double, and three queens—awaits with robes, flowers, and chocolates. You'll awaken to the aroma of a heart-healthy breakfast, with entrees ranging from banana-pecan pancakes and waffles to egg soufflés and French toast. Afterward, you'll want to venture out and see the sites that make Staunton so special. Nearby attractions include the P. Buckley Moss Museum, Grand Caverns, and the Museum of American Frontier Culture. Across the street is 300-acre Gypsy Hill Park, where you can play golf, tennis (rackets and balls provided), or swim. The Statler Complex, owned by country music's award-winning Statler Brothers, is right down the street.

Thornrose House has lovely gardens gracing its acre of grounds. The wraparound veranda with rocking chairs is perfect for an afternoon tea. The sitting room has a fireplace and a comfortable window seat in the bay window. School-age children are welcome.

Lexington and Rockbridge County

Applewood Inn & Llama Trekking $$
Buffalo Bend Road, Lexington
(540) 463-1962, (800) 463-1902
www.applewoodbb.com

Before moving to Virginia in July 1996, Linda and Christian Best operated a bed-and-breakfast in the Berkshires of western Massachusetts. But they had a dream of incorporating a llama-trekking business into their inn and their land in the Northeast was too small. They searched and found the perfect spot on 36 acres above Buffalo Creek in November 1995. After two months of renovating and llama buying, the Applewood opened for its first guests on Labor Day weekend, 1996.

The llamas aren't the only unique thing about Applewood Inn. Their lodge-style inn was designed as a passive solar home. Those unfamiliar with this system don't need to fear cold rooms and tepid water. There's always plenty of hot water, and the average temperature of the inn is 72 degrees.

There are four guest rooms scattered through the inn. The Quilter's Room is located on the ground floor and is decorated with a four-poster queen-size bed, love seat, gas-log fireplace, and large bath with Jacuzzi-shower combination. The room is decorated with a variety of hand-quilted items and adjoins a small porch with swing. This room is wheelchair accessible. The European Room is also on the ground floor and has a queen-size bed. Artwork from Germany, France, and Holland adorns the walls, and a gas-log fireplace adds a homey touch. Through the adjoining French doors is a small porch. The Hillside Room is decorated with an antique queen-size four-poster bed, a small gas-log fireplace, and wildlife prints. The private bath has a separate vanity area and a large whirlpool tub and shower. The room opens onto a large porch. The Autumn Room also opens onto the large porch and has an antique queen-size bed and private bath with corner shower.

There are many common areas throughout the house, including second-floor enclosed porches, the dining room with views of the mountains and llama pastures, and the Common Room, a nice place to relax and enjoy the fireplace in winter. There is a TV and VCR and a library of movies. From May through October you can sunbathe around the in-ground pool located just east of the house.

Breakfast is healthy and delicious, with homemade whole-grain breads and preserves, fruit, corn pudding, omelets, and other hot dishes. It is served in the dining room or on the porch. Linda and Christian can also prepare a four-course dinner as part of a long weekend package. Served on Sunday only; be sure to give advance notice. Complimentary snacks and beverages are available to guests all day long.

Applewood Inn is surrounded by 900 acres of woods and pastures with miles of trails. Chris and his llamas can take you on several different guided treks into the woods for a very reasonable fee. You lead your own llama, who carries your lunch, binoculars, and other gear so that you can just enjoy the walk. These animals are friendly and curious and can make an ordinary hike into something special. There's also fishing and other outdoor recreation nearby, and the area is perfect for cross-country skiing in winter. There's plenty to do for those who would rather find an antiques bargain than cast a line. Lexington is only 10 minutes away.

Smoking is permitted outdoors. Dogs are allowed in the European Room, and children older than 6 are welcome in the Quilter's Room, but please call ahead.

A Bed & Breakfast at Llewellyn Lodge $
603 South Main Street, Lexington
(540) 463-3235, (800) 882-1145
www.llodge.com
This charming 1940s brick Colonial home is in the heart of Lexington, within walking distance of all the city's historic sights. Ellen and John Roberts are your hosts. Ellen's a gourmet cook who has been a part of the airline, travel, hotel, and restaurant industries. John Roberts is a native Lexingtonian, born in the Stonewall Jackson House, once a hospital, now a museum.

The warm and friendly lodge has been welcoming weary travelers for more than 20 years. Refreshments are served upon arrival, while the comfortable living room with its large fireplace is a perfect setting for a good conversation. Each of the six

bedrooms is distinct, designed to meet the needs of a variety of guests. All rooms have king down bedding and a ceiling fan, and some have televisions. There also is a well-stocked guest refrigerator, free DSL Internet access, and Wi-Fi. Highlights include a large room with king-size bed and two rooms with double and twin beds. The screened gazebo is a great retreat for reading or relaxing.

Ellen's award-winning breakfast awaits you each morning—fantastic omelets, Belgian waffles, Virginia maple syrup, homemade muffins and breads, bacon, sausage, ham, juice, coffee, and teas. There are also low-carb options for the health conscious.

After breakfast, take on the great outdoors. John has a detailed *Trail & Outdoor Guide,* packed full of great advice on hiking, fishing, and other outdoor activities. The Lodge offers guided fly-fishing, golf, canoeing, horseback riding, and outdoor theater packages. The Robertses are happy to help you design a memorable outdoor adventure.

Smoking is not permitted in the guest rooms or dining room, and pets are not allowed, but a vet-attended kennel is close by. The Lodge is designed with adults in mind, although children ages 10 and older are welcome. Super winter rates, midweek discounts, and corporate rates are available.

The Bed and Breakfast Association of Virginia is a statewide association of more than 200 member inns. For a free copy of the directory, to purchase gift certificates for the member inns, or for information regarding innkeeping in Virginia, call (888) 660-2228.

Brierley Hill   **$$**
985 Borden Road, Lexington
(540) 464-8421, (800) 422-4925
www.brierleyhill.com
Guests at this bed-and-breakfast inn rave about the wonderful food and beautiful accommodations, not to mention the

breathtaking views from the large veranda. Situated on eight acres of hillside farmland, the inn is quiet and romantic, and the hospitality is second to none.

The inn is decorated throughout with Laura Ashley wall coverings, fabrics, and linens. Each of the five guest rooms has an elegant bed (three are canopy beds, and one is a medieval-style four-poster bed), a private bathroom, and sitting area. The Deluxe King Room has an additional daybed, fireplace, and TV. A two-room suite has a fireplace, Jacuzzi, and private patio looking out toward spectacular views. The inn has central air-conditioning, and a fireplace in the dining room warms the winter chill.

Owners Joyce and Ken Hawkins serve a full "no lunch" breakfast. You are likely to find eggs Florentine or raspberry-stuffed French toast alongside your country-style bacon. Homemade scones and muffins and fresh-ground coffees are also served daily. Pleasant days find breakfasts served on the veranda, while chilly mornings find you in front of a crackling fire. Take an afternoon break from your activities and relax with a refreshing drink and homemade cookies every afternoon.

You can relax in the serenity at Brierley Hill by lounging on the veranda or strolling down a country road. If you're up for a little more adventure, you can go sightseeing in historic Lexington or take advantage of special packages for theater, horseback riding, winter getaways, and specials for midweek stays. Children older than 12 are welcome. Smoking is restricted to the veranda or garden. No pets are allowed.

Cottage Farm Bed & Breakfast $$
3147 Glasgow Highway, Buena Vista
(540) 258-1252, (800) 895-7457
www.cottagefarm.com
In 1890 Briscoe Girard Baldwin purchased this 1871 Victorian mansion perched on 70 acres for $10,999.10. Over the years he sold off all but the house and the four acres surrounding it. The house stayed in the Baldwin family until 1964 and then changed hands five times until Ken and

Denise Gorsky purchased the property in 1998.

Their three guest rooms are named after ladies who once lived here, and the rooms are decorated in the fashion of their times. The Mary Baldwin Suite is a two-room suite divided by back-to-back fireplaces. A queen-size bed, ceiling fans, southern yellow pine floors, and floor-to-ceiling windows accent the suite. The bathroom contains a claw-foot tub and shower. The Margaret Paxton Room is a comfortable room with a queen-size bed, southern yellow pine floor, fireplace, sitting area, ceiling fan, and a whirlpool tub in the bathroom. The Mary Briscoe Room is great for families. It's a large room with a queen-size bed, fireplace, ceiling fan, and southern yellow pine flooring. Common rooms include a guest parlor with comfortable seating and TV.

The Gorskys serve a full country breakfast in the formal dining room. As a sampling, breakfast begins with juice, seasonal fruit, baked goods, and entrees as varied as egg nests Provencale and pineapple upside-down French toast. A wide selection of gourmet teas or freshly ground coffee is available.

Children older than 12 are welcome, but pets are not. Smoking is permitted in designated areas only. The inn gives special midweek corporate discounts, so be sure to ask when you make reservations.

The Hummingbird Inn $$$
30 Wood Lane, off Alt. Highway 39
Goshen
(540) 997-9065, (800) 397-3214
www.hummingbirdinn.com
This unique Victorian Carpenter Gothic, "born" in 1780 and completed in 1853, has been nationally recognized for its country charm and elegance. Owners Pat Miller and Dick Matthews have done a beautiful job redesigning the interior. Its five guest rooms, furnished with antiques, are colorful and spacious, and each has a private bath (two have double Jacuzzis). The Eleanor Room, with a king-size bed, fireplace, and large double-headed shower,

was named to commemorate Eleanor Roosevelt's stay here in 1935.

Full country breakfasts include original entrees, homemade bread, and foods unique to the area. A four-course dinner, served on Saturday only, is available with 48-hour notice and costs $35 per person. Typical entrees include steak or medallions of pork tenderloin in a peppercorn-mustard sauce. Dinner includes a bottle of wine. A simpler "picnic basket" dinner ($45 for two) is available to guests on Friday, and the innkeepers will prepare a "Day Pack" lunch for those exploring the area.

The house features wraparound verandas on the first and second levels, original pine plank floors, and a rustic den, solarium, and living room. Lovely perennial and rose gardens line the property, and a deck overlooks Mill Creek.

During Goshen's boom days in the late 1800s and early 1900s, the inn was directly across from the town's railroad station, and the steps from the tracks to the inn's private road are still in place.

Five minutes away is the gorgeous Goshen Pass, a popular spot for kayaking, picnicking, and sunbathing in warm weather. This place is not to be missed when the rhododendron are in bloom! Just 25 minutes away is historic Lexington, with its fine restaurants and shops, the Virginia Horse Center, George Marshall Museum, Stonewall Jackson House, and other historic sites. Also nearby are the Jefferson Pools, where guests can "take the waters."

The Keep Bed and Breakfast $$$
116 Lee Avenue, Lexington
(540) 463-3560
www.bedandbreakfast.com

This bed-and-breakfast inn in a gorgeous Victorian home sits on a quiet corner in the heart of Lexington's historic residential district. Owners Bea and John Stuart offer guests two suites and a double-bed room, each with a private bath. Don't expect a lot of froufrou here—the decor is elegant and understated. The Stuarts put on a lavish breakfast, complete with linens on the table, and also serve dinner upon request.

At tea time, the owners are always happy to share tea or coffee with their guests. "We like to spoil nice people," says Bea.

Summertime travelers to Lexington will certainly appreciate the central air-conditioning at the Keep, which is a short walk from museums and shops in downtown Lexington. The inn does not allow children younger than 12 but does welcome small, well-behaved pets on request.

Lavender Hill Farm $
1374 Big Spring Drive, Lexington
(540) 464-5877, (800) 446-4240
www.lavhill.com

Sarah and John Burleson's 200-year-old farmhouse sits on the banks of Kerrs Creek and has three light, airy guest rooms with private baths. One of the queen-size rooms can be rented as a suite; it connects to a second room with a double bed. The inn is decorated throughout with art from local artists.

Horseback trips led by Virginia Mountain Outfitters are a unique aspect of a stay here. Trail rides and riding workshops are geared to all levels of riding experience. The inn was designed with animal lovers in mind. Visit the Burlesons' sheep roaming the pastures or play fetch with their dogs. The farm is also conducive to birding, fishing, and hiking, and is a great starting point for a biking trek. Horse (or other livestock) boarding is available for guests in the farm's barn, built in spring 1997.

John is a great chef who loves to cook with herbs and vegetables grown on the farm. Four-course dinners are optional and require reservations.

A Horse Lovers Holiday package is available, including a two-night stay, breakfast, dinner, and picnic lunches both days, along with the use of horses, tours, and all instruction. Other packages include the Horse Owner's Vacation, which includes use of a horse, or you can board your own horse for $20 per night. The unique Wool Workshop gives lessons in spinning, weaving, and processing wool, from novice to expert levels. Instruction is held at the nearby Saville Hill Farm Fiber Arts Studio.

Guests can get special theater packages during the summer months, when the local Lime Kiln Theatre puts on its outdoor evening plays and Sunday night concerts. The Burlesons will purchase tickets and pack a gourmet picnic dinner to take along to Lime Kiln, where the bucolic grounds are conducive to sipping wine and feasting. They are also willing to create packages according to guests' interests.

The Burlesons don't allow pets or smoking inside the house. But they do welcome children accompanied by "well-behaved adults."

---

i

Some inns accept credit cards to hold your reservation; others may require payments or deposits in advance. Make sure you understand the reservation and cancellation policies at the time of booking.

Magnolia House Inn   **$$$$**
501 South Main Street, Lexington
(540) 463-2567
www.magnoliahouseinn.com

In 1868 master builder William Pole, who built Lee Chapel at Washington and Lee, took hammer in hand and crafted this Victorian house located in the heart of historic Lexington. Since then, the house has seen history, quite literally, pass it by. Robert E. Lee cantered this way almost daily on his horse, Traveler, as they took their daily ride through town and into the nearby hills. Jim and Jan Decker now own the home and have created a beautiful surrounding, complete with a cottage garden and flowers framing the front door.

Inside, the owners have decorated the common rooms simply but tastefully, with area rugs and warm tones on the walls. The four guest rooms reflect this simple elegance, with the Shenandoah Suite being the largest and most luxurious accommodation. It includes a large bedroom with couch and reading area, a smaller sitting room with a twin bed, private bath, and a private enclosed porch with a tree-framed

view of House Mountain. It's furnished with a queen-size sleigh bed, Empire sofa, and flame-stitch wingback chair. There is also a fireplace. The Equestrian Suite includes a large bedroom, separate sitting room with a single brass bed, full bath, fireplace, and a private porch. A queen-size four-poster bed, antique dresser, recliner, and overstuffed chair round out the furnishings. The Garden Room has a queen-size bed and Victorian furnishings and overlooks the inn's magnolia tree, while the Sunshine Room overlooks Main Street and also has a queen-size sleigh bed.

A full breakfast is served in the dining room, after which guests can enjoy local nature hikes or visit VMI, Washington & Lee University, the Virginia Horse Center, or area museums. The inn is a no smoking facility, and invites children older than 12 to stay.

Steeles Tavern Manor   **$$$$**
Highway 606 and US 11
Steeles Tavern
(540) 377-6444, (800) 743-8666
www.steelestavern.com

Leave the kids home and prepare to be pampered. Let innkeepers Eileen and Bill Hoernlein worry about the details while you enjoy a romantic getaway. Try breakfast in bed. Robes, extra towels, a complimentary snack basket, and a stocked refrigerator are just a few of the extras here, all designed so that couples need not ask for anything. Guests have all the privacy they want.

The inn has five guest rooms, each with a private bath, double-size Jacuzzi, and TV/VCR. Each room is named for a flower— dahlia, buttercup, wisteria, hyacinth, and rose—and has a king- or queen-size bed and a sitting area. The house and guest rooms are tastefully decorated in antique furniture, quilts, and lace. A romantic cottage is also available to rent.

The Hoernleins bring out their fine china, light the candles, and put on classical music, creating a special atmosphere for a sumptuous country breakfast. If you're an early riser, Eileen will have hot coffee waiting at your door each morning. Afternoon tea is served between 4:00 and 5:00 P.M. Evening sherry is also available.

Hospitality in the small town of Steeles Tavern on Lee Highway (US 11) dates back to 1781, when David Steele provided lodging to travelers between Staunton and Lexington. The home Steele's descendants built in 1916 underwent extensive restoration in 1994. In 1995 the Hoernleins opened its doors as a highly rated inn, completing the circle. The inn sits on 55 acres and has a stocked fishing pond and views of the Blue Ridge. Children, pets, and smoking are not permitted. Weekend packages are available.

Stoneridge Bed & Breakfast $$
Stoneridge Lane, Lexington
(540) 463-4090, (800) 491-2930
www.webfeat-inc.com/stoneridge
Located in the heart of the Shenandoah Valley on 32 secluded acres of fields, woodlands, and streams, Stoneridge is just minutes away from historic Lexington. The original house, built in 1829 and rumored to have been a stagecoach stop for weary travelers, offers a glimpse of antebellum life.

The Stallard family continues Stoneridge's long tradition of warm and friendly hospitality. Over the years, several additions and modern amenities have been added, including central air, ceiling fans, Jacuzzis, gas-log fireplaces, private baths, and a recently completed 360-square-foot guest-friendly kitchen. Step through the Adams-style double doors and find restored rooms with high ceilings, intricate moldings, elaborate mantels, and heart-of-pine floors. There is a guest library with an extensive collection of books, mounted water fowl, satellite television, and a cozy fire. In the evening, partake in a glass of sherry in the living room, decorated with old musical instruments, original French oil paintings, and a grand piano. Enjoy a bottle of Virginia wine from Stoneridge's wine list while relaxing on the porch and watching the sun set over the mountains. Jim would be pleased to help you with your selection.

The inn has five lovely rooms, each with a private bath. Sandy's talent for decor enhances the uniqueness of each room. The Wilma Evans Matthews Room, in the original 1829 part of the house, is named for a former owner of Stoneridge and has a queen-size rice-carved mahogany bed, marble-faced fireplace, and a view of the mountains. Also in the original house is the Kathryn Cross Room, featuring a queen-size iron bed, sitting room, and view of the meadows and mountains. The Sweet Alice Suite has a large bedroom with a queen-size iron bed, a Jacuzzi, and a gas-log fireplace. The suite also includes a reading room, a private balcony, and a small second room with a single bed, ideal for a third person. The Kingsley Newman Room, the inn's largest, has a roped, carved queen-size bed, a Jacuzzi opposite the gas-log fireplace, and a private porch that opens onto the newly constructed 600-square-foot patio. The John Howland Room has a private balcony, Jacuzzi, private entrance, gas-log fireplace, and a view of the mountains.

In the morning, enjoy a cup of coffee on the front porch or patio while breakfast is being prepared. Breakfast is served around 8:30 in the dining room of the 1829 home. Seasonal fruit salads and Evelyn's homemade baked goods, including cranberry-orange scones, banana bread, pumpkin bread, buttermilk biscuits, or fruit muffins, start your breakfast. The main course may consist of lemon-poppy waffles with a blueberry compote, cinnamon-pecan pancakes with honey-mapled bananas, crème brûlée French toast with four-berry coulis, or John's fluffy omelets, as mentioned in the August 2003 issue of *Gourmet* magazine, topped with a morning Chardonnay sauce.

During your stay, you may visit historic Lexington, Natural Bridge, the theater at Lime Kiln, Stonewall Jackson House and Cemetery, the Marshall Museum, and the Lee Chapel. Stoneridge is convenient to the Virginia Military Institute, Washington and Lee University, The Blue Ridge Parkway, Buffalo Spring Herb Farm, and Rockbridge Vineyard. Enjoy lunch or dinner in one of the area's fine restaurants or, if you decide to stay close to home, inquire when you make your reservation about having a four-course dinner at Stoneridge prepared for you by Chef John. In the early evening you may enjoy exploring the grounds of Stoneridge and find remnants of a restored spring house and a time-worn corn crib or watch the deer, turkeys, and songbirds that call Stoneridge home. Sit on the spacious front porch or back patio and watch the sun set. Smoking is not permitted except on the porch, patio, or grounds.

Sugar Tree Inn   **$$$**
Highway 56, Steeles Tavern
(540) 377-2197, (800) 377-2197
www.sugartreeinn.com
Innkeepers Jeff and Becky Chanter maintain a unique inn less than a mile off the Blue Ridge Parkway near Steeles Tavern. The narrow, winding driveway takes you back to a scenic mortise-and-peg timber and stone lodge, from which you can see 40 miles across the mountaintops and watch wildlife as close as 100 feet or less. At an elevation of 2,800 feet and set on 28 wooded acres, this inn actually feels a part of the surrounding landscape. In spring, the woods are a riot of trillium, rhododendron, laurel, and dogwood blossoms, and in autumn you don't just look at the fall colors, you walk among them.

The Main Lodge is constructed from 175-year-old timbers that were rescued from six buildings in the valley, and the Inn features 12 rooms spread out among four buildings; each features private baths, incredibly comfortable beds, and wood-burning fireplaces. A full country breakfast is included with each stay, and four-course dinners are available with advance reservations.

This Select Registry property is located in the middle of the George Washington National Forest, so outdoor activities abound. Nearby Lexington and Staunton provide historical and cultural opportunities, while Luray Caverns, Natural Bridge, and Monticello are all less than an hour away.

ROANOKE VALLEY
Roanoke and Salem

Down Home Bed & Breakfast   **$**
5209 Catawba Valley Drive, Catawba
(540) 384-6865
www.downhomebb.com
Owners Dave and Lucy Downs like to say their fieldstone and wooden lodge–like bed-and-breakfast is "twixt tooth and knob"—between well-known hiker climbs Dragon's Tooth and McAffee's Knob, that is. There's plenty of local activities to keep everyone busy: Hanging Rock Civil War Battlefield, Valhalla Winery, and downtown Roanoke. But the Downses provide a little something extra for trekkers. An Appalachian Trail access point is less than 2 miles away, and hikers coming off the AT can expect a warm welcome and a special discount.

After a hard day of rock scrambling and bargain hunting, everyone can relax in the pool or on the sunny deck. There's a TV in the living room and a library filled with nature and travel guides. If the urge for a midnight snack hits you, don't worry: The Downses have a centrally placed fridge filled with complimentary goodies and drinks.

Have a restful sleep after your exertions in one of two nicely appointed bright rooms. The Peace and Plenty Room is decorated in Pennsylvania Dutch style, complete with an 1848 family quilt. The Woods Room is filled with earth tones and a hiking motif. Both rooms have queen-size beds, private baths, and beautiful views.

In the morning a full breakfast awaits you, with homemade muffins or biscuits, fruit, juices, coffee, tea, and a rotating hot entree.

Children older than 12 are invited, but the owners ask that you keep your pets at home.

The Inn at Burwell Place   **$$$$**
601 West Main Street, Salem
(540) 387-0250
www.burwellplace.com
Upon completing graduate school at Vir-

ginia Tech, Cindy MacMackin left the area for a career in hospitality in the nation's capital. Twenty years later she has fulfilled her wish to return to the Roanoke Valley. She's putting her years of experience to work as owner of this turn-of-the-20th-century mansion at the southern end of the Shenandoah Valley. Since acquiring the inn, the MacMackins remodeled and redecorated to create a rich, elegant atmosphere.

The home is decorated throughout with late-19th-century period antiques in walnut and cherry. Six hundred yards of silk fabric and antique handmade Oriental rugs adorn the rooms. There are one bedroom and two suites available, and most with cable TV and VCR, robes, slippers, hair dryers, and "white noise" machines. Each of the bedrooms' private bathrooms still has its original fixtures and tubs. The suites have Jacuzzis.

After a continental breakfast of cereals, fresh fruit, croissants, and other favorites, visit the sights of Salem. The historic downtown area is full of antique shops. Roanoke College and Salem's Farmers' Market are within walking distance, and a short drive will take you to Dixie Caverns, the Blue Ridge Parkway, Mabry Mill, Peaks of Otter, Natural Bridge, and historic downtown Roanoke. Return after a day's exploring to rest on the veranda, or spend your day relaxing out back in the gorgeous formal English gardens.

The inn specializes in hosting weddings and receptions. Pets are not permitted, and smoking is not allowed inside the inn. Children older than 12 are welcome. Roanoke College events such as parents' weekends or commencement require a minimum two-night stay.

EAST OF THE BLUE RIDGE
Loudoun County

Owners Jeff and Gail Bogert deeply believe in architect Frank Lloyd Wright's philosophy, "A hill and house could live together each the happier for the other." They have fulfilled this ideal at Buckskin Manor. Surrounding the house are ponds, gardens, fields, and woods.

This large farmhouse set in hills close to the West Virginia border has four guest rooms. The Squire is an elegantly rustic room perfect for families with a queen-bedded room, sitting area, private bath with Jacuzzi, and garden views, and fieldstone walls accentuate the decor. An additional bed can be set up for a $40 fee. Rose's Room is done in soft shades of rose and pink and holds a double four-poster bed, fireplace, and views of the pond and gardens. Helen's Room, rented in conjunction with the Rose Room, is an old-fashioned room with twin beds and private bath. You are indeed tucked away at the top of the manor in the Garret. It's decorated with a double antique four-poster bed, separate sitting room, private bath, and views of the pond and gardens. Guests wanting a bit more privacy can stay in the nearby cottage. There's a fully equipped kitchen, a dining room, common room with TV and VCR, and a four-poster queen-size bed, double Jacuzzi, and separate tile shower. Outside are private gardens, a grill, and a picnic table.

A full country breakfast gets you ready for the day. The area caters to outdoor enthusiasts and history buffs, with fishing, boating, horse trails, and several Civil War battlefields nearby. Harpers Ferry is right down the road. The area is perfect for cross-country skiing. Buckskin also has its own large pond stocked with largemouth bass and bluegill for the younger anglers. There's also a pool and rocking chairs back at the manor. Smoking and pets are not allowed; older children are invited to join you.

Buckskin Manor Bed & Breakfast   **$$$$**
13452 Harper's Ferry Road, Purcellville
(540) 668-6864, (888) 668-7056
www.buckskinmanor.com

Leesburg Colonial Inn   **$$$**
19 South King Street, Leesburg
(703) 478-8503, (800) 392-1332
www.leesburgcolonialinn.com

The Colonial Inn is set in the heart of historic downtown Leesburg, just 30 minutes from Washington, D.C., and 15 minutes from Dulles International Airport. Parts of the building, including the beautiful stone-framed entrance, date to the late 1700s.

The decor has been selected to pay tribute to the inn's Colonial past; each of the 10 guest rooms have 18th-century-style American furniture, wood floors, fine rugs, and impressive period pieces such as rustic farm dressers. All the rooms have private baths, telephones, cable television, and individual heat and air-conditioning. Some rooms have fireplaces, whirlpool baths, and adjoining rooms.

Rates include a breakfast at Georgetown Cafe and Bakery.

The Norris House Inn $$$
108 Loudoun Street SW, Leesburg
(800) 644-1806, (703) 777-1806
www.norrishouse.com
Formerly a Federal-style home built ca. 1760, this inn, now with a charming Queen Anne addition, has been voted the best inn in Leesburg numerous times by the *Leesburg Today* readers' survey.

This inn in the heart of the city's historic district has six rooms, five with private baths. Guests have access to the common rooms, including the stately dining room, parlor, library, and veranda overlooking the award-winning gardens. Rooms are appointed with antiques and a variety of canopy, brass, and feather beds. All bedrooms are air-conditioned, and fireplaces are found in the library and dining room.

The Norris House has been operating as a bed-and-breakfast since 1981. Carol and Roger Healey purchased the property in 2003 and have been renovating and adding new features. Guests are treated to a full breakfast with a hot entrée. Other amenities include DSL wireless connections for laptops.

Popular for weddings, the Norris House can accommodate a guest list of up to 75. The inn is not suitable for small children.

Smoking is restricted to the gardens. Nearby sites include Oatlands Plantation and Balls Bluff National Battlefield. A shuttle service to the C+O Canal is provided for biking enthusiasts.

The Red Fox Inn $$$$
2 East Washington Street, Middleburg
(540) 687-6301, (800) 223-1728
www.redfox.com
This ca. 1728 inn began as a tavern, serving as a stopping point for traveling colonists, including a young surveyor named George Washington, who was known to stop in around 1748. During the Civil War, the house became both a Confederate headquarters and a hospital for soldiers. The pine service bar still used today was constructed from the field operating table used by an army surgeon. In 1887 the building once again became a tavern and has since been offering food and lodging. Today, however, visitors are more likely to be city-weary travelers looking for a country hideaway.

The Red Fox Inn's lodging options include the original building as well as three nearby historic properties—the Stray Fox Inn, the McConnell House Inn, and the Innkeepers Cottage. In all, the inns offer 23 rooms and suites decorated in beautiful period furniture such as canopy and poster beds. All rooms have private baths, cable television, four-poster beds, and telephones, and some have sitting areas. One enormous suite comes equipped with a king-size bed, a large sitting room, and its own grand piano.

Fresh flowers, cotton robes, bedside sweets, and a morning paper are among the extras. Breakfast is continental style, served in the Red Fox Restaurant, which also serves lunch, Sunday brunch, and dinner (see our Restaurants chapter). Packages and catering are also available. An art gallery is housed in the main building, and the garden courtyard is popular for weddings.

Fauquier County

The Ashby Inn $$$$
692 Federal Street, Paris
(540) 592-3900
www.ashbyinn.com

Yes, Virginia, there is a Paris in the Piedmont. Adding to the charm of this Fauquier County village is the Ashby Inn and Restaurant, which occupies a home dating back to the 1820s and serves some of the best food outside the Washington Beltway.

Six guest rooms in the main building are decorated with studied, elegant simplicity to let the magnificent view of the mountains reign. Most of the furnishings in these rooms date back to the 1800s. Of these, the Fan Room with its two skylights, fan window, and private balcony is among the most coveted. Four other delightful larger and grander rooms occupy the former one-room schoolhouse, each with its own private porch facing the Blue Ridge. Each suite has a four-poster bed, fireplace, Oriental rugs, wing chairs, phones, televisions, and double bathrooms. Quilts and blanket chests impart a country feel in all rooms, but you won't find creaky floors or clanking pipes. Everything at the Ashby Inn is first class. Oriental rugs have even been added to each room. Discounts for weekday stays are available. There are four unique dining rooms at The Ashby Inn; one is an enclosed porch looking out onto perennial gardens. Others include a converted kitchen with walnut beams and a fireplace, and in the summer you can sit out on the covered patio overlooking the lawns. Dinner, prepared by Christopher Carey, is served here from Wednesday through Saturday, while the Sunday brunch buffet is known throughout the region.

Hosts Roma and John Sherman are busy during dinner hours at the restaurant, but you may get to know them over breakfast—a feast reserved for guests. Roma is an avid horsewoman and John is a former House Ways and Means Committee staffer and former speechwriter.

1763 Inn and Restaurant $$$
10087 John Mosby Highway, Upperville
(540) 592-3848
www.1763inn.com

Bernie and Megan Kirchner are the second generation to operate this inn, a complex of six old farm buildings on 50 acres turned into a heavenly getaway steeped in history and comfort. The stone house restaurant dates to 1763 and was once owned by George Washington. This cozy restaurant in the main farmhouse overlooks a pond with swans and is decorated with items gathered during the Kirchner family's travels. The restaurant menu is German-American (see our Restaurants chapter).

Sixteen bedrooms are dispersed among the main house, stables, log cabin cottages, and a stone barn atop a hill. Each room is distinctively decorated. Naturally, there is a George Washington room, but you also will find a German and a French room, each furnished in the style of those countries. Another room includes a museum-size portrait of FDR that once hung in the Mexican embassy. Most have hot tubs and fireplaces.

Other amenities include a swimming pool and a fishing pond. Nearby activities include horse country events such as horse shows, steeplechases, and fox hunts as well as antiques shopping in Middleburg.

Rappahannock County

Belle Meade Bed & Breakfast $$$
353 F.T. Valley Road, Sperryville
(540) 987-9748
www.bellemeadeinn.com

You can expect understated luxury and comfortable elegance at this turn-of-the-century Victorian inn. Renovated in 1994, the inn has four guest rooms, each with a

Suites and cottages with kitchenettes are great for extended stays and can save you money on lunches and dinners out.

scenic view and a private bath. There's also a cottage with a private bath, deck, and porch.

A hearty breakfast starts a relaxing day here. The 138 acres are gorgeous in any season—fall foliage, winter vistas, and spring flowers are especially enticing—and hiking and birding are popular pastimes. The inn has a 60-foot swimming pool, a hot tub, and a pond. If you plan ahead, owners Susan Hoffman and Mike Biniek will serve you a candlelight dinner for $35 a person, or a bag lunch for $10 a person. Massages by a licensed massage therapist can be arranged.

The nearby 1914 Belle Meade Schoolhouse has been recently renovated and is perfect for weddings or other gatherings.

Attractions in the area include Old Rag Mountain, a popular hiking destination (see our Recreation chapter). The Skyline Drive and Luray Caverns are nearby, as are many fine restaurants and wineries.

Bleu Rock Inn $$$$
12567 Lee Highway, Washington
(540) 987-3190, (800) 341-2538
www.bleurockinn.com

Situated on 80 acres in Rappanhannock County, this country inn is in a renovated farmhouse with five guest rooms, each with a private bath. The Inn overlooks lush meadows, a pond, and tall shade trees with a vista of the mountains beyond.

Several acres are carefully tended vineyards that supply wines for the inn. After a glass of wine in the lounge, you can dine fireside in one of three dining rooms. An open-air terrace overlooks the vineyards of cabernet sauvignon, chardonnay, and seyval grapes.

You can stroll through pastures where horses graze, or try your hand at catching bass, catfish, and bluegill from the pond. The Bleu Rock Equestrian Center is on the premises and is the headquarters for the Rappanhannock Hunt. Guests can board their own mounts or rent one of Bleu Rock's, and can take advantage of the center's lessons, steeplechase course, and polo ring. Polo matches are held here

every Saturday in the summer, and you can ask the pro for a polo lesson. The non-horsey set can take advantage of Rappanhannock County's ample opportunities for skiing, biking, canoeing, golfing, hiking, and caving. Wineries and historical sites are not far from the inn.

Jo Mariea and Calvert Clark are the owners and operators of Bleu Rock Inn and have made sure the inn's cuisine is as special as its grounds. Every morning Chef Eric Smith whips up a delicious breakfast for overnight guests. It begins with juice and freshly ground coffee, followed by biscuits, muffins, and croissants. Next is fresh fruit and homemade waffles, fluffy omelets, or another hot entree. The full-service restaurant serves French-American food, and brunch and dinner showcase the amazing range of Chef Smith's talents. The ever-changing menu could include salmon baby biscuits, mussels billi bi, crabmeat pissaladiere, Black Angus fillet, Alsatian choucroute garni, and grilled lamb tenderloin. Desserts are scrumptious and can include crème brûlée, and dark chocolate and peanut butter mousse cake. Casual dress is fine. After dinner you can retire to the Bleu Horse Pub for a drink and live music on Friday and Saturday nights. While the Inn is open daily, the pub and restaurant are closed Monday and Tuesday.

Well-behaved dogs are allowed, and children may be accommodated with prior notice. The Inn is closed Monday and Tuesday.

Caledonia Farm–1812 $$$$
47 Dearing Road, Washington
(540) 675-3693, (800) BNB-1812
www.bnb1812.com

Set in rolling hills, with a magnificent mountain backdrop, Caledonia Farm is a restored Federal farmhouse with a companion summer kitchen dependency, constructed entirely of native Virginia fieldstone. You literally walk into history when you enter the front door. The hand-laid masonry is considered some of the best stonework in America, and the interior mantels and window wells were crafted by Hessian soldiers who remained in the area as journeymen carpenters after the Revolutionary War. Two-foot-thick walls, 32-foot exposed ceiling beams, and pine floors transport you back into time, and it really wouldn't be much of a surprise if George Washington walked in and took a seat before the fire. The flint-lock rifle hanging over one of Caledonia Farm's six working fireplaces was used by the first owner during the Revolutionary War.

Guests aren't the only ones admiring the home: Caledonia Farm is on the National Register of Historic Places. Phil Irwin has been the owner and proprietor of the farm for more than 20 years, making it one of the area's oldest continually operated bed-and-breakfasts, and he strives to make your visit a memorable one. He can arrange hot-air balloon rides, history tours, riding lessons, carriage rides, theater tickets, and restaurant reservations. Riders are welcome to bring their own mounts and board them in Phil's stable. Locally, 700 miles of riding trails run next to the property and through adjacent Shenandoah National Park. There's also a hot tub for a relaxing soak, as well as lawn games, bikes, a piano, and a well-stocked library. Many people are fascinated by Phil's scale model railroad set, which he proudly shows off to guests.

There are two suites available, one a honeymoon suite with fireplace. Both rooms are bright and decorated with double beds and period pieces and have private baths. In the morning a full country breakfast with all the fixings is served in the breakfast room by candlelight, and there are complimentary snacks and beverages available all day.

Children older than 12 are welcome. Pets must stay at home, and smoking is outside only. Midweek discounts and packages are available. There is also a cabin that rents per week.

Foster–Harris House $$$$
189 Main Street, Washington
(540) 675–3757, (800) 666–0153
www.fosterharris.com

Patrick and Rita Corbett's turn-of-the-20th-century frame home is right on Main Street in this little tourist town. The house offers five air-conditioned guest rooms, each with a private bath, queen-size bed, and a wonderful view of either the mountains or the perennial gardens. The Mountain View Suite has a whirlpool tub big enough for two and a wood-burning stove for winter evenings. The Garden Room has mountain views and overlooks the inn's herb and flower gardens.

The Corbetts prepare a full breakfast every morning and greet you with cookies, tea, and lemonade on your arrival. Smoking and pets are not allowed.

Area attractions include orchards, vineyards, fairs, antiques shops, and local theater. Hiking, biking, and horseback riding are available, too.

The Gay Street Inn $$$
160 Gay Street, Washington
(540) 675–3288
www.gaystreetinn.com

At the end of a quiet, dead-end street sits this 150-year-old stucco home, a restored farmhouse with three guest rooms and a suite, resident dog and cat, and lovely gardens out back. All rooms have views of the mountains, private baths, and Colonial wallpaper from the Shelbourne Museum Collection.

One room has a canopy bed and a working fireplace. The suite has a full kitchen and a television and is a great option for families; it is also available for short-term rental for those who want an extended stay. Children and pets are welcome here. A portable crib is available on request.

Innkeepers Donna and Robin Kevis prepare a marvelous morning feast, which sometimes includes frittata, smoked turkey sausage, home fries, and homemade Gay Street Inn muffins served in the inn's breakfast room.

The Gay Street Inn is charming, homey, and convenient to Washington's shops and restaurants. The Shenandoah National Park is nearby, as are caverns, wineries, and other natural attractions.

Heritage House $$$$
291 Main Street, Washington
(540) 675-3207, (888) 819-8280
www.heritagehousebb.com
Cynthia Brown's elegant inn dates back to 1837 and is said to have been used by Confederate Gen. Jubal Early as headquarters during the Civil War. It has served as an inviting bed-and-breakfast since 1985, and is a minute's stroll from shops, historic landmarks, and the famous Inn at Little Washington. The great outdoors are at your back door here, including Shenandoah National Park and the Skyline Drive. Not far away are the Rapidan, Rose, and Thornton Rivers and other well-known trout streams.

Each of the five guest rooms has either a king or queen bed, features a private bathroom and air-conditioning, and is comfortably decorated with antiques and reproductions. The Garden Suite features an enclosed sun porch overlooking the summer garden and the Blue Ridge Mountains. All rates include a hot gourmet breakfast served each morning in the dining room.

The Inn at Little Washington $$$$
Middle and Main Streets, Washington
(540) 675-3800
www.relaischateaux.com/site/us
If you want to be pampered beyond your wildest dreams and eat food more delicious than you thought possible, then the Inn at Little Washington should certainly be No. 1 on your list. Situated in a quiet Rappahannock County town, it is one of the top-rated inns in the United States. Praise has come from far and wide, including *USA Today, People* magazine, the *New York Times,* and the *San Francisco Chronicle.*

Since 1987, the Inn has been a member of Relais & Chateaux, the prestigious organization of the world's finest hotels and restaurants. It was the first establishment in the *Mobil Travel Guide*'s history to receive five stars for its restaurant and five stars for its accommodation and is the first inn to receive AAA's 5 Diamond Award for both food and accommodation.

Reinhardt Lynch and Patrick O'Connell are the owners. Lynch takes care of the day-to-day operations at the Inn—little stuff such as making sure the 3,000 requests for Saturday-night dinner are narrowed down to 65 diners. O'Connell causes all the commotion with his culinary masterpieces. The prix fixe dinners include five to six courses. (The price does not include alcohol, tax, or gratuity.) Diners select from 11 entrees and 15 desserts. Some of the Inn's specialties include seared duck foi gras on polenta with country ham and huckleberries and local rabbit braised in apple cider with wild mushrooms and garlic mashed potatoes.

The Inn's 12 guest rooms and suites feature queen or king-size beds, two with Jacuzzi baths and separate showers, one with a fireplace, and three with private balconies. The separate Guest House has a guest room and a one-bedroom suite, both with king-size beds and a parlor and kitchen in the suite. Located across the street is the Mayor's House, which has a king-size bed, fireplace, Jacuzzi bath and separate shower, a sitting room with a fireplace, and a courtyard garden. The Presidential Retreat, 17 miles from the Inn, is a Victorian farmhouse on a private estate with two master bedrooms, living rooms, kitchen, parlor, and a wraparound porch.

The interiors are sumptuous and comfortable, designed by Joyce Evans, a London set designer. She paired richly layered fabrics, fine art, and period antiques to create the luxurious environment. Other wonderful touches include the silk fringed lampshades in the dining room and the 17th-century wooden floor from a French chateau in the Inn's living room. Enjoy afternoon tea with sweets and savories, 24-hour room service, and pick up a picnic lunch to take to nearby Shenandoah National Park.

Of course, luxury doesn't come cheap. The least expensive rates are $370 to $550 for a room, $550 to $690 for a suite, and $890 for the Mayor's House, while a stay at the Presidential Retreat can range from $1,100 to $2,400. That's a night. Bear in mind that Fridays are $145 additional and Saturdays, $245. Dinner reservations are guaranteed for overnight guests. The Inn is very popular, so advance reservations are a must.

Middleton Inn $$$$
176 Main Street, Washington
(540) 675-2020, (800) 816-8157
www.middletoninn.com
Middleton Inn is an elegant historic country estate in a rural setting with mountain views. The house, which has an impressive center hall and high ceilings throughout, was built in 1850 by Middleton Miller, who designed and manufactured the uniform worn by Confederate soldiers. The house has eight working fireplaces, including one in every bedroom, and each of the five guest rooms has a private marble bath.

Sharing a five-acre knoll with the house are three other original buildings—the summer kitchen, the smokehouse, and the slave quarters. The latter is now a two-story guest cottage with a working fireplace and Jacuzzi.

Owner Mary Ann Kuhn, a former CBS producer and *Washington Post* reporter, serves a full gourmet breakfast with fresh fruit, homemade breads, and a hot entree, which might be eggs Benedict or raspberry pancakes.

For the past five years, Middleton Inn has received AAA's Four-Diamond Award. The inn combines the best of town and country, with cattle grazing in an adjoining pasture and shops just 2 blocks away. Washington and the surrounding area are rich in antiques and craft shops, natural wonders such as the Skyline Drive, and small-town festivals that pull visitors into the spirit of the place.

Sunset Hills Bed & Breakfast $$$$
105 Christmas Tree Lane, Washington
(540) 987-8804, (800) 980-2580
www.sunsethillsfarm.com
Betty and Leon Hutcheson never dreamed of running a bed-and-breakfast when they bought 25 acres high on Jenkins Mountain in 1981. They just had a dream of building

> *The American dogwood is the state tree. Visit in the spring and you'll see mountains dotted with its pretty white blooms.*

a beautiful house, commissioned by Frank Lloyd Wright protégé Kamal Amin. Isolated and full of briars, a road had to be built to the land so that the contractor could reach the mountaintop. But it was worth the wait when the house was unveiled in 1986. Made of stone and full of windows and fanciful shapes and overhanging roofs, with beautiful landscaping, the Hutchesons decided their home was too beautiful not to share with others, so they opened a bed-and-breakfast.

Sunset Hills Farm is truly wonderful, set high on a mountain with views of the Skyline Drive and the surrounding working orchards of the farm. Friendly Belgian horses roam the pastures, and deer often wander onto the grounds. Even a bear has been known to come and sample some fruit on the sly. You can even watch a video of the furry poacher on the farm's Web site.

Three guest rooms are available. The extra-large Gazebo Room comes with a king-size bed, its own sitting area, and an enormous marble bath with Jacuzzi tub and twin sinks. The room offers private access to a deck and screened-in gazebo. The Sunrise Room has a queen-size bed, and the bathroom has a private marble bath and shower. The Stone Room has a queen-size bed, with a Rappahannock County natural fieldstone wall with stone collected from Jenkins Mountain. There is a private marble tub and shower. Guests are encouraged to relax in the Great Room or take in the sauna.

Breakfast is an affair, complete with dishes made with fruit from the on-site apple and peach orchards. Guests may be served Smithfield ham, brandied peaches, apple butter and biscuits, eggs, waffles, or pancakes. Afternoon tea is also served, either outside or in the Great Room.

Spend your day touring the orchards, petting the horses, riding a bike, playing golf, or visiting nearby (yet so far away) Washington, D.C. Sunset Hills Farm is a nonsmoking, adult-only bed-and-breakfast.

Culpeper County

Fountain Hall Bed & Breakfast   **$$$**
609 South East Street, Culpeper
(540) 825-8200, (800) 29-VISIT
www.fountainhall.com
George Washington, the first county surveyor of Culpeper, referred to the town as "a high and pleasant situation." It still is, and Fountain Hall enjoys an enviable location in this charming village, once part of a large tract owned by Virginia's royal governor, Sir Alexander Spotswood. Hosts Steve and Kathi Walker have decorated the six large, sunlit guest rooms with antiques but provided the modern conveniences of a telephone and private bath in each. Some rooms have whirlpool tubs and outdoor porches.

Breakfast in the sunny morning room is a leisurely affair of fresh croissants topped with country preserves, plus cereals and juices.

Formal gardens are perfect for strolling. The streets of Culpeper beckon history and antiques buffs. You can hike, fish, and ride horseback nearby. Golf and canoeing packages are available.

Inn at Kelly's Ford
16589 Edwards Shop Road, Remington
(540) 399-1779
www.innatkellysford.com
Just around the corner, the land opens up, presenting an expansive estate with stately buildings and white fences sprawling across rich green hills. Located on the historical site of Kelly's Ford Civil War Battlefield, the Inn is set on a 500-acre estate. The Main House, originally built ca. 1779, served as a home for the Kelly family during the Civil War. Bill and Linda Willoughby opened the Inn at Kelly's Ford in 2000 as an elegant place to dine and stay the night.

The Main House was restored in 1999 and has two bedrooms, each with a queen-size bed, fireplace, and a balcony view of the Kelly's Ford Battlefield and the Rappahannock River. Three cottages house six large suites that include a Jacuzzi, wet bar, refrigerator, king-size bed, and queen sleeper sofa, as well as a fireplace and balcony or patio. Two of the suites, the Jackson and the Meade, contain conference tables. A unique option is the Silo, which has been converted into a two-level suite with a queen-size bed, private bath, picture windows, an indoor fountain, gas fireplace, two wet bars, a spiral staircase, and stone patio. The Inn has a great equestrian center, where you can take a horseback ride or a lesson, for any level of experience. They've got miles of scenic country trails, a lighted arena with clubhouse, and a large outdoor show ring. The Inn also offers swimming in its heated pool, or you may relax in the outdoor Jacuzzi. Take a hike along the river and picnic at the Inn's wooded park, equipped with picnic tables and grills. There is also space for lawn games, including volleyball, croquet, horseshoes, and bocce ball.

A restaurant in the Main House overlooks the countryside. A large stone hearth, candelabra, and pewter plates add to the atmosphere. Entrees include venison, filet mignon, pheasant, and seafood selections. Dinner is served Wednesday through Sunday and reservations are recommended. Brunch is offered on Sunday. If you want something more casual, take the stairs down to cozy Pelham's Pub, where you can warm up by a large fire while enjoying a bowl of homemade soup or sandwich. The Pub is open daily for lunch and dinner (see our Restaurants chapter).

Madison County

Graves Mountain Lodge   **$$$$**
Off Highway 670, Syria
(540) 923-4231
www.gravesmountain.com
This inn is known far and wide for its deli-

cious, homemade, family-style meals, served in a large dining hall on long wooden tables. Room prices include three meals, which is a blessing because you wouldn't want to miss one of these country spreads (see our Restaurants chapter for more information). The atmosphere at meals sets the tone for the entire Graves Mountain experience—informal family fun in the midst of friendly and easygoing folks. Relax in one of the inn's rocking chairs or take a long hike on one of the many easily accessible trails. Whatever your activity choice, you will find lots of country hospitality here.

Graves Mountain is family owned, and its perch on the edge of Shenandoah National Park puts it close to a host of outdoor activities. Fishing, hiking, and hunting are popular pastimes. The inn also offers swimming in a junior Olympic-size pool, horseback riding on more than 100 miles of scenic trails, hayrides on Friday and Saturday night, volleyball, softball, and horseshoes. The recreation center has books, magazines, games, a piano, and a television for rainy days. Both adults and children can participate in interactive programs in farming and animal care. Self-guided tours of the cannery, where Graves makes dozens of specialty preserves, relishes, jams, and spreads, is another rainy-day option. The gift shop sells mountain crafts, souvenirs, and jewelry.

The lodge has several accommodation styles. The Ridgecrest Motel has 22 rooms and two conference rooms, and Hilltop Motel has 16 rooms, some with televisions. Ridgecrest and Hilltop are modern accommodations. The Old Farm House, built in the early 1800s, has seven rooms with half-baths and a portico to the shower house. You can still see the original hand-hewn logs and mud chinking in the Old Farm House, though it has been renovated. Eleven cottages are in the vicinity of the lodge. The cabins include the Lower Cabin built in the 1920s and used as a Boy Scout camp. The Upper Cabin is in a secluded area. Wildwind, originally a one-room schoolhouse, overlooks the Robinson River.

Blackwood and Greenwood are cabins. The lodge closes the Sunday after Thanksgiving and reopens the third weekend in March. Reservations are required for overnight stays.

The Inn at Meander Plantation $$$$
2333 North James Madison Highway, Locust Dale
(540) 672-4912, (800) 385-4936
www.meander.net

In the heart of Jefferson's Virginia, the Inn at Meander Plantation offers the charm and elegance of Colonial living. The stately mansion, built in 1766 by Joshua Fry, is the centerpiece of an 80-acre estate. Converted to a bed-and-breakfast inn in 1993, the house contains seven sun-drenched bedrooms, each with a private bath. Four-poster queen-size beds are piled high with plump pillows atop down comforters. There is also a Groom's cottage near the house that allows pets.

Throughout the house are private nooks for reading, and guests gather in the parlor, once often visited by Thomas Jefferson and the Marquis de Lafayette. A baby grand piano awaits for impromptu concerts.

A full plantation-style gourmet breakfast is served daily in the formal dining room or under the arched breezeway. Full dinners and picnic lunches can also be arranged. White rockers line both levels of the expansive back porches, providing peaceful respites for sipping afternoon tea. The boxwood gardens are dotted with secluded benches and a hammock. Croquet, volleyball, badminton, and horseshoes are set up on the lawns, and the woods are made for strolling. Overnight boarding for horses is available at the stables. Cheese, fruit, and champagne await you on your return.

The innkeepers are Suzanne Thomas and Suzie Blanchard. Suzanne, a former newspaper publisher, finds time now for freelance writing. Suzie continues her career as a food writer and can teach a special cooking class for guests.

They also can arrange massages and hot air balloon rides.

The inn is in a bend of the Robinson River, 9 miles south of Culpeper. The best of the countryside is close at hand, including wineries, antiques shops and historic sites.

Greene County

The Lafayette Hotel $$$$
146 Main Street, Stanardsville
(434) 985-6345
www.thelafayette.com

This historic landmark built in 1840 is a full-service bed-and-breakfast and a delightful restaurant. The Georgian-style building has three levels with 11-foot ceilings and sweeping colonnaded porches. The frame is of hand-hewn mortise-and-tenon beams with 15-inch-thick walls made of local red brick. Large windows provide a view of the Blue Ridge Mountains and the quaint town of Stanardsville.

The Lafayette was built as a stagecoach line hotel and served as a hospital for the Confederacy during the Civil War. In the 20th century it has been a private residence, a boarding house, apartment building, and home to several businesses, including the area's first telephone exchange, newspaper, and post office. Innkeepers Whitt Leford and Nick Spencer began renovations in 1996 and continue to carefully restore this special Virginia landmark.

Accommodations include a wheelchair-accessible guest room on the first level along with the restaurant. The second floor has five guest rooms decorated in 19th-century furnishings and warm country house decor. The rooms have queen-size beds and comfortable sitting areas, as well as their original fireplaces and individually controlled heating and air-conditioning systems. A full breakfast is included for two people. Dinner packages are available.

The Lafayette is on Highway 33, just 10 minutes from the entryway to the Skyline Drive and Shenandoah National Park.

South River Country Inn $$$
301 South River Road, Stanardsville
(434) 985-4473, (877) 874-4473
www.southrivercottage.com

South River Country Inn is in a 1900 restored farmhouse on a working farm of more than 100 acres in the South River Valley. Huge trees and flowers surround the house and rolling meadows, and the inn is just a few minutes from the Skyline Drive and the Blue Ridge Parkway. Here you can relax and enjoy all the warmth and comforts of life on a farm without having to do any of the chores. There's a stocked trout stream on the grounds just waiting for a well-cast fly, and cows and chickens to pet and watch.

South River Country Inn has special midweek corporate rates and is set up to cater to its business guests. Internet, fax, copying, and mailing facilities are available for free or a nominal fee.

South River Country Inn offers extremely flexible accommodations. There are four private bedrooms with queen-size beds, and three additional sleeping rooms that can be used in conjunction with these rooms to provide private suites for families with children or for family groups traveling together. Stars & Stripes features a patriotic theme, queen-size iron bed, private bath with whirlpool tub and shower, and satellite television with digital stereo music. Morning Glory is done in yellow and blue with a queen-size bed, private bathroom with whirlpool, and satellite television. Country Garden has a queen-size bed, deluxe private bathroom with double whirlpool tub and shower, and satellite television. Bird's-Eye View is a three-room suite ideal for families and has one queen-size bed, one trundle bed, and one double bed. It includes a private bathroom and satellite television with digital stereo music. It's also available as a single room. The entire cottage can sleep up to 12 and is a perfect place for a family reunion, a group getaway, or a small business retreat. There are also a den and kitchen available for all guests to use. The den has satellite television and a game table, and the kitchen has all new, modern appliances, including a microwave and dishwasher. In the summer you can take a dip in the Inn's new swimming pool.

Weather permitting, breakfast is served on the back veranda or on the front porch. These are real country breakfasts, with French toast, blueberry pancakes, eggs, sausage, bacon, ham, fried potatoes or apples, and a variety of homemade breads and muffins. In case of inclement weather, breakfast is served in the kitchen, den, or enclosed back porch. South River Country Inn invites children, but pets are not permitted.

Orange County

Greenock House Inn $$$
249 Carolina Street, Orange
(540) 672-3625, (800) 841-1253
www.greenockhouse.com
Greenock House offers a restful, relaxing setting with gourmet meals, genteel company, and wraparound porches dating from the 1880s. The house sits on five acres within the small town of Orange, which secludes the inn from the town. Specimen trees overlook the house, including black walnut, cypress, spruce, catalpa, magnolia, maple, oak, and white ash, including one ash said to be more than 200 years old.

The grounds are ever changing, as owners Lill and Rich Shearer and Andria and Brett Conyers are constantly designing, renovating, and planting a variety of gardens, including herb, vegetable, flower, and a special woodlands shade garden. Nature lovers will enjoy wandering around the inn's lawns. Bird-watchers can spy many types of birds from hummingbirds to yellow-bellied sapsuckers to bluebirds, and there are even binoculars for your use. Wildlife abounds, including groundhogs, raccoons, wild turkeys, and resident cats.

Those less active can find a hidden nook or sit in the sun and read a book. The library has a nice collection of books, as well as board games and puzzles. Musi-cally inclined guests can jingle away on the antique upright grand piano. The inn is also close to Civil War battlefields (Chancellorsville and the Wilderness), Montpelier, Monticello, Ash Lawn–Highland, art galleries, antiques shops, golf courses, and even skydiving.

The five guest rooms all have central air-conditioning and private baths and have either a queen- or king-size bed. Rooms have televisions, fireplaces, or double whirlpool tubs. Considering the owners used to own restaurants before opening the inn, the specialty at Greenock House is the cuisine.

You can sit on the wraparound porch and enjoy the country breezes along with your evening hors d'oeuvres that could be Spanish tapas, English tea, or maybe Chinese dumplings. Experience a candlelight five-course prix fixe dinner in the formal dining room. In the morning, indulge in a gourmet breakfast, including one of the pastry chef's sinful desserts.

Smoking is allowed outside, and older children may be accommodated with prior arrangements for whole house rentals.

Mayhurst Inn $$$$
12460 Mayhurst Lane, Orange
(540) 672-5597, (888) 672-5597
www.mayhurstinn.com
Lt. Gen. A.P. Hill used Mayhurst Plantation as his headquarters during two winters of the Civil War. Even Robert E. Lee was here on that May morning when Hill christened his daughter Lucy "Lee" Hill. Stonewall Jackson and the Army of Northern Virginia camped nearby for six months. In fact, he reviewed the troops from the rooftop cupola. It's no wonder this 1859 mansion is listed on the National Register of Historic Places. Today, Mayhurst Inn is a fully restored 9,400-square-foot Italianate Victorian plantation manor house situated on 37 acres of gardens, manicured lawns, and forests. (Walking paths will take you by several 200-year-old trees.) Explore the ca. 1829 summer kitchen, one-room schoolhouse, and smokehouse, or stop by the pond to fish for bass.

Inside, an oval spiral staircase will lead you to all four floors. Take refreshments (wine and cheese are served daily at 4:30 P.M.) on the porch or in the library or parlor, or take in the view from the cupola. There are eight renovated accommodations to choose from. Each has a private bath and fireplace and is decorated with antiques, but each has its own distinct personality. The teal, olive, and tan Generals' Room pays homage to the three Confederate generals who stayed here. The Madison Room, decorated in Dolley Madison's favorite shade of scarlet, is so named because the original builder, John Willis, was a relative of the Madisons and is buried at nearby Montpelier. Other rooms include the Magnolia, the Garden, Piedmont, Southern Charm, and Italian Suite with a two-person Jacuzzi tub. The suite also features a four-columned custom-made queen-size bed, a sofa bed, a sitting room, and its own balcony.

Innkeepers and owners Jack and Pat North serve a three-course breakfast each morning with freshly baked bread and muffins, juice, fresh fruit, and rotating entrees, including Belgian waffles, made-to-order omelets, French toast, crepes, and eggs Benedict. Breakfast is usually served by the fireplace in the dining room but is frequently served on the veranda or patio. There is also a "pampering menu" available for special occasions. Mayhurst is a popular site for weddings and can accommodate 50 guests indoors or 250 outside.

The Shadows $$
14291 Constitution Highway, Orange
(540) 672-5057
www.theshadowsbedandbreakfast.com
This restored 1913 stone inn is surrounded by old cedars on 44 acres on Highway 20, just 3 miles from Montpelier. Innkeepers Barbara and Pat Loffredo invite you to forget about the hassles of the modern world and enjoy a relaxing stay in their Craftsman-style house. Curl up in front of the large stone fireplace with a cup of cider or select a good book from the library. Hold hands on the porch swing or chat with other guests during afternoon tea. Whatever your choice, the pace is slow and quiet.

Four artfully decorated guest rooms are individually named and creatively appointed. The Blue Room has a queen-size pre–Civil War walnut bed and a daybed, and its natural cedar bathroom features a vanity, claw-foot tub, and pedestal sink. The Rose Room is full of frills and lace, with a full-size high-back oak bed and a private upper deck. The Peach Room is an Edwardian delight with a king-size burled walnut bed and a private hall shower. The Victorian Room, with a full-size iron and brass bed, has a private hall bathroom with a tub/shower.

In addition, the Loffredos have lovingly restored a cabin, just a few steps away from the house. The two-room Rocking Horse Cabin is decked in country crafts, has a gas-log fireplace, a queen-size bed, and private deck.

A memorable country gourmet breakfast is served each morning. Entrees have included French toast, garden vegetables and cheese frittata, soufflés, and poached pears. Reservations are accepted and require one night's deposit. Children 10 and older are welcome to stay at the inn.

Sleepy Hollow Farm $$
16280 Blue Ridge Turnpike, Gordonsville
(540) 832-5555, (800) 215-4804
www.sleepyhollowfarmbnb.com
This cozy 18th-century house is filled with nooks and crannies; bedrooms feel like private hideaways. Flower and herb gardens surround the house, and the broader surroundings include woods and rolling fields where cattle graze. Beverley Allison and her daughter, Dorsey Allison-Comer, run the inn, which has been the Allison family home for decades.

The atmosphere here is casual and comfortable, with family pets to greet you when you arrive. In their rooms, guests find a welcome basket stocked with Virginia peanuts, fruit, and homemade chocolate-chip cookies. The formal dining room is very pretty and overlooks the herb garden and distant rolling hills.

The brick farmhouse has four guest rooms, all with private baths. The main floor has two bedrooms, one with fireplace and whirlpool tub, the other with a four-poster bed and dressing room . Upstairs is a small bedroom, known for its peacefulness, and a two-bedroom suite perfect for families. The cottage has two suites, one with a great room, Franklin wood-burning stove, whirlpool room, and full kitchen. The other is equipped with a fireplace and small refrigerator and microwave. Each have televisions and VCRs.

Sleepy Hollow caters to children, and a babysitter easily can be arranged. Pets, with prior arrangements, also are welcome in the cottage for a fee.

Rates include a full country breakfast, and homemade goodies always are available on the sideboard in the formal dining room.

Sleepy Hollow is a beautiful location for small weddings. And it's close to the Skyline Drive, Montpelier, and Monticello.

Willow Grove Inn $$$$
14079 Plantation Way, Orange
(540) 672–5982, (800) 949–1778
www.willowgroveinn.com
If you want to live and breathe history, consider this antebellum mansion with formal gardens and sloping lawns. Willow Grove Inn, listed on the National Register of Historic Places and designated a Virginia Historic Landmark, was built by Joseph Clark in 1778. A brick addition was added in 1820 by the same craftsmen who had just completed work on Thomas Jefferson's University of Virginia. The mansion, the exterior of which is a prime example of Jefferson's Classical Revival style, fell under siege during the Civil War. You can still see trenches near the manor house, and a cannonball was recently removed from its eaves. Generals Wayne and Muhlenberg also camped here during the Revolutionary War.

Tucked into 37 secluded acres, this 18th-century plantation retains its original Colonial atmosphere. Fine American and English antiques decorate the manor

house, and English boxwood, magnolias, and willows grace the lawns.

Owner Angela Mulloy has figured out how to help her guests unwind. A newspaper and pot of fresh coffee will be at your door in the morning, along with freshly baked muffins if you want something before the hearty plantation breakfast.

Rates include breakfast and dinner, which is served in distinctive dining rooms offering varying atmospheres—Clark's Tavern is dark, cozy, and casual, while the Dolley Madison Room is formal and resplendent in delicate china and crystal. (See our Restaurants chapter for more information on the restaurant.)

Antique furnishings, wide pine flooring, and original fireplace mantels preserve the traditional character of each of the inn's five rooms and cottages. Furnished with antique beds and heirloom quilts, each of the five rooms in the manor house is named for a Virginia-born president, while each of the five cottage rooms is named for its original functions (Summer Kitchen, Schoolhouse). You'll also find fresh flowers, down pillows and comforters, and coconut milk baths in your private bathroom.

The original tenant farmer cottage is perfect for families. It can sleep six and has a sitting room, cable TV, and two private decks.

Albemarle County

Chester Bed & Breakfast $$$$
243 James River Road, Scottsville
(434) 286–3960
www.chesterbed.com
Scottsville is a historic town, and the Chester Bed & Breakfast has been around to see quite a bit of that history. This beautiful home was built in 1847 by Joseph C. Wright, a retired landscape architect from Chester, England. Situated on seven acres of a historic arboretum, Chester's grounds contain a natural lily pond, garden patio pond and fountains, large stands of English boxwoods, more than 50 different varieties of trees, shrubs,

and flowers, and reputably the largest holly tree on record in Albemarle County.

During the last month of the Civil War, Northern Gen. Philip Sheridan and his troops occupied Scottsville. The house was then occupied by Major James Hill, the local Confederate army commander who was on the brink of death from battle wounds. Sheridan and his aide, George Custer, visited Hill with the intent to arrest him. Certain Hill was dying, Sheridan decided to leave Hill to his fate and left the home empty-handed. However, Major Hill survived and after the war became editor of the *Scottsville Courier.*

Current owners Craig and Jean Stratton keep this part of history alive by hosting occasional Civil War reenactments and encampments on the grounds. Chester has five guest rooms, and all are appointed with Oriental rugs, four-poster beds, wood-burning fireplaces, private baths, down comforters, plush towels, and fresh flowers. For those seeking a bit more room and privacy, Chester's Cottage Suite is available. An inviting sitting room provides a cozy place to relax in front of the fire or watch a movie, and there's a four-poster bed in the bedroom. You can watch the sun set from the rocking chairs on your private porch. Mornings begin at tables in the fireside dining room, set with crisp linens, Villeroy and Boch china, and fresh flowers.

Breakfast varies daily and may include fresh fruits and juices, homemade breads and muffins, breakfast soufflés, Canadian bacon, cinnamon orange French toast, and coffee and tea. Five-course candlelight dinners are available upon request for parties of six or more. Menus may include freshly made garden soups, spring green salads, homemade breads, rosemary-grilled pork tenderloin, seasonal vegetables, flourless chocolate cake, and fresh fruits. Wines are served with each course. Craig and Jean can also make suggestions for dining in either Scottsville or nearby Charlottesville.

Nature lovers will find Chester's grounds a sanctuary for a wide variety of Virginia wildlife. Deer, hawks, tree frogs, hummingbirds, and many species of nest-ing birds can be seen. Many varieties of unusual birds have been spotted at Chester, and a bird census is conducted twice yearly by a local wildlife group. You're also sure to spot the Stratton's pets: Lucy Rose, a gentle hound, Susie, her canine companion, Casey, a golden retriever, and, lording it over all of them, a dignified silver tabby cat named Doc. Unfortunately, guests' pets aren't allowed, but older children are.

High Meadows Vineyard Inn $$$
55 High Meadows Lane, Scottsville
(434) 286-2218, (800) 232-1832
www.highmeadows.com

In 1832, 100 years after the settlement of Scottsville, surveyor Peter White built the Federal portion of High Meadows. Fifty years later, businessman Charles Harris created the Victorian portion of the inn. In 1985, Peter Sushka and Jae Abbitt planted a vinifera vineyard and began restoring High Meadows, and Rose Farber and Jon Storey joined the partners and owners in 2000. The renovation was magnificent, and the interior gives visitors the same glimpse of Federal-era life as nearby Monticello, Montpelier, or Ash Lawn–Highland. High Meadows is also Virginia's only inn that is both on the National Register of Historic Homes and has a renaissance farm vineyard.

All rooms are furnished in original and reproduction furniture and include accents of both the Federal and Victorian eras, and many have working fireplaces, claw-foot tubs, and unusual window arrangements. Seven rooms are in the main inn: High View, Vineyards View, Fair View, Music Room, Meadows View, the Surveyor's Suite, and the Scottsville Suite. There are three contemporary carriage houses close to the main inn. The Cedar Carriage House has a queen-size canopy bed, fireplace, shower, VCR and movie library, and vaulted ceilings. The French Country Carriage House is decorated with a 7-foot round bed next to a slate fireplace, balcony, kitchen, skylights, VCR and movies, French brandy, sundeck, and a hot tub. The World at Glenside Carriage House is a very private two-room cottage with a queen-size canopy bed, stone fireplace, sitting room with VCR and movies, sundeck, hot tub spa, and kitchen. There are also two rooms in the 1920s-era Morningside Garden Cottage. The Wild Rose Room has a king-size bed, separate sitting room with double soaking tub and shower, and a living room with a fireplace. The Abbitt Magnolia Suite contains a queen bed, sunken two-person Jacuzzi, and private outdoor deck.

High Meadows is recognized for its cuisine, and its restaurant is open to the public. In fact, the Inn is included in *Gourmet* magazine's Restaurant Hall of Fame. Diners can enjoy a private candlelight dinner in one of several historic dining rooms. A prix fixe dinner menu offers entree choices changing nightly, with dinner often preceded by Virginia wine tastings and hors d'oeuvres. Four- or six-course meals are highlighted by fresh herbs, seasonal vegetables, exotic mushrooms, and imported cheeses. Overnight guests are treated to a private breakfast with freshly squeezed orange juice, a variety of fresh-baked breads and muffins, fresh fruit, eggs, and coffee or tea. Guests can also have one of the inn's unique European Supper Baskets delivered to their room. The basket contains soup and appetizer, salad, a hot entree, dessert, fresh-baked bread, wine, poetry, and candles.

High Meadows is close to Monticello, the University of Virginia, wineries, Michie Tavern, the Blue Ridge Parkway, kayaking on the James River, and the Waltons Museum in nearby Schuyler. Scottsville, with its antiques stores and restaurants, is a leisurely amble away.

Inn at Court Square $$$$
410 East Jefferson Street, Charlottesville
(434) 295-2800, (866) 466-2877
www.innatcourtsquare.com
An architectural gem, the Inn at Court Square is in the oldest building in historic downtown Charlottesville. Built in 1785 and beautifully restored by owner Candace DeLoach, the inn has five guest rooms, each containing antique furniture, furnishings, and decorative objects. If something in your room catches your eye, have a chat with Candace: Guests have been known to purchase the beds they slept in during their visit.

All rooms are equipped with working fireplaces and private baths, and some have whirlpool baths. A hearty breakfast served in the antique-filled dining room sets you up for a day of exploration.

The pedestrian mall with its great shops and restaurants is a short walk away, and a free trolley takes you to the UVA campus. Monticello, Ash Lawn–Highland, and a plethora of recreation activities are close by. Children are welcome, and there's private off-street parking for guests.

Inn at Monticello $$$$
1188 Scottsville Road, Charlottesville
(434) 979-3593
www.innatmonticello.com
Norman and Rebecca Lindway invite guests to "spend the day at Thomas Jefferson's beloved Monticello. Spend the night with us." This country manor house was built in the mid-1800s in the valley of Jefferson's Monticello Mountain. On the grounds of the house are dogwoods, boxwoods, azaleas, and beautiful Willow Lake. Sit back and enjoy the view from one of the rockers on the porch or join in a game of bocce ball on the manicured lawn.

Inside are five elegant bedrooms, all of which are furnished with period antiques and reproductions. The beds are made with crisp cotton linens and down comforters. Some rooms have special features, such as a working fireplace, four-poster canopy bed, or private porch. Each room is air-conditioned and has a private bath.

The aroma of freshly ground coffee will lure you from your warm bed. The ever-changing, large gourmet breakfast menu includes such delicious entrees as fresh blueberry stuffed French toast, nutmeg buttermilk pancakes with fresh fruit, or homemade scones. Guests can purchase the Inn's new cookbook and replicate the delicious recipes at home.

The inn is less than 2 miles to Monticello and convenient to Michie Tavern, Ash Lawn–Highland (the home of James Monroe), Montpelier (the home of James and Dolley Madison), and many vineyards. Children 12 and older are welcome. A two-night minimum stay is required on weekends and holidays.

The Inn at Sugar Hollow Farm $$$$
Highway 614, 3 miles off Highway 810, White Hall
(434) 823-7086
www.sugarhollow.com

Dick and Hayden Cabell are the innkeepers at this 70-acre wooded farm in the Moorman River Valley at the edge of the Shenandoah National Park. The serene country setting offers mountain views and the comforting sound of rushing woodland streams.

The new inn was custom-built in 1995 and has seven distinctive bedrooms, with cozy corners for reading and relaxing as well as several comfortable common areas. Each bedroom has a different theme, ranging from woodland to Colonial, and each has a private bath. Three rooms have double whirlpool tubs in the private baths. Wood-burning fireplaces warm you in four of the bedrooms, and one bedroom has a modern gas fireplace. The oak-beamed country-style family and dining rooms open to a broad, bluestone terrace offering a grand view across the gardens and fields to Pasture Fence Mountain and the Blue Ridge. An upper deck overlooks a large herb and flower garden, which features a fountain and swing for two. A library/TV room, sunroom, and reading nook are other relaxing options.

A full country breakfast features egg specialties or French toast or homemade blueberry pancakes, side dishes, fresh fruit, a choice of juices, gourmet coffee, and freshly baked muffins or pastries. Complimentary soft drinks, coffee, and tea are always available.

Exploring the outdoors tops the list of activities here. The nearby Shenandoah National Park offers two hiking trails with free access only 2 miles from the inn that lead to the Appalachian Trail at the top of the Blue Ridge. Nearby roads serve as favorite biking routes for both road and mountain bikers. Fifteen of Virginia's fine wineries are within a 45-minute drive of the inn and offer tours and tastings. Children older than 12 are welcome.

Inn at the Crossroads $$
5010 Plank Road, North Garden
(434) 979-6452, (866) 809-2136
www.crossroadsinn.com

Surrounded by beautiful countryside 8 miles south of Charlottesville, the Inn at the Crossroads commands spectacular vistas of the foothills of the Blue Ridge. It is near many of the region's finest natural attractions, including Crabtree Falls, Devil's Knob Mountain, and the James River.

The aptly named inn and one-time tavern, built in 1818, sits at the crossing of two Colonial roads: a north-south route linking Charlottesville with Lynchburg (now U.S. Highway 29) and an east-west pike connecting the James River with the Shenandoah Valley (now Highway 692). The three-story Federal-style home is on the National Register of Historic Places and a Virginia Historic Landmark. Through the years, Crossroad Tavern served as a meeting place, polling center, post office, and trading post. The location makes for easy access to Charlottesville as well as many of the surrounding attractions.

All the rooms and cottages have private baths and individually controlled heat and air-conditioning. The main inn has five rooms. There are three rooms with queen-size beds and two two-room suites with king-size beds. The summer kitchen cottage, built in 1824, is ideal for families. The cottage sleeps four and has a housekeeping kitchen. Children older than 12 may stay in the main inn, and children of any age are welcome in the cottage. A full breakfast is included in the room price.

Silver Thatch Inn   **$$$$**
3001 Hollymead Drive, Charlottesville
(434) 978-4686, (800) 261-0720
www.silverthatch.com

Built in 1780 by Hessian soldiers, the Silver Thatch Inn's central house brings to mind the architecture of Colonial Williamsburg. The house is an immaculately restored white clapboard building surrounded by dogwoods, magnolias, and pines.

In the 19th century, the inn served as a boys' school, then a tobacco plantation and, after the Civil War, a melon farm. A wing was added in 1937, and a cottage was built in 1984 to complement the main building.

Owners Jim and Terri Petrouits have decorated the inn with early American folk art, quilts, reproduction furniture, and antiques. The seven guest rooms are named for Virginia-born presidents. The Thomas Jefferson Room has a pencil-post, queen-size canopy bed and fireplace. All rooms have private baths and several have fireplaces. Guests will find fresh, homemade cookies waiting for them in their rooms. Guests enjoy a full country breakfast.

The Silver Thatch Inn has a restaurant with three dining rooms, a sunroom, and a bar where guests can have a glass of wine or beer before dinner from Tuesday through Saturday. The wine cellar has earned the Wine Spectator Award of Excellence for more than a decade. The menu changes frequently but always includes a vegetarian special and entrees such as grilled filet mignon to satisfy conventional tastes. Two of the more exotic items on the menu are artichoke hearts with roasted vegetable marina sauce and sea bass with crab blini. (See our Restaurants chapter.)

Silver Thatch is a short drive from the University of Virginia, Monticello, Montpelier, and Ash Lawn–Highland. The Skyline Drive and the Blue Ridge Parkway are a half hour away. Guests have access to an outdoor swimming pool.

200 South Street Inn   **$$$$**
200 South Street, Charlottesville
(434) 979-0200, (800) 964-7008
www.southstreetinn.com

This inn is actually two restored houses in downtown Charlottesville. The restoration was completed in 1986, and every detail of 200 South Street was meticulously re-created or renewed, including the classical veranda and a two-story walnut serpentine handrail. The larger of the two buildings was built in 1856 for Thomas Jefferson Wertenbaker, son of Thomas Jefferson's first librarian and close friend, and remained a residence until the 20th century. In the following years, the building was believed to have housed a finishing school for girls, a brothel, and then a boarding house before it was transformed into the inn.

Innkeepers Brendan and Jenny Clancy have decorated the 19 rooms with lovely English and Belgian antiques. You can choose a room with a whirlpool bath, a fireplace, a canopy bed, or a private living room suite. Every room has a private bath.

A complimentary continental breakfast with home-baked breads, cakes, and coffee, afternoon tea, and wine are available to guests. The inn is only steps from the finest restaurants, shops, and entertainment in the area, 1 mile from UVA and 4 miles from Monticello. It's hard to leave the comforts of 200 South Street, though; the library, sitting room, upstairs study, veranda, and garden terrace beckon.

Nelson County

Acorn Inn   **$**
2256 Adial Road, Nellysford
(434) 361-9357
www.acorninn.com

This cozy, art-filled bed-and-breakfast provides a creative and inexpensive home base for exploration of the area's many offerings. Skiing and golf at Wintergreen Resort, winery tours, cycling, hiking, fishing, and a host of mountain sports are all close to Acorn Inn.

Innkeepers Martin and Kathy Versluys lived in many Latin American countries before they opened Acorn Inn, so the masks, baskets, tapestries, and most of her photographs are primarily from Mexico and South America. But there are also several shots from trips to Turkey and various European countries. The bedrooms are decorated with wall-quilts made by a Nelson County artisan.

Three different lodging styles are available: the Inn, Acorn Cottage, and the Farmhouse. The Inn, once a horse barn, offers 10 comfortable rooms, each with a double bed and original stall doors. An 880-square-foot meeting room with kitchenette is ideal for corporate retreats, weddings, and reunions. Guests are charmed by the colorful folk art and a relaxed Scandinavian atmosphere. The common room features a beautiful Finnish soapstone bake oven. The oven is by the Finnish company Tulikivi (which is Scandinavian), but an interesting fact is that the soapstone all came from Nelson County, back during the few brief years that Tulikivi was quarrying nearby. Ladies' and gentlemen's bathrooms are shared in the inn.

Acorn Cottage, with its own kitchen and bath, is perfect for honeymooners or families with small children who want more privacy. Two guest rooms in the Farmhouse—which also is the home of the Versluys—are available during the busiest seasons. These two rooms share a bath. Since Martin is from the Netherlands, visitors can't help but notice Acorn Inn's European accent, in carpentry, design, and language. He has cycled and "adventured" all over the world, so the photos, folk art, inspiration, conversation, and atmosphere spread far and wide.

A continental breakfast each morning features a delicious variety of homemade breads, muffins, and fruit cobbler along with fresh fruit, juice, coffee, and tea.

Afton Mountain Bed and Breakfast $
10273 Rockfish Valley Highway, Afton
(540) 456-6844, (800) 769-6844
This 1848 pre-Victorian farmhouse near

the Blue Ridge Parkway is an English country-style inn. The inn, within a half hour's drive of Charlottesville, Monticello, and Wintergreen Resort, used to be the county's tax preservation office.

Today, innkeepers Dan and Orquida Ingraham have decorated their five guest rooms with antiques. Each room is air-conditioned and has a private bath. Two wicker-furnished porches offer views of the countryside, while the parlor and living room are comfortable settings for reading, parlor games, and television. Refreshments are served each afternoon.

Breakfast in the formal dining room starts with freshly baked muffins or breads and juice, followed by a second course of seasonal fruits and then the main course, which could include stuffed cinnamon French toast or lemon pancakes. The broiled grapefruit is the house specialty. Coffee and tea are available to early risers on the antique buffet outside the rooms.

Fresh-cut flowers from the garden grace the inn's interior, and guests may stroll through the rose garden or the plantings along the two stream banks or take a dip in the inn's pool. Wine Lovers, anniversary, ski, and Valentine's Day packages are available. Children are welcome.

Harmony Hill $
929 Wilson Hill Road, Arrington
(434) 263-7750, (877) 263-7750
www.harmony-hill.com
Looking for the tranquil respite from a fast and hectic life of the Northeast, Joanne and Bob Cuoghi bought 17 acres of rolling farmland in Nelson County. Wanting to share what they found, they decided to design and build a log home. Trudy, their daughter-in-law, named it Harmony Hill. Deer, raccoons, and other wildlife frequent the grounds, and hawks perch in nearby trees awaiting a passing meal. There are plenty of shady and sunny spots to lounge in and watch the world go by . . . slowly.

The owners begin their pampering at your arrival, greeting you with a quick smile and a cool drink. Fresh flowers and fruit baskets are waiting in your room. Satellite TV and VCRs are available, and an in-room massage can be arranged with a local certified massage therapist.

The interior of Harmony Hill showcases Joanne's skills in arts and crafts. Stencils, faux wall finishings, and quilts bring a bright and unique look to the common areas and guest rooms. The five guest rooms all have private baths and are named after local rivers and mountains. Each of the second-floor bedrooms features a window seat, offering a view of the fields and hills surrounding Harmony Hill. The Tye River room decor is accented in yellow and green and is furnished with a queen-size mahogany bed. The Oak Ridge room is warmed by a fireplace. The burled walnut bed brings a touch of art deco. A standard-size whirlpool bathtub adds luxury to the bath. The Piney River room is decorated in elegant simplicity with a rocking chair, handcrafted four-poster bed, and a standard-size whirlpool tub in its private bath. The Blue Ridge room, warmed by its brown color scheme and a cozy fireplace, completes the four rooms on the second floor. The James River room, on the first floor, is huge, some 400 square feet. This room is a favorite of both newlyweds and families. It features striking log walls, a cherry king-size bedstead, a large sitting area with convertible sofa, fireplace, and full bath.

Harmony Hill offers several unique packages. The "Honey, I'm Sorry" special, the Valentine special with breakfast in the room, and the Murder Mysteries are some of the guests' favorites. Joanne also teaches a quilting workshop for guilds or groups of six to eight. Breakfast is a treat and is served in the dining room, which is filled with Joanne's beautiful collection of antique kitchen appliances and porcelains. Guests are served a full breakfast with special offerings such as coco banana bread, cantaloupe bread, pumpkin bread pudding, or egg in a cloud.

There are roads to bike and nearby rivers to canoe, kayak, and tube. Or visitors can drive right up the road and visit the Waltons' Museum, Monticello, Ash Lawn–Highland, historic downtown Charlottesville, or Nelson's six wineries. The Blue Ridge Parkway and Wintergreen Resort are a short drive away.

Children are welcome, but the Cuoghis ask that you leave your pets at home.

The Mark Addy $$
56 Rodes Farm Drive, Nellysford
(434) 361-1101, (800) 278-2154
www.mark-addy.com

Beautifully restored, The Mark Addy offers the richness and romance of a bygone era. The inn is a former estate house, Upland, that began as a four-room farmhouse before the Civil War and was expanded from 1884 to 1902.

The eight rooms and one suite are decorated in individual themes: Oriental, English, Victorian, or the military-style Colonel's Room. Each has a private bathroom with either a double whirlpool bath, double shower, or an antique claw-foot tub with shower. Five porches and a hammock are available for lounging. Public rooms include a dining room, a parlor, a library, and a sitting room with cable TV, VCR, games, and phones.

Breakfast is a hearty meal. Innkeeper John Maddox takes pride in his cuisine de grandmere.

Nearby attractions include the Skyline Drive, Monticello, wineries, Wintergreen Resort, and all the shops, museums, restaurants, and social activities of the university city of Charlottesville. For those who are happiest when browsing through curiosity shops, Tuckahoe Antique Mall is just a few miles away. But antiques lovers won't have to travel far: The inn opened its own antiques and gift shop in one of the outbuildings. For the more adventurous, canoeing, hiking, and rafting are minutes away. Children older than 12 are welcome.

The Meander Inn $$$
3100 Berry Hill Road, Nellysford
(434) 361-1121, (800) 868-6116
www.meanderinn.com

The Rockfish Valley of Nelson County is

the setting for this country farmhouse on 50 acres of horse-grazed pasture and woods. The Count Alain San Giorgio, a native of Monaco, and his wife Francesca, bought this ca. 1914 Victorian home in 1999.

It's located just 100 yards from the Rockfish River. Contessa Francesca San Giorgio, who is Japanese-American, has decorated many of the rooms with oriental wall hangings, ornaments, and furnishings. Alain, whose Monaco ancestors can be traced back more than 700 years, has added his collection of antique military prints, which grace the stairway to the guest rooms.

Five guest rooms are available furnished with Victorian, French, Japanese, or country antiques, and each has a private bath. All rooms have queen-size beds.

You will be treated to a delicious full-country breakfast. Afterward, you can settle down for a quiet read in the library or get comfortable in the sitting room. Enjoy a picnic by the river or relax on the wide front porch and take in the gorgeous views.

Alain and Francesca share a love of horses and horseback riding. This 40-acre property is home to their four Arabian horses, and they offer their boarding facilities to those traveling with horses. Among their many packages is a horse-lovers package, including horseback riding for two and a tour of the barn with 11 Arabians horses and Peruvian Paso. As the inn's name suggests, you can meander along the Skyline Drive and behold the spectacular scenery. Among the activities within easy reach are skiing, canoeing, horseback riding, tennis, golf, fishing, hiking, swimming, and biking.

Pets are not allowed at the inn, but well-behaved children are welcome. Smoking is permitted outdoors only. A two-night minimum stay is required on most weekends.

Amherst County and Lynchburg

Babcock House $$
250 Oakleigh Avenue, Appomattox
(434) 352-7532, (800) 689-6208
www.babcockhouse.com

The front five rooms of this restored Victorian home were built in 1884 by Samuel Patterson Coleman Jr. The house was sold in 1908 to H.C. Babcock for $1,815. Adding the rooms to the rear of the original five, the Babcocks used the house as a family dwelling and boarding house until it was converted to a bed-and-breakfast in 2000 by Jerry and Shelia Palamar. The Babcock House was also the boyhood home of outdoor author Havilah Babcock.

Each of the five bedrooms and one suite is furnished with antiques and period reproductions. All rooms have private baths, cable television, ceiling fans, and air-conditioning. Telephones, coffeepots, hair dryers, complimentary beverages, and bottled water are also provided for guests' convenience. The Bradley Suite is named after one of Annie Laurie Babcock's children and features a light and airy sitting room with an antique fireplace and queen-size sofa bed. The bedroom area features an oversized queen-size pine cottage bed with a hand-crocheted bedspread. The Abbitt Room is named after Dr. Julian Abbitt, an earlier owner of the Babcock House, and is decorated with an iron queen-size bed, yellow walls, steamer trunk, and Oriental carpet. The Annie Laurie Room is named after Annie Laurie Babcock, the last Babcock descendant to reside here, and contains a four-poster queen-size bed and the original claw-foot bathtub. The Rebecca Room is furnished with a full-size bed and a daybed, perfect for a small family. The Havilah Room is named after Dr. Havilah Babcock himself and has Persian blue walls and Oriental carpet; it is furnished with a sleigh bed. The Bryon Room is on the first floor, is wheelchair accessible, and boasts natural stained floors and a queen-size bed.

A full gourmet breakfast is included with your room rate and may include stuffed French toast, puffed apple pancakes with orange sauce, blueberry pancakes, homemade muffins and bread, breakfast meats, fresh fruits and juices, and coffee. Meals are served on tables set with linen, china, and silver. The Babcock House restaurant is open for lunch, Tuesday through Friday, and take-out lunches are available for guests any day of the week, including a romantic picnic lunch. Candlelight dinners are available by reservation, and the menu may include roast pork tenderloin with garlic, apples, and thyme; grilled tuna with tomato, olive, and herb compote; or roast duck.

Guests at Babcock House can find plenty to keep them busy. Appomattox Courthouse, the site where Robert E. Lee tendered the Confederacy's surrender to Ulysses Grant to end the Civil War, is right down the street. Also close by are Sweet Briar College, Longwood College, and the Booker T. Washington Museum. Children are welcome.

Dulwich Manor Bed and Breakfast $$
550 Richmond Highway, Amherst
(434) 946-7207, (800) 571-9011
www.thedulwichmanor.com
You will know your journey is over when you turn onto the winding country lane and see the inviting porch of this estate, set on 97 secluded acres in Amherst County. Flemish bond brickwork and fluted columns decorate the outside of this late-1880s English-style manor house. Nestled in the countryside and surrounded by the Blue Ridge Mountains, Dulwich Manor abounds with beauty and country appeal.

Hosts Mark and Gail Moore have a serene getaway. Period antiques decorate the rooms, and the living room and study each have a large fireplace to set a cozy, relaxed mood. The six bedrooms are reminiscent of an English country home—beds are canopied brass or antiques—and you can choose a room with a fireplace or window seat for relaxing afternoons or evenings. The Scarborough Room also offers a king-size Victorian bed and an oversize Jacuzzi. The Erin Room has a standard-size Jacuzzi and features a carved oak queen-size bed.

Each day begins with a full country breakfast, including fresh fruits and juices, inn-baked muffins and breads, country sausage, herb teas, and hot coffee. Take a stroll after breakfast and see the natural beauty of the Washington and Jefferson National Forests. The Blue Ridge Parkway is nearby for hiking, picnicking, or photographing the view. Natural Bridge and Caverns, Peaks of Otter, and Crabtree Falls are scenic spots for a lunch. This area of the country is also full of history: Washington, Jefferson, and Patrick Henry were all born near here. Monticello, Ash Lawn–Highland, and Poplar Forest are all within a short distance of Dulwich.

Pets and children are not allowed. Smoking is allowed outside only.

Franklin County

The Claiborne House Bed and Breakfast $$
185 Claiborne Avenue, Rocky Mount
(540) 483-4616
www.clabornehouse.net
English-style gardens surround the 1895 Queen Anne Victorian Claiborne House, an elegant home in Franklin County. This tranquil getaway is nestled between the Blue Ridge Parkway and Smith Mountain Lake. The best place to enjoy the scenery is from the 130-foot wraparound porch furnished with white wicker furniture.

Victorian-era furnishings add charm to the interior. The 10-foot walnut ceilings and 9-foot windows make the parlor and dining room delightful. Guest rooms are inviting, decorated with a personal touch and filled with period antiques. Enjoy the Sierra Suite with its king-size four-poster bed, sitting area, and a separate entrance from the gardens. The quaint Blue Ridge Room features a queen-size lacy canopy bed with walnut armoire. All five guest rooms have private baths. Breakfast is a bountiful meal that may include fresh berries or other homegrown fruits in season.

Enjoy your morning cup from the porch with its old Southern–style hanging ferns as you listen to the native birds and watch playful squirrels hop from treetop to treetop in the ancient maples and oaks. Stroll through the lovely English gardens or have some quiet moments by the three-level water pond and fountains.

Tony and Shellie Leete are your hosts and can help you plan a day in the area. Smith Mountain Lake offers year-round activities—fishing, golf, boating, tennis, and biking—on its 500 miles of shoreline. Booker T. Washington National Monument is just minutes away. Ferrum College and its Blue Ridge Farm Museum, Mabry Mill, Peaks of Otter, Mill Mountain Zoo, and Roanoke's historic Farmer's Market are all within a short drive.

NEW RIVER VALLEY

Montgomery County

L'Arche Bed and Breakfast $$
301 Wall Street, Blacksburg
(540) 951-1808
www.larchebb.com
An elegant 1900-to-1903 Federal Revival-style home takes you away from it all—right in the heart of downtown Blacksburg. Vera Good opened this renovated landmark, just a block from Virginia Tech, in 1993. Five comfortable guest rooms are decorated with fluffy comforters and handmade quilts. Each features a private bath, queen-size bed, and fresh flowers. The Country Room will accommodate a family with two children.

Guests may read, chat, and relax in the drawing room, and the two cavernous dining rooms overlook the gardens. Share a table for two on the wide porch or sit under the Jeffersonian gazebo. Recreation

is close at hand: white-water rafting on the New River, boating at Claytor Lake State Park, or picnicking by Cascades Waterfall. You'll find horseback riding, horse shows, and carriage rides at Dori-Del Equine Center. Nearby Virginia Tech and Radford University provide cultural and athletic events.

Breakfast at L'Arche is an event. The inn serves fresh fruit, home-baked breads, muffins and cakes, homemade granola, and spiced teas. The morning repast may also include French toast, fluffy omelets, or pancakes and waffles. Special dietary needs can be accommodated. The adjoining Vera's Tea Garden serves traditional tea and light lunches, dinners, and receptions.

Reservations are strongly encouraged. A two-night minimum stay is necessary on football weekends, commencement, parents' weekend, or other special events at Tech. Smoking is permitted outside on the grounds. Gift certificates are available.

The Oaks Victorian Inn $$$$
311 East Main Street, Christiansburg
(540) 381-1500, (800) 336-6257
www.bbhost.com/theoaksinn
Massive oak trees, believed to be more than 300 years old, surround this estate in Christiansburg, which has been widely recognized for lodging excellence. A green lawn stretches for what seems like miles, and the home itself stands like a fairy-tale castle. Major W. L. Pierce built the buttercup-yellow Queen Anne Victorian for his family, completing it in 1893. The home remained in the Pierce family for almost 90 years.

Margaret and Tom Ray converted the Oaks into a country inn. The luxurious manor is well suited for both leisure and business travelers. Guest rooms have queen- or king-size canopy beds with Posturepedic mattresses, fireplaces, and window nooks. Other amenities include telephones with private lines and dataports, TVs and VCRs, minirefrigerators stocked with complimentary refreshments, decanters of sherry, and valet service on request. The private baths in each room are stocked with plush towels, fluffy terry robes, and English toiletries. The garden gazebo houses a Hydrojet hot tub. The inn also has a large library of VHS movies to choose from.

In 1997 the Oaks was selected by the National Trust for Historic Preservation for the cover of its guidebook and was one of 52 properties chosen for the 1998 engagement calendar. The inn has been a member since 1993 of the Select Registry, an international organization where membership is by invitation only. In 2004 the Oaks received its 10th consecutive Four-Diamond Award from AAA. Guests from 50 states and 34 countries have visited.

Each morning, guests wake to freshly ground coffee and a newspaper. The breakfast menu is varied and features such specialties as spinach or asparagus quiche Provençal; Belgian waffles served with butter-pecan ice cream, blackberries, a homemade sauce made with grapefruit and Grand Marnier and topped with toasted almonds and coconut; fresh fruit in honey and Amaretto; and a variety of fresh breads. A bounty of fresh fruits and juices are available as well.

Take some time after breakfast to lounge on the wraparound porch with its Kennedy rockers and wicker chairs. Investigate the books and games in the parlor. Nearby, you can hike on the Appalachian Trail and boat or fish on Claytor Lake. The historic Newbern Museum, Mill Mountain Theatre, Center in the Square, Smithfield Plantation, and Chateau Morrisette Winery are a short drive away. The Oaks' Victorian Christmas each December is a special event.

Gift certificates are available. Advance payment and a two-night minimum are required for special-event weekends at local universities. Corporate rates are available Sunday through Thursday.

Pulaski County

Homestead Inn on Claytor Lake $$$$
2652 Brown Road, Draper
(540) 980-6777
Innkeeper Diane Whitehead has redecorated and revitalized this lakeside home, which she opened to guests in 1999. Little extras and special touches make the Homestead Inn unique. From the beginning of your stay, when Diane greets you at the door with a specially created nonalcoholic drink, you will see how intent she is on pampering her guests.

The home is decorated throughout with antiques, reproductions, and collector's pieces. The lovely living room, with fireplace, is a wonderful place to gather with friends or family to relax, read, play cards, or chat. Most rooms in the cozy old house have a spectacular view of the lake. The brick and stone wraparound porch provides a magnificent view.

Each of the five upstairs guest rooms and one suite on the main floor have all the comforts of home, including color televisions, VCRs, and private phones. Beds vary in size from a king-size to two twin-size beds. All have private baths. A gourmet breakfast is served whenever you want it. Sit out on the porch or deck, or stop by the dining room for frittatas and elegant French toast. They also have an excellent homemade buffalo sausage. Guests also are invited to call ahead to request dinner.

Numerous recreational opportunities are available at the inn. Spend your afternoon on the 550 feet of private white sand beach along the lake. The cabana building is perfect for picnics and parties. You can rent small paddleboats. Nearby is an 18-hole PGA golf course and the New River Trail. A short drive will take you to historic downtown Pulaski, Wilderness Road Regional Museum in Newbern, or the Blue Ridge Parkway.

The inn is open year-round. Advance reservations are suggested. Well-behaved children are allowed.

ALLEGHANY HIGHLANDS

Alleghany County

Firmstone Manor $$
6209 Longdale Furnace Road
Clifton Forge
(540) 862-0892, (800) 474-9882
www.firmstonemanor.com

Stone gates welcome you to Firmstone Manor, named after the man who built it in 1873. Driving up the arched drive lined with flowering plum trees offers a view of the splendid 10,000-square-foot Victorian with a classic gazebo. A myriad flowers and exotic shrubbery enhance the charm of this elegant inn set near the southern tip of Virginia's beautiful Shenandoah Valley.

The magnificent entrance hall will take you back in time to when Ulysses S. Grant was president and Virginia's first hot-blast iron furnace was established at Firmstone, which has been superbly restored by the new owners. Explore Firmstone Manor's 18 rooms, many decorated with original fixtures, art, and furniture. Have lunch in one of the outdoor garden rooms, or just sit on the swing at the gazebo and enjoy cool mountain breezes.

The new owners, Barbara Jarucka and Charles Towle, have renovated and upgraded the manor, putting in a flagstone maze and stone wall surrounding the front of the property. They also planted a variety of flowering bushes and started a fruit tree orchard. There's outdoor seating areas in shaded spots for intimate picnics, and fountains along the grounds.

The inn has five large bedrooms and a two-room suite, a library, game room, and sitting areas. Four of the bedrooms have beautiful hand-painted marble or wood and tile carved fireplaces.

There are three cottages on the property. Two are one-bedroom cottages with living rooms and small kitchens. The third is two rooms and a kitchenette. Pets and children are welcome.

At Firmstone, a full gourmet breakfast is served, varying with what is in season.

The manor also caters to guests' requests for their favorite foods. There are no set hours for breakfast, so you may sleep in and have breakfast served in your room, the dining room, or on the gazebo, where you can enjoy a splendid view of the mountains. Picnic lunches can be provided upon request, and Sunday dinners, too, since many places are closed. Relaxing activities here include croquet on the side lawn beneath century-old shade trees or strolling the 12 acres of grounds rich with the wildflowers and songbirds that make their home at Firmstone Manor.

There's plenty of unspoiled beauty, and artists often come here to paint the landscape. Recreation sites are plentiful in the area. One mile west of the manor, Longdale National Recreation Area has a variety of trails and a mountain lake for swimming. Outdoor enthusiasts and photographers will want to see the North Mountain Trail. Firmstone is at the foot of North Mountain, a challenging and highly rated spot for hikers and mountain bikers. Also, nearby Lexington offers shopping in many small boutiques.

Firmstone Manor hosts gatherings, such as family reunions and retreats, and provides a special romantic setting for weddings.

Weekly rental rates for the cottages are $300 to $450.

Milton Hall Bed & Breakfast Inn $$
207 Thorny Lane, Covington
(540) 965-0196
www.milton-hall.com

The Hon. Laura Marie Theresa Fitzwilliam, Viscountess Milton, built this manor in 1874. Lord Milton was ill and Lady Milton hoped the peace and tranquillity of the countryside and beautiful mountain scenery would help return him to health. Today, Milton Hall still stands on 44 acres just west of Covington, in the community of Callaghan. Surrounded by the Allegheny Mountains, the house, with its gables, buttressed porch towers, and Gothic trimmings, is a contrast to its rustic surroundings. The inside is not as ornate, and, while it is spacious, it is more of a large country home than a mansion.

A roomy living area and equally large dining room each have two sets of French doors opening to the gardens in the south lawn. Each of the six guest bedrooms has a private bath, and two baths have claw-foot tubs. There is also a library upstairs. Some rooms feature queen-size beds and fireplaces. The second-floor master bedroom suite has a sitting area. All rooms have cable TV.

Owners Mike and Laurie Finnegan, Jean Daniels, and Kathleen More serve a full breakfast in the dining room. Picnics or elegant basket lunches are available to sightseeing guests. Plenty of attractions are nearby—Lake Moomaw, national forests, and state wildlife management areas are just a few. There is also the famous Humpback Bridge, Virginia's oldest standing covered bridge, within walking distance. The bridge is the nation's only surviving curved-span covered bridge. Children older than 8 are welcome.

Bath County

Fort Lewis Lodge   **$$$$**
River Road, Millboro
(540) 925-2314
www.fortlewislodge.com
In 1754 Col. Charles Lewis built a stockade to protect the southern pass of Shenandoah Mountain from Indian raids. This frontier outpost became a vast 3,200-acre farm, situated deep within the Allegheny Mountains. For more than 200 years, this area has remained virtually unchanged. The spectacular scenery and rushing mountain streams are enough to take your breath away. About 18 years ago, John and Caryl Cowden moved from Ohio to manage and operate the farm. Today they are your hosts at this mountain retreat. They have restored the old redbrick manor house and the Lewis gristmill, dating back to 1850, adding a guest lodge.

The large gathering room is framed with massive beams of oak and walnut. The observation tower, which is actually an enclosed stairway leading to the top of an adjoining silo, provides 360-degree views of the grounds; the silo also has three bedrooms. The lodge's 12 bedrooms are decorated with wildlife art and handcrafted walnut, cherry, red oak, and butternut furniture, much of it made by local craftsmen from wood cut right on the property. Each guest room has a private bath. Historic hand-hewn log cabins are also available to guests for $210. These romantic hideaways feature queen-size beds, sleeper sofas, large stone fireplaces, and rocking chair porches. There are also little extras such as refrigerators and coffeemakers. All the cabins have private baths.

Among many of Fort Lewis's happy surprises is Riverside House, a short three-minute drive away, on the upper tract. Peaceful and secluded, it offers all of the amenities of the lodge with an added bonus: a picturesque view of the river and some of the finest fishing on the grounds. Hugged with porches, it has ample areas to enjoy the scenery or to just curl up with a good book. The five spacious guest rooms are elegant and feature individual bathrooms. For the purist, spring water flows fresh from the tap.

Meals are served in the 19th-century Lewis Gristmill. Two meals are included in the room rate under the Modified American Plan, and all dishes are homemade and scrumptious. A full country breakfast includes freshly baked breads, eggs, sausage, bacon, fruits, and French toast with locally made maple syrup. The buffet dinners include fresh vegetables from the farm's garden. You may also have a box lunch prepared to take along with you.

Outdoor activities are abundant here, with more than 2 miles of the meandering Cowpasture River flowing through the valley for swimming, tubing, and sport fishing (it's catch-and-release) for smallmouth bass and trout. Several state-stocked trout streams are nearby. Miles of marked trails and old logging roads allow you to stroll along or explore.

Hidden Valley Bed & Breakfast $$$
Hidden Valley Road, Warm Springs
(540) 839-3178
www.hiddenvalleybedandbreakfast.com
Hidden Valley Bed & Breakfast started life as Warwickton, a brick mansion built by James Woods Warwick in 1885. This columned mansion is on the National Register of Historic Places and is a Virginia Historic Landmark. The house sits on a large acreage bordered by the unpopulated beauty of the George Washington National Forest, and the Jackson River runs in front of Hidden Valley and is teeming with trout.

Ron and Pam Stidham have re-created the interior of the house to closely match what James Warwick would have known. A formal living room, music room (complete with piano), foyer, and upstairs hall are furnished with period pieces, knickknacks, and area rugs. The three guest rooms continue the trick of transporting you back into time. The Library Room is decorated in vibrant tones of green and red and a hunting and fishing motif. The room holds two double beds and is perfect for a small family. The School Room was once actually the Hunt School for local children and now has a gorgeous four-poster canopied bed and an armchair. The Garden Room has an antique rosewood bedstead and Empire wardrobe. All rooms have private baths, although they are located in the hallway. The Stidhams have not forgotten those on a working holiday. All rooms have desks, and the inn has a fax and dataport at your disposal. You can opt to stay in the summer kitchen, located next to the house and built for the movie *Sommersby* as a replica summer kitchen. It's one large open space, with a gas fireplace, kitchen, two twin sofa beds, and a king-size bed, and is perfect for families.

A full country breakfast is served in the formal dining room and includes fresh baked goods, fruit, coffee, tea, and a variety of hot entrees.

You don't have to leave Hidden Valley grounds to have a great trip. Biking, trail hiking, hunting, and fishing are all available on-site. A quick trip in the car will take you to area museums, shops, and battlefields. The Allegheny Highlands Arts and Craft Center and Cass Scenic Railroad are nearby.

Children older than 6 are permitted, and pets may be accommodated with prior permission. Smoking is permitted on the porches.

King's Victorian Inn $$
RR 1, Hot Springs
(540) 839-3134
www.kingsvictorianbandb.com
Nestled in a grove of old maple trees, this 1899 Victorian mansion is the perfect place to take it easy after a day of exploring the Alleghany Highlands. Set on three acres of land 1 mile north of Hot Springs, it's secluded without being isolated. There's an inviting veranda with rockers just made for reading, or you can chat with owners Liz and Richard King about the best fishing hole in the area.

The Kings provide six guest rooms, all furnished with Victorian furnishings, including carved four-poster beds and Oriental rugs. Four of the rooms have private baths, and two rooms share a bathroom. There is also a honeymoon cottage with a fireplace, as well as a four-bedroom guest cottage and the Kings Cottage at the Cascades, which is a two-bedroom cottage with a fireplace. The cottages are wonderful choices for families. Breakfast is not included for those in the two larger cottages.

After a full breakfast there's a full day of activities ahead of you. There's excellent trout and fly-fishing nearby in local streams and Lake Moomaw, along with hiking, biking, horseback riding, and ice skating in the winter. Culture buffs will want to check out the Garth Newel Music Center, noted for its excellent summer chamber music series. McDowell Battlefield and history-filled Lexington are a short drive away. You can even visit the nearby Homestead resort and learn the history of the spas that give the town its name.

Older children are invited to enjoy the Kings' hospitality. No smoking or pets are allowed.

Three Hills Inn   **$$**
Route 220 N., Warm Springs
(540) 839-5381
www.3hills.com
In 1913 Miss Mary Johnston was in a financial bind. Her Civil War novels were selling poorly and her groundbreaking feminist novel, *Hagar*, had just received decidedly mixed reviews. An independent and spirited woman, Mary took her savings and her resolve and poured them into her home, Three Hills. In 1917 she and her two sisters opened their mansion as an inn. It soon developed a following because of the magnificence of the building, the breathtaking view of the Alleghenies, and the charm of its hostesses. Mary continued to write novels (which sold quite well) and shock men with her views on equality until the day she died. Three Hills passed from the Johnston family in 1955 and has continued to receive guests ever since then. The inn is on the National Register of Historic Places and is now operated by Charlene and Doug Fike.

The Fikes had never heard of Mary Johnston when they bought the house, but they continue her tradition of graciousness and courtesy. They have also kept their rooms as grand as Mary herself would have. The Fikes welcome groups of all sizes and budgets into a variety of suites and rooms, and all rooms have private baths and TVs. There are four Master Suites appropriate for families, and all include one or two bedrooms, sitting room, and kitchenette, and most include mountain views. The three Hotel Rooms include a bedroom and private outside entrances. There is also a Garden Cottage available, which can sleep four. A new conference center, which can do outdoor concerts, seats 100 inside the amphitheater.

Sixty percent of Bath County is set aside for preservation and conservation, which is great news for visitors. Explore the area by hiking, hunting, fishing, canoeing, or swimming in George Washington National Forest, Gathright Game Management Area, Douthat State Park, and Lake Moomaw. Expect to find stocked streams, along with turkey, deer, bear, and small game.

Nearby Garth Newel Music Center presents music festivals and concerts throughout the year. The Warm Springs Pools, which are the namesake of the area, have drawn people for 200 years and are less than a mile from Three Hills.

Children of all ages are welcome here, and cribs and roll-away beds are available. The Fikes can accommodate some pets with advance notice for a small additional fee. Smoking is restricted to the veranda and grounds.

Highland County

Mountain Laurel Inn   **$**
Main Street, Route 250, Monterey
(540) 468-3401, (800) 510-0180
www.va-bedandbreakfast.com
The Mountain Laurel Inn is in the small rural town of Monterey, which was once the Shawnee tribe's hunting grounds. Winding mountain roads lead you to the town and through the least populated county in Virginia.

The inn is the original Arbogast house, a turn-of-the-20th-century Victorian completely renovated in 1997. Owner Pat Adams provides four spacious guest rooms all individually furnished with king-, queen-, or full-size beds and private baths. Fireplaces and a wide porch invite guests to laugh over a card game or nod over a book in the evening. Coffee and tea are available at dawn for early risers, and a full breakfast is served each morning, featuring fresh-baked breads and muffins, seasonal fruit, and special daily entrees. Pat can also cater special events, meetings, and family celebrations.

Because of the low population in the area, you can enjoy some of the most beautiful and pristine woodlands and streams in the entire state. Excellent bird-watching, hiking, mountain biking, fishing, and caving are in the area, and Snowshoe Ski Resort in West Virginia is only 40 miles away. Bargain hunters will delight in the local antiques and craft stores. There are several interesting festivals every year, including the Maple Sugar Festival, celebrating the area's maple sugar industry.

Pets and smoking are not allowed. Older children are welcome.

RESORTS

The Blue Ridge resorts have lured visitors from all over the world, including Hollywood. Mile-high Mountain Lake Resort was made famous by the movie *Dirty Dancing*, and Bernard's Landing on Smith Mountain Lake was the site of Bill Murray's zany flick *What About Bob?* Many of the stars of Jodie Foster and Richard Gere's *Sommersby* stayed at the Homestead while filming nearby in Bath County. Of course, you will find other resorts with great amenities that Hollywood has not discovered yet, and you can even see one of the seven natural wonders of the world.

The listing that follows, from north to south and east to west, tells you about the resorts' histories, amenities, and what sets each apart. Unless otherwise noted, major credit cards are accepted.

SHENANDOAH VALLEY

Bryce Resort
1982 Fairway Drive, Basye
(540) 856–2121, (800) 821–1444
www.bryceresort.com
Bryce Resort offers an intimate, family-centered experience. This small resort sits on the western lip of the Shenandoah Valley in the Shenandoah Mountains. On a map you will find it in Shenandoah County near the West Virginia border.

Bryce is especially attractive to golfers and outdoor enthusiasts. Popular as a winter skiing recreation getaway (see our Skiing chapter), it is also unique for its mountain boarding and grass skiing. Yes, we said "grass," in which participants glide down the resort's hills on short, treadlike skates during the summer and fall months. Grass skiing requires considerable physical strength and agility and is offered to those 10 and older. (You'll pay $27 for a first-time package, which gets you instruction, a lift

ticket, equipment, and protective gear—knee and elbow pads and a helmet. Experienced folks pay $24.)

Bryce's 18-hole golf course is a par 71, 6,260-yard mountain layout. Facilities offer a driving range, putting green, club and cart rentals, professional instruction, individual club storage, and a fully stocked golf shop. Cart and greens fees range from $35 during the week to $50 on weekends; the price lowers to $30 and $40 after noon. Adjacent to the entrance of Bryce is Stoney Creek Lilliputt, a miniature golf course, which is open Memorial Day through Labor Day. Admission is $4.00 for adults and $3.00 for children 12 and younger.

The whole family can enjoy Lake Laura, a 45-acre man-made private lake with its own sandy beach and grassy picnic area, offering swimming, boating, and fishing. The beach is also open Memorial Day through Labor Day; admission is $4.00, free for children younger than 3. Canoes and paddleboats are available to rent, $10.00 an hour.

From Memorial Day through Labor Day, the resort's T. J. Stables provides daily one-hour guided trail rides for $25.00 and pony rides for kids ages 3 to 6 for $5.00 (closed Wednesday). During the spring and fall, the stables are open on weekends only, as weather permits. They are closed December through March.

Tennis is another favorite activity at Bryce Resort, which has lighted outdoor courts and a well-stocked pro shop. Court time is $10 an hour. Reservations are required.

Lodging options include studio condominiums, and two- to four-bedroom town houses, private homes, and chalets that sleep anywhere from six to 14 people, all privately owned and rented through real estate agencies. The decor can be quite interesting, often reflecting the history of this colorful and friendly valley. All condo units are furnished with kitchenettes, and most town houses have full kitchens, private Jacuzzi baths, fireplaces, and washer/dryers.

Lodging prices vary according to seasons and accommodations. Aspen East Condominiums, located on the ski slopes, have great fireplaces, bedrooms, and baths and rent for $220 for the two-night minimum stay, plus $50 for each additional night. Two-bedroom town houses on the golf course rent for $145 nightly or $800 per week. The Creekside Village town houses rent for $135 a night or $700 weekly. Houses rent from $400 to $475 for the first two nights and $75 for each additional night.

The resort is on Highway 263, 11 miles west of Interstate 81 off exit 273. Sky Bryce Airport is a five-minute walk from the resort.

Natural Bridge Resort
**U.S. Highway 11 S., Natural Bridge
(540) 291-2121, (800) 533-1410
www.naturalbridgeva.com**

Natural Bridge is a Virginia Historic Landmark and is listed on the National Register of Historic Places. Built in the shadow of one of the seven wonders of the natural world, Natural Bridge Resort isn't posh in the same sense as some of the other great resorts of the Blue Ridge, but it's definitely worth seeing and staying at overnight because of its unique character. Many make the trip just for the unique Easter Sunrise Services as well as for the nightly Dramas of Creation, a spectacular light and sound show. Both are held under the 23-story-high, 90-foot-long limestone arch that gives this resort its name.

The story of Natural Bridge, a 36,000-ton structure carved by Mother Nature millions of years ago, is a historian's delight. Early on, the bridge was worshipped by the Monacan Indians. Thomas Jefferson was the first American to own the bridge, which he purchased from King George III in 1774. George Washington surveyed the bridge as a lad. In fact, you can still see the spot where he carved his initials. Colonists made bullets by dropping molten lead off the bridge into the cold creek water below. During the War of 1812, soldiers mined the nearby saltpeter cave to make explosives.

Additional attractions here are the massive caverns—some folks say they're haunted, with ghostly voices still heard as late as 1988—and the Natural Bridge Wax Museum, which houses lifelike figures including a gallery of American presidents.

Speaking of haunted, Natural Bridge also has the Haunted Monster Museum and a toy museum. (See our Attractions chapter.)

A huge gift shop, open daily year-round from 8:00 A.M. to dark, sells such tasty fare as homemade fudge and rock candy; it also carries collectibles, Virginia-made gifts and foods, and handmade Monacan Indian crafts. For lunch or a snack, try the deli in the gift shop during the fall and summer, or Creekside at the Summerhouse Cafe from April through October. An attraction added in recent years is the Monacan Indian Living History Village, where visitors can learn about the ways of life for these indigenous people, from canoe building and hide tanning to cooking. The Village is open April to November.

For recreation, the tennis courts, indoor heated swimming pool, and 18-hole Mini-link Indoor Golf Course are popular features. Admission to the bridge costs $10.00 for adults, $5.00 for children 5 to 12. Cost to get into the caverns or wax museum is $8.00 each for adults, $5.00 for kids. Or you can purchase a three-way combo for $18.00 ($8.50 for kids). Children younger than 5 get in free.

Natural Bridge has welcomed travelers since 1833. The current hotel, the Natural Bridge Inn and Conference Center, was built in 1963 and features Colonial-style decor, spacious rooms, and beautiful mountain views. Between the hotel and the cottages, which are grouped on hilltops across the street from the hotel, there are 180 rooms. The cottages, open from late March to mid-November, are one-level brick buildings with four to six guest rooms each. Some rooms are equipped with high-speed Internet access.

Nightly room rates are $47.25 to $73.95 for a cottage, and $51.95 to $129.95 for a hotel room. For a balcony room, expect to pay an additional $10.00 per night, $5.00 for a room with a view of the mountains. There are also two suites that rent for $159.00 to $175.00. Personal checks are accepted for advance deposits only.

Meals in the Colonial Dining Room in the hotel are both delicious and plentiful, and the service is first class. The Colonial Dining Room serves breakfast and dinner daily, as well as its signature Friday evening seafood buffet, Saturday evening prime rib buffet, and Sunday Southern-style lunch buffet. Reservations are strongly recommended for these popular weekend meals.

Natural Bridge is 13 miles from the Blue Ridge Parkway, 39 miles north of Roanoke, and just minutes from Downtown Historic Lexington. From I-81, take exit 180. Follow US 11 south. At the intersection of US 11 and Route 130, the Natural Bridge gatehouse is straight ahead.

EAST OF THE BLUE RIDGE

Lansdowne Resort
22050 Woodridge Parkway, Leesburg
(703) 729-8400, (800) 541-4801
www.lansdowneresort.com

At the northern end of the Blue Ridge, not far from D.C., lies Lansdowne, a beautiful full-service resort flanked by breathtaking countryside and the Potomac River.

Accommodations include 305 deluxe guest rooms and suites in a nine-story center tower complex with two five-story wings. The rooms provide panoramic views of the Potomac River, the mountains, and the resort's lovely golf course. The rooms feature warm, rich fabrics, triple-sheeted beds, hair dryers, coffeemakers, spacious work areas, and marble-accented bathrooms. Rooms also are equipped with two-line phones, voice mail, and dataports for those who want to combine business with leisure.

A perfect place for a conference or a corporate board meeting, Lansdowne offers 25 meeting rooms including a ballroom, a 126-seat tiered amphitheater, and boardroom, all equipped with audiovisual equipment.

After the work is done, why not take a break on the 18-hole championship golf course, designed by Robert Trent Jones Jr. The scenic 7,057-yard, par-72 course features lush green fields, woods, and centuries-old rock walls and concludes with a dramatic finish on 18. The 100-foot change in elevation will challenge novices and intrigue old pros over this 610-yard, par-5 signature hole. Lansdowne also has a well-equipped pro shop, a driving range, and chipping and putting greens.

After an afternoon on the links, step into the full-service spa at the health club. The Lansdowne Health Club includes four outdoor tennis courts, racquetball and volleyball courts, steam room and sauna, whirlpools, indoor and outdoor swimming pools, walking and jogging trails, and Cybex exercise equipment to help release that stress.

Of course, you will want to partake in the food offerings here. The Lansdowne Grille specializes in prime steaks and is open daily for lunch while dinner is served every night but Sunday (see our Restaurants chapter). There is a lounge area and two private dining rooms as well. The Riverside Hearth is the conference dining room and seats more than 200 people. It is open daily for breakfast, lunch, and din-

As adult-oriented and lavish as most of these resorts are, many gear themselves toward the whole family by offering family vacation packages and a wide assortment of kid-friendly activities, especially in the summer, when school is out.

ner. The Sunday brunch here is the most sumptuous feast around, especially on holidays. The Fairways Deli, open seasonally, offers sandwiches and snacks near the outdoor pool, and Stonewalls Tavern, near the resort's living room, has a casual atmosphere with its fieldstone fireplace, red-felted billiard tables, darts, and large-screen televisions. (There's even a cigar menu with stogies from Ecuador, Dominican Republic, Honduras, and Jamaica.)

Boar's Head Inn
A Country Resort at the University of Virginia
200 Ednam Drive, Charlottesville
(434) 296-2181, (800) 476-1988
www.boarsheadinn.com

Nestled in the foothills of the Blue Ridge Mountains, Boar's Head Inn offers the grace and charm of times past with all the luxurious amenities of a full-service resort. The Boar's Head Inn, a AAA-rated Four-Diamond resort, is set on a 573-acre country estate in Charlottesville. The Inn has 170 guest rooms and suites, 12 private function rooms, a grand ballroom, three restaurants, four outdoor swimming pools, a championship golf course, a modern sports club, and a luxury spa. *Tennis Magazine* rates Boar's Head one of America's top 50 tennis facilities—there are 20 courts, including six for indoor play, and two squash courts, one being the only regulation doubles squash court in Virginia. Private lessons, clinics, men's and women's interleague play, a junior tennis academy, and squash instruction are all available.

At Christmas, the staff drapes the Inn in pine boughs, ribbons, and sparkling lights and serves hot cider by the fireside. The winter holiday season is busy with cooking demonstrations, wine tastings, lectures, elegant afternoon teas, gingerbread house workshops, and the Teddy Bear Tea for children.

Birdwood Golf Course has long been ranked one of the Mid-Atlantic's top 100 courses by *Washington Golf Monthly.* Designed by Linsay Ervin, Birdwood is an 18-hole, par 72 course of 6,865 yards of memorable drives, chips, and putts. Birdwood also offers practice greens and a three-tiered driving range. Lessons and clinics are available to adults by appointment, and young people ages 8 to 18 can learn the basics of the game at the summer Junior Golf Academy.

If you prefer your fitness indoors, try the state-of-the-art fitness center, chock full of bikes, treadmills, steppers, ellipticals, free weights, a power rack, and Cybex equipment. Nationally certified aerobics instructors teach a variety of classes, including interval training, water aerobics, yoga, and Cycle Reebok. An outdoor heated, 25-meter Junior Olympic pool provides six lap lanes for fitness and competition swimming.

Afterward, be sure to pamper yourself with a visit to the spa for an aromatherapy massage or a craniosacral session. Try hydrotherapy, a body wrap, or choose between an array of facials and manicure and pedicure treatments.

The Inn's architectural style recalls an earlier era, but its facilities offer all of the modern amenities. Guest rooms include four-poster beds, oak and walnut accents, opulent window treatments, and Italian Anichini linens. The antique reproduction desks have been modernized with data-port outlets.

The history of the Inn, which takes its name from the old English symbol for festive hospitality, is a colorful one. Three decades ago the Inn's founder, John B. Rogan, moved an 1834 mill to its present spot from near Thomas Jefferson's historic Monticello. The mill, with its massive hand-hewn beams, is the heart of the resort and home to the Old Mill Room, one of Virginia's highest-rated restaurants. The Old Mill Room recently received its 17th consecutive Four-Diamond rating from AAA. Boar's Head Inn's renowned executive chef and his international staff create culinary masterpieces for guests who enjoy gracious service and a wonderful wine selection, all in an intimate atmosphere (see our Restaurants chapter). A less formal dining experience can be enjoyed in Bistro 1834, where an expansive veranda with a stunning view of the Virginia countryside can be enjoyed on sunny days.

Casual family dining is the specialty at the Cafe at the Sports Club. The menu focuses on homemade soups and salads, sandwiches, and wraps, and even a pasta bar on Thursday nights. Outdoor seating is available in warm weather. Or eat course-side at the Birdwood Grill—enjoy burgers, sandwiches, chili, or soup while you take in the great views of the Blue Ridge.

Daily rates range from $188 to $675, but Boar's Head Inn also offers seasonal packages, including the traditional bed-and-breakfast package, several spa packages, and packages including golf and tennis, visits to historic sites such as Monticello, and official winery tours.

From Interstate 64, take exit 118B to U.S. Highway 250 W. The Inn is 1.5 miles on the left.

Keswick Hall at Monticello and Keswick Club
701 Club Drive, Keswick
(434) 979-3440, (800) 274-5391
www.orient-express.com

On the east side of Charlottesville is yet another beautiful resort. This is Keswick Hall, which rests on 600 acres of lush Virginia countryside known as Keswick Estate. The 48-room luxury hotel is a prime example of Italianate architecture. Keswick has a long and fascinating history: It is the site of Broad Oak, a pre–Civil War mansion, which was replaced by Villa Crawford in 1912. Twice the location of the Virginia State Open Golf Tournament, Keswick became a country club in the 1930s and was closed for 10 years. In 1990 it was purchased by global entrepreneur Sir Bernard Ashley, who tripled the size of the building and added the Keswick Golf Club. Ashley is the cofounder of the internationally known Laura Ashley fashion company and founder of Ashley House, Inc.

Orient–Express Hotels acquired Keswick in 1999. While the signature flowery Laura Ashley print fabrics still adorn much of the rooms and furnishings, the new owners have curtailed the cool British flavor in favor of a more American-style inn. Gone are the wrought-iron gates barring people from the premises. Visitors are met by personable housemen who take their luggage and usher them inside to attentive staff.

Consistently named by Andrew Harper's *Hideaway Report* as one of the best small inns in America, Keswick Hall offers a step back to a simpler time. Public rooms at Keswick Hall are traditional yet elegant, decorated with overstuffed furniture, antiques, paintings, sculptures, art books, and rare editions. Fires burning in warm hearths, silver dishes full of nuts gracing heirloom buffets, and decanters shining with colorful liqueurs complete the inviting setting. Long hallways adorn either side of the Great Hall entrance, which features stone flooring brought over from European villas. Flanking the main fireplace are large overstuffed chairs and sofas with rich fabrics from Laura Ashley's archival designs. Like most elegant American great houses, public rooms at Keswick Hall serve different purposes. The Crawford Lounge, formerly the entrance hall for Villa Crawford, is the perfect setting for cocktails or afternoon tea. The yellow Morning Room, elegant Drawing Room, and the cozy Lounge are places where guests can enjoy a midnight game and a glass of sherry before bed. Furnishings are a blend of antique and contemporary designs. With 8,000 square feet of meeting and conference space, Keswick is one of the best for meetings, executive retreats, corporate gatherings, and private parties.

The rooms at Keswick are decorated by themes and vary a great deal. A large number of guest rooms have canopied four-poster beds with feather pillows, as well as Abergere club chairs, antique memorabilia, hand-painted armoires, ottomans, antique furnishings, and fitted carpets with Aubusson designs. Again, signature Laura Ashley fabrics and wall coverings brighten each room. Bathrooms are generous proportions and feature separate, glass-enclosed showers.

Dining is a special aspect of the

Keswick Hall experience. Newly opened Fossett's seats 74 and provides for a breathtaking setting with its expansive three-sided floor-to-ceiling windows with spectacular views of the golf course and estate. Interiors are warm and refreshing, accented with historical Virginia botanical art and original landscape. John Brand joined Keswick Hall as executive chef in the fall of 2003. Chef Brand uses his own version of American Regional cuisine and emphasizes his freedom to experiment with distinctive favors and ingredients. John has honed his culinary skills for the last 17 years while working at some of the most prestigious resorts and hotels in the country. He comes to the Hall from The Little Nell, a Relais & Chateau and Mobile five-star property in Aspen, Colorado, where as executive sous chef he helped oversee the hotel's award-winning restaurant, Montagna. Complementing the fine food are wines from an extensive cellar, which includes selections from Virginia as well as some of the top vintages from producers all over the world.

Guests can come for breakfast, including a Sunday brunch from 11:30 A.M. to 2:30 P.M. Afternoon tea complete with warm scones and lemon curd also is very popular. You could choose to have your lunch at the Palmer Room at the Keswick Club, which provides casual dining for guests and Club members. The food is lighter fare than what's served in the dining room. This facility offers expansive views of the golf course and seats about 50.

Guests at Keswick Hall enjoy privileges at the exclusive Keswick Club, with its 18-hole Arnold Palmer–designed signature golf course, now Audobon certified. New in the summer of 2002 was an infinity pool with constantly moving water, a pool common in five-star hotels. Guests can enjoy the Club's open-air pavilion, from May to October, with its Olympic-size swimming pool, five tennis courts lit for night play, and a separate children's wading pool and play area. If you're still not done, the fitness center offers a variety of fitness activities, including aerobics, water exercises, personal training, out-door hot tub and Jacuzzi, sessions in the sauna, steam, or whirlpool. The spa has recently been expanded to include four new treatment rooms offering a full range of massage and beauty treatments.

Lodging rates range from $310 to $725 for a master suite, which includes a traditional afternoon tea. Weekly rates vary depending on the season. Call and ask about their many packages.

From Charlottesville, go east on Bypass US 250 east on Highway 22, and right onto Highway 744 until you reach a stop sign. Keswick is directly ahead.

Wintergreen Resort
Highway 664, Wintergreen
(434) 325-2200, (800) 325-2200
www.wintergreenresort.com

Wintergreen Resort, an 11,000-acre resort along the spine of the Blue Ridge, enjoys a reputation as one of the most environmentally conscious facilities in the Blue Ridge and has won awards for its conservation efforts.

Wintergreen consistently ranks among the Top 50 Favorite Family Resorts named by *Better Homes and Gardens* and the Top 10 Family Mountain Resorts chosen by *Family Circle* magazine. The resort and its Wintergreen Nature Foundation were even recognized with a Phoenix Award given by the Society of American Travel Writers for its environmental achievements.

Tennis Magazine has named Wintergreen one of its Top 50 Tennis Resorts for the past 16 years. *Golf Digest* rated the resort's Stoney Creek course the second-best in Virginia and the 34th-best resort course in the country. While Stoney Creek occupies the valley, giving guests the unique opportunity to play golf and ski on the same day (see our Skiing chapter), the resort's mountaintop Devils Knob Course has the highest elevation in the state at 4,000 feet.

Tennis buffs have their pick of 19 composition clay courts and three indoor courts for all-season play. Outdoor court rates range from $12 to $16 for singles, and tennis clinics, workouts, and ball-machine rentals are available. Registered guests can play the outdoor courts for free midweek, and reduced rates are available on weekends.

As for other activities, the options are many. Swimmers can take advantage of an indoor pool at the Wintergarden Spa and Fitness Center, and eight (!) outdoor pools. Water enthusiasts also have 22-acre Lake Monocan for swimming, canoeing, and paddleboating. Or you can learn basic kayaking skills in a kayaking clinic. Bikes can be rented for $7.00 an hour for riding on the bike trails that surround the lake and golf course, offering spectacular views of the Blue Ridge. The rentals are available weekends in May and September, and daily Memorial Day through Labor Day. You can pick up a Wintergreen trail map at the Wintergreen Nature Foundation's office in the Trillium House for $3.00. For a ride that can include the little ones, there are standard road bikes available to ride on the paved bike trails that wind through Stoney Creek.

Wintergreen offers horseback riding, pony rides, riding lessons, hacks for more experienced riders, and wagon rides daily except Monday, from mid-March through November. A new program that has been very popular in the summertime is the "Sunset Dinner Trail Ride," which includes a horseback trail ride to Lake Monacan, chef-prepared dinner, and a ride back as the sun sets over the Blue Ridge. There are fishing and fly-fishing retreats. Still looking for something to do? You're in luck. There's an exciting facility at Wintergreen. The Out of Bounds Adventure Center offers a host of fast-paced activities including paintball target shooting, miniature golf, a 25-foot climbing wall that offers beginner to expert routes, and a park for inline skaters, BMX riders, and skateboarders. Or you can hop on a mountain bike with full suspension and fly down Wintergreen's 4.5-mile downhill track, a quick trip to the valley. Out of Bounds operates from May to October. Children younger than age 13 must be accompanied by an adult. Purchase an all-day combo pass for $39, or a season park pass for $120 (with equipment rental, the pass is $180).

Special events, such as the Spring Wildflower Symposium, are featured throughout the year and include holiday celebrations such as a Blue Ridge Mountain Christmas, with horse-drawn carriage rides and candlelight dinners.

In summer, Camp Wintergreen offers a variety of children's programs for toddlers to teens. The program introduces youngsters to the beauty and wildlife of the Blue Ridge. Babysitting services are also available.

Wintergreen Resort has been undergoing $35 million in upgrades over the last six years, including the new Out of Bounds Center, upgrades to skiing, which resulted in two new high-speed six-passenger lifts and the Plunge, a 900-foot snow tubing hill, a revolutionary 100 percent computerized snowmaking system, and a complete remodeling and expansion of the spa. A new wing added to the spa is set to open in July 2005, which will double the size. The spa and fitness center feature a state-of-the-art exercise room and sauna and personal fitness training. You can schedule a Swedish massage after all the day's activities, or a mountain mud wrap or skin-softening salt glow.

In 2002 the Lookout was completed, offering light fare in a casual atmosphere with a big stone fireplace and large windows overlooking the mountains. During ski season, you can get a bowl of chili and sit on the wraparound deck as you watch the excitement at the Plunge tubing park or the ski slopes.

If you're interested in golf, you may want to visit the 18-hole Ellis Maples–designed Devils Knob golf course, which recently underwent extensive upgrades. The Devils Knob clubhouse features a pro shop, locker room, restaurant lounge, and snack shop. The nationally ranked Stoney Creek golf course offers 27 holes designed by Rees Jones, while the Wintergreen Golf Academy offers intensive analysis and improvement through personalized training in a three- or five-day program. Ask about the portable computerized digital video, designed to help

While many a typical visit to a resort could cost a pretty penny, it's still possible to visit some of these posh establishments, stroll through shops and view the well-landscaped acreage, and sit down for a light meal at one of the more casual eateries with minimum impact to your wallet.

golfers improve their strokes right on the practice tee.

The Tennis Pavilion at Devils Knob has turned tennis into a year-round sport at Wintergreen. The complex features three indoor Deco-Turf courts, locker room facilities, a larger clubhouse and pro shop, and indoor viewing deck, stadium seating, and a lounge for the Wintergreen Tennis Academy. The new changes could be among the reasons *Tennis Week* placed Wintergreen in its Gold List of the Top 100 tennis resorts in the world. The Wintergreen Tennis Academy consistently places in TennisResortOnline's top 10 tennis camps in the world.

Wintergreen Resort offers full-service conference, meeting, and retreat facilities. The year-round resort is also becoming a popular site for family reunions, parties, receptions, and weddings.

Dining at Wintergreen Resort is an exceptional experience. Wintergreen has seven restaurants in all, ranging from elegant to casual. The Copper Mine features gourmet dining, a unique open-pit copper fireplace, and a cozy, romantic atmosphere. For dinner you can dine on roast rack of lamb or twin lobster tails. The Devils Grill Restaurant, located at the Devils Knob Golf Course, features a fabulous mountaintop view and serves dinner during the winter. Choose from its freshly prepared seafood or hand-cut steaks. Or, you can try the full-service Devils Grill Lounge for a sandwich or burger while watching a game on one of three televisions. Families and groups also like dining at the Edge Restaurant, where they can pick from such

lunch and dinner items as spicy buffalo wings, barbecue, and pasta dishes. It also has a large-screen television and live entertainment. There's also a restaurant in the Wintergreen valley. Have a nice dinner at the Stoney Creek Bar and Grill while enjoying the panoramic views of the Stoney Creek Golf Course. The grill serves a blend of casual American fare with an emphasis on fresh, seasonal ingredients. Lighter fare is offered in the lounge. Children's menus are available at the Copper Mine, Devils Grill, Stoney Creek Bar and Grill, and the Edge. The Copper Mine and Devils Grill also provide vegetarian options. During ski season, the Blue Ridge Terrace Grill, an outdoor grill, and Pryor's Porch Cafeteria in the Mountain Village and the Lookout, offer quick meal choices near the skiing action. (See our Restaurants chapter.)

Wintergreen has 300 rental homes and condominiums, ranging from studio size to six-bedroom. Most have fireplaces and fully equipped kitchens, and many have spectacular views from decks and balconies. Daily rates for a studio condominium range from $136 to $154 during the spring and fall, $154 to $181 during the summer, and $126 to $199 during the winter. Various packages are available, including golf, tennis, family, sports, and romantic getaways.

The resort is 40 miles southwest of Charlottesville, bordering the Blue Ridge Parkway. From I-64 take exit 107, US 250 W. to Highway 151 S. to Highway 664. Then just follow the signs to Wintergreen.

Bernard's Landing Resort and Conference Center
775 Ashmeade Road, Moneta
(540) 721-8870, (800) 572-2048
www.bernardslanding.com
The word "tranquility" springs to mind when describing Bernard's Landing. This serene place is the only resort on the Blue Ridge's most popular lake, Smith Mountain Lake, although a rash of motels are planned. The second largest lake in Virginia with 500 miles of shoreline, it has become a watery playground for people from all over the East Coast. The resort's majestic

view of Smith Mountain and magnificent fiery orange sunsets sinking into the calm water have drawn artists and photographers from around the world.

Bernard's Landing was built in 1981 on what was once a prosperous farm worked by slaves of the Parker family. The family home, an original brick plantation house, still stands at the center of Bernard's activity as a clubhouse. Appalachian Power (now American Electric Power) filled the lake in 1966, submersing 22,000 acres and making many Franklin, Bedford, and Pittsylvania county farmers instantly wealthy. Bernard's was built on the widest part of the lake and is one of few places where you can view the full expanse of the 7-mile-long Smith Mountain Lake.

For its 1990 production of *What About Bob?*, Walt Disney Productions searched the entire United States for a lake resort with just the right combination of qualities to portray the out-of-the-way vacation spot that still had luxurious amenities. A staff of 100, including actors Bill Murray and Richard Dreyfus, stayed nearly six months for the filming of the popular comedy. Many of the guests were so impressed with the lake's pristine beauty, they stayed even longer. That's because Bernard's has become known as the place where people come to get away from it all. Although friendly, Franklin County residents grant you privacy, whether you're sailing, swimming, or just absorbing the silence.

The well-planned waterfront community sits on its own peninsula and is designed to take advantage of its natural surroundings, mainly mountains reflected in the sparkling lake. As you drive up, the resort impresses you with its huge expanse of lawn that separates the buildings. There is a sandy beach for swimming and sunbathing, an Olympic-size swimming pool, a separate children's wading pool and play area, and a smaller pool near the conference center. There's also a clubhouse, fitness center with bikes, treadmills, Jacuzzi, spa and sauna, six tennis courts, two racketball courts, a volleyball court, and a basketball court. If you want more than a

splendid view, there's plenty to keep you entertained.

Smith Mountain is an angler's paradise. Nationally known for its striped bass fishing, the lake boasts the state's record striper, weighing 45 pounds (this record seems to get broken every year). If you're into fishing (see our Fishing section in our Recreation chapter), Bernard's operates four marinas and rents fishing, pontoon, and ski boats, as well as canoes and kayaks, right at the dock. The Virginia Commission of Games and Inland Fisheries manages an adjoining 5,000 acres for hunting enthusiasts.

The resort's restaurant, the Landing, serves gourmet meals and is the most popular spot on the lake for fine dining. The Landing packs many a picnic lunch for boaters and consistently earns *The Roanoker* magazine's "Best Restaurant on the Lake" award. The chef and owner, Andy Schlosser, likes to describe it as "New York with a southern touch and island flair." Probably every resident at the lake has enjoyed the sumptuous Sunday brunch, truly worth a tasting trip. Other dining can be found at the Castaways, located on the deck adjacent to the Landing restaurant. This lakeside bar and grill offers outdoor dining with everything from fun burgers to gourmet pizza. It's enclosed and heated in cold weather. There's always the BLT Cafe, where during the peak season, you can grab some fresh barbecue, burgers, grilled chicken, and homemade ice cream.

Bernard's Landing completely redecorated its conference center in the spring of 2002, adding new wallpaper, carpet, furniture, and new audiovisual equipment. The conference center is available for business meetings, conventions, retreats, weddings, and reunions. The four event areas can accommodate up to 150 guests with a full range of services including food, theme parties, entertainment, golf outings, and lake cruises.

Bernard's rental facilities include one- to three-level townhouses, single-level homes, and one- to three-bedroom condos. They feature fireplaces, decks, skylights, cathedral ceilings, kitchens, living, and/or dining rooms. Some have wrap-around decks and steam or Jacuzzi baths. Nightly rentals in peak season range from $125 for a one-bedroom condo to $260 for a three-bedroom townhouse, for a week-day. During the off-season (early October to mid-May) you can rent the same for $95 to $230 a night.

It is a 45-minute drive from either Roanoke or Lynchburg to Bernard's Land-ing. From Roanoke, drive south on U.S. Highway 220 to a left on Highway 697 at Wirtz. Follow this road to its intersection with Highway 122 and turn left. Continue for approximately 7 miles, then turn right on Highway 616 at NBC Bank. Drive 7 miles, then turn left on Highway 940, which will dead-end at Bernard's. From Lynchburg, take U.S. Highway 460 W. to Highway 122 and drive about 25 miles to Highway 616. Turn left and follow above directions to Bernard's.

NEW RIVER VALLEY

Mountain Lake Resort
115 Hotel Circle, Mountain Lake
(540) 951-1819, (800) 346-3334
www.mountainlakehotel.com
Let Mountain Lake Resort "Put You on Top of the World," as the slogan goes. And they mean it! If you saw the majestic sandstone lodge at the top of the moun-tains in the movie *Dirty Dancing*, you saw Mountain Lake Resort. The beauty of this grand old hotel was forever captured in 1986 after Vestron Pictures, searching for a genteel, romantic, 1960s-era resort, saw an ad for Mountain Lake in an airline mag-azine. The rest is history. Everyone wants to know where Patrick Swayze slept when he stayed here, and the room stays booked.

But there's far more history than that to Mountain Lake, one of only two natural freshwater lakes in Virginia and one of the highest natural lakes in the East. It was formed when a rock slide dammed the north end of the valley, creating a 100-

foot-deep lake fed by underground streams that rarely allow the water tem-perature to rise above 70 degrees.

The first report of a pleasure resort here was in 1857, and the first hotel was wooden. In the early 1930s William Lewis Moody of Galveston, Texas, purchased the property and built the present huge hotel from native stone. His elder daughter, Mary, who died in 1986, loved to sit under the great stone fire-place in the lobby, which is still inscribed with "House of Moody." Mary ensured her beloved Mountain Lake, where she stayed each summer, would keep its 2,600 acres of natural paradise in perpetuity by establish-ing a foundation in her name.

When you sit in a rocking chair on the great stone front porch overlooking the lake, you can't help but feel refreshed and renewed at this haven for body and spirit. Summer offers the opportunity to relax in cool mountain air, and in the autumn few fall foliage vistas can compare to Mountain Lake's. The air is rare, and so is the experi-ence!

Open the first Friday in May through November, the resort offers boating, fish-ing, hiking, biking, tennis, swimming, and lawn games. They also have an indoor sauna and spa. And the Activities Barn offers games, snacks, and several nearby shops featuring Appalachian arts and gifts. Mountain Lake celebrates the fall season with an Oktoberfest every weekend from mid-September through October.

Mountain Lake's 20 miles of hiking and biking trails crisscross the property and lead to many breathtaking views. Adult and children's bikes and helmets are avail-able to rent. The terrain is said to be some of the most challenging in the mountain biking scene and earned the resort a spot in two major national cycling events—the Eastern Regional Finals of the American Mountain Bike Challenge and the Misty Mountain Hop.

Mountain Lake is a great place for fish-ing—it's stocked annually with rainbow trout and also has bass and sunfish. Check out the resort's tackle shop and the fully equipped fishing boats and canoes. You can also get a guided fishing tour or a fly-fishing lesson. Other water activities include paddleboats, kayaks, and a daily pontoon boat tour of the lake. There's a kiddie pool and snack bar in the new recreational complex. If that's still not enough, there's archery, tennis, croquet, volleyball, badminton, bocce ball, and more. Take the kids on a pony ride, a horse-drawn carriage ride, or a hayride.

All right, Mountain Lake also has activities designed to teach us all a little something. Explore the heavens as part of the astronomy program, a joint effort with nearby Virginia Tech. Portable telescopes are set up on the hotel lawn, and at 4,000 feet above sea level, the resort is the perfect stargazing place. Or check out the Natural History Museum and Visitor Center, which offers displays, books, and maps covering the ecology and natural history of the area. Your kids will enjoy the interactive children's exhibits. In the summer, Mountain Lake offers a wilderness camp for children ages 6 to 12.

The food is consistently superb in the restaurant, where guests lucky enough to get window tables will see a panorama of bluebirds, snowbirds, and redbirds scolding spoiled squirrels, who are awaiting handouts from guests. Neat attire is requested for evening meals, which are a gourmet's delight. Brunch is $17.95 to $18.95, and dinner is $25.00 for non-overnight guests. Many Virginia Tech parents make the 17-mile trip just for the meal, which can be booked with a reservation.

Accommodations include the 50-room hotel in which room amenities may include a fireplace and a whirlpool, the 16-room Chestnut Lodge nestled among the trees, and, in the summer, 13 wooden cottages with fireplaces. Prices for couples range from $160 nightly to $235 in the hotel, with an additional charge for each child. There are also two- to five-night packages that include lodging, meals, and activity vouchers. Cottage rental prices range from $165 a night to $695. With the grand opening of its nine new luxury cottages in 2003, Mountain Lake is once again a year-round resort. The Blueberry Ridge Cottages offer one-, two-, three-, and four-bedroom options, with full kitchens, dining rooms, private decks, and living rooms with vaulted ceilings. Just a five-minute walk from the landmark hotel, the cottages surround the resort's 1,500-square-foot Executive Retreat Center. Most guests stay on the Modified American Plan, which includes lodging, breakfast, dinner, and use of all facilities and equipment. Personal checks are accepted.

To get there, take the US 460 bypass around Blacksburg to Highway 700. Follow this road for 7 steep, winding, scenic country miles straight up to Mountain Lake.

ALLEGHANY HIGHLANDS

The Homestead
US 220, Hot Springs
(540) 839-7785, (800) 838-1766
www.thehomestead.com
The Homestead, one of the South's major resorts, is grandly situated on 15,000 acres in the Allegheny Mountains. It has been one of America's highest-rated resorts for more than 30 years, yet it's as homey as its name suggests and famous for its afternoon teas in its long, wide great hall. Thomas Jefferson and 21 other presidents strolled these grounds, and Lord and Lady Astor honeymooned here. On December 29, 1941, three weeks after the attack on Pearl Harbor, 363 Japanese diplomats, along with many Japanese citizens in the United States, were placed at the Homestead for a three-month internment.

The Homestead has been pampering guests since the late 1700s, when the aristocracy of Virginia went to the mountains instead of enduring the lowland heat with the common folk. In those days, it was fashionable in high society to move from one mountain spring to another en masse. Originally valued for medicinal purposes by Native Americans, the springs around the Homestead became centers of social activity, and the Homestead has stood for more than two centuries, as one of the

CLOSE-UP

The Sport of Kings

Some may argue that golf has been the crown jewel at the Homestead for more than 77 years, but in 1998 the real "sport of kings" arrived at the Bath County resort.

That's when Duane Zobrist Jr. brought his falcons, hawks, and owls to the Homestead, making it one of the first resorts in Virginia and only the third on the East Coast to offer falconry.

"There is one resort in Vermont, the Equinox, and one in West Virginia, the Greenbrier, that has such falconry programs," said Zobrist, founder of the Falconry and Raptor Education Foundation. Zobrist's West Virginia–based non-profit foundation also runs the program at the Greenbrier.

"We take out small groups and show them our hawks, owls, and falcons and explain all about them. We talk for about 30 minutes, then we do flying demonstrations, where the birds fly free and usually return to the falconer," he added with a good-natured laugh.

"Then we put a glove on each of the students, put a falcon on their fist, and take their picture. People have just been enthralled."

And educated, too.

Falconry traces its beginning to China nearly 4,000 years ago. Back then, hunting game with trained birds was an effective way to put meat on the table. But as the centuries passed by—and the gun arrived—falconry became much less widespread.

Although sportsmen marveled at watching their winged companions take flight, hunting was no longer the pri-

mary goal. Training falcons to respond to command became known as sport for noblemen. It was indeed called the "sport of kings," most likely because only royalty was allowed to own many of the rare birds.

Even in modern times just finding information on the sport can be hard to come by.

"I became interested in falconry when I was nine years old," Zobrist said. "That was because my dad always wanted to do it, but he could never find any books on falconry here. Whenever he would travel abroad, he would bring back a book. That's why he always wanted to go to England."

Like father like son. The young Zobrist even trained in England.

"I was going to be a lawyer," he said. "I had finished up my undergraduate work in Utah at BYU, but I really had a desire to work with falcons. I wanted to find out if there was some way to turn my avocation into a vocation."

He will be the first to tell you that he opened his foundation on "a wing and a prayer."

"I had no clue how it would do," the Homestead's director of falconry said. "But now through small groups—of five to six people in a group—we are educating 6,000 people a year, plus we also go into schools, too."

Homestead guests may sign up to get the royal treatment. Beginner lessons are $85; $60 for children ages 5 to 15. Call (800) 838-1766 for more information.

most prominent springs in Virginia. The lineage of the Homestead as a resort and its tradition as a place to "take the waters" can be traced back to 1766. The spa of today was built in 1892.

In 2001 the Homestead had completed a thorough, multimillion-dollar restoration including the complete refurbishment of all its rooms and suites. September 2001 brought the grand opening of a fabulous new ballroom expansion and meeting facility. The 20,000-square-foot structure brought the meeting space at this resort to 72,000 square feet. The construction is among the most significant additions to this National Historic Landmark Resort in its 238-year history. The elaborate 14,000-square-foot ballroom is the finest grand ballroom and meeting facility on the mid-Atlantic coast. This expansion of the Garden Wings hosts 1,000 guests for dinner and up to 1,200 when arranged theater-style. The new ballroom features classical columns, adding a touch of elegance to the traditional mahogany paneling and floors, 22-foot ceilings, and special high-tech lighting that helps illuminate the facility while magnificent chandeliers light the way through the hallways and corridors. The adjoining lobby is similar to a garden room or French *orangerie* with large, plant-filled windows. French doors open onto an exquisite landscape. Guests get a breathtaking view of the Allegheny Mountains through the floor-to-ceiling bay windows of the new center.

There were also restorations to the Great Hall and the Jefferson Parlor, and the Washington Library was established. The exterior grand staircase connects the Great Hall to the casino and surrounding expanisve lawns. The Jefferson Parlor features an octagonal floor plan, custom furniture, and a series of specially commissioned murals depicting the history of Hot Springs. Adjacent is the Homestead's first-rate business center and travel agency. The Tower Library renovation showcases more than two centuries of American resort history, including a fascinating photo exhibit of famous resort visitors. The library is impres-

sive, complemented by an awesome bay window as well as mahogany paneling. Equally impressive is the Wine Room. With its 11-foot ceilings, the room's redwood walls and racks can hold 3,900 bottles. A highlight is the 400-piece, 35-square-foot stained-glass window, reflecting Italian-tile floors.

The Homestead did a multimillion-dollar renewal of its celebrated 109-year-old European-style spa. This luxurious facility features a state-of-the-art beauty salon, complete with facials, manicures, pedicures, and other salon services. Many spa and beauty products are Homestead signature items available for purchase. The fitness center, weight room, and aerobics rooms complete the spa. The reception area features vaulted ceilings, hardwood floors, and beautifully detailed woodwork.

An outdoor swimming pool along with a children's pool with a fountain opened in the summer of 2001, as well as a new pool house and a pool bar. The Homestead's magnificent spring-fed indoor pool, constructed in 1903, has also undergone extensive restoration. The two covered pools at Warm Springs, called the Jefferson Pools when the Homestead acquired them in the 1880s, and the sheltered drinking spring have been preserved in their natural condition. Mrs. Robert E. Lee's special chair is still at the women's pool. Legions of visitors swear by the springs' curative properties.

Since 1994, golf, which is king at this resort, also has received lots of attention. The Homestead course has undergone more than $1 million in improvements, overseen by architect Rees Jones, and the resort's legendary Old Course was completely restored. One of the three 18-hole courses has been the site of the U.S. Amateur and boasts the oldest first tee in continuous use in the United States. *Golf Digest* and *Golf* magazine rank the Cascades Course among the top in the nation. In 2001 *Golf Digest* recognized the entire resort in its first ever "Top 75 Resorts" feature, while *Golf* magazine awarded the Homestead a Gold Medal ranking, reserved for the "best of the best" in the hotel and hospitality worlds. John D. Rockefeller used to spread his wealth here by tossing shiny dimes into the pool of water in back of the first tee for the caddies to fight over. President William Taft nearly created a scandal by playing the "frivolous" game of golf on the Fourth of July holiday here at the turn of the century. Golf carts are included in the rates, which range from $110 to $265 for guests for the champion course. A nice touch after the game is a visit to Sam Snead's, where the food is presented in a casual atmosphere amidst Snead's memorabilia (including 35 framed golf balls that are among Snead's holes in one).

There are more than 20 specialty shops. Those who enjoy shopping won't be left out of the fun as they browse through the specialty boutiques that sell everything from clothing to logo sports gear to unique gift items. Children have a place to go too, as there is a playground and clubhouse, KidsClub, located on Cottage Row, offering a host of fun indoor and outdoor activities (see our Kidstuff chapter). Tennis is also superb at the Homestead, with six courts, including four all-weather ones. Clinics and private lessons are also available for all ages and skill levels, mid-March through mid-November, or you can register to play in a tournament!

Fishing is another favorite sport (permits cost $20), as are skeet, trap, and sporting clays at the Shooting Club, where a round of 25 birds costs $40. The resort now has 100 miles of hiking trails throughout its beautiful 15,000 acres. Travel through quiet forests and along pristine streams by foot or by mountain bike. For another kind of riding, the Homestead has an equestrian center with more than 50 horses and offers both English- and Western-style riding. A ride on a buckboard is another pleasant option. Indoor entertainment includes bowling and movies.

Winter brings a whole new round of sports with skiing (see our Skiing chapter) and ice-skating. Skating sessions are $10.00, $8.00 for children. Some winter weekends are priced for the budget-minded pocketbook. Bring the kids!

Aside from its Olympic-size skating rink, the Homestead expanded its winter sports season by unveiling its new multi-million-dollar snowmaking system in 2003. The resort now has the capability to open in December with consistent snow over its nine downhill runs, half pipe area, and tubing park. Guests can choose among cross-country skiing, snowshoe tours, guided snowmobile tours, and snowboarding.

Accommodations at the Homestead are classic. The complete refurbishment of all its 506 guest rooms and suites was complete by fall 2001. Traditional furnishings, plush patterned carpets, and floral draperies reflect the elegant Georgian architecture and create a warmth and elegance in these spacious rooms. Each wing of this landmark has been carefully decorated with its own theme. Daily room rates in the high season, April through November, start at $145 per person per night. During the value season, October through December 21, rooms start at $99 per person per night.

Dining options are varied, ranging from the elegance of the Homestead's famous Dining Room, which serves continental cuisine prepared under direction of their new Executive Chef Josef Schelch. A bountiful breakfast is served daily, and live music and dancing are offered in the evening. The 1766 Grille offers French and American cuisine and another fine dining choice with an intimate atmosphere and views of the casino and grounds. The Casino Club Restaurant is located adjacent to the first tee of the Old Course and offers a relaxed option for meals, serving dinner only on Friday and Saturday in the summer. The Mountain Lodge Restaurant is open seasonally, serving skiers and others trying to get in from the cold. The Cascades Club Restaurant is 4 miles south of the Homestead, offering a casual lunch experience, and is particularly suitable for players who have just finished a round of golf.

For even more variety, the Homestead added the Cottage Café. Located on Cottage Row, this 1950s soda fountain–style restaurant features outdoor dining. Guests also may stop by the Homestead Market, where gourmet deli foods are prepared for elegant dinner parties. A favorite with the ladies are the teas served in the elegant Great Hall.

From I-81, take Mt. Crawford/Highway 257 exit W. to Highway 42, then go south to Millboro Springs. Take Highway 39 W. to Warm Springs and US 220 S. to Hot Springs. Ground service is available from Roanoke Regional Airport. Ingalls Field, Hot Springs, is nearby, serving private and corporate aircraft.

SOUTHWEST VIRGINIA

Doe Run High Country Property Management
Mile Post 189, Blue Ridge Parkway, Fancy Gap
(276) 398-2212, (800) 325-6189
www.doerunlodge.com
Just across the border of Floyd County, in Patrick County, Doe Run and its High Country Restaurant are nestled in the most beautiful part of the Blue Ridge Parkway. With Groundhog Mountain as the midpoint on this road of pastoral beauty, your senses will be overwhelmed by what this resort has to offer.

The resort has an outdoor heated swimming pool and saunas, available in season. In 2001 massage therapy was added to the resort's options, with your choice of Swedish or deep tissue massage, set up by appointment.

Doe Run was built to match the beauty of the environment. The chalets are constructed of wood beams and stone, and floor-to-ceiling windows allow magnificent views. Each large suite has a fireplace, two

If you are in the mood for a day trip, the Greenbrier is just a hop, skip, and jump away in West Virginia. A National Historic Landmark, this resort is set on 6,500 acres and features three championship golf courses. For details, check out www.greenbrier.com or call (800) 624-6070.

bedrooms, two full baths, and a living/dining area. The chalets and villas are furnished and have complete kitchens. Millpond Hideaway, designed for executives and honeymooners, is styled after an old gristmill, complete with an attached water wheel. With marble floors, a double whirlpool tub, a luxury shower, full-suite stereo and TV, a raised natural stone fireplace, and a balcony and patio overlooking the millpond, this is the perfect setting to kick back and enjoy life for a while.

The historic Log Cabin dates back to 1865 and was moved to the lodge from another site. The exterior remains primitive, but the interior features a queen-size bed, a double whirlpool bath, full stereo sound, a natural stone fireplace, and a TV/VCR. The Executive Suite is a modern chalet with a whirlpool tub, a luxury shower, and full-suite stereo and a TV.

High Country Restaurant offers breakfast to its guests on Saturday and Sunday mornings. The restaurant has great views of the Piedmont.

Nearby attractions include Groundhog Mountain Overlook, a championship 18-hole golf course, Mabry Mill, Pucketts Cabin, Chateau Morrisette Winery, Lover's Leap Park, and Old Mayberry Store.

In-season rates range from $119 on weekdays to $234 for weekends.

RESTAURANTS

Blue Ridge dining has come a long way since the days of country ham, fried chicken, peanut soup, and apple pie. Sure, plenty of old-fashioned restaurants still offer hearty, conventional Southern fare. But the most exciting happenings in regional dining have involved innovative chefs preparing Virginia-grown food in wonderful and surprising new ways.

It's fusion food we're seeing at the upscale restaurants. This cuisine combines local ingredients with international influences to create an array of gastronomical treats. Of course, not everything works, but when the experiments of our regional chefs do succeed, it's pure eating pleasure.

Many of these cutting-edge restaurants tend to be concentrated in the Charlottesville area and the northern foothills region of the Blue Ridge. Others are in remote rural areas such as Eagle's Nest in Crows or Chateau Morrisette in Floyd County. Highly acclaimed dining spots include the internationally renowned Inn at Little Washington and the Bleu Rock Inn, both just an hour from the "big" Washington Beltway; L'Auberge Provencale in White Post; Lansdowne Resort in Leesburg; the Homestead in Hot Springs; and the Joshua Wilton House in Harrisonburg. These just scratch the surface, though.

A large number of chefs rely primarily on local products for their dishes. Virginia farm-raised trout is commonly pan-fried or smoked; Chesapeake Bay blue crab, both hard-shell and soft-shell, is served in season; and locally raised rabbit, veal, bison, venison, and poultry are prepared in a variety of ways. Virginia-grown fruits and vegetables are too numerous to name, but most notable are the region's peaches and apples. And, of course, one of the fastest-growing areas of Virginia's agriculture is grapes, which are made into dozens of varieties of wines at the state's 80 wineries.

Because of the vastness of the region we have attempted to cover in this guide, we were unable to list every good restaurant in every city, town, and village. We hope your favorite is included. But if it is not, drop us a line with your suggestions. We update this book periodically and may add your favorite to this list.

Most restaurants accept major credit cards for payment; we indicate those that do not.

The restaurants profiled in this guide are listed alphabetically under regional sections, then by counties.

Bon appetit!

PRICE CODE

Readers may be able to challenge our pricing guidelines for the restaurants listed below. Personal choices and menu changes will prove us wrong in some cases. Still, we created this code to provide you with a basic idea of the cost of entrees not including desserts, alcoholic beverages, sales tax, or gratuity.

$	Less than $20
$$	$21 to $35
$$$	$36 to $50
$$$$	More than $50

SHENANDOAH VALLEY
Frederick County

Cafe Sofia $$
2900 Valley Avenue, Winchester
(540) 667-2950
This lovely restaurant serves the only Bulgarian food in the Shenandoah Valley and some terrific seafood dishes as well. One of its most popular dishes is pierogies—seafood or chicken sauteed with vegeta-

bles, wrapped in a puff pastry with cheese and baked. The Bulgarian goulash was featured in an issue of *Bon Appetit*. Of course, you'll also find staples such as homemade moussaka, goulash, baklava, and homemade Bulgarian yogurt. The restaurant is filled with old-world touches. An antique woodstove heats the entrance in the winter months, while family needlework decorates the walls. Special decorating touches include handmade tablecloths, hand-embroidered menus, framed embroidery pieces, and an extensive doll collection. It is open for lunch and dinner Tuesday through Friday and dinner only on Saturday. You will need reservations on Friday and Saturday.

Cork Street Tavern $$
8 West Cork Street, Winchester
(540) 667-3777
www.jesara.com
This historic building, dating back to the 1830s, sits on one of the oldest streets in Winchester. In fact, Lord Fairfax and his agent gave the street its name in 1759. The building itself survived heavy shelling from three battles during the Civil War. As you might expect, the original tavern still has that rustic atmosphere. However, you can take a quick leap into modern day in the new section that was added in 1995. It's a sports lover's dream with five televisions. Be warned: You might want to wear your Washington Redskins jersey. Cork Street Tavern is extremely popular with the locals for its barbecued ribs, but you can also choose broiled trout, swordfish steak, and pasta dishes. Beverages range from Virginia wines to microbrews. The Tavern is open daily for lunch and dinner.

Tucano's Restaurant $$
12 Braddock Street, Winchester
(540) 722-4557
Once you step through the door at Tucano's, you leave behind the historic district of Old Town Winchester and enter a little corner of Brazil. This is cozy fine dining with a "neat casual" dress code. Candlelight adds a romantic atmosphere

for what the family-run business calls Brazilian international cuisine. Among the favorites on the varied menu is the Mouqueca Baina, white fish, shrimp, clams, and mussels in a special Brazilian sauce. Veal Bellaboca, the Italian favorite, includes stuffed veal served with potatoes and fresh vegetables. The locals keep coming back because the staff makes an effort to remember the customers and their favorite meals. It's open for lunch and dinner Monday through Friday with dinner only on Saturday. Reservations are accepted.

Violino Ristorante Italiano $$$
181 North Loudoun Street, Winchester
(540) 667-8006
Marcella Riccardo and Chef Franco Stocco serve classical dishes of Northern Italy in this romantic restaurant in downtown Winchester. Choose a traditional favorite or sample some of the chef's creations. The pansotti with lobster tail is a favorite. The menu offers about 15 to 20 homemade pastas, plus there are more than 20 vegetarian items on the menu. You will need to call three or four days in advance if you would like to try the seven-course, three-hour Best of Violino's tasting menu. On Friday and Saturday, musicians from Shenandoah University add to the romantic atmosphere with a little classical music. You also may eat outside on the patio. Violino serves lunch and dinner Monday through Saturday. Reservations are strongly recommended.

Wayside Inn $$
7783 Main Street, Middletown
(540) 869-1797
www.waysideofva.com
Opened in 1797, this elegantly restored 18th-century inn has been in operation for more than 200 years. Excellent regional American cuisine is served in seven antique-filled dining rooms, one of which is the old slave kitchen. Special features on the menu are peanut soup, spoon bread and country ham, a variety of game and seafood dishes, and homemade

desserts. Unless you have a reservation, expect to wait on weekends for a table, as this is a favorite with locals. Wayside serves brunch on Sunday.

Clarke County

L'Auberge Provencale $$$$
U.S. Highway 340, 1 mile south of U.S. Highway 50, White Post
(540) 837-1375
www.laubergeprovencale.com
One of Virginia's most celebrated French restaurants, L'Auberge is just over an hour's drive west of Washington, D.C., in the gentle hill country of the northern Shenandoah Valley. Expect superb authentic cuisine fashioned from the Provence region of France. The five-course prix fixe menu costs $75 a person and has plenty of options for each course. A recent menu included *Le Homard Roti Au Gnocchi de Patisson,* otherwise known as oven-roasted lobster served with butternut squash gnocchi and a brown butter sage sauce. Other choices featured shiitake-crusted venison, Provencale breaded veal cutlet, triple lamb chops, spiced rubbed duck breast, Chilean sea bass, and seared Scottish salmon. But every meal is a unique occasion as the menus are often planned around locally available produce and game and served in three distinct dining rooms. Speaking of national recognition, L'Auberge Provencale was recently reviewed in the *Washington Post,* while Chef Jeff Wood was nominated for the prestigious James Beard Award. An excellent wine selection, including vintages from local vineyards, adds to the upscale experience. The restaurant serves breakfast to inn guests daily and dinner Wednesday through Sunday. Reservations are required for weekends.

Warren County

Main Street Mill $
500 East Main Street, Front Royal
(540) 636-3123
www.mailstreetmill.com
You can't miss the barnlike building just across from the visitor center, but what's inside will surprise you. Artist Patricia Windrow's *trompe l'oeil* murals of farm animals and Civil War scenes are disturbingly realistic. The simple lunch and dinner meals, ranging from chicken to blackened hamburger, are well prepared and nicely presented. Steak, seafood, pasta, and ribs also are on the menu. Main Street Mill is open for lunch and dinner daily. Dress is casual.

Shenandoah County

Hotel Strasburg $$
213 South Holliday Street, Strasburg
(540) 465-9191
www.hotelstrasburg.com
This wonderfully restored Victorian inn dates back to 1895. The antique furnishings are for sale, so the decor is always changing. The restaurant has a strong following in the northern Shenandoah Valley and is known for its generous portions, courteous service, and delicious meals. Dinner specialties include a mixed grill, veal, various pasta dishes, plus one of the favorites, Appalachian chicken. Attire ranges from casual to coat and tie. Reservations are strongly recommended on the weekends. The restaurant is open for lunch and dinner on weekdays, breakfast, lunch, and dinner on Saturday and Sun-

day. Brunch also is served on Sunday. (See our Hotels and Motels chapter.)

Southern Kitchen $
Congress Street on U.S. Highway 11
New Market
(540) 740-3514
If you're hungry for traditional southern food, nothing fancy, this is the place. Established in 1955, Southern Kitchen is known for its peanut soup, fried chicken, and barbecued ribs of beef. It's open daily for breakfast, lunch, and dinner.

The Spring House Tavern $$
325 South Main Street, Woodstock
(540) 459-4755
www.jesara.com
Word has it that an underground spring used to be on this property, and town folk came to fetch spring water from the lady who lived here. Folks still come here for refreshment, though the spring is now closed. Lunch and dinner are served daily. Specialty entrees include steak, pasta, and seafood. Some say the ribs are the best in the valley.

Page County

The Brookside Restaurant $
2978 U.S. Highway 211 E, Luray
(540) 743-5698, (800) 299-2655
www.brooksidecabins.com
The fresh air and natural setting in Luray will give you a hearty appetite, which will serve you well for the daily all-you-can-eat homestyle lunch and dinner buffets at the Brookside. On the weekend and holiday Mondays, you can get the breakfast buffet. The salad bar includes goodies you might remember from Grandma's kitchen, and the melt-in-your-mouth breads, pastries, and desserts are made fresh daily. The Brookside is open daily for breakfast, lunch, and dinner from mid-January through mid-December. (See our Hotels and Motels chapter for information on Brookside's nine luxury cabins.)

Rainbow Hill Eatery $
2547 US 211 W, Luray
(540) 743-6009
www.shentel.net/rainbowhill
This place is popular with golfers who play Luray's courses in spring, summer, and fall. The atmosphere is casual. You can eat in or take out from a menu that includes salads, sandwiches, homemade soups and pies, beer, wine, and cocktails.

Rockingham County

Blue Stone Inn $$
US 11, Lacey Spring
(540) 434-0535
Locals, including professors from James Madison University, love this place and are willing to stand in long lines for a table, so plan your visit early or late. Specialties are tender steaks and fresh farm-raised fish such as Lacey Spring trout. The atmosphere is rustic tavern-style with deer heads mounted on the wall—some credited to owner Mike Olschofka, whose grandfather bought the restaurant in 1949. It's open Monday through Saturday for dinner.

Calhoun's Restaurant and
Brewing Company $$
41 Court Square, Harrisonburg
(540) 434-8777
www.calhounsbrewery.com
Calhoun's Restaurant and Brewing Company opened in 1998 in Harrisonburg's Court Square. Calhoun's touts itself as the Valley's premier microbrewery, and all their beers are craft-brewed by their brew master, Eric Plowman, right on location. The beer selections may change occasionally, but they can be anything from the light-bodied India Pale Ale to the Oatsmead Stout dark and full-bodied big beer, and many varieties in between. The menu includes such fare as jumbo lump crab cake, catfish stuffed with shrimp, and prime rib. There's a kids' menu, too. The establishment has a banquet facility to

accommodate large groups such as business meetings or weddings. There's also a regular calendar of live acoustical performances. Open seven days for lunch and dinner, with a popular brunch on Sunday.

El Charro $$
1570 East Market Street, Harrisonburg
(540) 564-0386

This is a good Mexican restaurant with locations also in Dale City and Fredericksburg. The menu is standard Mexican fare: burritos, enchiladas, and tacos. Be sure to try the delicious homemade chips and salsa, available in three degrees of heat. Service is fast, and the staff is courteous. El Charro is open every day for lunch and dinner.

Joshua Wilton House $$$
412 South Main Street, Harrisonburg
(540) 434-4464
www.joshuawilton.com

The restaurant inside this beautifully restored Victorian home serves the most exquisite food in town and is easily one of the state's finest dining spots. It's hard to believe the place was once a fraternity house for James Madison University students. Craig and Roberta Moore gutted the whole building and started over, creating a beautiful, romantic place to have dinner—and spend the night.

The wine list of more than 240 selections includes a variety of American and imported wines at very reasonable prices. The food is eclectic regional with emphasis on fresh produce and local products. The a la carte menu changes regularly, but specialties include a smoked salmon appetizer on apple potato cake topped with dill crème fraîche and salmon roe and a tasty crème brûlée. Reservations are recommended. Dinner is served Tuesday through Saturday. (See our Bed-and-Breakfasts and Country Inns chapter for information on an overnight stay here.)

L'Italia Restaurant $$
815 East Market Street, Harrisonburg
(540) 433-0961
www.litaliarestaurant.com

Gervasio and Veronica Amato own this restaurant right off Interstate 81 in Harrisonburg. The pasta and sauces are all homemade, and many of the entrees are prepared with a light touch for fat- and cholesterol-watchers. One of the outstanding offerings is gnocci, tiny dumplings filled with ricotta cheese and topped with a tomato and meat sauce. L'Italia's Staunton restaurant, run by Gervasio's brother, Emilio, is at 23 East Beverley Street. Lunch and dinner are served Tuesday through Sunday.

Pano's $
3190 South Main Street, Harrisonburg
(540) 434-2367

Within the French provincial exterior is a casual, wood-paneled family restaurant offering 106 entrees at lunch and 110 at dinner. Meals are nicely done, and the prices are right, too. Pano's is open daily for lunch and dinner. Choose from pasta, seafood, poultry, beef, and salads, prepared in simple American style. The specials change daily. Seniors receive a 10 percent discount.

The Village Inn $$
4979 South Valley Pike, Harrisonburg
(540) 434-7355
www.shenandoah.org/villageinn

The dining room at this small, family-owned motel serves simple, delicious American-style meals. The Inn has a gorgeous view of the mountains and is one of the highest-rated restaurants in the area. The Inn serves breakfast Monday through Friday and dinner every day except Sunday, and buffets are offered most meals. Alcohol is not sold.

Augusta County

The Beverley $
12 East Beverley Street, Staunton
(540) 886-4317

This restaurant has been around for 35 years and is known for its luscious homemade pies and generous afternoon teas. It's a small, family-owned place where you can also get real whipped potatoes and country ham on homemade bread. Traditional English tea is served from 3:00 p.m. to 5:00 P.M. on Tuesday and Thursday and includes sandwiches, cake, cheese, fruit, scones, and other pastries. The Beverley is open Monday through Friday from 7:00 A.M. to 7:00 P.M. and Saturday from 8:00 A.M. to 3:00 P.M.

Capt'n Sam's Landing $$
2323 West Main Street, Waynesboro
(540) 943-3416

If you love seafood, come dine with the captain. Surrounded by a nautical decor, you can indulge in fish, crab, oysters, lobster, scallops, and clams prepared in a variety of ways. The steak and chicken dishes are good, too. All entrees are served with a trip to the salad bar (or one hot vegetable) and a choice of french fries, baked potato, or sweet potatoes. Don't miss the week-long Shrimp Feast that's held the second week every month—all the shrimp you can eat is prepared nine different ways. The adjacent pub serves fresh popcorn and a special menu. Capt'n Sam's is open for dinner every day except Sunday. Reservations are accepted for parties of six or more.

The Depot Grille $$
Train Station, 42 Middlebrook Avenue
Staunton
(540) 885-7332
www.depotgrill.com

This popular dining spot in the old freight depot portion of the restored C & O train station has a 50-foot antique oak bar. On the menu are fresh fish, crab cakes, seafood combination platters, salads, and a "lite bites" selection. Daily specials, tasty desserts, and a children's menu round out the choices. The Depot Grille has a full bar, including a selection of beers and wines from around the world. The restaurant is open for lunch and dinner daily.

Edelweiss German Restaurant $
US 11 and US 340 N, Staunton
(540) 337-1203
www.edelweissrestaurantva.com

Edelweiss offers authentic German cuisine in the rustic setting of a log cabin. German-born owner and chef Ingrid uses many of her mother's recipes to prepare specialties such as sauerbraten, roast beef that is brine-marinated for up to five days, and schnitzel, thinly cut, tender breaded pork. If you are new to German food, ask for the sampler. You can try five different items to see what you really like. Fresh vegetables are served family style. For dessert the house specialty is *schwarzwalder kirschtorte* (Black Forest cake). If you enjoy beer with your meal, you'll find a nice selection of imported light and dark beers and German wines. Attire is casual, and a half-price children's menu is available. The restaurant is open for breakfast, lunch, and dinner every day except Monday.

Pampered Palate Cafe $
28 East Beverley Street, Staunton
(540) 886-9463

This is another great watering hole smack in the middle of the most interesting shopping area downtown. Here you'll find gourmet deli sandwiches such as roast beef and Brie on French bread, bagels, stuffed potatoes, quiche, iced strawberry tea, and cappuccino served with luscious desserts. You can get a continental breakfast, too. The place sells a lot of wines, including the best Virginia ones, as well as gourmet coffees, gift baskets, and imported candies. Wine tastings are offered, too. The cafe is open Monday through Saturday.

The Pullman Restaurant $$
Train Station, 36 Middlebrook Avenue
Staunton
(540) 885-6612
www.thepullman.com

Step back in time as you enter this authentically restored turn-of-the-20th-century train station. The building is furnished with antique lighting fixtures. The menu features updated versions of old-time railroad dining car fare, including a variety of steaks, seafood, sandwiches, and lighter meals. There is an elegant Sunday brunch. You can sit along the train station concourse and watch the trains pass (Amtrak stops Wednesday, Friday, and Sunday), and be sure to visit the elegantly appointed bar room. The Pullman is open for lunch and dinner daily.

Rowe's Family Restaurant
and Bakery $
Richmond Avenue, Staunton
(540) 886-1833
www.mrsrowes.com
They opt for fresh-cut flowers instead of linen tablecloths. Oh, it may not be fancy, but if you're in the mood for some down-home country cooking, Rowe's is the place to be. Locals are willing to wait in line—sometimes as long as 45 minutes—to savor the hospitality, homemade food, and bargain prices. Baked pork tenderloin with homemade mashed potatoes has been a local favorite since the Rowes opened the restaurant 57 years ago. Williard Rowe came up with the idea in 1947, but the customers really started lining up after his wife, Mildred, came down to show him how to cook. Mildred passed away in 2003, but the family continues to carry on in the established tradition. It's a friendly atmosphere, and most of the people who work there have been there for years. Of course, all the food is homemade: ham, cubed steak, chicken, even the pies are made from scratch, including everything from apple pie to coconut cream. There is not a full bar, but beer and wine are available. Located right off Interstate 81 at exit 222, Rowe's draws a lot of business from tourists following the New York to Florida corridor, but there is ample parking close by. Rowe's is open daily from 7:00 A.M. to 8:00 P.M. Reservations are allowed if you have a party of six or more. You may take home their frozen entrees and fresh-baked pies and cakes.

Scotto's Italian Restaurant
and Pizzeria $
1412 West Broad Street, Waynesboro
(540) 942-8715
Join in the casual family atmosphere at

Scotto's, where the owners take great pride in their Italian heritage and in the art of true Southern Italian cooking. The homemade dishes, including chicken and veal Parmesan and gourmet pizzas, are all reasonably priced and available for take-out or delivery. Lunch and dinner are served every day.

South River Grill $$
23 Windigrove Lane, Waynesboro
(540) 942-5567
www.southrivergrill.com
Open seven days a week for lunch and dinner, South River offers a varied menu. Favorites include prime rib and shrimp, St. Louis–style barbecued ribs, hand-patted burgers, homemade soups, and an inexpensive children's menu. South River's atmosphere is pure Blue Ridge, with large picture windows, lots of plants, and a fireplace. The restaurant also offers off-premises catering. Reservations are suggested.

Weasie's Kitchen $
130 East Broad Street, Waynesboro
(540) 943-0500
The down-home cooking and laid-back setting draw many regulars and tourists to this former Dairy Queen. Opened by Mary Eloise Roberts—known as Weasie—more than a decade ago, this dining spot finds success in Weasie's basic Southern recipes. Weasie passed away, and the restaurant is now owned by Joyce and Blair Campbell. Breakfast is the big draw, with homemade biscuits and gravy the most requested items. Desserts, all home-made, are also popular. Breakfast, lunch, and dinner are served daily. Credit cards are not accepted.

Wright's Dairy Rite $
346 Greenville Avenue, Staunton
(540) 886-0435
www.dairy-rite.com
This is the place where world-famous musicians the Statler Brothers hung out while they were growing up. The country quartet even mention the restaurant in

"Carry Me Back," although some might not know that "Hamburger Dan's" is a reference to this still-popular local eatery. Just drive up to the curbside speakers, place your order, and a server brings your meal out to your car. You can also eat indoors or call for takeout, but the unique curbside service will carry you back to the 1950s. The Wright family opened Dairy Rite in 1952 with two ice cream machines. Today you can satisfy that craving for a juicy burger and fries with fresh, homemade food that's quick and tasty. Dairy Rite makes its own onion rings every day, as well as barbecue and slaw. With their homemade vegetable soup, "nothing comes out of a can," they make just enough chicken, egg, and tuna salad to serve for the day. Also popular is the Super Burger, around for 40 years now. Or try chicken, shrimp, or a foot-long hot dog. Dessert is the hardest part—you have to choose from a plethora of ice cream treats including sundaes, cones, and floats. An Insider favorite is the milkshakes, which come in nine flavors, including raspberry, cherry, butterscotch, and banana. (The fruit shakes have bits of real fruit.) And—shades of the '50s—you can even get a malted shake. This is a place you can drop in for lunch, dinner, or a late snack. Dairy Rite is open from 9:00 A.M. to 10:00 P.M. Sunday through Thursday and 10:00 A.M. to 11:00 P.M. on Friday and Saturday. Who knows, you might even see one of the Statler Brothers. They still drop in from time to time.

Lexington and Rockbridge County

The Colonial Dining Room   **$$$**
US 11 S, Natural Bridge
(540) 291-2121
www.naturalbridgeva.com
An oasis of good family food, the Natural Bridge Village restaurants are as popular with the locals as they are with visitors at this gigantic tourist attraction. Known for

its Friday night seafood buffet, Saturday prime rib buffet, and Sunday brunch, the Colonial Dining Room serves quality food daily, including dinner and breakfast seven days a week. The menu offers a variety of Virginia fare (since this is a major tourism spot), such as red-eye gravy and grits, and other all-American favorites such as banana pudding and pecan pie. You'll feel comfortable dressed in after-church garb or Bermuda shorts. Waitresses, some with more than 30 years' experience, offer service that is second to none. (See our Resorts chapter.)

Maple Hall   **$$$**
US 11 N, off I-81 at exit 195,
6 miles outside of Lexington
(540) 463-4666
www.lexingtonhistoricinns.com
Fine dining in an elegant atmosphere describes the Maple Hall experience. This antebellum mansion is full of gorgeous antiques and restorations. The seasonal menu allows for the freshest and most delicious cuisine imaginable. Some favorites include filet mignon, sesame chicken, and pasta a la carbonara. It's open seven days a week for dinner only. Breakfast is served to overnight guests. Reservations are requested.

Southern Inn   **$$$**
37 South Main Street, Lexington
(540) 463-3612
This charming historical restaurant has been a tradition in Lexington since the 1930s. The Inn, in the heart of downtown, specializes in Virginia wines. Visit this family restaurant for sandwiches or contemporary American cuisine, including mahimahi, tuna, sirloin, or pasta. All desserts are homemade. Southern Inn is open seven days a week for lunch and dinner.

Willson–Walker House   **$$$**
30 North Main Street, Lexington
(540) 463-3020
www.willsonwalker.com
The beautiful architecture of this ca. 1820 Greek Revival town house sets the scene

for an elegant dinner or brunch. However, you are welcome whether you wear a coat and tie or dress casually. The interior has period antique furniture and artwork. Opening from the foyer are two main dining rooms, each with a fireplace with a faux-marble mantel and two portraits, ca. 1840. The menu of regional American cuisine affirms why the Willson-Walker House has been featured in *Conde Nast* and *Blue Ridge Country* magazines. The menus change seasonally and lists such tempting dishes as North Carolina potato-crusted trout, poultry, pork, and ribeye steak. A four-course prix fixe dinner is available for $20 per person. Desserts are ever changing; however, the chef's special upside-down apple pie is usually available. There is also a children's menu. A daily luncheon special is available for $5.00 or you may order from the menu, which includes items that comply with Weight Watchers' point system. Second-floor banquet rooms are available for private parties. You also may dine outdoors on the veranda from May to October. Lunch and dinner are served Tuesday through Saturday, except from January to March when lunch is not served on Saturday. Reservations are recommended.

ROANOKE VALLEY

Roanoke

Alexander's $$$
105 South Jefferson Street, Roanoke
(540) 982-6983
Excellent food and renowned service make this restaurant well worth the trip into downtown Roanoke. It always has been considered one of Roanoke's finest throughout its evolutions of location and hours. The menu goes through several revisions each year, and you are always sure to find a delicious selection. Bread and desserts are freshly made. Don't miss the delicious house-made desserts, such as glace au chocolat. Alexander's beef dishes are especially popular, as is its seasonal mixed grill of pork, lamb, and

chicken. Grilled tuna, pan-seared salmon, and veal Alexander are other favorites. Whatever you find on the menu will be gourmet, made of only the finest, freshest ingredients and served with flair. Dinner reservations are recommended. Lunch is served Wednesday only; dinner is served Tuesday through Saturday. The restaurant has a beautiful dining room for private parties and receptions.

Awful Arthur's Seafood Company $$
108 Campbell Avenue, Roanoke
(540) 344-2997
www.awfularthurs.com
Seafood lovers, cast your anchor at Awful Arthur's on the historic Roanoke City Market. The decor is nautical and basic, just like the food. The main attraction is the large raw bar serving an assortment of items you'd expect on a real visit to the ocean. The Captain's Sampler offers a bit of it all, with oysters, shrimp, clams, crab legs, crawfish, and mussels. Fresh is the only language spoken by the chef, and you can expect everything to taste like it just arrived from the dock. Appetizers include the standard oysters Rockefeller and fried calamari. Also expect surprises such as seafood pizza. In addition to the array of seafood, you'll find other dinner favorites such as beef fillets. If dinner isn't on your agenda, at lunch you can get a terrific sandwich or fresh fish of the day. A full wine list specializes in Virginia varieties with California and Oregon and pricey French vintages represented, too. A nice selection of microbrews is available at Awful Arthur's as well. Awful Arthur's is open for lunch and dinner. Attire is casual. A second Awful Arthur's is at 2229 Colonial Avenue.

Beamers $$
315 Market Street
Roanoke City Market
(540) 345-5000
OK, this is a "must" for all Hokie fans! This popular spot and the one located on 2509 Market Street in Christiansburg are named for the 1999 coach of the year, Frank

Beamer, football coach at Virginia Tech. Autographed Tech posters and players' jerseys decorate the walls of the building that fronts the popular city market street. Tables are covered in maroon cloths, of course, and the 15 televisions are all turned to a game, preferably a Virginia Tech game. Beamers claims that their "portions are substantial, enough to satisfy a football player's appetite," and they are surely correct. Try the Beamer Burger, a signature dish, or a Carolina barbecue or Maryland crab cake sandwiches. There's the more extensive fare of steaks, prime rib, and seafood. You can wash it all down with a Godiva chocolate martini or the Hoki-rita! Before coming to Beamer's, the executive chef did a 20-year stint at the White House.

Billy's Ritz $$
102 Salem Avenue SE, Roanoke
(540) 342-3937

Housed in a century-old hotel building with a screen door that slams when you enter, this traditional American grill is just 1 block from Roanoke's historic farmers' market. You can join the happy-hour crowd at an oak bar and dine in casual elegance in any one of four unique rooms amid a collection of art and antiques—or have your meal in the open-air courtyard. Although known for its great steaks, variety of salads, grilled fish, and teriyaki dishes, Billy's Ritz excels at a variety of other cuisine as well. The mixed grill is sure to please, and don't miss the prime rib on weekends. Wine is available by the bottle or glass from an extensive list. The star of the dessert list is molten chocolate cake. Dinner is served every night. Reservations are recommended for large groups, especially on the weekends.

Carlos Brazilian International Cuisine $$
4167 Electric Road, Roanoke
(540) 776–1117
www.carlosbrazilian.com

Hundreds of faithful *feijao preto* (black bean) lovers come from all over the Shenandoah Valley to partake of the magic that is Carlos Brazilian's international cuisine. When you ask the Roanoke Valley's leading gourmands to list their favorite restaurants, Carlos will always make the list. Carlos's time spent working in many different restaurants has manifested itself in a menu quite unlike anything even lovers of Brazilian food have seen. What Carlos does with simple fare, such as black beans and angel hair pasta spiced with international flavor, packs the place for both lunch and dinner on Roanoke's bustling City Market. Carlos is open for lunch Monday, Thursday, and Friday and dinner Monday through Saturday.

Corned Beef & Co. $$
107 South Jefferson Street, Roanoke
(540) 342-3354
www.cornbeefandco.com

Probably the most successful deli operation in town, Corned Beef & Co.'s hearty fare, served up by two former fraternity brothers who graduated from Roanoke College, is known both for its great food and downtown atmosphere. Now it's also known as the only restaurant in town with a brick pizza oven in its new expansion. A huge sports bar also has been added. The name says it all—don't look for anything pretentious here. What you will find is good, basic deli sandwiches (Jazzbo, All-American Combo) served quickly in a first-class atmosphere of marble and mahogany. There is also outside deck seating. It's open for lunch and dinner Monday through Saturday, 'til 2:00 A.M. Thursday through Saturday for the wee-small-hours crowd. (See our Nightlife chapter.)

El Rodeo Mexican Restaurant $
4301 Brambleton Avenue, Roanoke
(540) 772-2927

260 Wildwood Road, Salem
(540) 387-4045
www.elrodeo.com

This popular family restaurant will whisk you away to Mexico with its south-of-the-border decor and ethnic foods. Ingredients are printed on the menu for those unfamiliar with Mexican food. Expect the cuisine—

fajitas, taquitos Mexicanos, La Chicana, enchiladas de pollo (chicken enchiladas), and more—to be on the mild side. Select from vegetarian, children's, and lunch-only menus as well. The chef is always willing to accommodate your substitutions. El Rodeo, one of five Roanoke locations, is open for lunch and dinner every day.

 Save room for dessert, especially during strawberry, peach, and apple seasons. These Virginia-grown fruits—spectacular on their own—become even more delicious in a dessert dish.

The Library $$$
3117 Franklin Road, Roanoke
(540) 985-0811

The Library, one of the most elegant and exclusive dining establishments in the Roanoke Valley, is rated among the top seven restaurants in Virginia. It also is a recipient of the Dirona designation, one of 568 restaurants in North America to bear this distinction of quality. The decor is that of a well-stocked library, adding to the memorable dining experience. French cuisine, served by candlelight, includes such classics as veal Princess, veal with shrimp and crab and a béarnaise sauce; and English Dover sole with spaghetti squash, beurre blanc, and almonds. Desserts include mousse for traditional tastes and fresh fruit Romanoff for something a bit different to close an exquisite meal. A full wine cellar features French, Virginia, and California wines. Dinner is served Monday through Saturday. Reservations are recommended.

Lily's $$
At the Wyndham Roanoke Airport Hotel
2801 Hershberger Road, Roanoke
(540) 563-9300
www.wyndham.com

This casual restaurant in the Wyndham Roanoke features an array of steaks, seafood, and pasta dishes as well as children's menus. The breakfast buffet also is

quite popular. It's open every day, and reservations are suggested.

Luigi's $$$
3301 Brambleton Avenue, Roanoke
(540) 989-6277

This Italian gourmet restaurant was established after the tradition of Mama Leone's restaurant in New York City. Naturally, the spaghetti is wonderful; coupled with the other pasta selections, it's an Italian gourmet's delight. Some of the special treats include veal Luigi's, shrimp scampi, and the popular Cappuccino L'Amore, a blend of gin, brandy, rum, creme de cacao, and Galliano liquors topped with a cinnamon stick, clove, and whipped cream. Homesick Northerners can get real Italian desserts such as cannoli and spumoni. Luigi's is definitely a cut above any other Italian restaurant in town, both for food and service. Each dish is prepared by your special order, so count on a leisurely dinner with a lot of attentive service. Dinner is served daily. Luigi's is open until midnight Friday and Saturday. On weekends Luigi's averages about 200 customers per night.

Macado's $
120 Church Avenue, Roanoke
(540) 342-7231

3247 Electric Road, Roanoke
(540) 776-9884

209 East Main Street, Salem
(540) 387-2686
www.macados.com

At Macado's the decor is as interesting as the food, and both keep the restaurant packed with a younger crowd. A big hot-air balloon hangs from the ceiling, and pictures and keepsakes from local or nationally known bands decorate the walls. You'll see the Three Stooges riding in an airplane, a section of a real classic car on the wall, old toys, posters, nostalgic collectibles, and antiques. The extensive menu could take your entire lunch hour to read. It specializes in a delicious array of hot and cold deli sandwiches; the salads and chili are exceptional, too. Macado's has several locations in the Roanoke and New River Valley including Blacksburg, Radford, and Salem. Macado's is open daily for lunch and dinner and stays open until the wee hours.

Mediterranean Italian & Continental Cuisine $$
213 South Williamson Road, Roanoke
(540) 982-7160

A Turkish touch by owner Ihsan Demirci has turned this restaurant into a Mediterranean delight. Pasta is the main attraction—it's delicious, plentiful, and inexpensive. Lovers of fettuccine Alfredo and stuffed shells will be delighted to see their favorite Italian dishes prepared just right. Health-food lovers also are treated to an array of pasta dishes with fresh vegetables, seafood, and chicken. The chicken Saltimboca, a tender breast of chicken with prosciutto and mozzarella cheese smothered in a light sauce of Marsala wine and onions, makes watching your weight bearable in this den of delights. Veal dishes are another attraction, especially the veal Frances, tempting fillets of veal dipped in a light egg batter and pan-browned in white wine and lemon sauce. Spaghetti is the side dish, of course. The Mediterranean is open Monday through Friday for lunch and dinner; dinner only is served on Saturday.

Mill Mountain Coffee and Tea $
112 Campbell Avenue SE, Roanoke
(540) 342-9404

4710 Starkey Road, SE, Roanoke
(540) 989-5282

17 East Main Street, Salem
(540) 389-7549

700 North Main Street, Blacksburg
(540) 552-7442

Botetourt Commons, Daleville
(540) 966-1102
www.millmountaincoffee.com

Success breeds success, and nowhere is this more true than with restaurants. Although Mill Mountain Coffee and Tea really isn't a full-service restaurant, it is one of the most popular hangouts in the Roanoke Valley (see our Nightlife chapter). All locations offer a delicious variety of baked goods, and all except the Campbell Avenue location offer lunch menus that include soups, salads, and sandwiches. They copy the famous Seattle coffeehouse concept—a cozy atmosphere for mingling—which Roanoke Valley restaurant patrons have enthusiastically embraced. The draw, of course, is the multitude of coffee, tea, and Italian soda flavors readily available for refill. Another appealing aspect is having a quiet place to go to talk or conduct business. All you have to do is place your order, sit down, and enjoy the company. All coffees are freshly roasted on the premises.

Nawab Indian Cuisine $$
118-A Campbell Avenue, Roanoke
(540) 345-5150
www.nawabrestaurant.com

Nawab, in the heart of Roanoke's downtown historic district, offers a richly varied Indian menu of fresh, natural ingredients, wholesome sauces, and flavorful spices. Choose from a versatile selection of natural foods—all can be prepared mild, medium, hot, or Indian hot with freshly ground herbs and spices. Try one of the tandoori specialties, such as tandoori chicken tikka or boti kebab. The tandoor is a special pit oven made from clay and fueled with charcoal. All meats, poultry, and seafood marinade overnight, then are skewered and broiled in the tandoor, giving them a delicious and unique flavor. Vegetarians will be in heaven here with numerous meatless dishes to choose from. The vegetable dorma will make your mouth water with its nine fresh vegetables cooked in a blend of spices and cream and sprinkled with nuts. The palak paneer is made of spinach with Indian cheese cubes cooked in mild spices and herbs. For dessert try kheer, traditional Indian rice pudding with nuts, flavored with cardamom and rose water. Nawab is open daily for lunch and dinner. There is a lunch buffet daily, and lunch specials are served within 10 minutes. Children's portions are available on some items at half price.

Roanoke Weiner Stand $
25 Campbell Avenue, Roanoke
(540) 342-6932

In 1916, when Prohibition caused the decline of Salem Avenue by forcing its saloons to close their doors, brick-paved Campbell Avenue took over as Roanoke's main thoroughfare. The road was exciting and new, with streetcars and electric streetlights. And the Roanoke Hot Weiner Stand opened for business at the location where it would remain for more than 87 years. Harry Chacknes opened the stand with a six-burner stove, a kitchen that measured 13 by 7 feet (including counter space), and six stools. And right in the heart of the Magic City, you could get a steaming, plump hot dog for just a nickel. Almost eight decades later, times have changed. What once cost you five pennies now runs you $1.45. The original six stools increased to 19 in 1988 when the Weiner Stand became a part of Center in the Square. The place even traded up for a more modern stove after using the old one for 86 years. But some things haven't changed a bit. The stand is still in the Chacknes family. Harry's wife, Elsie, ran it in the 1960s. Now his nephew, Gus Pappas, is the owner. Elsie's nephew, Mike Brookman, runs the stand at 3601 Brandon Avenue, (540) 345-0095. And while John Liakos is not actually a blood relative, he is certainly a part of the family after working here for more than 43 years. You can still get that delicious, plump hot dog. And we don't think the friendly conversation and warm, honest smiles will ever leave the kitchen of the Roanoke Weiner Stand. It's open for breakfast, lunch, and dinner Monday through Saturday. Credit cards are not accepted.

The Roanoker Restaurant $
Colonial Avenue at Interstate 581 and
Wonju Street, Roanoke
(540) 344-7746

This restaurant has held high standards for 63 years, and it shows. It's busy every day of the week, filled with loyal customers whose parents and grandparents ate here. Run by the Warren family all these years, the Roanoker is frequented by customers who have come to expect quick service and farm-fresh quality food. Noted for its Virginia mountain hospitality, the Roanoker also serves stir-fry entrees and extensive salads. The Roanoker has been voted Best Place to Eat with Your Mother, and it is! Breakfast is a crowd pleaser; menu favorites include red-eye gravy and ham with biscuits and grits. The restaurant serves breakfast, lunch, and dinner Tuesday through Sunday.

Texas Tavern $
114 West Church Avenue, Roanoke
(540) 342-4825
www.texastavern.com

As soon as you open the door to this 74-year-old white brick Roanoke landmark, you can smell the hamburgers and hot dogs sizzling on the grill. You will notice that the nickel countertop is dented and dull. Men in industrial-white T-shirts, work pants, and aprons shout "hello" over the bubbling chili and chattering customers. The staff is neighborly and will shoot the breeze with you—that is, if they have the time. A sign reads, "WE SERVE 1,000 PEOPLE 10 AT A TIME." Never mind. You didn't come here for pamperin'—you came for some of the best chili this side of Texas. The Tavern is a great place for a quick, hot lunch or a midnight snack. It serves all the standards—hot dogs, hamburgers, the Cheesy Western, and, of course, chili. And if you order a nice cool drink, you won't get a Styrofoam cup or even an aluminum can. Only glass soda bottles and straws are found here. Texas Tavern is near three (pay) parking lots, which is a bonus, since they have little parking space of their own. It is also just a few blocks away from the farmers' market and Center in the Square. The restaurant is open 24 hours a day, seven days a week. (See our Nightlife chapter.) Credit cards are not accepted.

309 Market Street Grille $$
309 Market Street, Roanoke
(540) 343-0179
www.roanokeonline.com

Dining at 309 Market Street is like having your favorite meal with an old friend. If there's one thing that stands out about this place, it's the repeat business it enjoys as a downtown Roanoke favorite on the historic city market. It's especially popular as a lunch spot for urban professionals. It serves lunch and dinner in a sunny, contemporary dining room under a skylight. Menu specials include gourmet burgers and bison along with seafood salad and chicken fingers. Burgers are popular choices—the Burgundy Burger has a hint of fine wine, the Tex-Mex Burger is well seasoned with jalapeños, hot sauce, and cheese, and the favorite is a top-of-the-line gourmet burger with bacon and Swiss. Dinner selections include traditional favorites such as filet mignon and chicken teriyaki. Also available to please the vegetarian taste is grilled vegetables and polenta. All dinner selections include a salad, hot bread and butter, fresh steamed vegetables or seasoned rice, and baked potato, onion rings, or fries. It's open for lunch Monday through Saturday. Dinner is served Tuesday through Saturday. There is live entertainment on Friday and Saturday evenings.

Wildflour Cafe and Catering $
Towers Mall, Roanoke
(540) 344-1514

Wildflour II Market and Bakery $$
1212 Fourth Street SW, Roanoke
(540) 343-4543

If you're going to eat lunch at either of the Wildflour restaurants, be sure and get there before 11:30 A.M. The small Towers Mall operation's healthy and homemade food was so popular in Roanoke that the owners expanded to a new location in Old Southwest with Wildflour II Market and Bakery. But it's still tough to get a seat because the food is so fabulous. The folks here cook from scratch early, so the smell of fresh baking bread lures people who've been thinking about eating there since morning. The breads du jour, of the European-style hearth variety, are arranged in a flower pot at the cash register for all to smell and admire. The best red beans and rice we've ever eaten comes out of this place—we could eat it every day and not tire of it. The salads are varied and gourmet. As a nice touch, the owners take the time to chat and get to know everybody, yet they run extremely efficient operations. Wildflour is open Monday through Saturday for lunch and dinner.

Salem

Mac and Bob's $
316 East Main Street, Salem
(540) 389-5999

If you want to go to *the* hangout in Salem, this is it! Directly across from Roanoke College, Mac and Bob's (see our Nightlife chapter) is without a doubt the place for both locals and college kids to eat in Salem. It offers casual dining with good service. You can get your basic burger and sandwiches fixed the way you want. Along with wholesome salads and terrific desserts that appeal to everyone, there is also a full menu of pasta, fresh fish, steak, ribs, and chicken. New chef Robert Lowe has been developing an upscale menu featuring filet mignon, crab cakes, and homemade soups and desserts.

Catawba

The Homeplace $
4968 Catawba Valley Drive, Catawba
(540) 384-7252

"Down-home cooking that makes you want to eat all your veggies" is the slogan of this grand old farmhouse and family restaurant just outside Roanoke. The home-style food is served family-style in bowls placed right at your table. Fried chicken, mashed potatoes and gravy,

Some of your best meals in the Blue Ridge may be in the least formal settings. Browse the local newspaper for small-town fund-raisers or celebrations. The locals whip up their finest recipes for these occasions and love to feed visitors.

pinto beans, apples, and hot biscuits are menu staples here. Leave room for homemade fruit cobblers for dessert. A neighborly and courteous staff will make you feel right at home. Thursday is Barbecue Night, but you can still order the regular fare. Always plan on a wait of at least 20 minutes, since Roanokers pack the place on weekends. You won't mind waiting on the big front porch, where you can pet the farm felines. Dinner is served Thursday through Sunday. If you're dieting or watching your cholesterol, don't go near this place! They all eat the way Grandma and Grandpa used to, before we knew everything that was bad for our arteries.

EAST OF THE BLUE RIDGE

Loudoun County

Back Street Cafe   **$$**
4 East Federal Street, Middleburg
(540) 687-3122
Tutti Perricone reigns over this tiny eatery a block off Main Street and makes sure that her patrons are well fed and undisturbed, no matter how famous they are. The mostly Italian menu contains some wonderful fish and pasta dishes, and the daily specials are innovative and tasty. The outside deck is great for people-watching in good weather. On Friday nights, Tutti engages one or two jazz musicians and can sometimes be persuaded to sing with them. Back Street Cafe serves lunch and then opens again for dinner Monday through Saturday. It also operates a sizable catering business.

The Coach Stop   **$$**
9 East Washington Street, Middleburg
(540) 687-5515
www.coachstop.com
This casual dining restaurant features regional cooking with dishes such as Virginia ham, locally grown trout, and fresh prime rib. The Coach Stop is known for its homemade onion rings, which come thinly sliced and piled high. Nightly specials often take advantage of in-season regional seafood—shad roe, soft-shell crab, and the like. A children's menu is available, and reservations are strongly suggested for weekend nights. It's open daily for breakfast, lunch, and dinner.

The Green Tree   **$$$**
15 South King Street, Leesburg
(703) 777-7246
www.leesburgcolonialinn.com
This famous watering hole, surrounded by the enchanting homes, historic buildings, shops, and museums of Leesburg, specializes in authentic 18th-century recipes and does its own baking. The original building was constructed in 1768, when it was opened as an inn and tavern. Try a house specialty, such as Robert's Delight (choice beef rolled in sweet herbs and spices) or Jefferson's Delight (liver presoaked in milk, sauteed with onions on top), while listening to 18th-century music. You must try the bread pudding soaked in hot rum for dessert. It's open daily for lunch and dinner, with brunch served on Sunday. Reservations are preferred on the weekends.

Johnson's Charcoal Beef House   **$$**
401 East Market Street (Route 7)
Leesburg
(703) 777-1116
This is a great place to bring the kids—with the restaurant's pleasant family atmosphere, good food, and kids' and senior menus—plus you won't have to spend a lot. They serve country breakfast, lunch, and dinner seven days a week. Enjoy a thick, juicy steak, fresh seafood specials, Virginia country ham, and delicious, homemade desserts, all prepared

fresh. You'll feel like you're visiting your cousins in the country with the extensive gun collection on display.

Lansdowne Grill at Lansdowne Resort $$$$
44050 Woodridge Parkway, Leesburg
(703) 729-4073
www.lansdowneresort.com
Located near historic Leesburg, this scenic resort bordering the Potomac River is in the heart of Loudoun County's famed "hunt country." Whether you are in the mood for a romantic dinner or a sandwich after a round of golf, Lansdowne can suit your taste with four distinct dining areas, two restaurants, a tavern and a deli.

The Lansdowne Grille
The Grille, which specializes in prime steaks, is open daily for lunch and Monday through Saturday for dinner. In addition to the main dining room, there is a lounge area and two private dining rooms. For nine years the Grille received the *Wine Spectator* Award of Excellence for its wine list and has received the Gold Cluster Award for promoting Virginia wines. Service is excellent, and you can expect leisurely dining. The menu usually consists of six steak entrees and seven seafood choices. Steaks run from a petite filet mignon to the porterhouse in red wine reduction. Chesapeake crab cakes are another favorite. You can count on the vegetables being local. Following the main course, there is an array of fine desserts, plus pressed coffee, postdinner libations, and a cigar menu. Be forewarned: The Grille is a cell-phone-free environment. Reservations are required.

Riverside Hearth
This dining room can seat 218 guests, and quite often it's filled to capacity, especially for its renowned Sunday brunch. Riverside features a unique kiosk-style service with exhibition cooking. It is open daily for breakfast, lunch, and dinner. Like the Grille, it features a panoramic view of the golf course. Reservations are required.

Fairways Deli
The Deli is located at the turn of the golf course and adjacent to the outdoor pool. It offers unique sandwiches, snack items, and beverages. The Deli is open seasonally.

Stonewalls Tavern
Located off the resort's living room, the Tavern offers a casual atmosphere complete with billiards, darts, a massive fieldstone fireplace, jukebox, and large-screen televisions.

Lightfoot Restaurant $$$
11 North King Street, Leesburg
(703) 771-2233
www.lightfootrestaurant.com
Step into this restaurant and you've stepped into a piece of history—a restored historic old bank building with preserved vaults in tact. The building stands at the intersection of past and present, offering a taste of both. Classic architecture and thoughtfully prepared meals of fish, duck, beef, pork, and chicken will make this a truly memorable dining experience. The menu is modern contemporary American. Attire is business casual and reservations are recommended. The restaurant is open daily for lunch and dinner.

Mansion House Restaurant $$$
Holiday Inn at Carradoc Hall
1500 East Market Street, Leesburg
(703) 771-9200
www.leesburgvaholidayinn.com
This historic mansion provides a wonderful warm atmosphere and an experience not to be missed. There's a wide variety of entrees including specialty potato and sweet corn chowder with fresh lump crabmeat. On Sunday, from 7:00 A.M. to 2:00 P.M., enjoy an elegant brunch. Guests refer to the restaurant as "Leesburg's best-kept secret."

Red Fox Tavern $$$
2 East Washington Street, Middleburg
(540) 687-6301, (800) 223-1728
www.redfox.com

The Red Fox serves delicious traditional Virginia fare such as peanut soup and crab cakes, along with continental seafood, beef, and game dishes. Built in 1728, the tavern, believed to be the oldest continuously operating dining establishment in the Old Dominion, sits in a lovely 18th-century stone building in the middle of Middleburg, Hunt Country's premier antiquing and equine center. The restaurant serves lunch and dinner daily. Reservations are recommended.

Tuscarora Mill Restaurant   **$$**
203 Harrison Street SE, Leesburg
(703) 771-9300
www.tuskies.com
In a restored grain mill in Leesburg's historic Market Station complex, this restaurant serves regional American cuisine with international influences. Try the roasted salmon with stir-fry veggies. It's open for lunch and dinner daily.

Fauquier County

Ashby Inn & Restaurant   **$$$**
692 Federal Street, Paris
(540) 592-3900
www.ashbyinn.com
The Ashby Inn, one of the finest restaurants in the state, is nestled in the east end of Paris, Virginia. This Paris boasts a population of 61, but the Ashby Inn has been known to host more than that number for one of its famous brunches.

The small village was renamed from Punkinville to Paris in honor of the Marquis de Lafayette, who visited the area numerous times, including his last stop in the early 1820s. During the Civil War, Paris changed hands many times and was a critical property for John Singleton Mosby and his Confederate raiders. When innkeepers Roma and John Sherman moved to town in 1984, they took great care to renovate and preserve the early architecture of the 1829 residence.

The heart of this bed-and-breakfast inn is the kitchen. Many refer to the inn as a

"restaurant with rooms" (see our Bed-and-Breakfasts and Country Inns chapter). As the Shermans note, the daily menu is "limited, intelligent—and guided more by tradition than trend." Seasonal foods, including asparagus, shad, raspberries, soft-shell crab, lamb, and local game, set the tempo. On a recent evening, diners could choose among seven delectable main courses, ranging from braised oxtail on lemon polenta to grilled filet mignon with au poivre sauce. The inn's jumbo lump crab cakes are regarded as the region's best. Breads and desserts are all homemade. Herbs, cut flowers, and much of the summer produce come from the Shermans' own garden. Sunday brunch specialties include made-to-order omelets and Smithfield ham. The inn's wine list also changes regularly, but you most likely will find a tasty selection of sauvignon blancs and pinot noirs. There are four dining areas, including a converted kitchen complete with its walnut beams and a fireplace. *Washingtonian* magazine called Ashby Inn the "best place for a romantic date." Reservations are necessary.

The Depot Restaurant   **$$**
65 South Third Street, Warrenton
(540) 347-1212
Inside this historic restored train station you will find both American and Mediterranean cuisine, including salads, seafood, a Middle Eastern eggplant dish, veal piccata, and rack of lamb, and desserts including baklava, chocolate mousse, tarts, and pies. The airy dining room has 14 French doors that overlook a garden and restored caboose. Train memorabilia, such as lanterns and crossing signs, add to the classic decor. The Depot is open Tuesday though Saturday for dinner.

Fantastico-Ristorante Italiano Inn/
Lounge–Piano Bar   **$**
380 Broadview Avenue, Warrenton
(540) 349-2575
www.fantastico-inn.com
The Italian food here attracts plenty of locals who come for fresh seafood, veal,

lamb chops, and homemade pasta—served in the northern Italy tradition that emphasizes light wine sauces, capers, rosemary, olives, and the like. The Lounge–Piano Bar opens at 4:30 P.M. Tuesday for open-mike night, while Michael Heavens Band plays Thursday. Fantastico-Ristorante is open Monday through Friday for lunch and dinner and Saturday and Sunday for dinner only. Reservations are recommended.

Napoleon's   **$$**
67 Waterloo Street, Warrenton
(540) 347-4300
www.napoleonsrestaurant.com
Napoleon's serves continental cuisine. A regular menu is complemented by three daily specials that take advantage of whatever is fresh and good. Specialties include seafood croustade, a variety of seafood served in a puff pastry with cream sauce, and filet en croûte, a fillet wrapped in puff pastry, baked, sliced, and served with a Madeira sauce. Desserts are homemade. You can dine outside on the terrace during warm weather or inside by the fireplace during cold months. It's open for lunch and dinner Monday through Saturday and for brunch on Sunday. Reservations are suggested.

1763 Inn   **$$$**
10087 John Mosby Highway, Upperville
(540) 592-3848
www.1763inn.com
Megan and Bernie Kirchner have decorated their historic inn (which is as old as the name implies) with antiques and original art. The restaurant is divided into small, intimate dining rooms, one overlooking a lake where swans reside. The cuisine is contemporary American and nicely done, right down to the freshly made breads and desserts. The French-trained chef uses local produce and herbs from the herb garden. It's a delightful place to stay as well as dine (see our Bed-and-Breakfasts and Country Inns chapter), and history buffs can browse through the Civil War memorabilia in the sitting room

next to the bar. The dining room serves breakfast to inn guests every day. It's open Wednesday through Saturday for dinner. Sunday brunch is served from 11:30 A.M. to 2:30 P.M. Reservations are requested.

Rappahannock County

Bleu Rock Inn   **$$**
12567 Lee Highway (US 211), Washington
(540) 987-3190
www.bleurockinn.com
Owned by Jo Mariea, the Bleu Rock Inn is situated on 80 acres about an hour from the Washington, D.C., Beltway. The Inn's three dining rooms have fireplaces, and in warm weather, the terrace is a wonderful place to have dinner, drinks, or dessert. The food is French-American with an international flair; menus change weekly. It's open Wednesday through Sunday for dinner. The English pub is most popular in the winter with a full-service menu from 4:00 P.M. to midnight. Reservations are suggested. (For more information about an overnight stay at the Inn, see our Bed-and-Breakfasts and Country Inns chapter.)

Many of the restaurants that serve wine now offer selections from Virginia wineries. Ask for recommendations to go with your meal. It may well influence you to visit the winery.

Four & Twenty Blackbirds   **$$$$**
650 Zachary Taylor Highway, Flint Hill
(540) 675-1111
This wonderful restaurant is on the border of the Shenandoah Valley region, a short drive from Front Royal. For the past six years, it has made the *Washington Post's* top 100 and was in *Zagat's* top 40. Owners Heidi Morf and Vinnie DeLuise prepare creative American cuisine. The menu changes completely every three weeks so

that the cooks can take advantage of the best available seafood and local produce. The first-floor dining room is small but offers privacy for romantics; the tables are in nooks with screens of lace or floral prints. For dinner, guests can select from four appetizers, eight entrees, and three desserts. Appetizers have included apple-smoked bacon with corn relish and fried oysters on a bed of lemony shaved fennel and topped with spicy roasted bell peppers. Entrees have included beef fillet kebabs in a red wine sauce sparked with bleu cheese and walnuts and served with lemony sauteed potatoes and snow peas. Desserts are homemade and fabulous. The restaurant serves brunch on Sunday and dinner Wednesday through Saturday beginning at 5:30 P.M. Reservations are suggested. Four & Twenty Blackbirds is wheelchair accessible.

The Inn at Little Washington $$$$
Middle and Main Streets, Washington
(540) 675-3800

A little more than an hour's drive from the city, this highly acclaimed country inn is a favorite of Washington, D.C., media stars and politicians. Celebs can be spotted here several times a week; Paul Newman even spent his 64th birthday here.

In July 2004, Chef Patrick O'Connell created a special dinner for the Club des Chefs des Chefs. This exclusive club is made up of personal chefs to the heads of state from 25 nations, including to the king of Spain, the queen of England, the king of Thailand, and President George Bush.

So it should come as no surprise that you will spend big money for exquisite regional American cuisine complemented by a 15,000-bottle wine cellar. The restaurant, which has been praised worldwide, celebrated its 27th anniversary in 2004. O'Connell and Reinhardt Lynch recently completed a $5 million renovation and expansion that added a bar, and a lounge and has only enhanced what has been called the "most beautiful kitchen in the world." (It's hard to believe that this crown jewel had once been a garage.) Today, the kitchen houses a massive 16-foot Vulcan range, custom made in France. Adjacent is a combi oven, equipped with a brain capable of remembering 78 recipes. For a surcharge of $450 on top of the dinner charge, up to 12 people can dine in the kitchen and watch O'Connell and his staff in action. The menu changes daily, and guests are served a seven-course meal for a fixed price. O'Connell said he is not satisfied if a dinner is "good" or "fine"—he wants his meals to be among the best his diners have ever experienced. People worldwide who visit the Inn say it serves some of the best food in the world—no small claim. The menu also varies with the seasons: venison in the fall, lamb in the spring. Wondering how fancy a menu this five-star restaurant has? Try the chilled goose foie gras with rhubarb Riesling sauce and fleur de sel. Other favorites have included boudin blanc on sauerkraut braised in Virginia Riesling, seared duck foie gras on polenta with country ham and huckleberries, and local rabbit braised in apple cider with wild mushrooms and garlic mashed potatoes. A vegetarian menu also is available. Their desserts are artistic creations of beauty and flavor. Try the Seven Deadly Sins, chocolate desserts of varying intensity, or the house-made sorbets arranged on a painter's palette. The wine list is impeccable, and for an additional $60 a person, the sommelier will pair a by-the-glass selection to match your courses.

On Saturday, dinner costs $158 per person, not including tax, tip, or wine. Monday, Wednesday, and Thursday the price is $118; Friday, it's $128. The restaurant is open for dinner every day except Tuesday, but during the busy months of May and October, dinner is served every day. A 10-course tasting menu is offered, paired with wine. Reservations are required and, in fact, can be hard to come by. (See our Bed-and-Breakfasts and Country Inns chapter for information on the inn.) The Inn is wheelchair accessible. Guests may dress comfortably; women usually wear cocktail dresses or pants suits.

Culpeper County

Hazel River Inn Restaurant   **$$**
195 East Davis Street, Culpeper
(540) 825-7148
www.hazelriverinn.com
At first glance, the thing you might notice about this establishment is its large hardware sign painted like a banner across the top; however, don't judge too harshly. The building that houses the Hazel River Inn Restaurant has a distinguished history. The corner brick building is said to be the oldest commercial building in Culpeper's Historic Downtown, occupying part of the 1759 plat of the town. The building is listed on the Virginia Register of Historic Places. The original building area has handmade brick, hand-hewn and pegged timbers, and wide pine floors. The rear portion was built about 1790, while the front dates back to 1835. The first level on the corner of East Street and East Davis Street has been used as a stable and a tobacco warehouse, among other businesses. The lower level was used as a Civil War jail for both the North and South armies.

Today you will find casual, fine dining and an international wine list. The menu features dinner entrees such as roasted stuffed quail, hazelnut veal medallions, seafood grill, Virginia bison tenderloin served with bourbon mustard glacé, and grilled duck breast with carmelized mango. The dessert choices are just as adventuresome—don't leave without trying the homemade hazelnut ice cream. The restaurant is open Thursday through Monday with a fixed-price Sunday brunch. It is closed Tuesday and Wednesday. On the weekends a piano player performs in the restaurant, with more live entertainment downstairs in the pub.

Inn at Kelly's Ford   **$$$**
16589 Edwards Shop Road, Remington
(540) 399-1779
www.innatkellysford.com
The Inn at Kelly's Ford may be a little difficult to find because it requires navigating several very small country roads, but it certainly is worth the trip. The sight of this expansive estate with its stately buildings and white fences sprawling across rich green hills will leave you breathless. Located on the historic site of the Kelly's Ford Civil War Battlefield, the Inn is set on 150 acres, part of a larger 500-acre estate. Dining takes place in the Main House, originally built circa 1779 and serving as a home for the Kelly family during the Civil War. Bill and Linda Willoughby opened the Inn at Kelly's Ford in 2000 as an elegant place to dine as well as stay the night.

The intimate 30-seat restaurant overlooks the scenic countryside. A large stone hearth, candelabra, and pewter plates add to the atmosphere. Start your meal with an appetizer of duck terrine with goose liver, followed by a sumptuous entree of loin of venison with cranberry sauce or an angus filet mignon with roquefort sauce. Pheasant as well as several seafood selections round out the menu, but don't forget to choose a delicious homemade dessert. Menu items do vary depending on the seasons and the chef's decisions. Dinner is served Wednesday through Sunday and reservations are recommended. Brunch is served on Sunday. If you've been out exploring all day and want something more casual, take the stairs down to the cozy and cheerful Pelham's Pub, where you can warm up by another large fireplace while enjoying a bowl of the homemade soup of the day, onion rings, a burger, crab cake sandwich, or lasagna. While you're there, you can try your hand at the billiard table or watch a game on the television. You can even learn a little Civil War history by taking in the large mural of a Civil War battle, as well as all the memorabilia and photos along the walls, including one of John Pelham. The Pub is open daily for lunch and dinner. There is also live acoustic music on Friday and Saturday evenings. (See our Bed-and-Breakfast and Country Inns chapter for more on the Inn.)

Kirstens   **$$**
219 East Davis Street, Culpeper
(540) 829-8400
This is a lively little place in the heart of

Culpeper, located in what's called the Taft building. A mixture of modern and old style, the cafe has hardwood floors, a purple ceiling, a brick wall on one side, and dark green wallpaper with yellow swirls on the other. There are dark wooden chairs and tables, a fireplace, and wood posts. A large picture window and door at front and back ends of the building provide natural light throughout the restaurant. The bar at the other door has the cold ones. Come to Kirstens for a Reuben or club sandwich, soup and salad, or pizza for lunch, or for a favorite dinner item such as tomato basil chicken or beef tips. There's usually a steak special and a pasta du jour. A children's menu is also available. Breakfast, lunch, and dinner are on tap Monday through Saturday. Breakfast and lunch are served only on Sunday.

It's About Thyme $$
128 East Davis Street, Culpeper
(540) 825-4264

A small but very cute place, It's About Thyme sits on one of the busiest streets in downtown Culpeper. Its wide glass front with wrought-iron trim, flower boxes, and colorful awning draping over iron chairs and tables on the sidewalk patio invite you in. The food here is European country-style and includes cooking with a lot of herbs. The menu may vary, but a favorite is the roasted pork with sauerkraut and creamy potatoes. Or you could try the nut-crusted salmon or the penne with veal. There's ravioli filled with lobster or smoked chicken, depending on the chef's whim. The variety of flavors is shown in the beef choices on the menu—from an old-fashioned pot roast with peppercorns to beef that is marinated and grilled with chow-chow and Havana hot sauce. There are always plenty of specials—for dinner and lunch. Also unforgettable is the decor. A huge mural of Lake Como and Palazzo Pitti in Florence decorate the walls, while a wood-burning oven, vintage oak tables, and the rough wood and pressed ceiling finish off the catchy façade. Lunch and dinner are served Tuesday through Saturday.

Madison County

The Bavarian Chef $$
U.S. Highway 29, 5 miles south of Madison
(540) 948-6505
www.thebavarianchefatrestaurant.com

This restaurant a few miles north of Charlottesville serves huge portions of family-style German cuisine. The food is extraordinary, especially the sauerbraten and homemade desserts, which include a Bavarian nutball and Tiroler apfelstrudel with vanilla sauce. You can also order conventional American seafood dishes. Reservations are suggested. The restaurant serves dinner Wednesday through Sunday.

Bertines North $$
206 South Main Street, Madison
(540) 948-3463
www.bertinesnorth.com

It looks like a stately old Virginia home with a wraparound porch and towering shade trees, but step inside and you'll feel like you've landed in the Caribbean: The inviting aroma of chef Bernard Poticha's special gumbo fills the air as you take in the colorful walls, a deep-sea blue in one dining room, salmon pink in the other. Steel band reggae plays lightly in the background. Bernard's wife, Christine, is happy to discuss the colorful art they use to decorate their 12-year-old restaurant. Sea fans adorn the walls; large shells surround the fireplace; there are original paintings by a Caribbean artist, still others by the artist's two sons, a mantel filled with Haitian wood carvings, and more brought back from the Potichas' 10-year stay in the Caribbean. The couple, who met and married in Chicago, settled in St. Martin, where they ran a popular restaurant and guest house. When their son was born, they decided to move back to the States, so they brought their combination of Creole, Cajun, Italian, and French recipes to the foothills of the Blue Ridge.

Their crab cakes and "steak on a hot rock" are local favorites, and you can order Jamaican-style jerk chicken by request.

But those in search of a real Caribbean treat might be enticed to sample the conch stew, blackened swordfish, or shrimp curry. Bernard has flavorful spices on most of the Creole selections, but he also offers a dish of his homemade hot sauce if you prefer to pep things up a bit. Beer and wine complement the meals, or you can have Key lime soda or nonalcoholic ginger beer. Save room for dessert: Bertines offers homemade pecan pie, coconut tart, chocolate mousse, rhubarb cake (in season), and a delightful Key lime pie. In the warmer months, dining is also available on the front porch. Dinner is served beginning at 6:00 P.M. by reservation Monday through Friday. The couple say the restaurant will be "open until closing," but the last service is usually around 9:00 P.M.

Graves Mountain Lodge $$
Off Highway 670, Syria
(540) 923-4231
www.gravesmountain.com
Folks come from miles around for this abundant Southern fare. Long pine tables seat locals and travelers, many of whom stay in the lodge's overnight accommodations (see our Bed-and-Breakfasts and Country Inns chapter). Using foods fresh from the Graves garden, chefs prepare country-style favorites such as Southern fried chicken, pan-fried trout, and tasty Virginia ham. Meal prices include the whole spread, beverage to dessert (which you will want to be sure to save room for). Saturday and Sunday nights and Sunday lunch are buffet-style; otherwise, it's family-style service. You can count on getting plenty to eat—too much, if you're not careful. These meals are popular, so call well in advance for reservations.

The Lodge welcomes families and has plenty to do for everyone. After dinner, if you're not too full to leave your chair, take a hike on one of the trails that crisscross the Lodge grounds or drop a pole in a nearby fishing spot. Or just sit back on one of the many porch rockers while the kids play games in the recreation room. The

Lodge is closed from the first Sunday after Thanksgiving until March 19.

The Grille at Prince Michel $$
US 29, Leon
(540) 547-9720, (800) 800-WINE
www.princemichel.com
In 2003 Prince Michel made an extensive renovation to its formal restaurant and now features the best of wine country cuisine in a casual atmosphere. The ambience of the restaurant leaves no doubt that you have arrived in Virginia wine country. The furniture is created from reclaimed oak wine barrels, while Prince Michel, Madison, and Rapidan River wine bottles line the length of one wall. Even the large windows in the banquet room overlook the Prince Michel's vineyards.

Executive Chef Bob Heck brings wine country cuisine to Central Virginia. A graduate of Baltimore International College, School of Culinary Arts, Heck has worked in professional kitchens for 20 years with chefs such as Jan Birmbaum, Roland Passot, and Todd Muir. All three are known to pair bold flavors and outstanding wine in a symbiotic relationship. The seasonal menu, developed by Heck, changes to highlight the local cuisine, including Muskrat Farms Rabbit. The lunch menu items range from roasted butternut squash soup sprinkled with curried cashews to the eclectic prosciutto and asparagus wrap with Boursin cheese to a taste of home-style Bell Evans Farm chicken pot pie. For dinner, start with Prince Edward Island steamed mussels simmered in Graves Brothers apple cider and Prince Michel Pinot Grigio with Nodines applewood smoked bacon and sage. The entrees include a sesame-crusted tuna loin, pan-seared and served medium rare on Wasabi potato cake and spinach with a ginger lemongrass broth and Black Angus sirloin served with bleu cheese scalloped potatoes, grilled asparagus, and onion jam on the side.

For customers looking for a special Sunday treat, the Grille is serving a brunch buffet with delights such as applewood smoked bacon, grits with garlic and cheese, crab cakes, chicken piccata, and made-to-order omelets.

The Grille is open Thursday through Saturday for lunch and dinner and on Sunday for brunch.

Greene County

Blue Ridge Cafe $$
8315 Seminole Trail, Ruckersville
(434) 985-3633
www.blueridgecafe.com

If you are looking for good American cuisine in a relaxed atmosphere, drop by Blue Ridge Cafe right off US 29. Shawn Hayes, owner of the cafe, serves a mixture of American grill with an international flair. Besides burgers, you can order barbecue ribs, steaks, crab cakes, seafood, Mediterranean salads, and pan-seared flounder. Past specialties have included lobster scampi and steak imperial. The Blue Ridge also has a full bar. The cafe is casual with black carpet and white walls in high gloss and black crown molding. Decor also includes oak tabletops and lots of mirrors and plants, which gives it a fresh, open feeling. Visitors include tourists as well as businesspeople meeting over power lunches, so you'll feel comfortable in jeans or a suit. The cafe is open for lunch and dinner seven days a week. Sunday brunch, a local favorite, is served from 10:00 A.M. to 2:00 P.M. Reservations are requested for parties of seven or more.

The Lafayette $$
146 Main Street, Stanardsville
(434) 985-6345
www.thelafayette.com

Whitt Ledford and Nick Spencer decided to give the folks in Greene County a place where they can go and feel special, so the partners from Charlottesville began remodeling the stately 1840 building on Main Street. During the Civil War, it was used as an office for the Confederate army during the Battle of Stanardsville. The new owners tried to make the interior look as it might

have appeared in 1840. While the dining room has a formal feel, you will be comfortable whether you are decked out in coat and tie or wearing khakis and a polo shirt. The menu features a variety of regional American dishes including mountain trout almondine, braised duckling, and lamb chops. Save room for the homemade desserts. Wine, cocktails, and beer are available. Lunch and dinner are served Tuesday through Saturday, with a popular brunch served on Sunday.

Vinny's New York Pizza & Pasta $
US 29 in Countryside Square Shopping Center, Ruckersville
(434) 985-4731

In 1988 Vinny decided to leave Long Island and set up shop in Greene County, and for the past 16 years, customers have been willing to make the drive from Albemarle and Madison Counties to savor the authentic Italian dishes and gourmet pizzas. One of their trademarks is the 18-inch pizza, one of the largest made in town. The family-owned restaurant caters to a family crowd and includes special selections for children younger than 12. Adults may choose from a wide variety of pizzas, pastas, salads, calzones, and heroes. Dinners also range from steak and eggplant parmigiana to veal cutlet. Beer and wine are available. The restaurant is open daily for lunch and dinner.

Orange County

Palladio Restaurant $$$$
17055 Winery Road, Barboursville
(540) 832-7848
www.palladiorestaurant.com

Visiting the Barboursville Vineyards is a real treat, and what can make it even more special is a delicious meal at the Palladio Restaurant. This warm and cheerful restaurant features Northern Italian cuisine and uses fresh seasonal produce and the finest regional and imported ingredients. The entire staff travels to Italy annually to retain the authenticity, and in 2002 executive chef Melissa Close spent time cooking at Piemonte's renowned Ristorante da Guido, one of Italy's top five restaurants. Here at Palladio you can enjoy lunch Wednesday through Sunday, and dinner Friday and Saturday. You can choose a two-, three- or four-course lunch, with or without pairings of suggested wines, or a four-course dinner with or without suggested wines. The four-course dinner with wines will run you $75. Start off with antipasti, such as smoked salmon over celeriac salad and mosto olive oil or a chilled shrimp salad served with shaved fennel, baby rucola, and orange vinaigrette. The next course could be potato gnocchi with Gorgonzola and walnuts, or homemade fettuccine with pine nuts, goat cheese, and pear tomatoes, just to name a few. The main course choices include pan-seared tuna served with polenta, asparagus, and black olive tapenade; roasted duck breast; and chicken and veal dishes. Very popular is the Guest Chef Series. On select Saturdays through the year, chefs from other restaurants are invited to create a four-course dinner, paired with a superb Barboursville vintage with each course. Reservations are required for dinner.

Willow Grove Inn $$$$
14079 Plantation Way, Orange
(540) 672–5982, (800) 949-1778
www.willowgroveinn.com
Limoges china, crystal chandeliers, Chippendale chairs . . . you get the picture. This elegant plantation home, built in 1778, is now a full-service inn with a sensational restaurant. The regional American cuisine is the most contemporary thing about this magnificent place. The menu changes frequently depending upon the season, but four-course meals have included such items as bourbon molasses-glazed quail with herbed sweet potato cakes or smoked Rag Mountain trout with horseradish cream. Desserts are homemade and truly scrumptious. The friendly bartender will help guests select an appropriate wine for dinner. The menu suggests a particular

wine for each entree and offers a full range of dessert wines, after-dinner liqueurs, and dessert coffees. Reservations are recommended. Dinner is served Thursday through Saturday, with brunch also offered on Sunday. Clark's Pub also serves entrees.

Charlottesville

Aberdeen Barn $$$
2018 Holiday Drive, Charlottesville
(434) 296–4630
www.aberdeenbarn.com
This is a well-established restaurant known for its roast prime rib and charcoal-grilled steak. But you can also have lamb chops, Australian lobster tail, crab cakes, shrimp scampi, and other seafood delights here. The atmosphere is candlelit and intimate, and the Sportsman's Lounge has live entertainment several nights a week. Reservations are suggested. Dinner is served from 5:00 to 10:00 P.M. daily.

Baja Bean Co. $
1327 West Main Street, Charlottesville
(434) 293–4507
www.bajabean.com
On the Corner near the Rotunda, this California-style Mexican restaurant serves up lighter meals than the typical Tex-Mex fare. When owner Ron Morse moved here from San Diego, he brought the healthier California sensibility with him. The vegetarian specialties for lunch and dinner are especially popular. A full bar offers 11 Mexican beers and 24 brands of tequila. All dishes are freshly made, including hot and mild salsas. The festive restaurant is decorated with banners and T-shirts from Puerto Vallarta,

Just as in our big-city counterparts, expect a three- to seven-course dinner at a fine restaurant to be an event in and of itself. So don't make a date for dinner and a movie. Enjoy the time to savor the meal.

Cancun, Cozumel, and other Mexican hot spots. Baja Bean Co. is open daily for lunch and dinner; expect to wait for a table on weekends. Reservations are not accepted. (Also see our Nightlife chapter.)

Biltmore Grill $
16 Elliewood Avenue, Charlottesville
(434) 293-6700
One of the most attractive things about this restaurant is the wisteria-covered arbor that shades an outdoor dining area. A popular restaurant for UVA students, the place serves pasta dishes, unusual and hearty salads, and much more. You'll find a wide selection of imported and domestic beer. The dessert menu includes such yummy items as a Tollhouse Cookie Pie, grasshopper pie, and warm apple crisp. The Biltmore is open daily for lunch and dinner. (Also see our Nightlife chapter.)

Blue Bird Cafe $
625 West Main Street, Charlottesville
(434) 295-1166
Enjoy innovative cuisine in a casual, eclectic atmosphere at this cafe in the historic downtown area. Whether you choose to dine outdoors on the patio or inside, you'll find the experience enjoyable. A diverse menu includes fresh seafood, hand-cut prime beef, poultry, and pasta dishes. This is the home of what the menu touts as "World Famous Blue Bird Crab Cakes." Fine French, American, and Virginia wines are served, as are domestic, imported, and microbrewery beers. Full bar service and cappuccino and espresso complement your meal, which simply must include one of the delicious homemade desserts. The Blue Bird is open for lunch and dinner daily. Brunch is served on Saturday and

Sunday. Dinner reservations are accepted. Ample parking is available.

The Boar's Head Inn
(Old Mill Room) $$$$
(The Cafe) $$
U.S. Highway 250 W., Charlottesville
(434) 296-2181, (800) 476-1988
www.boarsheadinn.com
The Boar's Head Inn's Old Mill Room is a restored 1834 gristmill serving regional fare accompanied by a nationally recognized wine list. The menu changes about four times each year, but some of the chef's specialties are grilled filet mignon, pork tenderloin, and tandoori-dusted Maine lobster. Sunday brunches here are impressive: omelets and Belgian waffles made to order, pastries, breads, cheeses, smoked fish, breakfast meats, and egg dishes, among other items. Reservations are required in the Old Mill Room for dinner and are suggested for lunch and breakfast. It's open daily. The less formal cafe offers guests elegant dining in a casual atmosphere. There is a healthy, all-American menu for lunch and dinner Monday through Saturday, plus a weekday evening light-fare lounge menu. Boar's Head has been rated a Four-Diamond restaurant for the past 16 years. (See our Resorts chapter for more information on the inn.)

Bodo's Bagel Bakery and New York
Sandwich Shop $
Preston Avenue and Harris Street
Charlottesville
(434) 293-5224

Emmet Street and US 250 bypass
Charlottesville
(434) 977-9598
Some of the best bagels in town. Sandwiches emphasize fresh, simple ingredients with some unusual twists such as a hummus and sprouts sandwich. Most everything is good but take note of the Caesar salad, "everything" bagel, and delicious soups. Atmosphere is lively and loud, with great music playing all day long. Both kids and adults love this place

Some of the wineries, such as Barboursville and Chateau Morrisette, feature charming restaurants where the ambience combines with succulent dishes that pair nicely with their vintages.

because of its easy rhythms and wonderful food. Both locations are open daily for breakfast, lunch, and dinner.

The Brick Oven $
1966 Seminole Trail
Rio Hill Shopping Center, Charlottesville
(434) 978-7898

A favorite with locals, the Brick Oven is the place to go for the most creative ideas in pizza. This modest restaurant, inside the Rio Hill shopping center, is cozy and spacious inside, always packed with a talkative, energetic crowd of couples, families, and college kids. Not only is there a variety of meat topping pizzas such as the Puaka Tunu (roasted pig), with as much meat as you can stand—pepperoni, ham, bacon, sausage, prosciutto—there's also the big cheese, topped with mozzarella, Parmesan, Swiss, cheddar, and tomato sauce. You can also get a no-cheese pizza, several selections of veggie pizzas, or three pizzas with chicken. Too tame? Try the Tu'i Tonga, a pizza topped with grilled chicken, pineapple, cheddar cheese, and bacon with the house ranch dressing as the sauce. They also let you create your own—go crazy with your choice of a base: basil pesto, ranch dressing, barbecue, creamy ricotta cheese, or, of course, tomato sauce. Not in the mood for pizza? There's lasagna, baked ziti, and other delicious pasta choices along with crab cakes and steak. But be prepared to wait, especially on a weekend night, unless you have reservations. While there, take a peek at their unique oven. All the pizzas are cooked in a wood-burning brick oven. Did we mention the Brick Oven has one of the town's favorite salad bars with more than 25 items, including pasta salad and soups?

C & O Restaurant $$
515 East Water Street, Charlottesville
(434) 971-7044
www.candorestaurant.com

For more than 25 years, dining at this celebrated establishment has been noteworthy. In fact, William Rice, editor-in-chief of *Food and Wine* magazine, said, "I can con-fidently assure you that not since Jefferson was serving imported vegetables and the first ice cream at Monticello has there been more innovative cooking in these parts than at the C & O Restaurant." Well, in 1997 owner Dave Simpson changed the setup to what has been called a marriage of both worlds. It's a little less formal and a lot less expensive, with a new menu.

The C & O has three areas for dining, including upstairs and the third-floor mezzanine. A new patio allows for warm-weather dining outdoors. On the lower floor, you'll find the bistro, a boisterous and lively place. Although it changes frequently, the menu has featured rainbow trout in parchment with oven-roasted tomatoes, pan-seared liver with pommery mustard sauce, and butternut squash ravioli with wild mushroom broth. Crème brûlée and walnut tarts are favorite dessert choices. The C & O has maintained its extensive wine list, including some very old wines. The restaurant is open daily for dinner. There is also a late-night menu with soups, salads, desserts, and coffee served until 2:00 A.M. Reservations are recommended.

Carmello's $$
400 Emmet Street, Charlottesville
(434) 977-5200
www.restaurantsdiningmenu.com

It's no wonder that a variety of professionals found Carmello's. It's right across the street from University Hall, the site that hundreds of UVA alumni visit regularly to watch their alma mater play basketball. But it's a combination of quality Northern Italian cuisine, reasonable prices, and an atmosphere of comfortable elegance that keeps Carmello's alumni coming back for more. Along with daily chef's highlights, there are between 40 and 50 items on the menu, including veal, fish, and chicken, all served with pasta. Carmello's also offers an extensive wine list. It's open daily for dinner. Lunch is available Monday through Friday with a brunch served Saturday and Sunday. Reservations are recommended.

College Inn $
1511 University Avenue, Charlottesville
(434) 977-2710
www.thecollegeinn.com

This University Corner landmark serves a wide assortment of Greek, Italian, and American dishes. As the name suggests, it's a popular dining spot and watering hole among the university crowd but also caters to a loyal following of Charlottesville natives and tourists. The restaurant is open daily for breakfast, lunch, and dinner. The inn also offers free delivery to a limited area.

Coupe deVille's $
9 Elliewood Avenue, Charlottesville
(434) 977-3966

This is a busy place that attracts scores of UVA students. The food is inexpensive but sophisticated. You can get fresh pasta that's made locally, along with sandwiches, seafood, and homemade soups. A rotisserie cooks Peruvian-style chickens. You can dine indoors or outdoors on the garden terrace (even in the rain, since there's an awning). Coupe deVille's is open weekdays for lunch in the spring and summer and Monday through Saturday for dinner. There is also live entertainment from 10:00 P.M. to 2:00 A.M. most nights.

Court Square Tavern $
Fifth and Jefferson Streets
Charlottesville
(434) 296-6111

This bar on historic Court Square is a watering hole for lawyers and other professionals in town. No wonder. It has between 135 and 150 bottled beers from around the world and a huge array of beers on tap as well as hard apple cider. The tavern-style menu includes, among others, homemade soups, sandwiches, and grilled bratwurst.

The British pub atmosphere features antique mirrors and engravings, a stained-glass window, and copper-topped bar. The tavern is open from lunchtime until midnight Monday through Saturday.

Escafe $
227 West Main Street, Charlottesville
(434) 295-8668
www.escafe.com

This popular restaurant, next to the Omni Hotel, serves American cuisine with Asian accents. The menu, which changes seasonally with daily specials, includes vegetarian dishes, fine aged meats, and seafood complemented by an extensive wine list. Escafe is a bistro, where most entrees are priced between $10 and $18. Co-owner and chef Sean Concannon is a graduate of the Johnson and Wales Culinary Arts School. Escafe is open Tuesday through Sunday on the Historic Downtown Mall. They specialize in private parties.

Hamiltons' $$
101 West Main Street, Charlottesville
(434) 295-6649
www.hamiltonsrestaurant.com

The husband-and-wife team of Kate and Bill Hamilton each had spent nearly a decade working in the food industry when they decided it was time to go into business for themselves. Six years ago, they opened their own stylish contemporary American restaurant on the Historic Downtown Mall, and Hamiltons' quickly won raves as one of the best restaurants in town. The decor is striking. It's light, some would say hip. But Bill Hamilton says their goal was to create a cross-cultural atmosphere with their decor and food. The menu changes every two weeks or so but always includes fresh seafood, meats, and pasta, complemented by an eclectic wine list. If Nasi Goreng is on the menu, try it. The spicy Indonesian-style stir-fry includes shrimp, grilled chicken, and smoked pork. All desserts and breads are made in-house, and there is a full bar. Patio dining is available when the weather permits. Hamiltons' is open for lunch and dinner Monday through Saturday. Reservations are recommended. Tables book well in advance on the weekends, and the lunches are very popular, too.

The Hardware Store Restaurant　$
316 East Main Street, Charlottesville
(434) 977-1518, (800) 426-6001

The Grand Old Hardware Store Building, a city landmark since 1895, houses this restaurant that offers a huge variety of food. Inside the central dining area, you'll see the same ladders and shelves that belonged to the old hardware store, which operated continuously from 1895 to 1976. This was the original sales area. On the Water Street end of the restaurant, the hardware store's offices have been transformed into dining rooms, and you can see the original typewriters and adding machines used by the store's clerical workers decades ago. A city block long, the Hardware Store building—also home to an art gallery, book shop, and jewelry store—also has a new entrance on Water Street, conveniently across from a parking garage. The restaurant, open for lunch and dinner Monday through Saturday, is known for its generous portions in beverages, sandwiches, and salads. Ribs, pasta, mesquite-grilled chicken, and crepes are also on the menu. If you simply want to satisfy your sweet tooth, choose from pastries or order a treat from the old-fashioned soda fountain. You'll find plenty of free parking at the Water Street door.

HotCakes　$
1137-A Emmet Street, Charlottesville
(434) 295-6037
www.hotcakes.biz

No, it's not a pancake house. HotCakes, in the Barracks Road Shopping Center, has a bakery, gourmet take-out counter, and an eat-in lunch menu. The prices are high, but the food is worth it. Homemade pastries, pies, and cakes are fabulous. Many local residents buy take-home meals or use the popular catering service. Families of UVA students also call to have birthday cakes and care packages delivered to students. HotCakes is open daily for lunch and dinner. It stays open until 8:00 P.M. on Friday and Saturday and 6:00 P.M. on Sunday.

The Ivy Inn　$$$
2244 Old Ivy Road, Charlottesville
(434) 977-1222
www.ivyinnrestaurant.com

Transport yourself back to Jefferson's time at the Ivy Inn. Fine china, tablecloths, and candlelight set the stage for wonderfully elegant regional food with international influences. This manor house, with its high ceilings and Virginia Colonial-style decor, was rebuilt in 1817. Dine in one of several inviting rooms either upstairs or downstairs; whatever your choice, you'll want to linger over these relaxing meals. Warm-weather days will take you outside for romantic patio dining.

The menu features modern American cuisine with European flair. A specialty of the house is rack of lamb, served a variety of ways, depending on the season and the mood of the chef. It's tender and savory, with delicate flavors you will enjoy. Desserts are, of course, homemade, so save room. The Inn is closed Sunday. You'll find the Inn just off the US 250 bypass, 1 mile west of the University of Virginia.

L'Aventura　$$
220 West Market Street, Charlottesville
(434) 977-1912

This cozy little place next to the Vinegar Hill Theater bills itself as Italian country cooking and is one of the few restaurants on Charlottesville's Historic Downtown Mall that you will find open on a holiday such as New Year's Day. Choose from such succulent items as grilled rack of lamb with eggplant and zucchini caponata and grilled polenta to daily fresh pasta and grilled pizza specials. The restaurant, owned by Ann Porotti and David Wyatt, was the winner of the 2001, 2002, and 2003 *Wine Spectator* Awards for their wine list.

Little John's　$
1427 University Avenue, Charlottesville
(434) 977-0588

Be it lunchtime or the middle of the night, Little John's is the place to go if you've got a hankering for a New York–style deli sandwich. Open 24 hours a day, Little John's is on the Corner, a short walk from the Rotunda at UVA. Specialties are the Nuclear Sub (a combo of coleslaw, turkey, barbecue, and mozzarella) and the Baby Zonker (a bagel with cream cheese, bacon, tomatoes, and onions).

Martha's Cafe $
11 Elliewood Avenue, Charlottesville
(434) 971-7530

This is a popular place on the Corner, and it's no wonder. The food is freshly made, interesting, and reasonably priced, and the atmosphere is casual. Martha's has been around since 1976. The menu emphasizes chicken and fish, and nothing is deep-fried. It's known for its crab cakes, but another popular item is the sesame chicken salad with peanut-garlic dressing. The cafe is situated in an old house with an enormous elm tree out front. You can dine indoors or, in spring or summer, outside on a cobblestone patio under the elm tree. As with most of the restaurants on crowded Elliewood Avenue, you need to park in the centrally located parking garage. Martha's is open daily for lunch and dinner, with a brunch on Saturday and Sunday.

Michie Tavern $$
683 Thomas Jefferson Parkway
Charlottesville
(434) 977-1234
www.michietavern.com

At Michie Tavern, a 200-year-old converted log house called the Ordinary serves a sumptuous lunch buffet of fried chicken, black-eyed peas, stewed tomatoes, coleslaw, potato salad, green bean salad, beets, homemade biscuits, corn bread, and apple cobbler every day of the year. It's a taste of early America with recipes dating back to the 1700s. Even the servers are dressed in attire from the eighteenth century. Lunch costs $13.50, not including beverage, dessert, or tax. Children younger than 5 eat for free.

Monsoon $
113 West Market Street, Charlottesville
(434) 971-1515

Born in Taiwan and raised in Southeast Asia, owner and chef Lu-Mei Chang fuses the strong, direct flavors of the Orient to create startlingly delicious cuisine. The flavors are simple and the ingredients fresh—lemongrass and basil are staples. A personal favorite is Pad Thai, rice noodles and vegetables seasoned with tamarind juice and fish sauce and served with either seafood, chicken, beef, or vegetables—you won't be disappointed with this choice. Squid is tenderly cooked and expertly seasoned in all the dishes—a great seafood choice. The drinks list is extensive, with lots of exotic teas, Asian sodas, and beers. And a note about the decor: It's one-of-a-kind, 1950s and '60s decor, with original lamps on each table and smoky-colored graffiti art by artist Steven Keene from floor to ceiling. Some tables and chairs are even covered with his work, which creates an artsy yet intimate atmosphere. It's open for lunch Monday through Friday and dinner every night. Outdoor seating is available.

Northern Exposure $
1202 West Main Street, Charlottesville
(434) 977-6002
www.northernex.com

You'll find wholesome American food, or "big" food as the managers call it, at this spot, a short walk from the University of Virginia and a few minutes' drive from the Downtown Mall area. They also pride themselves as having the only rooftop dining in town. The menu is diverse, with dishes ranging from homemade pizza to New York strips. Pasta dishes include ravioli, lasagna, and linguine. The restaurant's biggest seller is broiled bistro steak sauteed in red wine with garlic and served with fresh mushrooms. The atmosphere is casual. A large patio is great for outdoor dining when weather permits. The restaurant's theme is New York, with photos of famous New York landmarks on the walls and items such as Bronx cheesecake (it's actually made in the Bronx) on the menu. Homemade desserts include tiramisu and Key lime pie. A children's menu is also available. Northern Exposure is open daily for lunch and dinner and for Sunday brunch. There is free parking in the back.

Rapture $$
303 East Main Street, Charlottesville
(434) 293-9526
Take a stroll down the Historic Downtown Mall of Charlottesville and you'll find this colorful place with its bright purple neon sign. Inside you'll find more wild decor in dramatic purple, black, and red. The atmosphere is laid-back, the food good and varied—from a tasty bowl of French onion soup, to thick pork chops and hearty hamburgers, to several choices of spicy Thai bowls. This is a good place for dinner and a fun evening, as there are billiards and nightlife available. You can play a game of pool in the back of the restaurant, next to the bar, or climb the winding metal steps to the upstairs, where there are four more tables. The restaurant expanded to include a dance floor and dance club, where double-feature movies are shown free on Sunday.

Rococo's $$
Hydraulic Road and Commonwealth Drive in the Village Green
Charlottesville
(434) 971-7371
The quest to find the restaurant most favored by locals would bring many a visitor to Rococo's, an elegant but casual Italian restaurant featuring homemade ravioli, fettuccine, mesquite-grilled seafood and meats, gourmet pizza, and more. Since 1988 Rococo's has emphasized the freshest ingredients and creative interpretations of traditional Italian dishes. Some of its specialties are wild mushroom pizza, free-range chicken marsala marinated in balsamic vinegar and rosemary, and house specialty tortellini bellisima. Desserts, such as cheesecake and chocolate toffee ice-cream pie, are homemade and fabulous.

The restaurant has an award-winning wine list and a full-service bar. It's open

for lunch Monday through Friday, brunch on Sunday, and dinner every night. Reservations are accepted and families are welcome.

Saigon Cafe $
1703 Allied Lane, Charlottesville
(434) 296-8661
The atmosphere is relaxed and comfortable at Charlottesville's first Vietnamese restaurant. Some of the specialties of the house are Vietnamese egg rolls served with fish sauce and grilled lemon chicken. The soups are especially noteworthy. Chinese lunch specials are amazingly inexpensive. Saigon Cafe is open daily for lunch and dinner.

St. Maarten Cafe $
1400 Wertland Street, Charlottesville
(434) 293-2233
www.stmaartencafe.com
This is a favorite of UVA students—a place to forget your troubles and imagine you're far away on a tropical island. It has a late-night menu from 11:00 P.M. to 2:00 A.M. The cafe serves a lot of fresh seafood and burgers, and all the soups are made from scratch. St. Maarten Cafe, on the Corner near the college campus and hospital, is open every day until the wee hours; Sunday brunch is also served. It gets crowded on Tuesday, when a double-wing special brings in crowds of UVA students.

Silver Thatch Inn $$$
3001 Hollymead Drive at US 29 North Charlottesville
(434) 978-4686
www.silverthatch.com
The menu changes every six weeks or so at this exquisite, candlelit restaurant in a beautiful ca. 1780 inn (see our Bed-and-Breakfasts and Country Inns chapter). The Silver Thatch serves upscale regional American cuisine, with an emphasis on fresh produce. Two typical entrees are grilled breast of duck and grilled certified Angus filet mignon. There is also a vegetarian dish on the menu. The wine list is all-American, with an emphasis on those from California and

Virginia, and the recent addition of vintages from Washington and Oregon. Desserts are homemade, beautifully presented, and mouthwatering, such as passion-fruit cheesecake and tiramisu. Reservations are recommended. Dinner is served Tuesday through Saturday.

Southern Culture $$
633 West Main Street, Charlottesville
(434) 979-1990

This hip cafe and restaurant serves southern coastal cuisine. Try the seafood-okra gumbo and sweet potato fries. The bright and lively atmosphere creates an exciting place for dining and chatting with friends or a loved one. The bar is a lively gathering place for intellectuals and artists of all sorts. The restaurant and bar are open daily for dinner and drinks and Sunday for brunch. Free parking is available. A patio opened in the spring of 2002.

Spudnut Coffee Shop $
309 Avon Street, Charlottesville
(434) 296-0590

You can't say you've had a true taste of Charlottesville until you've stopped by this popular doughnut shop. For 35 years, Richard F. Wingfield has been up before dawn, kneading, shaping, and baking his unique breakfast treats. Oh, Spudnut serves a few sandwiches—your basic tuna salad, egg salad, and BLT—but what keeps customers coming back to this well-worn shop are Wingfield's spudnuts. "They're made with potato flour," says Wingfield's daughter Lori Fitzgerald. "Potato flour is more difficult to work with than wheat flour, and it takes a little longer, but my dad is quite a baker." Every morning except Sunday, he creates nine different kinds of spudnuts, including glazed, cinnamon, chocolate, and coconut, plus a few honeybuns, too. While the shop can seat 15 to 20 people, most customers stop by on their way to work. "I'd say 95 percent of what we do is take-out," Fitzgerald says. "But we do have a group of people who come in regularly . . . some have been coming in for 30 years." Lori and her sister

Glenda, a nurse, have been helping out in the shop most of their lives. "I have gone off to school," Lori says, "but I came back. I like to work with my dad." Spudnut is open from 6:00 A.M. to 2:00 P.M. Monday through Friday and 6:00 A.M. to noon Saturday. A dozen spudnuts will run you about $4.81, tax included. You can also quench your thirst with coffee, hot chocolate, soft drinks, or whole milk.

Starr Hill Restaurant, Brewery, & Music Hall $
709 West Main Street, Charlottesville
(434) 977-0017
www.starrhill.com

At the site of the old Blue Ridge Brewery, Starr Hill opened in the fall of 1999 with a fresh take on contemporary American cuisine. A seasonal menu features local and organic products. Items range from gourmet pizzas to filet mignon. The restaurant also features award-winning microbrews and an on-site brewery. Its smooth ales make a good pairing with almost any dish, and their popularity is reflected by the fact that they can be found on many of the menus of area establishments. The Music Hall offers both national and regional acts of all musical genres. A truly unique experience, Starr Hill is the only locale for hundreds of miles that provides excellent cuisine, award-winning microbrews, a locally owned art gallery, and musicians of worldwide renown all under one roof.

Tastings $$
502 East Market Street, Charlottesville
(434) 293-3663
www.tastingsofcville.com

This restaurant, wine bar, and wine shop combo is run by William Curtis, who also owns the popular Court Square Tavern nearby. You can stop first at the bar and sample a wine to order with your dinner or simply drink and munch on a few crackers. Foods are straightforward, fresh, and deeply satisfying. The wood grill adds a delicate flavor to meats and fish. Year-round entrees include crabmeat casserole, and in the summertime, strawberry rhubarb pie is the seasonal favorite. Most times the menu will incorporate an array of Pacific Northwest–grown wild mushrooms. You can select your dinner wine from more than 2,000 in the shop or order a half or full glass from a list of about 125 wines. Better yet, Curtis will prepare a flight of three wines to sample during dinner. Lunch and dinner are served Tuesday through Saturday. Reservations are appreciated.

The Virginian $
1521 University Avenue, Charlottesville
(434) 984-4667
www.restaurant.com
A University of Virginia tradition for generations. You still feel like you have stepped into a timeless college restaurant where professors discuss department politics at one table while students quaff beer at another. Large wooden booths are the only way to dine here, so don't plan on sitting together if you come with a big crowd. The food is good, with an ambitious menu offering everything from burgers and pasta to New York strips, crab cakes, grilled dishes, and Sunday brunch with choices that include eggs Benedict, omelets, and French toast. The Virginian is open daily for lunch and dinner.

Vivace $$$
2244 Ivy Road, Charlottesville
(434) 979-0994
Open nine years in July 2004, Vivace is a favorite Italian restaurant in a town with lots of great restaurants. Cozy and warm and decorated with Italian family pictures, it's "like your grandmother's dining room," says co-owner Beth Lippmann. She ought to know since she did the interior decorating. She and co-owner/husband Tom Lippmann found the real Catholic confessional in an antiques store in Ruckersville. The quaint little room has now become the wine room. Dine outside on the patio when the weather is nice or have a beverage in the new lounge, nicely appointed with a large, curvaceous bar, big windows,

and nostalgic University of Virginia student life posters on the wall. Of course, there are many choices of pasta, from simple marinara sauce to pesto and Salsiccia (grilled Italian sausage and marinara), or try the *gnocchi di patate Fiorentina* (Italian potato dumpling in a parmesan and spinach cream sauce), or the grilled tenderloin smothered in a tomato, garlic, and herb ragout served with garlic mashed potatoes and broccolini. There are also private dining rooms that can seat 10 to 12 people.

Nelson County

The Blue Ridge Pig $
Highway 151, Nellysford
(434) 361-1170
Some claim this is the best barbecue in the Blue Ridge. Local carpenters and farmers line up next to golfers and skiers from nearby Wintergreen Resort for these tasty meats and sandwiches. The offerings are just as diverse as the clientele—choose from pulled pork or sliced beef barbecue, ribs, and smoked turkey, all fired in a large hickory-burning smokehouse that sits behind the restaurant. Side dishes garner their share of praise as well—oniony potato salad laden with a delicate dill sauce and spicy baked beans are made on-site. With a gas station on one side and a car wash on the other, the Blue Ridge Pig is not lacking for atmosphere. Actually, the small dining area is quite pleasant, with rustic chairs, benches, and tables. You'll have to decide whether to eat inside or out, but the hardest decision you will have to make is what to eat. For that reason, many travelers make this a regular stop. About 40 minutes from Charlottesville and Waynesboro and 15 minutes from Wintergreen Resort, the Blue Ridge Pig is certainly worth a detour from U.S. Highway 64, US 250, or US 29. The Pig is open daily for lunch and dinner.

The Copper Mine Restaurant & Lounge $$
Wintergreen Resort, Highway 664
Wintergreen
(434) 325-8090
www.wintergreenresort.com
From casual to elegant, Wintergreen Resort provides four impressive dining options. Wintergreen's chefs specialize in using only the freshest ingredients of the season, and the menus offer a delectable array of entrees and appetizers to satisfy all tastes. Enjoy informal, relaxed breakfasts, elegant gourmet dinners, and spectacular Sunday brunch buffets at Wintergreen's signature restaurant. The Copper Mine offers continental fare paired with an ambience of an open-pit copper fireplace. Sample the steak au poivre, tender filet mignon served with a brandied peppercorn cream sauce, roast rack of lamb with a rosemary and garlic rub, or one of many other dishes. Vegetarians should fear not, as there are several options available. Breakfast and dinner are served daily. Lunch is served on weekends during ski season. Brunch is offered on holiday weekends throughout the spring and summer. Brunch and dinner reservations are required. The restaurant is wheelchair accessible.

Devils Grill at Devils Knob Golf Clubhouse $$
Wintergreen Resort, Highway 664
Wintergreen
(434) 325-8100
www.wintergreenresort.com
Located in the Devils Knob village, this is the newest of the Wintergreen restaurants. Superb mountaintop views await you at this traditional clubhouse restaurant, which features a wide array of popular and innovative menu items. Dishes range from grilled eggplant steak to filet mignon, all prepared with a contemporary Southern flair. Lunch, dinner, and patio dining are offered in the spring, summer, and fall. During ski season, dinner is served Wednesday through Sunday. A children's menu is available and dinner

reservations are required. This restaurant is wheelchair accessible. For a more casual meal, visit the lounge, where you can enjoy a burger or hearty sandwich and a cold beverage while watching the game on three televisions.

The Edge $$
Wintergreen Resort, Highway 664
Wintergreen
(434) 325-8080
www.wintergreenresort.com
This restaurant is perfect for a relaxed family dinner, complete with mountain views and seasonal evening entertainment and dancing. Ever-popular specialties such as spicy buffalo wings, Virginia barbecue, chicken salad, and tasty pasta dishes will please the palates of everyone in your crowd. No reservations are required. The Edge also provides box lunches and dinners for those attending the Wintergreen Performing Arts mountain concerts.

Lovingston Cafe $
165 Front Street, off Highway 29
Lovingston
(434) 263-8000
This unpretentious cafe in the heart of Lovingston serves an array of good old-fashioned American eats, including great burgers, grilled chicken breast sandwiches, pizza, pasta, fish, and soup. It's a nice place to unwind on your way to or from Charlottesville, which is just a few miles to the north. The restaurant is open for breakfast Friday through Monday and daily for lunch and dinner. There is also a breakfast buffet on the weekends.

Stoney Creek Bar & Grill $$
Wintergreen Resort, Highway 664
Wintergreen
(434) 325-8110
www.wintergreenresort.com
Located in the heart of the Stoney Creek valley, the Stoney Creek Bar & Grill offers a distinctive alfresco dining experience combining the splendor of the Blue Ridge Mountains with spectacular panoramic views of the Rockfish Valley and Stoney

Creek Golf Course. The menu is a unique blend of casual American fare with an emphasis on fresh, seasonal ingredients. Specialties include a variety of hand-cut steaks with a choice of sauces. Open for lunch and dinner in the spring, summer, and fall, and evenings during the winter. Reservations are required for dinner. The restaurant offers a menu for children 12 and younger.

Lynchburg

Charleys $
707 Graves Mill Road, Lynchburg
(434) 237-5988
www.charleysrestaurant.net
There is always something special going on at Charleys that will appeal to businesspeople as well as families. The menu is as varied as the atmosphere and includes fajitas, fresh seafood, chicken cordon bleu, and prime rib, as well as soups, salads, and sandwiches. The restaurant is open for lunch, dinner, and late-night dining daily. You can usually catch live entertainment on Friday night. Reservations are suggested for parties of six or more.

Clayton's $
3311 Old Forest Road, Lynchburg
(434) 385-7900
Clayton's is a casual restaurant with table service by a friendly staff. You can have breakfast and lunch daily and dinner twice a week. Choose from chicken Tina (boneless chicken breast wrapped in bacon with mushroom sauce), grilled marinated shrimp, a grilled vegetable sandwich, plus two hot specials daily. The restaurant is open for breakfast and lunch daily. Dinner is served Wednesday and Friday.

The Farm Basket $
2008 Langhorne Road, Lynchburg
(434) 528-1107, (800) 842-0477
www.thefarmbasket.com
Don't miss the Farm Basket while you're in Lynchburg! Regardless of your age or nature, it's the kind of place that will fascinate you for hours with its shopping opportunities. Then it will amaze you once again with its tiny restaurant that's always packed with locals and others who keep coming back for the homemade food prepared by cooks who are creative in both new and old recipes. The white-meat chicken salad with grapes on a homemade yeast roll will melt in your mouth. Have dessert—the chocolate tarts are delicious—on the deck overlooking Blackwater Creek. They will also prepare a box lunch. It's open daily except Sunday.

Historical Community Market $
12th and Main Streets
Downtown Lynchburg
(434) 495-4486, (434) 455-4483
Since 1783, folks have come to the Market to buy, sell, and exchange goods. This old-world tradition continues with vendors who still sell a variety of wares: specialty handmade crafts, a large variety of garden delights, farm-fresh produce, home-baked goods, local honey, herbs, specialty breads, jams and jellies, and a number of other scrumptious treats.

The Market is open Monday through Saturday from 7:00 A.M. to 2:00 P.M. and features nine unique restaurants and craft shops. Enjoy home-cooked food at Irene's Country Cookin', visit Moore's Famous Hot Dogs for their mouthwatering treats, or grab a fresh deli sandwich at Booley B's. But there's also the chance for some international cuisine. Try Philippine Delight's stir-fry and kabobs, American Pie and Bakery, or El Roi International House of Spices vegetarian and Indian cooking. Delicious foods, unique crafts, and year-round special events are all available in one location.

Meriwether's $$
4925 Boonsboro Road, Lynchburg
(434) 384-3311
www.meriwethers.com
At the site formerly occupied by Emil's Swiss Restaurant, Meriwether's has taken the casual dining crowd by storm. The restaurant was started by the husband-

and-wife team who ran the much-acclaimed food service at Randolph–Macon College, Marie Meriwether-Godsey and her husband, Ed Godsey. They have offered upscale catering to the Lynchburg crowd for years. They even served Mikhail Gorbachev and Lech Walesa at nearby Poplar Forest. A typical Virginia meal includes real Southern ingredients such as grits and plantation tenderloin with bearnaise sauce. Signature dishes include produce from as many local farmers as possible. The menu changes seasonally. The Market Shop offers packaged gourmet treats, fine wines, T-shirts, cups, jockey caps, and flower arrangements. Meriwether's is open Monday through Saturday for lunch and dinner.

Smith Mountain Lake Area

Dudley Mart & Restaurant $
Highways 670 and 668, Wirtz
(540) 721-1635
Frequented by locals and close to the Smith Mountain 4-H Center, this revamped country school built in 1931 is now home to one of Smith Mountain Lake's most delightful dining surprises with an old-fashioned flair. The homemade barbecue and roasted chicken are worth the trip, and it's a great place for a quick meal while you're touring the lake. Fridays are famous for the walleye fish fry, while prime rib is a Saturday specialty. You'll find the kinds of odds and ends and groceries you would in old-timey country stores, and takeout is available. Stop by daily for breakfast, lunch, and dinner.

The Landing Restaurant at Bernard's
Landing Resort $$
773 Ashmeade Road, Moneta
(540) 721-3028
www.thelanding.net
If you want the finest dining and best view on the lake, this premier restaurant at Bernard's Landings has them. It's truly a

special place, worth the 45-minute drive from Roanoke or Lynchburg. Everything on the menu is a delight. If you're going to the lake to experience it the way Insiders do each weekend, don't miss this dining opportunity. Nothing can match the gentle lake breezes as a pleasant distraction from the everyday world. The Landing is open for lunch and dinner Monday through Thursday; breakfast, lunch, and dinner are served Friday and Saturday; and brunch and dinner are served on Sunday.

Virginia Dare Cruises and Marina $$$
Highway 853, Moneta
(540) 297-7100, (800) 721-3273
www.vadarecruises.com
Glide across gorgeous Smith Mountain Lake while enjoying some of the best food around. You can ride on the luxurious *Virginia Dare*, a 19th-century sidewheeler. Bask in the sun on an afternoon cruise or relax with a cocktail while watching the sun set across the lake on your way to the Smith Mountain Lake Dam. A substantial meal often ranges from sliced top round beef with au jus to stuffed chicken in a light cream sauce. Trips feature narration by the captain. The cruises run April through December, but times vary. Call for reservations and specific information on specialty cruises, charters, and sight-seeing tours. Once back on land, you can stop by portside for burgers, kabobs, and your favorite libation. Located near the Smith Mountain Lake State Park, *Virginia Dare* Cruises is accessible by land and water. This is a wonderful experience for lake lovers of all ages. Reservations are required.

White House Restaurant $
Highways 608 and 626, Huddleston
(540) 297-7104
www.virginiasbestkeptsecret.com
A pleasant restaurant specializing in family fare, White House is open year-round for lunch and dinner. Breakfast is served in the busy summer season. Here you'll find great food at great prices. Salad, pastas, hand-cut steak, prime rib, barbecue, ribs,

chicken, and seafood are all on the menu. Daily chef specials feature seafood and real mashed potatoes. The owner's motto is that it's a "place where neighbors and friends dine." Try the hand-dipped ice cream and the game room. Be sure to check out this place near Smith Mountain Lake State Park.

Bedford County

The Bedford Restaurant $
U.S. Highway 460 W, Bedford
(540) 586-6575
For delicious down-home cooking, try the Bedford Restaurant. Have a real country-style breakfast with eggs, tenderloin, toast, and chipped beef gravy over home-made biscuits. The lunch menu offers a variety of sandwiches. For dinner, try the honey-dipped chicken, cooked to order, ribeye steak, seafood platter, or pork barbecue. The restaurant is open daily.

Franklin County

Blue Moon Restaurant $
U.S. Highway 220, 1 mile north of Rocky Mount
(540) 483-2070
Remodeled in 2002, Blue Moon is a family restaurant featuring charcoal-grilled steaks, fresh seafood, Italian specialties, and more. Sirloin and ribeye steaks are cooked to your preference and served with sauteed mushrooms. Fresh shrimp scampi or frog legs (for the more adventurous diner) are offered along with a surf 'n' turf special for those who can't decide. Blue Moon is open Monday through Friday for lunch and dinner and Saturday for dinner.

Olde Virginia Barbecue $
35 Meadowview Avenue, Rocky Mount
(540) 489-1788
Come discover the most succulent pork,

beef ribs, and chicken barbecue in the county. This restaurant, a local landmark, has created its own Olde Virginia Barbecue Sauce and is a favorite hangout for the Franklin County crowd. You've just never tasted better barbecued chicken and ribs anywhere else, and people who don't even like coleslaw can't believe how great the Olde Virginia's real Southern variety tastes. Children have their own menu. The restaurant's open seven days a week for lunch and dinner.

NEW RIVER VALLEY
Blacksburg

Bogen's Steakhouse $
622 North Main Street, Blacksburg
(540) 953-2233
www.bogens.com
Probably the most popular local restaurant with the college crowd and business people, Bogen's slogan is "Casual with Class." The food is inexpensive, and the atmosphere is great. The menu features gourmet sandwiches, deluxe burgers, charbroiled steaks, spicy barbecued ribs and chicken, and tempting seafood. To top it off, get one of the outrageous ice cream desserts—sky high and wonderful! Bogen's opens for dinner, and the lounge is open until late night (see our Nightlife chapter).

Krazy May $
1600 North Main Street, Blacksburg
(540) 951-2828
A relaxing family atmosphere surrounds you as you dine in this college-town favorite. The menu consists of American favorites and treats such as burgers, seafood platters, duck, homemade cheesecake, and crème brûlée. It's open for dinner Monday through Friday and Sunday; dinner only is served on Saturday. Reservations are suggested.

Christiansburg

The Farmhouse $$
285 Ridinger Street
Christiansburg
(540) 382-4253, (540) 382-3965
www.g3.net/farmhouse
Exceptional service is a trademark of this authentic farmhouse-turned-restaurant. The farmhouse was part of an estate built in the 1800s and opened as a restaurant in 1963; an old train caboose was added in the early 1970s. The staff extends Southern hospitality to its diners, who include families, corporate executives, and college students. The rustic setting, decorated with both antiques and country furnishings, adds to the ambience. The menu is full of such favorites as prime rib, jumbo ocean shrimp cocktail, steak, and the famous Farmhouse onion rings. A separate children's menu is available. The Farmhouse is open seven days a week for dinner. It also serves a buffet on Sunday. Reservations are accepted for eight or more; otherwise, it's first come, first serve.

The Huckleberry $$
2790 Roanoke Street, Christiansburg
(540) 381-2382
Convenient and luxurious, this restaurant is near I-81 and several hotels in the Christiansburg area. Two lounges, Whispers and Sundance, offer Top-40 and country-and-western entertainment in beautiful decor (see our Nightlife chapter). Your hosts, the VanDykes, offer homey settings, some next to fireplaces that roar on cool nights. The succulent barbecued items are slow-cooked in "the finest hickory-smoking oven money can buy." The restaurant also guarantees the high quality and freshness of its beef. You can choose from baby back ribs, Dijon chicken, filet mignon, and broiled lobster tail. A varied wine list includes several Virginia vintages. The Huckleberry dessert specialties are ice cream fantasies—drinks made with real ice cream, cream, fresh fruits, nuts, candies, and fine liqueurs. Kids have their own menu here, too. It's open Monday through Saturday for dinner.

Stone's Cafeteria $
1290 Roanoke Street, Christiansburg
(540) 382-8970
A longtime favorite with locals and tourists alike, Stone's gives you real country food as fast as you can go through the cafeteria line to get it. Lovers of dishes such as fried chicken, greens, mashed potatoes, and pinto beans will be in their glory, both when they taste and when they pay. Stone's is open for breakfast, lunch, and dinner Monday through Saturday.

Giles County

Macado's Restaurant and Delicatessen $
510 East Main Street, Radford
(540) 731-4879
www.macados.com
One of a chain of family-owned restaurants throughout the Blue Ridge, including locations in Roanoke and Blacksburg, Radford's Macado's offers a fun dining alternative in the New River Valley. Macado's is popular both with students and professionals for its overstuffed sandwiches and unique, antiques- and collectibles-filled decor. Macado's is open mid-morning to the wee hours daily.

Mountain Lake Resort Restaurant $$
115 Hotel Circle, Pembroke
(540) 626-7121, (800) 346-3334
www.mountainlakehotel.com
If dining in absolutely gorgeous surroundings is your idea of a great evening, as it is for many from nearby Virginia Tech, then you should drive the 7 winding miles up one of the highest mountains in Virginia to Mountain Lake. This 2,600-acre paradise was the setting for the movie *Dirty Dancing*, and that glorious scenery wasn't designed in the prop room. For miles all you see are tall trees, rolling hills, beautiful wildflowers, and a clear mountain lake. And as if that weren't enough, the dining

is out of this world. (See our Resorts chapter.)

The elegant atmosphere matches the outstanding cuisine. It may include chilled blackberry soup, sauteed shiitake mushrooms, London broil Madeira, or red snapper with pecan butter, if the chef is in a gourmet mood, or you may get Swiss onion soup, top round with horseradish, and chicken Polynesian. Breakfast is a buffet of Giles County country favorites such as Appalachian buttermilk pancakes, biscuits and gravy, or local produce. Sunday brunch is popular for special events from May to October, and weekends in November, when Mountain Lake is open. The prices are low for the high quality of the food. Reservations are important, since guests of the resort dine there as part of their stay.

Floyd County

Blue Ridge Restaurant Inc. $
113 East Main Street, Floyd
(540) 745-2147
Lunchtime regulars and those just passing through will find plenty of friendly faces here. The generous servings and honest-to-goodness real food—real mashed potatoes, and pinto beans that are always soaked dried beans, not canned—are well known in the area. Choose from such delicious country-style favorites as hotcakes, country ham, grilled tenderloin, and fried squash. Children have their own dinner menu at a reduced price. The restaurant is open daily for breakfast, lunch, and dinner.

The Restaurant at Chateau Morrisette $$
Meadows of Dan
(540) 593-2865
www.thedogs.com
Built to resemble a French castle, Chateau Morrisette, a family-owned winery in the Rocky Knob district, produces world-class Virginia wines and also has a charming restaurant. Founded in 1978, the winery is

small enough to remain in the family and yet large enough to produce several varieties of award-winning wines. The winery's restaurant serves both American and international cuisine in an elegant old-world atmosphere. Although the fabulous wines are the highlight of Chateau Morrisette, luscious menu items such as grilled honey-soy chicken on an organic green salad with raspberry vinaigrette and fresh fruit will please your palate as well. The Jazz on the Lawn events are reminiscent of a Monet painting of a French picnic. Visitors are welcome to tour the facilities, sample the wines, and enjoy a light meal surrounded by the magnificent Blue Ridge Mountains. The restaurant is open for lunch Wednesday through Saturday, with brunch on Sunday. Dinner is served on Friday and Saturday evening. Reservations are requested.

ALLEGHANY HIGHLANDS

Alleghany County

The Cat & Owl Steak and Seafood House $$
Off Interstate 64, exit 21, Lowmoor
(540) 862-5808
www.catandowl.com
Rail memorabilia and antiques create a timeless atmosphere as you dine in this beautiful home remodeled by owner-operator Bruce Proffitt, whose father and uncle opened the Cat & Owl 32 years ago. A concourse covers the walkway, giving it the appearance of a railroad passenger depot. This steak and seafood restaurant has a Victorian atmosphere that will please the eye and a wide selection of tasty dishes that will delight the palate. Steaks are USDA Choice and prepared on an open charcoal broiler. The Cat & Owl was opened more than a quarter of a century ago to serve Chesapeake & Ohio railroad workers in nearby Clifton Forge. There already was a C & O Restaurant in Clifton Forge, so the restaurant was named Cat &

Owl to symbolize the first letters of the railway's name. You'll enjoy the decor, including a barber chair, player piano, and a machine once used to crank out personalized pencils. Selections such as charbroiled shrimp, filet mignon, and fresh tuna steak have kept the Cat & Owl popular. Finish off your meal with delicious banana fritters. The restaurant is open Monday through Saturday for dinner. Reservations are suggested.

Eagle Nest Restaurant $$
4100 Kanawha Trail, Covington
(540) 559-9738
www.eaglenestrestaurant.com
At Eagle Nest, established in 1930, you can have a gourmet meal on a deck overlooking a waterfall, somewhat like dining in Frank Lloyd Wright's private home. The nature lover and adventurous tourist will love this place that's in the middle of practically nowhere (about 1 hour west of Roanoke and 10 minutes from White Sulphur Springs, West Virginia). It's one of the most intriguing places in the entire Blue Ridge. In an ancient log cabin decorated with antiques, beside that breathtaking waterfall outlined in purple irises and a pool filled with trout and ducks, you'll see chubby felines (the restaurant's charity cases) roaming the mountain crags 70 feet straight up. The scenery alone makes this place one you won't forget. But nothing about the food is forgettable either.

Dinners may be international in flavor one day, or traditional, with fresh brook trout, the next. The soup may be cream of leek, cream of broccoli, or clam chowder. Select from a full complement of house wines, including their own Virginia table wine under the Eagle Nest Label with Horton Wineries. The Horton Vineyards received gold ratings for two wines in the 1994 and 1995 Governor's Cup Wine Competition. Eagle Nest is also among an elite group of award-winning Virginia wine retailers and restaurants. They are Covington's only honoree as a Three Cluster top

award winner in the Virginia State and Wine Marketing Program. The waitstaff provides impeccable service. This is an experience anyone in love with the Blue Ridge shouldn't miss. The restaurant is open for dinner seven days a week. Reservations are requested.

Imperial Wok $
348 West Main Street, Covington
(540) 962-3330
A Chinese restaurant of high caliber, Imperial Wok is a favorite of Covington residents and is known miles around for its quality. The more popular dishes include the Seafood Delight, chicken and shrimp combo, General Tsao's Chicken, and mixed vegetables with shrimp. Another favorite is the Happy Family meal, which is made with chicken, beef, pork, shrimp, and fresh vegetables. It's open daily for lunch and dinner.

James Burke House Eatery $
232 Riverside Street, Covington
(540) 965-0040
Stop at this restaurant in a historic home (ca. 1817) for continental breakfast or lunch. The menu includes soups, sandwiches, salads, and desserts, all homemade and delicious. Especially popular are the quiche, Greek salad, and homemade chicken- and tuna-salad sandwiches. The restaurant is open Monday through Saturday.

Lakeview Restaurant at
Douthat State Park $
Highway 629, Clifton Forge
(540) 862-8111
This historic landmark is a vision of rustic beauty. The casual dining area has high-beamed ceilings and a large gorgeous fireplace. The porch overlooks a 50-acre lake stocked biweekly with trout. Try the sandwich menu for lunch, and the pleasing a la carte Wednesday through Sunday. Lakeview Restaurant is open daily for lunch and dinner.

Bath County

The Casino Club Restaurant $$
The Homestead, Hot Springs
(540) 839-7894
www.thehomestead.com
Adjacent to the first tee of the Old Course, the Casino Club restaurant offers a relaxed setting with a view of the practice green, tennis courts, and lawn game area. It features regional American cuisine, Southern favorites, and assorted desserts. The restaurant hours are from 11:00 A.M. to 3:00 P.M.

The Homestead Dining Room $$$$
The Homestead, Hot Springs
(540) 839-7563
www.thehomestead.com
The world-renowned Homestead (see our Resorts chapter) offers elegance and sophistication with dinner and dancing in the resort's famed Dining Room. The menus change daily, featuring continental cuisine prepared under the direction of the executive chef, Josef Schelch. He uses fresh Virginia products enhanced with quality ingredients from around the globe. The trademark entrees are complemented with distinctive wines. The resort has won the *Wine Spectator's* Award since 1993 for having one of the most outstanding wine lists in the world. The Dining Room also serves a bountiful breakfast buffet daily, while live music and dancing are provided nightly. Jacket and tie are required in the evening for men. Reservations are required

Sam Snead's Tavern $$
The Homestead, Hot Springs
(540) 839-7666
www.thehomestead.com
Sam Snead's Tavern is housed in a historic old bank building complete with the original vault, which houses the tavern's wine collection. The restaurant is named after native and lifetime Hot Springs resident, the late Sam Snead, a heralded professional golfer. The menu features the finest of Tavern favorites such as certified Angus steaks, juicy smoked ribs, and fresh Virginia Allegheny Mountain trout. The memorabilia from Snead's legendary golfing career makes the Tavern a unique experience.

1776 Grille $$$$
The Homestead, Hot Springs
(540) 839-7552
www.thehomestead.com
You will want to get dressed up to appreciate the fabulous setting and gourmet dining at this restaurant at the Homestead. French and American cuisine are favorites at the 1776 Grille, featuring an intimate atmosphere with views of the perfectly manicured grounds and mountains beyond. Tableside preparation and unparalleled presentation along with live music, special desserts, and superb wines make this the Homestead's unique "fine dining" choice. And men, jackets are required for evening dining. Reservations are a must.

The Waterwheel Restaurant $$
The Inn at Gristmill Square
Warm Springs
(540) 839-2231
www.gristmillsquare.com
Continental cuisine is served in the setting of an old mill here. This area, composed of restored 19th-century buildings, is full of rustic beauty. The restaurant's fresh smoked trout is a favorite. Appetizers may include a pâté Maison country loaf of sausage, chicken livers, and pork tenderloin blended with brandy and spices and served with house chutney. Entrees include an all-American grilled rib eye, swordfish, and pasta of the day. Guests are invited to descend past the grinding waterwheel to the well-stocked wine cellar. Dinner is served daily; there's also a Sunday brunch. Reservations are recommended.

Highland County

Highland Inn   **$**
Main Street, Monterey
(888) 466-4682
www.highland-inn.com
This historic inn is a memorable setting for dinner. Formerly the Hotel Monterey, this three-story landmark is one of the few mountain resorts of its size still in operation in Virginia. Candlelight and classical music set the mood. Local fresh mountain trout, maple-mustard pork tenderloin, and pecan-crusted chicken are three of the creative choices. Be sure to leave room for the maple pecan pie, made rich with Highland County maple syrup—simply delicious. The inn is open for dinner Wednesday through Saturday, with a buffet served on Wednesday night. Lunch is available Friday and Saturday, and stop by for brunch on Sunday.

NIGHTLIFE Ⓨ

The Blue Ridge may be known more for its scenic mountains than its rock and roll—but that trend is changing, thanks in part to the Dave Matthews Band. There has always been a marvelous collection of musicians performing in and around the Blue Ridge, but the quintet from Charlottesville put a national spotlight on the area's nightlife scene.

It used to be you could drop by Trax in Charlottesville and see the local band for less than five bucks. Today, the Grammy-winning stars are playing in sold-out arenas around the world. Their success has brought other acts to the region who want to play in Dave Matthews's backyard, and it is not unusual to see representatives from record companies scouting the local clubs for the "next Dave Matthews Band."

Now, it's true, most visitors to the Blue Ridge don't come for late nights or the bar scene. Daytime activities are so plentiful and enjoyable that most folks don't miss the lack of night-prowling opportunities that are more common in metropolitan areas.

However, clubs in the college towns of Charlottesville, Harrisonbug, and Roanoke are sure remedies for the in-bed-at-a-reasonable-hour syndrome. You just need to know where to look, and we can point you toward some of the hot spots.

SHENANDOAH VALLEY

Frederick County

The Daily Grind
3 South Loudoun Street, Winchester
(540) 662-2115
This shop on the walking mall serves lunch in its outdoor cafe as well as hosts a variety of bands in the evening. A Celtic orchestra performs here on the first Friday of each month, with no cover charge.

The Exchange
218 South Loudoun Street, Winchester
(540) 678-0600
www.exchangecoffeehouse.com
If you are looking for something a little different, drop by this coffeehouse. It's nonsmoking and nonalcoholic, and there's no cover charge. The Exchange is open Friday and Saturday night with a variety of musical offerings, ranging from folk and jazz to blues, rock, and even classical guitar. There's live entertainment on Saturday starting at 8:00 P.M. Sunday is set aside for the Gathering, a meeting for informal worship and prayer. While there, you might want to sample their own creation, a Coffee Zinger (espresso, soda, and vanilla ice cream). A full lunch menu of sandwiches and salads is also available.

Jimmy's Steak and Seafood Grill
Route 50 and Interstate 81, Milwood Pike
Winchester
(540) 667-1249
www.jimmysgrill.com
Since 1962 this local restaurant has been a popular spot for the local crowd, with a wide selection of bottled beer and local microbrews. Just pull up one of the bar stools or sit back in one of the comfy chairs in the lounge and enjoy the happy

If you're looking for big-time entertainers, the Nissan Pavilion at Stone Ridge is just a few miles east of Fauquier County in Bristow. This outdoor amphitheater hosts the biggest names in the business from late spring to early fall. Among the recent performers were Dave Matthews Band, Toby Keith, Ozzy Osbourne, and Jimmy Buffett. Call (800) 551-SEAT for tickets or visit www.nissanpavilion.com.

hour at 5:00 P.M. If you are in the mood for a little music, Jimmy's has been known to host live bands on Friday and Saturday evenings. Bugsy Cline and the Blue Devils were one of the recent acts. The music runs from 9:15 P.M. to midnight. There is usually no cover. Banquet rooms are available for special events and private meetings. Jimmy's serves breakfast, lunch, and dinner.

Rockingham County

Biltmore Grill
221 University Avenue, Harrisonburg
(540) 801-0221
This is a restaurant by day, a place where college kids come to hear music by night. OK, you can have a meal here in the evening, too, but local bands—and beer— help pack the place when James Madison University is in session. If you're looking for dinner, it's a good idea to come early and beat the crowds. The entertainment usually starts about 10:00 P.M. If you work up enough nerve, Friday is karaoke night. DJs rule on Thursday.

Buffalo Wild Wings
1007 South Main Street, Harrisonburg
(540) 438-9790
www.buffalowildwings.com
The college crowd—and the locals—are wild about this one. If you are in the mood for chicken wings, go early. This restaurant is right across the street from James Madison University, so by 10:00 P.M., the place is packed. No wonder. Along with good food, this sports bar has 30 televisions and 20 different beers on tap. Karaoke is on tap Thursday. There is another Buffalo Wild Wings in Charlottesville, at 1935 Arlington Boulevard, with karaoke on Thursday and a DJ on hand for special events.

Calhoun's Restaurant and Brewing Company
41 Court Square, Harrisonburg
(540) 434-8777
www.calhounsbrewery.com
The Valley's only microbrewery opened in the heart of downtown Harrisonburg in 1998. Friday is usually your best bet for jazz. The best part, there's no cover. When weather permits, there is outdoor dining upstairs on Sunday from 3:00 to 9:00 P.M., accompanied by a little jazz. Check your watch—happy hour is 4:30 to 6:30 P.M. Monday through Friday.

Casey's Lounge
1400 East Market Street, Harrisonburg
(540) 433-2521
The action is at Casey's Lounge in the Sheraton Four Points Hotel (see our Hotels and Motels chapter). Formerly known as Scruples, this bar has undergone more than a name change. A remodeling job has turned the nightspot into a true sports bar with 11 screens for viewing your favorite game.

Dave's Downtown Taverna
121 South Main Street, Harrisonburg
(540) 564-1487
www.davestaverna.com
What with their snazzy dance floor, Dave's Downtown Taverna is a great place to spend some time out on the town. Stop by for jazz on Wednesday and singer/ songwriter nights on Tuesday and Thursday, free of charge. On weekends you'll find regional and national bands for a cover charge. Enjoy the Greek and American cuisine, including souvlaki, gyros, and a veggie pita, among other dishes. There's a full-service bar, and besides the stage, other nice touches include the 100-year-old refinished wood floor and the trademark spiral staircase. The split dining area can accommodate families who want to eat and those who drop in to listen to music. A banquet room seats up to 70 people. The Taverna closes at midnight.

Encounters Lounge
Highway 644, Harrisonburg
(540) 289-9441
www.massresort.com
After a cool night on the slopes, you can warm up to a little dance music at Encounters Lounge at Massanutten Resort. This glass-walled club serves light meals throughout the day. During ski season, you can sit back and sip a hot toddy while listening to live regional bands on Friday and Saturday nights. There's a pretty good size dance floor here, too, if you are so inclined. The cover, if any, will usually range from $5.00 to $10.00. On Wednesday, Encounters plans to add a little acoustic music, while Thursday is karaoke night. The resort also hosts five annual outdoor festivals throughout the year, including a summer jam in July, a blues festival in August, and a bluegrass festival in September. The Cool Summer Nights series, which features everything from bluegrass to electric rock, is staged Wednesday nights from July through August.

Main Street Bar and Grill
153 South Main Street, Harrisonburg
(540) 432-9963
www.mainstreetrocks.com
Here's where the college students hang out. Just a couple of blocks from the James Madison University campus, Main Street has been "the place to go" since 1997 with a restaurant, dance club, and concert hall. There is usually something going on every evening from Tuesday through Saturday. Mega DJ weekends usually create long lines from the college crowd. Jackall, Confederate Railroad, Blue Oyster Cult, the Wailers, O.A.R., and Quiet Riot are just a few of the big-name acts who have performed here. The local bands usually bring a $5.00 cover charge, while the national acts are more in the $15.00 to $18.00 range.

The Pub
1950-A Deyerle Avenue, Harrisonburg
(540) 432-0610
www.dothepub.com
Here's the perfect spot for your honky-tonk tailgate party. Nashville has even sent some of its stars to perform at the Harrisonburg hot spot, including Tracy Lawrence. There are also plenty of chances for you to be the star on karaoke nights. Karaoke is king on Tuesday, Thursday, and Sunday, while the bands take over Friday and Saturday. If sports is your game, grab a cue and try out the pool tables, or you can sit back and enjoy the view on one of the big-screen TVs. The Pub's grub includes quesadillas, wings, subs, and burgers.

Augusta County

Byers Street Bistro
18 Byers Street, Staunton
(540) 887-6100
www.byersstreetbistro.com
This is a happening place, what with bands playing Friday and Saturday night, karaoke on Tuesday, and open mike night on Wednesday. There's rarely a cover for these primarily local bands, and the bistro is open from 5:00 P.M. until midnight. There is a nonsmoking section, and the private banquet room can seat up to 100 people. For dinner, choose from sandwiches, gourmet pizzas, pitas, and wraps to something more extensive such as smothered sirloin, grilled pesto tuna, and baby back ribs, to name just a few of the entrees. You will find specials on any given night, such as wings on Monday, baby back ribs on Wednesday, and pizza takeout night on Sunday. For those with little ones, a children's menu is available.

Clock Tower Tavern
27 West Beverley Street, Staunton
(540) 213-2403
The Clock Tower is the perfect night-on-the-town spot, what with the great back room and stage area. Bands, primarily local, play Friday and Saturday night starting between 8:30 and 9:00 P.M. With rarely a cover charge, the spot is popular with students and local residents alike. If the family is what you are bringing out, stop in for

some great food in the restaurant area, complete with handsome wood floor and wood tables. A large Cat's Meow-style replica of the street decorates the far wall, and old pictures of historic Staunton hang around the rest of the building. Catch your favorite sports show or news broadcast from one of the five televisions. Choose from entrees of steamed spiced shrimp, filet mignon and pasta specialties, or specialty pizzas. A kids' menu offers grilled cheese, PB&J, or hamburgers. A wide selection of domestic and imported beers as well as wines are available, as is a late-night menu.

Luigi's
111 North Augusta Street, Staunton
(540) 886-5016
This is a popular spot with Mary Baldwin College students and the Staunton crowd. Pizza and subs are on the menu, while a live local band comes in to play alternative or acoustic sets every Tuesday. It's actually an open mike night, so bring your guitar. There is a nice PA system, but if you prefer to go unplugged, that's OK, too. But be prepared to wait. What started out as a small group of homegrown musicians has now grown to a crowd of 30 different people who play everything from bluegrass to rock and roll. There's no cover charge. There is a side room with a pool table, dart boards, TVs, jukebox, and Golden Golf Tee.

Mill Street Grill
1 Mill Street, Staunton
(540) 886-0656
www.millstreetgrill.com
This cozy restaurant is in the enchanting old converted gristmill in the historic White Star Mill Building. On Wednesday the downtown eatery serves up jazz . . . most often by a unique band called Splaat. This band has a revolving membership, so you never know what combination will be playing when. It gives true meaning to the old saying that a band never sounds the same way twice. During the school year, a quartet from James Madison University has been known to drop in and perform for the Sunday brunch crowd.

Mulligan's Pub & Eatery
Country Club Road, Staunton
(540) 248-6020
Mulligan's Pub & Eatery in the Holiday Inn right off I-81 offers live bands playing classic rock Friday and Saturday nights and karaoke on Thursday. Locals might know Mulligan's as the 19th hole at the Staunton Golf and Conference Center, but don't be afraid to take a swing at the nightlife. The cover is $5.00.

Lexington and Rockbridge County

The Drama of Creation
Natural Bridge of Virginia
(800) 533-1410, (540) 291-2121
www.naturalbridgeva.com
For a truly breathtaking and religious experience, attend Natural Bridge of Virginia's Drama of Creation (see our Attractions chapter), held nightly from April through October and on Saturday only from November to March. This 45-minute program combines classical music and special lighting under Natural Bridge to tell the Biblical story of Creation. Cost is $10.00, $5.00 for ages 6 to 15.

Lime Kiln Theater
Lime Kiln Road
Box Office, 2 West Henry Street
Lexington
(540) 463-3074
www.theateratlimekiln.com
Without question, the most exciting nightlife in Lexington in the summer happens at the outdoor Lime Kiln Theater (see our Arts chapter). The Sunday Night Concert Series draws huge crowds to hear Celtic rock, bluegrass, rock, folk, jazz, and swing. From Tuesday through Saturday, Lime Kiln Theater stages a play with a theme that relates in some way to the culture of the Southern mountains. Concert tickets range from $12 to $26.

Lime Kiln has great picnic spots for dining before the performances.

The Palms
101 West Nelson Street, Lexington
(540) 463-7911
www.thepalmslexington.com
The Palms is a downtown restaurant and bar with five big-screen TVs. This is a popular college hangout, but locals also feel at home here. This full-service bar is probably best known not for who has performed here but who has eaten here. Among the list of patrons are Jodie Foster, Debra Winger, Chris O'Donnell, and Rob Morrow.

ROANOKE VALLEY

Cheers
1650 Braeburn Drive, Salem
(540) 389-4600
Cheers is a lively, classy bar with a raised dance floor that stays full every weekend night. Every Wednesday night the stage is packed with wanna-be stars singing and dancing to karaoke music. Live entertainment on weekends includes both local and regional bands. Cheers also has geared up for football season with a whole series of sports packages. With 12 TVs set to different channels, you can come in on Sunday and root for your favorite pro team; on Saturday cheer for the college of your choice. (Be aware, however, that you are in the heart of Virginia Tech territory.) Monday nights everyone will be out in force for the NFL game of the week. The party goes on until 1:00 A.M. . . . or whenever the crowds leave. There is no cover charge.

The Coffee Pot
2902 Brambleton Avenue, Roanoke
(540) 774-8256
Established in 1936, the Coffee Pot is the "oldest continuing functioning roadhouse in the South." Events ranging from birthday parties to weddings and everything in between have been held here. The Coffee Pot offers live music five or more nights a week. It's mostly local bands, but

some national acts have been known to drop by, too, playing everything from bluegrass and blues to rock 'n' roll. The fun starts around 9:30 P.M., with the music running until 2:00 A.M. There is generally no cover, except when a national touring act drops by. Blues, jazz, and rock 'n' roll lovers alike will enjoy the variety and talent of the musicians that frequent this club.

Corned Beef & Co.
107 South Jefferson Street, Roanoke
(540) 342-3354
Corned Beef & Co. is known as Roanoke's best nightspot, and the crowds on Friday and Saturday nights are definitely an indication of this distinction. You will usually find a DJ pumping out music of the '70s, '80s, and '90s and keeping the dance floor packed. Bands play here on occasion as well. If you need a break from dancing, you can head upstairs to the rooftop deck, where many of Roanoke's VIPs have been spotted lounging and sipping drinks.

The city-block-long club has six bars and 40 TVs. You can even flex a few muscles with the virtual golf simulator, championship pool tables, shuffleboard, or a good old-fashioned game of darts.

Downstairs, large brick ovens turn out wood-fired pizzas that are absolutely delicious. (See our Restaurants chapter.) Corned Beef & Co. partners with a local radio station to host special events (like pre-concert parties and St. Patrick's Day celebrations) almost monthly. It's closed Sunday.

Mac and Bob's
316 East Main Street, Salem
(540) 389-5999
Mac and Bob's (see our Restaurants chapter) has been a favorite of Salem residents and Roanoke College students alike for 20 years. The 50-foot bar and 11 TVs are great for getting together with friends and watching the big game.

Mill Mountain Coffee & Tea
112 Campbell Avenue, Roanoke
(540) 342-9404
www.millmountaincoffee.com

A more sedate place to congregate is Mill Mountain Coffee & Tea, in the heart of the downtown City Market. You can sip cappuccino or Italian iced tea while you people-watch from the tables outside on the sidewalk or tables in the two alcoves by the huge windows at the front of the shop. They've got some of the best coffee and tea du jour in the Blue Ridge, along with yummy desserts. Everybody who's anybody meets here for both business meetings and fun. Bluegrass lovers will want to stop by Wednesday. The open jam night is the longest-running old-time jam in the area.

The same goes for the other Mill Mountain locations at 4710 Starkey Road in Roanoke and 17 East Main Street in Salem. (See our Restaurants chapter.)

The Park
615 Salem Avenue, Roanoke
(540) 342-0946

For an alternative experience, do the Park and mingle with Roanokers both gay and straight. Many consider it the best place in town to dance because of its all-night Saturday hours and spacious dance floor. DJs spin dance club and Top-40 remixes from 9:00 P.M. to 4:00 A.M. Friday through Sunday. You also will find a comedy or impersonator show on Sunday. You'll find people from your office right alongside the drag queens. (Good luck telling who's who!)

The Pine Room at Hotel Roanoke
110 Shenandoah Avenue, Roanoke
(540) 985-5900

If you're looking for an elegant evening away from the throngs of 20-somethings you typically find in the Downtown Market area, try the Pine Room in posh Hotel Roanoke & Conference Center (see our Hotels and Motels chapter). A gorgeous setting and marvelous service are indicative of facilities at this five-star hotel. The Pine Room offers live weekend entertainment, billiards, and atmosphere. Friday and Saturday nights and Sunday afternoons bring a variety of soft rock.

Roanoke Star
Milepost 120, Blue Ridge Parkway
Roanoke
(540) 342-6025, (800) 635-5535

Many dates end, or begin, at this incredible illuminated landmark overlooking Roanoke near Mill Mountain Zoo (see our Attractions chapter). The star, a 100-foot-high metal structure, is magnificent itself, but the nighttime view of Roanoke is breathtaking. *The Roanoker* magazine readers called it the "Best Place to Propose Marriage," and you often hear about newlyweds returning on their anniversary to this special spot. Don't miss this truly unique experience.

Texas Tavern
114 West Church Avenue, Roanoke
(540) 342-4825

This no-frills lunchtime landmark in downtown Roanoke is also a favorite spot for a midnight snack. Voted "Best Late Night Food" by Roanokers, Texas Tavern will satisfy the heartiest late-night appetite. (See our Restaurants chapter.) A local landmark since the 1930s, Texas Tavern is open 24 hours a day.

EAST OF THE BLUE RIDGE
Culpeper County

401 South Nightclub
401 South Main Street, Culpeper
(540) 829-6445
www.lordculpeper.8m.com

Called "Culpeper's Hottest Nightstop," there is something to do here every night of the week. This club, downstairs at the Lord Culpeper Restaurant and Hotel, has three pool tables, plus foosball, video games, and darts. If you want to dance, drop by on the weekend. There is usually a DJ spinning records on Thursday and Friday, while the live bands drop by on

Saturday. If you want to be the star, Wednesday is karaoke night. This tapestry brick building first opened on December 21, 1933, but has undergone big renovations thanks to Bo and Libba Chase. If you order a meal in the restaurant, you'll get free admission in 401 South.

Rex's Sports Bar
110 East Davis Street, Culpeper
(540) 825-3955
Here's the place to stop and watch the big game. You won't miss a minute of the action with the widescreen TV or seven smaller ones anchored near the ceiling. With its pennants, caps, and jerseys decorating the walls, it's clear the owner is a true fan. The bar even hosts parties for big events, such as the Super Bowl or Daytona 500. If you prefer your entertainment live, Rex's books a wide variety of regional bands on Friday. Cover is around $5.00. Or just sit back, listen, and sample some of the deli-style subs and sandwiches.

Charlottesville

Baja Bean Company
1327 West Main Street, Charlottesville
(434) 293-4507
www.bajabean.com
You can be the star at this Mexican restaurant (see our Restaurants chapter). There's an open mike night on Monday, while Steve Miller hosts karaoke on Tuesday. You also might catch a little live music from a local trio if you are in town on the third Thursday of the month. There is no cover.

Biltmore Grill
16 Elliewood Avenue, Charlottesville
(434) 293-6700
This popular eatery was listed as one of the Top 100 college bars in the country in the October 1997 issue of *Playboy* magazine. When the nearby University of Virginia is in session, you may hear everything from acoustic guitar acts to rock

bands. During the school year, you'll find DJs on Saturday, and live bands on Friday. The Biltmore serves interesting salads, desserts, and pasta dishes, too. (Also see our Restaurants chapter.)

Durty Nelly's
2200 Jefferson Park Avenue
Charlottesville
(434) 295-1278
Durty Nelly's is a gritty little joint that serves sandwiches and has live music, usually local rock 'n' roll, folk, or country bands, Tuesday, Thursday, Friday, Saturday, and Sunday nights. Schedules often change with the seasons, so call ahead if you're headed their way. There is usually a cover charge, around $4.00.

Grammy-winning Dave Matthews purchased five of the Albemarle County farms that billionaire John Kluge gave to the University of Virginia. The $5.3 million sale includes 1,260 acres south of Charlottesville. Matthews plans to preserve agriculture and forest land on the farms with an emphasis on organic farming.

The Gravity Lounge
103 First Street, Charlottesville
(434) 977-5590
www.gravity-lounge.com
One enters the semilit neon aqua rooms with a low ceiling and wonders, is it a bar? A coffee shop? A bookstore? One of the new nightspots on the Charlottesville Downtown Mall bills itself as just such a combo. And with its low-key atmosphere, it can be the perfect place to enjoy a beer—or a cup of coffee—and watch a live performance. There's music every night of the week, from every genre—often local and regional musicians, but Leon Russell has played here as have John D'earth, Devon Sproule, and Paul Curreri. Cover ranges from $5.00 to $20.00, depending on who's performing. Need to check your e-mail? There are four iMacs that you can

rent for $5.00 an hour while your companion browses through an enticing arrangement of books—from cookbooks and history to the latest John Grisham novel. The graystone floor and serpentine walls are nice touches, as is the artwork decorating the walls to give this place a fourth venue: art gallery. If you are hungry, there's the soup of the day, meat loaf, and specialty sandwiches.

Michael's Bistro and Taphouse
1427 University Avenue, Charlottesville
(434) 977-3697
You might catch a lot of University of Virginia students at this restaurant. It's right across the street from the campus. Music is on tap a couple nights a week when UVA is in session, ranging from jazz and folk to rock and acoustic. The cover charge is usually in the $3.00 range, depending on the band.

 If you're making a trip to Charlottesville in the summer, you can hear top local bands from across the region playing every Friday from 5:30 to 8:00 P.M. at the outdoor amphitheater on the Historic Downtown Mall. Fridays after Five starts in mid-April and runs through September. The shows are free.

Miller's
109 West Main Street, Charlottesville
(434) 971-8511
Miller's on the Downtown Mall, an excellent jazz club and restaurant, offers live music every night. Trumpet player John D'earth, who toured with Bruce Hornsby, plays here regularly. You'll also hear blues and acoustic. An outdoor patio is great in the summer if the heat isn't too withering. Cover charge is usually less than $5.00. (Oh yes, Dave Matthews used to tend bar here.)

Orbit Billiards & Cafe
102 14th Street, Charlottesville
(434) 984-5707
It may be tough to find a table here even when live music isn't on the schedule. Aside from pool and sandwiches, Orbits tries to book occasional local shows ranging from bluegrass and folk to fusion and country up to four nights a week. The music starts around 10:00 P.M. and lasts until 2:00 A.M. There is no cover charge, unless it's a big act.

Outback Lodge
917 Preston Avenue, Charlottesville
(434) 979-7211
www.outbacklodge.com
This small club in Preston Plaza packs a wide mix of local, regional, and national acts throughout the year. While most of the music leans to the blues side, Outback also has been known to bring in funk, rock, and alternative music on Wednesday through Saturday nights. James Cotton, Buddy Miles, and Koko Taylor all have played at the Outback. Outback added Down Under, a dance club that rocks the downstairs on the weekends. The cover charge varies, but it's usually between $6.00 and $10.00.

The Prism
214 Rugby Road, Charlottesville
(434) 97-PRISM
www.theprism.com
We talk about the Prism in our Arts chapter but mention it again here because it is such a great place to hear live bluegrass, folk, and other acoustic music. The Prism occasionally brings in nationally (and sometimes internationally) known musicians such as John Hartford and Tony Rice. Alison Brown brought her quartet to start off the 2004–2005 season (admission was $22). The Prism also provides a forum in which the area's top folk, acoustic, and bluegrass musicians can perform, so cover charges will vary. The first hour of every Saturday night show is broadcast live on local radio. Just remember, this is not a nightclub, so there is no alcohol and smok-

ing is not permitted. The Prism is closed during the summer months.

Starr Hill Music Hall
709 West Main Street, Charlottesville
(434) 977-0017
www.starrhill.com

Opened in 1999, this concert space has become the premier music venue in Charlottesville, bringing in regional and national acts of all musical genres. Situated upstairs above the Starr Hill Restaurant and Brewery, this smoke-free club provides entertainers with an intimate setting and great acoustics. Fans can sit back, listen, and sample some of the brewery's award-winning microbrews. The people who play here want to keep coming back, but the club also has built a reputation for being on the cutting edge with a lineup of fresh new talent. They like to bring in quality acts on the rise. Norah Jones played to a sold-out audience in June 2002. The prices will vary from $5.00 to $25.00, with the lineup often reflecting who is passing through on the festival tour circuit. Jerry Jeff Walker, Dar Williams, and Ben Taylor, the son of James Taylor and Carly Simon, were all recent visitors.

Nelson County

Dulaney's Lounge
U.S. Highway 250, Afton
(540) 943-7167

Regional and local bands play every Friday and Saturday night at this lounge at the Inn at Afton (see our Hotels and Motels chapter). There may be a few oldies or beach music sets, but you usually will hear Top-40 sounds. The cover charge varies. The inn is 3 miles east of Waynesboro just off Interstate 64 at exit 99.

The Edge
Highway 151, Wintergreen Resort
(434) 325-8080
www.wintergreenresort.com

After a cool morning on the slopes or a warm afternoon on the links, the Edge is the perfect place to take off the edge. Relax and take in the mountain views in this family-oriented restaurant at Wintergreen Resort. There is seasonal entertainment and dancing, mostly on the weekends, and there is no cover charge.

Lynchburg

Cattle Annie's
4009 Murray Place, Lynchburg
(434) 846-2668, (434) 846-3206
www.cattleannies.com

Cattle Annie's is a country-western entertainment complex. The place features a 4,500-square-foot dance floor and offers dance lessons and live entertainment throughout the week, Tuesday through Saturday. Top-name country bands, like Confederate Railroad, are featured every month, and fans of '70s Southern rock will occasionally find their icons performing in concert at Cattle Annie's as well. You can take center stage on karaoke Tuesday, while Wednesday is line dancing night. Friday will appeal more to those who prefer rock and Top-40 dance music, while Saturday is usually the night for country.

Jazz Street Grill
3225 Old Forest Road, Lynchburg
(434) 385-0100

For unique atmosphere and some hot live jazz, try Jazz Street Grill, located in the Forest Plaza West Shopping Center. This New Orleans Cajun-style restaurant hosts talented jazz musicians every Friday and Saturday night. They have big holiday celebrations—Cinco de Mayo, Mardi Gras, New Year's Eve, and Halloween—when the staff dresses up and they offer drink specials.

T. C. Trotters
2496 Rivermont Avenue, Lynchburg
(434) 846-3545

If you are searching for the college crowd in Lynchburg, look no further than T. C. Trotters. Wednesday night is College Night, and the bar serves up quarter drafts to those bearing a college ID. DJs start spinning the tunes at 8:00 P.M. The cover is usually $3.00, but if you have your college ID, you can get in for a reduced rate. On Friday and Saturday, young bands get a chance to get started. The music will vary from Top 40 to the blues. The action tunes up at 10:00 P.M. and runs through 1:30 A.M. Cover will run you between $3.00 and $5.00.

NEW RIVER VALLEY

Blacksburg

Bogen's
622 North Main Street, Blacksburg
(540) 953-2233
Bogen's (see our Restaurants chapter) doesn't have any live entertainment, but it's one of the popular hangouts. Although the restaurant is popular with college students, you can rub elbows with Blacksburg's young professionals as well. The last call is at 1:25 A.M.

Hokie House Restaurant
322 North Main Street, Blacksburg
(540) 552-0280
Hokie House, located right across from the Virginia Tech campus, is a local favorite. The restaurant has a sports bar upstairs and a casual bar and dining downstairs. It also has seven pool tables, shuffleboard, air hockey, Golden Golf Tee, and other video games to occupy those late-night hours. Thursday and Saturday nights during the school year you can order late-night breakfast from midnight to 3:00 A.M.

Sharkey's Grill
216 North Main Street, Blacksburg
(540) 552-2030
Sharkey's is home of the Super Mug (a 34-ounce beer mug) and is known for the "best wings and ribs in town." Happy Hour lasts from 11:00 A.M. to 9:00 P.M.! The local paper voted Sharkey's the best happy hour price in town. The restaurant has two

bars, five pool tables, and a jukebox. There are also five TVs, so you don't have to miss a minute of the game!

Woody's Baha Bar and Grill
218 North Main Street, Blacksburg
(540) 552-7471
This club used to be Preston and Company; it has a new name, but they are still serving up a mix of "hot stuff" food and music for the college crowd. You can find a DJ serving up dance music from Tuesday through Saturday. Special guest DJs come in from big cities to spin the latest hit music. The cover is around $3.00. Dance nights, the hours are 9:00 P.M. to 2:00 A.M.

Christiansburg

Huckleberry's Restaurant
2790 Roanoke Street, Christiansburg
(540) 381-2382
Huckleberry's (see our Restaurants chapter), on U.S. Highway 11 off the I-81 Virginia Tech exit, has two lounges with two dance floors that offer Top-40 and country entertainment. Country-music lovers should definitely stop here to boot-scoot on the largest dance floor around. On Friday and Saturday nights, there will be a country band in Whispers and a DJ in Sundance. The cost is about $7.00.

Floyd County

Floyd Country Store
206 South Locust Street, Floyd
(540) 745-4563
www.floydcountrystore.com
In Floyd County, you'll do your rocking and rolling country style at the legendary store's Friday night live jamborees (see our Attractions chapter). Here bluegrass and old-time musicians entertain crowds every weekend. Local and regional musicians are featured on Friday nights beginning around 6:30 P.M. The price is $3.00.

On Saturday, usually in late summer and early fall, some of the bigger names are booked, including the likes of the Little River Band. These 7:30 P.M. concerts will run up to $10.

Oddfella's Cantina
Locust Street, Floyd
(540) 745-3463
www.oddfellascantina.com
Only in the foothills of the Blue Ridge Mountains would you expect to find . . . Cuban music. Floyd County, long noted for its cultural diversity, has another place for the in crowd to meet and greet. Oddfella's is a restaurant that specializes in vegetarian fare and multicultural music. It's been called an "Age of Aquarius kind of place." You can usually find some sort of entertainment Wednesday through Sunday. Cellist Matt Hamovitz and bluegrass star Rhonda Vincent were among the recent guests. Irish is usually played the first Friday of each month, songwriters' night is Wednesday, and you can even hear a little instrumental music during Sunday's brunch. Reservations are required. There is usually no cover, but tips for the musicians are graciously accepted.

If big dance floors are a plus in your nightlife expectations, the New River Valley has the largest in the region at Huckleberry's in Christiansburg.

ALLEGHANY HIGHLANDS

Bath County

The Presidents Lounge
The Homestead, Hot Springs
(800) 838-1766
www.thehomestead.com
The Presidents Lounge at the Homestead (see our Resorts chapter) is an elegant place to gather before and after dinner. Adorning the walls are portraits of the 13 presidents who have visited the resort. Downstairs in the Sports Bar you will find big-screen and other TVs for viewing sporting events; you can also snack on finger food and play billiards and darts, or dance to the sound of Top-40 music in Players Pub.

SHOPPING

W hether you're looking for antiques, handcrafts, or the truly unique in clothing and housewares, the Blue Ridge region has a wonderful variety of choices. Of course, we have the usual shopping malls, Wal-Marts, and Kmarts. But most towns in the Blue Ridge have at least one quaint antiques shop and a place featuring the work of local crafters.

Some fine furniture makers in the region, such as E. A. Clore in Madison or Suter's in Harrisonburg, sell directly to the consumer.

This is also true for the shops selling fine handcrafts. Places such as the Blue Ridge Pottery on U.S. Highway 33 near the Skyline Drive specialize in ceramics that are crafted literally right next door.

Charlottesville is known for its fine downtown shops that sell crafts and other objets d'art from around the globe. In this Blue Ridge city you can just as easily find an African mask or Indian totem as a bar of American soap.

If you're visiting from out of state and want a made-in-Virginia souvenir, plenty of shops specialize in such products. Virginia Born and Bred in Lexington is one fine example, selling beautiful brass and silver items as well as folk art, woven goods, peanuts, jams, and jellies. Virginia Made Shop in Staunton and the Virginia Company in Charlottesville are others.

The following is a description of some of our favorite shops. This is in no way a comprehensive listing, and we may have inadvertently missed your favorite shop. Drop us a line and give us your Insider's perspective if you know of a top-notch place we've missed.

Also, in the retail world shops come and go, so call ahead if you have your heart set on a particular store. This seems especially true in the antiques trade. We've given you the businesses' phone numbers to save you possible disappointment at the end of a long drive.

SHENANDOAH VALLEY

Winchester and Frederick County

ANTIQUES

Millwood Crossing
381 Millwood Avenue, Winchester
(540) 662-5157
Collectors will have a field day at this old apple-packing warehouse on U.S. Highway 50 W. Inside are approximately 10,000 square feet of antiques and specialty shops. Wooden floors and hand-hewn beams add to the comfortable charm. Shoppers will find a range of antiques, collectibles, and reproductions, featuring American country pieces in pine, walnut, cherry, and oak. The shops include Buck's County Reproduction Furniture and Apple Shop, with local jams and jellies, and quilts. Millwood is a half mile off Interstate 81. It's closed most Mondays.

SPECIALTY SHOPS

Dancing Fire Gallery
15 East Boscawen Street, Winchester
(540) 722-2610
You can pick up one-of-a-kind gifts at Dancing Fire. Leslie Betz Malone took over this gallery and studio from potter Alicia White Daily in the late '90s. Malone, who has been working as an artist for more than 20 years, displays her own pottery and crafts in this bright and colorful shop.

Handworks Gallery
150 North Loudoun Street, Winchester
(540) 662-3927, (800) 277-0184
Handworks, located on the pedestrian-only Loudoun Street Mall, is one of the

finest places in the region to find hand-crafted jewelry, pottery, basketry, and textiles. The gallery operates on seasonal hours, so it is a good idea to call beforehand. It's closed Sunday and Monday.

Kimberly's
135 North Braddock Street, Winchester
(540) 662-2195, (800) 967-8676
www.kimberlyshome.com
This is just one of 200 shops, cafes, and services in the 45-block National Historic District of Old Town Winchester. Housed in Civil War General Sheridan's headquarters, Kimberly's sells fine European linens, home accessories, and stationery. The 5,000-square-foot shop also carries a wide selection of brand-name children's apparel and "Finger Follies," a collection of puppets. Just look for the giant apple on the front lawn.

MALLS

Apple Blossom Mall
1850 Apple Blossom Drive, Winchester
(540) 665-0201
www.simon.com
Anchored by the likes of Belk, JCPenney, and Sears, this indoor facility is home to more than 90 stores. It also includes a six-screen movie theater and a play zone for children.

Warren County

ANTIQUES

Front Royal Antique and Flea Market
Commerce Avenue, Front Royal
(540) 636-9729
If you follow Highway 522 from Winchester toward Front Royal on the weekend, you will find that traffic slows to a crawl at Commerce Avenue. That is the location of this big outdoor flea market, where you will find almost anything your heart desires. It is only up and running on Saturday and Sunday. It's closed January and February.

You can pick up antiques guides and brochures from chambers of commerce or visitor centers. Be sure to order your Blue Ridge Antique Guide by calling (800) 383-1758.

Shen-Valley Flea Market
Highway 522, Front Royal
(540) 869-1561, (540) 869-7858
Just outside of Front Royal is a smaller weekend flea market. It's a fun place to browse and you can make some good finds among the array of books, T-shirts, tools, glassware, and used furniture. The indoor and outdoor market operates year-round.

Warren County Fairgrounds
26 Fairgrounds Road, Front Royal
(540) 635-5827
www.warrencountyfair.com
If you want to shop year-round, regardless of the weather, the Warren County Fairgrounds offers an indoor facility for flea market shoppers. You will find furniture, collectibles, and bric-a-brac. The hours run from 9:00 A.M. to 5:00 P.M. on the weekends only. To get to the fairgrounds take Highway 522, 5 miles north of Front Royal.

SPECIALTY SHOPS

J's Gourmet
206 South Royal Avenue, Front Royal
(540) 636-9293
www.jsgourmet.com
For 13 years, J's has been serving its customers a taste of Virginia, and the world. Here you can purchase an assortment of wines from right here in the commonwealth and bottles from California, France, and Spain. The shop also carries exotic coffees, spices, breads, meats, and cheeses, and you can sample whatever assortment of goodies that the staff is preparing for the day.

Simonpietri's Gift and Pawn Shop
528 South Royal Avenue, Front Royal
(540) 636-1763
At the edge of town is this kitschy mixture of tourist items, plus crafts, guns, and musical instruments. The gift shop has been in business since the 1950s. Thirty years later, they added the pawn shop, and both areas are still going strong.

BOOKSTORES

The Royal Oak Bookshop
207 South Royal Avenue, Front Royal
(540) 635-7070
www.royaloakbookshop.com
There is a wonderful selection of new, used, and publishers' remainder books at Royal Oak. In business since 1975, this shop is open daily, but after Labor Day, it closes on Tuesday and Wednesday. If you happen to stop by after hours, you can sort through a selection of paperback and hardback books on the front porch to help get you through the night. They only cost 10 cents each.

Shenandoah County

ANTIQUES

Flea Market
164 Landfill Road, Edinburg
(540) 984-8771
From weekend to weekend, you never know what you might discover here. Everything from antiques to collectibles have been up for grabs, with 95 booths under one roof. This huge flea market is halfway between Woodstock and Edinburg. Just take exit 283 from I-81. It's open 7:30 A.M. to 5:00 P.M. Friday, Saturday, and Sunday.

Richard's Antiques
14211 Old Valley Pike, Edinburg
(540) 984-4502
Richard's has been specializing in fine country and formal antiques since the late 1980s. His 18th-century and early-19th-

century furniture are mainly Southern and mid-Atlantic pieces. He also carries wood and pewter accessories. The shop is a mile south of Edinburg on U.S. Highway 11.

Strasburg Emporium
160 North Massanutten Street, Strasburg
(540) 465-3711
www.waysideofva.com
Whether you're a serious collector or someone who just likes to drool over beautiful things, you must visit this 65,000-square-foot building that houses more than 100 booths of antiques and art dealers. The building used to be a silk mill. Today you'll find a lot of unusual items ranging from iron beds to estate jewelry. There is plenty of free parking.

SPECIALTY SHOPS

Christmas Gallery
9373 Congress Street, New Market
(540) 740-3000
No matter what time of year, it will feel like a holiday when you step inside this turn-of-the-20th-century shop. It's filled with twinkling lights and hundreds of ornaments. Since 1977, it has been selling handmade crafts, wreaths, and collectibles, such as Snow Babies and Dept. 56 villages.

Deanville Fallow Deer Farm
7648 Crooked Run Road, Basye
(540) 856-2130
Located near Bryse Resort, this is one of only two farms in Virginia that raise deer for the meat. The deer roam 25 acres of this 50-acre farm, which started in 1992. There's a little shop where you can purchase jerky and venison, vacuum-sealed in a variety of cuts. Kids can also get a bucket of corn to feed the deer, which get very excited when they see a car drive up. Approximately 120 in this herd, these fallow deer are smaller than white-tailed deer and have antlers that are more like moose antlers. They can be different colors, too—spotted, white, and chocolate-brown. The owners say the meat is

sweeter and doesn't have the wild, or "gamey," taste of other deer. While there, pick your own heirloom organic veggies, including old-time pole beans, tomatoes that run the gamut of colors from white to purple, and unusual pumpkins that come in every color but orange. There are 18 breeds of chickens that represent 13 different countries on this Virginia-certified organic farm. Children will delight in meeting Sugar, the pet chicken, who comes running when summoned. Deanville Farm is open 10:00 A.M. to 4:00 P.M. Friday through Monday from April through November.

Shenandoah Valley Crafts and Gifts
9365 Congress Street, New Market
(540) 740-3899
Since 1983, this old-fashioned business has carried a great mix of Southern charm. You will find everything from country furniture to fireworks. There are also hand-loomed rugs, white oak baskets, quilts, and Virginia hams. You don't want to miss the Rock Shop.

BOOKSTORES

Paper Treasures
9595 South Congress Street, New Market
(540) 740-3135
www.papertreasuresbooks.com
This enormous bookstore used to be home to a car dealership. Since 1986 it has been a fascinating place to browse through 250,000 old books, magazines, and prints. Not only will you find used and rare books, but also hundreds of pieces of ephemera, maps, comic books, and record albums. The selection of old magazines includes *Collier's Weekly, The Saturday Evening Post, Ebony, Life, McCall's, Ladies' Home Journal,* and hundreds of other titles from the early 1800s to the 1990s. There also is a good selection of children's literature.

Page County

ANTIQUES

Bren's
24 East Main Street, Luray
(540) 743-9001
For more than a decade, Bren's has been offering a variety of items for the home decor. They specialize in it. There are plenty of antiques and estate jewelry, but you also will find gift books, Victorian accents, and natural products.

Mama's Treasures
22 East Main Street, Luray
(540) 743-1352
In downtown Luray, you will find an extensive collection of colorful glass and old costume jewelry at Mama's. The former clothing store now specializes in collectibles. You can also find some antique furniture and quilts here.

SPECIALTY SHOPS

Pine Knoll Gift Shop
3805 Highway 211, Luray
(540) 743-5805
Five miles east of Luray at the entrance to the Shenandoah National Park sits Pine Knoll. This old-time store is crammed with souvenirs. You will find knives, quilts, baskets, coonskin caps, American Indian moccasins and jewelry, jams and jellies, and fireworks, plus Blue Ridge pottery, rocks, and minerals. The fudge and peanut brittle are great.

Rockingham County

ANTIQUES

Chalot's Antiques
445 South Main Street, Mount Crawford
(540) 433-0872
www.svta.org/member
Chalot's is a mecca for lovers of fine old furniture. The building itself is a treasure, dating back to 1850. The shop has six showrooms of high-quality antiques; some

are set up with 18th-century beds and quilts. One room is called the Civil War Parlor and is decorated with pieces from that era. The store also has flow blue china, Victorian bric-a-brac, primitive accessories, and old glassware. It's closed on Wednesday.

Curiosity Shop Antiques
306 Spotswood Trail, Elton
(540) 298-1404
Farther east, in Elkton, is one of the area's finer antiques shops. Here you'll find antique furniture, folk art, primitives, quilts, and old tools for the discriminating buyer. The shop has been open for business since 1973. It's open Thursday through Sunday.

James McHone Antique Jewelry
75 South Court Square, Harrisonburg
(540) 433-1833
www.mchonejewelry.com
James McHone has been in the specialized antiques business for more than 15 years. This shop in downtown Harrisonburg deals with exquisite estate and antique jewelry. The store also features sterling flatware and a fine selection of diamonds. It's closed Sunday.

Rolling Hills Antique Mall
779 East Market Street, Harrisonburg
(540) 433-8988
It's one-stop shopping for bargain hunters. More than 60 area dealers have set up shop under one roof here in Harrisonburg. The 12,000-square-foot building has been divided into four rooms, with a variety of antiques and collectibles sprinkled throughout. You'll find primitives, coins, formal and country furniture, 100,000 postcards, and Depression glass.

The Shoppes at Mauzy
10559 North Valley Pike, Mauzy
(540) 896-9867, (866) 222-9173
www.MauzyShopping.com
This beautiful old building with a two-story porch used to be a stagecoach inn in the early 1800s. Today it is home to a collection of dealers that offer everything from

antiques and collectibles to "purposeful clutter." There is furniture, primitives, and country reproductions, as well as hand-crafted items including dried florals and candles. If you hit the right season, you may even be able to sample locally grown apples and fresh cider.

MARKETS

Dayton Farmers' Market
3105 John Wayland Highway, Dayton
(540) 879-3801
www.daytonfarmersmarket.com
It's definitely worth driving to the little town of Dayton, just 2 miles south of Harrisonburg on Highway 42, for this mini-mall where the merchants are incredibly friendly. Peddlers sell fresh poultry, seafood, beef, home-baked goods, cheeses, nuts, and dried goods. Specialty shops carry Early American tin lighting, pottery, quality antiques, and handcrafts, jewelry, and clothes. Among the array of shops, you'll find Swiss Valley Lace, the Cheese Place, Ten Thousand Villages, and Reflections of Yesteryear, which sells handcrafted furniture and Amish collectibles. Hank's will also serve up its special barbecue if you get hungry. It's open Thursday through Sunday.

Shenandoah Heritage Farmers' Market
121 Carpenter Lane, Harrisonburg
(540) 433-3929
Just south of Harrisonburg is a combination of an antiques mall, a produce market, and a collection of 20 specialty shops that sell just about everything, including crafts, bulk food, local souvenirs, Western wear, fishing gear, Amish-made furniture, and fudge. There are multiple dealers who offer everything from local antiques to estate sales. The shops include the Country Canner, which offers fruits, vegetables, and homemade soup in jars. If you work up an appetite, stop by the Dinner Bell Cafe for snacks or lunch fare throughout the day. The building itself is quite a treat. You can feed the goldfish in the pond by the entrance or watch a real waterwheel at work inside. It's closed Sunday.

HANDCRAFTS

Gift and Thrift
731 Mount Clinton Pike, Harrisonburg
(540) 433-8844
www.tenthousandvillages.com
After 21 years in downtown Harrisonburg, Gift and Thrift has moved to a bigger home with a spacious parking lot. Since opening in 1982 with the support of 10 Mennonite churches, the shop has raised $15 million to assist the Mennonite work both locally and abroad. Gift and Thrift is actually three shops under one roof. The gift shop, Artisans' Hope, features gorgeous handcrafts—weavings, clothing, ceramics, and the like—from around the world. Sales provide "vital fair income" to the Third World artisans who create the works. The thrift shop, World of Good, includes used clothing and household items. Sales from these reasonably priced items help benefit the community. Then in 2002, Gift and Thrift expanded to include Booksavers. Used books, textbooks, and magazines are collected from local folks, schools, and libraries and are sold in the store, to educational services, or to a recycling company. It's a great place to find a bargain and help a worthy cause at the same time.

Patchwork Plus
17 Killdeer Lane, Dayton
(540) 879-2505
www.patchworkplus/quilting.com
This is a fabric shop that also sells brilliantly colored hand-woven rugs and quilts. Look for the hitching post out front where buggy-riding Mennonites tie their horses while they shop. It's closed Sunday.

SPECIALTY SHOPS

Harper's Lawn Ornaments,
Water Gardens, Paths, and Ponds
2670 North Valley Pike, Harrisonburg
(540) 434-8978
www.harperslawnornaments.com
This is exactly what it sounds like—a concrete jungle. Canadian geese, bears, deer, frogs, even gargoyles are among the 1,000 different lawn decorations waiting at this unique shopping adventure. What started out as a hobby turned into the business for the Harper family, who have run this outdoor shop since 1962. There are fountains, benches, stepping-stones, statues, and thousands of concrete items made on-site. You also will find large fiberglass animals, plus ponds and liners, plants, artificial waterfalls, and fish food. If you need them, they will even sell you the fish. It's open Monday through Saturday year-round and on Sunday from May to August.

Ryan's Fruit Market
North Mountain Road, Timberville
(540) 896-1233
When the produce is ripe, Ryan's will have it ready and waiting. They specialize in fresh apples and peaches, and the shop should be open for business through mid-November. It's closed Sunday.

Showalter's Orchard and Greenhouse
17768 Honeyville Road, Timberville
(540) 896-7582
Here's a great place to partake of the region's sweetest crop of all—apples. Showalter's has its own cider mill and sells freshly pressed cider and many varieties of apples from late September through Christmas. The year-round greenhouse operation also sells just about anything that grows, from herbs to poinsettias. It's closed Sunday.

Suter's Handcrafted Furniture
2610 South Main Street, Harrisonburg
(540) 434-2131
www.suters.com
This family-run business has been around since 1839, when Daniel Suter, a skilled Mennonite cabinetmaker and carpenter, settled in the Harrisonburg area and began making furniture. Today the company carries on the tradition of quality craftsmanship. Suter's makes gorgeous Colonial reproductions in solid cherry, mahogany, and walnut, using the finest techniques. Choose your style—Duncan

Phyfe, Chippendale, Queen Anne, Hepplewhite, or Sheraton. There are showrooms here and in Richmond, or call for a brochure.

BOOKSTORES

Green Valley Book Fair
2192 Green Valley Lane, Mount Crawford
(540) 434-0309, (800) 385-0099
www.gvbookfair.com
People from all over flock to this book fair, held six times a year, usually for two weeks at a time. It all started more than 30 years ago with used and antique books sold in the Evans family barn. Locals would camp out just to be the first in line. Today, the Book Fair sells only new books in two buildings that cover 25,000 square feet of space. You never know what you might find with 500,000 books in a wide variety of fiction, nonfiction, educational books, cookbooks, and children's literature. The best part: These new books are sold at 60 to 90 percent below the publishers' retail prices.

MALLS

Valley Mall
1925 East Market Street, Harrisonburg
(540) 433-1875
www.simon.com
For those who prefer their shopping all under one roof, the Valley Mall houses 80 department stores and specialty shops, including Belk, Eddie Bauer, JCPenney, and Peebles.

If you have your heart set on a unique shop or store, always call ahead to be sure there will be someone there when you plan to go. Many shop owners are escapees from the big city or natives whose first priority is quality of life and second priority is running a retail establishment. Farming and other obligations might get in the way of their regular hours.

Augusta County

ANTIQUES

Dusty's Antique Market
2530 Lee Highway, Mount Sydney
(540) 248-2018
For 20 years, this old cinderblock building from the 1920s has hosted a variety of antiques. Today, more than a dozen dealers carry everything from oak and walnut furniture to tools, quilts, jewelry, and primitives. One dealer even has Fiestaware. Dusty's is open Thursday through Sunday or other times by appointment.

Jolly Roger Haggle Shop
27 Middlebrook Avenue, Staunton
(540) 886-9527
A fire burnt this former warehouse at the turn of the 20th century, but for more than 30 years, the renovated Wharf has been home to some of the most interesting antiques and collectibles in town. It is a virtual treasure chest of coins, china, old money, Civil War and American Indian artifacts, and much, much more. This multilevel shop also has estate jewelry on its list of offerings.

Once Upon a Time
25 West Beverley Street, Staunton
(540) 885-6064, (866) 877-8164
www.clockshop.stauntonweb.com
Long-case clocks, mantel clocks, wall clocks—this shop literally chimes with antiques of all varieties. It specializes in sale, restoration, and repair of antique and quality European and domestic timepieces. The store is open weekdays, but you might catch the proprietors on Saturday by chance or appointment.

Verona Antique Mall
307 Lee Highway, Verona
(540) 248-3532
Once a roller-skating rink, this 20-year-old building is home to 30 dealers and an American Indian museum. The shop carries a large variety of oak, pine, cherry, walnut, and other antique furniture, along

with quilts, linens, old books, china, coins, and vintage records. The museum represents a variety of tribes and features artifacts, headdresses, arrowheads, clothes, pottery, baskets, and rare pieces. It's right across from the firehouse. It's open Thursday through Monday.

SPECIALTY SHOPS

Andre Viette Farm and Nursery
994 Long Meadow Road, Fishersville
(540) 943-2315, (800) 575-5538
www.inthegardenradio.com
Andre Viette has one of the largest collections of perennials in the eastern United States, with more than 3,000 varieties of daylilies, peonies, irises, poppies, and many unusual plants for your garden. The Viettes moved their perennial farm away from encroaching development in New York to the wide-open spaces of the Shenandoah Valley in 1976. The owner of this 200-acre farm can be heard regularly on public radio, offering gardening tips on his call-in radio show, "In the Garden with the Viettes." The farm and nursery offers events May through December, including seminars, tours, and lectures; workshops in the fall; and a Christmas-decorating workshop in December.

Arthur's
13 East Beverley Street, Staunton
(540) 885-8609
For an elegant touch, try Arthur's. Since September 1986, this store has been dressing up local homes with a dazzling collection of lamps and Colonial Williamsburg reproductions and more contemporary pieces. There are plenty of home accessories, including items in brass, silver, and pewter.

The Cheese Shop
2366 Tinkling Springs Road
Stuarts Draft
(540) 337-4224
A number of Mennonite-operated businesses make shopping a real pleasure in the Stuarts Draft area, including the

Cheese Shop. This Amish-Mennonite family business since 1960 sells more than 30 varieties of cheese at great prices, along with nuts, dried fruits, and other bulk dried foods. The shop, just three-fourths of a mile north of Stuarts Draft on Highway 608, is closed on Sunday.

The Christmas Store & Museum
106 Rowe Road, Suite 102, Staunton
(549) 885-8174
Walk through the door and you step into Christmas past. Aside from a wonderful selection of Christmas ornaments big and small, what makes this specialty store unique is its museum. On exhibit are artifacts and ornaments spanning 1850 to 1960. From Shiny Bright ornaments to a child's sled, the collection includes pieces you would expect to find during the holiday season. But wait. If you came here to shop, you came to the right place. You can pick up Christmas collectibles from Snow Village, Heritage Village, Christopher Radko, even an authentic nativity scene from the Italian company Fontanini. There are also American and European decorations, ornaments, antique Santa reproductions, and American Christmas folk art. The shop is closed Sunday.

Elder's Antique and Classic Automobiles
114 South New Street, Staunton
(540) 885-0500
Peer through the big window and you can see sleek old Rolls Royces and other automotive beauties of yesteryear. You can see between 40 and 60 antique automobiles from 9:30 A.M. to 6:00 P.M. Open Friday and Saturday or by appointment.

The Emporium
101 East Beverley Street, Staunton
(540) 885-1673
www.emporiumgifts.com
For more than 20 years, this downtown shop has offered a large selection of toys and gifts for that special occasion. The Emporium is noted for its lamps, picture frames, and paper products, including Crane stationery. You can also find one-of-

a-kind gifts, including Nancy Thomas folk art and Mary Hadley pottery.

Golden Tub Bath Shop
20 East Beverley Street, Staunton
(540) 885-8470
If your bathroom needs a makeover, start here. Where else can you find 175 different shower curtains? This shop sells everything for the bath, including elegant soaps, towels, and accessories. There are Crabtree and Evelyn toiletries for her and Royal Lynne lotions for him. You can coordinate your entire bathroom or shop for unique gifts, including antique-style shaving mugs and brushes.

Grandma's Bait
24 East Beverley Street, Staunton
(540) 886-2222
Grandma's Bait has been providing clothing for Staunton's youngsters since 1981. From booties for the newborn to jeans for the 12-year-old, this shop carries a fine selection of quality brands and affordable prices. Sizes range from 0 to 16. Not only will you find sweaters, shoes, and slacks, the shop also carries fun things, too, such as jewelry, sunglasses, even stuffed Poohs, Teddys, and Elmos. The shop recently expanded its toy selection to include Little Farmer Toys, Melissa and Doug wooden crafts, dollhouses, and puzzles. Grandma's Bait also carries antique children's furniture and homemade quilts for the wee ones.

Holt's For the Home
16 East Beverly Street, Staunton
(540) 885-0217, (800) 420-4611
ww.holtschina.com
Since 1894, Holt's has been the area's top shop for fine china, crystal, glassware, and culinary supplies. Lenox, Wedgwood, Denby, Fiesta, and Oneida are just a few of the brand names that can be found here, not to mention the fine lines of Royal Worcester and Spode. The shop also carries kitchenware, ranging from Cuisinart to Oxo Good Grip. There are even beauty and bath products. Holt's is closed Sunday.

Honeysuckle Hill
100 East Beverley Street, Staunton
(540) 885-8261
You can find antiques, collectibles, and gifts in this downtown shop, but the star attractions are birdhouses. A Shenandoah Valley couple builds their own hand-painted birdhouses. They come in 50 different designs and can be personalized. It's closed Sunday.

Rockfish Gap Outfitters
1461 East Main Street, Waynesboro
(800) 851-6027
www.rockfishgapoutfitters.com
This is a fabulous place to pick up equipment for all your outdoor adventures, be they on a biking trail, camping trip, or a paddle down the river. Located just a few miles off the Appalachian Trail on U.S. Highway 250, the shop is a favorite restocking place for backpackers. Open daily, the store carries the best in tents and sleeping bags, including North Face and Mountain Hardware, and a plethora of backpacks, day packs, and fanny packs. They also carry Gary Fisher, Trek, and Cannondale bikes; kayaks and canoes by Old Town Perception and Wilderness Systems; as well as Gramicci and Patagonia clothing, to name but a few. You can even pick up cooking utensils and freeze-dried pizza or beef Stroganoff to rustle up a hearty feast on the trail. Open since 1988, this shop is truly a smorgasbord for the outdoor fanatic.

Rocky and Brenda's Gold and Silver
3287 Lee Highway, Weyers Cave
(540) 234-8676, (800) 296-8676
www.rockysgoldandsilver.com
People travel far and wide to find gems at bargain prices here in this shop, just north of Staunton. It's a true jewelry lover's delight. Not only can you find a wide assortment of gold and silver jewelry, Rocky and Brenda also carry flatware, antiques, collectibles, glassware, and coins. Rocky's is closed Sunday.

Silver Linings
16 West Beverley Street, Staunton
(540) 885-7808
This downtown shop is popular with tourists and locals alike. Once a store that catered to folk art, the owner has switched the emphasis to more of a boutique, specializing in unique wear for women. This "worldly boutique" carries both clothing and an assortment of accessories and silver jewelry.

Statler Brothers Gift Shop
1409 North Augusta Street, Staunton
(540) 885-7297
www.statlerbrothers.com
Staunton is home of the world-famous Statler Brothers, a quartet who started singing backup for Johnny Cash and went on to become a multi-Grammy Award-winning country group. Fans can stop by this new gift shop and purchase albums, cassettes, videos, CDs, T-shirts, sweaters, sweatshirts, hats, and all sorts of Statler memorabilia. The store is open 9:00 A.M. to 4:30 P.M. Monday through Friday.

Valley Framing Studio and Gallery
328 West Main Street, Waynesboro
(540) 943-7529
www.valleyframing.com
In downtown Waynesboro you will find this shop, which has been offering its award-winning custom framing services since 1983. The gallery has the Shenandoah Valley's largest inventory of limited-edition prints and other gifts. It also carries original art of the Blue Ridge, framed art, and everything from the historical art of Mort Kunstler to the figurative art of Steve Hawks. There are also collectibles here, including Terry Redlin's series of homes and havens. The studio is closed Sunday.

The Virginia Made Shop
54 Rowe Road, Staunton
(540) 886-7180, (800) 544-6118
Since 1984, Virginia Made has been offering an extensive collection of foods, wines, handcrafts, and other souvenirs from the commonwealth. Virginia peanuts are a big seller, as are the prints and pottery made by artists from across the state. The food brands range from Blue Crab Bay chowders to syrups from Winchester.

White Swan Gallery
107 East Beverley Street, Staunton
(540) 886-0522
www.whiteswangallery.com
Just down the road, you'll find this gallery where you can see and buy the work of regional artists, including the work of gallery owner and wildlife artist Laura Gilliland. Laura's art is as eclectic as her shop, which also sells American antiques, pottery, folk art, and collectibles. The gallery is open Tuesday through Saturday.

BOOKSTORES

The Bookstack
1 East Beverley Street, Staunton
(540) 885-2665
Book lovers of all ages can get their fill of best sellers and all types of new and even a few used books here. The shop, which has been around since 1978, also carries gift items, stationery, and souvenirs. The Bookstack nurtures the local literary crowd with open mike nights for writers, special events for children, and book signings by visiting authors.

MALLS

Colonial Mall
90 Lee Jackson Highway, Staunton
(540) 885-0315
www.colonialmallstaunton.com
You'll find more than 55 stores under the roof at this Staunton center. Anchoring the list are Belk, Goody's, JCPenney, and the Regal Cinemas.

OUTLET SHOPPING

The Virginia Metalcrafters
1010 East Main Street, Waynesboro
(540) 949-9432
www.vametal.com
You may have to fight for a parking place at the showroom and retail store located

next to the foundry. From 9:00 A.M. to 3:00 P.M. Monday through Thursday, you can watch through an observation window as craftsmen use the age-old technique of pouring molten brass into sand molds; the brass objects are later ground, sanded, and polished into faithful reproductions of 17th- and 18th-century pieces. The foundry reproduces candlesticks, lighting fixtures, fireplace tools, and other pieces from historic places, such as Colonial Williamsburg, Charleston, Newport, Monticello, Winterhur, and Old Sturbridge Village. Here, as in the location in the Waynesboro Village Outlet Mall, you can purchase seconds at a discounted price. The number at the outlet mall is (540) 949-8190.

Waynesboro Village Outlet Mall
601 Shenandoah Village Drive
Waynesboro
(540) 949-5000
Located right off Interstate 64 at exit 94, this attractively designed outlet mall houses dozens of specialty shops carrying discounted brand-name clothing, shoes, luggage, home furnishings, lingerie, and more. Liz Claiborne, Deck the Halls, Paper Factory, Virginia Metal Crafters, and L'Eggs/Hanes/Bali are but a few of the stores here.

Lexington and Rockbridge County

ANTIQUES

Antiques by Braford
18 Clay Brick Lane
Natural Bridge Station
(540) 291-2217
You'll find this exquisite shop down the road from Natural Bridge. The Brafords have a fine collection of 19th-century American furniture and pieces from Asia. The shop is closed Sunday.

Old South Antiques Ltd.
Highway 252, Brownsburg
(540) 348-5360
www.oldsthantiques.com
Here is one of the finest antiques stores in the Rockbridge County region, in the charming village of Brownsburg. The town is located 15 minutes north of Lexington via US 11 or Highway 39/252. Old South specializes in New England, Pennsylvania, and Southern antiques in original paint and refinished cherry, walnut, and pine. The shop is recommended by *American Country South* for its country-style wares and known for its large selection of American country furniture and accessories. The shop is open Thursday through Sunday.

SPECIALTY SHOPS

Artists in Cahoots
1 West Washington Street, Lexington
(540) 464-1147
www.artistsincahoots.com
This cooperative gallery of local artists and craftspeople have been in business since the 1980s. You'll find oil and watercolors, pottery, metalwork, handblown glass, photography, sculpture, hand-painted silk scarves, porcelain jewelry, stained glass, and decoys.

Cocoa Mill Chocolates
115 West Nelson Street, Lexington
(540) 464-8400, (800) 421-6220
www.cocoamill.com
If you're hankering for chocolate, head down to this shop. Hand-dipped scrumptious confections are sold individually or by the box, and the owners also have a mail-order service. This confectioner has even been featured in the *Washington Post* and the *Wall Street Journal* (in 2002). They're open every day except Sunday.

Pappagallo
23 North Main Street, Lexington
(540) 463-5988
A wide selection of sleek and funky dresses and exotic jewelry and accessories is what's carried by this shop. In business

for 20 years, Pappagallo offers everything from casual clothes such as T-shirts to trendy party dresses in a wide variety of styles. Accessories include handbags and purses, scarves, belts, and hair clips.

Peanut Butter and Jelly
121 West Nelson Street, Lexington
(540) 463-6166
This children's boutique opened up in spring 2003 and carries newborn to size 16 girls' and boys' clothing as well as gifts, toys, and jewelry. Owner Tammy Cash also carries belts and flip-flops for the college girls. The store is open 10:00 A.M. to 5:00 P.M. Monday through Saturday.

Sunday's Child
14 West Washington Street, Lexington
(540) 463-1786
Billed as a store of books, gifts, stationery, and greeting cards, this little place feels like much more—its subtitle is "world treasures for the children of yesterday, today, and tomorrow." It's the store of the magical and the mystical. Here you will find jewelry, fairy statues, posters, light-gathering wind mobiles, Mary Englebreit gifts, stuffed unicorns and other toys, bath oils, incense, Harry Potter memorabilia, and even lickable fairy dust (!).

Virginia Born and Bred
16 West Washington Street, Lexington
(540) 463-1832, (800) 437-2452
www.virginiabornandbred.com
Since 1986 this sophisticated shop has been selling Old Dominion wares, including fine brass work, Virginia metal crafts, linens, and Virginia pottery. You can pick up a fabulous gift basket as well as gourmet foods, wines, and garden products. Call and order their catalog.

BOOKSTORES

The Best Seller
29 West Nelson Street, Lexington
(540) 463-4647
If new and used books are your idea of a perfect afternoon of browsing, stop by the Best Seller. The shop, in its 33rd year, has 18,000 new and used titles. They also carry cards, stationery, local-music CDs, and maps. You can settle down with a good book at their cafe-style coffee bar. Their extensive children's section also includes educational toys.

The Bookery
107 West Nelson Street, Lexington
(540) 464-3377
You'll love visiting this store where the 40,000 books are stashed here and there throughout the place. New, used, and rare books focusing primarily on Civil War, Virginia, and local authors are found here as well as a wide variety of newspapers. Stop by on a Saturday and you may find an author ready to sign copies of his or her book. Be sure to request your special orders and out-of-print searches at this store. The Bookery also buys books from individuals and estates. Established 15 years ago, the Bookery is open Monday through Saturday from 9:00 A.M. to 6:00 P.M. and Sunday from 9:00 A.M. to 5:00 P.M.

Second Story Book Shop
19 Randolph Street, Lexington
(540) 463-6264
This bookshop shares space with the Lexington Historical Shop. It specializes in horse-related ephemera and books. A catalog of horse books is available. They are closed Sunday.

OTHER SHOPS

Buffalo Springs Herb Farm
Highway 606, Raphine
(540) 348-1083
www.buffaloherbs.com
Don Haynie and Tom Hamlin welcome you to the wonderful world of herbs in a big way. They are favored by the local garden club set for the way they have renovated this extraordinary 18th-century stone house and garden, which is open for herbal teas, luncheons, and tours by reservation. The plant house is stocked with herbs and garden accessories. They have

a large following for their herb workshops that are held throughout the season. A gorgeous gift shop in a big red barn sells herbal products, dried flowers, and garden books. The display gardens look like something out of Colonial Williamsburg. You'll see a culinary garden, springhouse tea garden, and foursquare heirloom vegetable and herb garden. Days and hours of operation are seasonal. It is closed January through March.

Wades Mill
55 Kennedy Road, Raphine
(540) 348-1400
www.wadesmill.com
This historic mill is located right next to Buffalo Springs Herb Farm. It's a working water-powered flour mill listed on the National Register of Historic Places. It's open from April to mid-December and produces and sells all kinds of bread flours, grits, cornmeal and bran, bread mixtures such as pesto bread and beer bread, as well as pancakes, waffles, and polenta. Admission to the mill is free, but they offer events and popular cooking classes, which do charge a fee. You can call ahead to set up a group lunch or dinner. Also ask for their free catalog.

ROANOKE VALLEY
Botetourt County

HANDCRAFTS

Amerind Gallery
1691 Roanoke Road, Daleville
(540) 992-1066
This unexpected gem in a rural area specializes in artwork of American Indians and Western artists. It is a member of the Indian Arts and Crafts Association and guarantees the authenticity of every American Indian handmade item in the gallery. A visit here is a veritable education in American art forms and cultures, expressed in superb original works, including a wide selection of the same beautiful silver jewelry you would find in New Mexico. The gallery is open Monday through Saturday.

Apple Barn Orchard and Apple Barn Store
1340 Apple Orchard Lane, Troutville
(540) 992-3636
www.applebarn-va.com
On US 11 you'll find this working apple farm and adjacent store owned by Al and Rachael Nichols. The Nicholses bought the property in 1969 and started a pick-your-own orchard with 300 apple trees. They built the big red barn on the property and in 1986 started their first retail business. You can still pick your own apples in season before you leave the picturesque setting or select prepackaged ones. On cold days and special occasions, you can enjoy hot, spiced, or slushy cider. The store also sells jellies, homemade apple butter, soup mixes, honey, specialty coffees, dressing mixes, and peaches, as well as apples in season, Amish-made furniture, and Beanie Babies. In the summer, the orchard and store are open seven days; off-season catch them Tuesday through Saturday.

Apple Barn II—Gifts and Collectibles
12 Boone Drive, Troutville
(540) 992-3551
www.applebarn-va.com
Located on the corner of Boone and US 11, this store is an outlet for Cat's Meow collectibles and was its number one national dealer. In fact, they did so well, the creator of Cat's Meow even came to the shop for a signing. This shop, also owned by the Nicholses, is a good place to find collectibles, including Snow Babies, Cherished Teddys, Precious Moments, and Ty Beanie Babies. Other collectible lines include Dept. 56, Buyer's Choice, Willow Tree Angels, Charming Tales, Possible Dreams, All God's Children, and Lizzie High dolls. From September to Christmas, the shop is open daily; other times of the year it's closed Sunday.

Cackleberry Ridge
81 Stoneybattery Road, Troutville
(540) 966-5646
This is the newest and fifth business opened by the Nicholses. Cackleberry is open daily and is a dealer for its large collection of Boyds Bears. They also sell Virginia-made products including Jim Shore's Heartland Collection and Lang and Bridgewater candles, as well as Toland flags and Ensco Growing Up Birthday Girl. You'll find home decor items as well as very nice Amish-made furniture in their building next door, including beds, tables, and cabinets. You won't want to miss the ice cram parlor and sandwich shop. There is ample parking and tour buses are welcome.

Old Country Store
Main Street, Buchanan
(540) 254-1130
Another shop owned by the Nicholses, this one sells country collectibles and Boyds Bears. You can also find wonderful Amish-made furniture here, everything from bookcases and toy boxes to pie safes, coffee tables, and hutches. When you've finished your shopping, be sure to cross the walkway that joins the store with the Apple Barn Gallery, a P. Buckley Moss dealership also located on Main Street (540-254-6677). Here you will find all the latest Roanoke Valley collectibles, including the Cat's Meow Roanoke collection of local landmarks. Both stores are closed Sunday.

ORCHARDS

Ikenberry
2557 Roanoke Road, Daleville
(540) 992-6166
This orchard has been in the Ikenberry family for four generations—100-plus years. Located on U.S. Highway 220, it is open every day except major holidays. Besides the apples you can buy, there's a retail market on the premises where you will find locally grown produce and seasonal produce such as pumpkins, sweet corn, and peaches. While you're at it, pick up some country ham, cider, homemade bread, pies, and cakes.

Craig County

Main Street Shops
326 Main Street, New Castle
(540) 864-7466
Here you will find several shops all rolled into one. In Ultimately Angels, the owner sells Victorian and angel collectibles plus her own handmade items that are very popular—little clothespin angels and birth-month angels. Each are made from clothespins and are complete with clothes and hair. She donates $1.00 from each angel to the American Cancer Society and the fight against breast cancer. There also is a Christmas section year-round, with ornaments and wreaths. Out of the Woods specializes in forest, fairies, and fantasy collectibles. It also includes jewelry, crafts, and art. Timi P. Beads features handcrafted jewelry and lampwork beads, while J. Clay Studio sells Jennifer Mulligan's pottery. Wild Birds caters to the feathered friends with bird feeders, food, and supplies. The stores are open Tuesday through Saturday.

Roanoke County

ANTIQUES

Roanoke Antique Mall
2302 Orange Avenue NE, Roanoke
(540) 344-0264
www.roanokeantiques.com
The Roanoke Valley is a treasure chest of top-notch, low-cost antiques. This mall on U.S. Highway 460 is Roanoke's largest antiques mall with more than 130 quality dealers and 25,000 square feet of timeless collectibles. It's open daily.

Vinton Antique Mall
107 South Pollard Street, Vinton
(540) 344-6847
Housed in a strip mall on the main street

through Vinton, this antiques shop is pretty large, with 30 dealers carrying "a little something for everyone." From antique furniture—higher-end pieces such as tables and wardrobes—to collectible art glass, jewelry, kitchenware, primitives, coins, and knives, you are sure to find what you need here. One dealer focuses strictly on antique clocks. The building itself was built in the 1940s as a furniture store and then operated as Sam's Variety Shop in the '50s and '60s. It's closed on Monday.

Wright Place Antique Mall
251 Wilderness Road, Salem
(540) 389-8507
This mall is home to 45 antiques dealers. What you'll find is a wide array of furniture, Highland furniture, folk art, antique books, glassware, gems, linens, pottery, and more.

HANDCRAFTS

Gallery 108, LLC
108 Market Street, Roanoke
(540) 982-4278
If fine handcrafts are what you seek, look no further than the historic City Market. Gallery 108 is located on the corner of Market and Salem Streets, across from Hotel Roanoke. It's a local artist cooperative and a retail gallery. They carry a wide selection of art and do corporate consulting, bridal registry, custom framing (there's the Framer's Workshop within the gallery), original artwork, glasswork, jewelry, enamels, sculpture, prints, and photography—and much more. They have several commissioned artists who do portraits. The six partners opened the gallery in 2001, and there are now 30 consignment artists. The hours of operation are Tuesday through Saturday.

Studios on the Square
126 West Campbell Avenue, Roanoke
(540) 345-4076
www.studiosonthesquare.com
You'll find the gallery on the first floor and the artist studios on the second and third floors. The public can come in and meet the 17 artists and see them demonstrate their work Monday through Saturday. Then you can purchase their wares, which include pottery, paper, fiber, wood, textiles, jewelry, baskets, stained glass, photography, and fine paintings. The gallery not only represents the artists in residence but carries the work of artists across the country. It's closed Sunday.

SPECIALTY STORES

The Binaba Shop
120 Campbell Avenue SE, Roanoke
(540) 345-7064, (800) 245-1277
www.binabashop.com
For something different, visit this little gem that is a volunteer-staffed, nonprofit shop, a joint venture between Kingdom Life Ministries, St. John's Episcopal Church, and Binaba's St. James Anglican Church as a way to help develop the cottage industries surrounding the village of Binaba in the West African nation of Ghana. Everything sold here is made in Africa, including masks from the Congo, baskets from Uganda, ebony, jewelry, bowls, handcrafted wood carvings of elephants, antelopes and the like, kuba cups, drums, and many other intriguing items. You can find Kisii stone carvings—made from soapstone—also known as Kisii stone because it comes from the Kisii highlands in the western part of Kenya near Lake Victoria. The shop started in 1998 and is open Monday through Saturday.

Fret Mill Music
21 Salem Avenue, Roanoke
(540) 982-6686
www.fretmill.com
Musicians, guitar enthusiasts, and anyone who appreciates fine stringed instruments should visit this music store. A wide selection of new and vintage guitars, mandolins, banjos, and fiddles is available. The store also sells amplifiers and hand percussion. Often you can walk in and find a seasoned musician trying out a new instrument, which is another compelling

reason to stop by! Fret Mill is closed Sunday.

The Gift Niche
101 Market Square, Roanoke
(540) 345-9900
If you're in the market for collectibles and gifts, stop in here. The shop is an author-ized Gold Paw dealer for Boyds Bear and Friends collectibles. They also carry the Seraphim Classics Angels and collegiate collectibles including Virginia Tech, Univer-sity of Virginia, and other Virginia schools. Not a Virginia college fan? Don't worry: They can special-order merchandise sporting the logos of out-of-state schools. These can include T-shirts, home decor, and even candles. The shop is going into its 20th year. It is closed on Sunday.

Gone Coco
32 Market Square, Roanoke
(540) 345-2604
For fun, contemporary clothing, jewelry, and gifts "for mother and daughter alike," try this intimate little shop. It carries cloth-ing in natural fabrics including cotton and linen. The fashion is fun but not too funky, so you can wear your new outfit to work. They also sell other accessories, soap, and incense. The shop is closed on Sunday.

La De Da
102 Church Avenue, Roanoke
(540) 345-6131
www.ladeda.net
This whimsical boutique for women's clothing caters to the young and young in spirit with flowing clothing, offering both work and play clothes. The store also sells eclectic furniture—from dining room tables to Indonesian pieces and unique kiln rugs.

PMD Screen Printing
650 Williamson Road, Roanoke
(540) 345-8337
PMD offers screen printing and embroi-dery. These are custom screens, any design. Specialty items such as key chains, lanyards, and pens are also available. It's open Monday through Friday.

Sam's on the Market
304 Market Street, Roanoke
(540) 342-7300
Specialty stores and boutiques abound throughout the Roanoke City Market. The Market Building and surrounding streets anchor the popular shopping area. At Sam's, you can buy uniforms, working clothes, and casual sportswear. They also do custom embroidery and alterations. The building that houses Sam's has an interest-ing history—recently renovated, it dates back about 95 years. In its previous history, though, it was a red-light district building with individual rooms upstairs. The renova-tion made the rooms into offices.

BOOKSTORES

Printer's Ink
4917 Grandin Road Extension, Roanoke
(540) 774-3500
This shop is a full-service bookstore, also carrying magazines, Hallmark cards, and jigsaw puzzles. Be sure to stop in, as the store has been in business for more than 30 years.

Ram's Head Bookshop
Tower Shopping Center, 2137 Colonial Avenue, Roanoke
(540) 344-1237
Ram's Head is a very popular place, being a large independent bookstore and the oldest independent bookshop in the Roanoke Valley. It celebrated its 40th anniversary in 2004, and visitors come back to visit from as far away as Los Angeles and New York. The shop has an excellent children's book room—probably more children's books than many kids-only bookstores. It also has a good Civil War section and sells stationery, notepa-per, and jigsaw puzzles. While there, be sure to climb the tall ladders that go all the way to the top shelves.

MALLS

Crossroads Mall
5002 Airport Road NE, Roanoke
(540) 366-4270

This mall has been a Roanoke Landmark since 1961. Anchor stores include Circuit City, Kmart, Goody's, Books-a-Million, and two movie theaters.

Tanglewood Mall
4420A Electric Road, Roanoke
(540) 989-4685
There are four main shopping malls in Roanoke. This one features a Belk, To the Rescue Museum, and a Carmike Theater featuring 10 movie screens with stadium seating.

Towers Shopping Center
2121 Colonial Avenue SW, Roanoke
(540) 982-6791
www.rappaportco.com/towers
This mall offers multilevel shopping near the center of town. The draws include Heironimus, Ram's Head Bookshop, and several restaurants.

Valley View Mall
4802 Valley View Boulevard, Roanoke
(540) 563-4400
www.valleyview.com
This mall, the largest shopping center in southwestern Virginia, has more than 100 stores and specialty boutiques, including Belk, Hecht's, JCPenney, Sears, Eddie Bauer, and a movie theater, Valley View Grande 16.

OUTLETS

Bacova Guild Factory Outlet
836 West Main Street, Salem
(540) 389-2667
www.bacova.com
You've seen the Bacova Guild's many silk-screened gifts, including mailboxes and doormats, in leading outdoor catalogs such as Orvis and L.L. Bean. Originally located in Bath County, the factory outlet moved to Salem in 1998. The Bacova Guild's owners provided every family in Bath County with a free silk-screened mailbox—a county trademark. The design department is still in Bacova, a charming village erected in the early 1920s as a lum-

ber mill's company town. In 1965 the village was totally restored by philanthropist Malcolm Hirsh. At the outlet store in Salem, you'll find every kind of mat you can imagine—accent rugs, area rugs, Orientals, anti-fatigue mats, kitchen rugs, and ceramics, as well as bath items and bedding, many with the wildlife motif.

Orvis Factory Outlet
31-B Campbell Avenue, Roanoke
(540) 344-4520
Fishing fanatics and lovers of the sporting life will enjoy this outlet, where they will find men's and women's clothing and gift items at a great discount price. There's casual and dress clothing, and hats, belts, and shoes. Many of these items are overstock, discontinued items, and samples. Summers are an especially good time to shop, since you can get discounts of up to 70 percent on winter items. You can also swing by the Orvis Outlet shop at West Salem Plaza Shopping Center in Salem (540-389-8190), offering the same great discount prices.

Orvis Retail Store
19 Campbell Avenue, Roanoke
(540) 345-3635
www.orvis.com
At this store you'll find the merchandise in the current catalog, which is men's and women's clothing, fishing rods and reels, and other gear. This store sells new items only, so there are no deep discounts.

EAST OF THE BLUE RIDGE
Loudoun County

ANTIQUES

The Old Lucketts Store Antiques
42350 Lucketts Road, Leesburg
(703) 779-0268
Seven miles north of Leesburg on U.S. Highway 15, you'll find this landmark building that dates back to 1910. It was once the town's post office, general store, and

the Lucketts family home. Today the restored facility houses 30 antiques dealers, carrying a mix of items ranging from country primitive and garden accents to quilts, kitchenware, and art deco.

SPECIALTY SHOPS

Designer Goldsmiths
203-A Harrison Street SE, Leesburg
(703) 777-7661
Located at Market Station, also known as the Wharf, this delightful shop is owned by Les and Stephanie Tompson, who specialize in goldsmithing, silversmithing, designing, and setting precious and non-precious stones. A custom shop, they make everything and they also do reproductions and repairs. The store is open Tuesday through Saturday.

The Finicky Filly
100 West Washington Street, Middleburg
(540) 687-6841
This cute shop carries very upscale women's clothing, accessories, and gifts, including women's reading glasses, jewelry, belts, scarves, handbags, cookbooks, candles, and lotion.

The Fun Shop
117 West Washington Street, Middleburg
(540) 687-6590
www.thefunshop.com
You've got to visit this place, established in 1956. It has an interesting array of gifts, greeting cards, and kids' clothing. It's actually a mini department store with everything from bed and bath linens to toys.

Hill High's Country Store
35246 Harry Byrd Highway, Round Hill
(540) 338-7173
West of Leesburg, you will find this country store where you can shop for crafts and rest from your shopping labors and travels with a deli sandwich or their specialty, a wedge of hot fruit pie. The store carries lots of country crafts and plates, wood furniture, baskets, and stuffed animals.

If you like to mix a little history with shopping, Leesburg's colorful Market Station at 180D South Street SE offers several shops in a delightful setting amidst renovated buildings that in the 1800s made up an area known as "the Wharf." The Wharf was home to grain and farm supply merchants, a blacksmith, a livery stable, an icehouse, McKimmey's Mill, and the W&OD Railroad depot. Today, five of the seven Market Station buildings are original structures from that 2-block area. If you need a break, there's a restaurant here, too.

The Irish Crystal Co.
102 West Washington Street, Middleburg
(540) 687-3422
www.buyirishcrystal.com
Since 1989, folks can find everything from paperweights to collector's items at the Irish Crystal Co. All things crystal, including fine crystal lamps, Waterford, and Christopher Radko, plus jewelry, stemware, lighting, and Christmas ornaments, are some of the great finds here.

Leesburg Emporium and Smoke Shop
205 Harrison Street SE, Leesburg
(703) 777-5557
The shop has been selling pipes, tobacco, premium cigars, and other smoking accessories since about 1980. It's located in the Wharf in what had been the stationmaster's house, which dates from 1915.

My Friends and Me
118 South Street SE, Leesburg
(703) 777-8222
www.myfriendsandme.com
Also at the Wharf, housed in an 1840s log house built of American chestnut, you'll find this cute little toy store. The shop has an exquisite collection of bears and dolls for all ages, including Madame Alexander dolls. It's open Tuesday through Saturday.

Red Fox Fine Art
1 North Liberty Street, Middleburg
(540) 687-5780, (800) 223-1728
www.redfoxfineart.com
Located appropriately enough behind the Red Fox Tavern, this gallery and studio specializes in 19th- and early-20th-century American sporting and animal paintings, and bronze sculpture. Red Fox Fine Art is on the second floor of the historic Red Fox Inn. It is open Monday through Friday.

The Sporting Gallery
11 West Washington Street, Middleburg
(540) 687-6447
www.sportinggallery.com
Opened in 1963, this is the town's oldest gallery. Located in the Duffy House (ca. 1820), the building features fireplaces, hardwood floors, and pine paneling and has been featured in *Architectural Digest*. This gallery specializes in fine sporting art, paintings, sculpture, antique prints, and books. Everyone from politicians to royalty have shopped here. The Gallery closes on Wednesday and Sunday.

The Tack Box
7 West Federal Street, Middleburg
(540) 687-3231
Here's another jewel that caters to the equestrian crowd and where you'll find delightful hunt country gifts for people and horses, including saddles, bridles, pillows, picture frames, and horse treats.

White Elephant
103 West Federal Street, Middleburg
(540) 687-8800
Be sure to check out this consignment shop that handles everything from antiques to clothing. It's not unusual to find treasures such as a pair of barely used Gucci shoes—and even more fun to speculate as to what Middleburg celeb might have worn them.

MALLS
Dulles Town Center
21100 Dulles Town Circle, Dulles
(703) 404-7120
www.shopdullestowncenter.com
This major shopping mall is located at the intersection of Highway 7 and Highway 28, right on the edge of Loudoun County. With more than 120 specialty shops and department stores, there's more than enough to keep you busy all day. The biggies include Hecht's, Lord & Taylor, Nordstrom, Sears, and JCPenney.

OUTLETS
Leesburg Corner Premium Outlets
241 Fort Evans Road NE, Leesburg
(703) 737-3071
www.premiumoutlets.com
Opened in 1998, this outlet center at the intersection of Highway 7 and the US 15 Bypass brought upscale outlet shopping to the northern edge of Virginia's Blue Ridge. The outdoor village setting includes 110 stores with everyday savings of 25 to 65 percent. Stores include Polo, Ralph Lauren Factory Store, Off 5th—Saks Fifth Avenue Outlet, Banana Republic Factory Store, Williams–Sonoma, Tommy Hilfiger, Nautica, Gap Outlet, Brooks Brothers Factory Store, Liz Claiborne, Nike Factory Store, Reebok, Rockport Factory Direct Store, Jockey, Kenneth Cole, Coldwater Creek, Waterford Wedgwood, and Mikasa.

Fauquier County

ANTIQUES
Fox Den Antique Mall
355 West Shirley Avenue, Warrenton
(540) 347-1162
This 30-dealer shop offers a diverse collection of antiques and collectibles and items on consignment. One specializes in primitive items, another in pottery, and another in African-American memorabilia.

You'll also find a wide variety of antiques. It's chock-full of furniture—everything from primitives from the late 1700s to furniture from the early and late 1800s. Show up the last Saturday of the month from March to October for the flea market in the parking lot.

church. Here you'll find new and used books, including fiction and nonfiction. They specialize in Civil War, Virginia, local, and regional books and authors; hiking maps; and trail guides. The store is open Friday through Sunday.

Rappahannock County

SPECIALTY SHOPS

Peter Kramer Cabinetmaker
311 Gay Street, Little Washington
(540) 675-3625
www.peterkramer.com
Peter Kramer has been a cabinetmaker for more than 30 years and has been making beautiful furniture in this lovely old town. Each of his creations is one of a kind, handcrafted from native American wood. Some of the furniture is rather whimsical, while other pieces are more classical.

Rush River Antiques
337 Gay Street, Little Washington
(540) 675-1410
www.rushriverantiques.com
Rush River features English and American antiques as well as fine arts. The shop itself is a showplace. The building was constructed in the 1700s. It's open Thursday through Monday.

Sperryville Emporium
11669 Lee Highway, Sperryville
(540) 987-8235
Off Highway 211, you'll find this series of connecting buildings where you can find everything from new solid wood furniture to apples, country hams, and honey.

BOOKSTORES

Old Sperryville Bookshop & Coffee House
44 Main Street, Sperryville
(540) 987-8444
www.geocities.com/oldbookshoppe
Greg and Nancy Ostinato own this unique shop housed in a century-old Gothic

Culpeper County

ANTIQUES

Culpeper Antique & Marketplace
137 South Main Street, Culpeper
(540) 825-5011
Sam Miller set up shop in this 14,000-square-foot building, which once housed a Leggett Department Store, and 50 dealers signed on to display their wares. Victorian-style antiques, including vintage clothing and furniture, can be found inside along with glassware and quilts. Hats are big. You'll find them hanging, perched, and placed throughout the marketplace. Free parking can be found behind the store.

MinuteMan MiniMall
Route 3 Germanna Highway, Culpeper
(540) 825-3133
Trains, planes, and toy automobiles. Just about any collectible you want is probably inside this 18,000-square-foot warehouse. Ed Reeves and his daughter had four vendors when they opened shop in 1992. Now there are 200, offering everything from Beanie Babies to reproduction furniture. There are lots of crafts, jams, and an entire room devoted to toy trains and accessories. Reeves said they aim for "nice stuff, reasonably priced." Don't be surprised if you are greeted by the owners' two cats.

Quail at the Woods Antiques
205 Main Street, Culpeper
(540) 825-2595
This shop in downtown Culpeper caters to the serious antiques collector. Beautiful furniture and fine china are among the exquisite works on display here. There is everything from mahogany Chippendale chairs from the 1870s to a sculpted

pewter lamp, ca. 1885. Bring your checkbook. One French candelabra from the 1800s recently carried a $3,350 price tag.

SPECIALTY GIFTS

Another Dimension Inc.
172 Davis Street, Culpeper
(540) 829-9062
www.anotherdimensiononline.com
This unique shop specializes in gifts and arts and crafts from different parts of the world. You can find everything from books autographed by local author Virginia Morton to crystal glass of Poland. The shop also carries a revolving collection of jewelry, local art works, toys for ages 3 and older, vibrant fabric bags, and wall hangings, including Dumbara weavings. The shop is closed on Sunday and Monday.

The Cameleer
125 East Davis Street, Culpeper
(540) 825-8073
If you are looking for a taste of the exotic, stop here. Owner Susan Berndardt has lived in or traveled through 32 countries, and she keeps her shop vibrant with different merchandise arriving on a regular basis. On a recent visit, this 12-year-old company had kilim rugs from Turkey, handmade stoneware from Poland, handcrafted candles from South Africa, soaps from France, jackets from Canada, possum down socks from New Zealand, leather purses from Columbia, and a 48-inch leather sculpted camel from India. It's a perfect place to find a gift for those who have everything.

Madison County

ANTIQUES

Blue Ridge Emporium
U.S. Highway 29, Madison
(540) 948-2255
www.bre-antiques.com
Nearly 80 antiques dealers have set up shop in this building, just 6 miles north of

Ruckersville. A word of advice: Wear comfortable shoes; it's much bigger than it looks. There are 16,500 square feet of antiques, collectibles, and crafts. Toys, furniture, old tools, Heritage lace, jewelry, and vintage clothing are just a few of the items in the emporium. It also houses a year-round Christmas shop, and the owners added a soda and snack shop up on the balcony.

Country Gardens
9373 Seminole Trail, 7 miles south of Madison
(540) 948-3240
This is a unique antiques shop that also specializes in period mantels and garden ornaments. The antiques alone are impressive, including a Scandinavian baking table that once belonged to Admiral Bull Halsey. The base dates back to the 17th century. The top lifts off so that the dough can be easily carried to the oven. The mantels, most from the Federal Period, are accompanied by a collection of andirons, fenders, and period fireplace tools. The owners also have expanded their collection of garden ornaments, with about 85 percent of those imported from England. Country Gardens is open Tuesday through Saturday.

SPECIALTY SHOPS

E. A. Clore Sons, Inc.
Highway 637, Madison
(540) 948-5821
www.eaclore.com
The Clore family has been making handcrafted furniture at its headquarters here in Madison since 1830. Nestled in a hollow three-tenths of a mile from Highway 673, E. A. Clore specializes in enduring Early American furniture in hardwood such as walnut, cherry, oak, and mahogany. Each piece, whether it's a Duncan Phyfe table or a computer desk, has a hand-rubbed finish. They sell directly from their factory to the consumer, and its showrooms are right there across from the shop. It's closed Sunday.

Handcraft House
2617 South Seminole Trail, Madison
(540) 948-6323, (800) 207-0534
This inviting handmade-gifts shop right on US 29 is the cat's meow, literally. It sells very fine crafts made by more than 300 artisans from across the nation, including central Virginia's largest selections of the popular Cat's Meow series. It's also the place to shop for rubber stamps and accessories. They also will teach you how to make your own personal gifts. Demonstrations and classes are held periodically on topics ranging from rubber stamping and embossing to making books and cards. If you would rather have someone else do the gift making, you can find country craft pottery, Gary Tavern puzzles, American Girl books, Yankee candles, and jellies from nearby Graves Mountain Lodge.

The Little Shop of Madison
320 South Main Street, Madison
(540) 948-4147
The Little Shop has been greeting customers in downtown Madison since 1978. Housed in a ca. 1859 building, this warm shop provides everything you need for quilt making. There are bolts and bolts of colorful cotton fabrics and the notions and patterns to piece them together. The staff is knowledgeable and friendly, plus they even offer lessons for all skill levels.

Plow & Hearth County Store
130 Commerce Lane, Rochelle
(540) 948-3659, (800) 866-6072
www.plowandhearth.com
If you want to give your home that country feel, here is your one-stop shopping store. Plow & Hearth, a nationally known catalog shopping mecca, has two shops here in its hometown of Madison. The owners, Peter and Peggy Rice, treat customers like neighbors. "We offer only products we use or would use ourselves." The County Store showcases many of their items, ranging from comfy leather chairs to gliders for your patio. There also are garden tools, bird feeders, gifts for your pets, and a selection of their famous peanuts and peanut brittle. Plow & Hearth also has a factory outlet store on the same property, closer to US 29. You can save at least 30 percent, maybe more, here on samples, discontinued items, and merchandise that has been returned from catalog sales.

Yoder's Country Market
Highway 230, Pratt
(540) 948-3000
www.yoderscountrymarket.net
People drive all the way to Pennsylvania to find the charm and country ways that are part of this little store in Madison County. Since 1985, Owen and Erma Yoder have been operating this cozy, down-home shop, selling fresh-baked breads, pies, and cakes and deli sandwiches featuring 75 different meats and cheeses freshly sliced for each customer. While you're at it, you can pick up some homemade salads—pasta, potato, coleslaw, and others—as well as pork barbecue and ham biscuits. If you're a whole foods and fresh grains kind of person, you've come to the right place. You'll find buckwheat flour, whole wheat bread flour, even rice and soybean flour, not to mention the full range of oat and wheat products. There are other baking ingredients from chocolate chips to carob drops and fructose. Buy your snacks here, too, as there are candies, crackers, and nuts, all tied up in baggies with the Yoder label. And the prices are unbeatable! From April through October Yoder's has four barbecues with chicken grilled right on the outdoor grill. Get yourself a plate and get comfy at one of the handcrafted picnic tables.

The lawn furniture is made by Amish and Mennonite people in Lancaster County, Pennsylvania, as well as locally, and it's for sale—gazebos, Adirondack chairs, swings, gliders, and more. The shop is open daily except Sunday. Like they say, "country people with country goodies."

Greene County

ANTIQUES

Country Morning Antiques
8315 Seminole Trail, Suite 2, Ruckersville
(434) 985-3958, (434) 985-7038
Doug Dye has been working full-time with antiques for more than 25 years. He started out doing restoration for museums, but for the past 11 years he has operated his own shop here in the Village Greene Shopping Center on US 29. He deals only with museum-quality pieces, including early American high-country antiques. Except for a few exceptions, most items are from the Colonial or pre–Civil War era. One, a Pennsylvania Dutch painted grandfather clock, sold the day after he brought it into the shop.

Country Store Antique Mall
14918 Spottswood Trail, Ruckersville
(434) 985-3649
Located on the corner of US 33 and US 29, this two-story mall is home to a dozen different dealers. The floors may creak, but there are plenty of hidden treasures inside this early 1900 building, and shoppers have been finding them here for 30 years. One visit uncovered two World War II army helmets. There are tons of books, plus wares ranging from antique to collectible. It's open daily except for Christmas and Thanksgiving.

Greene House Shops
Corner US 29 and US Highway 33
Ruckersville
(434) 985-2438
This three-story building at the intersection of two major highways houses 50 dealers of antiques, crafts, quilts, and all kinds of gifts. You can find just about anything here, ranging from furniture to glass bottles and locally made jellies. It's open every day and even accepts credit cards.

Joan Palmer Antiques
8332 Seminole Trail, Ruckersville
(434) 985-3602
This shop opposite County Morning Antiques on the northbound lane of US 29 has a good reputation for its 18th- and 19th-century furniture, oil paintings, and accessories. It's open Thursday through Monday.

SPECIALTY SHOPS

Blue Ridge Pottery
9 Golden Horseshoe Road, Stanardsville
(434) 985-6080
www.blueridgepottery.com
Housed in what was once the Golden Horseshoe Inn, ca. 1827, this popular shop and artist's studio off US 33 is just 2 miles from the entrance to the Skyline Drive. The inn, which sits along the old Spotswood Trail, used to serve travelers making the difficult climb over the mountains. Stonewall Jackson reportedly stayed here during the Civil War, using the inn as his temporary headquarters only a few weeks before he was killed. Alan Ward and his family now throw their stoneware pottery in a little studio right next to the Blue Ridge Pottery and welcome visitors. Ward's pottery, which is modeled after traditional Valley styles but painted with modern vibrant glazes, is sold in the shop along with home decor items, wine, and jewelry. The shop and studio are closed Monday in January, February, and March.

Boot'ville
8633A Seminole Trail, Ruckersville
(434) 985-4574
www.bootville.com
Howdy, partners. This Western-wear shop has been a popular spot on US 29 since 1982. As the name indicates, one of its two rooms is loaded with boots in all the major brands, including Durrango, Abilene, Sage, and Golden Retriever. While you're here, you might as well accessorize. There are plenty of belts, western shirts, even Stetson cowboy hats. If you need a little repair work, they also will clean and shape your hat or stretch your boots.

Crawford Saddlery
8629 Seminole Trail, Ruckersville
(434) 985-4262
www.crawfordsaddlery.com
Whether you are in the market for Western or English tack, this shop offers a fine selection of new and used saddles. In fact, there is just about anything in store for the horse lover on your shopping list, including blankets, riding apparel, Ariat English boots, Western jewelry, buckles, watches, and horse care products. The saddlery is owned by Joe Crawford, a rider who owns a dozen horses on his own farm in nearby Madison County.

Kelly's Korner Racing Kollectibles
8326 Seminole Trail, Ruckersville
(434) 990-0142
Jeff Gordon, Ricky Rudd, Dale Earnhardt Jr. If you know those names, you will be a fan of this neat NASCAR collectibles shop on US 29. John and Edith Kelly have stocked the shelves with all shapes and sizes of race cars, jackets, caps, T-shirts, key chains, flags, and windsocks. Right beside Early Time Antiques, this shop has a set of actual racing slick tires outside the front door. This pit stop is closed Monday and Tuesday.

Charlottesville

ANTIQUES

Antiquers Mall
2335 Seminole Trail, Charlottesville
(434) 973-3478
www.antiquersmall.com
Step inside this lovely brick building and you know you are not in your average antiquers mall. There are glass cases filled with estate sterling and Old Ivory Chintz, not to mention one case devoted to nothing but Tiffany. Farther back inside this two-story, 30,000-square-foot marvel are two massive 1865 great carved side chairs. They sell for $3,500. One shopper spotted *Recumbent Borzoi,* a small signed bronze sculpture by the French artist Paul

Gayrard. (A similar one sold at Sotheby's for $1,898.) Geared for antiques and high-end collectibles, the mall hosts 220 shops, offering everything from their own Antiquers Mall jams and jellies to a full-length mink from Saks Fifth Avenue. Daguerreotypes, Oriental rugs, Fiestaware, Steiff teddy bears, you name it. The snack shop even offers a step back in time with its old-fashioned Coke machine, along with horehound and licorice candies.

Consignment House Unlimited
121 West Main Street, Charlottesville
(434) 977-5527
The Consignment House has loads of great finds as it carries "anything antique or unique." With a prime location of the Downtown Mall, it has remained one of the area's busiest antiques shops since 1987. The antiques and high-quality designer pieces are big sellers along with Oriental rugs, pottery, and china. It has a plethora of nice furniture, ranging from hutches and tables to sofas and chairs.

De Loach Antiques
410 East Jefferson Street, Charlottesville
(434) 979-7209
De Loach is a charming place to find stylish and unusual decorative objects and antiques at very good prices. An eclectic selection of neoclassical, French, English, and American pieces are displayed here.

MingQuing Antiques
111 West Main Street, Charlottesville
(434) 979-8426, (434) 962-0586
Here you'll find Chinese antique furniture shipped directly from mainland China. As the owner says, they are things from another time and another world. They are open Thursday to Saturday.

Oyster House Antiques
122 East Main Street, Charlottesville
(434) 295-4757
www.oysterhouse.com
Oyster House on Charlottesville's Historic Downtown Mall is one of the area's largest importers and dealers of Chinese

antiques. It offers a wide range of altar tables, chairs, cabinets, screens, and traditional Chinese beds, to name a few. Also included at the shop are handmade folk carvings from Bali.

Sun Bow Trading Company
401 East Main Street, Charlottesville
(434) 293-8821
www.sunbowtrading.com
If you're interested in antique or 20th-century rugs from western and central Asia, stop by the Sun Bow Trading Company. Saul, the owner, has many a tale to tell about these tribal textiles and nomadic Oriental rugs and his journeys to find them. Since 1978, he's made more than 95 trips to everywhere from Kenya to Kashgar.

HANDCRAFTS

Cha Cha's
201-B East Main Street, Charlottesville
(434) 293-8553
www.chachawithme.com
Campy, kitschy boutique is how you might describe the inventory here, and the owner would be proud to agree. She sells eccentric, eclectic items for the home. You can buy leopard-print switch plates and retro-style clothes, rhinestone jewelry, pink flamingos, and Buddhist shrines. The merchandise changes constantly. If you are looking for funky, look here. They are open daily except some Sundays in the winter.

O'Suzannah
219 West Main Street, Charlottesville
(434) 979-2888
This store, centrally located on the Downtown Mall, is a boutique specializing in women's apparel, with a fresh, girlish flair. There is everything here from bathing suits and handbags to dresses and blouses. In 2003 O'Suzannah opened a second store right around the corner at 108 Second Street NW, (434) 979-7467. While the first store caters to fashion, this one is filled with all sorts of gifts, ranging from books and stationery to soaps and lotions.

Signet Gallery
212 Fifth Street, NE, Charlottesville
(434) 296-6463
www.signetgallery.com
The *New York Times* called Penny Bosworth's gallery a place "where craft . . . becomes art." The large shop carries handmade work by more than 300 artists and craftspeople from around the country. It is filled with jewelry, clothing, ceramics, glass, leather goods, toys, and garden ornaments. You'll find lamps by Janna Ugone, Simon Pearce glass, lambskin coats, and hand-painted frames. Sterling and 14-karat jewelry by David Yurman, enamel rings by Hidalgo, and 24-karat gold jewelry by Gurhan can also be found here. Jackson, probably the city's most well-known basset hound, is always around to greet visitors. Signet Gallery is one of the few stores in the historic district to have its own parking lot. Stop by Monday through Saturday.

SPECIALTY SHOPS

Andrew Minton Jewelers
192 Zan Road, Charlottesville
(434) 979-7672
Located in Seminole Square, Andrew Minton sells fine contemporary jewelry. The business started in 1978 and offers middle to upper-end merchandise, including watches, pearls, and diamonds. They also do custom design work and expert repairs and have a jeweler on the premises during all operating hours. Stop in any day but Sunday.

Blue Ridge Mountain Sports
1125 Emmet Street, Charlottesville
(434) 977-4400
www.brms.com
Those who love to venture outdoors will love to venture into this fabulous store at Barracks Road Shopping Center. You'll find all your gear for camping, canoeing, backpacking, hiking, and other outdoor activities. You'll find sleeping bags and tents by Eureka, Sierra Designs, and North Face, as well as gloves, jackets, hiking boots, and other outdoor footwear. There's also a

good selection of nature guides and books on hiking and camping. Blue Ridge Mountain Sports also has demonstrations and speakers, plans day hikes, and even sponsors the annual Banff Film Festival. The store won the national Trails for Tomorrow award from DuPont for the retailer who has done the most nationally for America's trails. The staff contributed to and sponsored work on the Rivanna Trails, the connecting trail around Charlottesville. This was the first of the 13 Blue Ridge Mountain Sports stores in the mid-Atlantic area.

Blue Wheel Bicycles
19 Elliewood Avenue, Charlottesville
(434) 977-1870
www.bluewheel.com
Come here to find fine bicycles at competitive prices—Gary Fisher, Lamonde, Fugi, and Seven Cycles are just some of the big brands you'll find. The shop, around since 1972, also sells a good selection of accessories, including essential clothing such as shoes, shorts, jerseys, and gloves. They also do a full range of bicycle repair services and sell pumps, lighting, tires, and tubes. The shop is closed Sunday.

The Cat House
102 Fifth Street SE, Charlottesville
(434) 984-2287
Here's a charming shop chock-full of clever gifts for the cat lover. There's something for the pet and owner alike, including stuffed animals, puzzles, clothing, jewelry, kitty-shaped backpacks, headbands and barrettes, mailboxes, gift wrap, and catnip toys.

Eljo's
3 Elliewood Avenue, Charlottesville
(434) 295-5230
www.eljos.com
For traditionalists, Eljo's has been selling preppie clothes since 1950. It offers the best of Southwick, Corbin, and Gitman, and in the summer you'll find Lacoste knits. This shop covers everything from sport coats and trousers to suiting. The store is closed Sunday.

Freeman–Victorious Framing
1413 University Avenue, Charlottesville
(434) 293-3342
www.universityprints.com
Not only do they do framing, they also sell antique prints and posters, mirrors, and other fine gifts. Freeman–Victorious also does artwork and frame restoration, as well as conservation framing, and offers free estimates. In business since 1938, Freeman–Victorious carries one of the largest collections of prints of the University of Virginia. It is closed Sunday.

The Gemstone Collection
413 East Main Street, Charlottesville
(434) 293-4367
The Gemstone Collection has a beautiful display of gems and minerals as well as designer sterling and gold jewelry. Custom designs are available, too.

Keller & George
1149 Millmont Street, Charlottesville
(434) 293-5011
Having opened in 1875, Keller & George is a staple in Charlottesville. Here you'll find the popular Jefferson cups along with fine jewelry and distinctive and unusual gifts. The store has a bridal registry and offers crystal, silver, and clocks as well as watches and diamonds. It's closed Sunday.

Les Fabriques
420 Shoppers World Court
Charlottesville
(434) 975-0710
Visit Shoppers World Shopping Center to find this small but treasured store. There's designer and bridal fabrics, buttons, and specialty threads. They specialize in natural fibers such as silk, wools, linens and cotton, and difficult-to-find materials. You'll find top-brand embroidery and sewing machines such as Pfaff and Elna. It's a great place to find patterns—besides Vogue, the store carries Burda, a German line, and Sewing Workshop, an artsy line from California. It's closed Sunday.

Levy's
2120 Barracks Road, Charlottesville
(434) 295-4270

For women, Levy's sells gorgeous, sophisticated sportswear downstairs and formal wear and snappy business suits on the upper level. Some of the lines they carry include Ellen Tracy, Lilli Pulitzer, Garfield and Marks, and Dana Buchman. Levy's is closed Sunday.

Market Street Wineshop
311 East Market Street, Charlottesville
(434) 296-3854, (800) 377-VINE

Just a few blocks off the Downtown Mall is a gathering place where everybody seems to know everyone else, but if you're a first-time visitor you'll receive the same friendly welcome as the regulars. The store has one of the state's largest selections of wine and beer, from the old and rare to the good and cheap. You can also find fresh-baked bread, plus meats, cheeses, and pasta. The shop has been so popular, the owners added another uptown store in the Shoppers World Shopping Center, near Whole Foods.

Mincer's
1527 University Avenue, Charlottesville
(434) 296-5687
www.mincers.com

Started as a tobacco shop on the corner in the 1950s, Mincer's sells a wide variety of university sportswear. You'll find sweatshirts, T-shirts, kids' things, soccer balls and footballs, folded stadium seats and cushions, ties, and UVA flags and banners.

Minda's Distinctive Clothing
& Accessories
2125 Ivy Road #3, Charlottesville
(434) 977-4576

You must visit this small but charming boutique to appreciate its eclectic and exciting offerings. Minda Gordon started the store 22 years ago and does her own importing. Each year she travels all over the world—to Bolivia, Equador, Peru—for handmade sweaters made from alpaca wool and gorgeous jewelry. She travels to India, Hong Kong, Bali, and Thailand (her native land), where Hmong artisans embroider jackets, and to Nepal for beautiful silk jackets. You'll find hand-painted batiks, hand-stamped clothing, linens and flax, wearable art in cotton knits, and inexpensive jewelry. There are delightful dresses for work and play in a variety of colors and styles. Minda's is closed Sunday.

Palais Royal Inc./Yves Delorme
311 East Main Street, Charlottesville
(434) 979-4111
www.yvesdelorme.com

Another outstanding specialty shop on the Downtown Mall is Palais Royal, which has the finest in French designer linens, robes, towels, and blankets. Come here for all of your bed and bath products. This shop serves as an outlet for items that have been discontinued, but you also may order new merchandise during your visit.

Plow & Hearth
1107-C Emmet Street, Charlottesville
(434) 977-3707, (800) 866-6072
www.plowhearth.com

Plow & Hearth sells beautiful outdoor ornaments and furniture made of wrought iron, cedar, and other sturdy materials, as well as a large variety of garden accessories. You'll find bird feeders, birdbaths, hammocks, benches, peanuts and peanut brittle, and fun things like toad houses. They also sell an assortment of shoes, mostly clogs, as well as some clothing—robes and shirts. The store is in the Barracks Road Shopping Center.

The Purcell Company Ltd.
107 West Main Street, Charlottesville
(434) 971-8822
www.purcellrugs.com

The Downtown Mall has several fine Oriental rug shops. This one specializes in Afghan tribal nomadic rugs. They also sell kilims and soumals, everything at wholesale prices. Have a worn or tattered rug that you hate to part with? Purcell's also does rug repair. The store also has expanded its selections to include decoupage boxes, pottery, imported tapestries, pillows, mahogany furniture, and teak furniture.

Ragged Mountain Running Shop
3 Elliewood Avenue, Charlottesville
(434) 293-3367
www.raggedmountainrunning.com
Known locally as the place to go for all your information on local races and training programs, Ragged Mountain has a great selection of running and aerobic shoes at competitive prices. You'll find Nike, Adidas, Brooks, and Saucony, among others. Also, there's a great selection of running apparel, such as shorts, sports bras, running jackets, and singlets—those sleeveless running shirts you see. Visit Monday through Saturday.

Scarpa
2114-A Barracks Road, Charlottesville
(434) 296-0040
www.thinkscarpa.com
Scarpa carries a vast selection of women's shoes, styles from collegiate casual to formal in all the top brands in all price ranges. Brands include Cole Haan, Donald Pliner, Stuart Weitzman, Kate Spade, and more. Scarpa includes accessories, handbags, jewelry, and even men's shoes.

Shenanigans
2146 Barracks Road, Charlottesville
(434) 295-4797
Walk into this store to be pleasantly surprised about what a great find it is for children's books, toys, stuffed animals, dolls from around the world, dollhouses and furniture, and children's music, including sing-along videos. There is everything here, from the latest Groovy Girl to nesting dolls from Matroyoshka. Collectors will love the Madame Alexander dolls and Steiff teddy bears. You'll also find gifts for babies.

Talbot's
1027 Emmet Street, Charlottesville
(434) 296-3580
www.talbots.com
Also at Barracks Road Shopping Center, Talbot's, a fixture since 1947, is a great shop where you'll find a premier selection of classic apparel and accessories for women in a comfortable, homelike atmosphere. There are suits, pants, dresses, cute tops, professional blouses, shoes, and handbags. (Roanoke has a Talbot's, too.) The adjoining store is Talbot's Petites.

Tap Tap
430 Valley Street, Scottsville
(434) 286-8880
Michael Ford decided to open Tap Tap after accompanying his father, Dr. Raymond Ford, on several of his many humanitarian trips to Haiti. Dr. Ford, a Charlottesville pediatrician, has been going to Haiti since the late 1990s to treat Haitian orphans. In fact, the Ford family has funded a new orphanage for more than 50 children just outside Cao Haitien. The younger Ford decided to join the effort by creating a market for Haitian artists. Tap Tap is full of original Haitian work, including wonderful and unique paintings, wood and stone carvings, and intricate beadwork. The prices are very affordable, ranging from $10 to $100. Tap Tap, by the way, is a Haitian taxi, usually a small pickup truck. The name comes from the children—orphans or runaways—who stand on the back, collect the money, and tap on the side when the drivers need to stop. The shop is closed Monday and Tuesday.

Timberlake Drugstore
322 East Main Street, Charlottesville
(434) 295-9155 (store)
(434) 295-1191 (soda fountain)
Timberlake may be small, but it's big in history. This shop has been around since 1890 and is one of the few places around with an old-fashioned soda fountain, which was completely renovated in 2001. The drugstore still sells cosmetics, fills prescriptions, and will develop your film, but it also offers a deli menu featuring old-fashioned thick milk shakes (vanilla, chocolate, strawberry, and cherry) available in regular or "extra thick." Or maybe you feel like a sundae, banana split, or an ice cream float. For those without a sweet

tooth, Timberlake's menu includes sandwiches, croissants, and breakfast foods. It's closed Sunday.

T. S. Eways
105 West Main Street, Charlottesville
(434) 979-3038
This shop carries a wide assortment of Oriental rugs, as well as antique and collector rugs. They also do restorations, cleaning, and appraisals. It's closed Sunday.

The Virginia Company
1047-B Emmet Street, Charlottesville
(434) 977-0080
www.thevirginiacompany.com
Virginia is best showcased in the Virginia Company, also in the Barracks Road Shopping Center. A great selection of gifts, food, wine, books, music, and much more, all with the Old Dominion mark of quality, are for sale here. You'll find the famous Jefferson cups, pottery, soaps, lotions, and T-shirts, as well as the popular Virginia product—peanuts. Both Virginia Diner and Hubs are among the brands sold here. The Virginia Company will also put together gift baskets.

Whimsies
2142 Barracks Road, Charlottesville
(434) 977-8767
True to its name, Whimsies has fanciful and spunky children's wear, including clothes for infants up through kids' size 16. There are play clothes and dress clothes and things in between.

BOOKSTORES

Barnes & Noble Bookstore
1035 Emmet Street, Charlottesville
(434) 984-0461
www.bn.com
Something is always going on at the area's largest bookshop. Aside from carrying more than 100,000 books, the store hosts readings, book signings, seminars, book groups, and two weekly story times for children. It's also a great place to sit back and read or enjoy a mocha latte in

Starbucks cafe. Since the shop is located in Barracks Road Shopping Center, it's usually easy to find a parking spot. But if a big author is booked for a discussion, you might have to walk a ways.

Blue Whale Books
115 West Main Street, Charlottesville
(434) 296-4646
The Blue Whale is among a collection of charming secondhand book shops. This gem right on the Historic Downtown Mall has a wide selection of used, rare, and out-of-print books. It specializes in scholarly, art, and Irish-related books. You also can find a fine selection of maps and prints, including engravings and lithographs.

The Book Cellar
316 East Main Street, Charlottesville
(434) 979-7787
This shop-within-a-shop specializes in quality used books and publishers' remainders. The Book Cellar is on the Downtown Mall, but to get to it you will have to go in the building that houses the Hardware Store restaurant. Before you get to the food, go downstairs. Here you can find just about everything from art to business-related tomes. There also is a Virginia room, which features books about Thomas Jefferson, the Civil War, and other works of regional interest.

Daedalus Bookstore
121 Fourth Street, Charlottesville
(434) 293-7595
If you are in the market for an out-of-print book, this is the place to be. There are nearly 100,000 books lining the walls in the three-story building just off the Downtown Mall. Don't be overwhelmed, though. Just tell the owner what you're looking for and he can point you to the right shelf. Allow a little extra time, because once you get in, you will marvel at all the choices.

Heartwood Bookshops
5 and 9 Elliewood Avenue
Charlottesville
(434) 295-7083

This used bookstore is really one store in two locations, both near the University of Virginia. At 5 Elliewood, Heartwood carries a large collection of secondhand scholarly and popular books, both in hardcover and paperback. Two doors down at 9 Elliewood is Heartwood's impressive collection of rare books, especially books on Americana and literature.

New Dominion Bookshop
404 East Main Street, Charlottesville
(434) 295-2552
Established in 1924, this shop is one of the cornerstones of the Historic Downtown Mall and one of the oldest booksellers in town. It truly caters to the hometown crowd and offers a wide selection of works by local authors. New Dominion hosts frequent book signings and discussions with regionally and nationally known writers, including John Grisham. (To put this in perspective, Grisham usually does book signings in only four towns each year: Charlottesville, New York, Los Angeles, and his hometown of Oxford, Mississippi.) New Dominion also offers exhibit space on its mezzanine for local artists to show their latest works, and it hosts monthly book discussions.

Quest Bookshop Inc.
619 West Main Street, Charlottesville
(434) 295-3377
The Quest is another long-standing member of the book community. For more than 27 years it has been specializing in books, both new and used, on human and spiritual development. It is the place to go if you are looking for reading material on holistic health, astrology, or Western religion. Visiting authors also stop by for discussion and workshops.

Read It Again, Sam
214 East Main Street, Charlottesville
(434) 977-9844
If you love a good mystery, and who doesn't, this is the bookshop for you. This shop has thousands of used and rare books, but what keeps the fans coming back for more is the wall full of nothing but mysteries. Read It Again celebrated its 10th anniversary in 2002, five years in Nelson County and the past five on the Downtown Mall.

University of Virginia Bookstore
Emmet Street, Charlottesville
(434) 924-3721, (800) 759-4667
www.bookstore.virginia.edu
Parking anywhere near the university is at a premium, but this bookstore is conveniently located directly on top of the parking garage on Emmet Street. What's better, the bookshop will give you 30 minutes' free parking if you make a purchase of $5.00 or more. With so much to choose from, that's not hard here. Not only is there a wide range of new and used textbooks, you also can find the latest in fiction, nonfiction, children's books, and magazines. The store also has a wide selection of computer-related books. While you're here, you might even want to pick up a few UVA souvenirs. There are plenty of T-shirts and other Cavalier collectibles. There's also a cafe here.

MALLS

Barracks Road Shopping Center
1117 North Emmet Street, Charlottesville
(434) 977-0100
www.barracksroad.com
Nearly 90 shops, restaurants, and grocery stores are situated along Emmet Street in what is one of the city's oldest and popu-

---

A 1994 survey by U.S. News & World Report *ranked Charlottesville third in the nation behind Seattle, Washington, and Austin, Texas, in book readers per capita. Countless writers also call the area home, including best-selling authors John Grisham and Jan Karon, and Pulitzer Prize winners Henry Taylor and Rita Dove. And you never know when one of them might be here for a local book signing. All told, there are more than 20 bookstores in the area.*

---

lar shopping centers. Big national chains such as Barnes and Noble and Old Navy bring in lots of customers, but so do the smaller unique shops, ranging from Lindt Chocolate to Albemarle Angler. The center is divided into three sections: the main shopping center, the island, and the north wing, an enclave of a dozen specialty shops. While searching for the unique, you also can come here to get your car serviced, buy groceries, do banking, mail letters, or even get a haircut. There is plenty of free parking, unless you happen to visit during the busy Christmas holiday season.

Charlottesville Fashion Square Mall
1600 Rio Road E, Charlottesville
(434) 973-9331
www.simon.com
If you'd rather do all your shopping inside in an air conditioned mall, plan a trip to Fashion Square. There are more than 65 shops and services here from Sears to Ann Taylor. Other major stores include Belk and JCPenney, as well as Abercrombie and Fitch and Eddie Bauer. If you have a sweet tooth, stop by the Kohr Bros. Frozen Custard stand, a very popular place indeed. The mall is at the intersection of US 29 and Rio Road.

Charlottesville Historic Downtown Mall
(434) 296-8548
www.cvilledowntown.org
We've already described some of the shops in the downtown pedestrian mall that specialize in exquisite handcrafts and antiques, as well as the delightful specialty shops, most of which are owner-operated. All told, there are nearly 120 stores and 30 restaurants in the historic area.

Nelson County

ANTIQUES

Afton House Antiques
31 Afton House Lane, Afton
(540) 456-6759
You'll find this antiques shop off Route 6

East. It offers fascinating collections of antique furniture—all periods—from country and Federal to Victorian and Empire. You'll also find arts, crafts, dolls, home furnishings, dishes, and country paintings. Check it out—Afton House also has a bed-and-breakfast, featuring a large cottage and a small cottage, and four bedrooms in the main house.

Four Brothers Packing House
4137 Pyebrook Highway, Colleen
(434) 263-8577
Farther south, at the crossroads of Highway 56 and US 29, you'll find the Four Brothers Packing House. They specialize in antiques, including furniture, glassware, and picture frames, as well as collectibles and American origin furniture. After shopping, you can take home some Thai food as well from their take-out menu. Four Brothers is closed Sunday and Monday.

Southern Star
Rockfish Valley Highway, Nellysford
(434) 361-1292
Located in the Valley Green Shopping Center, Southern Star has been dealing in antiques and folk art for 16 years. Featured are American period pieces from country to formal. The shop also caters to the dealer trade and has new inventory weekly.

Tuckahoe Antique Mall
4202 Rockfish Valley Highway,
Nellysford
(434) 361-2121
The mall on Highway 151 has a large selection of antiques with 50 shops under one roof. Surely, you'll find what you need or at least enjoy browsing for it. There's furniture, glassware, collectibles, toys, and many other items. It's open Thursday through Sunday.

HANDCRAFTS

Spruce Creek Gallery
1368 Rockfish Valley Highway,
Nellysford
(434) 361-1859
www.sprucecreekgallery.com

One mile south of Nellysford on Highway 151, you'll find this gallery, housed in the old Wintergreen Country Store, which was built in 1905 and is on the state register of historic buildings. The tin ceilings, wood floors, and counters of the old store compliment the gallery's collection of fine arts and crafts. It's open Thursday through Monday in January to May, seven days a week the rest of the year. The gallery sells traditional and contemporary art. More than 80 artists show their work here, including pottery, jewelry, paintings, baskets, fiber arts, stained glass, pastels and prints, stone and wood sculptures, and handmade clothing. The emphasis is on local artists. Spruce Creek also offers a framing service.

Valley Green Art Gallery
Highway 151, Nellysford
(434) 361-9316
www.valleygreengallery.com
Across from the Stedman House, in the Valley Green Center is this co-op. Founded in 1992, it's a cooperative for local artists to exhibit and show their work. There are 40 members, all residents of Virginia. Here you'll find handcrafts, jewelry such as handmade glass beads, sterling work, polymer clay. Other items include miniature furniture, stained glass, woven wearable art, original photography, and the paintings of various Virginia artists. Valley Green is open Wednesday through Monday. The gallery usually hosts two events a year—a summer celebration on the Memorial Day weekend and a Christmas open house on the Friday after Thanksgiving.

SPECIALTY SHOPS

Blue Ridge Mountain Sports
The Mountain Inn, Wintergreen
(434) 325-2156
www.brms.com
You'll find a nice selection of shops in and around Wintergreen Resort. The Mountain Inn in the resort has several nice spots,
including the Blue Ridge Mountain Sports store. The store, which came to Wintergreen in the early 1980s, is a great place to shop for quality outdoor sportswear and accessories—just perfect, since this is a resort that offers great outdoor activities. Some of the items you'll find include hats and gloves, hiking boots by Vasque and Montrail, outdoor clothing by Patagonia and Jansport, tents by North Face, and backpacks and day packs by Lowe Alpine. You can also rent movies here.

Stedman House
2788 Rockfish Valley Highway, Nellysford
(434) 361-2560
This home-decorating center located at the bottom of Wintergreen Mountain also sells beautiful furniture, art, antiques, and accessories. If they don't have what you're looking for, they can order the furniture you want. They also do design work for your house. It is closed Sunday.

Walton's Mountain Country Store
71 River Road, Faber
(434) 263-4566
It's hard to miss this stone building with the humongo sign in front on the intersection of Route 6 West and Route 29 South, in Nelson County. The building was constructed in 1930 and operated as a filling station and truck stop. In 1983 the Hamners, best known as John Boy Walton's family on the hit television show *The Waltons,* let them use the name for the store. If nothing else, you'll have to stop to quell your curiosity. Here you'll find all kinds of things that even the Waltons could have used—clothes, gifts, furniture, baked goods, and collectibles. There are even antiques, primarily from the 1920s—Victorian chairs and sofas. You can buy shot glasses (Mother Walton would have shaken her head), souvenir magnets, joke gifts, candles, cookie jars, bookends, and ceramic roosters and hens.

Amherst County

ANTIQUES

Antiques to Envy
10535 Wards Road, Rustburg
(434) 821-3771
This mall is 6 miles south of the Lynchburg Airport. It's Lynchburg's largest antiques and collectible mall with more than 60 dealers. It's open seven days and features more than 200 pieces of furniture and everything from primitives to Prussian glass, collector's books, pottery, jewelry, dolls, and toys. The store expanded in 2002 to bring the building to 10,000 square feet of space.

Sweeney's Curious Goods
1220 Main Street, Lynchburg
(434) 846-7839
One of the downtown shops, Sweeney's offers a little bit of everything. New and antique furniture, lamps, pictures, and candles are spread over the three floors of this shop. It's open Monday through Saturday.

HANDCRAFTS

Farm Basket Shop
2008 Langhorne Road, Lynchburg
(434) 528-1107
You can browse through the rooms of carefully chosen gift items from around the world. You can create custom invitations and announcements by computer. A mail-order catalog is available during the holiday season. If hunger strikes, stop for a cucumber sandwich at the complex's restaurant, which has some of the best homestyle food in the area. But be forewarned. They do not share their recipes! The Farm Basket's fruit is locally grown in their own mountain orchards. It's closed on Sunday.

Virginia Handcrafts, Inc.
2008 Langhorne Road, Lynchburg
(434) 846-7029
Part of the Farm Basket shopping complex, Virginia Handcrafts will keep you wandering around all day. It's a casual shop where browsers and their children are welcome. This unique store features a collection of American crafts, many of which are made by Virginians, including kaleidoscopes, game boards, pottery, jewelry, and handblown glass. These are displayed among planters, fountains, lamps, and much more. The atmosphere is just plain fun! The shop is closed on Sunday.

SPECIALTY SHOPS

Angler's Lane
Graves Mill Center, Route 221, Forest
(434) 385-0200
www.anglerslane.com
The perfect place for the fly-fishing enthusiast, Angler's Lane offers the best quality in fly-fishing equipment and outdoor and travel apparel. Whether you're going off to catch Virginia brook trout or to the Florida Keys for tarpon, the staff promises to be able to equip you for any fishing trip. You'll find a wide selection of products from Patagonia, Orvis, Ex Officio, Sage, and Scott. It is closed Sunday.

Lynchburg Community Market
1219 Main Street, Lynchburg
(434) 847-1499
www.lynchburgmarket.com
If you're in town Monday through Saturday, you need to stop on in the Lynchburg Community Market, established in 1783. It's the third oldest farmer's market in the country. You'll find specialty shopping and terrific eating. There are homemade crafts, Virginia-made goods, and baked goods. You'll also find a farmers' market—21 farmers bring their fresh vegetables spring, summer, and fall. Something is always going on at the Market, the hub of Lynchburg activity since the days of Thomas Jefferson. Jefferson scared local citizens by biting into a tomato, long thought to be a poisonous fruit. This market and the one in Roanoke are centerpieces of Blue Ridge life. There are events on Saturday throughout the year, including a spring garden show in late April, Christmas in July, a tomato fair, and a harvest festival in late October.

MALLS

River Ridge Mall
3405 Candlers Mountain Road
Lynchburg
(434) 237-1122
www.shopriverridgemall.com
Mall lovers, don't despair. This mall next to Liberty University is the area's largest. Home to more than 85 stores, the big ones include JCPenney, Sears, Hechts, Belk, Walden Books, and Value City, a super-discount store.

OUTLETS

Carolina Connection
525 Alleghany Avenue, Lynchburg
(434) 846-5099
For dancewear, gymnastics, and cheerwear you need to visit Carolina Connection. The store sells leotards, tights, and ballet shoes, predominantly for girls and women of all ages, but it does carry some men's lines as well. The store started in 1985 and is closed on Sunday.

Consolidated Shoe Store
22290 Timberlake Road, Lynchburg
(434) 237-5569, (888) 368-7996
Be sure to stop in at this shoe store that sells brands including Nicole, Madeline, Nike, Eliize, and Dexter, among others, at great discounted prices. The store is open Monday through Saturday.

Smith Mountain Lake

GENERAL AND SPECIALTY STORES

Atkins Lakeshore Gallery
175 Middle Valley Road, Hardy
(540) 721-7267
This gallery specializes in Civil War art and custom framing. You can also find handmade furniture, baskets and textiles, and lamps. The owners also do photography and framing. Visit Monday through Saturday.

Diamond Hill General Store and Garden Center
1017 Diamond Hill Road, Moneta
(540) 297-9309
On Highway 655 at the corner of Diamond Hill Road and Horseshoe Bend, you'll find this all-in-one shop. It's not simply a restored, living museum. It is also a gift shop, a Christmas shop, a New York-style deli, and an antique shop. Not only that, Carl and Christine Brodt added a garden center adjacent to the store. This landmark general store opened in 1857 as Debo's General Merchandise. The Debo family owned and operated the store for 135 consecutive years. The Brodts refurbished and reopened the store in 1992. Guests are invited to sign the register and sip fresh coffee around an old potbellied stove. Next door is the original post office building where James Debo presided as the first postmaster. In the old Debo residence you can find the wine shop and the year-round Christmas shop, specializing in Santas. The gift shop, featuring wood carvings, personalized signs, and Virginia pottery, is in the old general store, as is the antiques shop.

The Gazebo
16545 Moneta Road, Moneta
(540) 297-2255
www.gazeboatthelake.com
You'll need to stop in at the Gazebo, a unique crafts and consignment shop. More than 40 crafters display and sell their work here. It's an art gallery that also offers pottery. You can take a ceramics class, or you can bring your group here to celebrate a birthday by doing ready-to-paint pottery. They do the casting and have the supplies that are needed such as stencils. Your family can sit down and make a memory. And you don't have to have experience to do it. If you aren't interested in creating anything yourself, there are plenty of items to purchase. Browse among the hand-built pottery, thrown pottery, woodcrafts, handmade greeting cards, signs, tile trays and clocks, wooden toys, birdhouses, handmade jew-

elry, handmade doll clothes, and rustic garden benches made from old fences and other salvaged wood. Stop by Tuesday through Saturday.

Gifts Ahoy
16430 Booker T. Washington Highway,
Bridgewater Plaza, Moneta
(540) 721-5303
www.bridgewaterplaza.com
This shop will delight children and has the lake's most unique collection of gifts, greeting cards, and Beanie Babies and Boyds Bears. For those back at home, you can pick up home accessories such as Vera Bradley, Yankee and Colonial candles, bath and body items, and nautical gifts.

Smith Mountain Lake has two major shopping areas: Bridgewater Plaza on Highway 122, south of Hales Ford Bridge and home of the official Smith Mountain Lake partnership Visitor Center, and Village Square at the intersection of Highway 122 and Highway 655 in Moneta. Here you'll find enough interesting little shops to poke around in to suit your fancy. On summer weekends, live entertainment draws crowds; during the rest of the year, the steady seasonal stream of boats and visitors from around the world are often entertainment enough.

Hales Ford Store
14112 Booker T. Washington Highway,
Moneta
(540) 721-5504
About 2.5 miles south of Hales Ford Bridge, this store has souvenirs and just about anything else you need while enjoying the lake. They specialize in nautical gifts, floral designs, and pottery.

Ice Cream Cottage
16430 Booker T. Washington Highway,
Bridgewater Plaza, Moneta
(540) 721-1305

Take a break from your shopping and get a refreshing ice cream in a waffle cone or flavored shaved ice at this full-service ice cream shop. You can also choose milkshakes, banana splits, or frozen yogurt. The shop sells hot dogs, too. It's closed November through late March.

The Little Gallery
16430 Booker T. Washington Highway,
Bridgewater Plaza, Moneta
(540) 721-1596
www.thelittlegallerysml.com
Lovers of fine art will enjoy the Little Gallery, where you can find one-of-a-kind treasures and see the works of well-known artists as well as emerging local ones. The gallery, which began in 1988, features handblown glass, artist-made jewelry, pottery, and unique gifts.

Smith Mountain Flowers
14477 Moneta Road, Moneta
(540) 297-6524
They have flowers for any occasion. They can also special-order fruits, candies, and other gifts to satisfy your basket or boutique needs. This flower shop has been around since 1987. It's closed on Sunday.

Bedford County

ANTIQUES

Hamiltons
155 West Main Street, Bedford
(540) 586-5592
www.peterv.com
Yes, this little brick house by the oak tree sells antiques, but you'll also find books here because they're a publisher of books about the region, primarily nonfiction for adults. Look here for toy cars and trucks, too. The store opened in 1981.

The Peddler Antiques
Burnbridge Road, Forest
(434) 525-6030
This antiques store in a brick schoolhouse, open since 1972, is located on Highway

854 between Highways 811 and 221. Here you'll find 15 dealers in a large space. You can visit any day to pick up quality furniture, glassware, lamps, and antiques.

OUTLETS

Emerson Creek Pottery
1068 Pottery Lane, Bedford
(540) 297-7884
www.emersoncreekpottery.com
If you love pottery and enjoy seeing how it's made, travel to Emerson Creek Pottery's factory in Bedford County (take Highway 43 S. to Highway 725 E., about 10 miles from Bedford). The company's product line is sold in all 50 states and is becoming widely collected as fine art. A showroom here houses a permanent display of the pottery's private collection. Established in 1977 as a small studio of two artisans, the Emerson Creek Pottery now employs several people for each step of the pottery process. The distinctive hand-painted patterns are a part of what makes Emerson Creek so well known. The shop occupies an 1825 log cabin next to the factory. Along with great bargains, you'll find occasional unusual pieces, first runs, and specialties. Outside you can have lunch at the picnic table, wander through the flower gardens, or relax on a bench.

Franklin County

ANTIQUES

Blue Ridge Antique Center
20100 Virgil Goode Highway,
Rocky Mount
(540) 483-2362
www.spmarket.com/antiques.html
Here's a beautiful antiques center with a wide variety of wares in a climate-controlled environment, with well-lit, spacious aisles, wheelchair access, and clean restrooms. Browse among the items of 75 quality dealers and find glassware, china, lamps, toys, furniture, mirrors, linens, books, home decor accessories, and collectibles. The center also has a snack shop

and rest area when you need to take a break from your antiquing. For your special projects, Blue Ridge Antique Center carries a variety of antique replacement hardware, lamp parts, and accessories to accommodate your style, and polishes for use on just about any wood or metal there is. If you're still learning the finer points of this hobby, check out the extensive selection of collector's reference books and reproduction Victorian paper gifts. While the center opened with 12,000 square feet, it soon saw fit to expand to 24,000 square feet to create more dealer areas.

GENERAL STORES

Boone's Country Store
2699 Jubal Early Highway, Boone's Mill
(540) 721-2478
Don't leave Franklin County without a visit to Boone's Country Store. Run by German Baptists, the store has the most heavenly sticky buns, pies, cakes, rolls, and homemade entrees this side of Amish country. You must try the baked half-moon pies—made with dried apples, "like your grandmother used to make them." The store also sells homemade soaps and pillows, as well as gift items such as coasters, nightlights, figurines, framed prints and artwork, Thomas Kinkade artwork, magnetic notepads, mugs, books, and cards. They also sell quilting supplies and fabrics, and you can even take a quilting class at the store. Boone's has old barn siding as part of its construction, giving it that old-timey look, even though it opened in 1975. The store is closed Sunday and Monday.

HANDCRAFTS

From the Heart
265 Franklin Street, Rocky Mount
(540) 489-3887
Visit downtown Rocky Mount to find this little store with a unique assortment of gift items, toys, pottery, linens, and antiques. Some of the fun things you will be able to pick up include Fenton art glass, Boyds Bears, flags, Bridgewater candles, gift cards, and calendars. There is

something for everyone here, from electric tart burners to silver jewelry. From the Heart has a large inventory of collectibles, including clay works by Blue Sky and Willow Tree Angels.

OUTLETS

Southern Lamp & Shade Showroom
19858 Virgil H. Goode Highway,
Rocky Mount
(540) 483-4738
You'll be pleasantly surprised and a little in awe when you find this showroom on US 220. In business since 1989, it has a great selection of lamps and shades—everything from desk lamps to floor lamps—at less than retail prices. It's a large showroom that carries at least 1,200 lamps and 1,500 shades. It's well worth the visit if you're shopping for lighting.

NEW RIVER VALLEY
Montgomery County

ANTIQUES

Cambria Emporium
596 Depot Street, Christiansburg
(540) 381-0949
Cambria Emporium is the best place in Montgomery County to find tiny antique treasures and surprises. The big red three-story building in the historic Cambria area of the county is a landmark in itself, constructed in 1908 and operated as a surface wholesale company and then a dry goods and feed store. It was renovated several years ago as an antiques mall housing 15 dealers. Here, among 10,000 square feet of space, you can find every antique imaginable in a pleasant, old-time setting. It's open, airy, and uncluttered. You'll find glassware, furniture, dishes, quilts, vintage clothing, and fine china. Along with those, you'll run across small reminders of the past that will make you ooh and ahh! A counter sign reads, "IF IT AIN'T PRICED, IT AIN'T FOR SALE, FOLKS!" That's the spirit of Cambria Emporium.

Heirloom Originals
609 North Main Street, Blacksburg
(540) 552-9241
Heirloom is exactly that. Even the shop is the real McCoy. Dating back to 1872, it is the last little house on Blacksburg's historical Main Street. While there are no set hours, if you see a bright afghan on the porch, the shop is open. If the afghan's not there, just call. The owner said she is happy to come down and open the doors for you. For the business that's been around since 1967, here is beautiful furniture—no reproductions. Your hands will tremble in excitement as you look at the tables, chests of drawers, china cabinets, tea carts, tables, and other wonderful treasures. There's a fabulous collection of cut glass and open saltz.

SPECIALTY SHOPS

For the Birds
1702 South Main Street, Blacksburg
(800) 742-4737, (540) 953-3452
www.for-the-birds.com/birdfeeders.asp
For the Birds is filled with items both whimsical and practical, all bird-oriented, of course. The shop has bird feeders, houses and seed, books and tapes, binoculars, bird-themed clothing and gifts, and a large selection of garden items including birdbaths, fountains, and statuaries for your yard. Stop by Monday through Saturday.

Mish Mish
125 North Main Street, Suite 200,
Blacksburg
(540) 552-1020
www.mishmish.com
In downtown Blacksburg, a very special store started out as a hole in the wall several decades ago and has since grown to be one of the most popular art supply and overall neat-stuff stores in western Virginia. Everyone in the New River Valley is familiar with Mish Mish, which probably should be renamed Hodge Podge. Shoppers of any age could spend the entire day there looking at everything from the finest art supplies and watercolors to a

rainbow of Silly Putty. There is stuff for children and adults, and the store is particularly popular with Virginia Tech students. It's open till midnight during the school year.

MALLS

New River Mall
782 New River Road, Christiansburg
(540) 381-0004
www.shopnewrivervalleymall.com
Those who love malls will enjoy visiting this one, which offers 66 department stores and specialty shops. The bigger names include Peebles, Belk, JCPenney, and Sears. The mall will also win your heart with the use of free wheelchairs. Parents with young children will be glad to know that strollers are rented for $1.00 an hour. There's also a Regal Cinemas if you want to stop and take in a movie.

Radford

SPECIALTY SHOPS

Encore! Artful Gifts
1129 East Main Street, Radford
(540) 639-2015
www.encoreartfulgifts.com
Encore is the best place in the city to find unique gifts and original fine art. Merchandise ranges from the very unusual to the very trendy. Discover eclectic folk art, jewelry, toys that touch the senses, and truly unique cards, gift items, and packaging. You'll love the food line, which includes great basket fillers, items such as sauces, pestos, crackers, Bloody Mary mixes, and a great variety of 20 organic and regular coffee beans. The shop has received several small business awards from the Radford Chamber of Commerce.

Grandma's Memories
237 West Main Street, Radford
(540) 639-0054
This is one dandy antiques shop. They've got everything you could want, mostly

from 1900–1950. Items include glass, furniture—including bedroom and dining room furniture as well as small pieces—and an interesting assortment of postcards. Closed on Sundays and half days on Wednesday, Grandma's Memories got its start in 1974.

Pulaski County

ARTS AND HANDCRAFTS

Collector's Showcase and
Custom Framing
5635 Old US 11, Pulaski
(540) 674-0232
This shop offers custom framing and is also an authorized dealer of P. Buckley Moss and Thomas Kinkade. The store also carries Steif bears. Stop in any day but Sunday and Monday.

Fine Arts Center
21 West Main Street, Pulaski
(540) 980-7363
The Fine Arts Center celebrated its 25th anniversary in 2003. In this spacious setting you can view and purchase artwork created by artists in the New River Valley. Items include pottery, jewelry, cards, wood carvings, paintings, and rock sculptures, such as the popular "Women in Stone." Exhibits change about every six weeks, and the center is closed on Sunday except for receptions. There's also a small gift shop.

Theda's Studio
89 West Main Street, Pulaski
(540) 980-2777
Theda and Rudolph Farmer have been operating their portraiture business for more than 60 years. A trip to their shop is like taking a trip through time. Original tin-roofed ceilings and arresting pictures of brides from the '50s and '60s will take you back. The studio is open daily.

SPECIALTY SHOPS AND SERVICES

PJ's Carousel Collection
5223 Wilderness Road, Newbern
(540) 674-9300
www.pjs-carousel.com
Come browse this unusual shop that sells 8- to 10-inch tall carousel horses, or watch the production in the back of the building. This is one of the few companies left that make miniature carousel horses. You can take a tour and watch the painters do exquisite detailed hand-painting of the creatures. The carousel horses are made out of Gemwood and are limited-edition collector's items. Jim McDaniel, who had been a collector of the carousel horses for 10 years, bought the business five years ago after learning that the original owner had died and the business had all but stopped. McDaniel sells his horses to theme parks and to high-end gift stores— and to visitors like you. The production and shop are situated in one of the buildings where the company got its start—a house that's 130 years old. Originally the business started in 1980 when the first owner bought several carousel horse wood carvings, painted them, and took the pieces to several shows. It's open Monday through Friday.

Upstairs, Downstairs
27 West Main Street, Pulaski
(540) 980-4809
Don't miss this shop with its hand-painted furniture and lots of antiques on two floors. You'd find furniture like this for four times the cost in the metropolitan areas. The boutique sells estate jewelry, dolls, china, paintings, antiques such as furni-

There are more than 20 farmers' markets in the Blue Ridge. Find out more about them and their locations by contacting the State Farmers Market Representative at P.O. Box 1163, Richmond, 23218, (804) 786-3952.

ture, and smaller items including lamps and glassware. It's closed on Wednesday afternoons.

Floyd County

HANDCRAFTS

New Mountain Mercantile
114A South Locust Street, Floyd
(540) 745-4278
When you're traveling the Blue Ridge Parkway looking for a unique gift, don't miss this place, 6 miles from milepost 165.2. It's filled with many handmade items, with representation of more than 150 local and regional artists and craftspeople. You'll find an eclectic collection of artistic gifts and home and garden accessories. The artists' work includes pottery, stained glass, gemstone and sterling jewelry, wearable art, pressed-flower art and sun catchers, wood boxes, and bowls. You'll also find candles, cards, aromatherapy items, soaps, gift baskets, casual and dress natural fiber clothing, wind chimes, and water fountains, as well as Bent Willow furniture. The kids will have fun browsing, too, exploring Safari animals and toys, musical instruments, science kits, Groovey girls, kids jewelry, and hand puppets. The store is run by three savvy women, Theresa Cook, Kalinda Wycoff, and Christine Byrd, who know great buys when they see them. Their store also serves as a Floyd County information center of sorts. Their Here and Now art gallery features new exhibits monthly. New Mountain Mercantile rates as one of the outstanding handcraft stores in the Blue Ridge.

SPECIALTY SHOPS

County Sales
117A West Main Street, Floyd
(540) 745-2001
www.countysales.com
Lovers of bluegrass and old-time music will want to see the largest distributor of such music in the world. You can visit this

warehouse, which has been here since the early 1970s, or order merchandise from its mail-order store. Requests come in from the four corners for their old-time fiddle music and gospel albums. They sell cassettes, videos, books, DVDs, and CDs. The warehouse is open Monday through Saturday. Rebel Records is their recording label, which has an office in Charlottesville.

School House Fabrics
220 North Locust Street, Floyd
(540) 745-4561
Better than an outlet store, with more fabric than you could ever find in any retail store, School House Fabrics is a dream come true. Set in a renovated three-story schoolhouse built in 1911, the business opened in 1971 and is filled with everything from specialty fabrics to buttons and beads. What is amazing is how organized and well grouped this massive mania of yard goods is. Each room is arranged according to fabric. For example, a downstairs room is devoted to bridal fabrics, lace, veils, beading, and wedding goods. Out back, an extra building contains large reels of upholstery fabric, tapestry, and store remnants. You'll also find quilting fabrics, craft supplies, and books about sewing and quilting. Visit any day but Sunday.

GENERAL STORES

Poor Farmers Market
2616 Jeb Stuart Highway, Meadows of Dan
(276) 952-2670
www.poorfarmersmarket.com
Down the road a piece is another interesting general store, a combination grocery store, deli, and gift shop, just off the Blue Ridge Parkway. This hub for locals and tourists alike got its start when owner Felecia Shelor told a local farmer she'd buy his produce and then peddle it wholesale. The business boomed, and the store has grown 10 times its original size since 1983. You'll find all kinds of produce—including potatoes, cabbage, apples, and

other types—from farmers in the summertime. Its deli serves great lunches, with such favorites as fried apple pies and the Hungry Hillbilly sandwiches. While you can find tasty treats ranging from hoop cheese to horehound candy, you also can pick up a few gift items, including thimbles from all 50 states, linens, and books by local authors. The owner's life story is as interesting as the store: She rose from a life of poverty as a 15-year-old bride to a store owner with 15 employees. You'll love this place, and the prices are great!

ALLEGHANY HIGHLANDS
Alleghany County

HANDCRAFTS

Alleghany Highlands Arts & Crafts Center
439 East Ridgeway, Clifton Forge
(540) 862-4447
Visit the Alleghany Highlands Arts & Crafts Center in downtown Clifton Forge for fine arts and handcrafts. The center is a nonprofit organization run by a professional arts administrator and volunteer staff that encourage creativity and appreciation of the visual arts. Items for sale include pottery, wooden wares, baskets, jewelry, stained glass, needlework, drawings, fiber arts, prints, watercolors, and oil paintings. The center got started in 1984 and is housed in an old building that used to be the headquarters for Virginia Electric Power Company.

The Crafts Shop of Covington, Inc.
120 West Main Street, Covington
(540) 962-0557
Handcrafted textiles, glass, and other high-quality collectibles for you and your home are on display here six days a week. It's an antiques and crafters mall with 110 dealers selling a great variety of antiques and handcrafted items. You'll have to stop by, any day but Sunday.

Bath County

ANTIQUES

Quilts Unlimited
Main Street, Hot Springs
(540) 839-5955
www.quiltsunlimited.com
Lovers of quilts and high-quality, unusual quilted gifts and handcrafts should head for this cute shop. It handles new quilts and wall hangings along with a fine selection of regional handcrafts and jewelry. There are also delightful items for the children, including books, soft toys, like Pockets of Learning, and Kubla, Boyds Bears, and Vera Bradley, as well as wonderful wood puzzles.

SPECIALTY SHOPS

Classic Bath and the Homestead Collection
The Homestead, Hot Springs
(540) 839-7866
If you enjoy shopping for bath products, here's a perfect place to go. Classic Bath features unique bath, spa, and linen products and carries the Homestead Spa products including scrubs, oils, and gels. You'll also find fabulous lotions and perfumes. Also located in the same space is the Homestead Collection, a store that carries crystal, silver, classic home decor items, furniture, and accessories with Southern flair reminiscent of the Homestead.

The First Lady
The Homestead, Hot Springs
(540) 839-7612
This shop features ladies' dresses, designer sportswear, and accessories. Here you'll find casual and party outfits, suits as well as dresses, jewelry made by Brighton, shoes, purses, belts, sunglasses, and watches.

Hobby Horse
The Homestead, Hot Springs
(540) 839-7946
Take the children to this fun store, which is decorated in the fashion of a child's room with white and blue striped wallpaper and kites on the ceiling. Here you will find adorable casual and dress clothing for children. There's also a wonderful array of toys including dolls, stuffed animals, baby gifts, book shelves, toy chests, and decor items such as chairs, wall hangings, and clocks.

1766
The Homestead, Hot Springs
(540) 839-7743
You'll find your logo apparel and gift items here. There's lots to choose from, including umbrellas, sweatshirts and T-shirts, robes, golf shirts, wind shirts, golf balls, glassware, cookbooks, and Christmas ornaments.

Southern Taste
The Homestead, Hot Springs
(540) 839-7991
Visit Southern Taste for a complete range of items for the kitchen, including extraordinary wines—Virginia wines among them—culinary wares, gadgets, and serving pieces. You'll also find pottery as well as the Vietri line of dishes.

Highland County

ANTIQUES

High Valley Antiques and Collectibles
US 220, Monterey
(540) 474-5611
Seven miles north of Monterey, near the West Virginia line, you'll find this shop occupying a pre–Civil War era log cabin. The shop features glassware, pottery, some furniture, and a variety of collectible knickknacks. There are no regular hours; it's open by chance. Call first to see if you can swing by.

HANDCRAFTS

Gallery of Mountain Secrets
Main Street, Monterey
(540) 468-2020
This gallery is a treasure of traditional arts

and fine crafts. It's a very special store, down from the historic Highland Inn, that offers exquisite jewelry, pottery, wooden items such as the popular turned wood bowls, quilted items, decorative accessories, and graphics. It's open daily and is housed in an old store building constructed in the early 1900s and operated originally as a general store.

Highland County Crafts
Main Street, Monterey
(540) 468-2127
This shop gives a touch of country to all of its gifts, including handmade quilts and wormy chestnut furniture. It offers a Christmas corner with ornaments, stuffed snowmen, and wreaths. Highland County Crafts, which opened in 1973, also features maple syrup and homemade preserves. It is closed on Sunday, as well as Wednesday in the winter.

GENERAL STORES

Sugar Tree Country Store and
Sugar House
Off US 250, McDowell
(540) 396-3469, (800) 396-2445
www.sugartreecountrystore.com
This 19th-century country store features maple products, apple butter, pottery, and baskets. The building was constructed in the 1840s and originally built to be a country store. They make their own maple syrup and do copper kettle apple butter demonstrations. The store, in the scenic Bullpasture Valley, is a must-see during the annual Highland Maple Festival, when it has tours inside of the modern-day syrup operations. Highlights of the festival are outdoor demonstrations of old-time methods of making maple syrup in iron kettles. The country store offers maple products available by mail order, too.

SPECIALTY SHOPS

Ginseng Mountain Store
U.S. 220, Monterey
(540) 474-3663
This unique shop is open Thursday through Sunday, with fewer hours in the winter. You can get choice spring lamb cut to your specification, sheepskin products from the owners' farm, Highland County T-shirts and sweatshirts, wool earmuffs, and dusters, stoneware, wooden bowls, baskets, cherry kitchen utensils, and woven and braided rugs. You'll also find Jerry's Grilling Marinade, Hubs Peanuts, and local crafts and antiques at this shop that is 6 miles north of Monterey.

ATTRACTIONS

In addition to satisfying your soul with beautiful sights and friendly people, the Blue Ridge of Virginia will arouse your curiosity and pique your interest with its wide variety of attractions. You'll never grow tired of the scenic wonder of underground caverns, the historical insight of the region's many museums and historic homes, or the pure fun of many off-the-beaten-path destinations.

Maple sugar is celebrated at its own museum in Highland County. Alleghany County has one of the largest railroad archives in the United States, the province of the C & O Railroad Historical Society.

Historically, the Charlottesville area is one of the country's best-known tourist cities, with such attractions as Montpelier, Monticello, and Ash Lawn–Highland, the former homes of three of our greatest presidents. A half million visitors a year make the trek to the neoclassical mansion designed by the third president of the United States, Thomas Jefferson. Farther south is Jefferson's summer getaway at Poplar Forest in Bedford County. Also in Bedford is the National D-Day Memorial, which attracted nearly 300,000 people in its first six months. In the hills of Pulaski County, visitors stroll through an 1810 village in Old Newbern and see what life was like nearly two centuries ago.

History buffs will find the region's libraries an important source of information. In Lynchburg, Jones Memorial is one of the nation's foremost genealogical libraries. Virginia Tech's Carol Newman Library has the fifth-largest microfilm collection in the United States and Canada.

There's probably not a small town in the nation with as many military museums as Lexington, with its VMI Museum, George C. Marshall Museum, Stonewall Jackson House, and Lee Chapel. In Roanoke, To the Rescue Museum houses an international tribute to the millions of lives touched by the volunteer rescue squad movement and honors the father of the movement, Julian Stanley Wise.

Some museums honor forgotten geniuses, for example, the Cyrus McCormick Museum in Rockbridge County, dedicated to the inventor of the first successful reaper.

If it's other-world exploration you desire, you've come to the right region. The Blue Ridge boasts the highest number of caves of any mountain range in North America. So many miles of them exist under Virginia's outer skin that several have never been completely explored. In other words, no end has been found!

Most visitors to the area opt to tour one of the many commercial caverns; six of them are easily accessible from major interchanges of the Skyline Drive or Interstate 81.

Almost all the caverns have interesting histories peppered with stories of American Indians, soldiers, and adventurous children who stumbled across passageways leading to hitherto unseen wonders. But, unfortunately, some caves bear the scars of souvenir hunters, a practice that has been halted by the Virginia Cave Act. Explorers of wild caves now know to "take nothing but pictures, leave nothing but footprints."

Enjoy making your choices from the attractions listed in this chapter. Be sure to look at our Civil War, Kidstuff, Horse Country, and Wineries chapters for ideas of other things to do. Hours and prices may change, so be sure to call ahead. Good luck if you're trying to see it all!

PRICE CODE

The following is a price code for admission to attractions. The price listed is for adults. Children and senior citizens' admissions are usually lower.

$	Up to $5.00
$$	$5.01 to $10.00
$$$	$10.01 to $15.00
$$$$	More than $15.00

SHENANDOAH VALLEY

Frederick County

LIBRARIES

Handley Regional Library **Free**
Braddock and Piccadilly Streets, Winchester
(540) 662-9041
www.hrl.lib.state.va.us

Hundreds of history buffs travel here to do genealogical research in the library's archives, particularly on ancestors who fought in the Civil War. Aside from amassing a collection of more than 190,000 books, the library itself is also a magnificent structure. Listed on the National Register of Historic Places, the original building (it opened in 1913) was designed in the Beaux Arts style. Created to represent a book, the rotunda served as the spine with two wings representing the open pages. Corinthian columns stand guard in front, while the dome is covered with a copper top on the outside and stained glass on the inside. A new wing was added in 1979 called the "grandson leaning against the grandfather." There is also an impressive children's room on the second floor and an auditorium on the ground floor. The library is open from 10:00 A.M. to 8:00 P.M. Tuesday and Wednesday and 10:00 A.M. to 5:00 P.M. Thursday, Friday, and Saturday. The archives are open 1:00 to 8:00 P.M. Tuesday and Wednesday and from 10:00 A.M. to 5:00 P.M. Thursday, Friday, and Saturday.

MUSEUMS AND HISTORIC ATTRACTIONS

Abram's Delight Museum **$$**
1340 South Pleasant Valley Road, Winchester
(540) 662-6519
www.winchesterhistory.org

Abram's Delight, the oldest house in Winchester, was built in 1754 of native limestone with walls 2 feet thick. A restored log cabin on the lawn is from the same period. Abram's Delight is beautifully refurbished and furnished with period pieces. It's open Monday through Saturday from 10:00 A.M. to 4:00 P.M. and Sunday noon to 4:00 P.M. April 1 through October 31. You can save by buying a block ticket for entrance to this museum and two other historic sites in town, Stonewall Jackson's Headquarters and George Washington's Office Museum. Block tickets cost $10.00 for adults, $9.00 for seniors, and $4.00 for children. Family block tickets are $20.00.

Belle Grove Plantation **$$**
U.S. Highway 11, Middletown
(540) 869-2028
www.bellegrove.org

Belle Grove, ca. 1794, is an 18th-century plantation, working farm, and center for the study of traditional rural crafts. The National Historic Trust site was the home of Maj. Isaac Hite Jr. and his family for more than 70 years. Hite was a grandson of one of the first permanent settlers in the Shenandoah Valley. Thomas Jefferson was actively involved in Belle Grove's design, thanks to some family connections. Hite married the sister of James Madison, who was a close friend of Jefferson. In fact, James and Dolley Madison spent part of their honeymoon visiting the Hites at Belle Grove.

Belle Grove hosts a variety of special activities throughout the year, from the Cedar Creek reenactment in mid-October to the Living History weekend in November. A very nice gift shop is also at the site.

The plantation is open to the public April through October from 10:15 A.M. to 3:15 P.M. daily (1:15 to 4:15 P.M. Sunday). Belle Grove is a mile south of Middletown on US 11; take exit 302 from I-81, then head west on Highway 627 to US 11.

George Washington's Office Museum **$**
32 West Cork Street, Winchester
(540) 662-4412

Part of this old log-and-stone building was

used by Washington when he was colonel of the Virginia Regiment protecting the 300-mile-long frontier to the west. The Virginia Historic Landmark is open 10:00 A.M. to 4:00 P.M. daily (noon to 4:00 P.M. Sunday) April 1 through October.

Glen Burnie Historic House, Gardens $$
801 Amherst Street, Winchester
(540) 662-1473, (888) 556-5799
www.glenburniemuseum.org
The Glen Burnie Historic House is surrounded by six acres of beautiful formal gardens and furnished with the 18th- and 19th-century antiques, paintings, and decorative objects collected by art connoisseur Julian Wood Glass Jr. (1910–1992). The site traces its history to Col. James Wood, who settled on this land in the early 1700s and then donated portions of his homestead to establish the city of Winchester in 1744. Six generations of James Wood's descendants have lived in the house since that time. In 1997 the site was opened as a museum, with the Glen Burnie Historic House presented exactly as furnished and enjoyed by Julian Wood Glass Jr., the last James Wood descendant to live here. Visitors may explore all the gardens—which feature numerous fountains and sculptures—and take a docent-led tour of the house. There is also a small exhibition and video presentation about the site's history and a fully furnished miniature model of the house. Glen Burnie is open April 1 through October 31. The hours are 10:00 A.M. to 4:00 P.M. Tuesday through Saturday and noon to 4:00 P.M. Sunday. Members and children aged 6 and younger are admitted for free. If you would like to tour the gardens only, admission is $5.00.

Scheduled to open in April 2005, the Museum of the Shenandoah Valley is a new regional history museum dedicated to interpreting the art, history, and culture of the Shenandoah Valley. The 48,000-square-foot, $20-million museum will contain five exhibition galleries, a reception hall, a museum store, a tearoom, and a learning center. The new museum will open on the grounds of Glen Burnie and will transform the homestead of Winchester founder James Wood into a regional history museum complex open year-round.

Stonewall Jackson's Headquarters $$
415 North Braddock Street, Winchester
(540) 667-3242
www.winchesterhistory.org
Jackson used the private home of Lt. Col. Lewis T. Moore as his headquarters during the Civil War from 1861 to 1862. Jackson's office remains much as it was during his stay, and the house built in 1854 contains artifacts of Jackson, Turner Ashby, Jed Hotchkiss, and other Confederate leaders. The house is open from 10:00 A.M. to 4:00 P.M. daily (noon to 4:00 P.M. Sunday) April 1 through October.

If you plan on stopping by several sites, consider the block tickets. The block ticket will get you in Stonewall Jackson's Headquarters plus George Washington's Office Museum and Abram's Delight Museum. Block tickets cost $10.00 for adults, $9.00 for seniors, and $4.00 for children. Family block tickets are $20.00.

OTHER ATTRACTIONS
Patsy Cline Gravesite Free
1270 Front Royal Pike, Winchester
(540) 667-2012
Thousands of people come to Winchester each year to pay their respects to one of country music's most beloved singers, Patsy Cline. She was born on September 8, 1932, in nearby Gore and went on to star on the Grand Ole Opry. A year after "I Fall to Pieces" hit No. 1 on the country record charts, Cline was killed in an airplane crash in Tennessee in 1963. A bell tower was erected in her memory at the Shenandoah Memorial Park, where she is interred. Several local highways, including Highway 522, have been renamed in her honor. Those wishing to visit the grave should enter the north gate and take the first right to a bench on the left. Open sunrise to sunset, there is no charge to visit.

Clarke County

HISTORIC ATTRACTIONS

The Burwell–Morgan Mill $
15 Tannery Lane, Millwood
(540) 837-1799
www.clarkehistory.org
In 1782 Lt. Col. Nathaniel Burwell and Brig. Gen. Daniel Morgan decided to start a joint venture—a flour- and gristmill. During the Civil War, both armies bought feed and supplies from the mill. In 1876 a second floor was added, and the mill continued to operate until 1953. Today the mill is back in operation grinding meal and flour with the wooden gears dating back to the 1750s. Just as it did almost 200 years ago, the great wheel turns under a splash of water. You can watch them grind on Saturday, and you can even purchase cornmeal. The mill, on the National Register of Historic Places, is open for tours April through November from 9:00 A.M. to 5:00 P.M. Saturday and noon to 5:00 P.M. on Thursday, Friday, and Sunday. A donation is requested.

Historic Long Branch $$
Highway 624, Millwood
(540) 837-1856
www.historiclongbranch.com
This 400-acre estate in the heart of Virginia's hunt country has been owned by a series of famous men, including Lord Culpeper, Lord Fairfax, and Robert King Carter. In fact, George Washington helped survey the property. In 1788 Robert Carter Burwell inherited the land and began to build the mansion along the plans suggested by Benjamin Henry Latrobe, the architect who designed the U.S. Capitol. The property was handed down to Maj. Hugh Mortimer Nelson and Abram Hewitt, but by the 20th century, this large estate was declining. Harry Z. Isaacs, a Baltimore textile executive, bought the property in 1986 and in three short years restored it to its early grandeur. The estate is decorated with hand-painted wallpaper and 18th- and 19th-century antiques—the dining room chairs are identical to those in the White House. Long Branch is open for guided tours from noon to 4:00 P.M. weekends only from April through October. There is also a special weeklong Christmas tour the first week in December.

OTHER ATTRACTIONS

The State Arboretum of Virginia   Free
400 Blandy Farm Lane, Boyce
(540) 837-1758
www.virgina.edu_blandy
Also known as the Orland E. White Arboretum, this research center for the University of Virginia is on 170 acres of Blandy Experimental Farm. You can drive along a circular route or stroll through the grounds and enjoy a picnic lunch. Explore one of the most extensive boxwood collections in North America or rest beneath stands of beeches, magnolia, and maples. Printed trail guides and information on current programs are available at the Visitor's Pavilion. The Arboretum is open year-round from dawn to dusk. Admission is free. Guided tours are available by appointment.

Warren County

CAVERNS

Skyline Caverns $$$
U.S. Highway 340, Front Royal
(540) 635-4545, (800) 296-4545
www.skylinecaverns.com
Sixty-million-year-old Skyline Caverns, at the foothills of the Blue Ridge near the Skyline Drive, has a unique solarium entrance where green shrubs border the cave to create a most attractive welcome. Three running streams traverse the core of the cave; one is stocked with trout as an experiment in adaptation. Fat and thriving, the fish require chopped pork each week to make up for a lack of vitamin D. Another unusual aspect is anthodites, called "orchids of the mineral kingdom," the only such rock formations in the world. They grow at a rate of 1 inch every 7,000 years!

Skyline is noted for its simulated scenes of reality, such as the Capitol Dome, Rainbow Trail, and the Painted Desert. Two large gift shops, a snack shop, and picnic area are on the grounds. Kids enjoy the outdoor Skyline Arrow, a miniature train that carries them on a half-mile journey through the woods.

Skyline Caverns, near the north entrance of Shenandoah National Park, is open year-round, with hours depending on the season. From June 15 through Labor Day, the hours are 9:00 A.M. to 6:00 P.M. Admission is free for children younger than 6. Discounts are available for AAA, military, and seniors. Reservations are accepted but not required.

MUSEUMS

Warren Rifles Confederate Museum $
95 Chester Street, Front Royal
(540) 636-6982

Mosby's Rangers, Stonewall Jackson, Robert E. Lee, Jubal Early, J. E. B. Stuart, and Confederate spy Belle Boyd all saw action in Warren County. Uniforms, flags, pictures, and other relics of their feats are displayed here. The museum and gift shop, which is owned and operated by the Warren Rifles Chapter of the United Daughters of the Confederacy, is open from April 15 to November 1, weekdays 9:00 A.M. to 4:00 P.M. Discounts are available for groups or members of AAA or AARP.

Shenandoah County

CAVERNS

Crystal Caverns at Hupp's Hill $$
33231 Old Valley Pike, Strasburg
(540) 465-5884
www.waysideofva.com

Discovered in 1755, Crystal Caverns at Hupp's Hill is the oldest-documented and northernmost show cave in Virginia. Once operated as a commercial cave, it is now one of the area's newest attractions. After repairs were completed and exhibits prepared, the Crystal Caverns reopened June 27, 1998.

With many actively growing formations, it includes one of the Appalachian region's finest displays of microgours. An interpretive center in the caverns' entrance building contains informative exhibits explaining the cave's geology, paleontology, and use from prehistorical times to today.

Standard tours along the quarter-mile tour route are geared for small groups. For a step back in time, special lantern "illuminations" are conducted several times a year by costumed interpreters in period dress. By lantern light, they will tell you all about the caverns' occupants, including Native Americans, local settlers, truant children, servants, and Civil War soldiers.

The caverns, owned by the Wayside Foundation of American History and Arts Inc., are located in the same complex with the Stonewall Jackson Museum. A combination ticket offers discount rates to both attractions, plus the Museum of American Presidents and the Jeane Dixon Museum and Library on History Square. Crystal Caverns are open year-round from 10:00 A.M. to 5:00 P.M. Monday through Sunday. The last tour usually departs at 4:00 P.M. The caverns are closed six days a year, New Year's Day, Easter, Thanksgiving, Christmas Eve, Christmas, and New Year's Eve.

Shenandoah Caverns $$$$
Off I-81 at exit 269, south of Mount Jackson
(540) 477-3115
www.shenandoahcaverns.com

Shenandoah Caverns, taking its name from the Native American word for "daughter of the stars," was discovered in 1884 during the building of the Southern Railway. The grotto is an estimated 11 million years old and is the closest underground attraction to I-81. It opened on May 30, 1922—the same day Washington, D.C., presented the Lincoln Memorial. It's also the only one in Virginia with an elevator, an advantage to visitors who use wheelchairs, are elderly, or just plain tired. Bacon Hall, a formation named for its hanging slabs of striped iron oxide and calcite, has been featured in *National Geo-*

graphic. Other notable points on the tour are the Grotto of the Gods, Vista of Paradise, and Rainbow Lake.

A new 40,000-square-foot building was added in 2000 to house the owners' ever-growing collection of parade floats, American Celebration on Parade, (540) 477–4300. Inside this aboveground cavern are 22-foot bears from the Tournament of Roses parade and an American eagle that rode in the 2001 inaugural parade. Youngsters will be wide-eyed after seeing a 35-foot Rolls Royce and a 100-foot train. There are even sets from several staged events, including George W. Bush's first inauguration. The owners also had an eye on seasonal window displays from across the country. In 1996 they unveiled "Main Street of Yesteryear" on the second floor of the lodge. It's like stepping back in time as you view an array of antique department store windows filled with moving characters. Each of these Main Street storefronts is decorated as it would have been during the holidays. Nearby attractions include the Skyline Drive, New Market Battlefield and its Civil War museums, and the Meems Bottom covered bridge.

Shenandoah Caverns is open year-round; hours depend on the season. Admission gets you in to see the exhibit, the caverns, and American Celebrations on Parade. Group rates are available upon request.

COVERED BRIDGES

Meems Bottom Bridge   **Free**
Highway 720 off US 11,
Mount Jackson
Just north of Harrisonburg in Rockingham County and less than a half mile from busy I-81, visitors can step back in time at Meems Bottom Bridge. The 204-foot, single-span Burr arch truss crosses the north fork of the Shenandoah River 2 miles south of Mount Jackson on US 11. The bridge takes its name from the Meems family, who owned the Strathmore estate west of the Shenandoah River. The original 1892 structure was rebuilt in 1979,

Even if it's a warm summer's day, don't forget to take a sweater along when you visit any of the caverns along the Blue Ridge. The temperature in the caverns remains in the mid-50s year-round.

almost three years after arsonists burned it. It had been burned before, in 1862, when Stonewall Jackson went up the valley ahead of Union Gen. John C. Fremont, before the battles of Harrisonburg, Cross Keys, and Port Republic. The structure was rebuilt, only to be destroyed again by a flood in 1870. The one-lane bridge is open to automobile traffic and is a good side excursion from New Market, a major destination for Civil War buffs just 6 miles south of the bridge.

MUSEUMS

Jeane Dixon Museum and Library   **$$**
132 North Massanutten Street, Strasburg
(540) 465–5884
www.waysideofva.com
The Jeane Dixon Museum and Library tells the story of one of the most remarkable women of the 20th century. Best known as the seer who predicted the assassinations of John and Robert Kennedy, Martin Luther King, and Mahatma Gandhi, Jeane was also a devoted wife, real estate executive, wartime volunteer, devout Catholic, animal lover, and humanitarian.

Following her death in 1997, Dixon's family entrusted most of her personal estate to the Wayside Foundation, which opened the museum and library on March 1, 2002.

The new museum contains her artifacts, pictures, memorabilia, awards, honoraria, furniture, clothing, artworks, cherished mementos, and religious icons. The extensive research library contains hundreds of volumes on prophecy, paranormal studies, and presidential biographies, including books Mrs. Dixon authored as well as those she collected and studied. Her handwritten notes can be seen in the margins of her book on Nostradamus.

The museum is open May through October, Friday through Monday with tours at 10:00 A.M. to 2:00 P.M. The Jeane Dixon Museum and Library and the Museum of American Presidents are located on History Square.

Discounted combination tickets are offered for admission to both museums, plus Crystal Caverns and the Stonewall Jackson Museum at Hupp's Hill. All four are owned and operated by the Wayside Foundation.

Museum of American Presidents $
130 North Massanutten Street, Strasburg
(540) 465-5999, (540) 465-5884
www.waysideofva.com
New in 1996, this fascinating museum displays presidential artifacts, including James Madison's desk, on which he likely wrote the *Federalist Papers;* a lock of George Washington's hair; and many documents featuring presidential signatures. Many of the objects are part of Leo Bernstein's 60-year collection of artifacts, which had been housed in various banks and hotel lobbies. Combining education and entertainment, the museum displays biographical sketches of all 43 presidents. The one-room schoolhouse, a hands-on area for children, features reproduction Colonial costumes and toys. Admission is free for those younger than 6. Hours are 10:00 A.M. to 5:00 P.M. Friday through Monday. It's closed New Year's Day, Easter, Thanksgiving, Christmas Eve, Christmas, and New Year's Eve.

New Market Battlefield Historical Park and Hall of Valor Museum $$
8895 Collins Drive, New Market
(540) 740-3101
www.vmi.edu/newmarket
On May 15, 1864, a wavering Confederate line was reinforced with 257 teenage cadets from Virginia Military Institute. This museum, opened in 1970, chronicles their brave but tragic stand and has some interesting displays of VMI professor Stonewall Jackson (see the Civil War chapter). At the top of every hour, you can view one of three films, including the Emmy Award–winning film *The Field of Lost Shoes.* Also on-site is the 19th-century farm of Jacob Bushong, who had worked the farm for 30 years before the war turned his home into a makeshift hospital. You can see the original homestead along with a wheelwright shop, a blacksmith shop, a loom house, and a summer kitchen. The park is open 9:00 A.M. to 5:00 P.M. daily, except for holidays. Admission to the museum, farm, and battlefield are free for those younger than 5.

Stonewall Jackson Museum at Hupp's Hill $
33229 Old Valley Pike, Strasburg
(540) 465-5884
www.waysideofva.com
On October 20, 1864, two brigades of the second division of the Sixth U.S. corps were busy setting up their battle positions. Today those trenches are adjacent to a new interpretive center for the Civil War in the Shenandoah Valley. Once called Hupp's Hill Battlefield Park and Study Center, this facility reopened with all new exhibits on May 10, 1997, as the Stonewall Jackson Museum at Hupp's Hill.

The museum highlights Jackson's 1862 Valley Campaign and selected 1864 battles, with a collection of Civil War artifacts and hands-on reproductions, interpretive guides, the children's "haversack tour," and exhibits on the life of the soldier and valley civilian.

A children's room helps bring history alive. There are costumes to try on, wooden horses complete with cavalry tack to ride, and even a tent and camp furniture to play with. Discovery boxes allow children to explore history through games, puzzles, and artifacts.

The museum also contains an extensive in-house library for those interested in Civil War research.

Outside, there is a quarter-mile interpretive walking trail, where visitors can see the original trenches, including the federal gun positions and the Confederate entrenchments.

The Stonewall Jackson Museum is owned and operated by the Wayside Foundation of American History and Arts Inc. The public nonprofit organization also owns Crystal Caverns at Hupp's Hill and the Museum of American Presidents. Ask about a combination ticket, which will allow you to tour all the Wayside properties at a substantial savings over separate tickets.

Children younger than 6 can visit Stonewall Jackson Museum for free.

Stonewall Jackson Museum is open year-round from 10:00 A.M. to 5:00 P.M. Monday through Sunday. It is closed New Year's Day, Easter, Thanksgiving, Christmas Eve, Christmas, and New Year's Eve.

Strasburg Museum $
440 East King Street, Strasburg
(540) 465-3175
The two-story brick building that houses this museum was built around 1890 and began operating as Strasburg Steam Pottery, also known as the Strasburg Stone and Earthenware Manufacturing Company. The company operated for six years, until the rise of glass jars decreased the use of pottery for food storage. In 1913 the Southern Railway took over the building and used it as a railroad depot until the early 1960s. A group of local folks bought the building in 1966, and it was converted into the museum in 1970. The museum features several exhibit rooms; the newest one opened in May 2002—a pottery room with more than 150 pieces of pottery that date back more than 100 years. Another exhibit features railroad relics. Also on dis-

If you are planning a trip through Strasburg, maximize your sightseeing while minimizing your cost. Purchase a discount ticket to get into the Jeane Dixon Museum and Library, the Stonewall Jackson Museum at Hupp's Hill, the Museum of American Presidents, and Crystal Caverns. Check out www.waysideofva.com for details.

play are Civil War artifacts, old horse-drawn buggies, agricultural tools, blacksmith collections, machinery, and a sleigh. There's even a caboose people can climb in. Be sure to visit the gift shop, where you can pick up locally made pottery, baskets, and other items. The Strasburg Museum is open 10:00 A.M. to 4:00 P.M. daily May through October and is staffed completely by volunteers. Bus groups should call ahead.

Page County

CAVERNS

Luray Caverns $$$$
U.S. Highway 211, Luray
(540) 743-6551
www.luraycaverns.com
Each year nearly a half million people visit Luray Caverns, a U.S. Natural Landmark and the largest known cave on the East Coast, to see the colorful natural cathedral with the world's only Stalacpipe Organ. Stalactites are tuned to concert pitch and accuracy and are struck by electronically controlled, rubber-tipped plungers to produce music of symphonic quality. An hour-long conducted tour transports visitors through a wonderland of vast chambers, some 10 stories high. Memorable formations include the Fried Eggs, the enormous Double Column, and Pluto's Ghost. Placid, crystal-clear pools such as Dream Lake reflect the thousands of stalactites above. One of the largest chambers, the Cathedral, has been the setting for more than

400 weddings. A wishing well has produced more than a half million dollars for charity. Topside, you'll find three gift shops and a restaurant. A self-guided tour of the Historic Car & Carriage Caravan is included in the caverns admission.

The central entrance to the Skyline Drive is only 10 minutes from the caverns. Luray Caverns is open year-round at 9:00 A.M. with the last tour at 4:00 or 6:00 P.M., depending on the season. Children 6 and younger are admitted free. Group rates are available for a minimum of 20 people.

MUSEUMS

Luray Car and Carriage Caravan $$$$
US 211 Bypass, Luray
(540) 743-6551
www.skylinecaverns.com
This museum next to Luray Caverns grew from the car-collecting hobby of the caverns' president, H. T. N. Graves. Among the vehicles are Rudolph Valentino's 1925 Rolls Royce, a Conestoga wagon, an ornate sleigh, and an 1892 Benz, one of the oldest cars in the country. All 140 items, including cars, coaches, carriages, and costumes dating to 1725, are fully restored. Admission is included in your ticket to Luray Caverns. The caravan is open every day from 9:00 A.M. until one and a half hours after the last cavern tour.

OTHER ATTRACTIONS

Luray Singing Tower   Free
US 211 Bypass, Luray
(540) 743-6551, (888) 743-3915
Across from the Luray Caverns is a 117-foot tower containing a carillon of 47 bells, the largest weighing 7,640 pounds and the smallest 12 pounds. Free recitals are given on weekends at 2:00 P.M. during March, April, May, September, and October. From June through August, the bells peal at 8:00 P.M. Tuesday, Thursday, Saturday, and Sunday. Listen from outside on the grounds. There is no fee.

Rockingham County

CAVERNS

Endless Caverns $$$
Off I-81 at exit 257, New Market
(540) 740-3993, (540) 896-CAVE
www.endlesscaverns.com
On October 1, 1879, two boys and their dog chased a rabbit up the slope of Reuben Zirkle's farm. The rabbit disappeared under a boulder. The boys moved the boulder, and before their astonished eyes appeared a great shaft of Endless Caverns. More than 5 miles of passages have been mapped. No end has ever been found to the labyrinth of winding channels and vast rooms, which now are lighted artfully and dramatically for visitors. Snowdrift and Fairyland are two of the most popular formations. Of all the caverns, Endless is the one that makes you feel as if you're venturing into uncharted, rugged territory, and its outdoor scenery is most beautiful.

Just as interesting are the historic native limestone buildings constructed during the 1920s. On the wide porches of the Main Lodge, visitors are invited to rest, rock, and relax while enjoying a sweeping view of the Shenandoah Valley. The stone lodge is cooled in the summer and warmed in winter by air from the caverns. Nearby, Endless Caverns' 100-site campground sits at the foot of Virginia's Massanutten Mountains, adjoining George Washington National Forest.

On I-81, you can't miss the sign for Endless Caverns; it's the largest outdoor billboard in the Eastern United States, standing 35 feet high and 500 feet long.

Endless Caverns is open year-round except Christmas Day. The caverns open at 9:00 A.M. throughout the year. Closing hours vary: They are 9:00 A.M. to 6:00 P.M. from June 15 to September 4; 9:00 A.M. to 5:00 P.M. from September 5 to November 14; 9:00 A.M. to 4:00 P.M. November 15 to March 15; and 9:00 A.M. to 5:00 P.M. from March 15 through June 14. Admission is free for those younger than 4. A bottled water, Endless Caverns Premium Mountain Spring Water, is for sale in the gift shop along with fossils, rocks, glassware, and T-shirts.

MUSEUMS AND HISTORIC ATTRACTIONS

The Daniel Harrison House
(Fort Harrison)   Free
North Main Street, Dayton
(540) 879-2280

This historic 18th-century (ca. 1749) stone house, just north of Dayton, was a natural fort to which Daniel Harrison added a stockade and an underground passage to a nearby spring. What appear to be loop-holes set in the house's stone walls for fir-ing rifles at Indians gave rise to the name Fort Harrison. Free guided tours are avail-able. The house is open 1:00 to 4:00 P.M. on weekends from late May through Octo-ber and for special events in November to April. The house also hosts community events such as the Dayton Autumn Festi-val in October and the Christmas Craft Show at Thanksgiving, while special Colo-nial Dinners are held in May and October by reservation. Guided tours may be arranged at any time.

Edith Carrier Arboretum   Free
University Boulevard, Harrisonburg
(540) 568-3194
www.jmu.edu/arboretum

Commune with nature, right in the midst of a university campus. The Edith Carrier Arboretum, a 125-acre complex, is on the grounds of James Madison University, near the Convocation Center. Miles of winding trails lead through the oak and hickory forest. The grounds include a pond that supports aquatic plant and ani-mal life, daylilies and irises in Andre Viette's Bulb Garden, an antique and heir-loom rose garden, a rock garden, a bog garden, and the April Walk, where 52 vari-eties of daffodils are planted in plots of 50 to 150 bulbs. There are wildflowers, rhodo-dendrons, native shrubs, ferns, herbs, and rare and endangered azaleas. The arbore-

tum also hosts guided tours, workshops, children's activities, and crafts and bulb sales. The arboretum is open daily from dusk to dawn. There is no charge to visit.

Harrisonburg-Rockingham Historical Society Heritage Center $
382 High Street, Dayton
(540) 879-2681, (540) 879-2616
www.heritagecenter.com

This museum has a 12-foot electric relief map of Stonewall Jackson's Valley Cam-paign of 1862. The map fills an entire wall and lets you see and hear the campaign battle by battle. The museum also displays many artifacts of the Shenandoah Valley's history, a Civil War exhibit, and Valley folk art. The center also includes a genealogical library. The Heritage Museum Store sells genealogical and Valley-related books and gifts. Hours are Monday through Saturday 10:00 A.M. to 4:00 P.M. Admission is free for those younger than 5.

Lincoln Homestead
and Cemetery   Free
Highway 42, Harrisonburg

Abraham Lincoln's father, Thomas Lincoln, was born in Rockingham County, and his ancestors were buried here in a little cemetery 7.5 miles north of Harrisonburg. The house now standing at the old Lincoln homestead is privately owned, so please respect that when you visit the cemetery.

Reuel B. Pritchett Museum   Free
Highway 257, Bridgewater College
(540) 828-5462
www.bridgewater.edu

The Rev. Reuel B. Pritchett bequeathed his collection of rare artifacts to Bridgewater College in 1954. The 10,000-piece collec-tion features more than 175 rare books, including a three-volume Bible printed in Venice in 1482 and a medieval book of Gregorian chants made and hand-copied by a monk. There are also a cuneiform brick dating to 600 B.C., a Chinese Man-darin gown, a Kiowa chieftain's headdress, wooden carpentry tools, swords, coins, and glassware. The museum, in the lower level of Cole Hall, is open from 1:00 to 5:00 P.M. Monday through Friday. Admission is free.

Virginia Quilt Museum $
301 South Main Street, Harrisonburg
(540) 433-3818
Quilts represent a rich American heritage, combining practicality, skill, and creativity. Enjoy this history at the Quilt Museum, which displays beautiful works by both early and contemporary artisans. You will also learn about the role of quilts in American cultural life. The museum is open Monday and Thursday through Saturday from 10:00 A.M. to 4:00 P.M.; Sunday hours are 1:00 to 4:00 P.M. Children younger than 6 get in free. Group rates are also available.

SPORTING EVENTS

James Madison University   Free-$$$$
Harrisonburg
(540) JMU-DUKE
www.jmusports.com
Baseball is king at James Madison (JMU). In 1983 the Dukes became the first team in Virginia to participate in the College World Series. The squad also advanced to postseason play in 1980, 1981, 1983, 1988, 1995, and 2002. In 2002 Joe "Spanky" McFarland was named the Colonial Athletic Association's coach of the year as JMU advanced to its sixth regional appearance and its first since 1995. Along the way, JMU set a school record 43 wins and was ranked no. 22 in *Baseball America's* top 25 teams. First baseman Eddie Kim was named the conference player of the year, while Dan Meyer became the highest draft choice ever in JMU's 33-year history of baseball when he was picked 34th overall by the Atlanta Braves in the first round of the professional baseball draft. The Dukes play at the 1,200-seat Long Field/Mauck Stadium.

As football goes in the commonwealth, JMU's program is relatively young. That hasn't kept the Dukes from making their presence felt. In fact JMU won the National

Championship with a 31–21 win over Montana in 2004. The university fielded its first team in 1972, but the Dukes already have advanced to five NCAA playoffs, including the NCAA I-AA final eight in 1991 and 1994. Mickey Matthews, who was named the National Coach of the Year in 2004, took over as head coach in 2001. Among the notable stars who have worn the purple and gold are Gary Clark, a longtime wide receiver for the Washington Redskins, linebacker Charles Haley, who played for the Dallas Cowboys and the San Francisco 49ers, and Scott Norwood, a kicker for the Buffalo Bills. James Madison plays in the 14,000-seat Bridgeforth Stadium.

Basketball, both men's and women's, also has been a favorite with the locals. The crowds turned out in droves when feisty Charles G. "Lefty" Driesell led the men's program to five postseason appearances in eight years. When Driesell hung up his whistle in 1997, former JMU standout Sherman Dillard returned to take over head coaching duties at his alma mater. Dean Keener took over in helm in 2004. The Dukes have posted more than 560 wins since their first season in 1945; the best was a 24–6 record in 1981–82.

Since James Madison started out as a women's college, it's not surprising that the women's basketball program dates back to 1920. Madison hosted and played in one of the first national championship tournaments in the mid-1970s. After women's sports became governed by the NCAA, the Dukes earned semifinal bids in 1986, 1987, 1988, 1989, 1991, and 1996. In 2001 Bud Childers guided his squad to postseason matchup with Ohio State in the WNIT tournament. Both men's and women's basketball games are played in the 7,156-seat Convocation Center.

Other nationally ranked sports at the college have included field hockey, archery, women's lacrosse, and men's and women's soccer. The field hockey team won the national championship in 1994 and was a national semifinalist in 1995. The archery team also has three national titles, and in 2002 three archers qualified to compete in the World University Archery Championship in Bangkok, Thailand. The women's lacrosse team played in six NCAA tournaments and was a semifinalist in 2000 and quarterfinalist in 1997, 1998, 1999, and 2001. The university also has sported some top track-and-field athletes, including U.S. Olympians Juli Hemer in the 1,500 meters in 1996 and Tiombe Hurd in the triple jump in 2004.

James Madison University has 28 varsity sports. Thirteen receive NCAA scholarships, including four for men and nine for women.

The Valley League Baseball   **$**
Harrisonburg
(540) 568-6154
www.valleyleaguebaseball.com
One of the oldest amateur baseball leagues in the country, the Valley League is sanctioned by the NCAA because it features college players, many of whom go on to play professional ball. Mo Vaughn played here. Harrisonburg, Front Royal, Luray, Covington, New Market, Woodstock, Loudoun, Staunton, Waynesboro, and Winchester have franchised teams in the circuit. Starting the first weekend in June, the league plays 40 regular-season games, with the top two teams in each division competing in the playoffs. Front Royal, Luray, Loudoun, Winchester, and New Market make up the North Division, while Harrisonburg, Woodstock, Staunton, Waynesboro, and Covington represent the South Division. Games are scheduled for every day of the week, with most beginning at 7:30 P.M. Game schedules and directions are posted on the Web.

Augusta County

CAVERNS

Grand Caverns   **$$$$**
Off I-81 at exit 235, Grottoes
(540) 249-5705
www.grandcavern.com
Grand Caverns, within Grand Caverns

Regional Park, is one of the oldest and most spectacular caverns in the Shenandoah Valley. The public has been coming here since 1806, including Thomas Jefferson, who rode horseback from Monticello to see the site. During the Civil War, Gen. Stonewall Jackson quartered his troops within this massive stone fortress after the Battle of Port Republic. Union soldiers also visited the cave; their signatures still can be seen penciled on the walls. In better times the Grand Ballroom, which encompasses 5,000 square feet, was the scene of early-19th-century dances for the socially prominent. Cathedral Hall, 280 feet long and 70 feet high, is one of the largest rooms in Eastern caverns. Massive columns and the rare "shield" formations, whose origins are a mystery to geologists, are highlights.

It's open 9:00 A.M. to 5:00 P.M. daily April through Halloween, and on weekends from November through March. It's free for children younger than 3.

MUSEUMS

Frontier Culture Museum   **$$**
1290 Richmond Road, Staunton
(540) 332-7850
www.frontiermuseum.org
Somehow "museum" doesn't seem an appropriate word for the living, breathing outdoor Frontier Culture Museum. Authentic farmsteads have been painstakingly brought from Old World Europe and reconstructed here. Original gardens, hedges, pastures, and even road layouts have been duplicated, along with the old ways of survival. You can tour Scots-Irish, 18th-century German, American, and English farmsteads staffed with knowledgeable, articulate interpreters. Also authentic are the farm animals, including lambs, chickens, cows, oxen, pigs, draft horses, and kittens, making this a fine attraction for children.

The museum added an 18th-century forge, or blacksmith shop. This one-room, thatched-roof stone structure was brought over from Ireland. If you are lucky, you will catch the resident blacksmith demonstrating how the generations-old tools and equipment are used.

Throughout the year, the museum hosts more than 100 special events, such as Lantern Tours at Christmas and the creepy tales at Halloween.

The museum is open 9:00 A.M. to 5:00 P.M. daily for most of the year (10:00 A.M. to 4:00 P.M. January 1 through March 15). The facility is closed Thanksgiving, Christmas, and New Year's Days. Special rates are available for preregistered groups of 15 or more.

To find the museum, take exit 222 off I-81, then go west on U.S. Highway 250.

Waynesboro Heritage Museum $
Main Street, Waynesboro
(540) 943-3943
This historic building on the corner of Main Street and Wayne Avenue served the banking needs of the people of Waynesboro since 1908. Now it houses the city's historical treasures. You can still see inside the large walk-in vault, but all around are reminders of Waynesboro's past. There is a case of arrowheads and tools from the Indians who stopped by and planted crops. There is a bill of sale for a slave and notices from the tannery that closed when the chestnut blight swept through the area. There are reminders of war—shoes from Union and Confederate soldiers, a World War I canteen and pistol belt, a Japanese officer's sword taken from the beach at Iwo Jima during WWII. There's even a collection of international dolls, ranging from an Indonesian Rod Puppet

The Virginia Travel Guide *celebrated the 35th anniversary in 2004 of its popular slogan "Virginia is for Lovers." To get a free guide from the state, call (800) 932-5827 or order one at www.virginia.org. They also can be found at any of the state's 10 highway Welcome Centers.*

and Russian Nesting Matryoshkas to our own Colonial-era Applehead, Nuthead, and Corncob dolls. Hours are 10:00 A.M. to 4:00 P.M. Wednesday through Saturday. Donations are accepted.

Woodrow Wilson Museum
and Birthplace $$
18 to 24 North Coalter Street, Staunton
(540) 885-0897, (888) 4WOODRO
www.woodrowwilson.org
Woodrow Wilson's birthplace has been carefully restored to appear as it would have when he lived there as a child. Throughout the 150-year-old Greek Revival-style house are furniture and other personal items belonging to the Wilsons, including the family Bible in which Woodrow Wilson's birth was recorded. You'll also find an array of period pieces typical of the antebellum era.

The museum is a tribute to our nation's 28th president, who was born here in 1856. Displays chronicle his life as a scholar, Princeton University president, governor, and statesman. Seven exhibit areas include rare artifacts, photographs, personal possessions, and the furnishings of Wilson's study at Princeton. The displays do not shy away from the controversies Wilson generated in his lifetime, from the way in which he alienated wealthy trustees and alumni as Princeton's president to his lack of support for women's suffrage as America's president. Of course, the displays also highlight the reforms Wilson brought about as the nation's leader. The museum houses Wilson's beloved Pierce-Arrow automobile.

The museum and birthplace are open daily 9:00 A.M. to 5:00 P.M. (10:00 A.M. to 4:00 P.M. December through February except Thanksgiving, Christmas, and New Year's Days). Allow an hour and a half to tour the manse, museum, and gardens.

OTHER ATTRACTIONS

Natural Chimneys $
Off Highway 731, Mount Solon
(540) 350-2510
www.naturalchimneys.com

A mere 500 million years ago, layers of limestone began to form from sediment under an ancient sea that once covered the Shenandoah Valley. Today, seven of those rock formations can be seen at Natural Chimneys Regional Park. The "chimneys" range in height from 65 to 120 feet, but each includes a 12-inch band of lava about 6 feet up from the ground. One of the chimneys leans 13.5 feet, approximately the same as the Leaning Tower of Pisa. The park also includes campsites, a swimming pool, stage, and picnic shelters and hosts two jousting tournaments each June and August (see our Horse Country chapter). The park is open daily from 9:00 A.M. to dusk from March through October.

Lexington and Rockbridge County

CAVERNS

Natural Bridge Caverns   **$$**
US 11 S, Natural Bridge
(540) 291-2121, (800) 533-1410
www.naturalbridgeva.com
Here's a cavern with its own ghost! For more than 100 years, people have been hearing the plaintive voice of a woman deep within the limestone passages. The first time it happened in 1889, men working in the caverns abandoned their ladders, fled, and refused to go back. Their tools and lanterns were found in 1978. The last time the ghost was heard was 1988, when six people on the final tour of the day heard a distinct moaning sound, which continued throughout the guide's narrative. In all cases, it is documented that those present had an eerie feeling and fled the premises without hesitation. The caverns, at Virginia's Natural Bridge complex, offer a guided, 45-minute tour 347 feet underground. The pathways are winding and steep in areas, so walking shoes are suggested.

The Natural Bridge Gift Shop is the largest in the valley, with 10,000 square feet of space; the "rock" and "mineral" candies are sure to delight youngsters.

The cavern is open mid-March through November, 10:00 A.M. to 5:00 P.M. daily. Admission is free for those younger than 5.

MUSEUMS AND HISTORIC ATTRACTIONS

George C. Marshall Museum
and Library   **$**
VMI Parade Grounds, Lexington
(540) 463-7103
www.marshallfoundation.org
The Marshall Foundation was founded in 1953 at the suggestion of President Harry Truman to honor the memory of Gen. George C. Marshall. Marshall was the only American military hero to win a Nobel Peace Prize, for his plan to reconstruct Europe following World War II. Winston Churchill said of Marshall, "Succeeding generations must not be allowed to forget his achievements and his example." Marshall also was former Army Chief of Staff and Secretary of State and Defense. Presidents Johnson and Eisenhower dedicated the museum in 1964. Visitors can see a stirring movie and striking photographic display, including the hauntingly stark, black-and-white photos of the faces of children of war-torn Europe.

The museum is open from 9:00 A.M. to 5:00 P.M. daily. Admission is free for those younger than 18.

Lee Chapel and Museum   **$**
Washington and Lee University,
Lexington
(540) 458-8768, (540) 458-8095
www.leechapel.wlu.edu
Civil War buffs won't want to miss the beautiful Lee Chapel and Museum, the focal point of the campus where Confederate great Robert E. Lee served as president for five years after the war. Lee's remains are buried here, and you can see the famous Edward Valentine statue of a recumbent Lee. The museum traces the history of Washington as well as Lee. You can tour the museum in 45 minutes to an hour. The museum is open 9:00 A.M. to

5:00 P.M. Monday through Saturday from April through October and closes one hour earlier October through April. The chapel will be closed on Thanksgiving, the day after Thanksgiving, and from Christmas through New Year's. Sunday hours are 1:00 to 5:00 P.M. There is no charge.

McCormick Farm   Free
US 11 N to Highway 606 or exit 205 off I-81, Steeles Tavern
(540) 377-2255
This 635-acre farm, 20 miles north of Lexington, is the home of Cyrus McCormick, who invented the first successful mechanical reaper at age 22. McCormick Farm is part of the Virginia Tech College of Agricultural and Life Sciences and a Virginia Agricultural Experiment Station. Visitors may tour the blacksmith shop, gristmill, museum, and McCormick family home, all National Historic Landmarks. McCormick's 1831 invention launched a new era in agriculture, an age of mechanization that not only changed life on the farm but also made it possible for millions of people to leave the land and enter an industrial society. It takes 20 minutes to view. The site is open 8:30 A.M. to 5:00 P.M. daily.

Natural Bridge $$
US 11 S, Natural Bridge
(540) 291-2121, (800) 533-1410
www.naturalbridge.com
George Washington surveyed it. Thomas Jefferson once owned it. Today, anyone can see one of the seven natural wonders of the world right here in this small town near Lexington. This enormous rock bridge—now you see how the county got its name—is 90 feet wide and 215 feet tall. If you were able to weigh it, some estimate that it would be as heavy as 36,000 tons. The bridge has remained in private hands since Jefferson bought it for 20 shillings from King George III. If you plan your visit in the evening, you can take in the free *Drama of Creation* light and sound show that bounces off this mysterious formation. At the Natural Bridge park facilities is the Monacan Village, where you can watch

Monacan Indians tan hides, weave mats and ropes, make tools, and prepare their meals. You might even be able to lend a hand in turning a downed tree into a real canoe. You can tour the village complex from 9:00 A.M. to 5:00 P.M. April through November. It's free with your admission to the bridge. You can visit Natural Bridge from 8:00 A.M. until dark. Children younger than 5 are admitted free. Ask about the four-way combination ticket that will get you into the bridge, the wax museum, the toy museum (see our Kidstuff chapter), and the caverns. A fifth attraction was recently added. Professor Cline's Haunted Monster Museum is open seasonally for self-guided tours for a separate $8.00 admission.

Natural Bridge Wax Museum $$
US 11 S, Natural Bridge
(540) 291-2121, (800) 533-1410
www.naturalbridgeva.com
Speaking of natural wonders, where else in the Blue Ridge would you find Robert E. Lee, Daniel Boone, and Jesus? They are just three of the 170 creations in this wax museum at the Natural Bridge Park. After seeing the bridge aboveground and the caverns below, take a step back in time with these historical figures. Thomas Jefferson, George Washington, and the theatrical presentation of Leonardo da Vinci's *The Last Supper* are among the figures and historical scenes in the museum. Your tour also goes to the factory, where these life-size creations are made. The Wax Museum is open 10:00 A.M. to 4:30 P.M. daily from March through November and 10:00 A.M. to 4:00 P.M. weekends only from December through February. Children younger than 5 get in free.

Stonewall Jackson House $
8 East Washington Street, Lexington
(540) 463-2552
www.stonewalljackson.org
Stonewall Jackson House, owned and operated by Stonewall Jackson Foundation, is the only home the famous Confederate general ever owned. The house reopened

on June 1, 2004, after a $1.3 million renovation was completed. New paint and wallpaper take the home back to the way it appeared when Stonewall Jackson and his second wife, Anna Morrison Jackson, lived here from 1859 to 1861. It is furnished with period pieces, including many of Jackson's personal possessions. The house, which is listed on the National Register of Historic Sites, is open to the public daily for guided tours of the rooms. In addition to tours and exhibits, the Stonewall Jackson House sponsors a variety of educational programs through the Garland Gray Research Center and Library, on the office level of the museum. Educational activities include in-school programs, internships, lectures, workshops, and scholarly symposia. It is open 9:00 A.M. to 5:00 P.M. Monday through Saturday and 1:00 to 5:00 P.M. Sunday. The museum is closed on Thanksgiving Day, Christmas Day, New Year's Day, and Easter Sunday. Children younger than 6 are admitted free of charge.

Virginia Military Institute Museum $
VMI Parade Grounds, North Main Street,
Lexington
(540) 464-7232, (540) 464-7334
www.vmi.edu/museum
The Virginia Military Institute Museum, on the lower level of Jackson Hall on the VMI campus, brings the nation's history to life. Other exhibits tell American history through the lives and service of VMI faculty. Both Gen. Stonewall Jackson and Gen. George W. Custis Lee taught at VMI. While major renovations are under way, the museum still has a presence on the VMI campus. A temporary exhibit has moved to the George Marshall Museum (see our Civil War chapter). The entire collection will move back to the Jackson Memorial Hall in 2007.

ZOOS

Natural Bridge Zoo $$
US 11 N, Natural Bridge
(540) 291-2420
www.naturalbridgezoo.net

Next to Natural Bridge Village and Resort, this 25-acre zoo is also an endangered species breeding center. It has the largest petting area in Virginia and elephant rides for the kids. For two decades the zoo has been raising generations of endangered species, including four generations of the scarlet macaw, Siberian tigers, ring-tailed lemurs, and Himalayan bears. Elegant giraffes, graceful antelopes, huge camels, curious ostriches, and many monkey families make this collection of animals and birds Virginia's largest and most complete. The zoo has a white tiger named Mohan.

On weekends, children can ride Asha, the African elephant, for $4.00. Enjoy the thrill of mingling with tame deer, gentle llamas, and cute, fuzzy miniature donkeys. The family will enjoy large covered picnic pavilions and a well-stocked gift shop. Hours of operation are 9:00 A.M. to 6:00 P.M. seven days a week. It is closed December through March.

Virginia Safari Park $$
229 Safari Lane, Natural Bridge
(540) 291-1256
www.virginiasafaripark.com
Ostriches, emus, and llamas, oh my.

When you travel through this 180-acre drive-through park, you don't know what might poke its head in the window of your car looking for food pellets. Before it opened in 2000, this free-range park had been a breeding farm for zoos. Today, it is home to more than 500 exotic animals, including bison, yak, camels, zebras, kangaroos, elk, antelope, wildebeest, giraffes, even a Galapagos tortoise. While visitors must follow the Big Rule—stay in the car—there is a petting area where youngsters can get a hands-on look at some of the baby animals.

A bucket of feed costs $3.00, but beware, a hungry zebra might claim the whole thing. You might want to purchase four buckets for $10.00.

The park is open daily 9:00 A.M. to 5:00 P.M. from March 13 to May 29; 9:00 A.M. to 6:00 P.M. May 30 to September 6; and 9:00 A.M. to 5:00 P.M. from September 7 to

November 28. You must arrive one hour before closing time. Children younger than 3 get in free.

OTHER ATTRACTIONS

Boxerwood Garden $
963 Ross Road, Lexington
(540) 463-2697
www.boxerwood.org
Boxerwood Garden is an absolute horticultural treasure located just minutes from historic downtown Lexington. The late Dr. Robert S. Munger (father of world-renowned photographer Sally Mann) began this collection of more than 2,400 specimen plants spread over 15 acres when he started the collection. For more than 30 years, Dr. Munger collected rare and unusual trees and shrubs, tagged with its name and the date he planted it. Hundreds of varieties of dwarf conifers, magnolias, dogwoods, rhododendrons, azaleas, Japanese maples, and more adorn the grounds, along with an occasional (and equally unusual) piece of man-made art.

For years Boxerwood Garden was not open to the public. Only the privileged few gained access to the pristine natural sanctuary, named for Dr. Munger's 13 boxer dogs. Karen "K B" Bailey was one of those few; the doctor was her mentor for a number of years before his death, bestowing his knowledge on an eager and capable student. In 1997, after years of dedication to the garden, K B and co-owner Hunter Moehring purchased Boxerwood. They have opened the garden to the public in an attempt to preserve and continue the legacy of Dr. Munger. K B welcomes the opportunity to share her knowledge and horticultural techniques; guests are welcome to work in the garden alongside her.

Boxerwood Garden is open for self-guided tours from 9:00 A.M. to 4:00 P.M. Tuesday through Sunday from March 15 through November. Guided tours are available by appointment. A contribution of $5.00 per person is suggested.

Buffalo Springs Herb Farm Free
7 Kennedy Wades Mill Loop, Raphine
(540) 348-1083
www.buffaloherbs.com
This unique 18th-century farmstead offers nearly everything an herbal devotee needs. The "big red barn" has herbal products, dried flowers and designs, garden books, accessories, and a program room. There is a plant house and several themed gardens on-site. Visitors can enjoy a 1-mile hike to a waterfall or take a spiritual walk to meditate along the circular labyrinth. Buffalo Springs hosts Don Haynie and Tom Hamlin schedule various programs and workshops throughout the season as well. There is no fee except for special programs. The herb farm season runs from April through mid-December. Hours are 10:00 A.M. to 5:00 P.M. Wednesday through Saturday and 1:00 to 5:00 P.M. Sunday. The farm is closed during the winter.

Carriage Tours of Historic
Lexington $$$$
Lexington Visitor Center
106 East Washington Street, Lexington
(540) 463-5647
The Lexington Carriage Company will take you back in time to the 19th-century pace of this historic town. Horse-drawn carriages will transport you past sites like the Stonewall Jackson House, Lee Chapel, and Washington & Lee University and through the historic downtown and residential districts. Professional carriage drivers/tour guides narrate the tours. Be advised that carriage tours take 45 to 50 minutes and do not make stops along the way.

Tours begin across from the Lexington Visitor Center. They are offered daily from 10:00 A.M. to 5:00 P.M. from June through August and 11:00 A.M. to 5:00 P.M. in April, May, September, and October. Tours are cancelled in the event of inclement weather. Groups of 10 or more must make reservations. Discounts are available for groups of 10 or more and groups of 30 or more.

Haunting Tales $$
106 East Washington Street, Lexington
(540) 348-1080
www.ghosttour.biz

This 1.3-mile candlelight walk through the back streets and alleyways of historic Lexington is not for the skittish! Guides introduce visitors to some intriguing and chilling ghost stories while trekking after some of the town's long-departed residents. Witness firsthand the unexplained phenomenon that has occurred nightly in the Stonewall Jackson Cemetery since the tour began. Victorian-style seance recreations can also be arranged.

Tours are late May through October nightly. Admission is free for children younger than 3. Reservations are required.

Historic Garden Week $$$$
Various locations
(540) 463-3777
www.lexingtonvirginia.com

History and garden aficionados flock to Lexington in the spring for its incomparable Historic Garden Week. Each April (the date changes yearly), civic-minded residents open their historic homes and gardens to an appreciative public. Many of the residences are furnished with family heirlooms and gorgeous antiques and have ornate gardens.

Hull's Drive-In Theatre $
US 11, Lexington
(540) 463-2621
www.hullsdrivein.com

One of the last auto drive-in theaters left in Virginia, Hull's is worth a visit for a dose of nostalgia. From the well-groomed grounds to the syrupy snowballs, Hull's Drive-In is the only community-owned nonprofit operation anywhere. Nothing's changed since 1950. It's open weekends at dusk April through October. Those younger than 12 get in free.

W & L Mock Convention   Free
Washington and Lee University, Lexington
(540) 463-8460
www.mockcon.wlu.edu

This is an event worth waiting for every four years. Held only during presidential election years (look for the next one in the year 2008), Washington and Lee's nationally known Mock Convention has been called "the nation's foremost and most accurate predictor in presidential politics." The Convention has earned this reputation by correctly predicting the presidential nominee of the party out of power 17 of 23 times. In 2004 they correctly selected John Kerry as the Democratic nominee. It has been wrong only once since 1948, predicting Senator Edward Kennedy as the 1972 Democratic nominee.

The Convention itself is filled with political speeches, platform fights, and 1,700 student delegates who have spent months researching the attitudes of the states they represent. The result is an event that has been covered nationally and broadcast live around the world on C-Span. Harry Truman, Richard Nixon, Jimmy Carter, Bill Clinton, Dan Quayle, Newt Gingrich, Bill Bennett, Bob Dole, Michael Dukakis, and Mario Cuomo have addressed past Conventions.

Lest you get the idea that the Convention is all work, the event begins with a long parade of floats.

In the 1950s, Saturday night at the movies meant going to a drive-in. During their heyday there were more than 6,000 drive-in theaters across the United States. Today that number has dwindled to about 800. You can catch a part of Americana at several spots along the Blue Ridge, including Winchester, Fork Union, and Lexington.

Wade's Mill   Free
Highway 606, Raphine
(540) 348-1400, (800) 290-1400
www.wadesmill.com

This working water-powered gristmill, ca. 1750, is listed on the National Register of Historic Places. Not only does Wade's Mill offer a variety of stone-ground flours, but it also has pottery and basketry by local artists. The gift shop also carries tabletop and kitchenware from France and Italy. All products are available by mail. Cooking classes and other special events may also be arranged. The mill is open 10:00 A.M. to 5:00 P.M. Wednesday through Saturday from April to the Sunday before Christmas. It is open from 1:00 to 5:00 P.M. Sunday April through June and September through December.

ROANOKE VALLEY

Botetourt County

MUSEUMS AND HISTORIC ATTRACTIONS

Botetourt County Historical Museum **Free**
Court House Complex, Fincastle
(540) 473-8394
Botetourt County (pronounced BOT-uh-tot), named in 1770 for Lord Botetourt of England, once stretched to the Mississippi River, encompassing what is now parts of West Virginia, Wisconsin, Kentucky, Ohio, Indiana, and Illinois. Fincastle was the historic county seat. Starting out with 80 items in two rooms, the museum now is home to more than 800 artifacts in eight rooms. The museum, which attracts thousands of visitors annually, is sponsored by the Botetourt County Historical Society. Programs, especially those dealing with genealogy, are open to the public. The museum plays a cooperative role in historic Fincastle's annual fall Old Fincastle Festival, one of the largest festivals in the Roanoke Valley (see our Annual Events and Festivals chapter). Museum hours are 10:00 A.M. to 2:00 P.M. Monday through Saturday, 2:00 to 4:00 P.M. Sunday and upon request.

Roanoke and Salem

CAVERNS

Dixie Caverns **$$**
5753 West Main Street, Salem
(540) 380-2085
www.dixiecaverns.com
Dixie Caverns offers breathtaking netherworld formations along with a gift and pottery shop, antiques and collectibles shop, rock store, and campground. Tour guides first take visitors up the mountain instead of down into it, pointing out the spot where a dog fell through a hole and led to the discovery of the caverns. The pet's owners also found evidence that the Native Americans of Southwest Virginia used the cave for shelter and food storage. Some of the most popular formations on the cavern tour are the Turkey Wing, Magic Mirror, and Wedding Bell, where dozens of couples have been united.

Outside, there's also lots to do and see. The Dixie Caverns Pottery displays thousands of gifts in a shop open daily year-round from 9:00 A.M. to 6:00 P.M. Other shopping options include a rock and mineral shop, with its famous polished-stone wheel. The campground is open all year for RVs and campers. For anglers, the Roanoke River is nearby.

Summer hours are 9:00 A.M. to 6:00 P.M. daily. The caverns are also open the rest of the year from 9:30 A.M. to 5:00 P.M. daily. Admission is free for children younger than 5. Dixie Caverns is just south of Roanoke off I-81 at exit 132.

MUSEUMS AND HISTORIC ATTRACTIONS

Harrison Museum of African-American Culture **Free**
523 Harrison Avenue NW, Roanoke
(540) 345-4818
A regional Roanoke showcase for African-American culture, the Harrison Museum is on the Virginia Historic Landmarks Register as the first public high school for black

students in western Virginia. The museum's stated mission is to research, preserve, and interpret the achievements of African Americans, specifically in western Virginia, and to provide an opportunity for all citizens to come together in appreciation, enjoyment, and greater knowledge of African-American culture.

Since its opening in 1985, the museum has offered art and historical exhibits in its galleries and the Hazel B. Thompson Exhibition Room. The permanent collection of local artifacts and memorabilia has grown from a few objects to several thousand. Thanks to the generosity of donors, Harrison Museum owns an impressive African collection, which includes masks, bronze sculptures, paintings, furniture, and textiles. Schools and organizations may borrow several traveling exhibits and displays. One of its most popular undertakings is the annual Henry Street Heritage Festival held on the last Saturday in September (see our Annual Events and Festivals chapter). It's a festive celebration of African-American heritage; it was held on the Henry Street site for its first four years, then relocated to Elmwood Park in downtown Roanoke in 1994.

The Museum store and gift shop offers Afrocentric art, books, cards, jewelry, and African art. Museum hours are 1:00 to 5:00 P.M. Thursday through Saturday. For group tours contact the curator. Admission is free.

History Museum and Historical Society of Western Virginia $
Center in the Square, Levels 1 and 3
1 Market Square, Roanoke
(540) 342-5770
www.history-museum.org
The rich heritage of western Virginia unfolds in the galleries of the History Museum of Western Virginia. Travel back through time in the permanent exhibit "Crossroads of History." Prehistoric artifacts acquaint you with the way of life of American Indians who lived in the region before the frontier settlers arrived. Other changes in the region are documented

with exhibits of life during the Revolutionary and Civil Wars, Roanoke's rapid growth during the boom days of the N & W Railway, and on into the present. Changing exhibits focus on the events, industries, people, and cultures that have influenced the region. The Theatre History Gallery recalls Roanoke's golden age of stage and screen, including costumes from live theatrical performances and architectural elements from movie houses long gone.

The History Museum Gift Shop on the first floor sells historic-themed crafts, books, maps, and toys. The History Museum is open 10:00 A.M. to 4:00 P.M. Tuesday through Friday, 10:00 A.M. to 5:00 P.M. Saturday and 1:00 to 5:00 P.M. Sunday. Admission is free for children younger than 6.

October is one of the peak-season months for leaf peepers. Virginia has a new statewide fall foliage hotline, so call (800) 424-LOVE to get information on peak foliage dates.

O. Winston Link Museum $
Passenger Station, 209 Shenandoah Avenue, Roanoke
(540) 342-5770
www.linkmuseum.org
Roanoake's newest museum is a tribute to a photographer. The late O. Winston Link is perhaps best known for his black-and-white photographs of life along the tracks of the Norfolk & Western Railway, the last major railroad in the United States to convert from steam power to diesel. Link's camera captured a small-town way of life and a technology that had built America—both of which were about to disappear forever. The Link Museum aims to give visitors insight into the world in which he worked and into the unique genius of the man and his photographs.

In addition to his photographs, his cameras and lighting stands, as well as rail artifacts, are on display. Visitors can listen to some of Link's railroad sound recordings and view an array of books, magazines, and other publications from the United States, England, France, Germany, Japan, and elsewhere, showing the wide appeal of Link's photos throughout the world.

The Museum Shop, in the location of the old N & W coffeeshop, offers books, videos, sound recordings, and other memorabilia.

The Salem Museum and Historical Society   **Free**
801 East Main Street, Salem
(540) 389-6760
www.salemmuseum.org
The Salem Museum is in a National Historic Register building, the Williams-Brown House. That's easy. What was a little difficult for a while was finding the Williams-Brown House, ca. 1840, which was slated to be torn down until a group of Salem residents towed it from its original location to a safer destination just a quarter mile away. The two-story brick building is typical of those that served travelers in the mid-19th century. Run by volunteers of the Salem Historical Society, the museum focuses on a range of topics, from adventures and hardships of the Civil War to the leisure of a summer sojourn at the Lake Spring Resort Hotel. A gift shop and a gallery for rotating historical exhibits are also on the premises. Hours are 10:00 A.M. to 4:00 P.M. Tuesday through Friday and noon to 5:00 P.M. Saturday. Admission is free.

Science Museum of Western Virginia, Hopkins Planetarium and MegaDome Theater   **$$**
Center in the Square, Levels 1, 4, and 5
1 Market Square, Roanoke
(540) 342-5710
www.smwv.org
The Science Museum is a fun place for adults and children to explore the wonders of science through hands-on experiences. Permanent exhibits include a state-of-the-art weather gallery featuring a walk-through tornado, hurricane simula-

tor, and even a broadcast studio where you can give a weather report and see yourself on TV. The Science Arcade, with more than 45 interactive exhibits, lets you explore light, sound, and color in the physics gallery. Other permanent exhibits include the Digital Pathway of the 21st century, where visitors will experience the world of the supercomputer. Hardbottom Reef Tank, a 750-gallon marine aquarium, features fish native to the Atlantic coast. In the new Geology Gallery, children learn the difference between a rock and a mineral. From trilobites to dinosaurs to camels in North America, Life through Time explores the history of life on Earth through fossils that you can touch. Body Tech is a state-of-the-art exhibit designed to explore the "machinery" of the body. In the Illusions Gallery you will find that things aren't always as they appear.

You can explore the reaches of the universe in Hopkins Planetarium and experience giant-screen films (including IMAX films) in the MegaDome Theater, which will transport you to such places as Egypt, Africa, the Grand Canyon, and outer space.

In the first-floor Science Museum Shop, children delight in exploring the educational toys. Exhibits change frequently, ranging from roaring robotic dinosaurs and live reptiles to giant insects and the human body.

The museum is open 10:00 A.M. to 5:00 P.M. Tuesday through Saturday and 1:00 to 5:00 P.M. Sunday. Admission is free for those younger than 3. If you want to see the exhibits and the planetarium, it is an additional $2.00, exhibits and the MegaDome Theater is an additional $3.00. To see just the planetarium, it's $3.00, and to see just the MegaDome it's $5.00.

To the Rescue National Museum   **$**
Tanglewood Mall, 4428 Electric Road SW, Roanoke
(540) 776-0364
www.totherescue.org
To the Rescue, the only permanent national museum dedicated to volunteer lifesaving, brings an international spotlight to Roanoke as the birthplace of the rescue

Link to the Past

Several museums opened in the Blue Ridge in the last two years, all dealing with transportation. And while the O. Winston Link Museum in Roanoke is not nearly as large as the National Air and Space Museum's Udvar-Hazy Center, it is no less important or impressive. Link was a man who made his life following and taking pictures of steam trains and the people who made their lives on the trains. He knew that the steam train was a dying breed, so he set out to capture its glory before it was too late. His work was considered so important, even while he was doing it in the 1950s, that he was able to convince railway men to stop trains to get his pictures just right!

Located in the renovated and remodeled Norfolk and Western Railway passenger station, which is also the new home of the Roanoke Valley Convention and Visitor's Bureau, the O. Winston Link Museum takes up part of the top floor and all of the downstairs. It holds the largest collection of the world-famous photographer's original prints and an extensive display of N & W Railway artifacts. So far, the 15,000-square-foot facility houses 190 signed prints, 85 estate prints, and all 2,400 of his negatives. Although Link was from New York, he called Roanoke his second home. The city, and this station, was the hub of the railway that he followed

through Maryland, Virginia, North Carolina, and West Virginia. He followed the trains from 1955 to 1960, and in 2001 he was named one of photography's Grand Masters by *Vanity Fair*.

He turned down several offers to display his work from big-time museums. Instead, he wanted his photos displayed in a more fitting context. Before his death in 2001, he requested that a museum bearing his name be located in the old Roanoke station.

The museum is divided into the passenger level and the trackside level, with many galleries along the way. Halfway down the grand staircase, you can note the balcony view overlooking the N & W East End Shops, the place where Link's favorite steam engines were created. When you first get downstairs, an impressive full-scale photograph of an engine and workers forms the backdrop along the wall. The Scioto Gallery, containing published materials on Link, also includes interactive listening stations. Here you can select some of Link's audio recordings and listen to the sounds from along the railway.

The museum is open 10:00 A.M. to 5:00 P.M. Monday through Saturday and noon to 5:00 P.M. Sunday. Admission for adults is $5.00, seniors $4.00, and children under 11, $3.00.

squad movement. Julian Stanley Wise never forgot when, as a 9-year-old Roanoker, he stood helplessly by as two men drowned when their canoe capsized on the Roanoke River. He vowed then that

he would organize a group of volunteers who could be trained in lifesaving. He did.

In 1928 he and his crew of N & W Railway workers became the first volunteer rescue squad in America to use lifesaving,

---

The second Friday of every month, the Science Museum of Western Virginia opens its fourth-floor exhibits for free. You can even get discounted tickets to the MegaDome Theatre. Call (540) 342-5710 or visit www.smwv.org.

---

rescue, and first-aid techniques on victims. Later, they were the first to use iron lungs during the polio epidemics that struck the country. They pioneered the Nielson method of lifesaving and modern-day cardiopulmonary resuscitation.

Famous museum expert Conover Hunt, a Virginia native whose major project was the Sixth Floor, the JFK Museum in Dallas, oversaw the creation of the exhibit, which includes dramatic hands-on interactive videos and displays. The quality and brilliance shows. The exhibit features artifacts from the United States and abroad, including an American flag and helmet found at Ground Zero in New York City. To the Rescue also houses the VA Hall of Fame. In addition, exhibits include the National EMS Memorial, recognizing men and women who gave their lives while saving others. Hours of operation are noon to 6:00 P.M. Tuesday through Friday and 10:00 A.M. to 6:00 P.M. Saturday. Admission is half-price for EMS workers.

Virginia's Explore Park $$
3900 Rutrough Road, Roanoke
(540) 427-1800
www.explorepark.org
Virginia's Explore Park, a living history museum, nature center, and recreation park at Blue Ridge Parkway Milepost 115, allows visitors to experience the rich cultural heritage and natural beauty of western Virginia just minutes from Roanoke. The 1671 Totero Native American Village represents the height of Totero culture, and interpreters there demonstrate techniques and skills used prior to and during the first European contact. The site has

replicated several structures, a garden, and a dugout canoe construction area. A newly opened 1750s frontier fort interprets the lives of a Scots-Irish family in their fortified house. Several 19th-century buildings were moved from nearby counties and reconstructed in the park's 19th Century Area, including the Hofauger Homestead with farmhouse, storage shed/root cellar, and corn crib; the Wray Barn; the Houtz Barn; the Kemp's Ford School; and Slone's Gristmill. With the help of interpreters, visitors discover the lives of these people as well as the roles of the 19th-century blacksmith and a batteauman on the banks of the Roanoke River. In addition, visitors can enjoy fishing, canoeing, and kayaking in the Roanoke River, 6 miles of hiking trails, and 12 miles of biking trails winding through beautiful river-gorge scenery and wooded areas.

Regarding special events, here's the latest: Special events include Appalachian Folk Festival Labor Day weekend, Sleepy Hollow in October, and Holiday Traditions in December, as well as Senior Fest and Mother's and Father's Day events in the spring. The park also offers hikes, day camps, children's programs, canoe tours, and a series of workshops throughout the season.

If you get a little hungry during your visit, enjoy a meal at the authentic 1800s Brugh Tavern. Times vary, so call to be sure it's open, (540) 427-2440.

Virginia's Explore Park is open 10:00 A.M. to 5:00 P.M. Wednesday through Saturday and noon to 5:00 P.M. Sunday from May through October. Special event prices may apply. Group rates are available for groups of 15 or more.

Virginia Museum of Transportation $$
303 Norfolk Avenue, Roanoke
(540) 342-5670
www.vmt.org
This official transportation museum for the state is in a restored freight station next to the Norfolk Southern main line. Exhibits include the largest collection of museum rolling stock on the East Coast

(you can even climb aboard a caboose or a railway office car); antique autos, trucks, carriages, a trolley and rocket; an O gauge model train on 4 tiers of track; and a model circus train exhibit. The N & W Class J steam locomotive #611 and the N & W Class A steam locomotive #1218 are on permanent display.

Exhibits featured in the museum's main galleries include a replica 1940s passenger station, the exhibit African-American Heritage on the Norfolk & Western Railroad: 1930–1970, and early maps of Virginia. Other exhibits tell the story of coal transportation and the history of firefighting in Roanoke.

The museum celebrates America's independence in July with the Star City Motor Madness Classic Car Show and Corral the next day for classic automobile owners and lovers of classic automobiles. This event is similar to several nationally acclaimed events held across the country, including the Woodward Dream Cruise in Detroit, Michigan, and Hot August Nights in Reno, Nevada. Haunted Railyard in October gives young goblins an alternative twist on the Halloween haunted house. In the new year two events celebrate transportation heritage: African-American Heritage Celebration in February and the Gathering of the Eagles in April to celebrate aviation heritage.

New features of the museum include the Claytor Pavilion, which protects the outdoor exhibits, and Star Station, a children's playground.

Of special interest to history and railroad buffs is the museum's Resource Library and Archives, which includes photograph, film, periodical, and book rooms. It is also the repository for the Association of American Railroads' entire photograph collection.

The museum's gift shop sells prints by area artists, toys, books, souvenirs, and more. The museum is open 11:00 A.M. to 4:00 P.M. Monday through Friday, 10:00 A.M. to 5:00 P.M. Saturday, and 1:00 to 5:00 P.M. Sunday. Kids 2 and younger get in free.

SPECTATOR SPORTS

Salem Avalanche $
1004 Texas Street, Salem
(540) 389-3333
www.salemavalanche.com
As the top Class A affiliate for the Houston Astros baseball team, the Avalanche live happily in the sports-crazed Roanoke Valley City of Salem, where they have a state-of-the-art stadium. Major Leaguers such as Dwight Gooden of the New York Mets and Andruw Jones of the Atlanta Braves have played here in recent years. April through September, 140 games are on the agenda, half at home at the 6,300-seat Salem Memorial Baseball Stadium.

ZOOS

Mill Mountain Zoo $$
Off Blue Ridge Parkway, Roanoke
(540) 343-3241
www.mmzoo.org
On top of Roanoke's Mill Mountain, off the Blue Ridge Parkway and alongside the famous Roanoke Star, is an accredited five-acre zoo operated by the Blue Ridge Zoological Society of Virginia. One of its main attractions is Ruby the Siberian Tiger, who received local and national attention during a two-year fund drive to build a new habitat at the zoo. Thanks to donations, Ruby also has her own watering hole for use in the summertime. The tiger is just one of the 50-plus species exhibits of mammals, birds, and reptiles. Other animals include snow leopards, red pandas, Japanese macaques, and much more. Special events and educational programs are offered throughout the year, and the zoo is available for birthday parties and other private parties. The zoo is open daily, 10:00 A.M. to 4:30 P.M. except Christmas Day. Admission is free for kids younger than 2. Group rates are available. The Mill Mountain Zoo, in cooperation with the Roanoke Jaycees, operates a miniature train, weather permitting, for an additional $2.00 fee. The zoo has an outdoor cafe and a gift shop.

Picnic facilities, a wildflower garden, and a breathtaking overlook view of Roanoke are nearby. You can get to the zoo off Interstate 581; follow the signs off the Elm Avenue exit to Jefferson Street and take a left on Walnut Avenue.

OTHER ATTRACTIONS

Center in the Square   **Free**
1 Market Square, Roanoke
(540) 342-5700
www.centerinthesquare.org
This cultural complex in downtown Roanoke is a must-see attraction for arts and entertainment. The primary facility, an award-winning restoration of a former seed and feed warehouse, is on the Historic Farmers' Market, brimming with shops, restaurants, crafts, flowers, fruits, and vegetables. At Center in the Square, visitors can explore the Art Museum of Western Virginia, the History Museum & Historical Society of Western Virginia, and the Science Museum of Western Virginia and take in an evening or matinee performance at Mill Mountain Theatre.

Around the corner at Center on Church are the offices of the Arts Council of the Blue Ridge, providing resources to artists and information about the arts and cultural offerings in the region. Located a few blocks away at the Jefferson Center are two more Center in the Square organizations. Opera Roanoke stages grand operas and concerts of opera classics and favorites. Roanoke Ballet Theatre, the region's only nonprofit school of dance, also produces several innovative dance concerts each year.

Fifth Avenue Presbyterian
Church Window   **Free**
301 Patton Avenue NW, Roanoke
(540) 345-2500, (866) 345-2550
www.jeffcenter.org
The Rev. Lylburn Downing, pastor of Fifth

Avenue Presbyterian, an African-American church, commissioned a stained-glass window in the 1920s to honor Confederate general Stonewall Jackson. The Rev. Downing's parents had been members of the Sunday school class Jackson had established for slaves at his own church in Lexington. Although the church burned down in 1959, the unusual window was spared and then included in the rebuilt church in 1961, where it serves today as a symbol of racial harmony. The window may be viewed by calling for an appointment.

Jefferson Center   **Free**
541 Luck Avenue, Roanoke
(540) 345-2500, (866) 345-2550
www.jeffcenter.org
The Jefferson Center opened its doors in August 1993. Located in the beautifully refurbished Jefferson High School, which was built in 1924, it is now home to 21 nonprofit organizations as diverse as the Roanoke Symphony & Choral Society, a day-care center, the City's police academy, Mental Health Association, and Clean Valley Council. There is also a memorabilia room containing yearbooks, newspapers, and awards from the center's days as a high school. You'll also want to visit the recently renovated Shaftman Performance Hall, with its state-of-the-art acoustics and sound system.

The building itself was built in the English Classical Revival style. You will marvel at the sculptured ceiling in the old main entrance and the beautiful restoration of the marble and terrazzo floors. Fitzpatrick Hall won an award from the American Institute of Architects. The Fralin Atrium is stunning as well, with its chandeliers and a sculpture of Horace Fralin.

EAST OF THE BLUE RIDGE

Loudoun County

MUSEUMS AND HISTORIC ATTRACTIONS

Aldie Mill $
13401 John Mosby Highway, Aldie
(703) 327-9777
www.vaoutdoorsfoundation.org
For the first time in 26 years, the historic Aldie Mill opened to the public in the spring of 1997. Built in 1807, this five-story brick mill will be open from noon to 5:00 P.M. Saturday and 1:00 to 5:00 P.M. Sunday from late April through late October. Tours include a look at artifacts from the mill and early machinery used to grind grain. Corn-grinding demonstrations are held on weekends. In 1981 the mill was donated to the Virginia Outdoors Foundation by the Douglass family. Aldie Mill is on Highway 50, 1 mile west of Highway 15.

Dodona Manor, Gen. George C. Marshall Home
217 Edwards Ferry Road NE, Leesburg
(703) 777-1880
www.georgecmarshall.org
Gen. George C. Marshall served as U.S. secretary of state and is well known abroad for the Marshall Plan, a post–World War II reconstruction plan he drafted for Europe. He lived right here in Virginia. The home has been renovated; however, it will not be open to the public on a regular basis until the gardens have been completely renovated in 2005.

Loudoun Heritage Farm Museum $
21668 Heritage Farm Lane, Sterling
(703) 421-5322
www.loudounfarmmuseum.org
Loudoun County may be the fastest growing county in the nation, but it is paying homage to the rural history in this new museum. The Exhibit Hall, located in a 10,000-foot barn, opened in the fall of 2003. It showcases The Country People:

Three Hundred Years of Agricultural History in Loudoun County. The exhibit includes the Waxpool General Store and Post Office and an interactive play area where children's classes and programs are held. The classes meet Virginia's Standard of Learning guidelines. Characters from each time period, ranging from farmers and their wives to freed slaves and railroad workers, will explain their roles in developing Loudoun's farmland. There is no charge to walk the grounds in Claudmoore Park and enjoy the farm setting, animals, and nature trails. Just like a farmer's schedule, the grounds are open daily from sunup to sundown. The museum's farmhouse and Colonial road are listed on the National Register of Historic Places. The museum is open from 10:00 A.M. to 5:00 P.M. Tuesday through Saturday. Check out the Web page for a list of special events.

The Loudoun Museum $
16 Loudoun Street SW, Leesburg
(703) 777-7427
www.loudounmuseum.org
Follow the history of Loudoun County, from the days American Indians toiled the land to the time President John F. Kennedy, Gen. George C. Marshall, and entertainer Arthur Godfrey made their homes in Virginia's hunt country. You can also see Nicholas Minor's plans to develop a town in Leesburg, plus Civil War items from the nearby Battle of Balls Bluff. A video program helps put the experience in perspective. Books, maps, and toys are among the items for sale in the museum shop. Hours are 10:00 A.M. to 5:00 P.M. Monday through Saturday and 1:00 to 5:00 P.M. Sunday.

Morven Park $$
17263 Southern Planter Lane, Leesburg
(703) 777-2414
www.morvenpark.org
The Greek Revival mansion and estate, which was once the home of Virginia governor Westmoreland Davis, is listed on the National Register of Historic Places and is a

One Giant Hangar for Mankind's Machines

Ever since Orville and Wilbur Wright pushed their invention off a sand dune in Kitty Hawk, man—and woman—have been fascinated with flight. So it was fitting that to commemorate the 100th anniversary of their fateful first flight, fans from around the world came to Northern Virginia to pay tribute to those original pioneers and those who followed in their footsteps.

John Glenn, who twice soared into outer space, visited. John Travolta piloted his own plane in for the gathering of scholars and stars. Even a descendant of a German World War II fighter pilot was there as the Steven F. Udvar-Hazy Center was welcomed as the Smithsonian Institution's new branch of the National Air and Space Museum.

Before the Udvar-Hazy Center opened December 15, 2003, only 10 percent of the historic artifacts had been on display in the flagship museum on the Washington Mall. There wasn't enough room in the D.C. facility.

This brand-new colossal center in Loudoun County opened with 80 historic aircrafts on display. It will eventually hold 200 aircraft, 135 large space artifacts, and an array of smaller flight-related memorabilia. The structure will cover 760,000 square feet. The hangar itself is the length of three football fields. It is breathtaking—both when you first approach the facility and when you step inside. Some of the planes rest on the ground, while a third of them hang suspended overhead at two levels.

The $311 million facility is named for Udvar-Hazy, who donated $65 million to the project. The new center and its flagship building on the mall, which dates back to 1976, comprise the largest air and space museum complex in the world. Attendance is projected at three million people a year.

Such man-made wonders inside include the impressive black Lockheed SR-71 Blackbird, a reconnaissance aircraft and the fastest aircraft ever built.

Virginia Historic Landmark. The house is furnished with fine antiques and curios that the Davises collected on their travels around the world. On the grounds are gardens, an extensive carriage museum, and a Museum of Hounds and Hunting, which contains fox-hunting memorabilia from Colonial days (see our Horse Country chapter).

The estate, maintained through a trust established by the late Mrs. Davis, is one of the country's finest equestrian centers, staging fall and spring steeplechase races, horse shows, three-day events, foxhunts, and carriage competitions. Morven Park's mansion, gardens, Museum of Hounds and Hunting, and Mrs. Robert C. Winmill Carriage Collection are open to visitors from

noon to 4:00 P.M. Friday through Monday. It's free for those 4 and younger.

**National Air and Space Museum
Steven F. Udvar-Hazy Center
Air and Space Museum Parkway,
Chantilly
(202) 357-2700
www.nasm.si.edu/udvarhazy/**
Your trip to the northern end of the Blue Ridge is incomplete without a visit to this amazing new facility, which is fittingly located near Washington Dulles International Airport. When you approach the building, its size and shape will strike you as something out of a *Star Wars* movie. Stop just inside and take in the awe-inspiring

On its final flight from Los Angeles to Dulles, it arrived in one hour, four minutes, and 20 seconds!.

History abounds here, what with the B-29 Superfortress Enola Gay, which dropped the first atomic bomb during World War II—on August 6, 1945, on Hiroshima, Japan. Other specimens include the gigantic Air France Concorde, which began flying commercially in 1976, and the Space Shuttle Enterprise, which was the first space shuttle and served as a test vehicle for all the shuttles that followed. And, yes, the 1903 Wright Flyer, which made the historic flight, is represented.

Also on display are the space capsules Mercury 15B and Gemini VII, a Soviet MiG-21, and a helicopter flown in Vietnam, as well as flight suits worn by Charles Lindbergh and Amelia Earhart.

Adults and children alike can get a feel for flight in the flight simulator rides, watch shows dealing with flight and explorers' adventures in the IMAX Theater presentations, and go up into the Donald D. Engen Observation Tower to see jets taking off and landing at nearby Washington Dulles International Airport. Twice a day the museum's volunteer docents lead 90-minute tours of the center. Eventually, the center will have a restoration hangar, where visitors can watch aircraft and space artifacts getting restored, as well as four discovery stations with interactive activities.

But Udvar-Hazy already is filled with a sense of history that the old-timers understand and the promise of wide-eyed wonder that the youngsters feel. One young man gave a disapproving look as his mom approached. He wanted his photo taken alone with the sleek Blackbird. He puffed out his chest and staged a stern frown as the camera flashed. Yes, it is a place to remember the Wright brothers, John Glenn, and, who knows, maybe even a stern young pioneer of tomorrow.

setting of planes of all sizes resting and hanging in the huge open aviation hangar. The $311 million facility will initially display 80 aircraft and 65 large space artifacts. Don't forget to go up into the Donald D. Engen Observation Tower, where you can see jets taking off and landing at Dulles. The museum's opening on December 15, 2003, coincided with the 100th anniversary of the Wright brothers' first flight. As usual for the Smithsonian Museums, admission is free. However, parking costs $12.00 (after 4:00 P.M. it's free). The charge for the IMAX Theater show is $8.00 and $6.50 for children ages 2 to 12 and seniors 55 and older. The flight simulator costs $6.00 for a four-minute ride.

The museum hours are 10:00 A.M. to 5:30 P.M. every day. It is closed December 25.

The Naturalist Center   **Free**
741 Miller Drive SE, Leesburg
(703) 779-9712, (800) 729-7725
www.si.edu
You couldn't properly call this a museum because this center is so interactive. Here in this branch of the Smithsonian Institution visitors interested in natural history can delve into their own investigations. Visitors become amateur scientists, with access to the center's large collection of plants, rocks, fossils, insects, and animals, aided by scientific equipment, books, and references. This study gallery is for kids

(10 and older) and adults. A smaller exhibit with some hands-on activities has been set up to entertain younger children while older family members tour the main exhibit. (See our Kidstuff chapter.) Admission is free. Hours are 10:30 A.M. to 4:00 P.M. Tuesday through Saturday.

Oatlands Plantation   **$$**
20850 Oatland Plantation Lane
Leesburg
(703) 777-3174
www.oatlands.org
This magnificent Federal/Greek Revival-style house was built in 1804 by a descendant of Robert "King" Carter using bricks molded on the property and wood from a nearby forest. The 360-acre estate is renowned for its historic formal gardens in which something always seems to be blooming. Oatlands is a striking venue for spring point-to-point races and the annual spring and fall antiques shows. Tours are offered every hour from 10:00 A.M. to 4:00 P.M. daily, and from 1:00 to 4:00 P.M. on Sunday from April through December. Special Christmas candlelight tours are available Saturday evenings in December for $12.00. A garden-only tour costs $7.00. Children younger than 5 get in free.

Fauquier County

MUSEUMS

The Old Jail Museum   **Free**
Corner of Main and Ashby Streets
Warrenton
(540) 347-5525
The Old Jail Museum houses a variety of intriguing artifacts from Fauquier County history, including a war room, a kitchen, a hanging yard, and, some say, a ghost. Although Mr. McG. was nowhere to be seen on a recent trip to the second-floor cell where he died, there were plenty of artifacts and reminders that prison isn't a fun place. The museum is actually two jails—one built in 1808 and the other in 1823—and the hanging/exercise yard

between. The area used to be the center of activity in the early days with a pillory and stock and whipping post outside.

Today the entrance room to the 1808 jail houses a collection of local history. The kitchen, added in 1824, contains the original floor and displays a variety of utensils used during the time period. The war room used to be a maximum security cell but now houses artifacts from the Revolutionary War through World War II, including a German uniform and Civil War frock coat. Upstairs, originally the ladies' cell, is now an exhibition space that includes an old dental office.

The 1823 structure was used as a jail for 143 years. Here, you get a good look at what jail life was like. Three of the cells are open to the public; the fourth is now a storage room, but you can peek in and see if Mr. McG. is around. Downstairs also is a blacksmith display and a canal and tool room. If you climb the steep stairs to view the maximum security cell, you can see the graffiti prisoners scratched into the walls. Don't worry, the prisoner under the blanket is a mannequin. Venture out into the walled-in exercise yard. The gallows were here, but the small yard was also used as a garden, a space for chickens and pigs, a trash dump, and a privy. The museum is listed in the Virginia Landmarks Register and the National Register of Historic Places. The museum is closed on Monday.

Culpeper County

MUSEUMS

Museum of Culpeper History   **$**
803 South Main Street, Culpeper
(540) 829-1749
www.culpepermuseum.com
To coincide with the 250th anniversary of Culpeper County, the Museum of Culpeper History moved to a larger location in 2000. The museum's collection expanded to include dinosaur tracks discovered at a local quarry to memorabilia from the Civil War and World War II in the renovated

Williamsburg-style 4,000-square-foot site, where U.S. Highway 29 and U.S. Highway 15 converge. The exhibits tracing the history of Culpeper County from the age of the dinosaurs to the 20th century occupy a minimum of 2,500 square feet of the single-level building. Also on the new grounds is the recently restored Burgandine House, an 18th-century log cabin that museum officials believe is the oldest existing structure in the town. From June to September an American Indian family sets up a village with demonstrations on-site. Hours are 11:00 A.M. to 5:00 P.M. Monday through Saturday. During the summer it's open 1:00 to 5:00 P.M. Admission is free.

Orange County

MUSEUMS AND HISTORIC ATTRACTIONS

James Madison Museum $
129 Caroline Street, Orange
(540) 672-1776
www.jamesmadisonmus.org
This downtown museum offers several permanent exhibits, one celebrating the life and times of Madison and his important contributions to the American political system. Artifacts include furnishings from Montpelier, some of his presidential correspondence, and a few of Dolley Madison's belongings. Another permanent exhibit details the history of Orange; other exhibits change regularly. The museum is open on weekdays from 9:00 A.M. to 5:00 P.M., Saturday from 10:00 A.M. to 5:00 P.M., and Sunday from 1:00 to 4:00 P.M. The museum is closed January and February.

Montpelier $$
11407 Constitution Highway, Montpelier Station
(540) 672-2728
www.montpelier.org
The gracious home of President James Madison and his beloved wife, Dolley, opened for public tours in 1987. The restoration of Montpelier, which changed hands six times after Dolley Madison was forced to sell it to settle debts, is a work in progress.

In 2004 the Montpelier Foundation launched a complete restoration of the mansion, thanks in part to a $20 million donation from the Paul Mellon estate. (Mellon's contribution, by the way, is believed to be the largest single gift from an individual donor to a historic property.) It's out with the new and in with the old. Once completed, the home will be returned to the size, structure, form, and furnishings that the Madisons enjoyed in the 1820s.

The four-year renovation will remove all the alterations made to Montpelier since Madison's death in 1836. It's a whole new meaning to downsizing as the estate will decrease from 55 rooms to 22. Gone will be the wings added by the duPont family in the early 1900s.

Portions of the home will remain open to the public during the restoration process, allowing visitors to have the unique opportunity to see the restoration unfold. Periodically, there even will be special "hard-hat" tours of the mansion, in addition to a new guided walking tour of the grounds.

Fans of Marion duPont Scott should not despair. The restoration was one of the wishes of the last private owner of Montpelier. She bequeathed the property to the National Trust for Historic Preservation in 1983, and her legacy will live on.

There are plans to create the William duPont Gallery as part of a new visitor center complex on the estate. Highlighting the addition will be a re-creation of Marion duPont's famed Red Room, the Art Deco room that showcased all her horseracing memorabilia. The gallery also will include a great room inspired by the more formal rooms that William duPont Sr. added to Montpelier. Plans also call for an interactive exhibit on the duPont family history.

Montpelier was first settled by Madison's grandparents in 1723. After the completion of Madison's second presidential term, Dolley and James retired to the estate, where their legendary hospitality kept them in touch with world affairs. Madison was the primary author of the Constitution and one of the authors of the Federalist Papers. He was a proponent of freedom of religion and education in Virginia and served as second rector of the University of Virginia. His public life spanned 53 years and included services as a delegate to the Continental Congress, member of the Virginia House of Delegates, U.S. congressman, Thomas Jefferson's secretary of state, and U.S. president for two terms.

Montpelier was owned by the duPont family for decades before it was bequeathed to the National Trust for Historic Preservation in the 1980s. The duPonts built major additions to the home and planted elaborate formal gardens. The biggest challenge for Montpelier's new owners, the National Trust, was what to do about all the new rooms and interior changes. Visitors are encouraged to stroll through the grounds and see the barns, stables, bowling alley, and the garden temple Madison built over his ice house. Dolley and James Madison lie in a cemetery on the grounds along with a number of Madison family members.

One of the legacies of Marion duPont Scott, who made her home at Montpelier from 1928 until her death in 1983, is the annual Montpelier Hunt Races, which take place on the first Saturday in November. Montpelier had been one of the nation's top equestrian centers under Marion duPont's watch. Now, along with the steeplechase, the farm is again showcasing racehorses. In 2003 Montpelier opened its pastures to the Thoroughbred Retirement Foundation. The group, which finds good homes for retired racehorses, is using Montpelier's stables to house the rescued animals until they can be adopted. (See our Horse Country chapter.)

Montpelier is about 25 miles north of Charlottesville off U.S. Highway 20 near Orange. It is open daily from 9:30 A.M. to 5:30 P.M. April through October, and 9:30

A.M. to 4:30 P.M. November through March. Admission is free for those younger than 6.

Albemarle County

MUSEUMS AND HISTORIC ATTRACTIONS

Ash Lawn–Highland $$
1000 James Monroe Parkway off Highway 795, Charlottesville
(434) 293-9539
www.ashlawnhighland.org
This 535-acre estate was the home of James Monroe, our nation's fifth president, who fought in the American Revolution under George Washington and went on to hold more offices than any other U.S. president.

As ambassador to France, Monroe negotiated with Napoleon for the Louisiana Purchase, which doubled the size of the country. During his presidency, Monroe established the nation's first comprehensive foreign policy, later called the Monroe Doctrine, to prevent further European colonization of the Americas.

Ash Lawn–Highland is about 2 miles from Thomas Jefferson's Monticello, off I-64. The mansion holds many of Monroe's possessions, and his boxwood gardens, now occupied by magnificent peacocks, are carefully tended. Livestock, vegetable, and herb gardens and Colonial craft demonstrations depict life 200 years ago on the plantation.

Special events include summer musicals and operas performed in English, the Virginia Wine Festival in May, Plantation Days on the Fourth of July weekend, and Christmas candlelight tours.

The Monroe estate is owned and maintained as a working farm by Monroe's alma mater, the College of William and Mary. Ash Lawn–Highland is open daily 9:00 A.M. to 6:00 P.M. April through October and 11:00 A.M. to 5:00 P.M. daily from November through March. A special President's Pass costs $25 and also includes tours of nearby Monticello and Michie Tavern. Ash Lawn is closed Christmas Day, New Year's Day, and Thanksgiving Day.

Charlottesville/Albemarle
Visitors Center **Free**
600 College Drive off Highway 20 S,
exit 121, Charlottesville
(434) 977-1783, (877) 386-1102
www.charlottesvilletourism.org
A permanent exhibition shows aspects of Jefferson's domestic life at Monticello. Nearly 400 objects and artifacts, from his pocketknife to a porcupine-quill toothpick, are on display, many for the first time. You can view an award-winning film, *Thomas Jefferson: The Pursuit of Liberty,* daily in the exhibition theater, with additional showings in the summer. The center is open from 9:00 A.M. to 5:30 P.M. daily March through October and 9:00 A.M. to 5:00 P.M. the rest of the year. Admission is free. The museum shop is a great source of brass, porcelain, crystal, pewter, and silver pieces and reproductions made exclusively for Monticello.

Hatton Ferry **Free**
Highway 625, Scottsville
(434) 296-1492
www.avenue.org/achs
Long before steel bridges spanned the rivers of Virginia, ferries were needed to carry people and their cargo from one side of the riverbank to the other. The *Hatton Ferry* in southern Albemarle County is one of only two poled ferries still in operation in the United States. The *Hatton Ferry* started carrying cargo at its current location more than 100 years ago. When the Virginia Department of Transportation decided it was no longer needed as a public service, three groups got together to save the ferry as a historical artifact. The Department of Transportation, the Albemarle County Historical Society, and Albemarle County jointly maintain and operate *Hatton Ferry* on a reduced but fixed schedule. You can take a free historical ride across the James

River from 9:00 A.M. to 5:00 P.M. on Saturday and Sunday from mid-April to mid-October. Rides are contingent on water levels and conditions, so it is a good idea to call the historical society before you go.

Michie Tavern **$$$**
683 Thomas Jefferson Parkway
Charlottesville
(434) 977-1234
www.michietavern.com
Historic Michie Tavern (pronounced "micky") is one of the oldest homesteads remaining in Virginia and was originally set along a well-worn stagecoach route near Earlysville, about 17 miles away. To accommodate the many travelers seeking food and shelter at their home, the Michie family opened it as a tavern in 1784. In 1927 the tavern was dismantled piece by piece, moved by truck and horse and carriage, and reassembled on its current site. This historic move garnered the tavern a Virginia Historic Landmark designation.

Today, visitors to Monticello and Ash Lawn–Highland can still stop by the tavern for a hearty Southern-style meal. The tavern museum offers continuous tours of rooms decorated with 18th-century Southern furniture and artifacts. Next door, a 200-year-old converted slave house called the Ordinary offers a Colonial buffet of fried chicken, black-eyed peas, stewed tomatoes, coleslaw, potato salad, green bean salad, beets, homemade biscuits, corn bread, and apple cobbler from 11:30 A.M. to 3:00 P.M. daily for around $13.95. It's free for children younger than 5.

The Clothier, on the path to the General Store, is open 11:00 A.M. to 4:00 P.M. (It's closed in the winter.) The retail shop houses a collection of original and reproductions of Early American printed merchandise for sale, including currency, newspapers, stamps, books, and prints. The original Sowell House, ca. 1822, was relocated to Michie Tavern in 1993. The two-story stone and wood house is the first of several buildings highlighting early trades in what would become known as the Market Place. You can see how the house was built and get a glimpse into 19th-century rural life in Virginia.

Michie Tavern also houses the small Virginia Wine Museum in its basement. Next door in the Meadow Run Gristmill is a general store where visitors can buy Virginia wines, specialty foods, and crafts.

The Michie Tavern Museum is open year-round from 9:00 A.M. to 5:00 P.M. except Christmas and New Year's Day; the last tour goes out at 4:20 P.M. Admission to the museum is free for those younger than 6.

Monticello   **$$$**
970 Thomas Jefferson Parkway
Charlottesville
(434) 984-9822, (434) 984-9844
www.monticello.org

Thomas Jefferson's home, one of the country's finest architectural masterpieces, is such a popular tourist attraction that long lines are inevitable during the peak season of summer and early fall. Start early; you can always grab a snack at the lunch stand, which is open from 10:30 A.M. to 5:00 P.M. daily April through October.

Jefferson began construction of Monticello in 1769 when he was just 26, and he often longed to retire there during the most active part of his political career. Work on Monticello continued for 40 years, during which Jefferson made many alterations.

Jefferson's wide-ranging interests made him an avid collector of sculpture, maps, paintings, prints, Native American artifacts, scientific instruments, and fine furniture, and these objects kept his house quite cluttered. Today, Monticello is filled with original furnishings and many of Jefferson's other possessions. It gives one the feeling that he'll return from Washington at any moment.

Though he was our nation's third president, the author of the Declaration of Independence, and an international statesman, Jefferson apparently disliked politics. He wrote to his daughter Martha in 1800, "Pol-

itics is such a torment that I would advise every one I love not to mix with it."

Though he did not shirk his duty to his country and its fragile democratic system, he indulged his other interests at Monticello, especially horticulture and garden design. Included are ornamental and vegetable gardens, two orchards, a vineyard, and an 18-acre ornamental forest. He experimented with more than 250 varieties of vegetables and herbs, many of which are grown today in his 1,000-square-foot vegetable garden. Monticello's Thomas Jefferson Center for Historic Plants, the first of its kind in the nation, sells historical plants and seeds in the garden shop from April through October. The Garden Shop is open 9:00 A.M. to 5:00 P.M. March to November. There are two museum shops, one at Monticello and the other at the visitor center. They are open 9:00 A.M. to 5:30 P.M. Since it opened as a public attraction in 1923, Monticello has hosted 2.5 million visitors. The mansion and grounds are open daily from 8:00 A.M. to 5:00 P.M. March through October and 9:00 A.M. to 4:30 P.M. the rest of the year (closed Christmas Day). Written tour information is available in several languages.

The new stone, arched Saunders Bridge has opened, allowing visitors the option of walking all the way to the mansion. The bridge connects the Thomas Jefferson Parkway—a wooded walking and cycling path of just 5 percent grade—with the Saunders–Monticello Trail, which goes to directly to Jefferson's home.

Admission is free for children younger than 6. Group rates are available. It's possible to save on the cost of adult admission to Monticello, Ash Lawn, and Michie Tavern by buying a $25 President's Pass.

Rotunda and University
of Virginia   **Free**
McCormick Road, Charlottesville
(434) 924-7969
www.virginia.edu

Free historical tours of Mr. Jefferson's "academic village" are offered daily from the Rotunda, which Jefferson designed in the style of the Pantheon. Since 1825 the university has been renowned for its unique architectural design. In 1976 the American Institute of Architects voted Jefferson's design for the university the most outstanding achievement in American architecture.

Along with his authorship of the Declaration of Independence and the Statute of Virginia for Religious Freedom, the university was an achievement for which Jefferson wished to be remembered. He called it the "hobby of his old age," quite an understatement. Not only was Jefferson the principal architect, but he also helped select the library collection, hire faculty, and design the curriculum. He was one of the major financial contributors and succeeded in securing public funding for the school.

It was his ardent lobbying for public education in Virginia that led to the establishment of the university in the first place. Jefferson had studied at the College of William and Mary in Williamsburg, but he felt the state, which then encompassed West Virginia, needed a major university. He accomplished all this during his retirement at Monticello, from which he often watched the university's construction with his telescope.

The rotunda was completed in 1826, the year Jefferson died.

You can take a free tour of the central grounds from the Rotunda at 10:00 and 11:00 A.M. and 2:00, 3:00, and 4:00 P.M., except for three weeks at Christmas. Meet at the lower end of the East Oval Room. Reservations are not necessary. If you ask, tour guides will point out Edgar Allan Poe's former dorm room. Poe, by the way, left the university prematurely after running up a huge gambling debt he couldn't pay.

Scottsville Museum   **Free**
290 Main Street, Scottsville
(434) 286-2247
www.avenue.org/smuseum
The Albemarle County seat until 1762,

Scottsville is an old river town on the James River, about 20 miles south of Charlottesville on Highway 20. In and around the town are 32 authentic Federal buildings, one of the four or five largest concentrations of Early Republic architecture in the state. The town also has a local-history museum, originally a Disciples of Christ Church built in 1846, on East Main Street that opened in 1970. It's open 10:00 A.M. to 5:00 P.M. Saturday, 1:00 to 5:00 P.M. Sunday, and other times by appointment, from April through October. Donations are accepted.

University of Virginia Library   **Free**
Charlottesville
(434) 924-3017
www.lib.virginia.edu
When Jefferson designed the University of Virginia, the first library was housed in his famous Rotunda. Today there are 15 individual libraries on the campus, including the Special Collections Library, which opened in its gorgeous new space in August 2004. The Albert and Shirley Small Special Collections Library houses a premier collection of rare books and manuscripts underground (never fear—skylights provide excellent lighting). The collection, which includes a copy of the Declaration of Independence, houses more than 12 million manuscripts, 2.5 million items in the University archives, and 268,600 rare books, as well as approximately 4,000 maps, some 4,000 broadsides, and more than 125,000 photographs and small prints. University of Virginia is known

While visiting Charlottesville, be sure to stop in for a free guided tour of the Rotunda and Lawn. Tours are given year-round except for three weeks around the holidays in December and January. Tours meet at 10:00 and 11:00 A.M., 2:00, 3:00, and 4:00 P.M. at the Rotunda entrance facing the lawn. Call (434) 924-7969 for more information.

nationally for its collection in American history and American literature; its Virginiana collections, including Thomas Jefferson's papers and architectural drawings; the William Faulkner collection; and its collection of African-American materials. The aboveground part of the new building includes the Mary and David Harrison Institute for American History, Literature, and Culture. You will need to bring a photo ID to register to use the rare books collection.

Virginia Discovery Museum $
524 East Main Street, Charlottesville
(434) 977-1025
www.vadm.org

On the east end of the historic downtown mall is a dynamic place for children and their families. It was named one of the 50 best children's museums in the United States by *Child* magazine. You'll find hands-on exhibits and programs about science, arts, nature, history, and the humanities. (See our Kidstuff chapter.) Classes and summer camps include everything from computer operation to photography, juggling, dancing, and space exploration. The museum even has the real 18th-century Showalter Cabin from Rockingham County and costumes in which the children can play dress-up. Special exhibits change every few months. An art room with an array of materials invites children to create at their own pace, and a gallery space displays their creations for about three weeks. More than 42,126 people from 41 states and 13 foreign countries visited the museum in 2003–04. The facility is open Tuesday through Saturday from 10:00 A.M. to 5:00 P.M. and Sunday 1:00 to 5:00 P.M. ASTC members are admitted free. A family membership is $60 per year.

SPORTING EVENTS

University of Virginia   Free–$$$$
Charlottesville
(434) 924-UVA1, (800) 542-UVA1
(in-state)
www.virginiasports.com

There is always something to cheer about during the college season in Charlottesville.

A member of the competitive Atlantic Coast Conference, the University of Virginia fields 25 varsity sports.

Virginia finished in the top 31 each of the first nine years of the Sears Directors' Cup standings, which rank the success of Division I athletic programs in up to 20 sports.

Over the last 15 years, UVA has claimed five national championships in men's soccer, three in women's lacrosse, and one in men's lacrosse. In 1993 Virginia became the first school in NCAA history to win three consecutive national men's soccer titles. The Cavs topped that in 1994 by capturing their fourth national title in a row, followed by a fifth in six years. Women's soccer coach April Heinrichs led the U.S. women to a gold medal in the 2004 Olympics.

The women's lacrosse team captured national titles in 1991, 1993, and 2003, while the men's team won the 1999 NCAA championship.

The Virginia football team also has an impressive history with its 15th appearance in 2004, a 37–34 loss to Fresno State in the MPC Computers Bowl. In 1990 UVA climbed to number one in the regular season polls and played Tennessee in the 1991 Sugar Bowl.

UVA spent $86 million to expand its football stadium to 60,000 seats, but tickets are still hard to come by, especially on those Saturdays when Florida State and Virginia Tech come calling. True fans will be hard-pressed to pull themselves away from the television set on Sunday afternoon, too. Seventeen UVA graduates are continuing their athletic careers with the NFL. Heading a long list of pro players from the local ranks are quarterback Matt Schaub, running back Terry Kirby, linebacker Chris Slade, running back Tiki Barber, and his twin brother, defensive star Ronde Barber. Two former greats, Bill Dudley and Henry Jordan, have been inducted into the NFL Hall of Fame.

The men's basketball team won a share of the ACC regular-season championship in 1994–95 and advanced to the finals of the NCAA Midwest Region Tournament. Virginia has won two National Invitation Tournament championships (in 1980 and 1992) and reached the NCAA Final Four twice (in 1981 and 1984, when 7-foot 4-inch Ralph Sampson dominated the game).

The Virginia women's basketball team—coached by longtime favorite Debbie Ryan—won ACC Tournament titles in 1990, 1992, and 1993 and reached the NCAA Final Four three consecutive years, from 1990 to 1992. That was the Dawn Staley era. Staley, the Cavaliers' stellar point guard, is now a WNBA star for the Charlotte Sting and coach of the women's basketball program at Temple University. She also is the proud owner of three Olympic gold medals from the Games in Atlanta, Sydney, and Athens. Another alum, Val Ackerman, is president of the WNBA. The Cavalier women won their first ACC regular-season title in 2000 since winning six in a row from 1991 to 1996.

Both the men's and women's basketball teams will be moving into the $129.8 million John Paul Jones Arena when it is complete in 2006.

Nelson County

MUSEUMS

Oak Ridge Estate $$
2300 Oak Ridge Road, Lovingston
(434) 263-8676
www.oakridgeestate.com
Oak Ridge was the home of several prominent men, including Thomas Fortune Ryan, a Nelson County native who became one of the richest men in the country.

Robert Rives, whose son, Alexander, went on to become rector of the University of Virginia, built the original house around 1801. Some say Rives had 200 slaves to farm the land. Eventually the home passed on to William Porter Miles, a congressman

from South Carolina who helped design the Confederate flag. When Ryan bought the property in 1901, he turned Oak Ridge into a showplace. The nine-room house evolved into a 50-room Colonial Revival mansion. The grounds also included two schools, a movie theater, a greenhouse, formal gardens, a golf course, a race track, and a train station. However, the property slowly declined in the years following his death in 1928. But in 1989 John C. Holland purchased the property, and now his children are in the process of restoring the nearly 5,000-acre estate and its 50 outbuildings to the way it was during Ryan's time. Visitors can tour several rooms in the mansion, plus the Crystal Palace–style greenhouse, the train station, the Rives family cemetery, and Ryan's mausoleum. All tours are by appointment. Admission is free for those 7 and younger. Self-guided tours of the grounds are available for $5.00. The privately owned estate also is home to dozens of activities throughout the year, including music festivals, Civil War reenactments, and Camp Jeep.

Walton's Mountain Museum $
6484 Rockfish River Road, Schuyler
(434) 831-2000, (888) 266-1981
www.waltonmuseum.org
Earl Hamner Jr., whose early years were chronicled in the popular television series, grew up in tiny Schuyler. The museum dedicated to Hamner and *The Waltons* opened to great fanfare in 1992 in the same school where the Hamner youngsters learned their ABCs. The museum, made possible by a state grant and support from Hamner and community leaders, is actually a series of former classrooms that re-create sets from the television program. You'll find photo displays that juxtapose Hamner's real family with the television actors, and all manner of memorabilia. The school is a stone's throw from the old Hamner homestead.

From the first Saturday in March through the last Sunday in November (excluding major holidays), museum hours are 10:00 A.M. to 4:00 P.M. It is closed Easter, Thanksgiving, and the last Saturday in September. Children younger than 6 are admitted free.

Amherst County

MUSEUMS

Amherst County Museum and Historical Society　　　**Free**
154 South Main Street, Amherst
(434) 946-9068
www.members.aol.com/achmuseum
The Amherst County Museum, which opened in 1976, is housed in the German Revival–style Kearfott–Wood House. The house was built in 1907 by Dr. Kearfoot. It was renovated in 1999 and now has four exhibit rooms and a library. The Amherst County Pathways is a permanent exhibit on the history of the county. Two rooms offer changing exhibits and have featured displays on such topics as transportation and textiles. Also on the property is a one-room schoolhouse, a log cabin that had been used originally as a school in Amherst County. Or stop in the genealogy library and get started on tracing your family history. It's open 9:00 A.M. to 4:30 P.M. Tuesday through Saturday. Admission to the museum is free.

Lynchburg

MUSEUMS AND HISTORIC ATTRACTIONS

Anne Spencer House and Garden　　**$**
1313 Pierce Street, Lynchburg
(434) 845-1313
www.lynchburgbiz.com/anne-spencer
Anne Spencer was an internationally recognized African-American poet of the Harlem Renaissance period of the 1920s. Her poems are included in the *Norton Anthology of Modern Poetry.* Behind her home is the garden and accompanying cottage, built for her by her husband as a place

where she could write. Hillside Garden Club has beautifully restored the garden. Revered the world over for her intellect, Spencer entertained many great leaders and artists of her day, including Dr. Martin Luther King Jr., Supreme Court Justice Thurgood Marshall, scientist Dr. George Washington Carver, sports legend Jackie Robinson, Congressman Adam Clayton Powell (who honeymooned there), and the legendary singers Paul Robeson and Marion Anderson. House tours are by appointment only. The garden is open 24 hours a day, seven days a week. There is no charge to tour the gardens.

Jones Memorial Library　　　**Free**
2311 Memorial Avenue, Lynchburg
(434) 846-0501
www.jmlibrary.org
The Jones Memorial Library, opened in June 1908, is the second-oldest public library in Virginia. One of Virginia's foremost genealogical libraries, the Jones is known for its vast records: 30,000 volumes specializing in genealogical, historical, and Lynchburg holdings. The collection includes Revolutionary War records, family histories and genealogies, general works on the Civil War, enlistments, Virginia county and state court records, and census reports. Records from England, Ireland, and Scotland include heraldry information. A certified genealogist and a certified genealogical records specialist are both on staff to provide assistance for in-house research. This gem is probably one of the most underutilized treasures of the Blue Ridge.

The library is open 1:00 to 9:00 P.M. Tuesday and Thursday, 1:00 to 5:00 P.M. Wednesday and Friday, and 9:00 to 5:00 P.M. Saturday; it's closed Sunday and Monday.

**Lynchburg Museum at
Old Court House**　　　**$**
901 Court Street, Lynchburg
(434) 847-1459
www.lynchburgmuseum.org
The historical treasures of one of America's

legendary tobacco centers can be discovered in Lynchburg's 1855 Old Court House, now restored to its Greek Revival elegance and home of the Lynchburg Museum. From the native Monacan Indian tribes who inhabited the banks of the historic James River to the bustle of 19th-century industry and the tragedy of the American Civil War, relics of a developing community bear silent testimony to the struggle for a nation. Changing exhibits challenge visitors to reflect on Lynchburg's many contributions to the history of our country. Exhibits are open daily 10:00 A.M. to 4:00 P.M., but the museum is closed on holidays. Children 12 and younger get in free.

**Old City Cemetery Museums
and Arboretum** Free
**401 Taylor Street, Lynchburg
(434) 847-1465
www.gravegarden.org**
This cemetery, a Virginia Historic Landmark listed on the National Register of Historic Places, reflects 200 years of history and horticulture.

Four small museums interpret the life and times of the approximately 20,000 citizens buried in the cemetery—the Pest House Medical Museum, the Hearse House and Caretakers Museum, the Station House Museum, and an exhibit of Victorian mourning practices in the Cemetery Center.

The Confederate section serves as the final resting place for more than 2,200 soldiers from 14 states. Ninety-nine soldiers died of smallpox in the Pest House. The Pest House depicts conditions in the House of Pestilence quarantine hospital used during the Civil War. A second room in the Pest House Museum was furnished as Dr. John J. Terrell's office when he practiced medicine in the area in the 1800s.

Today, the Station House Museum is the only remaining C & O "standard station" of its size and style. The 1898 station interprets the importance of railroads in the city's history. It was dismantled and removed from its original site in Amherst County and placed within view of an active railroad.

Of the 20,000 citizens buried in the cemetery, 75 percent are African American, and one in three are children under the age of 4. Many self-interpretive plaques and a variety of brochures are available at the information gatehouse and throughout the recently restored cemetery. Antique roses and period plantings contribute to the horticultural significance and beauty.

The cemetery is free and open daily, dawn to dusk. The Cemetery Center and Research Library is open daily 11:00 A.M. to 3:00 P.M. It is closed Sunday during winter.

Guided tours are available by appointment for $4.00, $2.00 for students. There is a $30.00 minimum per tour.

The Virginia Heritage Music Trail was formed in May 2004. Follow the road signs along U.S. Highways 221, 58, 23, and 83 and Highway 40 to commemorate the state's bluegrass and country music heritage. Stops along the way include The Floyd Country Store and the Blue Ridge Folk Life Museum. Visit www.thecrookedroad.org for details.

Point of Honor $
**112 Cabell Street, Lynchburg
(434) 847-1459
www.pointofhonor.org**
This fully restored 19th-century plantation mansion is a remarkable example of Federal-style architecture where visitors can experience the lifestyle of one of Virginia's most remarkable families. Point of Honor is the home of Dr. George Cabell Sr., friend and personal physician to Patrick Henry. It was also home to Mary Virginia Ellet Cabell, one of the founders of the Daughters of the American Revolution. Newly re-created kitchen and stable buildings provide unique glimpses into an era now long past. Even the unusual name "Point of Honor" remembers fog-shrouded mornings of long ago when sword and pistol duels were fought on the lawn.

Tours of the house and gardens are available daily 10:00 A.M. to 4:00 P.M. Point of Honor is closed on holidays. Children younger than 6 are admitted for free.

SPECTATOR SPORTS

Lynchburg Hillcats $$
3180 Fort Avenue, Lynchburg
(434) 528-1144
www.lynchburg-hillcats.com
Lynchburg has had a baseball team in its midst for more than 100 years. Since 1966, the Hillcats have been entertaining fans east of the Blue Ridge as a Class A member of the Carolina League. The Lynchburg team has been affiliated with many clubs along the way, including the New York Mets and the Boston Red Sox. The team, which is now affiliated with the Pittsburgh Pirates, plays in the 4,000-seat Lynchburg City Stadium. Half of the 140 games per season are played at home.

Bedford County

MUSEUMS AND HISTORIC ATTRACTIONS

Bedford City/County Museum Free
201 East Main Street, Bedford
(540) 586-4520
www.bedfordvamuseum.org
Visitors can see a collection of artifacts and memorabilia showing the story of Bedford, a charming city at the foot of the Peaks of Otter, a Blue Ridge Parkway attraction. The exhibits begin with early natives of the region and progress through the mid-20th century. Here, you'll see American Indian relics, Revolutionary War and Civil War artifacts, clothing, flags, quilts, and more. This headquarters for the Bedford Genealogical Society and Library was built in 1895 as a Masonic Temple. It is the only example of Romanesque Revival architecture in Bedford. Hours are 10:00 A.M. to 5:00 P.M. Tuesday through Saturday.

National D-Day Memorial $
Highway 460 Bypass and Highway 122, Bedford
(800) 351-3329, (540) 587-3619
www.dday.org
Located in Bedford, the town suffering the highest per capita D-Day losses throughout the nation, the National D-Day Memorial commemorates the valor, fidelity, and sacrifice of the Allied Forces landing at Normandy on June 6, 1944. Of the 35 soldiers participating in the invasion from the community of approximately 3,200 people, 19 lost their lives. Since its dedication on June 6, 2001, the Memorial has hosted nearly 665,000 visitors.

With its three plazas, the memorial guides visitors through the complete D-Day experience, from planning to victory. The English Garden, featuring a floral version of the SHAEF patch and Order of the Day, commemorates the months of preparation that preceded the assault on Normandy. Next, visitors cross the middle plaza to arrive at a stylized tableau, complete with water, beach, landing craft, obstacles, and statues of soldiers in action. Air jets simulating enemy fire and a waterfall add to the realism of the depiction. Victory Plaza provides a conclusion to the D-Day experience with its Victory Arch rising majestically above the battle scene below and the flags of the 12 Allied nations flying high.

The Memorial is open daily from 10:00 A.M. to 5:00 P.M. It is closed Christmas Day, Thanksgiving Day, and New Year's Day, and seasonal weather closings are also possible. Mobility assistance, guided tours, and school programs are available, and a gift shop is on-site.

Thomas Jefferson's Poplar Forest $$
Fox Hole Drive, Forest
(434) 525-1806
www.poplarforest.org
Poplar Forest, Thomas Jefferson's personal year-round retreat, continues to be restored, and visitors are invited to get an

up-close perspective on the painstaking renovations. Archaeologists continue to explore the grounds for clues about Jefferson's plantation community and landscape. Various exhibits display artifacts discovered at the slave quarter site, Jefferson's "Wing of Offices" and other excavations. During the former president's time, this was a working tobacco farm spanning 4,819 acres. It was also the site of one of his most outstanding architectural achievements—an unusual octagonal home and its accompanying elaborate landscape. Thomas Jefferson and his wife, Martha, inherited the plantation from her father. Jefferson would travel two days by horseback to reach his retreat away from the bustle at Monticello, his home in Charlottesville. Family members often joined him on visits to his "Bedford estate," where he pursued his passions for reading, writing, studying, and gardening.

Poplar Forest's huge, 200-year-old tulip poplar trees are incredible to see on the beautiful grounds. The staff's enthusiasm for this cultural treasure is highly contagious. Open 10:00 A.M. to 4:00 P.M. every day except Tuesday April through November, Poplar Forest is open on major holidays except Thanksgiving. The last tour begins at 3:45 P.M. Group rates and tours are available by appointment. You can tour the grounds only for $3.00.

OTHER ATTRACTIONS

Elks National Home   **Free**
931 Ashland Avenue, Bedford
(540) 586-8232, (800) 552-4140
www.elkshome.org
A spacious retirement home used as a set in the Disney movie *What About Bob?*, the Elks National Home for retired members of this fraternal organization is best known for its annual Christmas light display. Men from every state work all year to give western Virginia's children a Christmas show worth driving to see. The rest of the year, the beautiful grounds are open for visitors.

Holy Land USA Nature Sanctuary   **Free**
1060 Jericho Road, Bedford
(540) 586-2823
www.holyland.pleasevisit.com
This 250-acre nature sanctuary represents the Bible Lands of Israel. Visitors can imagine the life, journeys, and deeds of Jesus Christ along a 3-mile trail in the beautiful Blue Ridge close to the Peaks of Otter. You have to use your imagination to envision the Biblical scenes outlined for Bible research and study, but many find inspiration from the visit. No admission fee is required to walk on your own. A fee is charged, however, for riding guided tours, which must be booked in advance. It's open 9:00 A.M. to 5:00 P.M. daily. There are varying fees for the wagon or riding tours, but they must be scheduled in advance.

Campbell County

Red Hill, Patrick Henry National
Memorial   **$$**
1250 Red Hill Road, Brookneal
(434) 376-2044, (800) 514-7463
www.redhill.org
Red Hill is the last home and burial place of the famous orator, first governor of Virginia, and champion of individual rights Patrick Henry. The Red Hill museum/visitor center and historic buildings showcase the world's largest collection of Patrick Henry memorabilia, including the famous Peter Rothermel painting, *Patrick Henry Before the Virginia House of Burgesses.* There is also a 15-minute introductory video on Patrick Henry and Red Hill.

You can visit Henry's house, law office, and other plantation buildings, and the grounds contain the Henry family cemetery and the national champion osage orange tree. Red Hill, which Henry called "one of the garden spots of Virginia," offers a breathtaking view of the Staunton River Valley. The memorial is open 9:00 A.M. until 5:00 P.M. daily except November through March, when it closes at 4:00 P.M. It is closed Thanksgiving, Christmas, and New Year's Day. A gift shop has a selection of Patrick Henry books and collectibles.

Franklin County

MUSEUMS AND HISTORIC ATTRACTIONS

Blue Ridge Institute and Galleries   Free
Ferrum College, Ferrum
(540) 365-4416
www.blueridgeinstitute.org
Visitors are often astounded that a small Methodist-related college in Franklin County, Virginia, has taken on the role of preserving a cultural heritage to the extent and level of visibility that Ferrum College has done. The result, the Blue Ridge Institute, along with the Blue Ridge Farm Museum and its Folklife Festival, places Ferrum among the nation's most important colleges culturally. Its archives contain thousands of photos, videotapes, phonograph records, vintage books, and manuscripts, all treasure troves of Appalachian scenes and people, Shenandoah Valley beliefs, southwest Virginia folktales, and African-American and Caucasian folk music from throughout Virginia. People of English, Scot, Irish, African, and German descent will be especially interested in the distinct identities reflected in Blue Ridge music, crafts, foods, beliefs, and customs formed after their forebears came to America. Both historical and contemporary folkways engage the visitor in the Institute's Museum Galleries. Two rotating exhibits showcase the rich texture of Virginia folk life in music, crafts, art, and customs. The Museum Galleries are the only facilities in the Commonwealth dedicated exclusively to the presentation of traditional culture. The Institute is open 10:00 A.M. to 4:00 P.M. Saturday and 1:00 to 4:00 P.M. Sunday, from mid-August to mid-May. It is closed on Sunday in the summer. The Archives are open by appointment, weekdays, 9:00 A.M. to 4:00 P.M.

Blue Ridge Institute Farm Museum $
Ferrum College, Ferrum
(540) 365-4416
www.blueridgeinstitute.org
The Blue Ridge Institute of Ferrum College, the State Center for Blue Ridge Folklore, presents the folkways of the region and Virginia as a whole through two unique museum facilities. The Blue Ridge Farm Museum, which presents the history and culture of early southwest Virginia settlements, features a ca. 1800 German-American farmstead with log house, outdoor oven, outbuildings, livestock, and gardens revealing the daily life of settlers who came from the German communities of Pennsylvania and the Shenandoah Valley.

All buildings are authentic and were moved from their original Blue Ridge locations. Heirloom vegetables flourish in the gardens, vintage breeds of livestock shelter by the barn, and costumed interpreters work at farm and household chores true to early life in the region.

The Farm Museum is open weekends from mid-May through mid-August, Saturday 10:00 A.M. to 4:00 P.M. and Sunday 1:00 to 4:00 P.M. mid-May to mid-August.

Booker T. Washington National
Monument   Free
Highway 122 Booker T. Washington
Highway, Hardy
(540) 721-2094
www.nps.gov/bowa/home.htm
Booker T. Washington was born into the legacy of slavery, spending the first nine years of his life in bondage on this small tobacco farm. It was from this unlikely beginning that Washington achieved international recognition as an educator, orator, unofficial presidential advisor, founder of Tuskegee Institute, and African-American leader. Begin your tour of his birthplace by watching the video presentation and seeing the exhibits at the visitor center. The monument includes 239 acres, with trails leading to reconstructed buildings and through scenic wooded areas. There also is a cemetery,

where you can see the markers for plantation owner James Burroughs and his son, Billy, who was killed in the Civil War. Visitors may take a self-guided tour along the farm trail. Guided tours are available daily in the summer and weekends in the fall.

This is the most famous attraction in Franklin County and with good reason. From the beautiful, restored farm and its animals to the hike up Plantation Trail, this monument offers a scenic, historic sojourn into a time when slavery was a way of life in America. The site is open daily 9:00 A.M. to 5:00 P.M., except for Thanksgiving, Christmas Eve, Christmas, and New Year's Day. Admission is free.

NEW RIVER VALLEY
Montgomery County

MUSEUMS AND HISTORIC ATTRACTIONS

Museum of Geological Science   Free
2062 Derring Hall, Blacksburg
(540) 231-3001
www.vtmnh.vt.edu/exhibits
Geology buffs won't want to miss this intimate museum on the campus of Virginia Tech University. You will be the first to know what's shaking, because along with gems and fossils, this museum houses a working seismograph. The exhibitions also include a full-scale model of allosaurus and the largest permanent display of Virginia minerals in the state. You also can pick up a few rocks, minerals, and fossils of your own in the gift shop. The museum is open 8:00 A.M. to 4:00 P.M. Monday through Friday during the school year.

Smithfield Plantation $
1000 Southgate Road, Blacksburg
(540) 231-3947
www.civic.bev.net.smithfield
Built by Col. William Preston in the 1700s, Smithfield Plantation has been extensively restored and is a Virginia Historic Land-

mark. It celebrated its 40th anniversary in 2004. It was the birthplace of two Virginia governors, James Patton Preston and John Buchanan Floyd, and was briefly the home of a third, John Floyd Jr. Hours are 1:00 to 5:00 P.M. Thursday through Sunday April 1 through the first of December. (Note that the last tour begins at 4:30 P.M.)

SPECTATOR SPORTS

Motormile Speedway $$
6749 Lee Highway, Radford
(540) 639-1700
www.motormilespeedway.com
The Motormile Speedway is a NASCAR-sanctioned 0.416-mile paved oval track running under the NASCAR Weekly Racing Series banner. The Late Model Stocks are the featured division of the speedway, with supporting divisions including Limited Sportsman, Late Model Trucks, Late Model Stock Cars, Pure Stocks, and Mini Stocks. Also competing on occasion throughout the year are Mini Cups. A family atmosphere prevails, and no matter what your preconceptions about racing, this is a sport for all ages to enjoy. Monster truck shows, car shows, concerts, kids' events, and other special activities are also held during the year.

Races are held every Saturday night from April through October.

Virginia Tech   Free-$$$$
US Highway 460 bypass, off I-81, Blacksburg
(540) 231-6726
www.hokiesports.com
Hokie football is big—make that BIG—in Virginia. Not only has Virginia Tech's success on the gridiron grown with each passing season, its contingent of loyal fans has skyrocketed. The Hokies added 11,170 more seats to their south end zone, pushing the capacity of Lane Stadium/Worsham Field to 65,115, but it's still hard to find a ticket, for any home game. Additional seating, a new dining facility, and a press box are part of another expansion project to the west side that started in 2004.

The nationally known Hokies have had unprecedented success from the 1990s to the present. The Hokies have played in 12 consecutive bowl games.

Coached by Frank Beamer, the Tech football team won Big East championships three times—1995, 1996, and 1999—and earned the right to play Florida State for the national championship in the 2000 Nokia Sugar Bowl in New Orleans. It was their second Sugar Bowl appearance.

At home, they're hard to beat. They knocked off Miami, the number two team in the nation in 2004, to record their 150th home win. In the past 11 years, they only lost at home 11 times. They even toppled Texas A&M in the midst of Hurricane Isabel.

Virginia Tech, which played its first gridiron game on October 21, 1892, had been an independent team for 26 years before joining the Big East in 1991. But on July 1, 2003, Virginia Tech, along with Miami, officially became members of the Atlantic Coast Conference in all its sports.

In its first year in the league, Virginia Tech won the ACC Championship, had the ACC Coach of the Year (Beamer), the ACC Player of the Year (Quarterback Bryan Randall) and advanced to the Sugar Bowl to play No. 2-ranked Auburn.

Among the Hokies' most notable football standouts were Michael Vick, the number one pick in the 2001 NFL draft and standout quarterback for the Atlanta Falcons. Defensive end Bruce Smith, who played for both the Buffalo Bills and the Washington Redskins, also was picked first in the NFL after winning the Outland Trophy as the top interior lineman in the country. Wide receiver Antonio Freeman helped lead the Green Bay Packers to back-to-back appearances in the Super Bowl, while Don Strock was a longtime starting quarterback for the Miami Dolphins. DeAngelo Hall was selected eighth overall in 2004 as five Virginia Tech players were drafted in the first five rounds of the NFL draft. All told, 25 Hokies were playing in the NFL during the 2004–2005 season.

But the players weren't the only ones getting national recognition. Coach Beamer—who instilled his famous "lunch box work ethic" on the Tech program— won the Paul "Bear" Bryant Award after the Hokies finished second in the nation in 1999. It was one of eight national honors he received that year.

Since 1958, Virginia Tech has had 116 All-Americans, most recently including Kevin Jones and Jake Grove in football and Matt Dalton in baseball. Thirty-one earned recognition on and off the playing field as Academic All-Americans. With a total of 21 varsity sports and 11 sporting venues, Virginia Tech provides generous opportunities for athletes—and fans—to get into the Hokie huddle.

Beth Dunkenberger was named the new coach of the women's basketball team in 2004, replacing Bonnie Henrickson, who guided the Hokies to their third straight NCAA appearance in four years. Tech advanced to the sweet 16 in 1999 and the final four of the WNIT in 2002. Two Hokies—Tere Williams and Ieva Kublina—were drafted to play in the WNBA.

While the men's team has been on the rebound, they have had stellar athletes as well, including Dell Curry and Bimbo Coles, who went on to play in the NBA. In 2004 Bryant Matthews was the leading scorer in the Big East and eighth in the nation. He also was invited to compete in the Slam Dunk Contest during the 2004 Final Four.

Virginia's golfers won the Big East championship three years in a row, from 2001 to 2003. They finished eighth in the nation in 2001. And the baseball squad has won conference or tournament titles seven times since the 1990.

Even the coaches make headlines. Cleopatra Borel, Virginia Tech's volunteer track and field coach, placed 11th in the shot put as she competed for her native Trinidad and Tobago in Olympia's ancient stadium during the 2004 Olympic Games.

OTHER ATTRACTIONS

Selu Conservancy and
Retreat Center Free
Radford University
(540) 831-7018
www.radford.edu
Selu (pronounced "say-loo") is Radford University's 380-acre "outdoor classroom" of woods, wetlands, and meadows bordering the Little River, 5 miles from campus. A hiking trail, a boathouse and dock, and the retreat center complement Selu's natural invitation to learning. In 2002 Selu opened the Barn, a science laboratory, and an observatory. A living history museum, called the Farm, is under construction and set to open in 2005. Visits to Selu must be set up in advance.

University Libraries Free
Virginia Tech Campus, Blacksburg
(540) 231-6170
www.lib.vt.edu
The University Libraries, established in 1872, include the Carol M. Newman Library (main building) and four branch libraries: Art and Architecture, Geo Science, Veterinary Medicine, and Northern Virginia Resource Center. Collections include 2.1 million printed volumes, 28,500 magazines or journals, 6.2 million microforms, 136,000 maps, government documents, and 13,700 films and videos. The Special Collections Department is a particularly rich depository in the history of southern Appalachia, the Civil War, science and technology, and railroad history.

Giles County

COVERED BRIDGES

Sinking Creek Bridge Free
Highway 601, Giles County
Near the beautiful Appalachian Trail in the New River Valley's Giles County stands a modified Howe truss built across Sinking Creek, just a half mile north of Newport. Built in 1916, the 70-foot Sinking Creek Covered Bridge was left in place when a modern bridge was built in 1963. The bridge is no longer used for automobiles. Visitors are welcome to explore the bridge—on foot, of course. This area also boasts two other covered bridges; however, they're located on private farms. To get to the bridge, take Highway 601, which is a half mile west of U.S. Highway 42.

MUSEUMS AND HISTORIC ATTRACTIONS

Giles County Historical Society
Museums Free
208 North Main Street, Pearisburg
(540) 921-1050
This museum complex consists of the Andrew Johnston House, the Doctor's Office, and the Historical Museum and Research Office. Johnston's House, a Colonial Georgian structure that dates back to 1829, is the oldest brick house in Giles County. The walls are 22 inches thick at the base, with log floor joists that measure 12 inches in diameter. Several pieces of the original furniture—many predate the Civil War—remain on display in the country home estate. The Doctor's Office, a much smaller structure, was added around 1857 to serve as a medical office for Andrew's son, Harvey Green I. During the Civil War, the 23rd Ohio Infantry Regiment used this office as headquarters for four days. Two officers in that regiment were future presidents—Colonel Rutherford B. Hayes and Major William McKinley. In 1993 the Andrew Johnston House and Doctor's Office were added to the Virginia Landmarks Register and the National Register of Historic Places. In November 1997, the two-story Historical Museum was dedicated. The upper level contains permanent and rotating exhibitions and a gift shop. Larger objects are on display downstairs. The complex is open from noon to 5:00 P.M. Wednesday through Friday and 2:00 to 5:00 P.M. Saturday and Sunday. The Research Office is open noon to 5:00 P.M. Thursday.

Pulaski County

MUSEUMS AND HISTORIC ATTRACTIONS

Wilderness Road Regional Museum   **$**
New River Historical Society
Highway 611, off I-81, Newbern
(540) 674-4835
Eighteen historical buildings comprise part of the 57 properties of the Old Newbern National Historic District, a neighborhood originally planned by early settlers. Seven are in the museum grounds. Newbern served as Pulaski County's seat from 1839 to 1893, when the courthouse was destroyed by fire. This interesting tour takes you through the historic buildings, some already renovated and some in the process, including a slave cabin, pre–Civil War church, buggy shed, and small weather-boarded barn. The museum is filled with historical artifacts relating to life in the New River Valley and some Civil War artifacts. The Annual Newbern Fall Festival is held the second weekend of October. Museum hours are 10:30 A.M. to 4:30 P.M. Monday through Saturday and 1:30 to 4:30 P.M. Sunday.

Pulaski County Courthouse   **Free**
52 West Main Street, Pulaski
(540) 980-7750
www.pulaskicounty.org
The Pulaski County Courthouse, originally constructed in 1896, has been restored after being destroyed by a fire in December 1989. The New River Heritage Exhibits offer a display detailing the local history of African Americans, including a profile of Mr. Chauncy Harmon. Mr. Harmon, his wife, Lucy, and several other teachers, with the support of the Virginia NAACP and Thurgood Marshall in the Supreme Court, Special Counsel for the NAACP, brought petitions for equalization in Pulaski schools in the 1950s. Their efforts led to one of only a handful of public school court cases in which the NAACP prevailed before winning *Brown v. the Board of Education*. The courthouse is open Monday through Fri-

day 8:30 A.M. to 5:00 P.M. The building is wheelchair accessible.

Pulaski Railway Station   **Free**
20 North Washington Avenue, Pulaski
(540) 994-4200
www.swva.net/pulaskichamber
In the late 1800s, Pulaski was a major stop along the Norfolk & Western Railroad route. N&W donated this railway station, constructed in 1886, to the town in 1989. The Raymond F. Ratcliffe Memorial Museum, located in the restored station, houses model railroads and exhibits artifacts from the town's history. The railway station is open from noon to 4:00 P.M. Tuesday through Thursday and 1:00 to 5:00 P.M. Saturday and Sunday. Donations are accepted.

SPECTATOR SPORTS

Pulaski Blue Jays   **$$**
Calfee Park, Pulaski
(540) 994-8624
www.pulaskirangers.com
The Pulaski Blue Jays baseball team, rookie team for the Toronto Blue Jays, plays at historic Calfee Park. Built in 1935, this unique ballpark has been pictured in *Sports Illustrated, National Geographic,* and *Life* magazines. It may be the ninth oldest professional minor league baseball parks in the country, but renovations include a new clubhouse. The Blue Jays play about half of their season at home against other Appalachian League teams like the Bluefield Orioles and the Bristol Sox. The season runs June through August.

Floyd County

Mabry Mill
Mile 176, Blue Ridge Parkway
(276) 952-2947
Undoubtedly the most scenic and most-photographed place on the Blue Ridge Parkway, Mabry Mill has been called one of the most picturesque water mills in the United States. Demonstrations on how the meal is ground are shown on Saturday

and Sunday. Grits, buckwheat, and corn-meal are sold in the gift shop along with items made in the blacksmith shop. Also stop by the Mabry Mill Restaurant. Meals are served from 8:00 A.M. to 6:00 P.M. The mill is open 9:00 A.M. to 5:00 P.M.

ALLEGHANY HIGHLANDS

Alleghany County

COVERED BRIDGES

Humpback Bridge   **Free**
Off Interstate 64, Alleghany County
Known as the "granddaddy of them all," Humpback is Virginia's oldest standing covered bridge and the nation's only surviving curved-span covered bridge. Built in 1835 as part of the Kanawha Turnpike, the graceful, 100-foot arched span rises 8 feet over Dunlap Creek. It is within viewing distance of I-64, off the Callaghan exit between Covington, Virginia, and White Sulphur Springs, West Virginia. Its hump design is unique in the Western Hemisphere. Only one other bridge, in France, is similarly constructed.

During autumn, the Humpback Wayside, between Virginia's breathtaking Allegheny and Blue Ridge Mountains, is a popular picnic area. Visitors can stroll through the bridge and wade in the shallow creek below to admire the structure's hand-hewn oak timbers.

Bath County

MUSEUMS AND HISTORIC ATTRACTIONS

Bath County Historical Society Museum   **Free**
Courthouse Square, Warm Springs
(540) 839-2543
The Historical Society offers a museum of artifacts related to the 210-year history of Bath County and its famed Hot, Warm, and Healing Springs. It also houses a nice collection of Civil War artifacts. The research library is one of the most comprehensive in the area, including books and photographs of Bath County, as well as other localities in Virginia and West Virginia. Established in 1969 as a nonprofit entity, the Bath Historical Society also publishes books of local and regional historic interest, which are for sale in the museum. There is no admission charge. The museum is open year-round from 9:00 A.M. to 4:00 P.M. Tuesday through Saturday.

Chesapeake & Ohio Historical Society   **Free**
312 East Ridgeway Street, Clifton Forge
(800) 453-2647, (540) 862-2210
www.cohs.org
This international railroad historical society deals with the history of the Chesapeake & Ohio Railway. Its predecessors and successors operated in Virginia, West Virginia, Kentucky, Ohio, Michigan, Indiana, and Ontario, Canada. The organization's archives division has one of the largest institutional collections devoted to a single railway, including more than 100,000 ink-on-linen original engineering drawings, 50,000 mechanical drawings, and more than 50,000 photographic images, dating from the 1870s to 1980s. A library contains thousands of books, magazines, and pamphlets devoted to railroad history in general and C & O history in particular. The Society also owns 19 pieces of historic original C & O railroad equipment, some of which is open for display by appointment, and some in storage awaiting restoration. Several passenger cars have been restored and are used to interpret the railway experience at special events in Clifton Forge and over several states. The premier restored passenger car is the dining car Gadsby's Tavern. The Society, which has more than 2,700 members in 50 states and 12 foreign countries, produces the annual Chessie Calendar, carrying on an unbroken tradition begun by the railway in 1934. The archives and shop are open 9:00 A.M. to 5:00 P.M. Monday through Saturday year-round.

Highland County

Highland Maple Museum   **Free**
U.S. Highway 220, south of Monterey
(540) 468-2550
www.highlandcounty.com
In the land of maples is a museum celebrating old-time sugaring. This replica of an old-time sugar house traces the history of maple-syrup making, from methods used by American Indians to today's modern techniques. The open-air museum is open anytime to walk through. Old-timers who can't otherwise get to the real sugar camps during Highland County's famed Maple Festival will find this especially interesting. There is no fee.

KIDSTUFF 👥

If your kids are looking for big metropolitan areas full of amusement parks, video games, and Disney-type make-believe, don't aim for the Blue Ridge. However, if you and your family are looking for a break from the artificial and searching for something real, you're heading in the right direction. Even the most jaded city children have been spotted making an amazing transformation from being bored to having some hidden chord struck by history and the beauty of the great outdoors.

The Blue Ridge offers adults and children many opportunities to experience and explore the kinds of places that don't exist anywhere else. We have natural wonders such as Shenandoah National Park, caverns and Natural Bridge in the Shenandoah Valley, and museums such as the New Market Hall of Valor, To the Rescue Exhibit, and the Science Museum in Roanoke. In the horse country stretching from Loudoun County to Albemarle County, children are thrilled to see horse shows, steeplechases, and fox hunts. Lexington's Virginia Horse Center has a plethora of events that children will enjoy. And the jousting tournaments at Natural Chimneys in Augusta County are a real treat—for all ages, actually. But parents be warned: Exposing your children to such events may lead them to begging you to buy a pony or horse.

PRICE CODE

As in our Attractions chapter, we have provided a general price guide for the activities that would appeal to the younger crowd. Dollar signs are used to indicate admission prices for the venues. In some cases, you will need to bring along extra cash to pay for rides, games, food, and, of course, souvenirs. If admission is free, we'll let you know.

$	$5.00 or less
$$	$6.00 to $10.00
$$$	$11.00 to $15.00
$$$$	$16.00 or more

SHENANDOAH VALLEY

Frederick County

Appleland Sports Center $-$$
4490 Valley Pike, Stephens City
(540) 869-8600
www.applelandsportscenter.com
South of Winchester is this miniature golf park and driving range. Kids can play miniature golf or take a swing in one of nine new batting cages, while parents try their luck on the driving range. There are 33 covered tees with a sand trap. A bucket of balls ranges from $6.00 to $9.00, while minigolf costs $5.00, $3.00 if you're between the ages of 6 and 12. For $1.00, you can take 15 hits in the batting cage. Try the par 3 golf course or take a spin on the go-kart track—$5.00 for NASCAR, $4.00 for Pacer. Weather permitting, Appleland is open from 9:00 A.M. to 10:00 P.M. daily from March through November. There's also a snack bar and a pro shop.

Belle Grove Plantation $-$$
U.S. Highway 11, Middletown
(540) 869-2028
www.bellegrove.org
Historic Belle Grove offers programs for families throughout the year. Visit during living history weekend, the second week in November, and you will find the place steeped in the late 18th century. Crafters in period dress demonstrate and sell their wares, exhibit various domestic animals, and play early Appalachian music. Or come in July for an old-fashioned ice cream social as well as music and 19th-century children's games. Other events

include the annual Easter egg hunt. The 1797 manor house is closed January through March.

Cedar Creek Battlefield Museum and Visitor Center $-$$
8437 Valley Pike, Middletown
(540) 869-2064, (888) 628-1864
www.cedarcreekbattlefield.org
For those who are interested in Civil War history and would like their children to appreciate it, the three-day reenactment of the Battle of Cedar Creek takes place every October at historic Cedar Creek, the very battlefield where the fighting took place. Tickets are available from the Cedar Creek Foundation. Children 5 and younger get in free.

Family Drive-In Theatre $-$$
US 11, Stephens City
(540) 665-6982
The Dalke family, which owns this theater along with the Community Theatre in Woodstock, marked its 92nd year in the movie theater business in 2004. Primary owner Tim Dalke started working in the company when he was 12, placing hand-bills on residents' doors and car wind-shields to advertise upcoming movies, as well as selling tickets and popcorn at the theater and cleaning the floors. Fewer than 10 drive-in theaters remain in Vir-ginia, including this one just 1 mile south of Stephens City. The Family Drive-In shows different double features on two screens on weekends during the summer, starting in early May.

Magic Valley $-$$
1107 Berryville Avenue, Winchester
(540) 667-5266
This smoke-free, gum-free, and sock-wearing playground is a great place to take the kids when the hotel pool is closed. Magic Valley features an indoor roller coaster. In fact, everything is indoors, including games, a moon bounce, race-track, ladders, tubes, slides, and a ball bin for running, jumping, and climbing. When the kids get hungry, there's no need to

leave—just grab a meal or snack at the snack shop. Adults accompanying children get in free. Game tokens are a quarter, ride tickets are $1.50, and speedway tickets cost $3.00. Package deals are available.

Shenandoah Apple Blossom Festival $-$$
135 North Cameron Street, Winchester
(540) 662-3863
www.thebloom.org
Winchester becomes a boomtown every spring during the Apple Blossom Festival (see our Annual Events and Festivals chapter). The sweet scent of apple blos-soms fills the air, and each year a different celebrity serves as the marshal of the fes-tival's showcase—the grand feature parade. With events sometimes running from 8:00 A.M. to 9:00 P.M. for five straight days, it's easy to find something to do. There's an arts and crafts festival on Sat-urday and Sunday, concerts, races, athletic events, a midway with carnival rides, and, of course, a circus. While some of the activities are free, you will need tickets for concerts and the circus.

Shenandoah Valley Discovery Museum $
54 South Loudoun Street, Winchester
(540) 722-2020
www.discoverymuseum.net
Dress up like a doctor in the mini-hospital emergency room or enjoy playing with the simple machine in the Apple Packing Shed. This hands-on, interactive museum for children features permanent displays, a take-apart room, climbing wall, even snakes. The museum is on the Loudoun Street Pedestrian Mall and is open from 9:00 A.M. to 5:00 P.M. Monday through Sat-urday and 1:00 to 5:00 P.M. Sunday.

Wayside Theatre $$-$$$$
7853 Main Street, Middletown
(540) 869-1782
www.waysidetheatre.org
Take a break with your kids from modern-day programming and go see a show at the historic Wayside Theatre (see our Arts

chapter). Wayside offers children's programs and children's theater, including comedies, dramas, and mysteries for the whole family.

Winchester Book Gallery
185 North Loudoun Street, Winchester
(540) 667-3444
A short walk down the pedestrian mall is this two-story bookshop, where you will find lots of information on regional and local history, including the Civil War. The entire upstairs level of the Winchester Book Gallery is devoted to children's books, and you might also find a few maps, dolls, and stuffed animals. Check it out from 10:00 A.M. to 5:00 P.M. Monday through Saturday.

Clarke County

Dinosaur Land $
U.S. Highway 522, White Post
(540) 869-2222
www.dinosaurland.com
Get your picture taken while you sit in King Kong's hand. The 20-foot replica of the movie icon is a crowd favorite at this outdoor prehistoric forest. More than 47 exhibits bring kids face to face with life-size reproductions of dinosaurs that roamed the earth during the Mesozoic era. Tours of the park are self-guided.

During the summer, the hours are 9:30 A.M. to 6:30 P.M. It closes at 5:30 P.M. from March to Memorial Day and at 5:00 P.M. in November and December. The park is closed in January and February.

Warren County

Front Royal Canoe Company $$$-$$$$
U.S. Highway 340 S, Front Royal
(540) 635-5440, (800) 270-8808
www.frontroyalcanoe.com
Front Royal is where the north and south branches of the Shenandoah River join in their rush to the sea. The waterfront

below the US 522 bridge draws boaters, swimmers, and anglers during warm weather. The Front Royal Canoe Company (see our Recreation chapter) can put you and your family adrift on any summer day. On the average, a day trip will run $34 to $50 for canoers; $22 to $32 for a kayak. If rowing is more effort than you want to expend, try tubing, where the river will do all the work for you. It costs only $16. Rent an extra tube to carry your lunch and spend the day lazily drifting; kids will enjoy swimming spots along the way. Self-guided rafting is available for $49 to $62, while landlubbers can take a self-guided horseback ride for $30 per hour.

Skyline Caverns $$$
US 340, Front Royal
(540) 635-4545, (800) 296-4545
www.skylinecaverns.com
One of three swift underground streams is stocked with fat trout that dart about in easy view in this underground wonder. Youngsters will also marvel at the cave formations inside Skyline Caverns, including the unusual anthodites or "cave orchids" for which Skyline is noted. Aboveground is the Outdoor Skyline Arrow, a miniature train that carries children on a half-mile journey through a real tunnel. (See our Attractions chapter.) It's free for children younger than 7.

Skyline Drive $$
3655 U.S. Highway 211 E, Luray
(540) 999-3500
www.nps.gov/shen
The Blue Ridge's greatest resource is its natural beauty, so this is a great place to introduce your children to nature. Starting at Front Royal, you can enter the magic world of the Skyline Drive, a road that squiggles along the crest of the mountains all the way to Waynesboro, where it joins the Blue Ridge Parkway (see our Blue Ridge Parkway and Skyline Drive chapter). The Drive and Parkway run through national parks, where deer and other wild creatures will be easy to spot from your car. The cost is $10.00 per car, $5.00 for pedestrians and bicyclists. To

make the experience even more special for your children (and you), plan to stay at one of the campgrounds or lodges in this unspoiled area.

Shenandoah County

Bryce Resort   **$$$$**
1982 Fairway Drive, Basye
(540) 856-2121
www.bryceresort.com
This Shenandoah County resort offers a wide range of family accommodations and activities (see our Resorts chapter), including skiing, grass skiing, and horseback and pony riding. Stony Creek Lilliputt is a miniature golf course adjacent to the entrance to Bryce. It is open daily in the summer. The kids will also like Lake Laura, a 45-acre lake, where they can swim, fish, and go boating. Have some fun on a paddleboat or teach them how to paddle a canoe.

Shenandoah Valley Music Festival $$$
221 Shrine Mont Circle, Orkney Springs
(800) 459-3396
www.musicfest.org
There is musical entertainment five weekends each summer at the Shenandoah Valley Music Festival (see our Arts chapter.) Held outdoors at the Pavilion on the grounds of the historic Orkney Springs Hotel, the festival hosts symphonic, Big Band, jazz, and folk. On symphony weekends, there are free concerts for kids. You can bring along an adult for $8.00.

Stonewall Jackson Museum at
Hupp's Hill   **$**
US 11 S, Strasburg
(540) 465-5884
www.waysideofva.com
For a more educational experience, the whole family should learn from a visit to this park conveniently located near the intersection of Interstates 81 and 66. This interpretive center illustrates nine battles of the Civil War, including the Battle of Cedar Creek and the role of the Shenandoah Valley. It offers hands-on exhibits and

activities. It even has a children's room with costumes to try on, wooden horses to ride, and a Civil War camp with a tent and camp furniture. Visitors are encouraged to learn about the era through touching, seeing, and experiencing what life was like during the Civil War period. (See our Civil War chapter for more information on Hupp's Hill.) There is also a walking trail and the only Karst walking trail in Virginia.

Page County

Down River Canoe Company $$$$
884 Indian Hollow, Bentonville
(540) 635-5526, (800) 338-1963
www.downriver.com
You also can explore the south fork of the Shenandoah with canoe, kayak, inner tube, or raft from Down River Canoe Company from April 1 to October 31. Daily rentals are $39 to $59 for a canoe, $28 to $34 for a kayak, and $12 to $14 for a tube. Rafts will run you anywhere from $49 to $119 depending on the size. Down River is open from 9:00 A.M. to 6:00 P.M. during the week and from 7:00 A.M. to 7:00 P.M. on weekends. It's a good idea to bring your bathing suit, foot protection, sunscreen, and a lunch.

Luray Caverns $$$$
970 US 211 W, Luray
(540) 743-6551
www.luraycaverns.com
Beneath the surface of the ground is the world's only stalacpipe organ. Luray Caverns (see our Attractions chapter) also features a Car and Carriage Caravan aboveground, which contains antique cars, carriages, coaches, and costumes dating back to 1725. The garden maze, with a half acre of 8-foot trees, is popular with the kids.

Luray Zoo $-$$
1087 US 211 W, Luray
(540) 743-4113
www.lurayzoo.com
Hours of endless facination can be had at

a setting with lots of wild and tame animals. The Luray Zoo has one of the state's largest reptile collections as well as a petting zoo with tame deer, llamas, and other creatures. All together, there are more than 300 animals in 90 exhibits. The Luray Zoo offers Animal Encounter Theatre, with two live animal shows a day. Crocodile Hunter Steve Irwin and his wife, Terri, visited in 1998. The zoo is open daily from 10:00 A.M. to 5:00 P.M.

Shenandoah River Outfitters $$$-$$$$
6502 South Page Valley Road, Luray
(540) 743-4159
www.shenandoahriver.com
Hook up with Shenandoah Outfitters for a leisurely day on the south fork of the Shenandoah River. Your kids will love the adventure! Rent canoes and kayaks from April to November. The first trip starts at 8:00 A.M., and the last departs at 1:00 P.M. You can rent a tube for the ultimate in lazy river fun from Memorial Day to Labor Day. Or try a more rigorous workout in a canoe for trips ranging from one to five hours. You can also rent a kayak for a day for $30. There is a tent campground. Seven river cabins also are available to rent year-round.

Rockingham County

Bull Pen $
1945 Deyerle Avenue, Harrisonburg
(540) 433-2243
www.bullpenamusements.com
Bull Pen is a great place to come for kids who hope to be the next Sammy Sosa or Mark McGuire. You can take a swing at 14 balls for $1.00. Aside from the batting cages, Bull Pen also has go-karts. Go-karts cost $4.75, but you must be 10 years old and at least 57 inches tall to take a drive. If not, you can ride with an adult. Bull Pen is open 10:00 A.M. to 10:00 P.M. six days a week in-season and 1:00 to 9:00 P.M. on Sunday.

Eastern Mennonite University
Planetarium $
1200 Park Road, Harrisonburg
(540) 432-4400
www.emu.edu/sciencecenter/
Eastern Mennonite University offers a more enlightening experience at its planetarium and museum. There's a half-hour program in the planetarium, then you tour the museum at your own pace. The 2:00 P.M. programs are only held on certain Sundays throughout the year, so call for an appointment. The cost is $2.00 for school groups. For others it's free, but donations are appreciated.

Funzone $-$$
100 Miller Circle, Harrisonburg
(540) 433-1834
Enjoy hours of fun and burn up some of that energy at Funzone, an old-fashioned roller skating rink. The rink is open Wednesday, and Friday through Sunday. There is usually a dance on Thursday during the summer. The hours vary, so call before you go.

George Washington and
Jefferson National Forests $
401 Oakwood Drive, Harrisonburg
(540) 432-0187
www.southernregion.fs.fed.us/gwj
For bigger adventure, the now merged George Washington and Jefferson National Forests are a stone's throw away with lakes for swimming, miles of hiking, and 25 campgrounds ranging from primitive to ones with electrical hookups, showers, and toilets. There's outdoor fun from one end of the Blue Ridge to the other. In fact, there's even an Eastern National Children's Forest Trail just 18 miles from Covington on Highway 613. The cost per car is $4.00 for picnicking or swimming. Fees vary from campground to campground, ranging from $5.00 to $25.00. (See our Recreation chapter for more on the National Forests.)

Harrisonburg Children's Museum $
30 North Main Street
Harrisonburg
(540) 442-9800
www. hcmuseum.org

Visit this place with your children, ages 2 to 12, and we are sure you will both agree that this is the coolest place for kids—hands down! The cost is just $3.00 (free for children younger than 2). The museum, which had previously jumped from various locations, finally settled in October 2003, in a prime spot at Court Square. Kids can have fun taking a house apart and putting it back together (the studs are right there), wiring it for electricity. Or they can dig in the dirt for vegetables, go shopping at the child-size market, use weights, list, calculator, and take them to the cute custom-made kitchen to cook up a feast. If drama's their thing, take them to the stage where there are movable scenes and a makeup table and even a sound effects computer. Once the museum opened in its new space, 7,000 visitors came through the doors in seven weeks. Science and the arts are the focus, and the museum offers storytelling, art classes, dance classes, and visits by doctors to talk about eyesight, skin, and other topics. The hours are Tuesday through Saturday from 10:00 A.M. to 2:00 P.M., Thursday from 1:00 to 6:00 P.M. and Friday from 5:00 to 8:00 P.M.

Hillandale Park
Hillandale Avenue, Harrisonburg
(540) 433-9168
www.ciharrisonburg.va.us

Explore a reproduction log cabin at Hillandale Park, or play basketball, practice archery, or jog. The Harrisonburg park has a 1.3-mile jogging and exercise trail, 12 picnic shelters, and a small playground. There is a $20 charge to reserve a shelter on weekends, $10 during the week; otherwise, the park is free.

Massanutten Resort $$$$
1822 resort Drive, Massanutten
(540) 289-9441
www.massresort.com

East of Harrisonburg is Massanutten Resort, with golf and great winter activities, including skiing, snow tubing, and snowboarding. Special programs help develop junior skiers into racers (see our Skiing chapter). The family-oriented resort offers a host of programs geared to children year-round. There are two recreation centers busy with kids in the summer. The children's program for ages 3 to 12 includes crafts and other classes. There is miniature golf, two stocked ponds for fishing, two outdoor pools, and two indoor pools. A skate park was added for inline skates and skateboards. You can even rent mountain bikes in the spring and summer for $6.00 an hour, $18.00 for the day. The fee includes the helmet.

Mulligan's Golf Center $
141 Carpenter Lane, Harrisonburg
(540) 432-9040
www.mulligansgolf.com

Play a round on the 18-hole miniature golf course while the adults practice on the driving range. The Golf Center is open daily from 10:00 A.M. to 9:00 P.M. You'll pay between $4.00 and $6.00 for a bucket of balls, while miniature golf runs $4.50 or $3.00 for ages 6 to 12. There's a pro shop, too, if you need new equipment. You can borrow kids' clubs for the driving range for those age 3 and older.

Purcell Park
Monument Avenue, Harrisonburg
(540) 433-9168
www.ciharrisonburg.va.us

Parents will be interested in several small parks in Harrisonburg, including Purcell Park with its picnic shelters, a 1.5-mile jogging trail, and a kids' castle. There also is a lake for catch-and-release fishing in the summer. Two lighted softball diamonds, a Little League field, Midget League football field, and tennis courts will attract the sports-minded youngster. Admission is free.

You Made It! $$-$$$$
163 South Main Street, Harrisonburg
(540) 434-4500
www.youmadeit.net

Walk in with your kids, pick a piece of pottery, and some paints, and begin to create! That's the goal of this "paint your own pottery studio," which provides materials for folks to make "one of a kind" gifts and mementoes. There is all kinds of creative decorating to be done on Christmas ornaments, vases, picture frames, mugs, bowls—more than 100 different shapes. Then consult their idea books for a design and pick from a wide array of colors, stencils, sponges, brushes, and more. You can make it on your own or ask for help from the staff. Workshops and parties are also possible. The cost of a piece can range from $6.00 to $50.00. You Made It! charges a studio fee of 50 percent for materials, glazes, and firing in the kiln. They ask for seven days to allow for the finishing of your piece for pickup. You Made It! is closed on Monday.

Augusta County

**Blue Ridge Soap Box
Derby Classic   Free
Main Street, Waynesboro
(540) 943-5569
www.brsoapbox.com**
Start your engines. Well, these racecars may not have engines, but they are powered by a lot of hard work and determination. After a brief hiatus, soap box racing returned to Waynesboro in 1994, and today it ranks as one of the largest races in the world. For one Saturday in mid-May, Main Street is blocked off so that kids ages 9 to 16 can show off how they cared for their own vehicles—not to mention their driving skills. The competition is friendly but tough. In fact, Mark Stephens, a representative from Waynesboro's 1997 competition, won the National Soap Box Derby championship in Akron, Ohio. And in 2000 a young lady named Loggan Quesenberry placed fourth in the world at Akron. It doesn't cost a thing to watch the race, which starts at 8:00 A.M. and is an all-day event. There is a registration fee to

enter the race. Derbies also are now held in Culpeper and Winchester.

**Frontier Culture Museum $$
U.S. Highway 250 W, Staunton
(540) 332-7850
www.frontier.virginia.gov**
Staunton's greatest attraction for children is its fascinating Frontier Culture Museum (see our Attractions chapter), where fields and livestock are tended exactly the way European and early American farmers used to do it. From cows to chickens to kittens, the animals will help make this a fun-filled day for children, and many festivals here throughout the year (see our Annual Events and Festivals chapter) are geared to families. Authentic farm areas have been re-created with costumed interpreters demonstrating life of the frontier culture.

**Grand Caverns $$$$
Off I-81 at exit 235, Grottoes
(540) 249-5705
www.uvrpa.org/grandcaverns**
It's a wonder this area doesn't fall into some subterranean passage. One of the oldest caverns in the Shenandoah Valley, Grand Caverns includes a 5,000-square-foot underground "ballroom." Look for the "shield" formations, too. (See our Attractions chapter.) Grand Caverns also has a swimming pool, miniature golf, a hiking trail, and a playground.

**Gypsy Hill Park
Churchville Avenue, Staunton
(800) 332-5219**
This is a favorite place for young and old. Athletes can choose between the lighted softball fields, Little League diamonds, tennis courts, a swimming pool, and horseshoe pits. There are the usual swings, picnic areas, and even a bandstand (free concerts are held here weekly in the summer), but the big draw to Gypsy Hill is the duck pond. You can buy food in the park to feed the ducks and swans, but don't let your fingers get too close. Another park attraction is the mini train, which runs on the weekends. The

Gypsy Express runs mid-April through Halloween. Cost is $1.00.

Humpback Rocks   **Free**
Near mile 5.8, Blue Ridge Parkway
(540) 943-4716
At nearby Humpback Rocks, the National Park Service has re-created a typical pioneer mountain farm as it might have appeared just before the turn of the 20th century. You can explore the farm and hike up the rocks for a heart-stopping view of the Shenandoah Valley and the Piedmont—all for free (see our Recreation chapter for more information). A picnic area and comfort station are nearby, where you can ask a ranger for information. The station is open from 9:00 A.M. to 5:00 P.M. from May to early November.

Shenandoah Acres Resort   **$**
Highway 660, Lake Road, Stuarts Draft
(540) 337-1911, (800) 654-1714
www.shenacres.com
Raft races for all ages are held the last weekend in July at Shenandoah Acres Resort. An excellent place for family fun, there's camping, horseback riding, tennis, and minigolf (see our Recreation chapter). For a day trip, you can enjoy the sand-bottom lake and picnic at one of many tables and grills surrounding the lake. The cost is $9.25 during the weekend, $7.25 on weekdays. Children ages 6 to 11 can get in for $5.75 and $5.00, respectively. The young ones get in free. Minigolf is $3.75, and horseback riding costs $11.00 for a 25-minute ride, $30 for the hour trail. The resort also has a snack bar.

Sherando Lake Recreation Area   **$-$$**
Off Highway 664, Lyndhurst
(540) 291-2188
www.southernregion.fs.fed.us/gwj
Just 14 miles south of Waynesboro, down a narrow but mostly flat country road, you'll find Sherando Lake, a recreation paradise nestled between two small, calm lakes. Being so surrounded by formidable mountains, one can mistakenly think she is miles from civilization. This area is family-

oriented with lots of outdoor fun, including roomy camping units, which are available on a first-come, first-served basis (see our Recreation chapter). With electrical hookup, the cost is $20 a night; tent camping is $15. You can enjoy a day of swimming or boating, stop for a picnic, then take a walk around one of the lakes or a longer hike up a mountain. There's also fishing here. A Virginia fishing license and trout stamp is required.

Virginia Metalcrafters
1010 East Main Street, Waynesboro
(540) 949-9432
www.virginiametalcrafters.com
Older children (and parents) will enjoy a visit to the showroom of Virginia Metalcrafters, where you can watch brass being molded. Artisans create a variety of items, including candlesticks, lamps, and trivets. Oh, and your parents might like to know that they can purchase these artworks at 25 percent below the suggested retail price. Virginia Metalcrafters is open from 9:00 A.M. to 5:00 P.M. Monday through Friday, 9:00 A.M. to 4:00 P.M. Saturday, and from 1:00 to 5:00 P.M. Sunday from April to December 22. There is no cost to visit.

Lexington and Rockbridge County

History is a major reason families come to Lexington and Rockbridge County—Civil War history (Robert E. Lee and Stonewall Jackson), World War II history (George C. Marshall), and natural history (Natural Bridge).

Carriage Tours of Historic
Lexington   **$$$**
Lexington Visitor Center
106 East Washington Street, Lexington
(540) 463-5647
The Lexington Carriage Company operates this nearly hour-long tour of many of Lexington's historic sites from April to October. Older children, especially those who've not

had the opportunity to get up close and personal with horses, will enjoy a ride on this forgotten mode of transportation. Carriage Tours do not make stops along the way, so parents of young or antsy children might want to consider the length of the 45-minute (or longer) tour.

Carriage rides cost $16.00, $14.00 for senior citizens, $7.00 for children ages 7 to 13, and it's free for those 6 and younger. (See our Attractions chapter.)

**George C. Marshall Museum
and Library** $
**VMI Parade Grounds, Lexington
(540) 463-7103
www.marshallfoundation.org**
This is a nice vacation for families or a perfect destination for school field trips. Large prescheduled children's groups can participate in "Try on a Piece of History." The museum staff coordinates this program in which pieces of uniforms are used to bring history alive. Older children and teens may gain perspective on the impact of war through a photographic display that includes black-and-white photos of the children of war-torn Europe. Admission is free for those 18 and younger. School groups are admitted free. The museum is open 9:00 A.M. to 5:00 P.M. daily and closed on major holidays (see our Attractions chapter).

Hulls Drive In $
**Route 11, 4 miles north of Lexington
(540) 463-2621
www.hullsdrivein.com**
Historic Hulls Drive-In has been in continuous operation since 1950. Hulls would not have stayed open except for strong community support from a nonprofit group, Hull's Angels, which began an effort in 1999 to keep the drive-in theater open. Now it is the nation's only nonprofit community-owned and -operated drive-in theater. Movies are shown the first week in April through the first week in October, on Friday through Sunday, rain or shine. The concession stand is one of the best around, where you can still get popcorn

> *The prices for kids' activities in the Blue Ridge can vary widely—from free activities such as hiking or visiting a park, to a couple of dollars in admission to small museums or attractions, to the hefty sums you can pay at the big-name resorts.*

for 75 cents. Children younger than 11 get in free.

Lime Kiln Theater $-$$$$
**Lime Kiln Road, Box Office, 2 West Henry Street, Lexington
(540) 463-3074
www.theateratlimekiln.com**
Lexington's professional outdoor theater presents musicals, plays, and concerts in "the most unusual theater setting in the United States"—a real kiln used 100 years ago. The productions are often family oriented, and each year there are some special shows scheduled for children. Outdoor shows run from early May to late October. A new indoor theater was added for year-round shows. Ticket prices range from $5.00 to $25.00. (See our Arts chapter.)

Natural Bridge of Virginia $-$$
**US 11 S, Natural Bridge
(540) 291-2121, (800) 533-1410
www.naturalbridgeva.com**
From Natural Bridge, one of the seven wonders of the natural world, to gigantic, breathtaking caverns and a wax museum featuring behind-the-scenes tours of how the figures are made, Natural Bridge of Virginia has something to please every child, not to mention a new Haunted Monster Museum. Not only are the natural surroundings sublime, but the resort also puts on an enthralling light and sound show nightly, *Dramas of Creation*. The show is held under the 23-story-high, 90-foot-long limestone arched bridge that gives this wonder its name. An attraction that will also peak children's interest as well as adults is the Monacan Indian Living History Village, where visitors can watch

canoe building, hide tanning, tool making, and other daily chores the Indians had to do to survive several hundred years ago. The village is open April to November (see our Resorts chapter).

The Toy Museum at Natural Bridge $$
6477 South Lee Highway, Natural Bridge
(540) 291-9920, (800) 869-7476
www.awesometoymuseum.com

"Wow. I had that." There's a pretty good chance you will say that at least once when you visit this new museum located at the entrance to Natural Bridge. In 2003 the Toy Museum moved from the Smokey Mountains region to a new and bigger home, bringing with it the "largest collection of childhood memorabilia on display in the world." In other words, it's a child's dream world. There are more than 45,000 toys, games, and dolls from the last century along with antiques dating back to 1740. The museum's artifacts are exhibited in two main themes. "American Patriots' Childhoods - America's History Told With Toys" displays play sets and toys depicting events from American history. "Memory Lane Stroll" features dolls and toys in Christmas scenes from each decade since 1946. Among the more popular toys, especially with the older crowd, are exhibits of Shirley Temple, Chatty Cathy, Rambo, and Masters of the Universe. Interactive tours run from 9:00 A.M. to 8:00 P.M. daily. Admission is $8.00, $5.00 for children ages 6 to 12, but you can save with a combination ticket to other attractions at Natural Bridge.

Natural Bridge Zoo $-$$
US 11 N, Natural Bridge
(540) 291-2420
www.lexingtonvirginia.com/natural_
bridge_zoo.htm

If your kids prefer to get out of the car to look at the animals, here's a good place to go. The Natural Bridge Zoo has the largest collection of birds and animals in Virginia: 400 all together. You'll see white tigers, giraffes, and camels, among many others. There's an animal petting area and even

elephant rides. Enjoy lunch on the picnic grounds, or make a stop for souvenirs in the Safari Shop. The zoo is open daily March through November. Cost is $7.50, $6.50 for seniors and $5.50 for children ages 3 to 12. Children younger than 3 get in free.

Stonewall Jackson House $
8 East Washington Street, Lexington
(540) 463-2552
www.stonewalljackson.org

Young visitors can watch an audiovisual exhibit to learn who Stonewall Jackson was, then take a guided tour of the furnished period rooms. Kids will also enjoy exploring the antique toy reproductions in the gift shop.

Admission is $6.00 for adults and $3.00 for ages 6-17 (see our Attractions chapter).

Sweet Things
106 West Washington Street, Lexington
(540) 463-6055

Lexington's homemade ice-cream parlor is a special delight for children of all ages. Choose from 24 flavors or buy some bulk candy for the road. You can even watch the homemade cones being made.

Virginia Horse Center $
Off Interstate 64 W at exit 55, Lexington
(540) 464-2950
www.horsecenter.org

The horse center hosts all kinds of horse shows, but the ones that are of particular interest to children are the pony club shows and mule and donkey shows. In addition, the center hosts rodeos and auctions, which are a delight for children of all ages! (See our Horse Country chapter.) Most events are free.

Virginia Safari Park $$
229 Safari Lane, Natural Bridge
(540) 291-3205
www.virginiasafaripark.com

Here's a concept: Stay in your car and drive through the park gawking at hundreds of exotic animals from all over the world as they roam free—just as if you were on a safari adventure! This drive-through zoo is on pasture and wooded land that stretches across 180 acres. You can even purchase a bucket of food to feed the animals from your car. There are also wagon rides available for an additional $5.00 per person on Saturday and Sunday, and the little ones will enjoy a petting zoo. Children 2 and younger get in free. The park operates daily from March to November, with the last car going through at 5:00 P.M.

Virginia Military Institute Museum $
VMI Parade Grounds, Lexington
(540) 464-7334, (540) 464-7232
www.vmi.edu/museum
This museum has a special display of a typical cadet's room in the barracks that always fascinates children. The Virginia Military Institute cadets in uniform and the Friday afternoon full dress parades are always of special interest to children. Throughout most of the year, except during breaks and exams, cadet guides give tours of the VMI Post. The current location of the museum is closed for major renovations until late 2007, but all of the exhibits still can be seen at its new temporary home in the Marshall Museum, beginning in 2005. While here, kids also can see examples of uniforms used when George C. Marshall was in charge (see our Attractions chapter). Both museums are on VMI's Parade Grounds.

ROANOKE VALLEY
Roanoke

Art Museum of Western Virginia $
Center in the Square, Levels 1 and 2
1 Market Square, Roanoke
(540) 342-5760, (540) 342-5768
www.artmuseumroanoke.org
The art museum offers special exhibits for children, such as cartoon originals. Its permanent collection of pictures and sculpture is worth a visit as well. The cost is $3.00 for children ages 3 and older, $7.00 for a family of four. (See our Arts chapter.)

ArtVenture $
Center in the Square, 1 Market Square
Roanoke
(540) 342-5760
This interactive art center for children is a creative explosion at the Art Museum of Western Virginia. Eight interactive stations interpret objects from the Art Museum collection. Bring the whole family to explore its creativity and imagination. The center is open Tuesday through Sunday. A family of four can visit for $7.00. It's free for artists 3 and younger.

B & D Comics
802 Elm Avenue SW, Roanoke
(540) 342-6642
The kids won't protest going into this shop. You are sure to find what you—er, your children—are looking for in this 1,000 square feet of retail that sells a wide variety of comics and games. Truth be told, there is a small section for children, but mostly the comics are for the older "kids."

Chuck E. Cheese's
4059 Electric Road, Roanoke
(540) 989-8193
www.chuckecheese.com
Bring out the earplugs for your basic loud and boisterous outing to a child's idea of Heaven. There are lots of rides and video games, and, yes, they do serve food. The pizza is quite tasty, a minimal comfort to long-suffering adults trying to hold a conversation above the happy, hollering kids and the Chuck E. Cheese show.

Community School Strawberry
Festival $
Elmwood Park, Roanoke
(540) 563-5036
www.communityschool.net
This 25-year-old event takes place 2 blocks down from the Chili Cook-off during the first weekend of May. Here children can sample homemade shortcakes and real whipped cream and assorted strawberry delicacies. There are bands and games, but you pay for only what you buy. (See our Annual Events and Festivals chapter.)

Festival in the Park $
Downtown Roanoke
(540) 342-2640
www.eventzone.org
This is a 10-day celebration of music, entertainment, food, and fun that attracts several hundred thousand people to sample an incredible array of festivity. It begins the Friday before Memorial Day. Special children's programming is ongoing, with theater, puppetry, and entertainment. There are different hands-on activities each year, including such things as fireman's foam from Sweden, plus regional, national, and international arts and crafts. There's a youth art show and the fabulous Children's Parade complete with Macy's-style balloons. Enjoy the Renaissance Fair where people dress in period costume and do demonstrations and music performances. And the little ones will also enjoy the petting zoo. Admission is free but select concerts and activities require purchase of a $10 button. Children 3 and younger can get into the concerts for free.

Good Things On the Market
City Market, 212 Market Street, Roanoke
(540) 343-2121
www.roanokeonline.com
You can find this candy store right across from Wertz's Restaurant. It is a must-see for children—and for the inner child of most grown-ups. There you'll find the childhood staples of gumdrops, licorice, and homemade fudge along with fancier, trendy candy and the latest gimmicks in the confectionery world, all packaged to delight any sweet tooth. Special gift items are available.

**Harrison Museum of
African-American Culture** $
523 Harrison Avenue NW, Roanoke
(540) 345-4818
www.harrisonmuseum.org
This museum, located in a renovated school, traces the history of the African-American experience. Its colorful displays of beautiful African artifacts are well worth a visit. Admission is free. The

museum is open Thursday through Saturday. (See our Attractions chapter.)

History Museum of Western Virginia $
Center in the Square, Levels 1 and 3
1 Market Square, Roanoke
(540) 342-5770
www.history-museum.org
This permanent exhibit offers the history of the area, emphasizing the railroad, which launched the city as a crossroads of transportation. Children enjoy seeing the miniature general store of yesteryear and an exhibit of vintage clothing. Special exhibits might range from D-Day to Elvis Presley's birthday. There's 15,000 years of history in 5,000 square feet of space. A gift shop on the ground level offers a treasure of books that are wonderful keepsakes. (See our Attractions chapter.)

Mill Mountain Theatre $$$-$$$$
Center in the Square,
1 Market Square, Roanoke
(540) 342-5740, (800) 317-6455
www.millmountain.org
Mill Mountain Theatre is a live, professional theater that operates all year on two stages. It's nationally known for its high-quality dramas, musicals, comedies, and regional premieres. Some performances are signed for the hearing-impaired and audio described for the sight-impaired. It's wheelchair accessible. The theater also offers theater classes for students as well as adults. Mill Mountain Players, a professional touring troupe, travels to schools and other venues throughout Virginia. (See our Arts chapter.) Plays range from $16 to $33.

Mill Mountain Zoo $
3 miles off Blue Ridge Parkway,
Roanoke
(540) 343-3241
www.mmzoo.org
You'll find the zoo right next to the large Mill Mountain Star, a 100-foot-high man-made metal star that glows at night and can be seen from all over the city. The zoo, which opened in 1952 around a children's nursery rhyme theme, has undergone

many changes during its existence. The zoo property was expanded to five acres in 1997 and a new snow leopard exhibit was completed. Each year, about 70,000 people come through to admire the 53 different species. These include four endangered species—tiger, red wolf, snow leopard, and white-naped crane. You can also see snakes and other reptiles, prairie dogs, wolverines, bald eagles, owls, snow monkeys, and red-tailed hawks. There's a nice picnic grounds where you can rest in the shade and eat lunch, a concession stand, and gift shop. Kids will especially love the Zoo Choo, a small train that travels around the park in the spring and summer (cost is about $2.00 to ride). The zoo also has events in the spring, summer, and fall, including the annual Zoodo held in late July, with food, music, and auctions (which you must be 21 to attend). The zoo is open daily all year. (See our Attractions chapter.) Children 2 and younger get in free.

Nuts & Sweet Things
City Market Building, 32 Market Square, Roanoke
(540) 344-3717
This store, in the City Market Building, which has been bustling with activity since 1922, is another place for candy lovers. The large festival marketplace showcases shops, gifts, food, crafts, and special events under a neon-light sculpture. At the center is a culinary arcade where more than a dozen restaurants offer a taste of American and international cuisine, so something is bound to appeal to the younger set. You'll find ice cream, homemade cake, and nuts.

Science Museum of Western Virginia and Hopkins Planetarium $$
Center in the Square, Levels 1, 4, and 5
1 Market Square, Roanoke
(540) 342-5710
www.smwv.org
This museum celebrated its 28th anniversary in 1998. Interactive exhibits ranging from colorful lasers to holograms keep the kids busy, and afterward you can catch

the latest Hopkins Planetarium show. Call ahead for show times. In the Mega Dome Theatre, there are large format films every day. There's an extra $2.00 for the planetarium show and $3.00 for the Mega Dome show. Both the museum and planetarium rate high on every child's list of what's fun to do in Roanoke. (See our Attractions chapter.)

To the Rescue National Museum $
Tanglewood Mall, 4428 Electric Road, Roanoke
(540) 776-0364
www.totherescuemuseum.org
This is the official national museum of the lifesaving movement. Here, children can fulfill all their emergency and rescue fantasies with interactive exhibits, a simulated car wreck, and documentary footage. Don't miss this gem in the city that gave birth to the volunteer rescue squad movement. The museum is open Tuesday through Saturday. (See our Attractions chapter.)

Virginia Museum of Transportation $$
303 Norfolk Avenue, Roanoke
(540) 342-5670
www.vmt.org
In this restored freight station is where Roanoke proudly displays its railroad heritage. Here the kids will find history larger than life as they stand beside steam engines and vintage locomotives. They can climb aboard a caboose or stroll through a railway post office car and the largest rolling stock collection in the East. A true delight is the gift shop, which is stocked with every child's dreams. The museum also added the Star Station, a new outdoor playground for the young ones. The museum is open daily. (See our Attractions chapter.)

Remember your camera when planning outings with kids. Their wide-eyed expressions are priceless, especially if you're going to a farm or horse show.

Virginia's Explore Park $-$$
Milepost 115, Blue Ridge Parkway
Roanoke
(540) 427-1800
www.explorepark.org
This park on the Blue Ridge Parkway provides a wonderful opportunity for children to explore the lives of inhabitants of the Roanoke Valley during the 17th, 18th, and 19th centuries. The park, which celebrated its 10th birthday on July 2, 2004, is a popular site for schoolchildren. Start with the Arthur Taubman Welcome Center for some background history, then begin your journey along the Salem Turnpike at the Totero Village, where culture, skills, and techniques used by American Indians before and during the first European contact in the Roanoke Valley are demonstrated. The "ati" houses are Totero-style dwellings based on archaeological remains from a site in nearby Roanoke County. Visitors also may explore a garden, where historically appropriate crops are harvested, and a dugout canoe construction area. Continuing along the Salem Turnpike, you will encounter Scots-Irish settlers at a 1750s frontier fort, where they struggle to provide for their families and protect their homes from the increasing danger of attack from French and Indian forces. Entering the 19th century, you can visit with a blacksmith as he forges iron at his shop, the miller as he grinds corn at Slone's Grist Mill, and the batteauman as he make repairs to his large, flat-bottomed river boat on the banks of the Roanoke River. (A batteau, by the way, was poled down the river to carry cargo and crops.) Domestic and farm life can be explored at Hofauger House, where meals are prepared over a hearth using vegetables and herbs harvested from the garden. It's also a good time to relax and listen to dulcimer music. The Hofauger House, Wray Barn, Houtz Barn, Kemp's Ford School, and Slone's Grist Mill are all historic structures that were relocated from the Roanoke area and constructed at the park. If you have time, you might want to check out the Brugh Tavern for a bite to eat. Explore Park is open on weekends in April and Wednes-day through Sunday from May through October.

EAST OF THE BLUE RIDGE
Loudoun County

Balloons Unlimited $$$$
2946 Chainbridge Road, Oakton
(540) 554-2002, (703) 281-2300
www.balloonsunlimited.com
The more adventurous children may enjoy a hot-air balloon ride, a great way to see the area around Loudoun County. Balloons are launched twice a day—around sunrise and late evening—from April through November. The hour-long ride costs $165; children younger than 12 pay half price.

Leesburg Animal Park $-$$
19270 James Monroe Highway, Leesburg
(703) 433-0002
www.leesburganimalpark.com
Spend some time with animals from around the world at this park that opened in the spring of 2000 but fomerly operated as the Reston Animal Park since 1980. There are many animals here for the kids to pet and feed—donkeys, llamas, goats, deer, sheep, and other exotic and domestic livestock. Stare in fascination at the Aldabra tortoises, ring-tailed lemurs, squirrel monkeys, and zebra. Have some fun on a hay ride or watch the wild animal show featuring primates, reptiles, and birds. In the spring you can help bottle-feed the babies and meet the newborn lambs and goats. There's a nice picnic area and a gift shop, as well as snacks and drinks available. The park is open in the summer. The hay ride is $1.00 and pony rides are $2.50. Oh, and here's a great birthday idea—call and schedule your party here with your new furry friends!

Morven Park $-$$
17263 Southern Planter Lane, Leesburg
(703) 777-2414
www.morvenpark.org

Leesburg's magnificent Morven Park (see our Attractions chapter) is the scene of many exciting horse activities, including steeplechases, horse shows, and carriage driving competitions. The carriage museum on the grounds has items of special interest to children, including small sleighs and carts and a marvelous toy carriage collection. In the summer, Morven Park offers a series of children's programs geared toward ages 6 to 10. These one-hour programs include a nature walk tour, where kids can learn to identify plants at Morven Park; visit Morven Park's Winmill Carriage collection to learn about transportation before the era of cars; and a tour of the mansion from a child's perspective—learning about life in the early 20th century.

My Friends & Me
118 South Street SE, Leesburg
(703) 777-8222
www.myfriendsandme.com
Doll and teddy bear collectors take note: If you are shopping in Leesburg's historic downtown, a shop that may be of interest is My Friends & Me. Known for its artist bears series, the shop also sells teddy bears and dolls for collectors of all ages. The shop is open from 11:00 A.M. to 6:00 P.M. Tuesday through Saturday.

Naturalist Center **Free**
741 Miller Drive SE, Suite G-2, Leesburg
(703) 779-9712, (800) 729-7725
Older children will enjoy a visit to the Naturalist Center, a part of the Smithsonian Institution's National Museum of Natural History. Children 10 and older can study natural history using the center's collections, scientific equipment, and books. Children become true scientists under the guidance and direction of the center's staff. A smaller exhibit with some hands-on activities has been set up for younger children, who must wait while older kids use the main study gallery. Take advantage of a part of the Smithsonian in the quiet Virginia countryside. It's open Tuesday through Saturday.

Oatlands Plantation **$–$$**
20850 Oatlands Plantation Lane
Leesburg
(703) 777-3174
www.oatlands.org
Oatlands Plantation, besides being steeped in history (see our Attractions chapter), has some marvelous activities for the children, including steeplechases in mid-May and festive Christmas celebrations. Oatlands is closed January through March.

Washington and Old Dominion
Railroad Regional Park **$**
21293 Smiths Switch Road, Ashburn
(703) 729-0596
www.nvrpa.org
The Washington and Old Dominion Rail Trail runs right through Leesburg and is a delightful place for biking and hiking. This multiuse trail begins at Purcellville and continues east toward Washington, D.C. For information on the trail, call the Northern Virginia Park Authority at (703) 352-5900 or write 5400 Ox Road, Fairfax Station, 22039. For those who didn't bring along a bicycle, call Bicycle Outfitters, (703) 777-6126. You can rent a bike for $5.00 an hour, $25.00 a day, or $75.00 a week.

Fauquier County

C. M. Crockett Park **$**
10066 Rogues Road, Midland
(540) 788-4867
www.fauquiercounty.gov
The C. M. Crockett Park—a 200-acre park with a 109-acre lake—offers a wide range of activities, from boat rentals, hiking, and fishing to special events on weekends at the park's Waterside Amphitheater, including magic shows and bands. Open from 7:00 A.M. until dusk, the park has five picnic shelters, plus areas to play volleyball or pitch horseshoes. Special events include a children's festival in October and Earth Fest in April. An entrance fee of $6.00 is charged on the weekends for nonresident vehicles.

Dominion Skating Center $
1550 North Main Street, Culpeper
(540) 825-3141
Ever wonder what your parents did for fun when they were young? Well, slip on a pair of roller skates and slide back in time. You can glide across the pecan hardwood floors at this 28-year-old skating rink. It's open from 7:00 to 9:00 P.M. Wednesday, and 7:30 to 11:00 P.M. Friday and Saturday. A good time for family fun is during the 2:00 to 4:00 P.M. sessions on Saturday and Sunday. Afternoon admission is $3.00, and if you don't bring your own skates, you can rent a pair for $1.00. At night the entry fee is $5.00. If you work up an appetite, don't worry: The snack bar offers pizza, hot dogs, chips, drinks, and ice cream.

Flying Circus Aerodome $$
Highway 644, Bealeton
(540) 439-8661
www.flyingcircusairshow.com
The Flying Circus, south of Warrenton, puts on a different air show every Sunday from May through October (see our Annual Events and Festivals chapter). These are precision aerobatics airshows complete with wing walking and skydiving. Rides are available at the shows, which feature antique open cockpit biplanes. The park has a concession stand and picnic grounds. The gates open at 11:00 A.M., with the shows beginning at 2:30 P.M. Admission is $10.00, $3.00 if you are between the ages of 3 and 12. The circus is right off U.S. Highway 17. Just follow the signs.

Marriott Ranch $$$$
5305 Marriott Lane, Hume
(540) 364-3741
www.marriottranch.com
Saddle up for a Western trail ride at the Marriott Ranch. Every day but Monday, you can take a guided trail ride of the farm's 4,200-acre Texas longhorn cattle operation. (See our Recreation chapter.) Reservations are required, and the minimum riding age is 10.

Sky Meadows State Park $
11012 Edmonds Lane, Delaplane
(540) 592-3556
www.dcr.state.va.us
Just west of Middleburg, Sky Meadows State Park offers camping, horse trails, picnic areas, fishing, and eight hiking trails, including a 3.6-mile stretch of the Appalachian Trail (see our Recreation chapter). There are even guided horseback trail rides on Saturday and Sunday. The 1,863-acre park is open daily 8:00 A.M. to dusk, and entrance fees are required. From April through October, the parking fee is $3.00 weekdays and $4.00 on weekends. If you would like to stay overnight, the camping fee is $9.00.

Warrenton Pony Show
U.S. Highway 29 Business, Warrenton
(540) 347-2675
Fauquier County is the hotbed of horse country with countless steeplechases and horse shows including the marvelous Warrenton Pony Show in late June (see our Horse Country chapter for specifics). The pony show is run completely by juniors with adult supervision. Admission is free.

Madison County

Graves Mountain Lodge
Off Highway 670, Syria
(540) 923-4231
www.gravesmountain.com
If the family gets hungry, stop in at Graves Mountain Lodge, just a mile away, for a magnificent country spread. The lodge is so popular, it's probably best to call ahead for reservations (see our Restaurants chapter). Graves Mountain Lodge also offers horseback riding, swimming, and hiking. You also can get grain from a dispensing machine to feed the farm animals. Horseback riding costs $25 an hour, and you must be 8 years old and 54 inches tall.

Albemarle County

AMF Kegler's $
2000 Seminole Trail, Charlottesville
(434) 978-3999
www.amf.keglerlane.com
Just down US 29 is AMF Kegler's, where bowling and an arcade should entertain all. Bowling is $5.00 an hour. They also have pool tables. A restaurant, lounge, and nursery on-site make this a fun family outing. Kegler's is open from 10:00 A.M. to midnight Sunday through Thursday, 10:00 A.M. to 2:00 A.M. Friday and Saturday.

Ash Lawn-Highland $$
Highway 95, Charlottesville
(434) 293-9539
www.avenue.org/ashlawn
Tour the home of President James Monroe or try to drop by when there's a special event (see our Annual Events and Festivals chapter). Children of all ages can come fly their kites and participate in contests during Kite Day at Ash Lawn, an early May occasion. If you are visiting in the summer, check out the music, puppetry, and drama for children at 11:00 A.M. Saturday from July to mid-August. Call (434) 293-4500 for admission to the outdoor Summer Saturday series. Don't forget to take along a picnic, and watch for the colorful peacocks. They roam all around the grounds.

Balloon Adventures $$$$
Boars Head Inn & Sports Club
US 250 W, Charlottesville
(800) 932-0152, (434) 971-1757
www.2comefly.com
Take flight in one of the largest passenger balloons in America—11 stories tall! Chief Pilot Rick Behr, a licensed commercial balloon pilot with more than 4,000 hours of experience, will fly you over scenic Charlottesville and surrounding green fields and woodlands of Albemarle County. Flights are every day at sunrise March 1 through December 1. Trips average an hour. Reservations are recommended, especially for weekends. Rates are $175 per person.

Charlottesville Fun Park
3350 Berkmar Drive, Charlottesville
(434) 975-4386
www.cvillefunpark.com
For more physical recreation, the Fun Park just off US 29 provides plenty of action. The park has go-karts, batting cages, miniature golf, an arcade, concessions, and a soft play center for younger kids. The park is open daily from 11:00 A.M. to 9:00 P.M. with extended hours on Friday and Saturday. Prices vary for individual activities. Go-karts—you must be 12 or older and stand 60 inches tall to ride alone—are $5.50. To get a little batting practice, you can take 15 swings for $1.50. Miniature golf rates are $5.00. Soft play, $5.00 for unlimited time, is only for children younger than 10. And quarters will get you tokens for the arcade games. Whew, that should keep you busy.

Charlottesville Ice Park $-$$
230 West Main Street, Charlottesville
(434) 817-2400
www.icepark.com
On the Charlottesville's Downtown Mall is the Charlottesville Ice Park (see our Recreation chapter). This indoor ice-skating rink—yes, you can skate year-round—rents skates and offers ice skating and hockey lessons. It's a newly renovated building, and your family should enjoy the unique experience ice skating on even the hottest days. Public skating times vary, so be sure to call ahead. You might even make it to one of the pickup hockey hours. Prices average about $3.00 to $7.50.

The Comic, Game, and Hobby Place
218 A. West Main Street, Charlottesville
(434) 984-1040
www.gamebit.com
Come in, sit down, and play. That's the kind of store you'll find on Charlottesville's Historic Downtown Mall. The shop more than doubled its size when it moved next

door to the ice park. There is also open miniature gaming every Saturday. Not counting the chess sets, you can buy games ranging in price from $2.00 to $200.00.

Community Children's Theatre $$
Charlottesville
(434) 961-7862
www.avenue.org/cct
Charlottesville has another organization that brings stage entertainment to kids. Around since 1953, the Community Children's Theatre arranges for professional shows to come to the Martin Luther King Jr. Performing Arts Center of Charlottesville and to the Piedmont Virginia Community College for one-night performances (see our Arts chapter). The Family Series brings in four professional stage productions a year, mostly geared for kids ages 3 to 11 and their families. The Sunday Series includes performances by musicians, dancers, and actors. Now a yearly tradition, the Missoula Children's Theatre drops by for a weeklong residency to work with children in kindergarten through 12th grade. The shows, which have included *Swiss Family Robinson* and *Roller-skate Express,* are well done and worth the effort.

James River Reeling and Rafting $$$
Main and Ferry Streets, Scottsville
(434) 286-4FUN
www.reelingandrafting.com
Just south of Charlottesville in Scottsville, the whole family can drift down the James River on a tube or try a faster pace in a canoe, kayak, or raft. James River Reeling and Rafting can outfit the whole family. Tubing costs $15.00, and you can rent a cooler tube for your picnic basket and beverages for another $5.00. Canoe trips range from the $35.00 4-mile float to the $86.00 overnight trip. (Find out more in the Recreation chapter.)

James River Runners Inc. $$$
10082 Hatton Ferry Road, Scottsville
(434) 286-2338
www.jamesriver.com

The scenery is exquisite and the experience of floating down the James River is truly relaxing. Just let the current carry your inner tube. The cost is $15.00, $6.00 for a cooler tube. Canoe rides are $18.50 per person or $37.00 per canoe. Overnight adventures cost $50.50 per person or $102.00 per canoe. James River Runners also has kayaks, ranging from $23.50 to $67.00, and four- and five-man rafts for $18.50 per person. (See our Recreation chapter for information.)

Monticello $$$
Highway 53, Charlottesville
(434) 984-9800
www.monticello.org
Charlottesville is steeped in history, and many children will enjoy the "old-fashioned" houses and odd furnishings of landmarks such as Monticello. The home of President Thomas Jefferson is open daily for tours (see our Attractions chapter). And be sure to ask why Jefferson cut a hole in the floor for his clock.

Old Michie Theatre $$-$
221 East Water, Charlottesville
(434) 977-3690
www.oldmichie.com
Just off the mall, the Old Michie Theatre entertains families with puppet shows and main-stage productions. Husband-and-wife team Frances Furlong and Steven Riesenman work hard to give children quality entertainment in a relaxed atmosphere. The puppet shows—held on Saturday—may range from *Johnny Appleseed* featuring marionettes from Czechoslovakia to the popular *Little Red Riding Hood.* They also teach drama classes for different ages and levels of interest. They even keep puppets in the lobby for young ones who can't sit still during performances. (See our Arts chapter.)

Panorama Trails $$
750 Miller's Cottage Lane, Earlysville
(434) 974-7849
www.panoramatrails.com
A novelty, really—a private farm that has

been opened up solely for mountain biking. Bring your kids and yourself for a fun day of riding through the woods and over wide-open meadows with a panoramic backdrop of the Blue Ridge Mountains, all right outside of Charlottesville. The farm provides more than 30 miles of single-track trails that traverse over 850 acres. There are some trails for beginners, but primarily this is for the intermediate and advanced riders, as it is all off-road and involves hills, rocks, roots, creek crossings, and clambering over logs. Purchase a day permit at several regional locations, including Extreme Sports, Blue Wheel Bikes, Downtown Athletic Store, and Blue Ridge Mountain Sports, all in Charlottesville, as well as the Bike Stop in Culpeper. While there, pick up a copy of the trail map. You can ride daily from mid-January to October 1, and the rest of the year, only on Sunday, Wednesday, and Thursday. To find Panorama Trails, take US 29 north of Charlottesville, turn west on Rio Road (Highway 631) and west on Earlysville Road (Highway 743) at the Rock Store. Go 2 miles and turn west on Panorama Road (Highway 844). The road dead-ends at the farm, so follow the driveway to the first drive on the right and park in the field across from the trailhead sign.

Soda Fountain at Timberlake's Drugstore
322 East Main Street, Charlottesville
(434) 296-1191
Step up to the soda fountain and order an old-fashioned milkshake. They come in vanilla, chocolate, strawberry, and cherry—regular or extra thick. This spot has been a Charlottesville tradition since the 1890s. You can treat yourself to a sundae, banana split, float, or cone or, if you're in the mood, try something from the deli menu, including homemade desserts. Since it's a drugstore, your parents can even get a prescription filled or drop off vacation film to be developed. The Fountain is open from 8:30 A.M. to 5:00 P.M. Monday through Friday and from 9:00 A.M. to 5:00 P.M. Saturday.

Splathouse $$$$
946 Grady Avenue, Suite 8, Charlottesville
(434) 977-5287
www.splathousepaintball.com
Here's something you might think is kinda insane, but your kids will jump at the chance to shoot each other with paint! The Splathouse touts itself as the East Coast's premier indoor paintball arena. The indoor course has a large maze of warehouse-size rooms, complete with 21,000 square feet of props, giving it the "urban decay" atmosphere. The rooms are connected by passageways. A three-hour session is $35 per player, which buys you 200 paint balls and equipment. Call ahead to reserve a session—available evenings and weekends—with a minimum of 10 players. Friday night is open game night, where you pit yourself against players of all ages and skills. There are also games with evenly matched teams and referees to oversee the action. Players must be 10 or older. Check out the Splat Store for your gear Monday, Wednesday, and Friday evenings.

University of Virginia Free-$$$$
Alderman and Massie Streets
Charlottesville
(434) 924-8821
www.virginiasports.com
If your kids are into sports, you've got a smorgasbord of events here (see our Attractions chapter). Athletic events at the University of Virginia run the full gamut from seven home football games to golf and rowing and are exciting outings for children. There are also sports camps for young athletes every summer led by members of UVA's coaching staff.

Virginia Discovery Museum $
524 East Main Street, Charlottesville
(434) 977-1025
www.vadm.org
The Downtown Mall in Charlottesville is a great place for family fun, and the Virginia Discovery Museum is the perfect place to start. Activities include hands-on exhibits, costumes, science programs, and an art room especially for children (see our

Attractions chapter). Hermit crabs have taken up residence in a new touch tank. Special events are held throughout the year, including a fun run for ages 3 to 12 each May. Ask about the log cabin. It is closed Monday.

Nelson County

Waltons Mountain Museum   **$**
Highway 617, Schuyler
(434) 831-2000
www.waltonmuseum.org
Even if your children haven't seen *The Waltons* reruns, they'll enjoy the Waltons Mountain Museum just west of Charlottesville (see our Attractions chapter). This museum is dedicated to Nelson County native Earl Hamner Jr., the creator of the hit TV show, and his wonderful family. The museum, in the school where the Hamners studied, is a grouping of sets from the series, with actual scripts, photos, and memorabilia. Kids can see a documentary video of Hamner and the cast. An anniversary celebration is held here the third weekend in October.

Wintergreen Resort   **$$$$**
Highway 664, Wintergreen
(800) 266-2444
www.wintergreenresort.com
Wintergreen Resort, about 50 minutes from Charlottesville, has loads to do for children—skiing, swimming, horseback riding, hiking, camp programs, craft workshops, canoeing—and plenty for parents as well (see our Resorts chapter). Wintergreen is such a family-oriented place that it was selected by both *Family Circle* and *Better Homes and Gardens* as one of the "Top Family Resorts in the Country." If you're looking for fun stuff to occupy your kids in the summer, you've come to the right place. From day camps where the little ones learn about the wonders of nature to actual campouts and Junior Explorers program, the fun is offered to kids ages 2 to 12. Your youngster can take lessons in

horseback riding, tennis, and golf. The Activities Department is located in the Treehouse and serves as the central point for family and children's activities including craft workshops, books, games, and special events. Talk about family fun, the outdoor pool is open daily mid-June to Labor Day. Or visit 22-acre Lake Monocan at Stoney Creek in the Valley. The lake is staffed daily by a lifeguard in the summer. Besides swimming, you can rent paddleboats, canoes, inner tubes, and fishing equipment. There's even standard road bike rentals, so the whole family can take a leisurely ride on the paved bike trails that wind throughout Stoney Creek. Bike rentals are available weekends in May and September, daily throughout the summer. Now, if you experience the problem of those teens and preteens who complain about nothin' to do in the summer, there's a hot new facility at Wintergreen. Just opened in 2001 is the Out of Bounds Adventure Center. There's paintball, in two-hour games played by teams on the ski slopes, a 25-foot climbing wall that offers beginner to expert routes, and a park for aggressive skaters, BMX riders, and skateboarders. Or you can hop on a K2 mountain bike with full suspension and fly down Wintergreen's 4.5-mile downhill track, a quick trip to the Valley. Don't worry, moms and dads, a helmet is included with the bike rental. There's also technical single-track trails for cross-country riding. Out of Bounds operates from May to October. Children younger than age 13 must be accompanied by an adult. Purchase an all-day pass for $49, or a season park pass for $120 (with equipment rental, the pass is $180).

Lynchburg

Lynchburg is the major metropolitan city in this part of the Blue Ridge, and history and shopping beckon in many forms for the children to have an enjoyable day.

**Pest House Medical Museum
and Confederate Cemetery** $
Old City Cemetery, Fourth and Taylor
Streets, Lynchburg
(434) 847-1465
www.gravegarden.org
Here children can take a tour of Dr. John
Jay Terrell's medical office with its 1860s
hypodermic needles and primitive medical
instruments. The amputating blades used
on Civil War soldiers always attract grave
attention and bring the war down to a
more human level that kids don't always
get from a textbook. While here you also
can see Victorian Mourning Museum,
Hearse House and Caretakers Museum,
and Station House Museum. Self-guided
tours are free, but guided tours with costumed guides cost $4.00, $2.00 for children. (See our Civil War and Attractions
chapters.)

Point of Honor $
112 Cabell Street, Lynchburg
(434) 847-1459
www.pointofhonor.org
This restored home of Dr. George Cabell
gives a slice of 19th-century life. Cabell
was the personal physican to patriot
Patrick Henry. The mansion was built in
1815 on a majestic location, commanding
an impressive view of the James River.
Children are fascinated to hear that the
name comes from the gun duels fought
on its lawn! The home is open daily.

**Red Hill: The Patrick Henry
National Memorial** $-$$
1250 Red Hill Road, Brookneal
(434) 376-2044
www.redhill.org
Most children have heard Patrick Henry's
"Liberty or Death!" speech of 1775, so a
visit to Red Hill is in order. Henry was Virginia's first governor after the commonwealth declared independence from Great
Britain. He served as governor of Virginia
from 1776 to 1779 and from 1784 to 1786.
Red Hill was home to Henry and eight of
his 17 children. Visitors can see the last

home and burial place of Patrick Henry—
including the original law office, kitchen,
and garden—as they were before his
death.

Thomas Jefferson's Poplar Forest $$
Highway 661, Forest
(434) 525-1806
www.poplarforest.org
This is Thomas Jefferson's retreat home. It
is being renovated and offers indoor and
outdoor views of painstaking historical
restoration through ongoing archaeologi-
cal digs. Kids are always fascinated with
Jefferson's solidly designed outdoor brick
privies. It is closed on Tuesday. (See our
Attractions chapter.)

Smith Mountain Lake

Bridgewater Plaza
Highway 122 at Hales Ford Bridge
Moneta
(800) 488-4516
www.parrotcove.com
Hales Ford Bridge is the center of life at
Smith Mountain Lake. At Parrot Cove or
Bridgewater Marina, you can rent pon-
toons and Jet Skis. Your family can even
rent a 51-foot-long houseboat at Parrot
Cove. Call ahead to reserve so you won't
be disappointed. They're not cheap; Jet
Ski rentals go for $200 an hour! If you
want to go fishing, look up some good
guides, such as Bob King, in the "Fishing"
section of our Recreation chapter. Fishing
licenses are available.
    You can call the Smith Mountain Lake
Chamber/Partnership at (540) 721-1203 to
learn the names of other guides. Although
you can do some impromptu lake expedi-
tions in your rented boat, you may want an
expert to show you where the action is.
The Plaza is home to the Smith Mountain
Lake Visitor Center, so stop in with your
questions or call (800) 676-8203. If it's
rainy, Bridgewater Plaza has a terrific
arcade with nearly 50 different video and
skill games offering tickets for prizes. The

ice cream parlor is right next door, and you can eat your treat either sitting on the deck on a pretty day or inside if the mercury is rising. There are several nice gift shops for browsing.

**Fun-N-Games Family
Entertainment Center $
Bridgewater Plaza, Hales Ford Bridge,
Moneta
(540) 721-5959**
This video arcade in a large complex will keep your kids busy. It has 50 video games and has been attracting both children and grown-ups for 12 years. You can save tickets and win prizes here. The arcade is open daily. If it's a particularly pleasant day, you can play 18 holes next door at Harbortown Miniature Golf. The course is elevated over the lake and provides a terrific view.

**Smith Mountain Lake State Park $
Off Highway 626 S
(540) 297-6066
www.dcr.state.va.us**
You won't be disappointed at this park. Relatively new, the beach is beautifully situated looking at the mountains, and a nearby campground and Turtle Island make an enchanting voyage from the beach for the little ones. Parking fee is $4.00 on weekends, $3.00 on weekdays.

Bedford County

**Bedford City/County Museum   Free
201 East Main Street, Bedford
(540) 586-4520
www.ci.bedford.va.us**
Children can soak up history effortlessly at the Bedford City/County Museum with its Civil War artifacts and other well-displayed items. Bedford is about 20 miles from the park at the lake. Open Monday through Saturday, donations are requested. (See our Civil War and Attractions chapters.)

**Elks National Home   Free
931 Ashland Avenue, Bedford
(540) 586-8232
www.elkshome.org**
At Christmas, one of the biggest displays of lights in the United States is showcased here at the Elks National Home. The retired Elks work on the exhibit all year, and it shows come December. There is no charge. (See our Attractions chapter.)

Franklin County

**Booker T. Washington National
Monument   Free
Highway 122, Hardy
(540) 721-2094
www.nps.gov/bowa/home.htm**
This place is centered around the famous educator's birthplace. The video on how a 9-year-old rose above slavery to become one of the most inspirational leaders of his time will fascinate everyone. The film addresses Washington's hard life and meager existence and is a historic sojourn into a time in America when slavery was a way of life. The site also has a beautiful restored farm—with lots of farmyard animals contained with split-rail fences—that will uplift you after viewing Washington's triumph over hardship. There is no charge. Two special events are held here each year: Juneteenth in the summer and the Christmas programs the first Friday and Saturday in December.

**Blue Ridge Folklife Festival $$
Ferrum College, Ferrum
(540) 365-4416
www.blueridgeinstitute.org**
At this festival, children can play games from the 1800s, see workhorses bigger than trucks, and eat fare such as funnel cakes with original recipes. It's wonderful, wholesome fun for the entire family, and even city kids are in awe when they leave. It is always the fourth Saturday in October.

Blue Ridge Institute Museum $
Ferrum College, Ferrum
(540) 365-4416
www.blueridgeinstitute.org
Here you can find an 1800 German-
American working farmstead with log
house, outdoor oven, outbuildings, pasture, and garden that demonstrates the
lifestyles of early colonists. Also visit the
Blue Ridge Institute with its many exhibits
and archives, which are internationally recognized for excellence. Exhibits have
included toys, walking sticks, canes, and
quilts. (See our Attractions chapter.)

NEW RIVER VALLEY

Blacksburg and Radford

Blacksburg Aquatic Center $
625 Patrick Henry Drive, Blacksburg
(540) 961-1852
www.blacksburg.gov
Here's another very nice pool in the heart
of Blacksburg. Not only can the kids
splash out some of that extra energy, but
you can relax in the sauna and hot tub.
The community center is located across
the street and has a basketball court and
weights. The pool is open daily during the
summer.

Radford Bisset Park Pool $
Main Street, Radford
(540) 731-3633
www.radford.va.us
If you're thinking about going swimming,
the city pool at Radford, home to Radford
University, is one of the nicest in the Blue
Ridge. The pool is open daily Memorial
Day to Labor Day. The park is located
beside the scenic New River and is a joy
for children and a peaceful backdrop for
adults to enjoy.

Virginia Tech   Free
Blacksburg
(540) 231-5396
www.vt.edu
The New River Valley is synonymous with
Virginia Tech, the state's largest land-grant
university. It's a 45-minute drive down I-81
from Roanoke. Tech in itself is the major
attraction in Blacksburg and one the children will enjoy touring. City children will
enjoy the perfect farm animals and agricultural experimental stations that raise
extraordinary farm livestock and hybrid
crops, the likes of which you won't see
anywhere else.
   The most popular spot at Tech is the
Duck Pond. Small children are enchanted
by the pampered fowl who lord over the
spot and hold court for visitors. Brazen at
times, they've no qualms about coming to
the kids to get a snack. These ducks are
definitely more intelligent than most and
definitely more aggressive! Bring your own
food if you would like to feed them.
   For kids who like to bike, Blacksburg
has some of the nicest bike trails in the
nation, so bring your bikes.

Giles County

Cascades Recreational Area $
Off Highway 623, Pembroke
(540) 265-5100
One of the biggest attractions in western
Virginia can be found right outside of
Blacksburg, 20 minutes from U.S. Highway
460, at this beautiful recreation area. College students and people from all over the
nation come to hike the trail to the fabulous Cascades waterfall. It's recommended
for children who can hike 4 miles and is
no—we repeat, no—fun for small ones.
Plan on keeping your eye on adventurous
children of all ages to prevent falls off the
waterfall. Parking fee is $2.00. (See our
Recreation chapter.)

Pulaski County

Claytor Lake State Park   **$**
Off I-81 at exit 101
(540) 643-2500
www.dcr.state.va.us
This lake south of Radford is a man-made body of water lined with clean, white sandy beaches, boat rentals, and a beautiful campground. It's a good base for sightseeing throughout the Valley. A concession stand is a good place to refuel after swimming. The fee to swim varies, but it will cost $4.00 to park.

Wythe County

Historic Millwald Theatre   **$$**
Main Street, Wytheville
(276) 228-5031
www.millwald.com
You can watch the latest movies in Virginia's oldest motion picture theater in continuous operation. This grand old building showed its first film in August 1928 and it's still going strong. During the summer Millwald hosts two shows nightly, with a 2:00 P.M. matinee on Sunday. From September to May, you can catch a 7:30 P.M. movie Sunday through Thursday. There are still two shows each on Friday and Saturday. The price is pretty reasonable. It's just around $3.50 for the young ones, about $6.00 for Mom or Dad.

Alleghany Highlands

The Homestead   **$$$$**
Highway 220, Hot Springs
(800) 838-1766
www.thehomestead.com
At the Homestead, children can join the resort's KidsClub, providing lots of fun every day, year-round. The programs are designed for children ages 3 to 12.

There's the literary center, where children can enjoy a large library of folklore and tall tales, or the stories of the resident storyteller, or enjoy a guest writer who visits and reads passages of his or her work. Or kids can enjoy the art and design center, where they will make everything from bird feeders and wreaths to jewelry, baskets, and T-shirts. Kids can also learn to weave, make masks, design label pins, and create treasure boxes. The Kidsclub is located in the Clubhouse on Cottage Row. There are half-day and full-day options available. The full-day price is $60, with lunch for the first child. There are many other attractions at the Homestead, including shops and restaurants. They can choose from a smorgasbord of fun outdoor activities as well. Visit the stable of 50 horses and enjoy a trail ride through the forest. Sign 'em up for a private tennis lesson or a clinic in-season. In need of fresh air and exercise? Take to the extensive grounds by hiking or biking the 100 miles of trails that wind over the 15,000 acres of the Homestead's property. Swimming options are many, with the famous indoor pool fed by natural streams, as well as the outdoor pool that is open in the summer. A new outdoor pool along with a children's pool with a fountain opened in the summer of 2001. Speaking of water, the Homestead in 2002 came up with an unusual set of spa programs—ones designed specifically for children younger than 16, to help kids become aware of the importance of health and wellness. Offerings include a kid's massage, a teen facial, a makeup session to learn the right way to apply makeup, and a pedicure involving a chocolate milk bath and manicure with strawberries and cream. Kids can also get coiffed in style by learning how to do a French twist or elegant updo, or receive a haircut.

The kids will have no problem being entertained no matter what they do. (See our Resorts chapter.)

THE ARTS

W hew! For a relatively sparsely populated region, the Blue Ridge of Virginia offers abundant and diverse opportunities for arts and cultural experiences. Listing the best and brightest is a difficult task, since they're all backed by energetic people who believe strongly in the causes they promote.

Fine arts, folk art, history, and pop culture blend well in these Blue Ridge counties. According to a recent study by Don Messmer and Roy Pearson, two professors at the College of William and Mary, the arts, humanities, and cultural institutions in Virginia represent a billion-dollar industry and are a major draw for tourism and economic development. And from the artistic endeavors along the Blue Ridge, it looks like that figure will continue to grow. Shenandoah Shakespeare has brought fans and journalists from across the country and beyond to the growing theatrical mecca in Staunton. When the much-honored theater company moved to town, the troupe built its own theater, Blackfriars Playhouse, the only exact reproduction of Shakespeare's famed stage in the world. Staunton theatergoers also have hopes of turning the old Dixie Theatre into a performing arts center, but it isn't alone in its efforts to save old movie palaces. The folks in Roanoke are raising funds to get the reels turning once again in the Grandin Movie Theatre, while Charlottesville had a grand reopening in 2004 of its famous Paramount Theater with a gala concert headlined by Tony Bennett. Speaking of expansion, three groups in Charlottesville have joined forces in an effort to build City Center for Contemporary Arts.

If music is your leisure choice, try Friday night flat-footing at Floyd Country General Store where fiddles, autoharps, and a 1940 jukebox hold forth. Or you can attend chamber music fests at Garth Newel Music Center in Bath County, where you'll probably rub elbows with jet-setters who patronize the Homestead Resort.

Theater opportunities range from movies to live performances. Worldly chic Charlottesville, home to numerous movie stars and directors, hosts the biggest names in the movie business during its annual Virginia Film Festival. More than 20,000 people show up to view film classics and hobnob with celebrities, who usually attend the opening gala.

No matter how small, nearly every community in the Blue Ridge has its own performing theater group, some comprised of as few as a dozen people, as in sparsely populated Giles County. In small-town Lexington, Lime Kiln Theater enjoys a national reputation for its open-air plays and musical performances in a magical setting. Middlebrook residents Robin and Linda Williams of public radio's *A Prairie Home Companion* with Garrison Keillor are regulars. Middletown's Wayside Theater, just south of Winchester, attracts patrons from Washington, D.C., to its summer performances, which often include big-name actors who love the area.

Museum buffs will find a surprising range and quality of offerings in the Blue Ridge. The works of world-famous artist P. Buckley Moss, "the people's artist," whose annual revenues have been estimated well into the millions, can be seen in her private retreat and museum at Waynesboro.

Not to be underestimated for the role they play in the region's arts and culture are the diverse programs underwritten by colleges and universities. The contributions of academic giants such as Virginia Tech in Blacksburg, Shenandoah University in Winchester, and the University of Virginia in Charlottesville are immeasurable.

The largest colony of artists-in-residence in the country, the Virginia

Center for the Creative Arts (affiliated with Sweet Briar College), is in the remote foothills of the Blue Ridge in Amherst County. And tiny Ferrum College in Franklin County is the nation's most important repository of Blue Ridge culture through its Blue Ridge Institute.

Enjoy making your choices from the attractions listed. Hours and prices may change, so be sure to call ahead.

SHENANDOAH VALLEY

Frederick County

THEATER

Shenandoah Summer Music Theatre
Shenandoah University
1460 University Drive, Winchester
(540) 665-4569, (877) 580-8025
www.su.edu/conservatory
Student actors, singers, and dancers perform four lively musicals June through August, Wednesday through Sunday, at the university. The recent playbill ranged from *Seussical* to *Carousel*. Tickets for individual performances are $23. A subscription to all four shows is $78 for Friday and Saturday nights, $75 for other nights and matinees, with discounts for seniors and children for matinees only.

Shenandoah University's Ohrstrom–Bryant Theatre
1460 University Drive, Winchester
(540) 665-4613, (540) 678-44327
www.su.edu
If you want to see the stars of tomorrow, check out the talent at this university. The Shenandoah Conservatory, the oldest of Shenandoah University's six schools, has audition requirements just to get in its competitive degree programs. In fact, it awards more than 64 degrees at the undergraduate, master's, and doctorate levels. Locals have reaped the rewards. The Shenandoah Theatre stages plays from October through April. Recent productions have included *Inherit the Wind*

and *Smokey Joe's Cafe,* along with children's theater productions. Strong voices and strong music have been a trademark of this university since its early days. Its music department includes the Conservatory Choir, Cantus Singers, Shenandoah Chorus, Music Theatre Ensemble, and Shenandoah Opera Chorus, to name a few. There are even dance recitals, too. Many of the concerts are free, while the theatrical productions are generally in the $12 range. The Conservatory Choir and Chamber Choir perform regularly at the Kennedy Center in D.C.

Wayside Theatre
7853 Main Street, Middletown
(540) 869-1776
www.waysidetheatre.org
The second-oldest professional theater in the state brings the best of Broadway to the valley. The company's professional actors from New York and around the country perform comedies, dramas, musicals, and mysteries in an intimate downtown theater. Among the recent productions were *Blithe Spirit* and *A Closer Walk with Patsy Cline*. Wayside stages a Christmas play every winter. The theater is in the middle of this little town, which you'll find by taking exit 302 from Interstate 81.

Tickets range from $20 to $26. Children 17 and younger pay $10. The theater is wheelchair accessible.

Warren County

Blue Ridge Arts Council Inc.
305 East Main Street, Front Royal
(540) 635-9909
www.blueridgearts.org
If you are looking for entertainment opportunities in the Warren County area, the Blue Ridge Council can point you in the right direction. Founded in 1987, the Council serves Warren, Rappahannock, Frederick, Clark, Fauquier, and Shenandoah Counties. This not-for-profit corporation's goal is to strengthen the

involvement in the visual and performing arts. It even sponsors several events throughout the year, including a summer concert series at the Front Royal/Warren County Amphitheater. You can catch these free outdoor shows on Sunday and Friday evenings. If you prefer a brush with the visual arts, there also are monthly exhibitions in the gallery.

Shenandoah and Page Counties

VISUAL ARTS

Art Studio Pottery
346 Endless Caverns Road, New Market
(540) 896-4400
www.artstudiopottery.com
You get great views inside and out at this studio overlooking the Blue Ridge Mountains and Shenandoah Valley. Artist Joan Cordner and other potters from the area feature their work in the studio in a picturesque log house. You are welcome to tour the studio and even watch the artist at work. The artwork on display includes stoneware, porcelain, earthenware, and salt-glazed and Raku pottery. The Pottery is open 9:00 A.M. to 6:00 P.M. daily.

MUSIC

Shenandoah Valley Music Festival
221 Shrine Mont Circle, Orkney Springs
(800) 459-3396, (800) 459-3396
www.musicfest.org
This outdoor summer music festival began in 1963 and features symphony pops, classical masterworks, folk, jazz, and Big Band music, all performed on the grounds of Shrine Mont Camp and Conference Center, the former Orkney Springs Hotel, a popular spa and mineral springs resort at the turn of the 20th century. Evening concerts are held on weekends between Memorial Day and Labor Day in a rustic open-air pavilion. Arts and crafts shows featuring regional artisans take place on the hotel's front lawn on select weekends.

Another festival tradition is the old-fashioned ice cream social held next to the pavilion before each concert. Don't worry about your attire. It's casual and relaxed. Admission prices and concert times vary. Tickets ranged from $16.00 to $23.00 for adults. Children's tickets were $8.00. You might want to call in advance, especially if you want seating under the pavilion. The show will go on, rain or shine. Many guests picnic on the grounds before concerts.

Rockingham County

VISUAL ARTS

Cleo Driver Miller Art Gallery
402 East College Street, Kline Campus Center, Bridgewater
(540) 828-5684
The state's first private coeducational senior college—founded in 1880—has a strong background in liberal arts. Its art gallery gives space for students and professional artists with revolving monthly exhibitions. Emory and Henry professor Charles W. Goolsby exhibited his monoprints from Italy recently. Bridgewater also hosts a wonderful series of musical concerts, the Lyceum Series, throughout the school year. Tickets are $10.

Sawhill Gallery
JMU campus, Duke Hall, Harrisonburg
(540) 568-6407
This free gallery exhibits five or six shows of diverse art during the year. The summer exhibition is traditionally geared for children. Sawhill is open seven days a week during the academic year, weekdays only during the summer. Gallery hours are from 10:30 A.M. to 4:30 P.M. Monday through Friday and 1:30 to 4:30 P.M. Saturday and Sunday. While Sawhill displays works of international, national, and regional interest, JMU also has other galleries that cater more to the students. Zirkle House Gallery features work of graduate and undergraduate students. Artwork Gallery and The

Other Gallery exhibit works by freshmen and sophomores, and Madison Gallery is devoted to graphic design.

THEATER

Court Square Theater
61 Graham Street, Harrisonburg
(540) 433-9189
www.courtsquaretheater.com
This renovated, historic building in the heart of downtown Harrisonburg is home to live performances, films, and concerts. When the facility opened in 1998, the Blue Ridge Theatre Festival moved in as the resident professional drama troupe. From May to October the company performs a series of plays. The Blue Ridge Theatre Festival also has staged shows in historical settings in Hungary, Romania, the Czech Republic, Moldavia, and at the Edinburgh Festival in Scotland. The local plays cost just under $15, or dinner-and-theater packages can be arranged with the Calhouns Restaurant and Brewery. Once a month, Court Square Theater hosts a popular music series that has booked 10,000 Maniacs, Leon Russell, and Seldom Scene, to name a few. Concert prices vary but are usually in the $15 to $25 range. The movies—which are more in the line of art-house films such as *Winged Migration*—cost about $5.50.

James Madison University Masterpiece Season Series
JMU campus, Wilson Hall, Harrisonburg
(540) 568-7000, (877) 201-7543
www.jmu.edu/masterpiece
This 22-plus event series features a wide array of shows. JMU faculty and staff put on theater, dance, and music performances. Professionals also come in to do family and encore shows, ranging from the Vienna Boys Choir and the Richmond Ballet to *A Chorus Line* and *Some Like It Hot*. Shows run September through April. Admission varies from $8.00 for the JMU productions to $25.00 for the road companies.

Latimer-Shaeffer Theatre
JMU campus, Harrisonburg
(540) 568-7000
In addition to James Madison theater, music, and dance department shows, this on-campus theater in Duke Hall also holds summer performances. Two children's shows in June and one family show in the summer round out the venue's offerings. Admission ranges from $5.00 to $10.00.

Augusta County

VISUAL ARTS

Artisans Center of Virginia
601 Shenandoah Village Drive
Waynesboro
(540) 946-3294, (877) 508-6069
www.artisanscenterofvirginia.org
If you want to see the best crafters from across the entire state, all you have to do is stop by this gallery. This 3,500-square-foot exhibition space opened in June 2000 to showcase the works of Virginia's finest artisans. Pieces selected must pass a tough juried process, and more than 130 artists are now represented at the Waynesboro facility. Each month, special exhibits highlight the works of individual artists. Pottery, baskets, furniture, sculpture, jewelry, glass, and metal works all are on view at this statewide showplace.

Shenandoah Valley Art Center
600 West Main Street, Waynesboro
(540) 949-7662
www.svacart.com
This nonprofit cultural center has been an all-volunteer organization since 1986. An affiliate of the Virginia Museum of Fine Arts in Richmond, the center provides a forum for artists of all diversities to exhibit their works. Housed in a beautiful old former residence downtown, the center holds art exhibits, music performances, workshops, and classes for children and adults. The galleries are open 10:00 A.M. to 4:00 P.M. Tuesday through Saturday and

2:00 to 4:00 P.M. Sunday. Admission is free.

Staunton-Augusta Art Center
1 Gypsy Hill Park, Staunton
(540) 885-2028
An old pump house at the entrance to the beautiful Gypsy Hill Park in Staunton is headquarters for this art center, an affiliate of the Virginia Museum of Fine Arts. It puts on seven exhibitions a year, displays art by area elementary and high school students every March and April, and exhibits works of local artists throughout the year. In addition, the art center offers classes and workshops for children. The third Saturday every May, the center hosts a huge outdoor art show of works by more than 100 artists. In the fall, the center is converted into an "arts for gifts" shop, where local crafters can display their wares. The center is open from 10:00 A.M. to 5:00 P.M. weekdays and 10:00 A.M. to 2:00 P.M. Saturday. Admission is free.

MUSEUMS

P. Buckley Moss Museum
150 P. Buckley Moss Drive, Waynesboro
(540) 949-6473
www.p-buckley-moss.com
The museum dedicated to this part-time resident of Augusta County resembles many of the large houses built by early-19th-century settlers. Since the early 1960s, Moss has found her inspiration and much of her subject matter in Shenandoah Valley scenery and in the area's Amish and Mennonite people. Although the artist was born in New York, she moved here in the mid-'60s.

Born with what later was diagnosed as dyslexia into a family of high achievers, Moss was ridiculed and taunted as a child for her lack of academic prowess. She hid her childhood sorrow in her painting, and eventually her family recognized her artistic genius. As a result, she now uses her foundation profits, guided by the worldwide Moss Society, to help needy children. Whenever she travels, she makes it a point

All aboard. On the second Friday of each month, Staunton hosts an ArtWalk from 5:00 to 7:00 P.M. If you don't have the stamina to walk about and view the exhibits at the local galleries, board the trolley and let it take you to your destinations. For details, call (540) 885-2323.

to visit pediatric hospital centers to encourage children.

The museum's displays examine the symbolism in her work and her sources. Guided tours are available. The museum and shop are just south of Interstate 64 at the Waynesboro West exit 94. The hours are 10:00 A.M. to 6:00 P.M. Monday through Saturday and 12:30 to 5:30 P.M. Sunday. Admission is free.

THEATER

Fletcher Collins Theatre
Deming Hall, Mary Baldwin College
Staunton
(540) 887-7189
www.academic.mbc.edu/theatre
Every academic year the theater department at this women's college produces five major plays, ranging from musicals by Gilbert and Sullivan to Shakespearean productions and several modern and experimental plays. With the arrival of Shenandoah Shakespeare in Staunton, Mary Baldwin's drama students have a classroom in Blackfriars Playhouse. Students are now offered a master's program on Shakespeare. Call for schedules. Admission prices range from $4.00 to $10.00.

Oak Grove Players
Quick's Mill Road, Verona
(540) 248-5000, (540) 248-5005
www.oakgrovetheater.org
This 50-year-old amateur theater company produces five plays every summer in the middle of a grove of oak trees 2 miles west of Verona. Founded in 1954 by

Fletcher Collins, the retired head of Mary Baldwin College's theater department, Oak Grove Players is one of the oldest amateur outdoor theaters in the country. The company, originally called the Theater Wagon of Virginia, went on the road to stage original and foreign productions in Canada and all across Europe. Today, Oak Grove does a series of local productions on its outdoor stage on Route 612 from June through August. A lot of patrons picnic on the grounds before the plays, which have ranged from *Oklahoma* to *Antigone*. Season tickets cost about $40 and can be purchased by writing to P.O. Box 3040, Staunton VA 24402. The theater on Route 612 also has hosted an annual music festival in August. The Oak Grove Players were the first to perform *The Nerd*, a play by the late Larry Shue, who still has family in Staunton.

P. Buckley Moss is known the world over for her paintings. Twice a year the artist opens up her Waynesboro home to meet her fans and autograph her work. It's a real treat, but be prepared. Moss has a large following, so you might have to wait in line for quite a while. To find out about signings and directions to her home, you can call the P. Buckley Moss Museum at (540) 949-6473.

ShenanArts Inc.
717 Quick's Mill Road, Verona
(540) 248-1868
www.shenanarts.org

ShenanArts is a nonprofit performing arts company that produces a variety of plays and musicals. The arts corporation also offers theater programs for youth, one of which led to a full-blown production of a rock opera, *The Wall*. Along with the Growing Stages productions geared more for young actors and audiences, the company also presents its On Stage series, which includes *Cabaret Nights* and productions

geared more for adults. Some of those works have included *The Elephant Man* and *Grace and Glorie*. Written by Lexington playwright Tom Zeigler, *Grace and Glorie* was staged here first before it went on to Broadway (with Estelle Parsons) and then film (with Gena Rowlands). ShenanArts has been staging its productions in a 250-seat converted IGA store, but plans are in the works to move the company into the old Dixie Theater once it has been renovated into a performing arts center.

Shenandoah Shakespeare
13 West Beverley Street, Staunton
(540) 851-1733, (877) MUCH-ADO
www.shenandoahshakespeare.com

A box or two may be the only props on their stage, just the way Shakespeare did it. A man may be playing a woman's role, just the way they did in the Bard's day. A woman might be playing a man's role . . . OK, women weren't allowed on stage until 1660, but Shenandoah Shakespeare likes to throw in a little fun. It began in 1988 when a troupe of 12 actors dressed in black slacks, black turtlenecks, and black tennis shoes decided to strip away 400 years of accumulated theatrical trappings and focus on the language of the plays. Today, this globe-trotting company of actors has won critical acclaim for their talents and for staging plays the way they were first seen in merry old England. Now they have brought more attention to their company. When the troupe moved its home base to Staunton in 2001, it decided to build quite a home, indeed. Their brand new Blackfriars Playhouse is the world's only exact replica of Shakespeare's long-gone arena. Oh, the company still tours far and wide, but if you are in luck, you will be able to see a top-notch play, by top-notch actors in a top-notch facility. The 2005 playbill includes *The Taming of the Shrew, Measure for Measure, A King and No King, Twelfth Night*, and *She Stoops to Conquer*. Tickets range from $15 to $28. Blackfriars Playhouse also hosts a concert series, which has included Suzy Boggs and George Winston.

Waynesboro Players
722 East Main Street, Waynesboro
(540) 949-8842
www.waynesboroplayers.org
This nonprofit amateur theater made up of actors from Waynesboro, Staunton, Augusta County, and surrounding areas has been around since the 1940s. They perform three plays a year and a musical in the spring at Louis Spilman Auditorium at Waynesboro High School. Tickets range from $9.00 to $10.00.

MUSIC

Jazz in the Park
Gypsy Hill Park, Staunton
(540) 337-6944
www.staunton.va.us/ae/music/jazzpark.htm
In 1988 three local jazz lovers—Phillip Nolley, Lew Morrison, and Lisa Morrison—decided to jazz up Staunton's music scene. They raised funds, made T-shirts, booked bands, ran concession stands, even performed a few concerts themselves. They built it and the fans came. Performers wanted to come. And sponsors soon followed. Today this popular concert series has become a favorite way for locals to spend their Thursday summer evenings. These free outdoor 8:00 P.M. concerts run from July through August and feature some of the best-known jazz performers in the region. The U.S. Air Force Airmen of Note were among the recent bands.

Shakin' at the Station
Johnson Street Parking Lot
(800) 332-5219
It seems almost everyone in Staunton turns out for this outdoor summer concert series. All kinds of bands, from rock 'n' roll to country, perform at a downtown location every Thursday from 6:00 to 8:00 P.M. Most recently Shakin' shook the Johnson Street parking lot near the refurbished train station. The music party runs mid-May through August.

Stonewall Brigade Band
3 Gypsy Hill Park, Staunton
(540) 332-3835
www.stonewallbrigadeband.com
This is reportedly the oldest continuously performing band in the nation. Formed in 1855, the band gave its first public concert before the Civil War. Today local musicians keep the tradition alive with free performances every Monday night at 8:00 P.M. during the summer months. If you went every week, chances are you still wouldn't hear the band's entire repertoire. Playing between 10 and 20 songs each show, the Stonewall Brigade Band performs nearly 150 different songs each season. There is one exception: Each show ends with the National Anthem.

Rockbridge County

VISUAL ARTS

Artists in Cahoots
1 West Washington Street, Lexington
(540) 464-1147
www.artistsincahoots.com
This well-filled gallery is run by a cooperative of local artists and crafters who somehow manage to put out beautiful works of art at reasonable prices. The collection encompasses paintings, prints, etchings, photographs, ceramics, jewelry, decoys, sculpted art glass, wood, and metal crafts. The Treasure Trove contains Sandage jewelry designs; the extraordinary metal and clay sculptures of Milenko Katic; Virginia clay jewelry and Lexington commemorative pottery by Maureen Worth; Margaret Carroll's expanded designs in stained glass; and new works by Joe Wilson, Marsha Heatwole, Bee Zwart, Elizabeth Sauder, and George Makinson. Feather-textured decoys by John Owen complete the array. The artists staff the shop themselves and chat with patrons as they create. The shop gift-wraps for free, ships purchases, and accepts most major credit cards. Founded in 1980, this gallery is open 10:00 A.M. to

5:30 P.M. Monday through Saturday and 11:00 A.M. to 3:00 P.M. most Sundays.

Nelson Fine Arts Gallery
27 West Washington Street, Lexington
(540) 463-9827
www.nelsonfineartsgallery.com
One might expect a scenic view of mountain ranges, even portraits of Civil War heroes. But step inside this new gallery in Lexington and you will find Byzantine-like paintings of religious icons. That's Bill Byers's style. The artist who has a doctorate from Columbia University is just one of eight artists who display their works in this cooperative gallery of local artists. Each month a new artist stages the spotlight. Dorothy Blackwell, Barbara Crawford, Paisley Griffin, Roy Rudasill, Lee Sauder, Jean Marie Trenmel, and Janet Weaver specialize in mostly paintings and sculpture. The gallery is open 11:00 A.M. to 5:00 P.M. every day except Wednesday and Sunday.

THEATER

Lime Kiln Theater
Lime Kiln Road
Box Office, 14 South Randolph Street
Lexington
(540) 463-3074
www.theateratlimekiln.com
The *Roanoke Times* called it "one of the most agreeable spots in the Western World." Performances at the outdoor Theater at Lime Kiln celebrate the history and culture of the southern mountains. What makes the place unique—even enchanting—is its setting in what was once a limestone quarry. After celebrating its 20th anniversary of outdoor plays, Lime Kiln became a year-round production company with the addition of a new space, the Troubadour. This building on the corner of Henry and Main Streets dates back to the turn of the century and was used by Washington and Lee University from 1935 to 1990. Now this historic stage with its 144 traditional theater seats will allow

Lime Kiln a place to hold a winter play season, a winter concert series, and special family events. *Stretch Marks* and *Grace and Glorie* kicked off the 2004 winter season. Plays cost between $15 and $19. Lime Kiln was best known for its annual musical, *Stonewall Country*, a rollicking tribute to local Civil War hero Thomas "Stonewall" Jackson. Robin and Linda Williams, favorites of Garrison Keillor's *A Prairie Home Companion* and longtime friends of Lime Kiln, wrote the music for *Stonewall Country*. Shows also have included *Smoke on the Mountain* and *The Wild Man*.

Lime Kiln's popular outdoor concert series in The Bowl always offers an eclectic slate of musicians. This Sunday-night series features nationally known musicians performing bluegrass to zydeco music. Tickets range from $15 to $25.

Lime Kiln has picnic areas with tables and grills, and vendors sell some food and drinks. The site is wheelchair accessible and has a big-top tent in case of bad weather, so performances take place rain or shine. Group rates are available.

Outdoor plays run Tuesday through Saturday, and concerts are performed on Sunday from Memorial Day through Labor Day. Performances begin at 8:00 P.M. nightly.

MUSIC

Lenfest Center for the Performing Arts
Washington & Lee University, Lexington
(540) 463-8000
www.lenfest.wlu.edu/index
W & L's Lenfest Center is the cultural heart of Lexington, offering lively arts, including national performers in concert, W & L's own University–Rockbridge Symphony Orchestra, and other music department performances. Since 1991 Lenfest has averaged more than 125 performances a year, everything from Rigoletto to Woody Guthrie. The center offers a Concert Guild Series, Theater Series, and Lenfest Series featuring performances to appeal to all artistic tastes.

ROANOKE VALLEY

Roanoke

VISUAL ARTS

Art Museum of Western Virginia
Center in the Square, Levels 1 and 2
One Market Square, Roanoke
(540) 342-5760
www.artmuseum.org
The Art Museum of Western Virginia emphasizes American art of the 19th and 20th centuries. The museum's growing collection of American masterworks includes pieces by John Singer Sargent, Winslow Homer, Childe Hassam, John Henry Twachtman, Frederick Frieseke, Maurice Pendergast, Maria Oakey Dewing, Robert Henri, and Robert Motherwell. Collections include works by Hudson River school of artists and contemporary American painters, printmakers, and photographers. The museum has also acquired a fine Japanese print collection. The museum also collects folk art and decorative arts from the southern mountains. The sculpture court holds impressive pieces. Museum education programs feature lectures, family days, tours, performances, classes, and workshops. Its rotating exhibitions are of regional, national, and international significance. ArtVenture is an interactive art center for the entire family. You can purchase regional and American crafts in the museum store. The museum is open 10:00 A.M. to 5:00 P.M. Tuesday through Saturday and 1:00 to 5:00 P.M. on Sunday.

Arts Council of the Blue Ridge
20 East Church Avenue, Roanoke
(540) 342-5790, (877) SWV-TODO
www.theartscouncil.org
The heart and soul of the cultural community in the Roanoke region, this council provides services and information to its more than 90 member organizations and artists throughout the Blue Ridge region since 1976. Programs include a quarterly newsletter; the City Art Show, a regional

Summer is a great time to see outdoor theater and music productions at unique venues such as Lexington's Lime Kiln Theater and the Ruins at Barboursville, once the estate of Virginia governor James Barbour.

juried art exhibition held annually; Art in the Window, which offers free display space for artists and children; the Perry F. Kendig Award for Outstanding Support of the Arts; the regional High School Art Show; and several after-school programs. The Council published *Arts History Science Zoo: A Shared Cultural View,* a community-wide cultural plan in the region. The Council publishes a regional cultural directory and maintains a kiosk advertising cultural events in downtown Roanoke. Office hours are Tuesday through Friday 9:00 A.M. to 5:00 P.M.

Center in the Square
1 Market Square, Roanoke
(540) 342-5700
www.centerinthesquare.org
This cultural complex in downtown Roanoke is the place to go for arts and entertainment. The primary facility, an award-winning restoration of a former seed and feed warehouse, is located on the Historic Farmers' Market. At Center in the Square, visitors of all ages will enjoy exploring the Art Museum of Western Virginia and the Science Museum of Western Virginia, and taking in an evening or matinee performance at Mill Mountain Theatre.
Around the corner at Center on Church are the offices of the Arts Council of the Blue Ridge, providing resources to artists and information about the arts and cultural events in the region. A few blocks away at the Jefferson Center are two more Center in the Square organizations. Opera Roanoke stages grand operas and concerts, while Roanoke Ballet Theatre, the region's only nonprofit school of dance, also produces several dance concerts each year.

The first Thursday of every month is minicultural fest in Roanoke. From 5:00 to 8:00 P.M., drop by the local art galleries to see new works on display during the free opening receptions. Refreshments are served at many of the galleries. If you need a ride, the free trolley starts at 5:30 P.M. at Market Square and runs until 8:00 P.M.

Eleanor D. Wilson Museum
Richard Wetherill Visual Arts Center,
Hollins University, Roanoke
(800) 456-9559
www.hollins.edu
The already creative Hollins University just got a little bit more so in 2004. The Richard Wetherill Visual Arts Center and Eleanor D. Wilson Museum opened with an official dedication ceremony on October 16. The 58,000-square-foot center was made possible by the vision and financial support of the late Eleanor D. "Siddy" Wilson. A graduate of the class of 1930, Wilson gave $2.9 million to name the center for her grandfather, a Philadelphia industrialist and civic leader. She also bequeathed $5.5 million for the project through her estate.

The Eleanor D. Wilson Museum, located in the new center, features three galleries, including two just for students' works. Not only will the third gallery allow Hollins to display works from its permanent collection but it also will bring in historical work, thanks to its affiliation with the Virginia Museum of Fine Arts.

The center includes studios and teaching facilities for art history, film, and photography. It allows Hollins to develop a program for sculpture and ceramics.

THEATER

Mill Mountain Theatre
1 Market Square SE, Roanoke
(540) 342-5740, (800) 317-6455
www.millmountain.org
"New York quality in the Blue Ridge" is how

this year-round professional theater has been characterized. Mill Mountain Theatre is nationally known for its high-quality dramas, musicals, comedies, regional premieres, and its annual new play competition, which attracts hundreds of new works from all across the United States.

The theatre's year-round productions include a holiday musical, the Norfolk Southern Festival of New Works, cutting-edge dramas, and musicals in the fall and summer. Mill Mountain is a leader when it comes to providing the live theater experience to people with special needs. Its accessibility program—including audio description for the sight-impaired and signed performances for the hearing-impaired—matches those of theaters in major metropolitan areas.

Mill Mountain produces free theater from October through May with its Center-Piece series. Each CenterPiece is a midday one-act play or comedy, and the public is invited to bring lunch and a friend to chill out for an hour.

Mill Mountain also offers theater classes for students and adults. The Mill Mountain Players—a professional touring troupe—travels to schools and other venues throughout the state.

Cork & Curtain, an annual gala and auction, attracts hundreds of guests from the mid-Atlantic region who bid on wines from private cellars and luxury items while enjoying tastings, an elegant seated dinner, and live music. Funds from the gala benefit the theater's programs. Mill Mountain's 400-seat Trinkle Main Stage is on the first floor of Center in the Square. Waldron Stage, a more intimate black box theater seating 115, is in Center on Church.

Mill Mountain Theatre celebrated its 40th anniversary in 2004. It attracts performers such as Donna McKechnie, the Tony Award–winning star of *A Chorus Line*, who chose this venue for a pre–New York tryout. Others, such as Robert Fulghum (who worked with the Theatre to develop a dramatization of his books), Sheldon Harnick, and Stephen Schwartz, have all been in residence at MMT.

Roanoke Civic Center
710 Williamson Road, Roanoke
(540) 853-2241
www.roanokeciviccenter.com
The Roanoke Civic Center has been the place to go for big-time entertainment. Whether you like major concerts—from Toby Keith to Incubus—touring Broadway productions, college or professional sporting events, or family fun at the circus, the Civic Center has been the social gathering place in southwest Virginia since 1971.

The coliseum can seat up to 11,000 fans for major events, while the smaller auditorium, which seats 2,440, has hosted Jerry Seinfeld, the Bolshoi Ballet, and the local Roanoke Symphony. The Center also has an Exhibit Hall, which has served as the venue for trade shows and conventions. Did we mention that the Miss Virginia pageant is held here each year?

MUSIC

Jefferson Center
541 Luck Avenue, Roanoke
(540) 343-3744, (866) 345-2550
www.jeffersoncenter.org
Once known as Jefferson High School in the 1920s, this stately building now schools hundreds of fans on the fine arts. This performing arts center, with its award-winning renovation of the 940-seat Shaftman Performance Hall, is home to classical concerts, contemporary performances, lectures, ceremonies, and gala events. Wachovia Performance Series, which has brought the likes of Joan Baez, Herbie Hancock, and The Blind Boys of Alabama, calls the center home. The series of seven productions, which usually is staged from September through April, includes an eclectic lineup of jazz, folk, comedy, operettas, you name it. Tickets range from $20 to $32.

Opera Roanoke
The Jefferson Center
541 Luck Avenue, Roanoke
(540) 982-2742
www.operaroanoke.org

Standing ovations are the norm for 28-year-old Opera Roanoke, southwest Virginia's professional opera company. Led by Artistic Director Craig Fields, the company engages up-and-coming singers in innovative productions. Opera Roanoke presents its performances in Shaftman Performance Hall at Jefferson Center, a state-of-the-art facility with superior acoustics and technical features.

Presenting repertoire ranging from Monteverdi to Bernstein, Opera Roanoke has elicited the praise of *Opera News* for "innovative" and "enthralling" interpretations of the masterworks. Operas here are performed in their original languages with supertitles—concurrent translations over the proscenium—so that every twist and turn in the plot is fully understood. Before each performance, an informal lecture, "Director's Notes," enlightens, educates, and entertains both the novice and opera buff. Tickets range from $16 to $66.

Roanoke Symphony Orchestra
541 Luck Avenue, Suite 200, Roanoke
(540) 343-6221, (540) 343-9127, (886) 277-9127
www.rso.com
Quality performances, superb musicians, innovative programs, and exceptional guest artists are the hallmarks of the Roanoke Symphony and Chorus. Music Director and Conductor David Wiley has led the organization to sold-out concerts and rave reviews. Wiley is also an accomplished pianist and composer.

The orchestra was founded in 1953 and is the only professional orchestra in Virginia west of the Blue Ridge Mountains. The RSO presents live performances throughout the year, including the Classics Series, consisting of classical symphonic and choral works at the Roanoke Civic Center; the Virtuosi Series, featuring chamber orchestra works in the more intimate Shaftman Performance Hall of the Jefferson Center; and the Pops Series, with world-class guest artists. Roanoke Symphony Orchestra also reaches out to the community and the region with its annual

Holiday Pops concerts, Music for Americans in Victory Stadium on the Fourth of July, annual chorus performances, and numerous concerts in other communities.

The Roanoke Symphony Chorus, a volunteer organization under the direction of John Hugo, began an association with the orchestra in 1999. Usually joining in on two concerts per year, the chorus covers everything from Beethoven's *Choral Fantasy* to Vivaldi's *Gloria*. Education is a major focus. It provides area youth with music instruction and ensemble training in its Youth Symphony Orchestra, the Junior Strings, and the Harp Ensemble.

The RSO has an impressive record of guest artists. Tony Bennett, Willie Nelson, Roberta Flack, Chet Atkins, Norman Krieger, Leon Bates, Bruce Hornsby, Lou Rawls, Ben E. King, Al Jarreau, Richard Stoltzman, and many other respected musicians have performed with the group. The RSO has also produced two CDs, including Beethoven's *Ninth Symphony* and an *American Piano Concerto*, featuring the *Piano Concerto No. 3* by David Wiley.

LITERARY ARTS

Literary Festival
Wyndham Robertson Library, Hollins University, Roanoke
(540) 362-6317
This small university in the foothills of the Roanoke Valley has fostered an amazing number of talented authors. Three alumni—Annie Dillard, Henry Taylor, and Mary Wells Ashworth—won Pulitzer Prizes. Margaret Gibson and Madison Smartt Bell were nominated for National Book Awards, and Margaret Wise Brown is known far and wide for her children's classics, including *The Runaway Bunny*. Others, such as Tama Janowitz (*Slaves of New York*) and Elizabeth Forsythe Hailey (*A Woman of Independent Means*), have seen their work turned into movies. Hollins also started one of the country's first writers-in-residence programs, and, word has it, Nobel Prize winner William Golding was living at the college when his *Lord of the Flies* became

a best seller. Nancy Parrish even penned a book about the university's literary reputation, *Lee Smith, Annie Dillard, and the Hollins Group*. Since 1960, Hollins has celebrated its success with an annual literary festival in early April. During the 44th event in 2004, there were readings by John McManus, Toi Derricotte, and Denise Giardina. All the events are free.

EAST OF THE BLUE RIDGE
Rappahannock County

VISUAL ARTS

Middle Street Gallery
Corner of Gay and Middle Streets
Washington
(540) 675-3440
This nonprofit artists' cooperative features museum-quality paintings, photography, and sculpture. Exhibitions change monthly, and classes are offered for adults and children. The gallery is open Friday through Sunday from 11:00 A.M. to 6:00 P.M. and by appointment.

THEATER AND MUSIC

Ki Theatre
Gay and Jett Streets, Washington
(540) 987-3164, (800) 258-8709
www.kitheatre.org
Ki Theatre is made up of Obie Award–winning playwright and performer Julie Portman and musician Paul Reisler. The two create original plays, which they perform at Ki Theatre and at locations across the country. Reisler scores the productions, and Portman writes and performs them.

Since 1986 their multifaceted Ki Community Arts has given the folks in Rappahannock a voice through their own concerts and performances. The organization offers a children's songwriting project and workshops on songwriting and storytelling for adults.

Call the box office to find out schedules and ticket information.

The Theatre at Washington
291 Gay Street, Washington
(540) 675-1253
www.theatre-washington-va.com
This theater is known for its professional dramatic and musical performances, including the noted Smithsonian at Little Washington chamber music series. The performances, which have ranged from the Yale Russian Chorus to the Alma Viator and Ben Jones's rendition of *Love Letters*, are usually held on the weekend. Jones, by the way, who hosts bluegrass bands at his own shop near Sperryville, starred as Cooter on the TV show *The Dukes of Hazzard*. The Rappahannock Association for the Arts also holds a monthly film series at the theater on Friday nights. Film nights cost $6.00. The main productions cost $15.00. Students 18 and younger only pay $5.00.

Culpeper County

Sara Schneidman Gallery
122 East Davis Street, Culpeper
(540) 825-0034
www.saraschneidman.com
You can't walk by this storefront gallery without the vivid colors catching your eye. Sara Schneidman, who had made a lucrative career selling stationery designed from her original paintings, recently added a new medium to her résumé—rugs. Her designs, in a kaleidoscope of brilliant green, fuchsia, and blue, have now been transferred onto handmade New Zealand wool rugs. The artist, who has lived in both Asia and Europe, recently opened this gallery in downtown Culpeper. Here she displays stationery, rugs, wall hangings, needlepoint pillows, and ceramics, along with the original watercolors that inspired them. Schneidman is a former picture editor for Time-Life Books.

Thistle Tree Forge
174 East Davis Street, Culpeper
(540) 829-8440

Some artists work in watercolor. Others like oil. Rich Schluter's medium of choice is iron. In his own 4,000-square-foot gallery in downtown Culpeper, Schluter displays the handcrafted furniture and household accessories that he created with hammer on anvil. There are mirrors, floor lamps, candle holders of various heights, even an iron candle-holding chandelier. This modern-day blacksmith also shares his exhibit space with others on a rotating basis. The Forge is open 10:00 A.M. to 5:00 P.M. Monday through Saturday.

Orange County

VISUAL ARTS

Art Center in Orange
129 East Main Street, Orange
(540) 672-7311
They will draw you in to see their art or take you out to see others. This Orange County center will do anything they can to help stimulate interest in the arts. They showcase the works of local and national artists with monthly shows, opening receptions, and gallery talks with the artists. Dedicated to encouraging an understanding of the arts, the center offers classes and workshops, and they even schedule frequent trips to galleries in Washington, D.C. Drop by 10:00 A.M. to 5:00 P.M. Monday through Saturday.

Ed Jaffe Gallery
108 West Main Street, Orange
(540) 672-2400
www.edjaffe.com
A traditional carver, Ed Jaffe exhibits his work in a museum-like setting. Sculpture, mostly done in marble and stone, and oil pastels by Jaffe are on display and for sale in this 5,000-square-foot studio and gallery situated in the heart of Orange. If the flag is out front, the gallery is open. In case the artist is working, just ring the bell and wait. Jaffe will show you around. It's usually open 10:00 A.M. to 4:00 P.M. Saturday.

Frederick Nichols Gallery and Studio
5420 Governor Barbour Street
Barboursville
(540) 832-3565
www.frednichols.com

Artist Frederick Nichols Jr. has his studio and gallery in a renovated general store across from the railroad tracks. He calls his work "photo-impressionism." He does enormous colorful landscapes of Blue Ridge scenes using either oil paint or a silk-screen process. A friendly fellow, Nichols will give tours through the gallery and studio. Nichols, who took top honors at an international print exhibition in Japan, expanded his exhibit space in 1998. He added the Nichols Gallery Annex to display the works of 30 artists from across the state. Both galleries are open 11:00 A.M. to 5:00 P.M. Thursday through Sunday and other times by appointment.

THEATER

Four County Players
5256 Governor Barbour Street
Barboursville
(540) 832-5355
www.fourcp.org

One of the oldest continuously operated community theaters in central Virginia, this 30-year-old theater company out of Barboursville produces Shakespearean plays, full-scale musicals, and children's productions. Most productions are performed at the Barboursville Community Center. But in August Shakespeare productions are staged in a most magical setting: the ruins of what was once the estate of James Barbour, governor of Virginia (1812 to 1814), secretary of war, and ambassador to the Court of St. James. Thomas Jefferson, a friend of Barbour's, designed the house, but it was destroyed by fire on Christmas Day 1884. Overgrown boxwoods tower over the ruins, adding to the air of enchantment about the place. The award-winning Barboursville Vineyards are within walking distance. Among the works staged recently was *Much Ado About Nothing*.

Call for a season brochure and ticket information. Admission prices are $18, $14 for seniors, and $12 for children.

Charlottesville

VISUAL ARTS

Biscuit Run Studios
981 Old Lynchburg Road, Charlottesville
(434) 977-5411

A father-and-son team produce stone-and-glass sculptures at this production and display gallery. Their works can be seen in front of many public buildings in the Charlottesville area and a few in Roanoke. David and Christian Breeden call their style "old-fashioned abstract." Sculptures range from 6 inches to 20 feet. Stop in and see the artists in action. The working studio is open daily by appointment.

bozART Gallery
211 West Main Street, Charlottesville
(434) 296-3919
www.bozartgallery.com

More than twenty artists make up this cooperative effort. They take turns staffing the space, and every month a different artist's work is featured in the front of the gallery. The rest of the exhibit area is devoted to the other members. A new show opens the first Friday of each month with a reception from 6:00 to 9:00 P.M. If you can't make it for the free food and drink, drop by to see the artwork from noon to 5:00 P.M. Wednesday through Saturday and 1:00 to 4:00 P.M. Sunday.

Fayerweather Gallery
Fayerweather Hall, Rugby Road
Charlottesville
(434) 924-6122
www.virginia.edu/fayerweather

This university gallery next to the University of Virginia Art Museum has regular exhibits by faculty, student, and contemporary artists, so it's naturally where the staff of the UVA art department likes to hang out. Big changes are in store, however, thanks to a $4.6 million general obligation bond. Renovations are under way and scheduled to be completed in 2006. Fayerweather is open Monday through Friday from 9:00 A.M. to 5:00 P.M.

Les Yeux du Monde at dot 2 dot
115 South First Street, Charlottesville
(434) 973-5566
www.lesyeuxdumonde.com
Lyn Rushton has always done her part to support the arts. She even opened a series of exhibitions in her own home, showcasing the works of some of the finest artists in the region. Her shows were so well received that she soon decided it was time to branch out. First at Starr Hill, Les Yeux moved to a bright new gallery on The Terraces just off the Downtown Mall. The new location and set hours may be more convenient for the average art buff, but her exhibitions remain anything but average. Les Yeux recently participated in a collaborative showing of Ted Turner's paintings with the University of Virginia Art Museum (no, not the media mogul). Turner, the first local artist to be honored with simultaneous shows across the city, is a former University of Virginia professor and one of the region's most multitalented artists. Richard Diebenkrum and Italo Scanga were among the more recent artists featured here. The gallery is open 10:00 A.M. to 6:00 P.M. Tuesday through Saturday and from 1:00 to 5:00 P.M. Sunday.

McGuffey Art Center
201 Second Street NW, Charlottesville
(434) 295-7973
www.mcguffeyartcenter.com
A renovated elementary school within walking distance of historic Court Square and the downtown pedestrian mall houses this arts cooperative begun in 1975 with city support. Its light, airy rooms have been transformed into 23 studios where you can sometimes watch artists and crafters work. Forty artists rent space in the studios, including potters, painters, sculptors, photographers, printmakers, stained-glass artists, a glassblower, and three dance companies. Treehouse Books,

which teaches the art of making paper, is in McGuffey. Once a month, a member artist is featured in one of three galleries. McGuffey exhibits shows in its Main, Hall, and Upper Galleries, and it has an excellent gift shop. Exhibits, tours, and gallery talks are available to the public from September through July. McGuffey offers classes in children's art, printing, painting, papermaking, and drawing. Hours are 10:00 A.M. to 5:00 P.M. Tuesday through Saturday and 1:00 to 5:00 P.M. Sunday.

Second Street Gallery
115 Second Street SE, Charlottesville
(434) 977-7284
www.secondstreetgallery.org
Looking for a space to showcase contemporary works, 11 area artists got together in 1973 and started the first artist-run alternative gallery in central Virginia. In 1991 the National Endowment for the Arts named Second Street one of two model art organizations in the country.

A free opening reception and gallery talk usually kicks off a new exhibit each month. Nearly 13,000 people visit the gallery annually to see the works by local, regional, even national artists. The exhibits range from paintings and photographs to sculptures and installations. During the opening receptions, the artists are usually on hand to give a gallery talk. In 2003 Second Street moved to its brand-new home at the City Center for Contemporary Arts on the corner of Water Street—and yes—Second Street. This new 2,050-square-foot gallery includes two exhibition spaces, the Main Gallery, and smaller Dove Gallery. More than 800 people attended its first opening in 2004, celebrating its 30 years with 55 artists. Second Street is open 11:00 A.M. to 6:00 P.M. Tuesday through Saturday and 10:00 A.M. to 5:00 P.M. Sunday.

V. Earl Dickinson Building for the Humanities and Social Sciences
501 College Drive, Charlottesville
(434) 961-5204, (434) 961-5376
www.pvcc.edu/finearts
Piedmont Virginia Community College

opened this $7.1 million facility in August 1998. A major boost to the arts in the Charlottesville area, this 36,000-square-foot multilevel building is home to a 500-seat theater, a black box theater for rehearsals and smaller productions, an electronic music lab, classrooms, artist studios with floor-to-ceiling windows, and a double art gallery with 140 feet of exhibition space. A smaller gallery in PVCC's main building also offers monthly exhibitions of students' works. The gallery hosts works by local, state, and national artists. The college also stages plays throughout the school year and hosts concerts and dance performances by students as well as visiting artists. There is no charge to stop by and view art exhibits, but fees will vary with staged shows, usually in the $6.00 to $17.00 range. The galleries are open 9:00 A.M. to 10:00 P.M. Monday through Thursday, 9:00 A.M. to 5:00 P.M. Friday, and 1:00 to 5:00 P.M. Saturday.

MUSEUMS

The Kluge-Ruhe Aboriginal Art Collection of the University of Virginia
400 Worrell Drive, Charlottesville
(434) 244-0234
www.virginia.edu/kluge-ruhe
Yes, right in the middle of the Blue Ridge, you will find a museum devoted solely to Aboriginal art from Australia. John Kluge, one of the richest men in the world, had a keen interest in Aboriginal art, and in 1993 he purchased the collection and archives of the late Edward L. Ruhe. When Kluge moved his main residence from Albemarle County to England, he gave his entire collection—some 1,600 paintings, sculptures, and artifacts—to the University of Virginia. Not only does this museum highlight the works and styles of artists with new exhibits each month, Kluge–Ruhe also hosts children's art programs, luncheon tours, demonstrations and workshops, guest lectures, films, and live performances. The museum is open 9:00 A.M. to 3:00 P.M. Tuesday through Saturday. Admission is free.

University of Virginia Art Museum
155 Rugby Road, Charlottesville
(434) 924-3592
www.virginia.edu/artmuseum
The University of Virginia's own modern museum has a permanent collection of more than 10,000 items, including ancient pottery, sculpture, and paintings. It also hosts special short-term exhibits, ranging from the art and writings of John Dos Passos to the *Mystical Arts of Tibet*. Richard Gere Productions helped put together the latter traveling exhibit of 108 art objects, including some from the Dalai Lama's own collection and artifacts from the Tibetan monastery Deprung Loseling. They also have exhibited works that ranged from photographs by Man Ray to paintings by Pablo Picasso. String quartets and other classical music groups also perform here at certain times during the year. The museum hosts lectures and workshops and arranges members' trips to other regional galleries. The museum is open Tuesday through Sunday from 1:00 to 5:00 P.M. Admission is free, but donations are welcome.

THEATER

Community Children's Theatre
Charlottesville
(434) 961-7862
www.avenue.org/arts/cct
Since 1953 this company has brought affordable family theater to the Charlottesville community. Professional actors perform in four productions a season. *Coyote Tales* opened the 2005 season. Tickets, usually less than $10, are sold at the door an hour before curtain and at other locations around town prior to performances. The theater offers children's workshops in the winter with an artist in residence. Performances are held at the Martin Luther King Jr. Performing Arts Center. Call for a brochure and a schedule.

Heritage Repertory Theatre
Culbreth Road, UVA, Charlottesville
(434) 924-3376
www.virginia.edu/drama/boxoffice/hrtseason

Since 1974, this highly praised professional theater produces a series of five plays from late June through early August at the University of Virginia. The productions vary from musicals and comedies to light dramas and thrillers. Superb acting, directing, and set design make this series well worth the effort. In conjunction with UVA's department of drama, Heritage served as the originating stage for two Broadway-bound productions: *A Few Good Men* with Tom Hulce and *The Roads to Home,* written and directed by Pulitzer Prize–winning Horton Foote and starring Jean Stapleton. Shows in 2004 included *Ragtime*—with a cast of 40 performers and 120 costumes—plus *Syringa Tree, True West,* and *Driving Miss Daisy.*

Tickets range from $20 to $30. Call after June 1 to receive a free brochure.

Live Arts
123 East Water Street, Charlottesville
(434) 977-4177
www.livearts.org
Live Arts had a moving tribute. After 13 years in its small space on East Market, the local community theater company held a parade. The company invited casts, crews, and fans to pick up the last few symbolic items from their old stage and march across the Downtown Mall to their new home in the brand-new City Center for Contemporary Arts. It's a huge facility that Live Arts shares with Second Street Gallery and Light House, a nonprofit group—including Oscar-winning filmmakers—that helps teens make their own movies. Their new abode, a four-story building, allows for a costume shop, scene shop, dressing rooms, rehearsal rooms, offices, an intimate 75-seat UpStage performance area, and large 200-seat Downstage theater, complete with orchestra and balcony chairs.

But as impressive as the new facility may be, the talent within is well deserving of its new surroundings.

The Live Arts Theater Ensemble produces everything from original plays to well-known Broadway musicals. The company began in 1990 and hosts theater, dance, poetry readings, performance arts, and musical events.

Its 2004 playbill included *Copenhagen and Jesus Hopped the A Train* in the UpStage theater and the Emmy-winning *Angels in America: Part One, Millennium Approaches* in the DownStage space. The 2004–05 season will include *Angels in America: Part Two, Perestroika* and Edward Albee's *The Play About Baby.*

Live Arts also holds labs and workshops for would-be actors and playwrights to hone their skills. There was even a directors' roundtable and a workshop on auditioning tips. Young actors also take center stage in the Latte series, Live Arts Teen Theatre.

Tickets, on average, run $13.00 to $15.00 for orchestra seats, $10.00 for balcony. The UpStage shows will run about $7.00, depending on the production. Every Wednesday, it's pay-what-you-can admission. Live Arts will validate for two hours of parking in the Water Street Parking Garage.

The Old Michie Theatre
221 East Water Street, Charlottesville
(434) 977-3690
www.oldmichie.com
Professional puppet shows and mainstage plays at this theater entertain young audiences throughout the year. A husband-and-wife team, Frances Furlong and Steve Riesenman, run the theater, now in its 15th season. Their drama school offers classes during the academic year and a full-day summer camp. The repertoire features classic and new plays for children, from *Little Mermaid* to *Beauty and the Beast.* Every fall, the main-stage selections include *The Legend of Sleepy Hollow.* Tickets for the puppet shows are $5.00. The other shows are $7.50. Those younger than 24 months get in free. Call for schedule and tickets. Ask about reduced group rates. They welcome birthday party groups.

University of Virginia Department of Drama
109 Culbreth Road, Charlottesville
(434) 924-3376
www.virginia.edu/drama
This is UVA's main student theater group, producing at least six high-quality major stage shows every academic year on two stages. The Culbreth Theater seats 595, while the smaller Helms Theater suits a more intimate setting of 160 to 200. Productions have ranged from *Macbeth* and *Fiddler on the Roof* to *Hair* and *A Raisin in the Sun*. Prices vary, so call the box office between 10:00 A.M. and 6:00 P.M. Monday through Friday for a schedule.

DANCE

Chihamba of Dancescape
201 Second Street NW, Charlottesville
(434) 961-8234
www.avenue.org/chihamba
The Chihamba of Dancescape celebrates and educates people about African cultures through music and dance. Ongoing programs include concerts, lecture demonstrations, and workshops. Dance performances often feature live African drumming, and classes are held at McGuffey Art Center.

The Miki Liszt Dance Company
201 Second Street NW, Charlottesville
(434) 973-3744
This nonprofit professional company performs locally, conducts workshops with guest artists, and offers lectures and demonstrations. Its mission is to expose audiences to new currents in dance performance while giving regional dancers the opportunity to create and perform new work. The company also sponsors the annual Community Children's Dance Festival in the spring. The troupe also hosts First Fridays Dance Series, featuring the work of local and guest dancers and choreographers on the first Friday of each month.

Wilson School of Dance
3114 Proffit Road, Charlottesville
(434) 973-5678
Juanita Wilson Duquette, who toured with the New York Dance Theater, operates her own dance studio, where she instructs advanced dancers and beginners in jazz, tap, ballet, swing, ballroom, hip-hop, and theater dance. For the past several winters, Wilson has worked with the Moscow Ballet to get hundreds of young dancers ready for their parts in the Russian troupe's local holiday production of *The Nutcracker.*

MUSIC

Ash Lawn Opera Festival
1941 James Monroe Parkway
Charlottesville
(434) 293-4500, (434) 979-0122
www.ashlawnopera.org
Every summer the festival's professional opera company stages a repertory of an opera and a classic musical at the restored home and gardens of President James Monroe. It's perfect for the opera novice; all the shows are sung in English. Those more in tune with the genre will enjoy the cast's skill. Members of the company have sung with companies across the United States, including the Metropolitan Opera. All performances are held in the estate's scenic Boxwood Gardens or, in the event of rain, under the pavilion. Other festival events include a music at twilight series—ranging from Mozart duets to toe-tapping Appalachian fare—Wednesday nights and children's programs on Saturday mornings. Opera tickets range from $15.00 to $24.00. Music at Twilight is $12.00 and $8.00 for students. Summer Saturdays cost $5.00. Picnicking is encouraged before the shows. In fact, you can even reserve a catered gourmet dinner if you don't want to pack your own basket. Ash Lawn–Highland also hosts a variety of events throughout the year. Call to receive a free brochure.

Old Cabell Hall
112 Old Cabell Hall, UVA, Charlottesville
(434) 924-3984, (434) 924-3052
www.virginia.edu/music/cabell.html
Situated at the south end of the famous college lawn, this auditorium has been restored to its turn-of-the-20th-century grandeur. Home to more than 80 concerts throughout the academic year, Cabell hosted the Albemarle Ensemble, Rivanna Quartet, and Oratorio Society. The beautiful, bowl-shaped concert hall seats 851 and has wonderful acoustics, making this a favorite venue for musicians. Offerings include a symphony series, artist faculty series, jazz ensemble, and the Tuesday Evening Concert Series, a Charlottesville tradition for more than four decades. Tickets range from $10 for a Glee Club concert to $22 for a full orchestra performance. Call between 11:00 A.M. and 5:00 P.M. Monday through Friday.

Prism
214 Rugby Road, Charlottesville
(434) 97-PRISM
www.theprism.org
This nonprofit volunteer organization presents folk, acoustic, and traditional music from around the world in a casual, smoke-free, alcohol-free setting. Formed in 1966, the Prism has brought a wide range of artists to town. Legend has it that Joan Baez stopped in to introduce a friend, a young unknown guitarist named Bob Dylan. It only cost 75 cents to go to an Emmylou Harris concert here. Of course, that was 1972. Today, the lineup has included the likes of Ani DiFranco, Allison Krauss, Bela Fleck, and Corey Harris. These concerts are staged on weekends from September through May. It's a happening place; call to hear an extensive recording of the events calendar or to reserve tickets. Weekend performances usually cost between $15 and $22.

Tuesday Evening Concert Series
108 Fifth Street NE, Charlottesville
(434) 924-3984, (434) 244-9505
www.tec.org

Since November 30, 1948, the Tuesday Evening Concert Series has given Charlottesville audiences the opportunity to hear some of the world's finest classical musicians perform in Old Cabell Hall. Over the last 50 years, the playbill has read like a list of Who's Who, including Grammy-winning cellist Yo-Yo Ma, soprano Dame Joan Sutherland, flutist Jean-Pierre Rampal, violinist Pinchas Zukerman, and Russian violist Yuri Bashmet. Today people travel from as far as Winchester and Richmond to attend the series. Because the series is so popular, tickets are hard to come by. Your best bet is to get a subscription to the entire series, but individual tickets—if there are any remaining—go on sale at the box office two weeks before each concert. The 2004-2005 season is sold out, but there is a waiting list for any returned tickets. Tickets are $24 for orchestra seats, $20 for full-view loge and balcony seats, $10 for student and partial-view seats.

The Westminster Organ Concert Series
190 Rugby Road, Charlottesville
(434) 293-3133, (434) 963-4690
www.avenue.org/organconcerts
Held every year at Westminster Presbyterian Church, this series of concerts offers organ music combined with other instruments and singers. Professional local and visiting musicians make these superb performances. The church's Taylor and Boody tracker-action pipe organ, styled after 17th-century German organs, was hand-crafted in the Shenandoah Valley and plays beautifully. The five-concert series is held Friday evenings at 8:00 P.M. September through April.

LITERARY ARTS

Virginia Festival of the Book
145 Ednam Drive, Charlottesville
(434) 924-6890
www.vabooks.org
Charlottesville confirms its status as Virginia's writers' capital with this festival. The event attracted more than 250 writers to four days of programs. Designed to cel-

ebrate the book in all its forms, the festival brought in a record attendance of 22,376. The 200 programs, which include book fairs, lectures, signings, panel discussions, and readings, are mostly free. John Grisham, best-selling author and Albemarle County resident, was the keynote speaker at the sold-out luncheon one winter. Also on the impressive list of writers who have attended past festivals are former U.S. Poet Laureate Rita Dove, Gay Talese, Lee Smith, Garrison Keillor, Tami Hoag, David Baldacci, Dorothy Allison, and Elizabeth Peters. The festival, which celebrated its 10th anniversary in 2004, is held in late March at various sites across the city.

Virginia Film Festival
UVA campus, Charlottesville
(804) 924-FEST, (800) UVA-FEST
www.vafilm.com
Late October brings leading actors, filmmakers, scholars, critics, and the public together to discuss film in a serious way. More than 80 classic and premiere films, including dozens of features from international festivals and not yet in American distribution, are shown at venues throughout Charlottesville, most followed by fascinating discussions with nearly 100 guest filmmakers and speakers.

Renowned actors and filmmakers who have participated in the festival include the late Jimmy Stewart, the late Gregory Peck, the late Robert Mitchum, Sissy Spacek (a Charlottesville-area resident), Charlton

Debbie Reynolds, who was nominated for an Academy Award for her role in The Unsinkable Molly Brown, *is the official spokesperson for the Blue Ridge-Southwest Virginia Film Office. The former Roanoke resident has starred on stage and screen for more than 50 years. You can hear her welcome address on the film office's Web site at www.blueridgeswvafilm.org.*

Heston, Sidney Poitier, Robert Duvall, John Sayles, Ann-Margret, Eva Marie Saint, Roger Ebert, Gena Rowlands, Sigourney Weaver, Sydney Pollack, Sir Anthony Hopkins, Nicolas Cage, and Sandra Bullock.

This stimulating and exciting event is well worth factoring into your fall vacation. More than 9,700 attended in 2003. Special discount hotel-and-event package rates are available. Admission prices are reasonable—$7.50, $6.00 for seniors—though premieres and galas cost more. The Academy Award–nominated *Shine* was among the list of premieres in 1996. Call to receive a free catalog and ticket information, usually available in September.

Nelson County

VISUAL ARTS
Spruce Creek Gallery
1368 Rockfish Valley Highway
Nellysford
(434) 361-1859
www.sprucecreekgallery.com
In 1998 a group of artists wanted to find a place to exhibit their wares, a space that could serve as a cultural focal point in Nelson County. The old Wintergreen Country Store seemed like a perfect spot, with its wooden floors and tin roof. Today the rural setting is home to more than 80 artists, with work ranging from paintings, sculpture, and pottery to jewelry, clothing, and fiber arts. The gallery hosts revolving exhibits and special events throughout the year. It's open 10:00 A.M. to 6:00 P.M. daily from June through December and 11:00 A.M. to 6:00 P.M. Thursday through Monday from January through May.

MUSIC
Wintergreen Performing Arts
Route 664, Wintergreen
(434) 325-8292
www.wintergreenmusic.org
Nelson County's hills are alive with the sound of music. And boy, do people like it. Since the Wintergreen Summer Festival

and Academy opened in 1997, thousands have flocked to the outdoor concerts on the slopes of Wintergreen's ski resort. A portable performing arts center, a tent that will seat up to 500, was added in 1998, and the summer recitals expanded to year-round concerts. Today the 55-member professional Wintergreen Festival Orchestra, conducted by David Wiley, stages a variety of musical fare at different sites across the county, most at the Evans Center. Whether you like Big Band, jazz, opera, or Beethoven, chances are there will be something on the schedule that appeals. Tickets range from $10 to $22. Seats are less expensive if they are on the lawn.

Amherst County

LITERARY ARTS

Virginia Center for the Creative Arts
Mount San Angelo, Sweet Briar
(434) 946-7236
www.vcca.com
Located on the beautiful Mount San Angelo Estate, this surprising artistic treasure is just outside of Lynchburg in Amherst County. It is the nation's largest continually operating working retreat for professional writers, artists, and composers. Artists who visit from abroad are often the leading creative forces in their own countries. Some of the most important exchanges between artists worldwide take place here. The Virginia Center for the Creative Arts is supported in part by the Virginia Commission for the Arts and is affiliated with Sweet Briar College, a private woman's college.

Because the VCCA is a working retreat for artists, the buildings are not normally open to the public. The VCCA holds special exhibits and meet-the-artist receptions in the Camp Gallery during the summer that are open to the public. Other public events, such as poetry readings with international writers-in-residence, are cosponsored with Sweet Briar College.

Lynchburg

VISUAL ARTS

Academy of Fine Arts
1815 Thomson Drive, Lynchburg
(434) 846-8451
www.lynchburgarts.org
An affiliate of the Virginia Museum of Fine Arts in Richmond, this 40-year-old center serves the region with live theater performances in its 500-seat theater; classes and workshops in drama, art, pottery, dance, and music; and exhibits by area artists in the center's two galleries. In 2003 the Lynchburg Fine Arts Center joined up with the Academy of Music Theater to create the new Academy of Fine Arts. More than 50,000 people come to the center each year to see plays, dance, concerts, and art exhibits. The costume shop has more than 4,000 costumes, which the public may rent.

Maier Museum of Art
Randolph–Macon Woman's College,
1 Quinlan Street, Lynchburg
(434) 947-8136
www.maiermuseum.rmwc.edu
Known for its collection of 19th- and 20th-century American paintings, the Maier Museum of Art at prestigious Randolph–Macon Women's College displays works by artists including Winslow Homer, James McNeill Whistler, Mary Cassatt, and Georgia O'Keeffe. Also featuring special exhibitions and programs, this tremendous community asset is well worth the visit for art lovers. The museum is open September through May from 1:00 to 5:00 P.M. Tuesday through Sunday, with summer hours from 1:00 to 4:00 P.M. Wednesday through Sunday.

OTHER CULTURAL ATTRACTIONS

Virginia School of the Arts
2240 Rivermont Avenue, Lynchburg
(434) 847-8688
www.vsaart.com
The Virginia School of the Arts, a non-

profit residential and day school for talented high school students, is dedicated to preparing young people for careers in dance and furthering their academic studies. Graduates often attend colleges or universities on full scholarship, and many have joined prominent professional companies. It is one of only six such schools for dance in America, and students come from throughout the United States. The students stage three shows a year at E. C. Glass High School. Its arts faculty includes professional performers who contribute greatly to Lynchburg's culture. Cost will vary from $10 to $120.

Bedford County

Sedalia Center
1108 Sedalia School Road, Big Island
(434) 299-5080
www.sedaliacenter.org
The Sedalia Center, "for the art of living and the living arts," is a regional, nonprofit organization offering programming in visual and performing arts. It offers classes, workshops, coffeehouse performances, and special events. The center's modern building is set on 14 acres in the foothills of the Blue Ridge near Big Island. Special events include a country fair, four music festivals, and the annual chili cook-off. Sedalia Center Stages are held the second Saturday of every month and are always a sure bet for great music—the summer season is held on the outdoor stage.

Franklin County

THEATER

Blue Ridge Dinner Theatre
Sale Theatre in Schoolfield Hall
Ferrum College, Ferrum
(540) 365-4335
www.ferrum.edu/brdt
Since 1979, the Blue Ridge Dinner Theatre

continues to operate on the three guiding principles of theater: discovery, wholesome family entertainment, and celebration. It also serves up a great luncheon or dinner in combination with everything from murder mysteries to great historical masterpieces. Adjacent to the Blue Ridge Institute, the Dinner Theatre also offers theatergoers tours of the facility. Ferrum's theater group, the Jack Tale Players, continues the legacy through acting out legends of the South. Members of the audience are invited to discuss issues related to the day's performance with guests and senior members of the BRDT staff at a free discussion series, the Greenroom Dialogues.

The company stages four to five shows in June and July. Prices will vary according to the productions. Generally, the dinner and theater shows are $23.60, or $11.80 if you just go to see the play. If you opt for a matinee with lunch, the cost is $19.80, or $9.90 for those who don't want a meal.

NEW RIVER VALLEY

Montgomery County

VISUAL ARTS

Armory Art Gallery
201 Draper Road, Blacksburg
(540) 231-4859, (540) 231-5547
www.gallery.vt.edu
One of several art galleries at Virginia Tech, Armory Art Gallery is operated by the school's Department of Art and Art History as an educational and outreach program. The 1,000-square-foot gallery, in the Old Blacksburg Armory, has a year-round rotation of exhibits by national or regional artists, work by student artists, and other shows of community interest. The gallery is open Tuesday through Friday from noon to 5:00 P.M. and Saturday from noon to 4:00 P.M.

Flossie Martin Gallery
200 Powell Hall, Radford University
Radford
(540) 831-5754
www.radford/edu/~rmuseum
This modern facility occupies 2,000 square feet on the beautiful Radford University campus. The combination gallery and museum features rotating exhibits of both regional and nationally known artists.

The gallery's roster has included Andy Warhol, Winslow Homer, sculptor Dorothy Gillespie, and a collection of narrative yarn paintings by Huichol Indians of the Mexican Sierra Madre. Radford University's art museum houses about 900 works of art, including the largest collection of pieces by New York artist Dorothy Gillespie and 250 works that had belonged to New York art dealer Betty Parsons. Gallery 205 is a more intimate gallery also inside Powell Hall. The hours are 10:00 A.M. to 4:00 P.M. Monday through Friday and noon to 4:00 P.M. Saturday and Sunday.

Perspective Art Gallery
Squires Student Center, Blacksburg
(540) 231-6040
Also at Virginia Tech, Perspective Gallery offers a range of artistic styles and media by artists ranging from internationally known professionals to students. The gallery, a facility of the University Unions and Student Activities, also offers talks and receptions where the public can meet featured artists. The gallery is open noon to 5:00 P.M. Tuesday through Friday and 2:00 to 8:00 P.M. Saturday and Sunday.

Radford University Art Museum
Downtown
1129 East Main Street, Radford
(540) 831-6780
In 1998 Radford unveiled a new cultural center in what had once been one of the premiere shopping stores in the downtown area. But a million-dollar transformation has given the Bondurant Center a boost, making way for a restaurant, several businesses, and space dedicated to the visual arts.

The Art Depot Gallery on the second

> *Lights! Camera! Action! The Blue Ridge has been the setting for many television programs and movies, including* Gods and Generals, The West Wing, Lassie, What About Bob?, Dirty Dancing, Sommersby, *and* The Waltons, *which was based on the Nelson County upbringing of its creator, Earl Hamner Jr.*

floor is dedicated to student works. It's open from 10:00 A.M. to 5:00 P.M. Monday through Friday and from noon to 4:00 P.M. Saturday. On the street level of the Bondurant Center is another exhibit space that features the work of Virginia artists. You can stop by this gallery from 9:00 A.M. to 7:00 P.M. Monday through Friday and from 10:00 A.M. to 6:00 P.M. Saturday.

Radford University stages ongoing exhibits here on the second floor throughout the year. The gallery hours are 11:00 A.M. to 4:00 P.M. Monday through Friday.

THEATER
Theatre Arts Department,
203 Performing Arts Building, Virginia
Tech, Blacksburg
(540) 231-5335
www.theatre.vt.edu
The New River Valley's cultural richness comes in great part from Virginia Tech's presence, and theater is no exception. They say the first play was staged on campus in 1876, but the academic theater program was launched in 1967. The only theater arts department in Virginia to have both its graduate and undergraduate programs accredited by the National Association of Schools of Theatre, Virginia Tech's has received more awards from the American College Theatre Festival than any other college or university in the Southeast. Three times, the university has advanced to the national theater festival at the Kennedy Center in Washington. The Theatre Arts Department at Virginia Tech stages four main stage productions during the school year, and two summer shows

and hosts four to six workshops. Recent works have included *Streetcar Named Desire, Far Away,* and *The Laramie Project.* The average cost is $6.50 to $8.00.

The school has three theaters: Haymarket Theatre at Squires Student Center, Black Box Theatre in the Performing Arts Building, and Squires Studio Theatre. All productions are open to the public.

OTHER CULTURAL ATTRACTIONS

The Montgomery Museum and Lewis Miller Regional Art Center
300 South Pepper Street
Christiansburg
(540) 382-5644
A Valley-wide project to promote Montgomery County's rich history and arts, this center is in a mid-19th-century home of American and Flemish bond brick made from local materials, with hand-hewn oak beams and rafters. A curious aspect of the manse portion of the house is a step-up feature in the back rooms, thought to be a carryover from Colonial days when some people believed that evil spirits bearing illness traveled the night air along floors.

New exhibits on Montgomery County and on the life and art of Lewis Miller are recent additions to the center. The house contains both historic and contemporary works, including exhibits and shows of southwest Virginia artists and crafters. It also houses a genealogical research area, historic small-press library, and archives. The Center is open 10:30 A.M. to 4:30 P.M. Monday through Saturday, or by appointment.

Radford University College of Visual and Performing Arts
Preston Hall, Radford University, Radford
(540) 831-5141
www.radford.edu/cvpa/
The university offers the public solo and ensemble music performances, theater, ongoing gallery exhibits, classical ballet, Big Band music, jazz, modern dance, and opera performances. The University Performance Series is held in Preston Hall and has brought in professional acts, ranging from Pancho Sanchez and his Latin Band to a Bulgarian production of *Aida.* The St. Petersburg Ballet also staged *Romeo and Juliet* here. Call the university for a schedule.

Pulaski County

VISUAL ARTS

The Fine Arts Center for the New River Valley
21 West Main Street, Pulaski
(540) 980-7363
This facility is the cultural hub of the New River Valley, featuring contemporary works, private collections, and amateur and professional artists. It is housed in a storefront building considered a prime example of Victorian commercial architecture. Built in 1898, the Center has been designated a Virginia Historic Landmark. Each summer the center produces free concerts in Pulaski's Jackson Park and Dublin's Sunken Gardens Park.

Floyd County

VISUAL ARTS

Old Church Gallery
110 Wilson Street, Floyd
(540) 745-2979
www.oldchurchgallery.com
In this 1850 Greek Revival building, art exhibits are adjacent to the history room. A century-old copper still used to make moonshine whiskey is on display, along with quilts, antiques, artifacts, and artwork. The gallery has an active quilter's guild and an arts and crafts workshop. The gallery is open 10:00 A.M. to 1:00 P.M. Saturday, and 2:00 to 4:00 P.M. Sunday from April through December.

OTHER CULTURAL ATTRACTIONS

Blue Ridge Music Center
Milepost 213, Fisher's Peak
(276) 236-5309
www.blueridgemusiccenter.net
The Blue Ridge Music Center opened its
16-week summer concert series at the
outdoor 2,500-seat amphitheater. The
series is designed to showcase traditional
Appalachian music, including old-time,
bluegrass, Piedmont blues, and gospel.
While most of the Sunday evening concerts are free, some do charge, so it's a
good idea to go online and order tickets.
Ricky Skaggs seats sold for $20.00 in
2004; other tickets range from $5.00 to
$20.00. Bring a lawn chair, blanket, and
picnic basket, but alcohol will not be
allowed on grounds. Located along the
Blue Ridge Parkway, the National Park
Service facility is operated by the National
Council for the Traditional Arts. Pickin' in
the Park is held from 5:30 to 6:30 P.M.,
before the 7:00 P.M. shows. The series runs
from June through mid-September.

Floyd Country Store
South Locust Street, Floyd
(540) 745-4563
www.floydcountrystore.com
The culture of mountainous Floyd County
doesn't get any better than this! At 6:30
P.M. Friday night, folks start showing up
with fiddles, harmonicas, banjos, and guitars, and what follows is a Floyd County
tradition. The flat-footing begins, old-
timers reminisce, and the music that is the
lifeblood of Floyd County mountain spirit
soothes the wounds of the work week. A
Gospel session starts the evening at 6:30,
followed by bluegrass at 7:30. In the
warmer months, don't be surprised if you
see musicians getting together for
impromptu jams in the parking lot. Admission is generally $3.00, but youths
younger than 12 get in for free.

ALLEGHANY HIGHLANDS

Alleghany and Highland Counties

Alleghany Highlands Arts & Crafts Center
439 East Ridgeway Street, Clifton Forge
(540) 862-4447
The two galleries' changing exhibits feature works by regional artists and those
from other areas. Among the fine regional
art and handcrafted products of juried
quality on sale here are pottery, watercolor, oil, prints, photography, baskets,
jewelry, stained glass, and needlework.
The center is open 10:00 A.M. to 4:30 P.M.
Monday through Saturday May through
December and during the same hours
Tuesday through Saturday January
through April.

Alleghany Highlands Arts Council
450 West Main Street, Covington
(540) 962-6220
www.alleghanyhighlands.com/arts4all/
The Alleghany Highlands Arts Council has
been bringing professional performing
arts events into the community since 1953.
Its performing art series has been called
one of the most successful entertainment
and cultural series in the state. The series
has included performances by the Barter
Theatre Troupe, Judy Collins, Marie
Osmond, and Leon Bates. The Young People's Theatre Series performs educational
theatre, musical, and dance productions.
The AHAC also provides ways for residents to become involved in the performing arts. The Alleghany Highlands Chorale

*The Jacksonville Center in Floyd fea-
tures artistic and cultural events. The
center, which opened in 1995, is owned
by a nonprofit corporation of Floyd
County volunteers. They stage festivals
for music, folklore, arts, and drama.*

gives two major concerts per year. The Alleghany Highlands Orchestra is a full orchestra of more than 30 members.

Historic Stonewall Theatre
510 Main Street, Clifton Forge
(540) 862-7407, (877) 301-3817
Country Music Hall of Famers Tex Ritter, Roy Rogers, and Gene Autry once performed in this grand old theater. Located on the eastern tip of what has been called the Golden Triangle of Country Music, other stars stopped by on their way to Kentucky and Tennessee, including Burl Ives, Tom Mix, Lash LaRue, and the original Drifters. In 1991 Appalfolks of America, a nonprofit corporation based in Clifton Forge, was given the theater as a charitable donation and what had become a twin cinema was converted back into a performing arts center. Today the 550-seat three-story building that dates back to 1904 hosts performances some Fridays and almost every Saturday. Stop by and you can hear a wide variety of concerts by country, bluegrass, gospel, and Junior Opry performers.

Stonewall also stages dramas by the Clifton Forge Players, the Stonewall Youth Theatre, and actors from nearby Lime Kiln, plus it has even hosted occasional variety shows and tributes to Martin Luther King Jr. and Elvis Presley. Most shows are in the $10 to $12 range, but prices are higher for the bigger-named acts. Robin and Linda Williams from Garrison Keillor's *A Prairie Home Companion* radio show and Grammy-nominated folksinger John McCutcheon are among past entertainers.

Bath County

MUSIC
Garth Newel Music Center
Warm Springs
(540) 839-5018, (877) 558-1689
www.garthnewel.org
Since 1973, from among the giant hemlocks, the hills of Bath County come alive with the sound of music. The importance of the Garth Newel Center to the culture of the Alleghany Highlands and western Virginia cannot be underestimated. Musicians, students, and awe-inspired audiences come together in this unspoiled mountain area to hear music by the likes of Beethoven, Bach, Mozart, Haydn, Schubert, Schumann, Brahms, and Dvorak in an enchanting mountain setting. The Center features the Garth Newel Chamber Players. It provides an intensive residential Chamber Music Fellowship Program in the summer for serious young musicians, who receive full scholarships. The architecture and acoustics of Herter Hall provide the perfect ambience for chamber music and create a unique sense of being outdoors while actually indoors! Before the performance, many visitors have made it a tradition to join friends for a picnic on the grounds of the 114-acre estate.

The Garth Newel Summer Chamber Music Festival begins in July with concerts every Saturday at 5:00 P.M. and every Sunday at 3:00 P.M. through Labor Day weekend.

Their Menu to Match the Music Series includes a gourmet dinner prepared by the resident chef on selected Saturdays following the concerts. The cost for dinner and concert is $65. In 2004 the Garth Newel Piano Quartet made its New York debut at Carnegie Hall.

Throughout the fall, winter, and spring, Garth Newel hosts Music Holidays weekends with guests in residence.

ANNUAL EVENTS AND FESTIVALS

Not a season passes in Virginia's Blue Ridge that some group isn't finding a way to celebrate. You will have plenty to do each month all around the 14-county region: craft shows, antiques sales, historic commemorations, agricultural fairs, horse shows and races, athletic competitions, and some of the best fun you'll find anywhere in traditional holiday observances. Imagine the Shenandoah Valley sky ablaze with fireworks on Independence Day, or conjure up a sense of patriotic pride as this history-rich region celebrates the birthdays of such famous Americans as Thomas Jefferson, George Washington, James Madison, and the South's famous generals, Robert E. Lee and Stonewall Jackson.

Let your taste buds lead the way as folks gather around to sample their favorite foods served with a big helping of fellowship. The Virginia Chili Cook-off in Roanoke is one such event, and the Highland Maple Festival in Monterey (with syrup-making demonstrations and plenty of maple-flavored goodies) is another. Other gatherings pay homage to such diverse edibles as garlic, apples in every form (especially apple butter!), wine, tomatoes, molasses, poultry, and more. Fall festivals usually feature the entire harvest—so save up your calories.

Music, running the gamut from hoedowns to symphonies, is almost always on the program. Don't miss the Old Fiddler's Convention—the original and largest such event—and other cultural extravaganzas. Many activities are held at the region's beautiful historic mansions, such as Montpelier, Monticello, and Ash Lawn–Highland.

The list that follows is a sampling of some of the bigger events—and a lot of smaller ones, too—that can entertain you for a weekend or longer. Where possible, we have given dates or approximate times of the month when these events occur. You should always call ahead to confirm times and specifics. Happy festing!

JANUARY

Virginia Special Olympics
Highway 664, Wintergreen
(800) 932-4653
www.specialolympicsva.com
Wintergreen Resort hosts this annual snow-skiing competition for more than 150 athletes with intellectual disabilities. Alpine races are on the agenda at this event, usually held in mid-January. There is no cost to watch.

Livestock Auction
7074 John Marshall Highway, Marshall
(540) 364-1566
On the second Saturday of every month, a horse auction is held at the Fauquier Livestock Exchange. You can bid on almost any type of horse, from draft horses to ponies and mules. Every Tuesday there are general livestock auctions. Such sales were once commonplace in rural America but are now a rarity. There's no cost to watch.

Hunt Country Winter Antiques Show
28050 Oatlands Plantation Lane
Leesburg
(703) 777-3174
www.oatlands.org
More than 73 selected exhibitors from New England to the Carolinas sell 17th- to 20th-century furniture, porcelain, jewelry, and other collectibles at the National Guard Armory during this three-day fair.

It's usually held either the second or third weekend of the month. Admission is $8.00.

Annual Charlottesville Antiques Show
235 West Main Street, Charlottesville
(434) 296-8018
More than 40 dealers display their wares at the Omni Charlottesville Hotel on the Downtown Mall for this show. Usually held the first weekend in January, the 2005 show marks the 21st year of the annual gathering. Admission is $5.50.

Founder's Day
Washington and Lee University
Lexington
(540) 463-3777, (540) 463-8768
Since 1871, Washington and Lee University has celebrated the birthday of Robert E. Lee with an event in Lee's Chapel. Robert Hartley spoke during the academic program in 2004. The free annual event always is held the Friday nearest the general's birthday, January 19.

FEBRUARY

Lincoln Day Ceremony
Highway 42, north of Harrisonburg
(540) 828-5605
On February 12, in celebration of the president's birthday, a free ceremony is held 2:00 P.M. at the site of the Lincoln homestead in the Shenandoah Valley. The hourlong ceremony features readings of Abraham Lincoln's famous speeches, including the Gettysburg Address and his second inaugural address. This annual event is sponsored by the president of Bridgewater College.

Loudoun County Civil War Roundtable
208 West Market Street, Leesburg
(540) 338-7550
Winter's a good time to drop by Thomas Balch Library to attend this ongoing meeting, which features a forum by various Civil War authorities. This group meets the second Tuesday of every

month, except July and August. For $20 the whole family can join the membership.

African-American History Month at Monticello
Highway 53, Charlottesville
(434) 984-9822
www.monticello.org
In keeping with the practice begun by Dr. Carter G. Woodson, the founder of black history commemorations who was also born nearby, Monticello celebrates the contributions of African Americans to the history of Virginia and our nation. Take a plantation community tour every weekend in February. Monticello Plantation life interpreters lead visitors along Mulberry Row, the plantation "street," where African-American slaves lived and labored, and the south dependencies, including the kitchen and cook's rooms. Other special events throughout the month include displays, lectures, workshops, and performances.

Shrine Circus
Roanoke Civic Center
710 Williamson Road, Roanoke
(540) 981-1201, (888) 397-3100
www.roanokeciviccenter.com
Three days in early February bring the Shrine Circus to the Roanoke Civic Center much to the delight of children and adults. Enjoy animals, trapeze artists, and lots of clowns. General admission runs at about $14.00 for adults and $8.00 for children.

MARCH

President James Madison's Birthday
Highway 20 S, Montpelier Station
(540) 672-2728
www.montpelier.org
Every year on March 16 Montpelier hosts a celebration to honor the birthday of the fourth president of the United States. There is a celebration at the newly restored Madison family cemetery, usually featuring the Marine Corps Band. Other events follow at the house. There is no charge.

Festival of the Book
145 Ednam Drive, Charlottesville
(434) 924-6890
www.vabook.org
Celebrate the book in all its forms with dozens of events and more than 100 writers. Programs for all ages include book fairs, storytelling, seminars, readings, and book signings at locations throughout the city (see our Arts chapter). Except for the luncheon and closing reception, most events are free at this festival that takes place near the last weekend in March. Past participants have included John Grisham, Tami Hoag, David Baldacci, and Garrison Keillor.

MDA Car Show
Roanoke Civic Center
710 Williamson Road, Roanoke
(540) 981-1201, (540) 772-3237
www.roanokeciviccenter.com
Since 1981, antique, late-model cars and trucks can be found on display at the Roanoke Civic Center in mid-March. Admission is $8.00 for adults and $3.00 for children. Free for those younger than 6.

St. Patrick's Day Parade
410 South Jefferson Street, Roanoke
(540) 342-2640, ext. 47
www.roanokespecialevents.org
Downtown Roanoke "sports the green" during this weekend parade that's fun for the whole family. There are bagpipes, a marching band, and a Celtic festival on the historic downtown market. It's free to watch.

Highland County Maple Festival
Various locations, Monterey
(540) 468-2550
www.highlandcounty.org
This festival, celebrated on the second and third weekends in March, takes place across Highland County, that rugged, gorgeous region bordering West Virginia, just west of Staunton. Begun in 1958, the Maple Festival has been named in the Southeast Tourism Society's Top 20 Events for the past 15 years. Look for 60,000 visitors to flock to

this rural area, which has a population of just 2,500. During the festival, you can visit local sugar camps and watch the actual process of syrup making. There's also a juried arts and crafts show, a maple queen contest and ball, dances, including the maple sugar hoedown, and plenty of opportunities to scarf down pancakes with maple syrup, maple donuts, and fresh fried trout. The events are free, but you'll pay for food.

Easter Egg Hunt
U.S. Highway 11, Middletown
(540) 869-2028
www.bellegrove.org
Celebrate the Easter holiday with the annual Easter Egg Hunt at Belle Grove Plantation on the Saturday before Easter. There are more than 3,200 candy-filled eggs and other games for kids. Activities are geared for children up to age 10. Cost is $3.00 per child, $5.00 for adults.

APRIL

Historic Garden Week
Locations throughout Virginia
(804) 644-7776
www.vagardenweek.org
This event, held in late April, celebrates its 72nd year in 2005. Charlottesville, Staunton, Harrisonburg, Roanoke, and the Front Royal areas are just a few of the popular touring regions. Prices may vary with locations, but tour block tickets usually range from $10 to $30 per event.

Victorian Festival
Beverly Street, Staunton
(540) 332-3972, (800) 332-5219
www.Stauntondowntown.org
It's the perfect setting in this town with its overwhelming number of Victorian homes, and in late April you can catch the Victorian Festival, opening with a ceremony on Historic Beverly Street on Friday at 5:30 P.M. Stroll down nineteenth-century streets, enjoy music by the Stonewall Brigade Band, and watch the grand procession with horse-drawn carriages, street

In Full Bloom

It's been called "America's Largest Open House."

For more than 70 years, Historic Garden Week has let you peek inside some of the most prominent homes across the state, giving visitors a chance to see how the other half lives or, at least, gardens.

For one week in April, the Garden Club of Virginia arranges three dozen tours of public and private homes and estates. Just as spring hits full bloom, you can wander through impressive lawns and paved paths of more than 250 gardens statewide.

Individual tours are held throughout the Blue Ridge, including Charlottesville, Lynchburg, Fauquier, Loudoun, Harrisonburg, Lexington, Orange, Roanoke, Staunton, and Winchester. Each local tour usually features five to six houses, many that are open only for Garden Week.

While the blooms are the main draw, some homeowners have been known to open their doors as well to show off their collections of antiques, artwork, and fine furnishings.

Highlights of the 2004 event included a visit to Seven Oaks mansion in Albemarle County. Seven Oaks, which is now owned by the manager of the Dave Matthews Band, was once the home of Nancy Langhorne Astor. Viscountess Astor was the first woman to sit in the British House of Commons. Her sister, Irene Langhorne Gibson, was a model for the fashionable "Gibson Girl." Both sisters used this 1860 estate as their home base when visiting family in the area. Seven Oaks, by the way, got its name for its seven huge oak trees. All were named for presidents from Virginia, but six were destroyed in 1954 by Hurricane Hazel. The one that weathered the storm, appropriately enough for Charlottesville, was "Thomas Jefferson."

On the other end of the historical time line, a stop on Harrisonburg's tour featured one of the first passive solar model homes in the Shenandoah Valley. Built in 1977, the house is filled with nearly 300 orchids and exotic bamboos. The owners also have an impressive collection of Hawaiian, Eskimo, and Japanese art.

To find out about next year's event, log on to www.vagardenweek.org or call (804) 644-7776. A 220-page guidebook is usually ready in February. To get one, send a $5.00 donation to Historic Garden Week, 12 East Franklin Street, Richmond 23219. The book will list all the tours, including times, dates, prices, contact numbers, and descriptions of the homes. Tours usually range from $10 to $30, with proceeds benefiting the restoration of historic gardens and grounds across the state.

entertainment, and Victorian dancers. Also featured at the event are the American Magic Lantern Show and the Virginia Hot Glass Festival. You'll see jugglers, magic acts, Victorian teas, Victorian reenactors, lectures and workshops, hot-air balloon rides, and Gypsy Express Mini-train rides. Don your most elegant frock for the grand ball on Saturday evening, and the Victorian bed race on Sunday.

Vinton Dogwood Festival
Various locations, Vinton
(540) 983-0614
www.vintondogwoodfestival.org
This community next to Roanoke celebrates spring in late April every year with a parade, band competition, an antique car show, music, food, crafts, bike races, a long-distance run, an evening of country music, and more. Most events are free.

Leesburg Flower and Garden Festival
King and Market Streets, Leesburg
(703) 777-1368, (703) 737-7154
Downtown Leesburg is transformed into a botanical garden with plants, gardening equipment, and supplies for sale as well as entertainment and food. Both King and Market Streets are blocked off for this festival on the third weekend in April. Cost is $3.00, free for those 6 and younger.

Graves Mountain Spring Fling
Highway 670, Syria
(540) 923-4231
www.gravesmountain.com
Rain or shine, Graves Mountain Lodge celebrates spring the last weekend of April with fly-fishing demonstrations, bluegrass music, cloggers, arts and crafts, hayrides, and horseback rides. Admission and parking are free. You also can sample some rainbow trout or have a hot dog and hamburger at the picnic area.

Thomas Jefferson Birthday Commemoration
Highway 53, Charlottesville
(434) 984-9822
www.monticello.org

Admission to Monticello's grounds and gardens is always free on April 13, the birthday of Virginia's best-known renaissance man—U.S. president, secretary of state, scholar, architect, collector, and horticulturist Thomas Jefferson. The morning celebration features a wreath-laying ceremony at Jefferson's grave site, with music by a fife and drum corps.

Charlottesville 10-Miler
Alderman Street, Charlottesville
(434) 293-6115
www.avenue.org/ctc/tenmiler
The city's largest foot race (fourth-largest in Virginia) is usually held the first Saturday in April, commencing at the University of Virginia's University Hall. If you would like to participate in the event, which celebrates its 21st year in 2005, call to get a brochure. It's free if you want to watch.

Dogwood Festival
McIntire Road, Charlottesville
(434) 961-9824
www.dogwoodfestival.org
This popular community event, which began in 1950 as an apple festival, was changed to the Dogwood Festival eight years later because it was always held at the height of the dogwood blooming season. It features a queen's coronation, fireworks, a carnival, and barbecue. It culminates in a grand parade that shows off Charlottesville at its springtime best. It's usually held for two weeks in mid-April. There is no charge for most events, but you will need some cash if you want to ride the carnival rides and eat the barbecue.

Doo Dah Day
Pleasant Valley Road, Winchester
(540) 662-7732
It's a family day of fun at this annual event on the last Saturday in April at Jim Barnett Park. There are games, food, live entertainment, and a parade. Spiderman even makes an annual appearance. It costs about $5.00 to get in.

Although many festivals are held outdoors, dogs are not always welcome participants. You might want to give the event organizers a call before you take Fido along for the ride.

Spring Garden Show
12th and Main Streets, Lynchburg
(434) 847-1499

This is a gardener's field day in late April at the Community Market, where landscapers, florists, and nursery operators display their products and where gardening techniques are demonstrated. Entertainment and food add to the festivities. The events are free.

Archduke Music Holiday
Highway 220, Hot Springs
(540) 839-5018, (877) 558-1689
www.garthnewel.org

A renowned cultural hub, the Garth Newel Music Center hosts this special weekend in late April for lovers of chamber music, gourmet meals, and fine wine. Enjoy the black-tie affair on Friday and other special activities throughout the rest of the weekend. Admission price is $65. Brunch and performance is $40.

MAY

Fridays After Five
Downtown Mall, Charlottesville
(434) 296-8548
www.cvilledowntown.org

This free outdoor concert series is held at the city's Downtown Mall amphitheater. Bands are usually local. This event is held 5:30 to 8:00 P.M. Friday through September.

Local Colors
Market Square, Roanoke
(540) 342-2640, ext. 33
www.localcolors.org

This local celebration of cultural diversity is held annually at the historic farmers'

market and on surrounding streets. More than 75 countries are represented in a parade of flags and through food, song, dance, music, artifact exhibits, ethnic dress, and international children's games. The event is held mid-month and is free.

Shenandoah Apple Blossom Festival
135 North Cameron Street, Winchester
(540) 662-3863, (800) 230-2139
www.thebloom.com

This five-day celebration, usually held the first full weekend of May, is a salute to the area's apple-growing industry. You'll find high-quality arts and crafts shows, numerous parades, live music, a 10K race, and a circus. (See our Kidstuff chapter.) Loni Anderson was the grand marshal for the 77th event in 2004, while other guests have included Sean Astin from *Lord of the Rings,* Kirk Cameron, Jackie Joyner-Kersee, and Whitey Ford. Some events are free. The circus costs $20.00 for adults, $9.00 for children 12 and younger.

Ash Lawn-Highland Virginia Wine Festival
James Monroe Parkway, Charlottesville
(434) 293-9539
www.avenue.org/ashlawn

In mid-May, take in one of the first major wine festivals of the year at the historic home of James Monroe. The festival features craft demonstrations, gourmet food, entertainment, house tours, and wine tastings from central Virginia wineries. The festival costs $10.00, $15.00 at the gate, but you will need a little extra to sample the food. Children younger than 7 pay $7.00.

Virginia Mushroom and Wine Festival
414 East Main Street, Front Royal
(540) 635-3185, (800) 338-2576
www.frontroyalchamber.com

This Main Street celebration started as a salute to the shiitake mushroom and grew to include more than 100 arts and crafts, food, wine tastings, live music, clogging, open-air theatrical performances, and rides for the kids. It's usually held the second weekend in May. The 18th annual event in 2004 cost $10.

Folk Arts and Crafts Festival
US 11, Weyers Cave
(888) 750-2722
The focus here is on local artisans, many of whom exhibit solely at this festival, but others from North Carolina, Pennsylvania, and Washington, D.C., also have attended. The show is usually held the first weekend in May at Blue Ridge Community College and includes foods ranging from country ham sandwiches to pork rinds. There's also live entertainment around the clock, including bluegrass, country, and Irish music. It's free.

Mayfest
46 East Main Street, Luray
(540) 743-3915
Luray's normally serene Main Street and the town park are transformed into a frenzy of activity the third Saturday in May in a celebration reminiscent of the old-fashioned street festivals. The street is lined with crafters, antiques dealers, and vendors with flowers, plants, and herbs. Food, live music by Shenandoah Valley bands, pony rides, llamas, arts activities, go-kart rides, dancers, and the performance of a traditional Maypole dance add to the fun. Historic buildings are open for tours too. Admission to the events is free.

Reenactment of the Battle of New Market
George Collins Parkway, New Market
(540) 740-3101
www.vmi.edu/museum/nm
This three-day event is centered around a skirmish and living history exhibit on Saturday and a full battle reenactment on Sunday closest to May 15, the date of the 1864 Civil War battle. The event is held at Battlefield State Historic Park. Cost is $8.00 in advance; $14.00 for two days, $18.00 for three days. Children younger than 6 get in free.

Memorial Day Horse Fair and Auction
US 11, Harrisonburg
(540) 434-0005
This 22-year-old tradition is the largest horse auction in the Shenandoah Valley. Held at the Rockingham County Fairgrounds, it also features Western wear and horse equipment. It's free, unless you have the high bid on a horse.

Ernest "Pig" Robertson Trout Fishing Rodeo
Lake Spring Park, Salem
(540) 375-3057
For the past 51 years, children have gotten a chance to land the big one at this fishing classic in early May. On the first Saturday, the fishing is reserved for kids ages 3 to 8, while the second Saturday of the rodeo, children ages 9 to 12 get to test their angling skills. The fun takes place from 9:00 A.M. to noon. Just bring your gear and bait. Children must be accompanied by an adult. Admission is free.

Antiques Expo
Off Interstate 64, Fishersville
(540) 846-7452
www.augustaexpo.com
This 15-year-old event is one of the largest gatherings of dealers and collectors in the region. Approximately 500 dealers from up and down the East Coast attended past events at Augusta County Expoland. The show is usually held the second weekend of May with another planned for October. General admission tickets are around $4.00 per day.

Wool Days
1290 Richmond Road W, Staunton
(540) 332-7850
www.frontiermuseum.gov
Sharpen the shears, the sheep are ready! The Frontier Culture Museum does it the old-fashioned way, from shearing to washing, carding, and spinning during the first week in May. It doesn't cost anything to watch interpreters shear the museum's flock of sheep, but you will have to pay the general admission to get in the museum. Last year it was $10.00 for adults $9.50 for seniors, $9.00 for students, and $6.00 for children ages 6 to 12.

Art in the Park
1 Gypsy Hill Park, Staunton
(540) 885-2028
This downtown Staunton outdoor art show features more than 100 local and national artists, including a large number of wildlife painters. The event, which also offers entertainment and food, is held at the city's beautiful Gypsy Hill Park usually the third weekend of May. It's free.

Blue Ridge Classic Soap Box Derby
Main Street, Waynesboro
(540) 943-5569
www.brsoapbox.com
Waynesboro plays host to one of the largest soap box derbies in the United States, usually the second weekend in May. Drivers ages 9 to 16 show their driving skills down Main Street in their own homemade cars. More than 168 boys and girls competed in 2004, with the winner advancing to the All-American Soap Box Derby Championship in Akron, Ohio. There's no fee to watch. Derbies are now also in Winchester and Culpeper.

Spring Wildflower Symposium
Highway 664, Wintergreen
(434) 325-8169, (434) 325-7451
www.twnf.org/wfs.html
Every May, Wintergreen Resort invites prominent specialists to lead workshops, lectures, and other educational programs about wildflowers. More than 45 field trips, lectures, and workshops are presented by well-known botanists, photographers, and artists. There are also guided hikes, wildflower sales, photography displays, and entertainment. The symposium is usually held the second weekend of May. Cost is $115 and does not include accommodations.

Culpeper Day
Davis Street, Culpeper
(540) 825-8628
www.culpepervachamber.com
This community-wide street festival is a tradition held the first Saturday of May featuring regional crafts, bluegrass, and country music and all types of food from shish kabobs to funnel cakes. Admission is free. The Museum of Culpeper also will be open for tours.

The Flying Circus
Highway 644, Bealeton
(540) 439-8661
www.flyingcircusairshow.com
The first weekend in May is usually the opening airshow for the Flying Circus at Bealeton, southwest of Warrenton on U.S. Highway 17 and Highway 644. Airshows, balloon rallies, and car shows are held on the grounds every Sunday through October. (See our Kidstuff chapter.) Admission is $10.00, $3.00 for those ages 3 to 12.

Delaplane Strawberry Festival
11012 Edmonds Lane, Delaplane
(540) 592-3556, (540) 364-2772
www.delaplanestrawberryfestival.org
Crafts, hayrides, clowns, games, pony rides, and a petting zoo are part of this strawberry harvest celebration held at Sky Meadows State Park usually on Memorial Day weekend. Sample strawberry shortcake and sundaes or take home fresh strawberries and jam. The cost is $15 per car.

Graves Mountain Festival of Music
Highway 670, Syria
(540) 923-4231
www.gravesmountain.com
This three-day bluegrass concert series, held the Thursday, Friday, and Saturday after Memorial Day, brings in folks from around the region to Graves Mountain Lodge. IIIrd Time Out, Rhonda Vincent, and Mac Wiseman were among the performers in 2004. Bring a lawn chair. The cost of a three-day pass is $70, or $60 in advance.

Dolley Madison's Birthday
Highway 20 S, Montpelier Station
(540) 672-2728
www.montpelier.org
This is an annual celebration on May 20 at Montpelier, 4 miles from Orange, including a birthday cake, garden tour, and free

admission to those who share the former
first lady's birthday.

Crozet Arts and Crafts Festival
Park Road, Crozet
(434) 823-2211
Claudius Crozet Park, 12 miles west of
Charlottesville, is the venue for this
nationally ranked show, always held on
Mother's Day weekend. It's a wonderful
opportunity to see and purchase a variety
of arts and crafts from more than 125
exhibitors. Admission fee is $4.00, $1.00
for children 6 to 12.

North-South Skirmish Association
Spring Nationals
U.S. Highway 522, Winchester
(540) 888-3349, (800) 662-1360
www.n-ssa.org
The North-South Skirmish Association
honors Civil War soldiers by staging
shooting competitions with authentic uniforms and original or reproductions of
firearms. You can watch mortar, cannons,
revolvers, carbine, and musket fire at the
109th national event in mid-May. There
also will be a ladies' dress competition at
Fort Shenandoah. Antiques, books, and
clothing will be on sale. Admission is free.

Neighborhood Art Show
Main Street, The Plains
(540) 253-5177
Collages, sculptures, ceramics, and paintings by artists young and old are displayed at Grace Episcopal Church Parish
House, usually the second weekend in
May. Admission to the Friday night gala
for this 57-year-old event is $10.00. Gen-
eral admission prices were $5.00 on Sat-
urday and Sunday.

Of Ale and History Beer Festival
US 11, Middletown
(540) 869-2028
www.bellegrove.org
Try unlimited samples of 35 specialty
beers at this annual microbrew and import
beer festival in mid-May at Belle Grove
Plantation. There is also live entertainment

*While many events are sponsored by a
facility or institution, other activities are
sponsored by church groups or organizations such as the Ruritans or Junior
League, and the telephone number
listed may be a private number or one
that is checked only occasionally. Plan
ahead and be patient, as it may take
time to get the information you need.*

and plenty of food. The cost is $18 at the
gate, $14 if you pay in advance.

Old Town Spring Festival
Main Street, Warrenton
(540) 347-4414
Country and bluegrass music, dancing,
clogging demonstrations, crafts, and a
petting zoo take over Main Street in historic Old Town Warrenton usually the third
Saturday in May. It's free.

Theater at Lime Kiln
Lime Kiln Road, Lexington
(540) 463-3074
www.theateratlimekiln.com
Memorial Day begins the summer outdoor
season at Lime Kiln, an outdoor theater
that's nationally recognized for presenting
original plays and musicals relating to Virginia's culture and history. Plays and concerts take place under the stars in an
enchanting setting, the ruins of an actual
lime kiln built in the 1800s. Plays are performed Tuesday through Saturday until
Labor Day. On Sunday nights, some of the
best and brightest in the music business
perform jazz, blues, folk, and bluegrass
music at Lime Kiln. Admission prices
range from $13 to $17 for plays and $12 to
$26 for concerts.

Haunting Tales
Streets of Lexington
(540) 464-2250
www.ghosttour.biz
Come experience Lexington at night—if
you dare! Narrated ghost tours of the
town run Memorial Day weekend through

October. Reservations are strongly recommended. Admission is $10.00 for ages 13 and older, $6.00 for ages 4 to 12, and free for children 3 and younger. Tours start at the Lexington Visitors Center at 106 East Washington Street.

Bonnie Blue National Horse Show
Highway 39 W, Lexington
(540) 464-2950
www.horsecenter.org
You'll see American Saddlebreds in action, from fine harness to country pleasure driving, at this major four-day event in mid-May at the Virginia Horse Center (see our Horse Country chapter). Most events are free for spectators.

The Virginia State Championship Chili Cook-off
Market Square, Roanoke
(540) 342-4716
Thousands of connoisseurs pour into Roanoke's historic farmers' market the first Saturday in May to indulge themselves. There is a fee if you want to enjoy the wine tasting or samples from the beer garden.

Community School Strawberry Festival
Downtown City Market, Roanoke
(540) 563-5036
This event takes place 1 block down from the Chili Cook-off during the first weekend of May. Be sure to save room!

Roanoke Festival in the Park
Roanoke
(540) 342-2640
www.roanokefestival.org
This 10-day celebration beginning Memorial Day weekend includes one of the East Coast's largest sidewalk art shows, a river race, concerts, fireworks, children's games, ethnic foods, bike and road races, and a children's parade. During the second week, a carnival is held at the Civic Center. Admission buttons are $15, $10 in advance.

An Evening of Elegance
2111 Memorial Avenue, Lynchburg
(434) 847-8688
www.vsaart.com
This annual fund-raiser for the Virginia School of the Arts is always held in early May. Internationally acclaimed dancers perform with local students at the E. C. Glass Auditorium. This gala benefits the Dame Margot Fonteyn Scholarship Fund. Tickets range from $20 to $100.

New River Valley Horse Show
off Highway 100, Dublin
(540) 674-1548
This is the largest such event in the New River Valley. It is held in May and includes various horse breeds. Admission is $5.00, $3.00 for children.

Art Museum of Western Virginia
Sidewalk Art Show
Market Square, Roanoke
(540) 342-5760
www.artmuseumroanoke.org
Sculpture, photography, watercolors, prints, and more are on display in the market district during Roanoke Festival in the Park weekend around the end of May. More than 200 artists attended the event, which celebrated its 46th anniversary in 2004. Admission is free.

Claytor Lake State Park Arts and Crafts Show
Dublin
(540) 980-7363
www.advance2000.com
This is a popular Memorial Day weekend event for the whole family. About 50 local craftspeople bring their best work to sell. Good Appalachian-style vittles such as hotcakes and apple turnovers are available, along with children's activities and live entertainment. There is a $3.00 gate fee to the park.

JUNE

Upperville Colt and Horse Show
Highway 50, Upperville
(540) 253-5760, (540) 592-3858
www.upperville.com

The oldest horse show in the United States was founded here in 1853 and continues the first week in June under the Oaks on both sides of Highway 50 at the Grafton and Salem farms. Designated as a World Championship Hunter Rider Show, this event was voted the Virginia Horse Show Association's Horse Show of the Year and is a designated World Championship Hunter-Rider show. Competition ranges from the Budweiser Upperville Jumper Classic to the Pony Prix. Also on the grounds are Jack Russell terrier races, sheepdog demonstrations, pony rides, arts and crafts exhibits, games for children, and food of all sorts. Daily admission will run around $10 per day, but children younger than 12 are admitted free when accompanied by an adult.

Strawberry Festival and Mountain Heritage Day
Court Square, Stanardsville
(434) 985-8327

This annual event in Greene County kicks off with a big strawberry breakfast, usually the first Saturday in June. But the festival offers plenty of activities for the entire family. There are two music tents, food vendors, a parade, a big band concert, craft demonstrations—many conducted by artisans in period dress—plus period games for children of all ages.

Vintage Virginia Wine Festival
Highways 624 and 626, Millwood
(800) 277-CORK, (888) 435-9746
www.vintagevirginia.com

Fifty-eight wineries and 30 restaurants take part in this early June weekend event on the grounds of Historic Long Branch Farm, once owned by the son of Thomas Nelson Jr., a signee of the Declaration of Independence and governor of Virginia during the Revolutionary War. More than 100 vendors display their arts and crafts at Virginia's largest wine festival, and other features include gourmet food; jazz, reggae, and pop music; rides; and children's entertainment. More than 40,000 people have attended these popular events. Admission is around $22, $18 in advance.

Shenandoah Valley Bach Festival
1200 Park Road, Harrisonburg
(540) 432-4582
www.emu/edu/bach

The second week in June is filled with professional concerts and events celebrating the works of Bach and Mendelssohn at Eastern Mennonite University. Concerts cost $18.50.

Bluemont Concert Series
Central and Northern Virginia
(703) 777-6306
www.bluemont.org

Enjoy music under the stars during this summer outdoor concert series held in Warrenton, Leesburg, Middleburg, Winchester, Culpeper, and Luray. Each town has a concert each week, beginning in mid-June. Musicians such as Grammy-nominated John McCutcheon and Robin and Linda Williams rotate venues. Call for a calendar of the family-oriented concerts. Admission is $5.00.

Hall of Fame Joust
Highway 936, Mount Solon
(540) 350-2510, (540) 568-2885

Four levels of competitors vie for jousting titles at Natural Chimneys Regional Park.

In mid-June, make your way to the 　ℹ️
James River to watch a fleet of flat-bottomed boats, called bateaux, pole
120 miles from Lynchburg to Richmond.
The eight-day Batteaux Festival commemorates the days when these trade
boats were the main vehicles to carry
cargo in the 18th and 19th centuries.

Look for this event about the third Saturday in June (see our Horse Country chapter). Admission is $6.00 per car.

Confederate Memorial Service
305 East Boscawen Street, Winchester
(540) 662-1937
The more than 2,500 Confederate soldiers buried in the Stonewall Jackson Cemetery are honored in this June 6 service sponsored by the Turner Ashby United Daughters of the Confederacy, Chapter 54. The event will celebrate its 139th annual service in 2005. There is no charge.

Greater Shenandoah Valley Fair
U.S. Highway 340, Waynesboro
(540) 943-9336
Hop on the amusement rides, buy cotton candy, listen to country music, or watch the automobile action at this weeklong event at the fairgrounds in late June. There is a lot of smashing and bashing in store during the championship demolition derby, but the main event is the stock car race on the Eastside Speedway oval.

Nelson County Summer Festival
Highway 653, Lovingston
(434) 263-5239, (800) 282-8223
www.nelsoncountysummerfestival.com
Held in late June, this is a family-oriented, upscale festival on the lovely grounds of Oak Ridge Estate south of Lovingston. It features two days of traditional and contemporary music, crafts, and wine from local wineries. Children will enjoy the animals, puppets, and Tom Sawyer's Fence Painting game. Cost is $15 at the gate, $10 in advance. Those younger than 12 get in free.

Miss Virginia Pageant
710 Williamson Road, Roanoke
(540) 981-1201, (540) 853-5483
www.missva.com
This annual event, which takes place the last weekend in June at the Roanoke Civic Center, produces the state's Miss America contestant. Young women from all over the state compete to win scholarships. Admission is $15 to $25.

Roanoke Valley Horse Show
1001 Roanoke Road, Salem
(540) 375-4013
www.salemciviccenter.com
Held in mid-June at the Salem Civic Center, this is one of the top all-breed horse shows on the East Coast. It usually attracts about 800 entries from across the United States. Admission is usually $8.00.

Festival Around Town
Pearisburg Community Center, Winona Avenue, Pearisburg
(540) 921-2644
This beautiful town near the Appalachian Trail hosts this all-day arts and music fete on the third Saturday of June. You can come celebrate early on Friday night when the Lion's Club hosts its kick-off barbecue dinner. Admission is free.

International Bass Bonanza
Covington
(540) 962-2178
This fishing event is held every year at Lake Moomaw in the Allegheny Mountains. The elusive largemouth bass is the featured attraction. There is no admission price to watch, but competitors must pay an entry fee, usually in the $100 range.

Chautauqua Festival in the Park
Downtown Wytheville
(276) 228-6855
www.angelfire.com/va3/chautauqua festival
In the late 19th century, the Chautauqua (pronounced sha-TAUK-wa) movement became a popular form of adult education and entertainment in the United States. In the 1920s, Wytheville was a stop on the Chautauqua circuit of traveling caravans with their tents and performances. The lectures, music, drama, and children's activities were popular until the Great Depression aided in its demise. But in 1985 the Chautauqua Festival was revived in Wytheville and has been a growing source of both entertainment and education. For nine days in late June at locations around this scenic southwest Virginia community,

you can sample food, participate in a hot-air balloon rally, watch a parade, hear concerts, go to the circus, test your taste buds in the pepper-eating contest, take in the art exhibits, or listen to the winners read from their works in the annual writing contest. Most events are free.

Newtown Heritage Festival
US 11, Stephens City
(540) 869-3087
Catch the 12th annual festival of crafts, art, artisans, parades, children's rides, food, and entertainment as Stephens City celebrates the heritage of Newtown. The free events take place throughout the small town of Stephens City. Look for the festival on Memorial Day weekend.

JULY

Shenandoah Valley Music Festival
221 Shrine Mont Circle, Orkney Springs
(540) 459-3396, (800) 459-3396
www.musicfest.org
Classical music is performed live in a concert series from July to August. Shows are performed in an outdoor pavilion next to the former Orkney Springs Hotel, a massive pre-Civil War building (see our Arts chapter). Get there early for the ice cream socials held before every concert. Arts and crafts shows are also held those weekends. Tickets run $16 to $23 for symphony concerts, and $15 to $24 for folk and jazz shows.

Ash Lawn Opera Festival
James Monroe Parkway, Charlottesville
(434) 293-4500, (434) 979-0122
www.ashlawnopera.org
This potpourri of music is highlighted by opera and musical theater productions throughout July and August, a Music at Twilight concert series with traditional and contemporary musical performances, and a Summer Saturdays family entertainment series. (See our Arts chapter.) Prices vary.

Fourth of July Celebration
Davis Street, Culpeper
(540) 825-4416, (540) 825-1093
Enjoy an old-fashioned parade, arts and crafts, games, and fireworks in downtown Culpeper and at the town's Yowell Meadow Park. It's free, but bring along some money for the covered-wagon rides.

Fourth of July Celebration
Cadet Street, New Market
(540) 740-3432
This Shenandoah Valley town hosts a big family celebration with a lot of music, food, games, a parade, and fireworks at Community Park at the south end of Cadet Street. Admission is free. There may be a small fee for parking.

Monticello Independence Day and Naturalization Ceremony
Highway 53, Charlottesville
(434) 984-9822
www.monticello.org
New citizens from the Charlottesville area are naturalized each Fourth of July on the grounds of Thomas Jefferson's Monticello. A fife and drum corps provides music at this moving event, attended usually by nearly 1,000 people. Past speakers have included then secretary of state Colin L. Powell and the Honorable Andrew Young, former U.S. ambassador to the United Nations. Admission to the outdoor ceremony is free. You will have to pay the general admission if you want to tour the house. (See our Attractions chapter.)

Frederick County Fair
US 11, Clearbrook
(540) 667-8739
www.frederickcountyfair.com
An old-fashioned country fete starts the last Monday in July and runs through Saturday at the county fairgrounds north of town. It features food, arts and crafts, concerts, a demolition derby, the Frederick County Fair Pageant, and a tiny miss pageant for 4- and 5-year-olds. Admission is $5.00.

CLOSE-UP
Ash Lawn Opera Festival

While a student at the University of Virginia more than 25 years ago, Priscilla Little had a bright idea of how to spend her summer vacation. Today hundreds of people organize their vacations around her grand plan.

Little, a singer who was working on her master's degree at UVA, enjoyed opera, but there were few places in the Charlottesville area, including Mr. Jefferson's university, where one could relish the stratospheric, high-speed coloratura of one of Mozart's arias. In other words, she was looking for a place to sing. So she founded the Ash Lawn Opera Festival.

"She came up here and asked if she could do a couple of one-act opera performances," said Judith Walker, general manager of Ash Lawn–Highland's festival. "They said yes, and she put on an all-local production."

Little did Little realize that her after-school project, which had blossomed into one of the most respected summer opera programs, would be recognized internationally. *Money* magazine named the festival one of the "20 top warm-weather opera companies in the world." That placed the Albemarle County company in the same league with Italy's La Scala Opera, Munich's Opera Festival, and Austria's Salzburg Festival. As grand as that may sound, Ash Lawn prides itself in taking the highbrow out of opera.

"It's a real easy way for people to experience opera for the first time," Walker said. "You can bring your bottle of wine and have a picnic before the show. It's outdoors, so you don't have to get dressed up, and all the songs are sung in English."

Set amid the relaxing centuries-old boxwood gardens at President James Monroe's historic home, the festival erases the intimidation factor for the opera novice. For the connoisseur, the

Camp Jeep
Oak Ridge Estate, Nellysford
(800) 789–JEEP
www.jeep.com/campjeep
It's a Jeep owners' paradise. The summertime gathering of owners and enthusiasts celebrated its 10th anniversary in 2004 at the Oak Ridge Estate in Nelson County. For three days in mid-July, participants meet for a wide range of family activities and live musical performances. One of the highlights is the Jeep 101, a course designed to teach off-highway driving and safety skills. Participants are paired with skilled drivers as they try to maneuver steep hills with large rocks, log crossings,

and sand. Once you master the course, there are plenty of trails to test your own vehicle. Approximately 2,500 Jeeps were registered for the 2004 event. Since its inception, 70,000 people from 48 states have participated. It's not cheap. The cost runs from $335 to $425, but register early. It has sold out every year.

Plantation Days at Highland
James Monroe Parkway, Charlottesville
(434) 293–9539
www.ashlawnhighland.org
At Ash Lawn–Highland, James Monroe's 535-acre estate, merchants, crafters, servants, and soldiers are depicted in a cele-

fully staged productions at Ash Lawn are a rare treat. Past cast members have performed at the New York City Opera, the Washington Opera, and the Metropolitan Opera.

"We spend two days auditioning in New York," Walker said, "and from 10:00 A.M. to 5:00 P.M. both days, we hear singers every four minutes. But we have been blessed with some exceptional singers. They come because they have the opportunity to sing the principal roles—at a very young age—that they wouldn't have the opportunity to sing at a major opera house."

The *Barber of Seville* and *Annie* were performed in 2004. But the festival includes more than opera. Its Music at Twilight series features a different musical performance every Wednesday night, ranging from Broadway show tunes to Appalachian hoedowns. There's something for the younger generation, too. Visiting puppeteers, storytellers, theater companies, and singers perform in the Summer Saturdays series for children. And there is even a free lecture series for those who want to know behind-the-scenes stories about the operas. Of course, that was Little's plan. Her first mini-festival in 1978 included two one-act operas, lectures, and a concert of African-American music. Her free performances drew 800 fans. Today, that number is closer to 10,000 each summer.

"Over the years, it evolved," Walker said. "In the beginning we borrowed lights from UVA. A lot of the costumes came from there. It was a real community effort, and it still is. We bring in 40 singers and musicians, and each one of them is housed by members of the community all summer long. That is very unusual."

Oh, and one of the other great things about going to Ash Lawn Opera Festival is that you don't have to fork out hundreds of dollars for a front-row seat at Salzburg. In recent years, tickets for Ash Lawn's operas and musicals ranged from $14 to $24. The 8:00 P.M. shows run from July through mid-August. For information on the Ash Lawn Opera Festival, call (434) 979-0122 or visit www.ashlawn opera.org.

bration of Early American life. More than 20 crafters and artisans in period costumes demonstrate and sell their work the first weekend in July. Visitors can also enjoy 18th-century music and games. Tickets are $5.00 in addition to the regular $9.00 admission fee.

Graves Mountain Fourth of July
Highway 670, Syria
(540) 923-4231
www.gravesmountain.com
Graves Mountain Lodge celebrates the Fourth of July with a fireworks display at dusk. Admission is free.

Fourth of July Firemen's Carnival
Park Road, Crozet
(434) 823-6178
Claudius Crozet Park, 12 miles west of Charlottesville, is the venue for this four-day festival with rides, games, food, fireworks, and a parade on Saturday. There is no charge, but it costs a dollar to park.

Orange County Fair
Highway 20, Montpelier
(540) 672-2271
www.orangecountyvafair.com
This late-July celebration of rural life features animal exhibits, country music, games, and food. You won't want to miss

the fiddle contest, draft horse pull, or the skunk drag races. Admission to the event is $6.00, $3.00 for children ages 5 to 12.

Fourth of July Celebration
Highway 664, Wintergreen
(434) 325-8180
www.wintergreenresort.com
The town of Wintergreen celebrates the holiday with a big three-day party for the entire family. Festivities begin Friday evening with a family campfire and sing-along. Saturday is filled with fun, including an arts and crafts fair, musical perform-ances, chairlift rides, workshops, an ice cream social, hayrides, and a volleyball tournament. It's more of the same on Sun-day, but the big attraction is a concert and the grand fireworks display. Blanket-style seating is recommended to watch the finale. With the exception of a small fee for workshop materials, most of the events are free.

Wintergreen Summer Music Festival
Highway 664, Wintergreen
(434) 325-8292, (800) 594-8499
www.wtgmusic.org
The Wintergreen Performing Arts Council stages a series of concerts ranging from chamber music to full orchestra in the John D. Evans Performing Arts Center at Wintergreen Resort starting in July. Ticket prices vary from $10 to $28.

Rockbridge Regional Fair
Highway 39 W, Lexington
(540) 463-6263
Come spend a day at this county fair held in late July at the Virginia Horse Center. It includes a variety of livestock, entertain-ment, carnival rides, food, concerts, a Confederate camp reenactment, and com-petitions. There's a minimal price to park but no admission charge.

Fourth of July Hot Air Balloon Rally
Virginia Military Institute, Lexington
(540) 463-5375
This Fourth of July event features the launching of 14 different balloons at the

VMI grounds throughout the weekend. There's also food, games, music, and fire-works. It's free.

Music for Americans
Roanoke
(540) 853-2889, (540) 345-4030
At Roanoke's Victory Stadium, this Fourth of July celebration features a performance by the Roanoke Symphony Orchestra, the community chorus, and fireworks. Admis-sion is free.

Virginia Commonwealth Games
Various locations, Roanoke
(540) 343-0987, (800) 333-8274
www.commonwealthgames.org
Produced by Virginia Amateur Sports in Roanoke during the third weekend of July, this sports festival is for men and women of all ages and abilities. This Olympic-style competition includes such sports as bas-ketball, karate, tennis, and chess as well as many others. Admission to opening cere-monies, held at the Roanoke Civic Center, is $15, $12 for those 12 and younger. Some of the sporting events are free, while oth-ers charge a minimal admission.

Vinton July Fourth Celebration
814 East Washington Street, Vinton
(540) 983-0613
The fireworks celebration is held at 6:00 P.M. every year at the Vinton War Memor-ial. Admission is free.

Salem Fair
1001 Roanoke Boulevard, Salem
(540) 375-4013
www.salemfair.com
For two weeks beginning in early July, this old-time country fair holds forth at the Salem Civic Center, both indoors and out-side. Carnival rides, Wild West follies, games, food, concerts, and livestock judging go on for the duration of the event. A bake-off attracts some of the best cooks in the Roa-noke Valley. General admission is free, but some events cost extra. The second-largest fair in the state draws 300,000 visitors.

Independence Celebration
Highway 661, Lynchburg
(434) 525-1806
www.poplarforest.org
This is not your typical Fourth of July party. At Poplar Forest, interpreters will portray the lives of local citizenry during Thomas Jefferson's time. The fun includes early-19th-century craft demonstrations, music, rides, and a lot of food. There is a $3.00 to $5.00 parking fee.

Bedford's Libertyfest
Centertown, Bedford
(540) 587-6061, (866) 586-2148
www.centertownbedford.com
Independence Day festivities are held throughout the town of Bedford, called the Patriotic Capital of Virginia. There will be crafts, children's activities, good food, beer, and wine from local wineries, not to mention the live concert and fireworks display. There also will be walking tours throughout the day at the D-Day Memorial.

July Celebration
600 Unruh Drive, Radford
(540) 731-5031
Radford's Glencoe Museum plays host to an old-fashioned Fourth of July with crafts and food vendors. After taking in the free activities, mosey over to Bissett Park, where the evening will be capped off with a fireworks display.

Madison County Fair
Highway 687, Madison
(540) 948-7073
Come on down to this old-fashioned county fair with a carnival, tractor pull, pet show, and fireworks. This event is usually in mid-July at the Young Farmers Grounds on Highway 687. There is a small admission fee.

AUGUST

Shenandoah County Fair
300 Fairgrounds Road, Woodstock
(540) 459-3867
www.shencofair.com

This weeklong fair in late August has been a tradition in Shenandoah County for more than 87 years. One of the larger fairs in the state, it is the only one with harness racing. Admission into the fair is $5.00 for adults, $2.00 for children, with entertainment ranging from tractor pulls and beauty contests to a demolition derby and concerts. Tickets to big-name concerts including the likes of Trick Pony, Ronnie Milsap, and Trace Adkins cost in the $21 to $26 range. Of course, there are carnival rides, too, to go along with food galore. There's even an "old-fashioned" baking contest.

Attending local festivals is fun, but sitting in traffic is not. Sometimes these annual events in small areas create traffic jams—fields are turned into parking lots with civilians directing cars. But people usually remain upbeat, so kick back, plan your next excursion, and smile.

Warren County Fair
US 522 N and Highway 661, Front Royal
(540) 635-5827
www.warrencountyfair.com
Since 1957, the Warren County Fairgrounds has hosted this annual family festival in late July, early August. It's an agricultural cornucopia with hogs, rabbits, goats, and cattle. But along with the usual fair fare, there are some top-notch concerts featuring national acts. Admission to the fair varies each day, usual in the $4.00 to $10.00 range, but the special concerts have been known to fetch $30.00.

Rockingham County Fair
4808 South Valley Pike, Harrisonburg
(540) 434-0005
www.rockinghamcountyfair.com
The *Los Angeles Times* named the Rockingham County Fair one of the 10 best rural county fairs in the United States. Virginia's largest agricultural county salutes its agrarian roots with exhibits, livestock,

and a tractor pull during the third week of August. Previous fairs featured country music stars Brad Paisley, Tracy Bryd, and Terri Clark. It's seven days of nonstop action with a rodeo, motocross, parades, bull riding, and a demolition derby. Admission is in the $5.00 range, with an extra charge for the main-stage concerts.

Natural Chimneys Joust
Highway 936, Mount Solon
(540) 350-2510, (540) 662-1937
Here's an anachronism. "Knights" from several states congregate to joust for a shining ring. Bluegrass music fills the air, and the seven castlelike towers of Natural Chimneys form a spectacular backdrop. The event, which has been held since 1821, takes place the third Saturday in August. (See our Horse Country chapter.) Admission is $6.00 per car.

Hot Air Balloon Festival and Airshow
Highway 644, Bealeton
(540) 439-8661
www.flyingcircusair.com
In mid-August, the Flying Circus near Warrenton hosts a weekend of aerial fun. You can even take a ride in the open cockpit of a biplane before or after the show. The 12-minute rides in a Piper Cub cost $30 per passenger. You can ride in a biplane for $50 for eight minutes, or for $100 you can take an aerobatic flight with loops and barrel rolls. Admission is $10.00; $3.00 for ages 3 to 12.

Lucketts Fair
Lucketts Community Center
42361 Lucketts Road, Leesburg
(703) 771-5281
Be sure to come to the Lucketts Fair, a summer tradition since 1972 during the last weekend in August. Enjoy bluegrass music, quality crafts including furniture, pewter, woven rugs, quilts, forged iron, stained and beveled glass, and many others, as well as antiques and old-time demonstrations in spinning and butter churning. For the little ones, there is juggling, music, magic, and old-fashioned games. After building up an

appetite, choose from a vast variety of down-home food, including barbecue platters, hand-churned ice cream, country ham sandwiches, roasted corn on the cob, and more. The price is only $4.00, and free for children younger than 5. Stick around for the fruit-pie baking contest in the afternoon.

Virginia Wine Festival
Long Branch Farm, Millwood
(540) 253-5001, (800) 520-9670
www.showsinc.com
The oldest wine festival in the Commonwealth is held in late August on the grounds of Long Branch Farm. It's an event featuring more than 50 of the state's finest wineries, food, arts and crafts, music, and wine lectures. Tickets to the 29-year-old festival are priced at $20, $16 in advance.

Shakespeare at the Ruins
Highway 777, Barboursville
(540) 832-5355
The Four County Players and Barboursville Vineyards in Orange team up to produce this annual theater, wine, and dinner evening. Enjoy a Shakespearean play staged outdoors at the historic ruins of Gov. Barbour's mansion in early August. Come 90 minutes early for a picnic, or call ahead to reserve a buffet dinner. Call for prices.

Oak Grove Folk Music Festival
Highway 612, Verona
(540) 885-3000
This annual festival, in its 27th year in 2005, is an intimate, family-oriented weekend where you can hear local and national folk acts under the trees at Virginia's oldest outdoor theater. Tickets were $15 for a Saturday session or $35 for a weekend pass. Food and beverages are available.

Albemarle County Fair
Off U.S. Highway 29, North Garden
(434) 293-6396
www.avenue.org/fair
This annual event is usually held at the end of August and features old-fashioned country fun with rides, games, contests, the Third Regiment of the Army of North-

ern Virginia Civil War Camp, live bands, food, and a variety of crop and animal exhibits. Tickets are $5.00 for adults and $1.00 for children ages 6 to 12.

Greene County Fair
241 Fairlane Drive, Stanardsville
(434) 985-8282
http://greenecountyfair.tripod.com
Enjoy food, music, exhibits, and rides at this annual fair held in early August. Along with the usual dairy, sheep, beef, and market hog shows, events include such acts as cloggers, country and bluegrass bands, plus frog-jumping, and horseshoe-pitching contests. Tickets to get in are $4.00 or $20.00 for a weekly pass.

August Court Days
Various locations, Leesburg
(800) 752-6118
More than 200 costumed characters interpret Leesburg's Colonial history in street vignettes in downtown Leesburg. A children's fair, music, and crafts are also featured. This Colonial-era street fair is held usually the third weekend of August. Look for troops representing the king to take on the buckskinners from the valley. The fest costs around $5.00, and children younger than 12 get in free.

Page Valley Agricultural Fair
Collins Avenue, Luray
(540) 743-3915, (540) 843-FAIR
Animal, crop, and homemakers' exhibits are part of this fair, which also includes a tractor pull, parade, demolition derby, and live music. It is usually held in mid-August. Admission to the fair is $6.00, half price for children.

Rockbridge Community Festival
Main Street, Lexington
(540) 463-3777
This 25-year-old festival is held along downtown Main Street in late August. It includes more than 170 exhibits and the usual festival activities such as music, arts and crafts, food, and live entertainment. It's free.

Vinton Old-Time Bluegrass Festival and Competition
Lee Avenue, Vinton
(540) 983-0613, (540) 345-8545
This event is held around mid-August every year at the Vinton Farmers' Market. Not only can you enjoy music by well-known musicians, but also you can listen to individual and band competitions. Don't forget to stop by and check out the crafts and carnival. It's free.

Steppin' Out
Main Street, Blacksburg
(540) 951-0454
www.downtownblacksburg.com/steppin
For more than 20 years, this major two-day festival has brought tons of people to downtown Blacksburg. Music and food are plentiful, as merchants seek ways to attract people to College Avenue, Draper Road, and Jackson and Main Streets. More than 170 craft vendors will line the streets selling jewelry, pottery, and fine art. This free event is always the first weekend in August.

Newport Agricultural Fair
Giles County
(540) 544-7469
One of the oldest agricultural fairs in Virginia, this Giles County community event has judged food and agriculture exhibits, livestock competitions, baking, sewing, pet shows, bluegrass music, and horseshoe and jousting tournaments happening the second weekend of August. Admission is less than $2.00.

Old Fiddler's Convention
1691 Fairfview Road, Galax
(276) 236-8541
www.oldfiddlersconvention.com
Step into the heart of country mountain music at the Fairview Ruritan's annual concert/competition five days in early August. The convention turned 69 in 2004. It's a day filled with the best of old-time and bluegrass music. If you know how to pick, you can call ahead to register. There are competitions in guitar, fid-

dle, mandolin, dulcimer, dobro, clawhammer banjo, bluegrass banjo, even autoharp, as well as best all-around performance. You will even see how to flatfoot-dance. And don't forget to bring along a little cash, because you will want to sample the great home cooking, too. Cost to get in during the week is $5.00, $8.00 on Friday, $10.00 on Saturday, and $30.00 for the whole shebang.

SEPTEMBER

Celebrating Patsy Cline Weekend
Various sites, Winchester
(540) 662-1326, (800) 662-1360
www.visitwinchesterva.com
A series of activities held September 4-6 pays tribute to the legendary country singer who was born in Winchester. Past events have included a buffet meal, a reunion dance with music provided by members of Patsy Cline's band, and a concert by George Hamilton III. The cost will vary depending on the events, but the proceeds go toward establishing a Patsy Cline Museum in Frederick County.

Taste of the Mountains Main Street Festival
Main Street, Madison
(540) 948-4455
www.madison-va.com/tastemtn.htm
Held the first Saturday of the month, this is a chance to watch craftspeople at work as they demonstrate basket weaving, woodcarving, glass blowing, chair caning, furniture making, quilting, spinning, barkbasket making, and beekeeping. You'll want to tear yourself away to listen to Appalachian tunes played on dulcimers and harps and watch the footwork of the clog dancers. A petting zoo for the kids and plenty of mountain-inspired food add to the fun. It's free. Since nearly a mile of Main Street has been blocked off for the fair, park at Madison High School on US 29 and ride the free shuttle.

Grand Caverns Bluegrass Festival
Off Interstate 81 at exit 235, Grottoes
(540) 249-5705
Grand Caverns Regional Park hosts the annual music festival in early September. Nationally recognized bands perform in the two-day event and other activities include arts and crafts booths, food, volleyball and horseshoe games, and half-price tours of the caverns. Past musical lineups have included the Nashville Bluegrass Band, James Armsworthy, the Orangeblossoms, and Alvin Breeden and the Virginia Cutups. Campers are welcome. Tickets are $18 or $31 for the weekend.

Apple Harvest Arts & Crafts Festival
Pleasant Valley Road, Winchester
(540) 662-3966, (800) 662-1360
www.visitwinchesterva.org
This fall festival at Jim Barnett Park features apple butter making and pie contests, live music, and arts and crafts galore. It is usually held the third weekend in September. Admission is about $4.00.

Bottle and Pottery Show and Sale
Purcell Street, Winchester
(540) 877-1093
www.fohbc.com
This early-September show and sale of antique bottles, pottery, postcards, and small collectibles, sponsored by the Apple Valley Bottle Collectors Club, has been an annual happening for 30 years. It's held at various venues. There's a $3.00 donation at the door.

Women's Four-Miler
Garth Road, Charlottesville
(434) 293-3367, (434) 293-6115
www.avenue.org/ctc/womens4
The largest women's race in the state of Virginia raises funds to help fight breast cancer. A total of 1,800 women signed up to run or walk the 22nd annual road race in 2004. Winners have been known to finish the 4-mile course in less than 25 minutes. The competitors, some breast cancer survivors, raised more than $30,000 for the Breast Resource Center at the Univer-

sity of Virginia. There's no charge if you want to come and cheer. It costs $20 to run, but don't delay; the race usually fills up by mid-July. The Four-Miler is held on Garth Road in front of Foxfield on the Saturday of Labor Day weekend.

Constitution Day Celebrations
Highway 20 S, Montpelier Station
(540) 672-7365
www.montpelier.org
Enjoy free admission on September 17 to tour Montpelier, the home of President James Madison, the father of the Constitution. This is an opportunity to better understand the man who contributed so much to the founding of our government. The daylong event commemorating the anniversary of our nation's charter includes music by a fife and drum corps.

Annual Orange Street Festival
Davis Street, Orange
(540) 672-5216
www.orangevachamber.org
For more than 20 years, Orange has blocked off 3 blocks along east and west Davis Street for its free street festival. On the first Saturday of the month, the streets are filled with crafts, food, children's rides, and live entertainment.

Virginia's Natural History Retreat
Highway 664, Wintergreen
(434) 325-8169
www.twnf.org
At Wintergreen Resort, natural science experts lead walks, field trips, lectures, and slide presentations during this event usually held in mid-September. Scientists, museum curators, and college professors lead programs on Virginia natural history, including slide lectures on bats, fossils, wetlands, birds, and reptiles at the Trillium House. Registration is $115 and does not include accommodations.

Edinburg Ole Time Festival
Various sites, Edinburg
(540) 984-9492
The town celebrates its anniversary with

cookin' and eatin', cloggin' and joggin', and walkin' and talkin'. This annual event sponsored by the local chamber of commerce is held over three days in mid-September and features crafts, demonstrations, antiques, concerts, dances, a walking tour, and a rubber-duck race. Prices vary according to the events.

Apple Harvest and Butter-Making Festival
Highway 741, Lovingston
(434) 263-5036
www.nelsoncounty.com
Enjoy apple butter and apple cider, cooked in giant kettles over an open fire at this fest, held at Drumbeller Orchard in late September and October. For more than 25 years, local orchards have staged special events throughout the harvest season. Admission is free.

Fauquier County Fall Farm Tour
Various sites, Fauquier County
(540) 347-4414, (540) 349-5314
The third weekend of September, seven farms in Fauquier County open their doors to allow visitors to see alpacas, llamas, sheep, ponies, dairy cows, cattle, and thoroughbred horses. This self-guided tour was awarded the Susan Allen Tourism Award for excellence in cultural tourism. An old-time barn dance was one of the treats in store at a recent tour. Brochures are available at the Fauquier Visitor's Center. The event is free, but bring some money for food. Burgers, hot dogs, and ice cream are longtime favorites.

Annual Rockbridge Food and Wine Festival
Theatre at Lime Kiln
Lime Kiln Road, Lexington
(540) 463-5375
This early September fest offers something for everyone: exotic autos, live music, seminars, food and wine tastings, and presentations by the Lime Kiln players. Admission is $15 in advance and $18 at the door.

Rockbridge Mountain Music and Dance Festival
Glen Maury Park
10th Avenue, Buena Vista
(540) 463-5214
This annual mid-September event at Glen Maury Park under the pavilion will turn 19 in 2005. Activities include fiddle and dance workshops, flat-flooting, old-time bands, and called dances. Admission is $9.00 per night.

Fincastle Festival
Roanoke Street, Fincastle
(540) 473-3077
www.hisfin.org/festival
Historic Fincastle celebrates its Scots-Irish roots at this free two-day festival held downtown the second weekend of September. Started in 1968, the festival also includes tours of the historic town, which was founded in 1745. Arts, music, games, and merchant open houses await thousands of visitors.

Henry Street Heritage Festival
Henry Street, Roanoke
(540) 345-4818
This is an annual celebration of African-American culture in a neighborhood close to downtown Roanoke the last weekend of September. The day includes ethnic food, music, entertainment, and children's activities in Elmwood Park. The events are free.

Olde Salem Days
Main Street, Salem
(540) 772-8871
This is a downtown celebration held the second Saturday in September. Its focus is on antiques and crafts with more than 400 vendors, and it's free. You'll also enjoy music, and antique car show, and children's activities.

Kaleidoscope
Various locations, Lynchburg
(434) 847-1811, (800) 732-5821
www.discoverlynchburg.org
This is Lynchburg's big annual fall festival that lasts nearly a month. It includes a

children's festival on the third Saturday, a major antiques show with 100 dealers, a riverfront music jamboree with barbecue, a craft show, bike race, and teddy bear parade. Thousands of runners participate in the 10-mile race. Admission to most events is free.

Boones Mill Apple Festival
U.S. Highway 220, Boones Mill
(540) 483-9542
www.franklincountyva.org
This tiny community rallies enormous resources to stage a major parade and social event along US 220. Look for major politicos among the common folk at this free event held the third Saturday of September.

Roanoke Symphony Polo Cup
Off Main Street, Salem
(540) 343-6221
www.rso.com
Come enjoy an afternoon of action with professional polo teams at Roanoke County's Green Hill Park. This early September event, sponsored by the Roanoke Symphony, includes a day of food, fashion, and fun. Admission is around $20.

Wine Festival
Bernard's Landing, Smith Mountain Lake
(540) 721-1203, (800) 676-8203
www.smithmountainlake.com
On the last Sunday in September, more than 16 of Virginia's best wineries converge at Bernard's Landing and Resort for a festival on the beautiful lake. Chamber music, wine tastings, and good food make this one of the area's more sophisticated festivals. Prices are $15.00 to taste or $8.00 for general admission.

OCTOBER

Fall Fly-In
491 Airport Road, Winchester
(540) 662-5786
Homebuilt, experimental, and vintage aircraft owners compete for prizes and share

their aviation interests with the public at the Winchester Regional Airport in early October. One year, visitors got to take a ride in a real B-17. Donations are accepted at the gate.

Fall Hunt Country Antiques Fair
28050 Oatlands Plantation Lane
Leesburg
(703) 777-3174
www.oatlands.org
More than 100 dealers exhibit antiques during this event held at Oatlands Plantation in mid-October. The $9.00 tickets do not include admission to the house.

Arborfest at the State Arboretum
U.S. Highway 50, 9 miles east of
Winchester
(540) 837-1758
www.virginia.edu/blandy
Celebrate multicultural gardening traditions the second Sunday in October at the State Arboretum with music, lectures, children's activities, entertainment, and the curator's fall tour of the arboretum. There is also an apple tasting and bulb sale. It's free, but there is a $5.00 parking fee.

Crozet Arts and Crafts Festival
Park Road, Crozet
(434) 823-2211
Claudius Crozet Park, 12 miles west of Charlottesville, is the venue for this nationally ranked show, always held the second weekend of October. This 20-plus-year-old event includes more than 125 crafters, music, and food, and a clown has been known to show up too. The cost is $4.00.

North-South Skirmish Association
National Skirmish
Off US 522 N, Winchester
(800) 662-1360
www.n-ssa.org
Members of the North-South Skirmish Association compete by live-firing Civil War firearms and artillery at breakable targets in the national event, held the first full weekend of October at Fort Shenandoah. A ladies' dress competition is also held, and

there is a large sutler area. Sutlers were people who followed the Civil War soldiers and sold goods. The modern-day sutlers will have books, period clothes, and antiques. Admission is free.

Shenandoah Valley Balloon Fest
US 50, Millwood
(540) 837-1856, (888) 558-5567
www.historiclongbranch.com
Take a ride in one of 25 hot-air balloons and see the fall foliage at its peak during this event on the third weekend in October at historic Long Branch, Robert Burwell's 1811 Greek Revival mansion. Other activities include an antique fire engine display, bluegrass music, hayrides, carnival rides, and mansion tours. Last year admission was $30 per carload or $10 per individual. Balloon rides are extra.

Battle of Cedar Creek Living History
and Reenactment
US 11, Middletown
(540) 869-2064
www.cedarcreekbattlefield.org
This reenactment is held on the site where the original Civil War battle was fought on October 19, 1864. The annual memorial takes place at Belle Grove Plantation on the weekend closest to October 19. Various symposiums and workshops are held throughout the days, and you also can watch two reenactments and artillery, infantry, and signal corps demonstrations. Admission is $10, $15 for a weekend pass.

New Market Heritage Days
Main Street, New Market
(540) 740-3212
The Shenandoah Valley town salutes its German, Scottish, and Irish heritage at this late-October weekend festival capped by a large parade. There are vendors from Maine to Florida, local crafts, a Civil War encampment, and two craft shows. It's free.

Page County Heritage Festival
Collins Avenue, Luray
(540) 743-3915
This Columbus Day weekend festival

October events attract many visitors already in the region for fall foliage. It's a great time to attend an apple-butter festival or grape harvest event—but plan early, as the Blue Ridge is busy in the Autumn.

brings to mind the old-time county fairs with music, clogging shows, wagon rides, apple cider, home-cooked food, and a steam and gas engine show. More than 170 crafters display their wares. The festival is held at the Page County Fairgrounds. A $6.00 admission will be charged.

Elkton Autumn Days Festival
B Street, Elkton
(540) 298-9370

This 18th annual outdoor festival is held the third weekend in October. Features include home-cooked food, a car show, square dancing, clogging, and live entertainment. More than 100 crafters also display their wares in front of Elkton Elementary School. There is no admission fee.

Aldie Harvest Festival
US 50, Aldie
(703) 327-6743, (800) 752-6118

This quaint village bursts with life in mid-October with a festival centering around the restoration of the town's double-wheel 1810 mill. More than 100 crafters and artists take part in the day's activities, which include a Civil War encampment, food, and music throughout the town. It's free.

Virginia Fall Foliage Festival
Broad Street, Waynesboro
(540) 942-6644, (540) 943-5187

This 33-year-old festival happens usually the first two consecutive weekends in October. Features include a 10K run, an arts and crafts show with more than 200 exhibitors, a chili cook-off, and a lot of good food made with apples, including apple dumplings, apple butter, and cider. There's also face painting and balloons for the kids. No admission is charged.

Graves Mountain Apple Harvest Festival
Highway 670, Syria
(540) 923-4231
www.gravesmountain.com/ appleharvest.htm

Celebrate apple-harvest season with the folks at Graves Mountain Lodge the second and third weekends of October. Festivities include arts and crafts, apple-butter making, hayrides, and horseback rides. You can also pick apples in the lodge's orchards. Don't miss the homemade Brunswick stew cooked in black kettles over an open fire each day. Admission and parking are free.

Fall Fiber Festival & Sheep Dog Trials
Highway 20 S, Montpelier Station
(434) 296-8533
www.fallfiberfestival.org

The stars are the sheep, llamas, angora and cashmere goats, and angora rabbits who provide the raw materials for the spinning, weaving, and shearing demonstrations. Sheepdog trials take place both days of the event, which is usually held the first weekend in October at Montpelier, home of James Monroe. Forty vendors also are on hand to exhibit and demonstrate their fiber crafts. A corner has been set up where children can learn to spin and weave. The parking fee is around $5.00.

Virginia Film Festival
Culbreth Road, Charlottesville
(434) 982-5277, (800) UVA-FEST
www.vafilm.com

Filmmakers, scholars, movie stars, and the public explored the cultural theme of "Speed" at the 17th annual Virginia Film Festival in late October 2004. More than 70 films, videos, and CD-ROMs are presented, along with guest speakers and free panels on how to break into the business. Past participants in the film festival included such stars as Nicholas Cage, Gregory Peck, Jimmy Stewart, Nick Nolte, Anthony Hopkins, Sigourney Weaver, Gena Rowlands, Robert Duvall, Charlottesville's own Sissy Spacek, and Jason Robards. While some receptions may cost in the $40.00 range, tickets to the movie screenings were $7.50 last year. Virginia native Sandra Bullock was the recipient of the Festival's 2004 Virginia Film Award.

Dayton Autumn Celebration
Main and College Streets, Dayton
(540) 879-9538
This Rockingham County town greets fall the first Saturday in October with live comedy and country music, 75 food vendors, 300 arts and crafts exhibits, and children's games. There is no cost. The festival also runs a free shuttle bus from satellite parking at Turner Ashby High School.

Annual Zoo Boo
Roanoke
(540) 343-3241
www.mmzoo.org
It's a Halloween party at the Mill Mountain Zoo that gets bigger every year. Children dress up and party among the animals. Admission is $6.75 for adults and $4.50 for children.

Affair in the Square
Campbell Avenue, Roanoke
(540) 342-5700
www.centerinsquare.org
This event combines entertainment, food, beverages, and dancing on every level of Center in the Square and has become an annual custom for many residents of southwest Virginia. It takes place the second Saturday of October. Admission is usually $70 per person.

Virginia Garlic Festival
2229 North Amherst Highway, Amherst
(434) 946-5168
www.rebecwinery.com
The five-acre Rebec Vineyards hosts this mid-October celebration, and several Virginia wineries participate. The wonderful food will please epicures. A Garlic Queen dressed in a giant bulb with sprouts shooting from her head has been known to make an appearance. You can also find music and arts and crafts. Admission with wine tasting for adults was $18.00, $14.00 for designated drivers, and $5.00 for chil-

dren ages 2 to 11. Tickets are a little more if purchased at the gate.

Amherst County Apple Harvest and Arts and Crafts Festival
US 29, Amherst
(434) 845-5606
More than 100 crafters display their works, along with apple products and special entertainment at Amherst County High School in late October. Admission is free.

Sorghum Festival
Highway 610, Clifford
(434) 946-2419, (800) 732-5821
Watch the experts make sorghum molasses at this annual event the first weekend in October. You can sample the sweets or sit back and listen to country and western music. There is plenty to keep you busy, including crafts, a tractor show, rides for the little ones, and food, including Brunswick stew and chili. All you pay is $1.00 to park your car.

Blue Ridge Folklife Festival
Ferrum College
(540) 365-4416
www.blueridgeinstitute.org
On the fourth Saturday of October, Ferrum College showcases regional folklife with this blockbuster festival. For its 31st event in 2004, visitors experienced the tastes, sights, and sounds of western Virginia folk culture as demonstrated by local residents. More than 50 Blue Ridge crafters demonstrate basket making, instrument making, tobacco twisting, and a variety of other folk arts. Many of these items are available for sale as well. The South's thriving auto culture is featured along with vintage steam and gaspowered farm machinery. There are horsepulling, mule-jumping, and log-skidding contests. The Virginia State Championship Open Water and Treeing Coon Dog contests are held throughout the day. A delicious variety of foods are always on hand, and there are three performance stages featuring music and storytelling. Many of these demonstrations are getting to be extinct as the old-timers die, so if you want to see the

Blue Ridge as it was, make it a point to go to the festival. It's crowded, but a lot of fun. The festival is held from 10:00 A.M. to 5:00 P.M. Admission, which includes a tour of the Farm Museum, is $7.00 for adults and $6.00 for children and senior citizens.

Smith Mountain Lake Fall Festival
Saunders Parkway Marina, Moneta
(540) 721-1203, (540) 297-5573
www.visitsmithmountainlake.com
On Columbus Day weekend, Smith Mountain Lake's six or so communities all host festivals, forming a virtual ring of events around the lake. You'll find arts and crafts shows, an antique car show, a flea market, traditional folkway demonstrations, and more. The events are free.

Charity Home Tour Gala
Various homes, Smith Mountain Lake
(540) 297-TOUR
www.smlcharityhometour.com
This national award-winning fund-raiser for local charities showcases the grandest homes on the lake. Homes are accessible by either land or water. Don't miss this event for show-and-tell for a good cause. It's held around the first weekend of October at 10 different homes each year. Tickets are $25 or $20 in advance.

Radford Highlanders Festival
Main Street, Radford
(540) 831-5324
www.radford.edu/festival
A joint partnership between the city of Radford and Radford University, this event celebrates the area's Scots-Irish heritage. Nearly 10,000 people were on hand as the festival celebrated its ninth anniversary in 2004. Appalachian traditions and activities include magicians, bagpipes, dancing, stilt walking, storytelling, food, Celtic and Appalachian music, a parade through downtown Radford, and, of course, traditional amateur heavy athletics at Moffett Field. The events are free and usually kick off the second weekend of October.

Newbern Fall Festival of Arts and Crafts
5240 Wilderness Road, Newbern
(540) 674-4835
Held at the Wilderness Road Museum in mid-October, this free event is filled with the spirit of the Appalachian Mountains through and through. Square dancing, antiques, crafts, and stagecoach rides are just a few of the activities you can find here.

Fall Foliage Festival
Downtown Clifton Forge
(540) 962-2178
The autumn glory of Alleghany County serves as an incredible backdrop for this arts and crafts festival held the third weekend in October. You can find music, craftspeople, an art show, homemade doughnuts and country ham, and various other activities featuring the Appalachian heritage. The festival is free.

Count Pulaski Festival
Downtown Pulaski
(540) 994-4200
Held in downtown Pulaski, this festival commemorates the renovation of the town's railway station. The event is a celebration of Pulaski's community spirit and pride. It includes activities such as a parade, boat and car shows, music, arts and crafts, and a railroad exhibit. Admission is free. Come hungry and bring the kids, too.

NOVEMBER

Christmas at Oatlands Plantation
28050 Oatlands Plantation Lane
Leesburg
(703) 777-3174
www.oatlands.org
Special Christmas events begin here the day after Thanksgiving and continue through Christmas. The mansion is dressed for the holidays, and living history presentations are staged on weekends. Call for events and times. Most programs in the day cost $10. Candlelight tours begin in mid-December.

Culpeper Christmas Open House
Davis Street, Culpeper
(540) 825-4416
Downtown Culpeper comes alive with Christmas activity in late November: carriage rides, caroling, stories, and refreshments. Kids will enjoy the trolley rides and pictures with Santa. To make sure you're in a festive mood, the open house launches the start of the downtown merchants' Christmas sales. There is no charge.

Montpelier Hunt Races
Highway 20, Montpelier Station
(540) 672-0027
www.montpelier.org
In 2004, the 70th running of this tradition of steeplechase racing and Southern hospitality was held on the grounds of the President James Madison's home in Orange County. Before the horses take center stage on the first Saturday in November, the Jack Russell terriers hurdle their way over their own obstacle course. There also is the famed Dolley Madison Tailgate competition, where racegoers can compete for the fanciest picnic setups and tasty dishes. Past judges have included food writers for the *Washington Post* and the *New York Times.* But the main attraction remains the steeplechase races, where horses and riders vie for thousand-dollar purses. Entry fee is around $15, less if you order tickets in advance. But you will need extra for parking. Parking costs $10.00, or $5.00 in advance. If you would like to reserve a spot right on the infield, expect to pay $30.00 to $40.00.

Stocked Market Holiday Bazaar
1001 Roanoke Boulevard, Salem
(540) 375-3004
www.salemciviccenter.com
More than 100 booths in the Salem Civic Center feature crafts and gifts during this mid-November event. Admission fees, usually less than $10, will get you in for three days.

Christmas at the Market
Main Street, Lynchburg
(434) 455-4485, (800) 732-5821
This colorful event is always held at the end of November at the downtown Community Market and City Armory. Come enjoy a variety of handcrafted Christmas items from more than 100 vendors. The kids will love the music and Mr. and Mrs. Santa Claus. Admission is free.

Franklin County Fall Arts and Crafts Festival
Rocky Mount
(540) 483-9211
This free festival is usually held the weekend before Thanksgiving. Downtown merchants gather together their best local wares for the event. It's usually held in the Armory, but if the National Guard is busy, the festival will move to the American Legion hall.

Living History Days
US 11, Middletown
(540) 869-2028
www.bellegrove.org
If you like to double your pleasure, early November is the perfect time to visit the historic Belle Grove Plantation. Your hosts will be decked out to take you back in history, or you can take some historical artifacts back home with you. It's the same weekend that dozens of antiques dealers will be on hand for their annual show in November. They call it their mini-version of *Antiques Road Show.* You can get an appraisal of your favorite antique for $5.00. While you're there, take in a tour of the house.

DECEMBER

Holiday House Tour
2 North Cameron Street, Winchester
(540) 667-3577
Tour five of Winchester's homes decorated for the holidays the first Sunday of the month. The tour includes a mix of old and new homes in and around Old Town.

Check by the Welcome Center in the Kurtz Building for locations and costs. In years past, the tour was $12, $10 in advance.

First Night Winchester
2 North Cameron Street, Winchester
(540) 535-3543

The town's annual New Year's Eve celebration of the arts features more than 20 different artists entertaining the public at sites throughout Winchester. It's a family-oriented, alcohol-free celebration. Buy a button for $7.00—$5.00 in advance—and you will have access to all the venues.

Christmas Candlelight Tour
336 Belle Grove Road, Middletown
(540) 869-2028
www.bellegrove.org

Belle Grove Plantation decked out in its holiday splendor is a grand way to celebrate the season. Local garden clubs provide the traditional decorations, including antique nativity scenes. The cost is $8.00, but if you time your visit right, you can take an evening tour with fireside refreshments and live music or stop by on Saturday or Sunday for an afternoon tea. Evening tours and teas, usually offered from mid- to late December, cost $10.

Candlelight Christmas Tour
46 East Main Street, Luray
(540) 743-3915
www.luraypage.com

Take a candlelight tour of Page County's historic bed-and-breakfasts the second weekend of December. About seven inns are included on this tour. Past events cost $12.00, $6.00 for ages 5 to 12. If you stay at one of the participating inns, it's free.

First Night Harrisonburg
Various locations, Harrisonburg
(540) 434-2319
www.firstnite.net

This is a nonalcoholic New Year's Eve community arts celebration for all ages. More than 20 musical, drama, and dance performances are staged at seven loca-

tions around the city. Simply buy a button for about $9.00, $7.00 in advance, and go to as many events as you like. Children younger than 5 get in free.

Woodrow Wilson Open House
18 North Coalter Street, Staunton
(540) 885-0897
www.woodrowwilson.org

Entertainment, birthday cake, punch, and holiday decorations are part of Woodrow Wilson's birthday party celebration on December 28 at his birthplace. There also are some special Victorian amusements geared for the children. It's free.

First Night Waynesboro
Downtown Waynesboro
(540) 943-7488
www.firstnightwaynesboro.com

A variety of music from classical to country can be heard at this New Year's Eve celebration for the entire family. Adults will enjoy line dancing, a visual arts display along Main Street, gospel and folk music, dramatic readings, cloggers, and magic tricks. A series of children's activities begin early in the afternoon with a parade, quilt painting, face painting, and pony rides. Participants are required to get a festival button for admittance in several of the venues. Buttons cost $5.00

Historic Staunton Foundation Christmas House Tour
120 South Augusta Street, Staunton
(540) 885-7676

This will be the 32nd year of the house tour, which last year explored five homes built between 1860 and 1917, in the Gospel Hill area, a National Register Historic district shown in the film Gods and Generals. Tickets can be bought in advance at various local shops including the Bookstack and Holt's for the Home, or you can purchase them on the day of the tour, at one of the houses. The $20 admission price gets you into all the houses on the tour. The tour usually takes place the first or second Sunday in December.

Christmas Open House at Morven Park
17263 Southern Planter Lane, Leesburg
(703) 777-2414

The mansion is decorated with turn-of-the 20th-century ornaments, the fireplaces are ablaze, and a 12-foot-tall Christmas tree fills the Great Room with its pine fragrance. It looks as if the late Virginia governor Westmoreland Davis and his wife might walk through the door at any moment. Because of renovations, the open house was not held in 2004 but will resume in 2005. The standard tour price was $7.00, $6.00 for seniors, and $1.00 for children ages 6 to 12.

First Night Leesburg
King and Market Streets, Leesburg
(703) 777-6306

This family event rings in the New Year with a candlelight procession to the courthouse. This celebration of the arts includes singing, puppet shows, storytelling, mimes, and plenty of food. Tickets are $8.00. Those 3 to 12 pay $3.00.

Christmas in Historic Old Town Warrenton
Main Street, Warrenton
(540) 349-8606, (800) 820-1021

Warrenton is full of holiday cheer with Santa visits, horse-drawn carriage rides, caroling, and more starting the first Friday in December and running every weekend until Christmas. There is a $1.00 to $2.00 charge for rides.

Yuletide Traditions at Ash Lawn–Highland
Highway 795 (James Monroe Parkway)
Charlottesville
(434) 293-9539
www.ashlawnhighland.org

Included in the holiday activities throughout December at the historic home of James Monroe is a Christmas by Candlelight evening tour. Cost runs around $12. After Christmas, you can attend afternoon holiday concerts at Ash Lawn–Highland.

Yuletide Traditions at Michie Tavern
683 Thomas Jefferson Parkway
(Highway 53), Charlottesville
(434) 977-1234
www.michietavern.com

An array of Christmas delicacies is served for a Yuletide feast in the Ordinary at historic Michie Tavern in mid-December. There also are candlelight tours and activities for the children during the weekend. The feast costs $29.50, $14.50 for children ages 10 and younger.

Yuletide Traditions Monticello
Highway 53 (Thomas Jefferson Parkway), Charlottesville
(434) 984-9822
www.monticello.org

The home of Thomas Jefferson holds guided holiday tours several evenings before Christmas, with period dancing in the parlor, food demonstrations in the kitchen, and refreshments in the museum shop. Last year the cost was $13.00, $6.00 for children ages 6 to 11. There's also holiday wreath workshops at the Monticello Visitor Center. Cost is $40.00.

First Night Virginia
Downtown Charlottesville
(434) 975-8269
www.firstnightvirginia.org

The first and the biggest of the First Night events in the state, this alcohol-free family-oriented New Year's Eve celebration of the arts is held in various locations in the downtown area from 3:00 P.M. to midnight. Nearly 100 acts are booked for the night's entertainment, ranging from blues to comedy to concerts, and it all ends with a gigantic fireworks display. Purchase a button—the cost is around $10.00 for adults and $5.00 for children younger than 12—and it will be your key to getting into all the events.

Family Wintertide Weekend
Downtown, Monterey
(540) 468-2550
www.highlandcounty.org

The county rolls out the holiday welcome

ANNUAL EVENTS AND FESTIVALS

mat the first weekend in December as local shops and galleries extend their shopping hours. A tree lighting ceremony is held on the courthouse lawn Saturday evening, followed by a Christmas concert at one of the local churches. Past Wintertide events also have included a craft show at the public library and an oyster dinner at the Blue Grass Ruritan building. And of course, don't forget to stop by and visit with Santa. Carolers, refreshments, and door prizes helped mark the 16th annual event in 2004.

Dickens of a Christmas
Market Square, Roanoke
(540) 342-2028
www.downtownroanoke.org
Roanoke's City Market is the place for carriage rides, chestnut roasting, ice carvings, hot cider, and holiday music on the first three Fridays in December. It's free. There is a charge for the carriage rides.

Ye Olde Salem Christmas
Main Street, Salem
(540) 375-4046
Early in December Salem celebrates the season with carriage rides, children's activities, food, and open houses. Also enjoy a parade and ice sculptures. The events are free.

Amos Alonzo Stagg Bowl
1001 Roanoke Boulevard, Salem
(540) 375-3004
www.salemciviccenter.com
Salem Stadium hosts the NCAA Division III football championship in mid-December each year. Admission is $10.00 in advance or $12.50 the day of the game for adults. Children and students get in for $5.00. The game is televised on ESPN.

The Living Christmas Tree
Thomas Road, Lynchburg
(434) 239-9281
Hear a spectacular 100-plus chorus and see more than 108,000 lights adorn a nine-tiered Christmas tree at Jerry Fal-

well's Thomas Road Baptist Church. In recent years the shows have grown even more elaborate with laser lights, dry-ice fog, and snow machines. The concerts are held two weekends in December. You can get in for about $16.

Christmas at Point of Honor
112 Cabell Street, Lynchburg
(434) 847-1459, (800) 732-5821
www.pointofhonor.org
This is a celebration of the joyous season as it would have been in the 1820s. Held in early December at Point of Honor, a mansion built by Patrick Henry's doctor, George Cabell, the event is an opportunity to revel in the color and aroma of festive greens. After you tour the house, cider and cookies are served in the Carriage House. Admission is free.

Patrick Henry Women's Auxiliary Christmas Tea
1250 Red Hill Road, Brookneal
(434) 376-2044
Enjoy Christmas tea, Colonial style, at Red Hill. Patrick Henry's home is decorated with period trimmings, and refreshments and holiday music add to the holiday mood. Admission is free.

Christmas Lights at Elks National Home
931 Ashland Avenue, Bedford
(540) 586-8232, (800) 552-4140
www.elkshome.org
Retired Elks work all year to get ready for one of the grandest displays of Christmas lighting in Virginia every December. Drive through and see years of innovative decorations by these retired fraternal associates. Nearly 100,000 visitors come by to see the collection of more than 50,000 lights. It's free to drive through.

Deck the Halls Open House
5240 Wilderness Road, Newbern
(540) 674-4835
Visit the Wilderness Road Regional Museum for a rustic Christmas to remember. It's free to enter.

THE BLUE RIDGE PARKWAY AND SKYLINE DRIVE

Imagine driving almost the entire length of an East Coast state without seeing fast-food restaurants, tractor-trailers, or glaring billboards. In Virginia this miracle is made possible by a scenic stretch of highway that begins in Front Royal as the Skyline Drive, runs the length of Shenandoah National Park, and becomes the Blue Ridge Parkway near Waynesboro. From Waynesboro, the Parkway meanders 469 miles, all the way to the Great Smoky Mountains in North Carolina, offering magnificent views of valleys, forests, and mountain ranges along the way.

Construction of the Skyline Drive began in 1931, spurred on by President Herbert Hoover, who spent many a weekend at his fishing camp in the area. As the story goes, Hoover was riding his horse along the crest of the Blue Ridge Mountains one day in 1930 when he turned to a companion and said: "These mountains are made for a road, and everybody ought to have a chance to get the views from here. I think they're the greatest in the world."

The road was built by local farmers, who were paid from drought relief funds. The Civilian Conservation Corps pitched in to build rock walls, picnic areas, and scenic overlooks. The 105-mile-long Skyline Drive was finished on August 29, 1939, during the administration of Franklin D. Roosevelt.

Today it costs $10.00 per vehicle to enter the Skyline Drive at any point. That fee and the 35 mph speed limit help keep the road free of commuters and speeders. Bicyclists pay $5.00. If you plan on being in the area for an extended stay, consider an annual pass for $20.00. A National Park pass is another option. This $50.00 pass will give you admittance to any national park. If you are 62 or older, a lifetime park pass costs $10.00.

Unfortunately, the crystal-clear visibility of a half century ago has given way to occasional hazy conditions brought on by worsening pollution, often caused by coal-burning power plants in the Ohio Valley and from as far away as northern Indiana. The haze is worst during summer months. Shenandoah National Park officials do a visibility check every day at 1:00 P.M. and post the results around the park by 2:00 P.M. If you want to know what the visibility is like before you go, contact one of the entrance stations that post the information daily: Front Royal, (540) 635-5258, or Rockfish Gap, (540) 943-8764. A weather recording is available at (540) 999-3500.

Just like Shenandoah National Park, the Blue Ridge Parkway is governed by the National Park Service but is a separate and distinct facility. The legislated purpose of the Parkway was to link Shenandoah National Park with Great Smoky Mountains National Park in North Carolina and Tennessee by means of a scenic highway. This goal was accomplished in 1936 and was recognized worldwide as a significant engineering achievement. The designers often took the long route, which would have been avoided by conventional highway builders, to provide access to scenic, historic, and natural features of the region. The route follows the mountaintops at an average elevation of 3,000 feet. Unlike the Skyline Drive, there is no charge for access to the Blue Ridge Parkway.

Both the Skyline Drive and the Parkway are very popular destinations. Shenandoah National Park officials estimate they have two million visitors a year during the peak seasons of summer and fall. When the leaves change colors in October, you can even see the cars lined up on the Rockfish Gap exit off Interstate 81 waiting to enter the Parkway and the Drive.

Along both the Skyline Drive and the Blue Ridge Parkway you'll find lodges, cabins, and campsites where you can spot deer, raccoons, and black bear from your doorstep. Waysides (grills and coffee shops) offer souvenirs. Drive slowly when you pull into the parking lot: Curious deer have been known to walk right up to the cars.

Of course, hundreds of restaurants, motels, hotels, and bed-and-breakfast inns pepper the area near the Skyline Drive and the Parkway, but this chapter includes only places on these scenic highways. The facilities in Shenandoah National Park are operated by ARAMARK, a concessionaire for the National Park Service. Some of the restaurants and accommodations along the Blue Ridge Parkway are privately owned and operated, which we have noted in individual listings. This is because the Parkway's boundaries are quite narrow in places, bordering private property where people live or make a living.

Accommodations, restaurants, and snack bars described in this section are organized from north to south. Locations are identified by mileposts, beginning with 0.6 at the Front Royal Entrance Station. The numbering system starts over when the Skyline Drive meets the Blue Ridge Parkway at Rockfish Gap.

For more information about the scenic highways, contact one of the following:

- ARAMARK Shenandoah National Park Lodges, P.O. Box 727, Luray 22835; (800) 999-4714, www.visitshenandoah .com, for accommodations and restaurants
- Shenandoah National Park Headquarters, 3655 U.S. Highway 211 E, Luray 22835; (540) 999-3500, www.nps.gov/shen
- Blue Ridge Parkway National Park Headquarters, 400 BB&T Building, Asheville, North Carolina 28801; (828) 298-0398 or (828) 271-4779, www.nps.gov/blri

These offices will send you directories and strip maps of the drives.

SKYLINE DRIVE
Visitor Centers

If it's your first trip to the Skyline Drive, you might want start off at one of the visitor centers. There's so much to see and do, and the friendly staff can get you started in the right direction. The centers can provide you with maps of the park, trails, and facilities, and they also sell books and more comprehensive guides to the area and its people. The park staff also will have the most up-to-date information about wildlife, changes in trail conditions, and upcoming ranger programs. The Skyline Drive has two visitor centers that are open from 8:30 A.M. to 5:00 P.M. daily from April to November 2. The hours are reduced in the winter. Both centers have restrooms, water fountains, and phones.

Dickey Ridge Visitor Center
Mile 4.6
(540) 635-3566
Near the Front Royal entrance to the Skyline Drive, this former dining hall was built in 1938 and converted into a visitor center in the 1950s. From here you have a view of Chester Gap to the east and Massanutten to the west. This center usually closes in the winter.

Harry F. Byrd Sr. Visitor Center
Mile 51
(540) 999-3283
Fifteen miles north of the Swift Run Gap entrance off U.S. Highway 33, this visitor center offers a scenic view of a large centuries-old meadow. Opened in 1966, the center is near the park's largest and most popular campground, Big Meadows.

Overlooks

It's a three-hour nonstop trip from Front Royal to Rockfish Gap. However, if you wish to stop and enjoy the view, which we recommend you do, there are more than 70 scenic overlooks along the 105-mile Skyline Drive. Aside from affording breathtaking views of the Shenandoah Valley to the west and the Virginia Piedmont to the east, several overlooks have picnic tables and access to hiking trails. Most will have signs explaining the views. Here is just a sample:

Stony Man Overlook
Mile 38.6, elevation 3,100 ft.
Look to your left and you can see what appears to be a man's face in the second-highest peak in the park, Stony Man Mountain. You also can see New Market Gap and the town of Luray. One of the larger overlooks along the drive, Stony Man has running water, flush toilets, and a picnic table. You also can hook up with the Appalachian Trail from here.

Franklin Cliffs Overlook
Mile 49, elevation 3,140 ft.
History buffs will find this spot interesting. From here you can look out over the Shenandoah Valley and see where Gen. Thomas J. "Stonewall" Jackson led his Confederate troops through what is now the little town of Stanley. His 25,000 men struggled up over the Blue Ridge through Fishers Gap in November 1862 on their way to victory in Fredericksburg. There are two placards here on Jackson and his campaign.

Hikes

One of the most popular activities on the Skyline Drive is hiking. There are nearly 500 miles of trails, including some 95 miles of the Appalachian Trail. Some of the most popular lead to waterfalls. Here are some of the favorites. See our Recreation chapter for more hiking information.

Limberlost Trail
Mile 43
Dedicated in September 1997, Limberlost is the park's first wheelchair-accessible trail. This gently winding loop is 1.3 miles long with a crushed greenstone walkway. The trail passes by old homesites and crosses Whiteoak Canyon Run. It includes a wooden boardwalk through the wetlands, a footbridge over the run, and many benches along the way.

Hawksbill Trail
Miles 45.6 and 46.7
There are two parking lots that lead to this 2-mile round-trip hike. Be prepared. It's a steep climb to the summit of Hawksbill Mountain, the highest point in the park at 4,051 feet. At the top, there is an observation platform, picnic table, and shelter.

Dark Hollow Falls Trail
Mile 50.7
This is one of the most heavily trafficked trails in the park. It will take you to the bottom of Dark Hollow Falls, a 71-foot waterfall that cascades over greenstone. It's a 1.4-mile round-trip hike from the parking lot.

Lodges

Skyland Lodge
Mile 41.7
(540) 999-2211, (800) 999-4714
This is the first lodging facility you reach when driving south on the Skyline Drive from the Front Royal entrance. George Freeman Pollock, one of the people instrumental in establishing the Shenandoah National Park, built a private resort, Stony Man Camp, with cabins and a dining hall on this site in 1894.

The Skyland facilities sit at 3,680 feet—the highest point on the Skyline Drive—and several of the 177 guest rooms overlook the Shenandoah Valley. Skyland offers a variety of lodgings, including rustic cabins, motel-style lodge rooms, and suites. Some are wheelchair accessible. Amenities include a glass-walled dining room and the Tap Room, which offers live entertainment nightly during the summer. Guest rooms do not have phones, but some have televisions. Service shelters have pay phones and ice and soda machines.

Skyland is a lively place for a family vacation. Adults can take guided horseback trips, and children may ride ponies. The playground has swings, bars, seesaws, and plenty of grass and dirt. An amphitheater serves as an outdoor classroom where the National Park Service conducts educational programs. Naturalists lead hikes along numerous trails near the lodge in spring and summer and offer evening programs on such topics as bird-watching, wildflowers, and acid rain. You can also gaze through a telescope at the brilliant stars. Skyland's gift shop is stocked with mountain crafts, photo supplies, daily papers, and magazines. The lodge has meeting rooms and audiovisual equipment to accommodate conferences.

Rates range from $79 to $110 per night for a single lodge unit on weekdays to $177 per night for a one-bedroom suite on weekends. Rustic cabin rooms are $52 to $97 per night on weekdays and $57 to $104 per night on weekends. The lodge is usually open from late March to the end of November.

The most popular month is October, that magical time of brilliant color in the Blue Ridge. Room rates are slightly higher this month. Reservations are often made a year in advance for these autumn nights. It's not a bad idea to make reservations well in advance for summer nights, too.

Big Meadows Lodge
Mile 51.3
(540) 999-2221, (800) 999-4714

Nine miles south of Skyland Lodge you'll come to a clearing, the only large treeless area in the Shenandoah National Park. The Byrd Visitor Center and the Big Meadows Wayside overlook the meadow, which was probably the result of fire set either by lightning or by Native Americans to encourage the growth of wild berries. The Park Service keeps the area clear to this day, and it's an excellent place for visitors to see a diversity of wildlife, including berries and wildflowers.

The resort is a short drive from the meadow. The main lodge was built in 1939 by mountain labor using stone from the Massanutten Mountains across the Shenandoah Valley. Paneling throughout the building came from native chestnut trees that grew in the Big Meadows area. This variety of tree is nearly extinct today because of the chestnut blight in the early 1930s.

The resort includes 11 rustic cabins and 70 motel-style rooms. The main lodge's 25 rooms offer the warm, cozy atmosphere of the historic lodge, while the cabins with fireplaces sit among the trees. The most modern units feature king-size beds, fireplaces, and sitting areas with televisions. The main lodge has an outdoor deck where guests can lounge by day and stargaze by night. For a quarter you can look more closely at the stars through a telescope.

The lofty central room of the main lodge is a casual place where you can relax and enjoy the valley view. Several board games are available, and a lot of comfortable sofas and chairs and a fireplace create a relaxed ambience. The dining room offers a tremendous view of the Shenandoah Valley. On a clear day you can enjoy the panoramic vista 40 miles across the entire Appalachian Range into West Virginia. The Tap Room, made cozy by a fireplace, is open from 4:00 to 11:00 P.M. with entertainment nightly.

Big Meadows Lodge offers naturalist activities and a children's playground, and Byrd Visitor Center, where exhibits illustrate the park's history and the folkways of its former inhabitants, is nearby.

The retreat is open from late April through October. Rates range from $60 per night in the main lodge on weekdays to $125 per night for a one-bedroom suite on weekends. Rates are slightly higher in October.

Cabins

Lewis Mountain Cabins
Mile 57.5
(800) 999-4714

For a tranquil experience, you can spend the night in one of the 10 cabins on Lewis Mountain, where rooms have no phones or televisions to disturb the peace. The heated cabins have furnished bedrooms and private baths, with towels and linens provided. Cooking is done in connecting outdoor areas equipped with barbecue pits, grills, and picnic tables.

The cabins are open from mid-May through October. Rates range from $61 per night on weekdays for a single-room cabin to $96 per night on weekends for a two-room cabin. Rates are slightly higher in October.

Potomac Appalachian Trail Club Cabins
118 Park Street SE, Vienna
(703) 242-0315, (703) 242-0693
www.patc.net

If you're game for a bit of backpacking, the Potomac Appalachian Trail Club maintains six cabins and seven three-sided shelters in the backcountry of the park. The shelters, which provide protection from the elements, are along the Appalachian Trail at intervals of 12 to 20 miles. You must have a valid backcountry camping permit for three or more nights. These free permits are available at any of the ranger stations, entrance stations, or the park headquarters on Highway 211 east of Luray and 5 miles west of the Skyline Drive.

The cabins provide a bit more comfort than primitive camping, and staying in one can be a gritty or sublime experience, depending upon your perspective. You must hike in, gather your own firewood, and draw your own water from a nearby spring. Each cabin has a table, woodstove and/or fireplace, bunks, and a pit toilet. There are mattresses and blankets, but you should bring your own sleeping bag or bedding. There's no electricity, so you must also have your own source of light. The cabins are equipped with pots, pans, and dishes.

Pets are allowed in park campgrounds but not in the lodges. Pets must be supervised and kept on a leash no longer than 6 feet while in the park. If you bring your pet for an overnight stay, it will cost you extra—$5.00 in the cabins and $3.00 per night in the campgrounds. Call (800) 933-PARK for details.

The cabins are Range View (Mile 22.1), Corbin (Mile 37.9), Rock Spring (Mile 41.1), Pocosin (Mile 59.5), Doyles River (Mile 81.1), and Jones Mountain (accessible from Criglersville, but not from the Skyline Drive). Most can accommodate up to eight people, while Jones Mountain sleeps 10. Cronin and Doyle River can house 12. Prices range from $18.00 to $28.00, with a $6.00 surcharge if there are 15 or more people in your party.

All cabins are locked, so you must get a key from the PATC by mail before your visit. For reservations or a complete guide with photos showing all the cabins in the PATC system (cost is $5.50 plus postage and tax), call or write the PATC at the address above. The cabins are popular, so reserve early.

Campgrounds

Shenandoah National Park operates five campgrounds along the Skyline Drive. All campgrounds have a 14-day limit, allow pets, do not accept credit cards, and are closed in the winter. Many sites accommodate tents, tent trailers, and recreational vehicles. However, water and electric hookups are not available for RVs. Shower and laundry facilities are near all but two of the campgrounds. For more information, refer to our Recreation chapter.

Mathews Arm Campground
Mile 22.2
(540) 999-3132

Mathews Arm, usually the last to fill up,

has 178 sites for self-contained vehicles only. Mathews Arm is available on a first-come, first-served basis. Cost is $16. There are no showers or laundry facilities.

Big Meadows Campground
Mile 51
(540) 999-3231, (800) 365-2267
The largest campground on the drive, with 227 sites, Big Meadows is also the most popular. It is a good idea to make reservations, especially in the summer and fall. Cost is $19 for RVs and $16 for tents per night. A campstore, laundry facilities, and a gas station are nearby.

Lewis Mountain Campground
Mile 57.5
(540) 999-3273
This 31-site campground is often full in pleasant weather, especially on weekends and holidays. It's first come, first served, so plan to arrive early. It costs $16 per site, per night. Amenities include a laundry and coin-operated concessions.

Loft Mountain Campground
Mile 80
(434) 823-4675
There are more than 200 sites at Loft Mountain, and you can usually find a spot except on the weekends. This, too, is first come, first served. The cost is $16 per night. There is a campstore nearby with coin-operated concessions and laundry facilities.

Dundo Campground
Mile 83.7
(540) 365-2267
This campground is open for any group. It's primitive tent camping with pit toilets, running water, picnic tables, and grills.

If you plan on driving the entire distance, be aware that there are only two places on the Skyline Drive that sell gasoline. You can refuel at Elkwallow and Big Meadows.

There are only seven campsites here with a maximum of 20 people per site. (You must have eight people to be considered a group.) The cost is $32 per night. Reservations are required.

Backcountry Camping

For those who prefer a little more seclusion, backcountry camping is allowed in most areas of the park, but permits are required. Tents may be set up as long as they are a half mile from the developed areas, such as picnic grounds or other campgrounds. Campers also should be a quarter of a mile from the Skyline Drive and other roadways in the park and be 20 yards from any trail or other backcountry campsites. If you prefer to rough it, be aware that campfires and glass containers are not allowed in the backcountry. Also, park officials recommend that you take along about 20 feet of rope. It's a good idea to hang your food from a tree in air-tight containers to discourage unwanted visits from bears. Permits are available at the entrances, visitor centers, or the main business office. If you have your trip planned out a month in advance, you can request a permit by mail. Call (540) 999-3500.

Places to Eat

Elkwallow Wayside
Mile 24.1
(540) 999-2253
Open from April to early November, this campstore has a small selection of groceries and camper supplies, a gift shop, gas station, and grill service.

Skyland Lodge
Mile 41.7
(540) 999-2211
One of the best views on the Drive is from the window tables in this glass-walled dining room, which offers full meals every day from late March through November.

Menus change, but dinner selections often include prime rib, trout, Virginia ham, or apple-smoked pork chops. The Tap Room has a limited bar menu to go with the beer, wine, and spirits dispensed daily from midday to late evening.

Big Meadows Wayside
Mile 51
(540) 999-2251

You can eat in or carry out at this wayside along the Drive. The breakfast menu features several tasty choices, including eggs and pancakes. Prices range from $1.50 to $4.00. For later in the day, the fare includes chicken breast fillet and an all-American burger. Here, too, the cost is easy on the pocketbook, with stuffed flounder listed at $7.60. Various other sandwiches and chicken orders are available for carryout. Big Meadows also offers a two-room camp store. One is for the tourists in search of T-shirts, regional cookbooks, games for kids, snacks, and a few tapes and CDs. The other room is a place campers can restock their supplies of groceries or pick up forgotten items, such as pots, pans, and ponchos.

Big Meadows Lodge
Mile 51.2
(540) 999-2221

Omelets, waffles, and blueberry pancakes are breakfast features. Lunch offerings include turkey wraps and a hearty Reuben. The dinner menu has savory fried chicken, beef, pasta, catfish, and trout. The restaurant is full-service late April through October. The Tap Room offers a limited bar menu well into the evening, with entertainment nightly.

Loft Mountain Wayside
Mile 59
(434) 823-4515

This grill/gift shop sells crafts, souvenirs, foodstuffs, and gas. The grill serves hamburgers, hot dogs, and the like. It's open weekends only April through mid-May, then daily from morning until early evening through November 3.

There are several picnic tables outside on a wooden deck, where you can enjoy a snack while you watch the deer.

Picnic Areas

If you decide to bring your own food, there are seven picnic facilities along the Skyline Drive with tables, restrooms, water fountains, and even fireplaces. From north to south are Dickey Ridge at mile 4.7, Elkwallow at 24.1, Pinnacles at 36.7, Big Meadows at 51.2, Lewis Mountain at 57.5, South River at 62.8, and Loft Mountain at 79.5. You may also find other picnic tables at overlooks, visitor centers, and lodges.

Fishing

Although streams are relatively small, a variety of fish inhabit the water in the Shenandoah National Park. Fishing regulations have changed significantly and may do so again, so it is a good idea to check with the visitor centers or entrance stations before you wet a line. They also will provide you with a brochure that includes updated rules and a handy list of park streams that are designated as "open for harvest." As of 2002 all the streams in the park are open to catch-and-release fishing unless designated as closed. Catch-and-release also is allowed in streams where you can keep your fish. Only artificial lures with single hooks are allowed in the park. No trout less than 9 inches long can be kept, and your creel limit is six trout per day. Fishing is allowed year-round, but residents 16 and older will need a Virginia State license. Nonresidents 12 and older must have licenses, too, but you can stop by Panorama Restaurant, Big Meadows, or Loft Mountain waysides or a local sporting goods store to purchase temporary passes. A five-day nonresidence license costs $6.50. Remember, you must carry your license with you when you fish, because game wardens will stop and check.

CLOSE-UP

Waterfalls

It's the second most-asked question in the Shenandoah National Park: "Where can I see a waterfall?" The question came up so often that the staff at the park was eager to find a quick reply.

"We asked Joanne Amberson if she would write a book for us," said Greta Miller, executive director of the Shenandoah Natural History Association. "She is a retired English professor who volunteers here at the park . . . and she likes to hike."

Amberson had trekked the paths to all of the waterfalls along the Skyline Drive many times.

"Since I was an ex-English professor, they knew I could write," she said. "It was a lot of hard work, but it was fun to do."

Amberson is used to putting up with hard work to do what she loves. For years the Rappahannock resident spent countless hours commuting from her home in Virginia to teach at Prince George's Community College in Maryland. When she retired, she signed on as a volunteer at the park. Today her long treks are mostly on foot.

Of course, asking Amberson which hike is her favorite is a lot like asking Florence Henderson which is her favorite Brady.

"They are all beautiful," she said. "The South River Falls has a sheer drop, and you can get fairly close to it. You can just sit there and see the whole mountain behind you. But for every person, a different falls would fit their personality. Jones River Falls is short, but it is exquisitely beautiful. Each one is unique, and each one has its own personality."

Far and away, Dark Hollow Falls is the most visited waterfall on the Skyline Drive because it is the closest to the Drive and requires the shortest hike—1.4 miles round-trip. Although Amberson describes it as a moderate climb, it descends pretty quickly alongside Hogcamp Branch, a small stream that gradually widens.

"The one thing they all have in common is that you have to walk down to see them," Amberson said.

And as they say in waterfall circles, those who walk down must hike back up to the car. In the summer the Dark Hollow Falls trail can be quite crowded with families, older folks, and people wearing shoes that give the impression that a hike was a spur-of-the-moment idea. For the climb back up, there are several places to sit and enjoy the ferns and wildflowers.

Horseback Riding

There is another way to traverse the miles of trails along the Skyline Drive—on horseback. Skyland Resort will take visitors on guided trips. The staff says their horses are safe and sturdy for adults, but you must be at least 4 feet 10 inches if you want to ride. The stables are open seasonally, so it's a good idea to call before you

"There are 15 major waterfalls in the park, but the book gives you nine hikes," Amberson said. "There is an arduous hike on one trail that would lead you to five more falls."

While only a true hiker will want to follow the steep and rocky path to those five smaller falls, the main hike to Whiteoak Canyon Falls is another of the more popular attractions. The round-trip hike of 4.6 miles leads to the second-highest falls, but even this hike seems to attract more experienced hikers. Most come prepared with hiking boots and water bottles. Although it is longer than Dark Hollow, this trail has a gradual decline through an old hemlock forest, where 400-year-old trees are bigger around than two people. You get a splendid view from the top of the cliffs directly across the falls as it cascades 86 feet down the canyon. You can sit here, even with the treetops, and listen to the splash of the falls.

"There must be an attraction between people and water," Amberson said. "It is all very refreshing. It makes you feel like sitting and meditating and contemplating."

While the falls are picturesque and peaceful, be advised that we're not talking Niagara here. In fact, in warm weather some of the falls will dry up to a trickle.

"In a dry summer the falls can have no water at all," Amberson said. "So the best time to go see them is in the spring and early summer...unless we have had a lot of rain. The Rose River Falls is perhaps the second easiest to get to (2.6-mile hike), but it is one that is good to go to in the spring. When there is a lot of water, it falls in four parallel streams. You are in the woods surrounded by hemlocks. It is just beautiful."

Also, if it's a dry season, you might want to postpone your trip to Overall Run Falls. Before you trek the 6.4 miles to the tallest falls in the park, be aware that your only view may be of Massanutten Mountain. Overall Run Falls will have little to no water in a dry summer, Amberson said.

The park's booklet is filled with such helpful hints for those who really want to see the falls.

"The book gives you a complete map of each hike, directions, and my statement on what is easy and hard," Amberson said. "Of course, it is all relative. What may be hard for one is easy for another, but I give my assessment."

Hike to Waterfalls in the Shenandoah National Park is available at each of the entrance stations on the Skyline Drive. For more information, call the Shenandoah Natural History Association at (540) 999-3582.

Oh, yes. The most asked question in the park is "Where can I get something to eat?"

make plans. Generally, the stables are open on weekends from March 31 to November 24. A one-hour ride costs $20 on weekdays and $22 on weekends. Reservations can be made a day in advance by calling the stables at (540) 999-2210. If you can only call during lunch or after hours, you can make reservations through the lodge office at (540) 999-2211.

BLUE RIDGE PARKWAY

Visitor Centers

Even if it's not your first trip on the Parkway, it might be a good idea to stop by one of the four visitor centers in Virginia. Mother Nature can alter the course of a trail or close a campground, so it's best to get the latest information. Each center has free maps, books for sale, exhibits, picnic tables, bathrooms, and updates on ranger programs. The centers are open 9:00 A.M. to 5:00 P.M. daily in the summer, weekends only in early spring and late fall, and they are closed in the winter. The James River center is open 9:00 A.M. to 5:00 P.M. weekends only. Besides the visitor centers, you could try the ranger's office in Vinton at (540) 767-2490. Another way to obtain general information about the Parkway is to call Plateau District office at (540) 745-9660. While most of the Parkway visitor centers and facilities are closed from the first of November to the end of April, this office remains open.

Humpback Rock Visitor Center
Mile 5.8
(540) 943-4716
This center is near the Rockfish Gap entrance to the Blue Ridge Parkway. Outside is an easy quarter-mile self-guided trail through a reconstructed farmstead. There's a group of log buildings, most dating back to the 1880s, that represents a typical pioneer homestead—a cabin, spring house, chicken coop, and barn.

James River Visitor Center
Mile 63.6
(434) 299-5496
From this center, there is a self-guided trail that will take you to the restored canal locks on the James River. Before railroads became the favored way to "ship" freight, engineers looked for easier ways to get their goods up river. In the mid-1800s, 49 miles of canals were built through the Blue Ridge. A footbridge will give you a good view of the river. Due to budget cutbacks, the center is only open 9:00 A.M. to 5:00 P.M. on weekends.

Peaks of Otter Visitor Center
Mile 86
(540) 586-4357
You can see a living history demonstration on weekends at the Johnson Farm, a homestead dating back to the 1800s. It has been restored to the way it looked in the 1920s. A trail around the farm is 2.1 miles. There also is an amphitheater, museum, naturalist program, nature walks, and a 23-acre lake near this popular center.

Blue Ridge Parkway Visitor Center
Mile 115
(540) 427-1800, (800) 842-9163
www.explorepark.org
This new facility located in Virginia's Explore Park is the only visitor center in the National Park System named specifically for this unique 469-mile park. The center, which opened in 2001, welcomes visitors to the Roanoke region, the largest metropolitan area on the Blue Ridge Parkway. You can learn about the Parkway, the National Park Service, and the Roanoke Valley at this educational and interpretive center. In addition to information services, touring exhibits are free to the public.

Rocky Knob Visitor Center
Mile 169
(540) 745-9662
This quaint center is in a converted gasoline station. It offers a series of activities, including a naturalist program, campfire talks, and guided hikes. The visitor center overlooks the Rock Castle Gorge, where three trail systems intersect. There is a strenuous 10.8-mile loop trail into the gorge.

Overlooks

If you don't like to hike, you can still see a lot of the great outdoors without ever leaving your car. According to the folks at the Roanoke headquarters, the road was designed to have an overlook at almost every mile. That means there are literally hundreds of overlooks scattered between Rockfish Gap in Virginia and Great Smoky Mountains National Park in North Carolina. Here are a couple of examples:

The Priest Overlook
Mile 17.6
The Priest is the tallest in what has been called the "religious mountains," including Little Priest, the Cardinal, the Friar, and the Bald Friar. There is a picnic table here and a half-mile trail to a scenic pedestrian overlook.

Yankee Horse Ridge Overlook
Mile 34.4
Word has it that this is where a Union soldier's horse fell and had to be shot. You can see a reconstructed spur of an old logging railroad by following the trail to Wigwam Falls. There's an interpretive sign and picnic table at this overlook.

Hikes

With more than 100 trails along the Blue Ridge Parkway, there is bound to be something to suit every hiker's fancy. Among the most popular trails are Humpback Rocks and Rock Castle Gorge (see our Recreation chapter). We also have listed a sample of easy, moderate, and difficult paths. Free trail maps are available at the visitor centers.

Falling Water Cascades National Scenic Trail
Mile 83.1
You can divide this trail into two parts or hike it as one continuous loop. It's a 1.6-mile moderate walk to see the cascades. Watch your step; the wet rocks can be slippery. Look for the thicket of rhododendron.

Flat Top Trail
Mile 83.5
This one's for avid hikers. The 2.5-mile hike to the summit leads to the highest of three main peaks in the area, Sharp Top, Flat Top, and Harkening Hill. This trail across Flat Top Mountain levels off at 4,001 feet. It's 4.4 miles to the peak's picnic area on Highway 43. Be sure to wear good shoes for hiking. It is a strenuous climb. This popular trail also has the distinction of being listed in the National Register of Historic Trails.

Sharp Top Trail
Mile 86
Another popular hike, this trail leaves the camp store and climbs to the summit of Sharp Top Mountain, an elevation of 3,874 feet with a 360-degree panoramic view. The 1.5-mile hike is strenuous but one of the best sites to watch the sun rise. Park officials report seeing numbers of hikers heading up the trail in the early morning hours. At one time, Sharp Top was thought to be the tallest peak in Virginia. A stone from the mountaintop even sits at the Washington Monument in D.C. with that distinctive but incorrect heading. If you would like to go to the top but don't think you are up to the hike, a bus will take you up most of the route, except for the last 1,500 feet.

Mabry Mill Trail
Mile 176.2
This is for the beginner who likes to see something more than nature. This easy half-mile trail takes you to E. B. Mabry's gristmill, sawmill, blacksmith shop, and other outdoor exhibits. You may even see actors re-creating old-time skills in the summer and fall.

Trails on the Skyline Drive and the Blue Ridge Parkway are very popular and well known. For a bit more quiet, check out the Jefferson National Forest, which has good hikes but are not often as well publicized.

Accommodations

Peaks of Otter Lodge
Mile 86
(540) 586-1081, (800) 542-5927
www.peaksofotter.com

Unlike the lodges in Shenandoah National Park, Peaks of Otter is open year-round. The lodge setting is idyllic, a valley surrounded by gentle mountains and facing a beautiful lake. Each room has two double beds, a private bath, and a private balcony or terrace overlooking the lake. The rooms have no televisions or phones.

The lodge's restaurant serves hearty Southern fare and has a sumptuous salad bar. The gift shop sells fine Virginia crafts, stationery, books, jellies, and more.

You can also camp at Peaks of Otter (see the listing below). Park rangers give talks on nature topics during the peak season, and hikers can trek along miles of well-marked trails near the lodge.

Rates are about $86 for two people per room weekdays or weekends, and slightly higher in October and on holiday weekends.

Rocky Knob Cabins
Mile 174
(540) 593-3503, (540) 952-2947
www.blueridgeresort.com

Seven cabins were built in the 1930s for the Civilian Conservation Corps workers who constructed much of the Blue Ridge Parkway. They have no fireplaces and no other source of heat, so it's understandable that they are only open from late May through the end of October. The cabins have completely furnished electric kitchens but no bathrooms. However, private showers and laundry facilities are in a bathhouse within 200 feet of each cabin. Rates are $56.00 and $8.00 for each extra person. You may make reservations by calling after 10:30 A.M. weekdays or in the evenings. Or you can write to: Rocky Knob Cabins, Route 1, Box 5, Meadows of Dan 24120.

Doe Run Lodge Resort and Conference Center
Off Parkway near mile 189, Fancy Gap
(276) 398-2212, (800) 325-6189
www.doerunlodge.com

This family-oriented year-round private resort in Fancy Gap sits on beautiful Groundhog Mountain and offers tennis, swimming, saunas, and golf. Choose from town-house villas, tennis center chalets, and single-family residences. Villas cost $169, while the chalets run about $139. See our Resorts chapter for complete details.

Campgrounds

The Parkway has nine developed campgrounds with tent and recreational vehicle sites (no water or electric hookups), including four in Virginia.

All campgrounds have restrooms (no showers), sewage dumping stations, and telephones. Grills and tables are provided at each site.

Campgrounds are open mid-May through October. You are limited to stays of 21 days in any one campground. Reservations are not accepted, but you probably won't need them. Do, however, plan to make camp early during the peak summer months or the fall foliage season.

All campgrounds charge $14.00 per site for up to six people and $2.00 for each additional person. Leashed pets are allowed. While the campground and other facilities typically don't open until May, if there has been a mild winter with little storm damage, there is a chance that the park superintendent may decide to open some facilities earlier in the season.

Drinking water and comfort stations are provided, but there are no shower or laundry facilities. Campgrounds have designated sites for trailers, but none are equipped for utility connections. The campgrounds do have sanitary dumping stations.

Shenandoah National Park's Most Visited Waterfalls

Fall	Height	Milepost
Overall Run No. 1	29 feet	22.2
Overall Run No. 2	93 feet	22.2
Whiteoak No. 1	86 feet	42.6
Whiteoak No. 2	62 feet	42.6
Whiteoak No. 3	35 feet	42.6
Whiteoak No. 4	41 feet	42.6
Whiteoak No. 5	49 feet	42.6
Whiteoak No. 6	60 feet	42.6
Cedar Run	34 feet	45.6
Rose River	67 feet	49.4
Dark Hollow Falls	71 feet	50.7
Lewis	81 feet	51.2
South River	83 feet	62.8
Doyles River No. 1	29 feet	81.8
Doyles River No. 2	63 feet	81.8
Jones Run	42 feet	84.1

Otter Creek Campground
Mile 60
(828) 298-0398, (434) 299-5125
It's a cool and peaceful setting here beneath the hemlock, oak, and pine trees. Otter Creek is the smallest campground, but there is room for 45 tents and 24 RVs.

Peaks of Otter Campground
Mile 86
(828) 298-0398, (540) 586-4357
Peaks of Otter, a half mile east of mile 86 on Va. 43, is one of the area's most popular campgrounds because of its beautiful lakeside setting. There are 82 tent sites and 59 sites for RVs or trailers. There are plenty of spots to picnic, with 62 tables on hand. Fishing is allowed, and there is a camp store and gas station nearby.

Roanoke Mountain Campground
Mile 120.5
(828) 298-0398, (540) 767-2492
If you are worried about finding a camping spot or want to avoid crowds, Roanoke Mountain is one of the lesser-used campgrounds. It's also handy if you would like to take a day trip to nearby Roanoke or Mill Mountain. It has 74 tent sites and spaces for 31 RVs.

Rocky Knob Campground
Mile 167.1
(828) 298-0398, (540) 745-9660
At 3,100 feet, this is the highest campground in Virginia's section of the Parkway. Rocky Knob has 119 sites for tents and RVs. There are 72 picnic tables, 15 miles of trails, and plenty of spots to fish

nearby. You might want to check out the Chinese chestnut trees.

Backcountry Camping

The Blue Ridge Parkway has one backcountry camping area near Rock Castle Gorge. Campers must apply for a free permit from the Rocky Knob Visitor Center. Call (540) 745-9662 or drop by the center at milepost 169. Campers may park their cars at the visitor center and pick up the trail from there.

Places to Eat

Otter Creek Restaurant and Craft Shop
Mile 60.8
(434) 299-5862
You can have breakfast all day long at Otter Creek, including bacon and eggs plus buckwheat, cornmeal, buttermilk, or just plain pancakes. If you would like a little something traditional for your dinner, there are the usual family favorites: fried chicken, hamburger steak, fish, and country ham. The restaurant is next to a year-round Otter Creek campground and small craft shop and is open May through October.

Peaks of Otter Lodge
Mile 86
(540) 586-1081, (800) 542-5927
Friendly service and hefty portions make this a popular dining spot among locals and travelers alike. Like the lodge, the restaurant is open year-round. Breakfasts are the stick-to-your-ribs sort, and lunch specials include big salads, burgers, and ham steak with buttered apples. The dinner menu offers Southern dishes such as barbecued ribs and country ham, as well as prime rib and tenderloin steak. Special buffets are prepared Friday nights and Sunday. The coffee shop prepares picnic lunches for guests wanting to eat outdoors.

Mabry Mill Coffee Shop
Mile 176
(276) 952-2947
www.blueridgeresort.com
A single menu is available throughout the day at this coffee shop at Mabry Mill, a famous pioneer attraction along the Parkway. Country ham, barbecue, and corn and buckwheat cakes are specialties, plus you can get breakfast any time of day. Mabry Mill is open from May through October.

High Country Restaurant
at Doe Run Lodge
Off Parkway near mile 189, Fancy Gap
(276) 398-2212, (800) 325-6189
www.doerunlodge.com
Open year-round, this privately owned restaurant serves dinner on Friday and Saturday and breakfast on Sunday. The menu is seasonal and offers such gourmet selections as salmon, venison, fresh rainbow trout from Doe Run's stocked pond, lamb, duck, steaks, and country ham. The hours are limited in the winter, but lodging is available year-round.

Picnic Areas

Of the 14 designated areas for picnicking along the Blue Ridge Parkway, six are in Virginia. They each include picnic tables, fireplaces, drinking water, and comfort stations. From north to south they are Humpback Rocks at mile 5.9, James River at 63.6, Peaks of Otter at 86, Smart View at 154.5, Rocky Knob at 169, and Ground Hog Mountain at 189.

Fishing

Fishing is allowed in certain spots along the Parkway, but it is a good idea to check with the local ranger for rules about creel limits and what type of bait is allowed. Regulations are usually posted at each fishing area, but they will vary from site to site. Designated "special waters" in

Virginia include Abbott Lake, Little Stoney Creek, and Otter Lake. In special waters, fishing lures are limited to a single-hook artificial lure. A Virginia fishing license is valid in all Parkway waters. No special trout license is required.

Activities

Explore Park
Milepost 115, Blue Ridge Parkway
(540) 427-1800, (800) 842-9163
www.explorepark.org

This living history museum and park on the Blue Ridge Parkway offers a whole series of outdoor activities. Along with historical re-creations that will stimulate the mind, there are ample recreational opportunities. You can explore history from a 1671 Native American village to restored 18th- and 19th-century buildings or explore nature through a series of trails for hiking and biking. Bring along a pole if you would like to fish. There is an $8.00 admission fee for the park. (For more details, see our Attractions chapter.)

THE CIVIL WAR

he War Between the States was, as the poet Walt Whitman described, "a strange, sad war." More Americans lost their lives in the Civil War (1861 to 1865) than in both world wars combined. And of all the states involved in the conflict, none suffered as much trauma as Virginia did, say some historians. Although the Old Dominion was one of the last states to leave the Union, its strategic geographic position among seceding states made it a natural battleground for clashes between the two armies. Beginning with the war's first major battle at Bull Run (First Manassas) and ending with the South's surrender in the tiny, peaceful village of Appomattox Court House near Lynchburg, 60 percent of the Civil War's battles were fought in Virginia. One borderline Shenandoah Valley city, Winchester, changed hands from Confederate to Federal control no fewer than 72 times. Thousands of men from both sides heeded the call to arms and never returned; 700,000 people died in the war, 400,000 of them victims of germs rather than bullets. Untold acres of family farms were laid to waste. Is it any wonder that 140 years later the War Between the States is not forgotten?

The Blue Ridge not only is the site of some of the bloodiest battles of the Civil War but also is home to one of the country's most noted Civil War scholars and authors, history professor James I. Robertson Jr. of Virginia Tech. He is past executive director of the U.S. Civil War Centennial Commission, and his book, *Civil War! America Becomes One Nation,* an illustrated history for young readers, probably best answers questions about the war in a way young and old can clearly understand. Robertson, whose book has been nominated for a Pulitzer Prize, teaches a Civil War class that is one of the hottest tickets on campus. His enthusiasm for Civil

War history comes as no surprise, since his great-grandfather was Gen. Robert E. Lee's cook. Robertson's book takes into account the political and socioeconomic mood of the 1860s and the events that set off a movement the South anticipated would be over within weeks but which, in fact, lasted four years and marked a turning point in American history. Robertson's biography of Stonewall Jackson, released in 1997, also was a bestseller. Robertson, who is the director of the Virginia Center for Civil War Studies at Virginia Tech, served as a consultant to Robert Duvall in the film *Gods and Generals.*

The fact the Confederacy even survived for the duration of the war was in large measure due to the military leadership of Virginia's Blue Ridge generals, Lee and Thomas J. "Stonewall" Jackson. As the story goes, Jackson's nickname came out of the battle of First Manassas. Gen. Barnard Bee of South Carolina pointed to Jackson's troops and shouted, "There stands Jackson like a stone wall." In addition to his legendary nickname, Jackson's Rebel yell became his battle signature. To this day, the U.S. Army regularly conducts staff rides into the Shenandoah Valley for its officers, following the course of Jackson's famed Foot Cavalry.

When discussing the role the Blue Ridge played in the Civil War, Robertson emphasizes the Shenandoah Valley's two important geographic characteristics: first as a spear pointing into the north and second as the "Breadbasket of the Confederacy." The number of major battles in the region attests to the constant wrenching for control of the Valley, which prompted Jackson, often called the "pious blue-eyed killer," to push his men so hard in the spring of 1862 that their shoes fell apart in the fields.

The war in the Blue Ridge is fraught with tragic moments in military history.

One of the most heartbreaking was the Battle of New Market on May 15, 1864, which is often retraced and its startling events reenacted. On that rainy Sunday afternoon, 247 Virginia Military Institute cadets advanced side by side with veteran Civil War infantrymen into hellish cannon and rifle fire. The soldiers forged onward with parade-ground precision, using each step to free the other from the furrows of mud caused by the heavy rainstorm. The Confederate commander of western Virginia, Maj. Gen. John C. Breckinridge, had enlisted the cadets to join his ragtag force of 4,500. The cadets marched forward, their muzzle-loading muskets slung over shoulders destined to bear a far heavier load, their VMI flag leading the way. Looming ahead was a battle that would go down in American history as one of the most valorous and one of the last Confederate victories in the Shenandoah Valley. As the smoke of the battle cleared, 10 cadets lay dead, including Cadet Thomas G. Jefferson, 17, descendant of our nation's third president. Another 47 cadets were wounded.

Visitors can retrace the soldiers' steps by touring the New Market Battlefield Historical State Park and its museum, the Hall of Valor, which has displays of Civil War muskets, uniforms, tintype photos, day-to-day accessories, and a replica of the type of cannon captured by the cadets. Many visitors find it to be one of the most stirring of all the Blue Ridge Civil War sites, fascinating young and old alike with its sense of history and urgency.

Beyond the Shenandoah Valley, southwest Virginia was also a region of vital importance to the Confederacy, Robertson points out. Through it ran the Virginia and Tennessee Railroad, the only lifeline between Richmond and the West. The lead mines at Austinville, the saltworks at Saltville, and the coal mines throughout the region provided the embattled South with essential natural resources. The May 1864 Battle of Cloyd's Mountain near Dublin in Pulaski County remains the largest engagement ever fought in south-

west Virginia. A future president, Col. Rutherford B. Hayes, was a hero of that battle. Today only a marker commemorates the site.

Roanoker Gary C. Walker, author of *The War in Southwest Virginia* and *Hunter's Fiery Raid Through Virginia's Valleys*, outlines in great detail the way the war was fought in this region of Virginia. He captures the mood of the area, geographically a third of Virginia, which broke away to rejoin the Union and form its own state, West Virginia. Walker's book on Maj. Gen. David Hunter, who was known for his unquenchable hatred of slavery, shows how Hunter wreaked his vengeance upon southwest Virginia before its secession. States Walker, "Civilian property became an official military target. Both men and women were arrested without charge. Routinely, Southern ladies and their crying babies were forced from their homes with nothing but the clothes on their bodies. Their manor houses were plundered and burned before their horrified eyes." In Hunter's books, one can almost smell the smoke, feel the perspiration drip from the brow, and hear the heart pound as the lines clashed and the men fell with hideous and gaping wounds.

Walker also is a consultant to the growing number of hobbyists who participate in Civil War battle reenactments all along the East Coast, including Roanoke County's reenactment of Hunter's Raid at Green Hill Park. A mid-October reenactment at Cedar Creek in Middletown, which includes open camps, drills, dress parades, demonstrations of military and civilian life, and a special education symposium, is part of an effort by the Cedar Creek Battlefield Foundation to save the battlefield's 158 acres from development. The visitor center, bookshop, and other annual battle reenactments also have helped stave off the bulldozers.

The Battle of Cedar Creek in 1864 marked the end of Confederate dominion over the Shenandoah Valley and its essential food supplies. It also marked the end of famed Gen. Jubal Early's career and of

Civil War Filming in Virginia

In fall 2001, filming took place in Lexington for the major motion picture *Gods and Generals,* starring Academy Award–winner Robert Duvall as Gen. Robert E. Lee. The film was based on the novel of the same name by Jeff Shaara and was written, directed, and produced by Ronald Maxwell. The film also starred Jeff Daniels and C. Thomas Howell. *Gods and Generals* is a prequel to the acclaimed film *Gettysburg,* which was based on a novel by Shaara's late father, Pulitzer Prize–winning Michael Shaara. Maxwell directed and produced that film, too.

In the film, more than 5,000 re-enactors participated in the re-creation of the struggles at Manassas I, Antietam, Fredericksburg, and Chancellorsville. Besides Lexington, the city of Staunton, Rockbridge County, and the Virginia Highlands Film Office also provided logistical support to the project while in Virginia. The film *Gods and Generals* contributed $1 million to acquire one of the Civil War battlefields.

the war weariness that had plagued the North. (A private trust fund was established in 1996 to preserve Early's home in Red Valley, Franklin County.) This battle also put to rest any hopes the Confederacy may have had for a negotiated peace. The victory freed Gen. Philip Sheridan and his men, including Gen. George Custer (who had the misfortune of tangling later with Chief Sitting Bull at the Battle of Little Big Horn) to play crucial roles in the final battles of the Civil War the following spring.

If you've never seen a battle reenactment, you're in for a real experience. Authenticity is a must. Sack cloth, shell jackets, and frock coats are required of all participants on the field. Eyeglasses must be of period construction. Only period footwear is allowed, preferably mule hide with square toes and wooden pegs. Uniforms must be woolen. Many of the soldiers carry their own original binoculars, pistols, and bayonet rifles. No, they don't use real bullets, but they do use real gun-

powder. To find out more about battle reenactments throughout the country, write to *Camp Chase Gazette,* P.O. Box 625, Morristown, TN 37814, or call (800) 634-0281.

Hundreds of monuments, museums, and battle reenactments await you in the Blue Ridge of Virginia. The region also has more than 300 historic markers that serve as on-the-spot history lessons. In the following pages, we list only actual sites where you can see or do something. For a complete list of Virginia Civil War battlefields and markers, write the State of Virginia, 1021 East Cary Street, Richmond 23219 or call (804) 786-2051. Another great guide is Robertson's book, *Civil War Sites in Virginia, a Tour Guide,* published by the University Press of Virginia. And our sister publication, *The Insiders' Guide® to Civil War Sites in the Eastern Theater,* describes tours anyone interested in the Civil War—including kids—will enjoy.

Unless otherwise noted, admission is free of charge.

SHENANDOAH VALLEY

Gen. Stonewall Jackson's Headquarters Museum
415 North Braddock Street, Winchester
(540) 667-3242

From this brick house, Jackson commanded his forces in defense of the strategic Shenandoah Valley. The French-style house contains artifacts of Jackson, his cavalry chief Gen. Turner Ashby, and others. From April through October, hours of operation are Monday through Saturday from 10:00 A.M. to 4:00 P.M. and Sunday from 12:00 to 4:00 P.M. It is open weekends only in November and December. Admission is $5.00 for adults, $4.50 for seniors, and $2.50 for children.

Old Court House Civil War Museum
20 North Loudoun Street, Winchester
(540) 542-1145
www.civilwarmuseum.org

This old courthouse has a storied history as long as the relics it now houses. The site was the home of the first courthouse beyond the Blue Ridge, but a fire destroyed the 1741 structure. The "new" courthouse was built in 1840 but was soon called into service as a hospital and prison to both Confederate and Yankee soldiers. Winchester exchanged hands more than 70 times during the war. Today the new is the Old. And the Old is the newest museum to pay tribute to those earlier times. Its exhibits include soldiers' graffiti and stories of the soldiers who left their marks on the walls, plus a collection of more than 3,000 relics. After renovations were completed in 2003, it opened with a reenactment of Stonewall Jackson's march after the First Winchester. The museum is open 10:00 A.M. to 5:00 P.M. Friday and Saturday and from 1:00 to 5:00 P.M. Sunday. Tours also are available by appointment. Admission is $3.00. Children 4 and younger get in free.

Stonewall Jackson Memorial Cemetery and National Cemetery
Several blocks east of business district, Winchester

These two cemeteries are located across the street from each other. Buried in the Stonewall Jackson Cemetery are 3,000 Confederate soldiers, including 800 who are unknown. Also buried here is Confederate Gen. Turner Ashby.

National Cemetery is one of the largest national cemeteries in Virginia and includes more than 4,500 Union soldiers, half of them unidentified. Some of the action of the Third Battle of Winchester in 1864 was fought in this vicinity.

Belle Grove Plantation
336 Belle Grove Road, Middletown
(540) 869-2028
www.bellegrove.org

Spared during the Civil War even though it served as Gen. Philip Sheridan's headquarters during the decisive 1864 Battle of Cedar Creek, Belle Grove was built between 1794 and 1797 with the design assistance of Thomas Jefferson. James and Dolley Madison honeymooned here. Today the house and grounds exemplify the home and working farm of a wealthy Federalist planter. From late March through October, the plantation is open Monday through Saturday from 10:00 A.M. to 4:00 P.M. and Sunday from 1:00 to 5:00 P.M. Admission is $7.00 for adults, $6.00 for seniors, and $3.00 for ages 6 to 12.

Cedar Creek Battlefield Foundation Reenactment
8437 Valley Pike, Middletown
(540) 869-2064, (888) OCT-1864
www.cedarcreekbattlefield.org

The Cedar Creek Battlefield Foundation is dedicated to the historic interpretation and preservation of this 1864 battlefield—a Civil War battle in which both Confederates and Federals claimed victory. Plan to stop at the visitor center overlooking the battlefield for a personalized presentation of the battle and a visit to the bookshop featuring the 1864 Valley Campaign. The Annual Reenactment and Living History is held in October by approximately 6,000 reenactors with artillery, cavalry, and infantry demonstrations daily as well as an afternoon battle. Admission to the 140th anniversary reenactment was $40 for the special three-day event. The cost will return to its normal rate in 2005, which is about $10. Children younger than 5 get in free. All proceeds go to the preservation of the battlefield. The hours of operation for the museum are Monday through Saturday from 10:00 A.M. to 4:00 P.M. and Sunday 1:00 to 4:00 P.M. from April 1 through November 1 only. There is no admission fee for the museum. For more information write: P.O. Box 229, Middletown, VA 22645.

Stonewall Jackson Museum at Hupp's Hill
33229 Old Valley Pike, Strasburg
(540) 465-5884
www.waysideofva.com/stonewalljackson
Adjacent to trenches built by the First and Third brigades of the Second division, Sixth U.S. Corps, on October 20, 1864, the Stonewall Jackson Museum at Hupp's Hill serves as an interpretive center for the Civil War in the Shenandoah Valley. It exhibits Jackson's 1862 Valley Campaign with an impressive collection of Civil War artifacts. Reproduction weapons and uniforms can be touched. The children's room features discovery boxes, costumes to try on, wooden horses to climb on, and a Civil War camp with tent and camp furniture. Hours of operation are 10:00 A.M. to 5:00 P.M. daily. The museum is closed on New Year's Day, Easter Sunday, Thanksgiving, Christmas Eve, Christmas, and New Year's Eve. Admission is $5.00 for adults, $4.00 for children ages 6 through 17, and free for children younger than 6.

Strasburg Museum/Train Station
440 East King Street, Strasburg
(540) 465-3175
The exhibits at the Strasburg Museum

include many high-quality Civil War and railroad relics. Here is where Stonewall Jackson used trains in the service of the Confederacy after he hijacked them in Harper's Ferry, West Virginia. The blacksmith, cooper, and potter's shop collections are especially noteworthy. While the museum exhibitions range from pottery collections to World War II displays, there are a few items from the Civil War era, including a family Bible. Hours of operation are 10:00 A.M. to 4:00 P.M. daily from May through October. Admission is $3.00 for adults, $1.00 for teens, and 50 cents for children 12 and younger.

Belle Boyd Cottage
101 Chester Street, Front Royal
(540) 636-1446
www.warrenhs.org
This cottage museum, dedicated to the famed Confederate spy, teenager Belle Boyd, depicts life in Warren County and Front Royal during the Civil War. Belle was famous for the information she gathered that helped Jackson win the Battle of Front Royal on May 23, 1862. The Cottage is maintained by the Warren Heritage Society, along with the Ivy Lodge and Gift Shop. The buildings are open from 10:00 A.M. to 4:00 P.M. Monday through Friday and from noon to 4:00 P.M. Saturday. Admission is $2.00 for adults, $1.00 for students, and free for those younger than 6.

Prospect Hill Cemetery
540 Prospect Street, Front Royal
(540) 635-5468
Within the cemetery you will find two significant memorials. The first one, Soldier's Circle Monument, stands over the graves of 276 Confederate dead. The second, Mosby Monument, is flanked by two Parrott rifled cannons and is a memorial to seven members of a Confederate group named Mosby's Rangers, who were illegally executed as spies in 1864.

Reenactments

It doesn't matter what the season, there is some type of Civil War–related activity planned every month of the year. There are mock battles, symposiums, lectures, demonstrations, drills—you name it. While some of these reenactments take place annually, others only occur at five- and 10-year anniversaries. The anniversary reenactments tend to be larger events, both in participants and onlookers, because they aren't able to do them every year. At a reenactment, the weekend warriors replay the battles. To help celebrate, there's usually cavalry demonstrations, music, authors, artists, and sutlers (also known as vendors) selling food, period merchandise, and antiques. Below is a listing of a few of the reenactments to watch for. Otherwise, you might consider purchasing a $28 subscription to the *Camp Chase Gazette*, a Civil War publication that publishes 10 times a year. The *Gazette* features articles that cover the Civil War reenactments, as well as articles about weapons, clothing and other topics of interest to reenactors. It also has a calendar listing of upcoming reenactments. Here are just some in our area.

April	Lee's Surrender at Appomattox Courthouse, (434) 352-8987
May	Battle at Kelly's Ford in Culpeper, (540) 399-1779
May	Battle of New Market in New Market, (540) 740-3101
June	Battle of Lynchburg near Appomattox, (434) 352-2621
August	Battle of Warm Springs in Warm Springs, (800) 628-8092
September	Battle of Stanardsville at Quinque, (434) 985-6663
October	Cedar Creek Battlefield near Middleton, (888) 628-1864

Warren Rifles Confederate Museum
95 Chester Street, Front Royal
(540) 636-6982, (540) 635-2219
Included in this museum is memorabilia from spy Belle Boyd and Generals Lee, Jackson, Early, and Ashby. The collection also has an abundance of other Civil War artifacts. From April 15 through November 1, the museum is open Monday through Saturday from 9:00 A.M. to 4:00 P.M. and Sunday from noon to 4:00 P.M.

Edinburg Mill
214 South Main Street, Edinburg
(540) 984-8400
Built in 1848 on the banks of Stoney Creek, the Historic Edinburg Mill operated as a gristmill until 1978 when it was converted to its present-day use as a restau-rant. In 1864 the mill was spared from being burned by Gen. Sheridan's soldiers when local women pleaded for the livelihood of the Shenandoah Valley. Aside from its Civil War history, the Edinburg Mill is also noted for its child ghost—Frankie. Killed on October 22, 1898, when his clothing became entangled in machinery at the mill, 11-year-old Frank Hottle is thought to still roam the large confines of the building. Many strange and unexplainable events have occurred over the years.

Herbert Barbee Confederate Monument
East Main Street, Luray
Herbert Barbee, an Italian-trained sculptor of international note, got the idea for this statue when, as a youth, he saw a Confederate sentry standing in Thornton Gap

during a snowstorm. The muzzle of the soldier's gun was pointed down to keep out the snow. With donations coming in from Virginia, Maryland, and even the northern states of New York and Pennsylvania, Barbee chose to place his creation in his hometown of Luray. It was different from other monuments because the soldier was ragged. He has no socks, his shoes have holes, and his clothes are tattered. When the statue was dedicated in 1898, many thought Barbee was crazy to place his monument on the outskirts of the town, but as the area has expanded, the Herbert Barbee Confederate Monument is now in the center of Luray.

New Market Battlefield State Historical Park and Hall of Valor Civil War Museum
8895 Collins Drive, New Market
(540) 740-3101
www.vmi.edu/newmarket

New Market Battlefield State Historical Park, owned and operated by Virginia Military Institute, offers a perspective on one of America's most dramatic eras and is one of Virginia's finest Civil War museums. Visitors can view cannons in a field where in 1864 6,000 Federal soldiers clashed with 4,500 Confederates, including the famous VMI cadet corps desperately recruited from the college to help the South's cause. It was the first and only time in American history that an entire student body fought in a pitched battle.

The Hall of Valor, focal point of the 280-acre battlefield park, presents a concise, graphic survey of the entire Civil War. Exhibits highlight significant events of the war chronologically. Visitors can view three films, including a stirring account of the cadets' baptism by fire, one about Stonewall Jackson, and the Emmy Award–winning *Field of Lost Shoes*. You will see a life-size artillery unit, a model railroad, exquisitely sculpted soldiers, and four battle scenes among the three-dimensional exhibits in the Virginia Room.

The ca. 1825 Bushong farmhouse, around which part of the battle raged, still stands with its reconstructed blacksmith shop, meat and loom house, wheelwright shop, oven, henhouse, and other artifacts of daily life in the 1860s. The home served as a hospital after the battle. The celebrated Shenandoah River flows nearby.

The park is open daily, except holidays, from 9:00 A.M. to 5:00 P.M. Admission is $8.00 for adults and $4.00 for seniors and children ages 6 to 12.

Fort Harrison
335 Main Street, Dayton
(540) 879-2280, (540) 879-2272

Guided tours are available of the home of Daniel Harrison, brother of Harrisonburg founder Thomas Harrison. The stone house was a natural fort used by settlers during Indian attacks in the 18th century, and it also served as a refuge from fighting during the Civil War. Admission is $2.00. The site is open May through October, on weekends from 1:00 to 4:00 P.M.

Harrisonburg–Rockingham Historical Society Heritage Center
Bowman Road and High Street, Dayton
(540) 879-2681
www.heritagecenter.com

The Heritage Center is the place to go to trace the history of Rockingham County, from the pioneer days up to 1950. New upgrades have kept up with modern history as a huge electrified map and audio cassette outlining Stonewall Jackson's Valley Campaign of 1862 has been replaced by a large-screen TV with digital narrative. The artifacts, photos, and paintings in the collection help illustrate significant events of the Civil War in Rockingham County.

In addition to its focus on the Civil War, the museum now showcases traditional arts of the Shenandoah Valley. Genealogy research is available, and many Civil War scholars take advantage of this free service. The Heritage Museum Store sells books on numerous topics, including the Civil War, local tales and legends, and genealogy. Admission is $5.00. The museum is open Monday through Saturday from 10:00 A.M. to 4:00 P.M.

Stonewall Jackson House
8 East Washington Street, Lexington
(540) 463-2552
www.stonewalljackson.org
Built in 1801, the only home Jackson ever owned is furnished with his personal possessions. Guided tours interpret Jackson's life as a citizen, soldier, VMI professor of natural philosophy, church leader, and family man. Guided tours of the home and restored garden are given every half hour. The museum shop specializes in books, prints, quilts, samplers, and reproductions of antique toys. Hours of operation are Monday through Saturday from 9:00 A.M. to 5:00 P.M. and Sunday from 1:00 to 5:00 P.M. It is closed Thanksgiving, Christmas, New Year's Day, and Easter. Admission is $6.00 for adults, $3.00 for ages 6 to 17, and free to children younger than 6.

Stonewall Jackson Memorial Cemetery
300 block of South Main Street
Lexington
(540) 463-3777
Marked by Edward Valentine's bronze statue of the general, Stonewall Jackson Memorial Cemetery contains the remains of the 39-year-old leader of battle, who died May 10, 1863, from wounds received at the Battle of Chancellorsville. Historians note the irony of the statue, which faces south, as probably the only time Jackson ever turned his back on his enemy. Approximately 144 other Confederate soldiers also are buried here. You will also see the graves of John Mercer Brooke, who developed the concept of the ironclad ship, the *Merrimac,* and William Washington (1834–1870), well-known artist of the Civil War period who is especially known for his painting *Battle of Lantane.*

Virginia Military Institute and Museum
VMI Parade Grounds
North Main Street, Lexington
(540) 464-7334, (540) 464-7232
www.vmi.edu/museum
Founded in 1839 as the nation's first state military college, VMI is known internation-

ally as the school of the citizen-soldier and often is called the "West Point of the South." In Civil War lore, it is known for the officers and men it contributed to the Confederacy. At the center of campus, in front of the cadet barracks, is a statue of Gen. Stonewall Jackson. Nearby are cannons from the Rockbridge Artillery. The famous statue *Virginia Mourning Her Dead,* a monument to the VMI cadets who fell at New Market, stands on the parade grounds. VMI Museum at Jackson Memorial Hall will be closed until 2007 for major renovations, but a temporary exhibit has moved into its own room at the George Marshall Museum. The Marshall Museum, also on the VMI Post, will feature rare and unique artifacts from the VMI collection, including the uniform Stonewall Jackson was wearing when he was mortally wounded, and Little Sorrel, the mounted hide of Jackson's war horse. The entire collection will move back to the Jackson Memorial Hall after the $3.3 million renovation is complete. While at the Marshall location, admission will be $3.00. The museum is open year-round, except holidays, daily from 9:00 A.M. to 5:00 P.M.

Washington and Lee University
Main Street, Lexington
(540) 463-8768
www.leechapel.wlu.edu
Robert E. Lee served as Washington and Lee's president in the five years after the Civil War. The focal point of the school's beautiful front campus is Lee Chapel, where the remains of Lee and most of his family are entombed. Edward Valentine, who created the statue of Stonewall Jackson in the Jackson Memorial Cemetery on Main Street, also sculpted the chapel's famous pose of the recumbent Lee. Lee's horse, Traveller, is buried just outside the chapel. A museum in the chapel's basement focuses on the last five years of Lee's life, and his office is preserved as he left it. The museum is open Monday through Saturday from 9:00 A.M. to 5:00 P.M. and Sunday from 1:00 to 5:00 P.M. The

museum closes an hour earlier in the winter. Admission is free, but contributions will go toward educational programs.

ROANOKE VALLEY

Hanging Rock Battlefield
Interstate 81, exit 141, at Orange Market via Highway 311, Roanoke
(540) 389-5118

Confederate Gen. Jubal Early waged a running battle with David Hunter's forces as the Union leader withdrew his troops from Lynchburg. Thanks in part to the efforts of the Hanging Rock Battlefield Foundation, there is a new park here with an interpreted battle trail.

Bikers and walkers can enjoy a 2-mile stretch that follows the route of an abandoned railroad from a trailhead on Kessler Mill Road in Salem to the Hanging Rock area. It was here where, in 1864, Confederate forces caught and defeated the retreating Union force in a 45-minute skirmish.

The Sons of Confederate Veterans Fincastle Rifles Camp No. 1326 capped off the new stop on the Civil War Trail with a bronze statue of a Confederate soldier. One of the markers on-site lists the Fincastle supporters and their ancestors who fought in the war.

EAST OF THE BLUE RIDGE

Balls's Bluff Battlefield Regional Park
Ball's Bluff Road, Leesburg
(703) 737-7800
www.nvrpa.org/ballsbluff.html

On October 21, 1861, a force of 1,700 Union soldiers crossed the Potomac River to meet an equal force of Confederates from the defenses of Leesburg. The battle resulted in 900 Union casualties, including their commander, Col. Edward Baker, a U.S. Senator and friend of Abraham Lincoln. The Confederacy lost 155 soldiers, including many local men serving with the Eighth Virginia Infantry. The Ball's Bluff battle resulted in the creation of the Joint Congressional Committee on the Conduct of the War, which investigated Union defeats and corruption in the Federal war effort. Battlefield Park's National Cemetery contains Union dead. The park is open from dawn to dusk daily, with free guided tours offered at 11:00 A.M. and 2:00 P.M. Saturday and 1:00 and 3:00 P.M. Sunday from May to October. To learn more about this site, follow the interpretive 1-mile trail maintained by the Northern Virginia Regional Park Authority.

Loudoun Museum
16 Loudoun Street, Leesburg
(703) 777-7427

The Loudoun Museum is the first stop on the Civil War Trail's new loop, "The Antietam Campaign Trail." At the museum, you will learn about another side of the Civil War era, illustrated in letters to the Lucas family.

Mars and Jesse Lucas were emancipated slaves who emigrated to Africa in 1830 but wrote letters to Albert and Townsend Heaton, their former masters in Purcellville. Six of their letters written between 1830 and 1836 are on display here. Other artifacts help illustrate how Loudoun was divided between Confederate and Union sentiments, even pitting brother against brother.

A Confederate officer's uniform is part of the permanent collection.

Museum hours are 10:00 A.M. to 5:00 P.M. Monday through Saturday, and 1:00 to 5:00 P.M. Sunday.

Aldie Mill
Highway 50, Aldie
(703) 327-9777

Built from 1807 to 1809, Aldie Mill was owned by Henry Moore during the Civil War. Moore sold provisions to both Union and Confederate forces in Loudoun County. It served as a common resting place for Union patrols because of the available feed for their horses. It was here in March of 1863 that Confederate Col. John Singleton Mosby and 17 of his men surprised and defeated 59 of the First

Vermont Cavalry. Mosby, known as the Gray Ghost, left his job as a Bristol lawyer to enlist when Virginia seceded. He organized a group of "partisan rangers" who went on a guerrilla rampage from Leesburg to Fairfax Courthouse. Aldie Mill also was the site of two other battles involving Mosby's troops in 1861. The mill is open from noon to 5:00 P.M. Saturday and 1:00 to 5:00 P.M. Sunday. Admission is $4.00, $2.00 for seniors and children.

Mount Zion Old School Baptist Church
Highway 50, east of Gilbert's Corner
(540) 687-6681, (703) 777-6247
At this 1851 church, Col. John S. Mosby held his first rendezvous with his men to initiate partisan activities behind Union lines. The church also was used during the Gettysburg campaign as a field hospital for hundreds of Union and Confederate cavalrymen. Church pews were broken up to make coffins for the Union dead, who were buried in the adjacent cemetery. During the war, the church was also used as a barracks and a temporary prison for local Confederate sympathizers arrested during Union sweeps through the area. The church was the site of a major skirmish between Mosby and the Union Cavalry in July 1864, which left more than 100 Union casualties. Mosby lost eight men.

Exchange Hotel and Civil War Museum
400 South Main Street, Gordonsville
(540) 832-2944
www.hgiexchange.org
This historic building started in the mid-19th century as Virginia's Exchange Hotel, a resting place for passengers on the Virginia Central Railway. During the Civil War, the hotel became the Gordonsville Receiving Hospital, and the Confederacy brought wounded soldiers here from nearby battlefields. The museum houses many good exhibits and artifacts, especially its medical displays. Special medical reenactments take place in the spring and fall. From April through November, the museum is open from 10:00 A.M. to 4:00 P.M. Monday through

While in the area, Civil War buffs may want to take a side trip to Manassas National Battlefield Park Visitor Center. You can take a walking tour of the battlefield, where Confederate troops fended off Union forces in two major battles in the early stages of the war. It's only a 25-mile drive from Leesburg along U.S. Highway 15 and Highway 234.

Saturday and from 1:00 to 4:00 P.M. Sunday. It is closed Wednesday. The cost is $5.00 for adults, $4.00 for seniors, and $1.00 for students.

Jackson Statue
Fourth Street, Charlottesville
This statue, created by Charles Keck, is of a bareheaded Jackson galloping forward on his favorite horse, Little Sorrel.

Lee Statue
Park between First and Second Streets, Charlottesville
The work of sculptors H. M. Shrady and Leo Lentelli, this is an equestrian statue of Lee.

University Cemetery
Alderman and McCormick Roads, north of UVA Football Stadium, Charlottesville
Even during the Civil War, Charlottesville was known for its health care facilities, many of which treated military patients. The remains of 1,200 Confederate soldiers lie in University Cemetery, most of them victims of disease. A bronze statue of a bareheaded Confederate soldier is at the center.

Daniel Monument
Intersection of Park Avenue, Ninth and Floyd Streets, Lynchburg
John Warwick Daniel was a member of Gen. Jubal Early's staff who went on to become a distinguished orator and U.S. Senator. This monument to the "Lame Lion of Lynchburg," so named for Daniel's wound at the Battle of the Wilderness, was created by Sir Moses Ezekiel, a famous postwar sculptor.

CLOSE-UP
Tours de Force

With more than 300 Civil War sites sprinkled across the Commonwealth, it could take weeks just figuring out what to see and how to get there. Well, Mitchell Bowman has been out with his shovel and hammer, making things a lot easier for tourists.

"We have sites across the state about the Civil War, where there have never been markers before," said Bowman, executive director of Virginia Civil War Trails Inc. "What we are doing is turning Virginia into one great big outdoor museum. All of our markers will explain what actually happened on that site."

Each of the markers is also linked by a series of trailblazing red-white-and-blue signs.

"The second thing we wanted to do was link entire campaigns and regions together so it will make it a lot easier to understand," he said.

An example of the signs linking Civil War Trails sites. MARY ALICE BLACKWELL

Lynchburg Museum at Old Court House
901 Court Street, Lynchburg
(434) 847-1459
The tragedy of the Civil War is apparent from the exhibits on display in this historical representation of Lynchburg's history. The city was at the center of Confederate supply lines, making it a frequent Union target. The museum is usually housed in Lynchburg's 1855 Old Court House. While the Greek Revival building is undergoing renovations, an exhibition has been moved to the corner of Court Street in the old toy store. The Court House is scheduled to

reopen in May 2005. The museum is open daily, except holidays, from 10:00 A.M. to 4:00 P.M. Admission is $1.00.

Pest House Medical Museum and
Confederate Cemetery
Old City Cemetery
Fourth and Taylor Streets, Lynchburg
(434) 847-1465
www.gravegarden.org
The Confederate section of the historic Old City Cemetery serves as the final resting place for more than 2,200 individually marked graves of Confederate soldiers

The partnership of federal, state, and local governments and private citizens spent four years and $2.2 million to create Virginia's Civil War Trails. In fact, they divided the state into six driving trails.

Along the Blue Ridge, you can follow Stonewall Jackson's exploits on the **Shenandoah Valley Avenue of Invasion** trail or you can see where Col. John S. Mosby slipped past Union forces along the **1861–1865 Northern Virginia Crossroads of Conflict** trail.

The trails give visitors an opportunity to walk in the soldiers' footsteps. The buildings still stand and the railroad still runs in the beautiful countryside of Fauquier County, where Jackson, not yet nicknamed Stonewall, hurried his troops onto train cars for the trip to Manassas in July 1861. March with Jackson west of Staunton into the rugged Allegheny Mountains, using the same backcountry dirt roads he did in 1862. Experience the horror with the citizens of the Shenandoah Valley as Union Gen. David Hunter orders the burning of fields, barns, and homes in 1864. Or wander among the soldier graves at Old City Cemetery in Lynchburg or others in Loudoun, Staunton, and Winchester. You can even travel to Appomattox Courthouse and stand in the reconstructed house where Lee surrendered.

Lee's Retreat, the **1862 Peninsula Campaign,** and **Lee vs. Grant: The 1864 Campaign** are the other three trails that link the state's history.

"We want to give people easy access to the sites," Bowman said. "We want them to be able to park their cars and go on a little hike, if they like."

You can obtain information and maps of Virginia's Civil War Trails by visiting www.civilwartrails.org or by calling (888) CIVIL-WAR.

from 14 states. Nearby is the Pest House Medical Museum. One room depicts conditions in the House of Pestilence quarantine hospital during the Civil War. The second room is furnished as Dr. John J. Terrell's office when he practiced medicine in the area in the late 1800s. A monument to the memory of the 99 soldiers who died of smallpox in the Pest House during the war is near the entrance to the adjacent Confederate section. Many self-interpretive tablets and a variety of brochures are available at the Information Gatehouse and throughout the recently restored cemetery. Antique roses and period plantings contribute to the horticultural significance and beauty. The museum and cemetery are open daily from sunrise to sunset for self-guided tours or by appointment. A new visitor center is open daily from 11:00 A.M. to 3:00 P.M. It is closed on Sunday from November to March.

Riverside Park
2240 Rivermont Avenue, Lynchburg
Here you will find a fragment of the hull of the canal boat *Marshall,* which transported

the body of Jackson from Lynchburg to Lexington for burial in 1863.

Southern Soldier Statue
Monument Terrace, center of downtown Lynchburg

Honoring heroes of all wars, a statue of a Southern infantryman stands at the top of Monument Terrace. It was designed by James O. Scott and erected in 1898.

Spring Hill Cemetery
Fort Avenue, Lynchburg

Buried here is Gen. Jubal Early, who saved the city of Lynchburg from destruction during 1864 when he ran empty railroad cars up and down the tracks to convince the Yankees that Confederate reinforcements were arriving for a major battle. The Union forces retreated, and Lynchburg was saved from the destruction of Gen. David Hunter.

Appomattox Court House National Historical Park
Off U.S. Highway 460, Appomattox
(434) 352-8987, ext. 26
www.nps.gov/apco

If you're going to Lynchburg to see Civil War history, just 20 minutes farther east will put you at Appomattox, where our nation reunited on April 9, 1865. A restored village is here, the same as the day generals Grant and Lee ended the war with a handshake. The 1,800-acre park includes 27 original structures, including the McLean House. Living-history exhibits are held during the summer. Appomattox hosts the famous Railroad Festival every autumn (see our Annual Events and Festivals chapter). The park is open daily from 8:30 A.M. to 5:00 P.M. Admission is $4.00.

Bedford City/County Museum
201 East Main Street, Bedford
(540) 586-4520

This interesting local collection includes a number of artifacts from the Civil War, including weapons, flags, photos, and personal effects. The museum is open Tuesday through Saturday from 10:00 A.M. to 5:00 P.M. Donations are requested.

Longwood Cemetery
Bridge Street, Bedford

A Civil War monument marks the final resting place of soldiers who died at one of five Confederate hospitals in and around Bedford. A tall obelisk stands over the single grave of 192 soldiers and a nurse.

NEW RIVER VALLEY

The Wilderness Road Regional Museum
5240 Wilderness Road, Newbern
(540) 674-4835
www.rootsweb.com/~vanrhs/wrrm

Operated by the New River Historical Society, the museum consists of six historic structures on a six-acre tract. The collection includes a number of Civil War displays, including a drum. The area is close to Cloyd's Mountain, site of southwest Virginia's major Civil War battle (May 9, 1864). Hours of operation are Monday through Saturday from 10:30 A.M. to 4:30 P.M. and Sunday from 1:30 to 4:30 P.M.

ALLEGHANY HIGHLANDS

McDowell Presbyterian Church
U.S. Highway 250 W, McDowell

McDowell is the site of the second major battle of Jackson's Valley Campaign; a roadside marker commemorates the event. Inside the village is McDowell Presbyterian Church, used as a hospital during and after the fighting.

WINERIES 🍇

Thirty years ago, you might have been right in fashion sipping a mint julep or iced tea on a summer afternoon in the Blue Ridge. Today, corks are popping from Leesburg to Pulaski.

In less than there decades, Virginia winemaking grew from a struggling cottage industry to a burgeoning international force. The industry transformation has been, and continues to be, remarkable. The state's winery count has increased from six in 1979 to 87 licensed wineries in 2004. Virginia is now the fifth-largest vinifera wine-producing state in the United States, producing almost 270,000 cases of wine per year. The Virginia wine industry generates more than $50 million in revenue for the state. Virginia wineries make more than 17 varieties of wine, though Chardonnay continues to be the most popular. However, the vinifera varieties of Cabernet Franc and Viognier continue to gain national and international reputations as superior Virginia wines.

These changes make it an exciting time to visit Virginia wineries. Visitors get a close-up view and firsthand taste of the fruits of our winemakers' labors. You can find out for yourself why *Wine Spectator* calls Virginia "the most accomplished of America's emerging wine regions" and why Virginia wines continue to win national and international awards at an impressive rate.

Since Thomas Jefferson tried to grow grapes at his home in Monticello, growers have suspected that Virginia soils and high elevations, which minimize summer heat and lengthen the growing season, would make ideal grape-growing conditions. The Shenandoah Valley, both climate- and soil-wise, has been favorably compared to Germany's Moselle Valley, a famous Riesling region, and the Piedmont is said to share many of the same characteristics with the Bordeaux region of France.

But it wasn't until the 1980s that the industry really took off, in part because of support from state officials. In 1985 the Virginia General Assembly created the Virginia Winegrowers Advisory Board to promote winemaking in the state. The Assembly also set up a research team to provide grape growers with the technical support necessary to produce a healthy crop.

The results of these efforts and the efforts of individual wineries are here for us all to enjoy. Winery tours in Virginia are wonderful in many ways. Not only do visitors get to taste a wide variety of wines, but they can do so in spectacular settings. Most have areas for picnickers, so take along lunch or brunch and make a day of it.

As you plan your winery tours, look at the maps in this chapter and consider visiting three or four wineries in a day. Around Charlottesville, Front Royal, and Middleburg, numerous day trip options are available. In Charlottesville, for example, Oakencroft, White Hall, King Family, and Autumn Hill vineyards are nestled together, as are Jefferson, Kluge, and First Colony. Each of these clusters make excellent day trips. Around Middleburg, you can visit Swedenburg, Piedmont, and Chrysalis, and outside Front Royal you'll find Oasis, Linden, and Naked Mountain vineyards.

We suggest you not try to do too much in one day; it is much better to savor each stop and each view. So chart your course carefully, and don't forget to call ahead to confirm winery hours, which can change.

If you're lucky, you'll be in the area when one of the wineries hosts a festival or open house. Spring and fall are big festival times. In May, Front Royal hosts the annual Virginia Mushroom and Wine Festival, and Mountain Cove Vineyards sponsors a Fiesta de Primavera with music, crafts, and tastings of new wines. Also, some unique Blue Ridge wine events include the Oasis Winery's Polo Wine and Twilight Dine at Bleu Rock Vineyard in the summer, Shakespeare in the Ruins at Barboursville Vineyards in August, the Garlic Festival at Rebec in mid-October, and a Civil War authors book signing at Gray Ghost Vineyards in November. All told, there are more than 300 events each year, ranging from barrel tastings to pig roasts. (See our Annual Events and Festivals chapter.) For a complete listing of festivals and events, we recommend an excellent annual guide to Virginia's wineries that is available free from the Virginia Wine Marketing Program, VDACS, Division of Marketing, P.O. Box 1163, Richmond, VA 23218; (800) 828-4637, or log onto www.virginiawines.org.

The following are some of the wineries of the Blue Ridge region, beginning with those in the Shenandoah Valley. Wineries are organized alphabetically within their geographic region. Many are still small family operations, created by people who do the planting, growing, and winemaking themselves, while others are now larger, multistaffed businesses, with vineyard managers and hired consulting winemakers. There are a couple of wineries we have not listed individually because they are not open to the public, but they are worth mentioning all the same. One of special interest to those who know about Virginia wine is Gabriele Rausse Winery in Charlottesville. Rausse has long been known as a premier winemaker in Virginia and has helped many a novice get a start. Rausse began making his own wine several years ago. Look for his Cabernet Sauvignon and Chardonnay in wine shops such as the Market Street Winery and the Gourmet Wine Shop in Charlottesville, as well as other retailers who offer a good variety of Virginia wines. Another winery is Blenheim Vineyards, also in Charlottesville. From land purchased by Dave Matthews of the nationally known Dave Matthews Band, another big name winemaker in Virginia is getting his chance to create his own wines. Another local favorite is Landwirt Vineyard in Harrisonburg.

SHENANDOAH VALLEY

Deer Meadow Vineyard
199 Vintage Lane, Winchester
(540) 877-1919, (800) 653-6632
www.dmeadow.com
Owner Charles Sarle made his first commercial wines in 1987, after retiring from a career as a mechanical engineer. He had been a home winemaker for 10 years. He and his wife, Jennifer, operate the winery on their 120-acre farm southwest of Winchester. They produce Cabernet Sauvignon, Chardonnay, Chambourcin, Golden Blush, made from 100 percent Steuben, and the blended semisweet Afternoon of the Fawn. This small, rustic vineyard is open March through December. Tours are offered from 11:00 A.M. to 5:00 P.M. Wednesday through Sunday and most Mondays and holidays.

Guilford Ridge Vineyard
328 Running Pine Road, Luray
(540) 778-3853
Owner John Gerba and co-proprietor Harland Baker planted these vines in the early 1970s and began winemaking in the mid-1980s. The Page County winery cultivates four acres of hybrid grapes to produce their Red Page Valley (Bordeaux-style red), et Delilah (Beaujolais-style red), and Pinnacles (crisp white). Visitors to the 80-plus-acre farm have an opportunity to see a variety of animals—llamas, peacocks, goats, sheep, and a potbellied pig—that make their home here. Call ahead to arrange a visit and purchases; tastings are offered to groups of eight or more from June to November by appointment only. There is a $3.00 fee for group tastings. Tours of the winery are not available.

North Mountain Vineyard & Winery
4374 Swartz Road, Maurertown
(540) 436-9463
www.northmountainvineyard.com
North Mountain Vineyard's 10 acres are situated on property in northern Shenandoah County that has been farmed since the late 1700s. The vineyard was established in

1982 when Dick McCormack planted some 8,000 vines of Chardonnay, Vidal, and Chambourcin. The Foster–Jackson family are now owners. At the winery building, which was built in 1990 and modeled after a European-style farmhouse, you can taste North Mountain's award-winning Chardonnay, Riesling, Vidal Blanc, apple blush, Chambourcin, and claret. Gourmet picnic fare is also available, including cheeses, pâtés, and homemade breads.

The winery's large picnic area and two decks overlook the vineyard. There are also a gift shop and a local art gallery at the winery. North Mountain is open for tours and tastings from 11:00 A.M. to 5:00 P.M. Wednesday through Sunday. Large groups should call ahead for an appointment.

Rockbridge Vineyard
35 Hillview Lane, Raphine
(540) 377-6204, (888) 511-9463
www.rockbridgewine.com

Shepherd and Jane Rouse own this expanding 17-acre winery, which is housed in a renovated 19th-century dairy barn. Shepherd was the winemaker at Montdomaine Cellars and Oakencroft Vineyard in Charlottesville. In just a few short years, Rockbridge Vineyard, between Staunton and Lexington, has brought home a series of gold medals and the Governor's Cup for its 1995 V d'Or dessert wine. In the 2002 competition, the V d'Or was a gold-medal winner. In 2001 Rockbridge won the Governor's Cup for its 1998 DeChiel Merlot. The 47-acre farm sits at a 2,000-foot elevation, so it is a wonderful spot on hot summer days. The breezy hillside is great for picnics, and the Rouses will even lend you a blanket if you want to find your own spot. There's also a deck and picnic tables available. Rockbridge produces Chardonnay, Riesling, Cabernet, Pinot Noir, Vidal Ice Wine, and several eastern varieties, including Vignoles, Traminette, Vidal Blanc, Chambourcin, and Concord. Tours and tastings are offered 11:00 A.M. to 5:00 P.M. Monday through Saturday and noon to 5:00 P.M. on Sunday. There is a tasting fee of $1.00 per person for groups of 10 or more.

Always call ahead before you visit a winery. Many are small, family-operated businesses that close in emergencies or during bad weather.

Shenandoah Vineyards Inc.
3659 South Ox Road, Edinburg
(540) 984-8699
www.shentel.net/shenvine

Established in 1976, the Shenandoah Valley's first winery grows 14 varieties of grapes on 35 acres. The winery itself is on the lower level of a renovated Civil War–era barn, which also houses a small gift shop and tasting room. Owner Emma Randel lives in the restored log house where her mother was born. In this peaceful setting with sweeping mountain views and a deck overlooking the vineyard, the winery produces Chardonnay, Riesling, Cabernet Sauvignon, Merlot, and several blends, including Shenandoah Blanc, Shenandoah Ruby, Sweet Serenade, Blushing Belle, Chambourcin, and Raspberry Serenade. In 1995 Shenandoah's Chardonnay was named one of the best white wines in the state. The winery is open for tastings from 10:00 A.M. to 6:00 P.M. daily March through November and from 10:00 A.M. to 5:00 P.M. December to February; it is closed Thanksgiving, Christmas, and New Year's Day. Tours are given hourly from 11:00 A.M. to 5:00 P.M. A large picnic area has wonderful views of surrounding mountains.

EAST OF THE BLUE RIDGE

Afton Mountain Vineyards
234 Vineyard Lane, Afton
(540) 456-8667
www.aftonmountainvineyards.com

This winery lies on a southeastern slope of the Blue Ridge at 960 feet, just minutes from the end of the Skyline Drive and the beginning of the Blue Ridge Parkway near Afton, a village known for its antiques and mountain crafts. The winery and its 11.5

Sip of the Tongue

Brut—broot
Cabernet Blanc—cab-er-nay blonc
Cabernet Franc—cab-er-nay fronc
Cabernet Sauvignon—cab-er-nay so-vin-yawn
Chambourcin—sham-boor-san
Chardonnay—shard-don-ay
Gewurztraminer—geh-vertz-tram-mee-ner
Merlot—mer-low
Pinot Grigio—pee-no gree-jee-oh
Pinot Noir—pee-no nwahr
Riesling—reez-ling
Sauvignon Blanc—so-vin-yawn blonc
Seyval Blanc—say-voll blonc
Vidal Blanc—vee-doll blonc
Viognier—vee-on-nay

acres of vineyards offer magnificent views of the Rockfish River Valley and the mountains immortalized in Edgar Allan Poe's "Tale of the Ragged Mountains." The winery sells breads, cheeses, and meats, which can be enjoyed from a scenic picnic area. Wines include Chardonnay, Cabernet Sauvignon, Gewurztraminer, Riesling, Sangiovese, Cabernet Franc, and Pinot Noir. The winery is open for tours and tastings from 11:00 A.M. to 5:00 P.M. Friday to Monday during January and February. From March through October, the winery is open from 10:00 A.M. to 6:00 P.M. daily except Tuesday. In November and December the winery closes at 5:00 P.M. Afton is closed Easter, Thanksgiving, Christmas, and New Year's Day.

Autumn Hill Vineyards/Blue Ridge Winery
301 River Drive, Stanardsville
(434) 985-6100
www.autumnhillwine.com
The setting for this small, award-winning winery is a high plateau northwest of Char-

lottesville. Owners Avra and Ed Schwab left Long Island for Virginia in the mid-1970s. Ed, who ran an interior design firm, had grown weary of the rat race. Deciding to try winemaking, the couple planted the first stage of their vineyards in 1979; they now have 13 acres of vines. Their European-style wines include Chardonnay, Cabernet Sauvignon, Cabernet Franc, Chardonnay Vintner's Reserve, Viognier, Merlot, white Cabernet Sauvignon, and Horizon Rouge (a Bordeaux-style blend). The winery is open to visitors only four weekends: two in April and two in October. There is a $6.00 tasting fee. Phone and Internet sales are available year-round.

Barboursville Vineyards
17655 Winery Road, Barboursville
(540) 832-3824
www.barboursvillewine.com
Barboursville wines have won more awards than any other vineyard in Virginia, including the 1997 Governor's Cup for its Cabernet Franc. Try the Chardonnay Reserve. It was selected as one of the top

25 Chardonnays produced in the United States, and it was recently served at the embassy in Paris. The Sauvignon Blanc 2000 was served with the first course at the James Beard Foundation Dinner in New York in December 2001.

The Zonin family, who owns the giant Italian wine firm, also owns this 900-acre estate, which includes a cattle farm and the imposing ruins of a mansion designed by Thomas Jefferson for Virginia governor James Barbour. The site is a registered Virginia Historic Landmark and has many prime picnic spots. The winery added Palladio Restaurant, an exquisite Italian restaurant that serves lunch Wednesday through Sunday and dinner on Friday and Saturday (see our Restaurants chapter). In the Guest Chef Series, chefs are invited to prepare their signature dishes to pair with Barboursville's wines. The estate's historic vineyard cottage, an 18th-century building with 21st-century amenities, may be reserved by Palladio guests. Barboursville produces more than 32,000 cases of wine a year from 130 acres of grapes. The wines at Barboursville are more in the European style, fresh and clean with subtle complexity, and include the popular Chardonnay, Sauvignon Blanc, Cabernet Franc, Pinot Noir, Barbera, Viognier, Merlot, Cabernet Sauvignon, Nebbiolo, Sangiovese, Pinot Grigio, and Barboursville Brut. Tours are available hourly from 11:00 A.M. to 4:00 P.M. on weekends. Tastings and sales are offered from 10:00 A.M. to 5:00 P.M. Monday to Saturday and from 11:00 A.M. to 5:00 P.M. on Sunday except major holidays. Other events include Opera in the Vineyard, with performances by the Virginia Opera, and Shakespeare in the Ruins.

Breaux Vineyards
36888 Breaux Vineyards Lane, Hillsboro
(540) 668-6299, (800) 492-9961
www.breauxvineyards.com
Friends of Paul and Alexis Breaux must have good taste. "I made some homemade wine and our friends and neighbors kept after us to make more," Paul Breaux said. So in April 1998, Breaux Vineyards became the 50th winery in the state. Ten months later, Breaux had won 15 medals in a series of wine competitions. When Paul and Alexis purchased their 400-acre farm in western Loudoun County, the property came with 18 acres of 14-year-old grapevines. They now have 65 acres of vineyards. Madeleine Chardonnay, named for his daughter, is one of Paul's favorites. The winery also produces Seyval Blanc, Vidal Blanc, Viognier, Cabernet Franc, Cabernet Sauvignon, Sauvignon Blanc, Merlot, barrel-fermented Chardonnay, and what is thought to be one of the state's first Late Harvest Vidal Blancs. One of their blends, a 2001 vintage called Alexis, won a gold medal at the State Fair of Virginia in 2003. Tours and tastings are available from 11:00 A.M. to 5:00 P.M. daily. The winery is closed on major holidays. There is a $3.00 tasting fee for individuals, $5.00 a person for groups of eight or more. Their Napa-meets-Mediterranean–style tasting room has been expanded and offers a view of their hillside vines on Short Hill Mountain. You may bring along a picnic or sample some of Breaux's light gourmet fare. Groups are asked to call and make advance reservations.

Burnley Vineyards and Daniel Cellars
4500 Winery Lane, Barboursville
(540) 832-2828
www.burnleywines.com
One of the oldest wineries in Albemarle County, Burnley Vineyards produces 13 wines that include Chardonnay, barrel-fermented Chardonnay, Cabernet Sauvignon, Riesling, Spicy Rivanna, Zinfandel, Peach Fuzz, and Daniel Cellars Somerset dessert wines. Lee Reeder and his father planted their first vines in 1976, the year after nearby Barboursville Vineyards opened. In 1984 father and son started the winery. Today the Reeder family produces about 6,000 cases a year from grapes grown on their own 30 acres and from a small, private vineyard in Luray. Their wines have won more than 100 awards in state, national, and international competitions.

Tastings are offered in a room with a cathedral ceiling and 60 feet of windows overlooking the countryside. The winery is open Friday through Monday from 11:00 A.M. to 5:00 P.M. in January, February, and March; from April through December, hours are 11:00 A.M. to 5:00 P.M. seven days a week. Group tours or evening visits can be arranged in advance. The $2.00 tasting fee is refundable on a purchase. Tours are given by appointment. Burnley also has a fully furnished guest house, which sleeps four people and can be rented nightly or by the week.

Cardinal Point Vineyard and Winery
9423 Batesville Road, Afton
(540) 456-8400
www.cardinalpointwinery.com

While the vineyard has been here for 18 years, Cardinal Point started selling its own wines in 2002. Owners Paul and Ruth Gorman grow 15 acres of vines on their 100-acre property. Mr. Gorman is a retired four-star army general, and he developed an interest in grape growing and wine-making when he lived in the Riesling area of Germany. Their son Tim studied viticulture and began making wine with their grapes. Daughter Sarah is an attorney who handles the winery's books. Bring in other son John, an architect who designed the facility, and the whole family is involved in the operation.

The tasting room is more of a modern-style facility, done in tan and red. The out-door terrace is a good place to sip a glass of wine and talk over the day's activities. Don't be surprised if you are greeted by a friendly dog when you enter the property. The wines produced at Cardinal Point include Cabernet Franc, Rockfish Red, Cabernet Sauvignon, and Meritage. Whites include Riesling, Barrel Select Chardonnay, A6 (blend of Chardonnay and Viognier), Aubaine (also Chardonnay), and a Rose. Tasting hours are 10:00 A.M. to 5:30 P.M. Wednesday through Monday. Cardinal Point is closed Thanksgiving, Christmas, New Year's, and Easter. The tasting is complimentary. The tour includes a video presentation of the activities that go on in the vineyard and winery.

Christensen Ridge Winery
Highway 698, Madison
(540) 923-4800
www.christensenridge.com

Winemaker J. D. Hartman owns this 211-acre property in Madison. From the seven-acre vineyard on his property, and from 10 acres at other vineyards, he is producing hand-crafted Tuscan Blend, Cabernet Franc, Merlot, Cabernet Sauvignon, Chardonnay, Vidal Blanc, and Viognier. Hartman's 2001 Chardonnay won a gold medal in the Grand Harvest Awards, one of only two Virginia wines to earn gold in the California competition. It also is one of two Christensen Ridge wines served at the Inn at Little Washington.

The property rents its 1700s log cabin, which sleeps two, and a modern six-bedroom house complete with pool. The house sleeps 12 to 16 and has a big country kitchen. J. D. Hartman is the innkeeper and the vineyard manager. You can stop by for tastings 11:00 A.M. to 5:00 P.M. on Friday, Saturday, and Sunday, and every day but Monday in October. The $2.00 tasting fee is credited to a purchase of $20.00 or more and includes a souvenir glass.

Chrysalis Vineyards
23876 Champe Ford Road, Middleburg
(800) 235-8804, (540) 687-8222
www.chrysaliswine.com

Ever since Jennifer McCloud opened her winery in Middleburg in 1998, she has been adding facilities—such as the tasting room complex, which has patio seating for 40, a new picnic pavilion, and a barbecue pit. With such facilities, Chrysalis often rents its space for weddings and other activities. The 209-acre Locksley Farm estate is on the banks of the Hungry Run in Loudoun County. Chrysalis has 51 acres in vines, including 25 acres of Norton, which is one of the largest plantings of Norton in the world. Chrysalis is particularly interested in the Norton, which is a native American grape and was internationally recognized in the 1800s.

With Alan Kinne and Brad McCarthy as consulting winemakers, Chrysalis Vineyards produces eight wines, including Chardonnay, Viognier (which won Best in Show in San Diego in April 2002), Sarah's Patio White, Sarah's Patio Red, Mariposa (a dry rosé), whole-cluster pressed Norton, estate-bottled Norton, Locksley Reserve Norton, Rubiana, Petit Manseng, Albarino, and five other private reserves. The winery is open daily for tastings from 10:00 A.M. to 5:00 P.M. There is a $3.00 tasting fee.

Farfelu Vineyard
13058 Crest Hill Road, Flint Hill
(540) 364-2930
www.farfeluwine.com

Located in Rappahannock County, Farfelu (pronounced far-fuh-loo) is Virginia's first winery.

The vineyard was planted in 1967 and produced its first vintage in 1975, when Virginia enacted its farm winery law. In 2000 John and Caroline Osborne purchased the winery from its founder and undertook a three-year revitalization campaign that renovated its 1860s dairy-barn-turned-winery, upgraded all the winemaking equipment, implemented ecofriendly, sustainable farming practices in the vineyard, and increased production from 600 cases to 3,500.

Farfelu now makes Chardonnay, Cabernet Franc, Syrah, a Bordeaux-blend called Muse, a Chardonnay/Viognier blend called Élan, two lightly sweet wines—Fou de Blanc (Crazy White) and Fou de Rouge (Crazy Red)—and Amour (a dessert wine). In keeping with its motto (Serious Wine for Un-Serious People), Farfelu offers a truly authentic experience. Its off-the-beaten-path 86-acre estate offers an expansive deck overlooking the vineyard, a large games meadow with horseshoes, bocce ball and badminton, a picnic pavilion with barbecue grills, and a hiking trail along the Rappahannock River. A rotating selection of Virginia-produced artisan cheeses and sausage is available. Come for tastings 11:00 A.M. to 5:00 P.M. Thursday through Monday. The $3.00 tasting fee includes a souvenir glass. Don't miss the annual pig roast in June or the End-of-Harvest Bonfire and Chili Fest in November.

First Colony Winery
1650 Harris Creek Road, Charlottesville
(434) 979-7105, (877) 979-7105
www.firstcolonywinery.com

As a descendant of George Washington's attorney general, Edmund Randolph, Randolph McElroy Jr. wanted to continue his family history within the wine business. Buying and opening a winery seemed like a natural fit for this Virginia native.

After establishing First Colony Winery in December of 2000, Randy hired a team of well-trained winemakers, viticulturists, and management. A strong foundation was laid with the first wines released in March 2002. The 2001 vintage proved to be promising, winning more than 20 awards at state, national, and international wine competitions. There are 50 acres of grapes involved in their production, with 15 acres on property. First Colony has a fourth-generation French winemaker, and their wines reflect Old World traditions. The wines produced are Chardonnay, Chardonnay Reserve, Vidal Blanc, Late Harvest Vidal Blanc, Viognier, Cabernet Franc, Cabernet Sauvignon, and Merlot.

Tastings are available 11:00 A.M. to 5:00 P.M. daily, and you can take a guided tour of the winery on the hour between noon and 4:00 P.M. First Colony is closed Thanksgiving, Christmas, and New Year's Day. There is no tasting fee for individuals, but groups of 10 or more should call ahead and expect to pay $5.00 a person, which includes a souvenir wine glass.

Gray Ghost Vineyards
14706 Lee Highway, Amissville
(540) 937-4869
www.grayghostvineyards.com

This small vineyard opened in the spring of 1994 on a 25-acre farm in Rappahannock County. Using grapes from their 11 acres of vines as well as from five other small Rappahannock vineyards, owners and winemakers Cheryl and Al Kellert produce Chardonnay, Cabernet Sauvignon, Reserve Chardonnay, Reserve Cabernet Sauvignon, Vidal Blanc, Seyval Blanc, Cabernet Franc, Victorian White, Victorian Red, Merlot,

Gewurztraminer, and Adieu (Late Harvest Vidal). Their Adieu, a wonderful dessert wine, has won more national and international wine competitions than just about any other winery east of California. The 2002 vintage received Best of the East Award from *Vineyard and Winery Management* magazine. The winery has a canopied picnic area and a gazebo and gardens. Gray Ghost also has a large display of logo wine glasses that are fun to browse. Tastings are available from 11:00 A.M. to 5:00 P.M. Saturday and Sunday in January and February, 11:00 A.M. to 5:00 P.M. Friday through Sunday from March through December, and on all Monday federal holidays. It's also open Monday through Thursday by appointment. Groups of eight or more should call ahead for an appointment.

Hickory Hill Vineyard
1722 Hickory Cove Lane, Moneta
(540) 296-1393
www.hickoryhillvineyards.com

Roger and Judy Furrow bought the property, called Toby Scruggs Farm, on the east side of Smith Mountain Lake, in 1992 when the former cattle farm became available after its 95-year-old owner passed away. Living in High Point, North Carolina, at the time, the Furrows had been experimenting with grape growing on the Smith Mountain Lake home of Roger's mother and making their own wine as a hobby. Now they have 4.5 acres of vines on the 43-acre farm in Bedford County. They opened in July 2002 and presented their wines, including Chardonnay, Cabernet Sauvignon, Vidal Blanc, Smith Mountain Lake Country Red, Smith Mountain Lake Mist (a white wine), and Smith Mountain Lake Sunset (a dessert-style wine made from Vidal and Chardonnay grapes).

The winery is in a renovated 1923 farmhouse, which had been the farm's homestead. The dining room has become the tasting room, decorated with artifacts and memorabilia found during the renovation. There are picnic tables and a screened-in porch with tables where you can relax and enjoy a glass of wine. Tours and tastings are available March through mid-December, Friday through Monday, from 11:00 A.M. to 5:00 P.M. and by appointment at other times. There is no tasting fee, but groups of 10 or more are asked to call ahead.

Hidden Brook Winery
43301 Spinks Ferry Road, Leesburg
(703) 737-3935
www.hiddenbrookwinery.com

Owners Eric and Deborah Hauck planted vines five years ago, and they opened in September 2002. He moved to the area when he was 18, whereas she is from New Brunswick, Canada, and has lived in Leesburg for the last 10 years. Enjoy a tasting in their large new log building, which also houses the winery. You can relax by the fire or enjoy the deck that overlooks the vineyards and mountains. Their wines include Chardonnay, Merlot, Cabernet Sauvignon, Vidal Blanc, Chambourcin, and Sweet Amber, a late harvest ice wine design. A small fee for tasting goes toward the cost of buying a bottle. The winery is open noon to 5:00 P.M. weekdays and 11:00 A.M. to 5:00 P.M. weekends. Hidden Brook is closed Thanksgiving, Christmas, New Year's Day, and Easter.

Hill Top Berry Farm and Winery
2800 Berry Hill Road, Nellysford
(434) 361-1266
www.hilltopberrywine.com

Like many couples, Marlyn and Sue Allen needed something to do after the kids went off to school. "We lived here for 22 years," Marlyn Allen said. "When the kids graduated from college, we decided we were going to do something we wanted to do." Ten years ago, they planted some berry bushes—a lot of berry bushes. In fact, they have six acres of blackberries alone, not counting their raspberries, plums, peaches, apples, and grapes. They usually open their gates for a pick-your-own blackberry day, but along the way Marlyn began to save a few berries to make some homemade wine. When friends tasted a sample of his blackberry wine, they encouraged him to make more.

So the Nelson County couple decided to give it a go. In March 1999, they opened their own small winery and released about 1,500 gallons of their "true to the fruit" wines. Today, the children have returned home, and three daughters help run the family operation. Their wines include blackberry, raspberry, apple, peach, plum, cherry, pear, cranberry, and even a blush made from Concord and Niagara grapes. The Allens have added a historical flair with a new line of wines made with honey, including Blue Ridge Mountain Mead, Rockfish River Cyser, Blueberry Melomel, and Strawberry Melomel. Hill Top is open for tastings 11:00 A.M. to 5:00 P.M. Monday through Saturday and 1 to 5 P.M. Sunday, with extended hours during the berry-picking season. The pick-your-own blackberry season is usually the entire month of August.

Horton Cellars Winery/Montdomaine Cellars
6399 Spotswood Trail, Gordonsville
(540) 832-7440
www.hvwine.com
In the early 1980s Dennis Horton searched the vineyards of southern France for grapes that would thrive in Virginia's warm climate. He settled on the Viognier, a variety used in some of the world's finest wines. He and his business partner, Joan Bieda, harvested the first crop from their 65 acres in Orange County in 1991 and made it into wine at Montdomaine Cellars, a noted Cabernet producer that Bieda and Horton later purchased. In 1993 Horton Vineyards made the first crush at its new underground stone cellars and offered tastings in a delightful vaulted-ceiling tasting room. Horton's Viognier and other Rhone varieties have done well in national competitions. Also included in its list of 38 wines are Chardonnay, Eclipse (red), Mourvedre, Dionysus (red), Cabernet Franc, Sparkling Viognier, peach, pear, blackberry, strawberry, blueberry, and raspberry. Plus, they make the only Vintage Port in Virginia. There's also a Pear Port and a wine called Rkatsiteli, a white wine whose grapes are widely grown in Asia but only in 10 acres in the United States, including Horton's six. The vineyard is open for tastings from 10:00 A.M. to 5:00 P.M. daily. Call ahead to receive an in-depth tour. Tastings are free, but a glass costs $3.00

For a great venue to sample wines produced in Virginia, check out the two big state wine festivals—Vintage Virginia Wine Festival, held the first weekend in June, and the Virginia Wine Festival, held in mid-August. Both have been going on for more than 20 years, and both are held at historic Long Branch in Millwood. Not only is there one of the largest selections of Virginia wines in one place, there are also samples of delicious Virginia-made food, great entertainment, and arts and crafts displays.

Jefferson Vineyards
1353 Thomas Jefferson Parkway
Charlottesville
(434) 977-3042, (800) 272-3042
www.jeffersonvineyards.com
This vineyard, between Monticello and Ash Lawn–Highland, is situated on the same stretch of rolling land once owned by Philip Mazzei, the 18th-century wine enthusiast who helped convince Thomas Jefferson to plant vines. Though Jefferson was never able to grow grapes successfully here, Jefferson Vineyards has been able to, cultivating 20 acres of European vinifera—the same variety that Mazzei tried to grow.

Today winemaker Frantz Ventre produces Cabernet Franc, Cabernet Sauvignon, Chardonnay, Pinot Gris, Merlot, Viognier, and Riesling at Jefferson Vineyards. Tastings are available from 11:00 A.M. to 5:00 P.M. daily, and tours are on the hour between noon and 4:00 P.M. There is a $1.00 fee for tasting. The winery has a small gift shop, a pleasant picnic table area under a grape arbor, and a deck with views of the surrounding mountains. The quaint, renovated barn that houses the tasting room can be booked for private parties.

King Family Vineyards
6550 Roseland Farm, Crozet
(434) 823-7800
www.kingfamilywineyard.com
This is the perfect place to enjoy a glass of wine—sitting at the long brick patio with wide views of the grassy fields and beautiful mountains. King Family Vineyards is one of the newest wineries in Virginia, but they made quick work of establishing a reputation as they won the 2004 Virginia Governors Cup for their Cabernet Franc, 2002 vintage. David and Ellen King are the owners of this family-run venture. The family moved here from Texas in 1996. He was a lawyer but now does the winery full time as does their son, Carrington, who obtained a horticulture degree.

They opened in October 2002 and offer two labels—the King family and a label under Michael Shaps's name. Shaps is the winemaker and a partner and has a strong reputation in Virginia winemaking tradition. There are 15 acres of vines on this 327-acre farm. Besides the Cab Franc, they offer eight other wines, including Chardonnay, Viognier, Merlot, Meritage, King Family Vineyards Roseland (a blend of Chardonnay and Viognier), and King Family Vineyards Crose (a rosé blend of Merlot and Cab Franc), as well as a late harvest Viognier and a late harvest Cabernet Franc. Stop by for a tour and complimentary tasting any day of the week, except for Thanksgiving, Christmas, New Year's Day, and Easter.

The King family has already started one annual event: Reds, Whites, and the Blue Ridge on July 4. They also have open house weekends leading up to Christmas and cooking classes. In the spring of 2005, they plan to start hosting polo matches on their wide and impressive fields. They have a catering kitchen and offer the site for rehearsal dinners and corporate dinners.

While they don't offer picnics, they encourage visitors to bring their own and enjoy the space. French bread and an assortment of cheeses can be purchased.

Kluge Estate Winery and Vineyard
100 Grand Cru Drive, Charlottesville
(434) 977-3895, ext. 55
www.klugeestate.com
Patricia Kluge, owner of one of the most famous homes in Central Virginia, started planting grapes in 1999 on nearly 100 acres of her 1,200-acre estate and soon opened the Kluge Estate Winery and Vineyard.

Her winery concentrates on quality, not quantity. Kluge decided to specialize in making a few wines and making them well, and brought in two French winemakers, Claude Thibaut and Charles Gendrot, to help oversee the process. Their Kluge Estate SP 2001 was made entirely of Chardonnay grapes in the methode champenoise. The grapes are hand-picked in small baskets and pressed in a champagne press before fermenting in stainless steel tanks. Kluge also makes a Cru, a Chardonnay-based aperitif, and a Kluge Estate New World Red, a Bordeaux-style wine made of Cabernet Sauvignon, Merlot, and Cabernet Franc and aged for 14 months in French oak barrels.

There were only 289 bottles of the estate's very first release in 2000, a New World Red. Each bottle was numbered and signed by Kluge and winemaker Gabriele Rausse and was sold for $495 in a special box made of American walnut designed by an Italian craftsman, Lord David Linley.

The winery was designed in the same 18th-century architectural style of the Kluge family home and chapel. Her estate also houses a private 18-hole golf course that was designed by Arnold Palmer.

A visit to the Kluge Estate Farm Shop is in itself a gourmet treat. Along with a room for wine tastings, the shop also has a separate coffee and tea bar. You also won't want to pass up sampling the delicious variety of prepared foods. They make their own jams, chutneys, and exquisite pastries and desserts created by New York chef

Serge Torres from Le Cirque restaurant. The shop also carries gardening accessories, including estate-grown plants.

Kluge Estate is open from 10:00 A.M. to 5:00 P.M. for tastings. There is a $5.00 fee to sample the wines.

Linden Vineyards
3708 Harrels Corner Road, Linden
(540) 364-1997
www.lindenvineyards.com

Linden has 30 acres of vines, about a third of them at two satellite vineyards. From this, Linden produces 5,000 cases a year of single-vineyard Chardonnay, as well as Sauvignon Blanc, rosé, claret, Seyval, single-vineyard Bordeaux blends, and Vidal Riesling. The latter is a blend of 64 percent Vidal and 36 percent Riesling. Well-designed and meticulously maintained, the winery was started in the spring of 1987. The comfortable tasting room offers a view of the vineyards against a mountain backdrop, and the grounds have picnic areas. A deck overlooking the vineyard is partly enclosed and heated by a woodstove in the wintertime. Tastings are available from 11:00 A.M. to 5:00 P.M. on weekends December through March and Wednesday through Sunday from April through November. The winery is also open some holiday Mondays but is closed Thanksgiving, Christmas, and New Year's Day. On weekends, there's a special cellar tasting that provides an in-depth tasting experience and information about the special bottling of single wines. The cost for this is $10 and it is offered every half hour. No limos or groups of seven or more are permitted. You can also take an educational tour of the vineyard and cellar beginning at 11:30 A.M. Saturday and Sunday.

Lost Creek Vineyard and Winery
43277 Spinks Ferry Road, Leesburg
(703) 443-9836
www.lostcreekwinery.com

This property touches the property of another new winery, Hidden Brook, and you'll notice the owners share the same last name. There's a reason for that—Bob and Carol Hauck, who own Lost Creek, are the parents of Eric Hauck, who owns Hidden Brook with his wife, Deborah. Lost Creek opened July 2002, after the Haucks bought the property in 1996. The parents have 52 acres, about 26 of which are planted in vines. The Haucks still run their fire-protection business while operating their winery. At first Mr. Hauck simply wanted to grow grapes and make his own wine, but friends kept telling him how great it was, so he decided to join the other winemakers.

The winery is located on a hill, between two very large horse farms, which makes it nice because you get a great view of the vineyards and the farms. Lost Creek produces 10 wines, including Chardonnay, Chambourcin, Merlot, Vidal Blanc, Cabernet Sauvignon, Rosé, and a Late Harvest.

You can relax in the spacious tasting room near the fireplace, or sit in the gazebo or on the patio in nice weather. There is a $3.00 tasting fee, which will be deducted from your first purchase. The Haucks serve gourmet cheeses from their cheese shop and some other light snacks for the tasting experience. Lost Creek is open Wednesday and Sunday from 10:00 A.M. to 5:00 P.M. all year.

Loudoun Valley Vineyard
38516 Charlestown Pike, Waterford
(540) 882-3375
www.loudounvalleyvineyards.com

This 32-acre vineyard on 55 acres of property has one of the best views in the area, and owners Hubert and Dolores Tucker have capitalized on it. Their glass-walled tasting room overlooks the Short Hill Mountains and the vineyard land, upon which Mosby's Rangers camped during the Civil War. The Tuckers produce Chardonnay, Pinot Noir, Riesling, Cabernet Sauvignon, Merlot, Zinfandel, Gamay (a Beaujolais style), late harvest Gewurztraminer, Nebbiolo, and Sangiovese. Tours are available from 11:00 A.M. to 5:00 P.M. on weekends January through March and Friday to Sunday April through December.

Loudoun Valley offers a complimentary tasting of four wines, but a complete tasting of all 13 to 15 wines will cost $4.00 per person. Groups larger than six should call ahead for an appointment.

Mountain Cove Vineyards and Winegarden
1362 Fortune's Cove Lane, Lovingston
(434) 263-5392
www.mountaincovevineyards.com
In 1974 Mountain Cove owner Al Weed became the first person in Central Virginia to plant grape vines. Weed left a career in investment banking and moved with his family to the Nelson County farm in 1973. He planted French hybrid grapes, believing they were more hardy and prolific than other vines. Today he produces Chardonnay, Skyline White, Tinto (red), blackberry, apple, and a tasty peach wine called LaAbra Peach. Weed built most of the winery and the rough-sawn oak tasting room himself. There is also a shaded picnic area and a performance pavilion. In 2002 the Nature Conservancy opened hiking trails just up the road from Mountain Cove, less than a mile away. The vineyard is open from noon to 6:00 P.M. Wednesday to Sunday from March through December, and it is closed January and February. There's a $5.00 fee for individuals in groups of 10 or more, which includes a souvenir glass. Groups are asked to call ahead. The vineyard is closed Christmas, Thanksgiving, Easter, and New Year's Day.

Naked Mountain Vineyard
2747 Leeds Manor Road, Markham
(540) 364-1609
www.nakedmtn.com
This chalet-like winery sits on the east slope of the Blue Ridge, east of Front Royal in Fauquier County. A picnic area on the eight-acre vineyard offers sensational views. Owners Bob and Phoebe Harper produce 7,000 cases annually of Chardonnay, Riesling, Sauvignon Blanc, and Raptor Red, a Bordeaux-blend of Cabernet Franc, Cabernet Sauvignon, and Merlot. They use traditional methods of winemaking, including fermentation and surlie aging in French oak barrels. The winery has a spacious tasting room on the second floor surrounded by a deck. Tastings are offered from 11:00 A.M. to 5:00 P.M. daily from March to December and on weekends during January and February. Naked Mountain is closed Thanksgiving, Christmas, New Year's Day, and Easter. Groups of 10 or more pay a $3.00 tasting fee per person and are asked to call ahead for an appointment.

Oakencroft Vineyard and Winery
1486 Oakencroft Lane, Charlottesville
(434) 296-4188
www.oakencroft.com
Felicia Warburg Rogan, president and owner of Oakencroft Vineyard and Winery, is also president of the Jeffersonian Wine Grape Growers Society, a group that won Charlottesville the title of Wine Capital of Virginia and initiated the annual Monticello Wine Festival in the early 1980s. The winery with its 13 acres of vines is situated on a bucolic farm west of the city, a beautiful site surrounded by rolling hills and overlooking a large pond. A big red barn houses the winery, tasting room, and gift shop. Oakencroft produces a variety of wines including Chardonnay, Cabernet Sauvignon, Merlot, Countryside White, and Countryside Red. Tours and tastings are given from 11:00 A.M. to 5:00 P.M. on weekends in March, 11:00 A.M. to 5:00 P.M. daily April through December. Call for appointments in January and February. The tasting fee is $1.00, but $3.00 will include the souvenir wine glass.

Oasis Winery
14141 Hume Road, Hume
(540) 635-7627, (800) 304-7656
www.oasiswine.com
This vineyard and winery sit on a spectacular stretch of land facing the Blue Ridge Mountains. From 100 acres of vines, Oasis produces two styles of Chardonnay, including their Oasis Barrel Select, which won a gold medal at the San Francisco International Wine Competition sponsored

by *Bon Appetit.* Oasis produces two bruts; one is Oasis Brut, which outscored Dom Perignon and was selected one of the top 10 champagnes in the world. The other is Blend of Gold. Their Meritage won a 2004 gold medal in Taster's International Wine competition. The other wines include Riesling, Merlot, and Cabernet Sauvignon Reserve. Tareq Salahi and his wife, Michaele, purchased the property in the mid-1970s and planted French hybrid grapes as a hobby. Salahi soon learned that the soil was well suited for grape growing and turned his hobby into a business. Although much of Oasis's wine is sold at the winery, it is also carried by some independent vintners and served by many restaurants in Virginia and Washington, D.C. Tastings are offered daily from 11:00 A.M. to 6:00 P.M., and tours are at 1:00 P.M. Tastings are $5.00 and include a sampling of up to eight wines and an Oasis wine glass. Reserve tastings are available for an additional charge. Large groups are welcome by reservations, and Wine Country Limousine Tours also are available. Indoor seating is offered or choose to sit outside on the 25,000-square-foot infrared-heated deck and pavilion, now equipped with a new misting system to help you stay cool on those warm summer days.

Oasis is a founding member of the BlueRidgeWineWay.com Association.

Old House Vineyards
18341 Corky's Lane, Culpeper
(540) 423-1032
www.oldhousevineyards.com
On a rainy Mother's Day in 1998, Allyson and Patrick Kearney decided to take a drive to look at some property advertised for sale. They bought the 75-acre farm with nothing in particular in mind. But in the meantime Mr. Kearney, who visited nearby Dominion Winery for a tasting, came back excited to tell his wife his new plans for the property, and they planted their first vines in April 1999. Now with 24 acres of vineyards, winemaker Doug Fab-

bioli, and a full-time vineyard manager, the couple opened their winery in June 2002. Tastings take place in a renovated 1820s farmhouse, where you can enjoy beautiful mountain views. The Kearneys rent out the grounds for weddings and other events.

The wines produced at Old House include Vidal Blanc, Chardonnay, Merlot, Cabernet Franc, Wicked Bottom, Chambourcin, and a late harvest Vidal. Tastings are offered Saturday from 11:00 A.M. to 5:00 P.M. and Sunday 1:00 to 5:00 P.M. through the year, and by appointment at other times. There is no tasting fee. They are closed Thanksgiving, Christmas, and New Year's Day.

Peaks of Otter Winery
2122 Sheep Creek Road, Bedford
(540) 586-3707
www.peaksofotterwinery.com
Nancy and Danny Johnson opened their small winery in 1996 and now operate it with the assistance of their son, Shannon, and his wife, Sharlene. The new winery actually is part of the 250-acre Johnson's Orchard, which has been in the Johnson family for five generations. Since more than 50 acres are devoted to fruit, the Johnsons specialize in "Fruit of the Farm Wine," producing more than 30 wines, including apple, peach, nectarine, pear, plum, fig, strawberry, crab apple, cherry, blackberry, blueberry, honey, peanut, apricot, elderberry, apple cinnamon, apple pepper, chili pepper, and even a grape! Peaks of Otter has the largest selection of different colored and shaped bottles of any around. You also can see some of the orchard's farm animals and take a self-guided farm tour. You can picnic in the pavilion, and there's a rental house available on the farm, which accommodates up to 12 to 14 people. The winery is open 9:00 A.M. to 5:00 P.M. daily August through October and noon to 5:00 P.M. April through December. Call for an appointment at other times.

Piedmont Vineyards and Winery
2546D Halfway Road, Middleburg
(540) 687-5528
www.piedmontwines.com
Virginia's first commercial vinifera vineyard is on Waverly, a 100-acre pre-Revolutionary War farm. Family-owned and -operated, these 25 acres of vines were planted in 1973. Today, owner Gerhard von Finck produces about 3,000 cases a year of Hunt Country Chardonnay, Special Reserve Chardonnay, Native Yeast Chardonnay, and Little River Red. Tastings are available from 11:00 A.M. to 5:00 P.M. every day except Thanksgiving, Christmas Eve, Christmas Day, New Year's Eve, and New Year's Day. A tasting fee of $3.00 is refundable with a wine purchase. Groups larger than six need to call ahead for an appointment. A picnic area is on the grounds for the use of visitors. While the Manor Home is a Virginia Historic Landmark, in 2002 Piedmont added a new addition to the winery, a new tasting room with a pergola. The restored 1915-vintage stable offers a 24-foot copper bar and indoor seating area with a fireplace. The terrace allows outdoor seating as well.

---

i *With so many wineries within easy driving distance, it's easy to visit several in one day. But don't overdo it. Even though the samples may appear small, they can add up. Make sure you have a designated driver.*

Prince Michel of Virginia Vineyards
154 Winery Lane, Leon
(540) 547-3707, (800) 800-WINE
www.princemichel.com
Prince Michel Vineyards, one of the premier producers in the state, sits just south of Culpeper. The vineyard is the state's first estate winery and offers overnight accommodations in four luxurious suites. It has an extensive museum about wine and a newly remodeled restaurant. The winery's owner, Jean Leducq, made his fortune in the industrial laundry industry and now lives in Paris. His dream to have his own winery came true in 1983 in the Blue Ridge foothills. His wines have become wildly popular, selling throughout the mid-Atlantic region. Prince Michel has more than 100 planted acres of vines and a 150,000-gallon production facility, one of the largest wineries in the state.

Now owned by the Leducq Foundation, founded by Jean and Sylviane Leducq in 1996 as a way to help fund cardiovascular disease research, Prince Michel underwent extensive renovations in 2003-04. Changes were made to the entire building, including the restaurant and gift shop. The restaurant, now called the Grille, and the gift shop have a whole new look, and the latter is even in a different location within the building.

The museum's diverse collection includes photos showing the process of grape crushing. Visitors will also find a collection of every Mouton Rothschild label from 1945 to 1984, many of which were designed by famous artists such as Picasso, Salvador Dali, and Georges Roualt.

A self-guided tour takes visitors throughout the winery and features displays that describe the winemaking process. The tour ends at the tasting bar and gift shop, which sells everything from elegant wine canisters to scarves, wine-related jewelry, and, of course, the wine itself. Visitors can sample wine or drink it by the glass at an attractive bar inside the gift shop.

Less than 20 years after its founding, Prince Michel has won more than 700 awards in competitions from California to Switzerland. Its Barrel Select Chardonnay won a gold medal in the 2002 Virginia Governor's Cup competition.

Some of the vineyard's award-winning wines include Chardonnay, Riesling, Gewurztraminer, Cabernet Sauvignon, Merlot, Merlot Cabernet, and Virginia Brut, a sparkling wine. Rapidan River Vineyards, also in Leon, is one of the Prince Michel family of vineyards. It produces fine Rieslings, Harmony, and Gewurztraminer (sold at Prince Michel) but is not open for visitors. Prince Michel is open for tours and tastings from 10:00 A.M. to 5:00 P.M. daily except major holidays. For $2.00 you can sample six of your choice of wines. Read more about the Prince Michel Restaurant in our Restaurants chapter or about the suites at Prince Michel in the Bed-and-Breakfasts and Country Inns chapter.

Rappahannock Cellars
14437 Hume Road, Huntly
(540) 635-9398
www.rappahannockcellars.com
John Delmare owned a winery in the mountains of Santa Cruz, California—Saratoga. Recognizing the promise in Virginia wines, Delmare moved his family's winery from California to the Blue Ridge Mountains in 1996. With careful tending of the vineyard and exacting knowledge of the cellar, he wanted to create rich, supple, and elegant wines at his innovative, state-of-the-art winery in Rappahannock. He did. In the first five years, Rappahannock Cellers won more than 125 medals in many national and international competitions. Its 2001 Cabernet Franc received the Best Wine of the East award at the Atlanta Wine Summit, while the 2002 Viognier was picked the Best Table wine award at the Virginia Wine Competition.

Nestled in the heart of Virginia's famous hunt country on the historic Glenway Farm, Rappahannock specializes in European-style wines, including Chardonnay, Seyval Blanc, Viognier, Meritage, Cabernet Franc, Cabernet Sauvignon, and Vidal Blanc.

The tasting fee is $3.50 and includes a souvenir wine glass. Tours and tastings are available 11:30 A.M. to 5:00 P.M. Sunday through Friday and from 11:30 A.M. to 6:00 P.M. Saturday year-round.

Rebec Vineyards, Inc.
2229 North Amherst Highway, Amherst
(434) 946-5168
www.rebecwinery.com
Richard Hanson has been making wine as a hobby for 37 years. In 1987 he decided to turn commercial. Rebec Vineyards is still a small operation producing about 2,500 cases annually from four acres of vines. Mountain View Farm had been home to Richard's late wife, Ella's, family since the mid-1800s. Built in 1742, the house is a Virginia landmark and a National Historic Landmark. It has been home to the family of Gov. William Cabel and U.S. Vice President William Crawford. Rebec wines include Chardonnay, Cabernet Sauvignon, Riesling, Gewurztraminer, Viognier, Landmark White, Landmark Sweet, Merlot, Pinot Noir, Sweetbrier Rosé, Autumn Glow, and Sweet Sofia.

Since 1991 Rebec Vineyards has hosted the Virginia Garlic Festival, an October event that features the crowning of a garlic queen, a garlic-eating contest, live music, good food, and a lot of Virginia wine. The winery, made of wood from a 250-year-old tobacco barn, is open for tours and tastings from 10:00 A.M. to 5:00 P.M. daily. From December to March, it's a good idea to call first. There is a tasting fee of $2.00 for groups of 10 or more.

Sharp Rock Vineyards
5 Sharp Rock Road, Sperryville
(540) 987-9700
www.sharprockvineyards.com
This six-acre vineyard sits in one of the most beautiful spots in Virginia, directly across an open field from popular Old Rag Mountain. Sharp Rock opened the winery in September 1998, and it produces a Chardonnay, a Chardonnay Reserve, a Sauvignon Blanc, Cabernet Sauvignon, Cabernet Franc, Malbec, and Chamois, a semi-dry white blend named after their late dog, Shamay. Hosts Jimm and Kathy East, along with business partner Steve Nausf, have maintained a small, hand-selected grape operation. With Jimm serving as winemaker, they produce about 800 cases of wine a year. They also operate bed-and-breakfast accommodations in the Carriage House and the Cottage, which dates to 1790. Many of the buildings on the 24-acre property have been restored, including the main house and

the one housing the winery. The winery and tasting room are in the barn rebuilt from old wood. The tasting-room floor was taken from a 250-year-old building in Charlottesville. Sharp Rock Vineyards is open for tours and tastings March through December, from 11:00 A.M. to 5:00 P.M. on Friday to Sunday. The tasting fee is $2.00 and is refundable with a wine purchase.

Smokehouse Winery
10 Ashby Road, Sperryville
(540) 987-3194
www.smokehousewinery.com
Here's a winery, opened in 1999, that does-n't quite fit the mold of all the rest. Instead of grapevines, owner John Hallberg raises beehives on his 15 acres. At Smokehouse Winery, he produces several traditional and nontraditional types of mead, which is a honey wine. Hallberg explains that it's a hybrid process, in between beermaking and winemaking. He produces Traditional Mead, Three Berry Metheglin (a spiced mead), Honeysuckle Metheglin, Juniper Berry Melomel (a fruit mead), Cassis Melomel, Crabapple Cyser, Braggot, and Old English-style Hard Cider. The flavors vary widely—some are sweet, some dry. You'll enjoy tasting them in the log cabin that is complete with a thatched roof, a reminder of Old England. There is also lodging available in a mid-19th-century log cabin located on the property.

Tours and tastings are available from noon to 6:00 P.M. on weekends February through December. Smokehouse is closed Christmas, Thanksgiving, and New Year's Day. There is no tasting fee.

Stone Mountain Vineyards
1376 Wyatt Mountain Road, Dyke
(434) 990-9463
www.stonemountainvineyards.com
Chris Breiner had his first press in 1998 and officially opened Stone Mountain Vineyards for tastings in June 2000. The vineyards, located in Bacon Hollow in Greene County, have 20 acres under vines on a 650-acre property. Breiner started the vineyards with his father, but Al

Breiner passed away in 2002. Breiner does his own winemaking with Gabriele Rausse as a consulting winemaker. In the 1970s, after seeing vineyards in Germany, Al Breiner decided they could grow grapes on his property near Dyke and bought an adjacent lot.

Stone Mountain produces 2,200 cases a year, and Breiner plans to increase it to 5,000. Wines include Chardonnay, Caber-net Sauvignon, Cabernet Franc, Pinot Gri-gio, Bacon Hollow Revenuers' Select, and a blush wine called Maquillage. Come by for a tour and tasting from 11:00 A.M. to 5:00 P.M. Friday, Saturday, and Sunday April through December, and 11:00 A.M. to 5:00 P.M. Saturday and Sunday in March. Stone Mountain is closed January and February. There is no tasting fee. You can enjoy a glass of wine while sitting on the large deck that wraps around the spacious tasting room and visit the wine cave. Breiner also plays upon the fact that Bacon Hollow was known for making moonshine, inscrib-ing on his bottle that "we're not the first to make alcohol, but we're the first to do it legally."

Stonewall Vineyards and Winery
Highway 721, Concord
(434) 993-2185
www.stonewallwine.com
This family-operated winery is halfway between Appomattox and Lynchburg. From their 14 acres of vinifera and French and American hybrids, owners Larry and Sterry Davis and their son, winemaker Bart Davis, produce Claret, Cabernet Sauvi-gnon, Chardonnay, Cayuga, Merlot, Brigade, Regiment, Mist, and Mirage. They also make a mead wine called Pyment that is a medieval blend of wine, honey, and spices. Using their own vines, purchased grapes, and grapes from leased vineyards, the Davises produce about 5,000 cases of wine a year. Stonewall Vineyards offers many ways to relax, as it has a patio, gazebo, and picnic grove. Tours and tast-ings are offered from 11:00 A.M. to 5:00 P.M. daily. There is a $1.00 tasting fee.

Swedenburg Estate Vineyard
23595 Winery Lane, Middleburg
(540) 687-5219
www.swedenburgwines.com
Named after its proprietors, Wayne and Juanita Swedenburg, this family-owned vineyard consists of 15 acres of grapevines on the 130-acre Valley View Farm, which has been under continuous cultivation for more than 200 years. The farm dates back to 1762. The winery produces European-style premium wines, including Cabernet Sauvignon, Pinot Noir, Chardonnay, a Rosé called Chantilly, and Seyval. The vineyard is open from 10:00 A.M. to 4:00 P.M. daily. There is a $3.00 tasting fee.

Tarara Vineyard & Winery
13648 Tarara Lane, Leesburg
(703) 771-7100
www.tarara.com
R. J. "Whitie" and Margaret Hubert own this 50-acre vineyard in Loudoun County and age their premium wines in a 6,000-square-foot cave at the edge of the Potomac River. Winemaker Robert Warren from Canada produces Chardonnay, Charval, Cameo, Merlot, Terra Rouge, Chardonnay Reserve, Chambourcin Reserve, Viognier, Pinot Gris, Cabernet Franc, Cabernet Sauvignon, and Wild River Red. Warren grew up working with his father and brother growing grapes for Welch's Grape Juice Company. Visitors can tour the cave and enjoy tastings from 11:00 A.M. to 5:00 P.M. daily. The tasting costs $5.00. Groups larger than eight should reserve in advance. Private tours and tastings cost $10.00 per person. The vineyard grounds have picnic areas, 6 miles of hiking trails, and a 10-acre lake. If you don't want to pack your own basket, gourmet picnics are available. Large groups (100 or more) can plan a catered picnic here, with a choice of two locations: the Meadow Pavilion or the Lakeside Pavilion. Both have a covered pavilion with ceiling fans and lights (2,100 square feet) and 20 picnic tables, with horseshoe pit, volleyball, or softball as options, depending upon location. You can also pick your own

blackberries and apples, in season.

The 476-acre farm offers a bed-and-breakfast facility with the choice of three rooms and one suite, all with private baths.

Unicorn Winery
489 Old Bridge Road, Amissville
(540) 349-5885
www.unicornwinery.com
Dave Whittaker's property is along the banks of the Rappahannock River and is a good stop for a picnic. You can also enjoy watching the koi-stocked pond while sipping a glass of wine on the shady two-tiered deck. The kids can stay occupied with bubbles or horseshoes. The grounds can be rented for a wedding or family reunion. Whittaker, who worked for IBM, became interested in running a winery when he toured several wineries during a trip to California. When he returned to Virginia, he attended many of the wine festivals and got to know the Virginia winemakers and vineyard growers. He opened Unicorn in 2000, and from six acres of vines on location and grapes from other vineyards, he produces Cabernet Sauvignon, Meritage, Merlot, Vidal, Viognier, Chambourcin, and his most popular, a blush wine called Slightly Embarrassed. Unicorn's winemaker is Bree Moore.

The winery is open for tastings from 11:00 A.M. to 6:00 P.M. Saturday and Sunday and Friday and Monday holidays, year-round. There is a minimal tasting fee for individuals, and groups of eight or more pay $3.00 a person and are asked to call ahead.

Veramar Vineyard
905 Quarry Road, Berryville
(540) 955-5510
www.veramar.com
You'll find this vineyard on a 100-acre estate in the middle of Virginia hunt country. It's a great place to go to enjoy the scenic outdoors through a picnic or walk, as the Shenandoah River is nearby. This small, family-run winery produces naturally dry, full-bodied wines, including Cabernet Sauvignon, Chambourcin,

Chardonnay, and Riesling. Veramar is a third-generation business. The Bogaty family has roots in the Italian Alps, where the family operated a vineyard. Come by for complimentary tastings 11:00 A.M. to 5:00 P.M. Thursday through Monday.

Veritas Winery
245 Saddleback Farm, Afton
(540) 456-8000
www.veritaswines.com

In 1999 Patricia and Andrew Hodson left their busy lives in Jacksonville, Florida, and bought a beautiful, sprawling 250-acre farm in Nelson County. They planted grapes soon after, recognizing a longtime dream, and were able to bottle their first wine two years later—something virtually unheard of in the winemaking business. The winery opened June 2002. Andrew, a former neurologist, and his wife, Patricia, who owned a medical billing service, claim they "are happier than we've ever been." The Hodsons, a charming couple who came to the United States from England in 1974, now have 25 acres in grapes. She grows the grapes; he makes the wine. Their current wines include Merlot, Cabernet Franc, Petit Verdot, Tannat, Chardonnay, and Traminette. They recently added Viognier, Sauvignon Blanc, and Petite Manseng to the list. The vineyards are beautiful, marching up the surrounding hills as you drive through the property to the winery. The newly finished tasting room is spectacular, with a wraparound deck that allows you to enjoy the view of the farm and the mountains in the background. Relax with a glass and a loved one at one of the large round picnic tables and enjoy a sunny afternoon. The winery is open 11:00 A.M. to 6:00 P.M. every day except Tuesday.

White Hall Vineyards
5184 Sugar Ridge Road, White Hall
(434) 823-8615
www.whitehallvineyards.com

It didn't take long for White Hall Vineyards to establish itself as a state-of-the-art winemaking facility. After planting vines in 1991, the facility opened for tours and tastings in 1996, just in time to showcase their award-winning 1994 wines. That first harvest earned eight medals at state wine competitions, and things only got better. The 1995 wines collected 12 more medals and the coveted Governor's Cup for their Cabernet Sauvignon. Their dessert wine Soliterre has been an award-winner, most recently receiving a gold medal from the 2002 Virginia Governor's Cup competition.

Brad McCarthy served as assistant winemaker at Horton Vineyards, Montdomaine Cellars, and Rockbridge Vineyard before becoming winemaker at White Hall. Owners Edith and Antony Champ had searched the East Coast for a spot to build a winery and grow grapes. Tony Champ was retired from the fiber industry in New York City, and both had always dreamed about operating a winery. They settled on White Hall, just outside Charlottesville, where they bought a scenic 300-acre tract of land with breathtaking views of the Blue Ridge Mountains. The winery produces Chardonnay, Merlot, Cabernet Sauvignon, Cabernet Franc, Gewurztraminer, Pinot Gris, and Soliterre from 30 acres of grapes. Tours and tastings are available Wednesday to Sunday from 11:00 A.M. to 5:00 P.M. White Hall is closed from mid-December to the first of March. The vineyard is closed on major holidays.

Willowcroft Farm Vineyards
38906 Mt. Gilead Road, Leesburg
(703) 777-8161
www.willowcroftwine.com

Small but selective describes this 13-acre vineyard on top of Mount Gilead. The winery is housed in a rustic barn with a splendid view of the nearby Blue Ridge. Owner Lewis Parker creates some of the Piedmont's finest Cabernet Sauvignon, Chardonnay, Riesling, Seyval, Cabernet Franc, Vidal, and Merlot wines, which have garnered quite a few international awards. The vineyard is open for tastings March through December from 11:00 A.M. to 5:30 P.M. Friday through Sunday, and some Monday holidays. You can also call for an appointment at other times. There is a $2.00 tasting fee, and groups of 10 or more must call ahead. Be sure to bring a lunch and enjoy the picnic area. Willowcroft also sells cheese and crackers.

Windham Winery
14727 Mountain Road, Hillsboro
(540) 668-6464
www.windhamwinery.com
They may have skipped a generation or two, but the Bazaco family is back in the wine business. Dr. George Bazaco's great-grandfather was a sheriff, but he also grew grapes in northern Greece. When young George went to study medicine in Italy, he also picked up a desire to grow grapes and make great wines. In the mid-1980s, George and his wife, Nicki, planted eight acres of grapes on their 300-acre farm in Loudoun County. They make Cabernet Sauvignon, Merlot, Cabernet Franc, Riesling, Chardonnay, Fume Blanc, and Vintner's Reserve (a red Meritage blend). Their newest wine, Doukenie, is a sweet blend of white grapes honoring Dr. Bazaco's grandmother. They release about 2,000 cases using the traditional European methods of winemaking. Tastings at Windham are a real treat. Bazaco's mother Hope offers up her homemade baklava so that visitors can have a little taste of Greece. The working farm is a beautiful spot for a picnic. A winery and tasting room building was added in 2001. The building also has a covered deck. The lake and weeping willow trees serve as a romantic backdrop for a picnic. The winery is open from noon to 6:00 P.M. Friday through Monday and by appointment.

Wintergreen Winery, Ltd.
462 Winery Lane, Nellysford
(434) 361-2519
www.wintergreenwinery.com
In the beautiful Rockfish Valley adjacent to Wintergreen Four Seasons Resort, this Nelson County vineyard offers spectacular views all seasons of the year. Part of the original Highview plantation built by the Rodes family, the land has been in agricul-

tural use since the early 1800s, producing tobacco, wheat, barley, hay, apples, and now grapes. Jeff and Tamara Stone are the new owners, and from 15 acres of vines (and another 15 from another vineyard) they produce Cabernet Franc, Merlot, Black Rock Chardonnay, Chardonnay, Cabernet Sauvignon, Riesling, Three Ridges White, Thomas Nelson White, Mill Hill Apple wine, and their very popular raspberry wine. The facilities are open for tours and tastings daily from 10:00 A.M. to 6:00 P.M. April to October and 10:00 A.M. to 5:00 P.M. from November to March. It is closed on major holidays. Wintergreen has a picnic area and gift shop. You can purchase picnic fare, such as imported cheeses, crackers, smoked trout, jams, and jellies. Tastings are complimentary, but groups of 10 or more must make reservations and pay a small fee.

SOUTHWEST VIRGINIA

AmRhein Wine Cellar
9243 Patterson Drive, Bent Mountain
(540) 929-4632
www.roanokewine.com
The biggest thing for AmRhein next to its opening in the summer of 2001 is winning the prestigious Governor's Cup in 2002 for its Viognier. Their Late Harvest Vidal Blanc was a Governor's Cup winner in 2003. The winery, which is located near the Blue Ridge Parkway, is owned by Russell and Paula Amrhein. The vines were first planted in 1995 and now there are a total of 25 acres from three vineyards. AmRhein means "on the Rhein River" and plays up the heritage of the owners, who specialize in German-style wine. The winemaker is

Not sure which wines to taste or purchase at a winery or festival because of the vast choices? Consider Cabernet Franc and Viognier, which are fast gaining international reputations as superb Virginia wines.

Steve Bolleter. Other wines include their Pinot Grigio, Traminette, Vidal Blanc, Chardonnay, Cabernet Franc, and Merlot.

Take some time out for a picnic and enjoy the scenic lake. Hours for tastings are Friday, Saturday, and Sunday noon to 5:00 P.M. April through December. Large groups (more than 10) are asked to call ahead. The tasting center features a self-guided tour.

Boundary Rock Farm & Vineyard
414 Riggins Road NW, Willis
(540) 789-7098
www.boundaryrock.com

Mary Risacher and Tony Equale invite you to drop by Boundary Rock Farm in Floyd County any day to do a tasting, but call first because they may be out working on the farm. It is a working farm, after all, with a seven-acre vineyard, all run by the family. And the tasting area you may also find to be unusual—their very own kitchen table. They've been at the 48-acre farm since 1991, a farm that got its name because of the 8-foot-tall rock that marks the property boundary at an odd triangle that cuts into their land.

They grow 15 varieties of grapes, including seedless white, red, and black grapes that they sell to the markets, and grapes they offer for self-picking for use in juices and jellies. Before opening a winery, Equale and Risacher grew grapes and sold them to other wineries such as Chateau Morrisette. At the time, they made wine for their own consumption. They decided to take the farm to the next level and produce wine for the public, opening as a winery in October 2000. As Equale says, it's difficult running a fruit farm unless you work in large quantities, and the winery gave them just "enough added value without extending ourselves too much." At this point they make 300 cases of wine a year and hope to double it in the future.

Some of their wines include Cabernet Franc, Chardonnay, Riesling, Vidal, Seyval Blanc, and a Chambourcin. Tastings are by appointment. There is no tasting fee.

Chateau Morrisette
Meadows of Dan
(540) 593-2865
www.thedogs.com

This remote winery commands a view from a 3,500-foot-high mountaintop farm bordering the Blue Ridge Parkway in Floyd and Patrick Counties. Since 1983 wines have been made here in a traditional European style, using a combination of stainless-steel tanks and oak barrels for aging and fermentation. Built of native stone and wood, Chateau Morrisette has an underground wine cellar, reminiscent of the Bourdeaux countryside. Facilities include a tasting room, restaurant, and large scenic deck with a view of Buffalo Mountain, the second-highest peak in Virginia.

Chateau Morrisette hosts a monthly "Black Dog" jazz concert series the second Saturday of each month from June to October. Live music, tastings, tours, and gourmet lunches make this an exciting event. Call ahead to confirm the time. The $17.50 in advance charge includes a tour, tasting, and commemorative glass, but the food is extra.

Wines include Chardonnay, Merlot, Black Dog, Black Dog Blanc, Sweet Mountain Laurel, Our Dog Blue, Cabernet Sauvignon, Pinot Noir, Cabernet Franc, Vidal Blanc, Blushing Dog, Red Mountain Laurel, Viognier, Chambourcin, and Frosty Dog. Tours and tastings are available from 10:00 A.M. to 5:00 P.M. Monday through Thursday, 10:00 A.M. to 6:00 P.M. Friday and Saturday, and 11:00 A.M. to 5:00 P.M. Sunday except major holidays. The tasting fee is $4.00 a person. There is gourmet picnic food available from Chateau to Go. The restaurant is open for lunch Wednesday through Sunday and for dinner Friday and Saturday.

Valhalla Vineyards
6500 Mount Chestnut Road, Roanoke
(540) 725-9463
www.valhallawines.com

Valhalla is another family-run operation, opened in 1998. Owned by Jim and Debra Vascik, the vineyards are at 2,000 feet, overlooking the Roanoke Valley. They also have a 200-foot-long barrel cave, which they put in 60 feet beneath the vineyards, where they age their wines. Valhalla produces Syrah, Cabernet Sauvignon, Gotterdammerung (a Cabernet Franc and Merlot blend), Valkryie (a Bordeaux red blend), Late Harvest Viognier, Merlot, Viognier, Sangiovese, Alicante Bouschet, Norton, and a Dry Rose. He is the grape grower while she makes the wines. In 2002 the Vasciks entered seven of their red wines in the Virginia Governor's Cup competition, and all seven entries won medals. Valhalla is open from April to December 24. Tastings are available from 4:00 to 7:00 P.M. Friday, noon to 5:00 P.M. on Saturday, and 1:00 to 5:00 P.M. on Sunday. The tasting fee includes a souvenir glass. It can run $5.00, $8.00, or $10,00 depending on the wines selected.

Villa Appalaccia Winery
752 Rock Castle Gorge, Floyd
(540) 593–3100
www.villaappalaccia.com
Susanne Becker and Stephen Haskill are willing to go the extra mile for their winery. The husband and wife are retired microbiologists. After a sabbatical in Northern California, the couple had planned on planting a few vines for their own enjoyment. Instead they filled four acres with 2,200 vines, eventually bringing their Sycamore Creek Vineyard to a total of 15 acres. This family-run vineyard puts an emphasis on Italian-style wines and produces 3,000 cases a year. The reds include Toscanello and Sangiovese. Pinot Grigio, Liciro, and Simpatico are three of their white wines made from Italian varietals. Other wines include Primitivo, Cabernet Franc, and Malvasia Bianca. Villa Appalaccia also features a Tuscan-style tasting deck with an inspiring view of the picturesque Rock Castle Gorge. Visitors are treated to Italian bread with pesto, cheese, and other Italian specialties. During the cooler months, you might want to stop by the tasting room to sample some minestrone along with the wines. The hours are 11:00 A.M. to 5:00 P.M. Thursday and Friday, 11:00 A.M. to 6:00 P.M. Saturday, and Sunday from noon to 4:00 P.M. Villa Appalaccia is not set up to handle large groups. There is a $3.00 tasting fee for select wines.

HORSE COUNTRY

Whether clearing fields or carrying soldiers from Bull Run to Appomattox, horses have played a vital role in the history of the Shenandoah Valley. Today, their workload may not be as physically demanding, but horses still have a major impact on Virginia's economy.

The Virginia Horse Center has brought more than 5 million visitors and millions of dollars to the Lexington and Rockbridge areas. Year-round events include everything from barrel racing to dressage.

East of the Blue Ridge, stretching from Loudoun to Albemarle Counties, is Virginia hunt country, an area devoted to the centuries-old sport of riding to the hounds and the accompanying lifestyle. Because of this singularity of purpose, the area has managed to keep development at bay, preserving large estates and horse farms.

Natural adjuncts to fox hunting are horse shows and steeplechases, activities that are easily accessible in this region and thrilling to watch. Attending a horse event not only gives you a chance to see beautiful country and fine horses but also to people-watch. The hunt country is crawling with celebrities from politics or the entertainment industry who have homes in the Middleburg/Upperville or Charlottesville areas. Even Virginia's most famous four-legged celebrity, Secretariat, is from nearby Caroline County. Here are some of the most popular places to catch the action.

FOX HUNTING

The area hosts more than a dozen historic hunts, which go out several times a week from fall through spring, including holidays. If you want to watch the blessing of the hounds or follow the chase by car, plan ahead. The best way to track down races is through *The Chronicle of the Horse,* a weekly publication that produces an annual hunt roster issue in September. *The Chronicle,* (540) 687-6341, www.chronofhorse.com, will send you a copy for $1.75. The roster lists race days and secretary numbers for all the hunts in the United States; the secretaries can tell you exact times and locations.

At least once a year, usually on the first Saturday in December, the Middleburg Hunt Club meets at the historic Red Fox Tavern in Middleburg and rides down Main Street, hounds and all. Call (540) 687-5452 for details.

HORSE SHOWS

It would be hard to drive through horse country without running into some type of weekend event. There are more than 400 horse shows held each year in Virginia. The Virginia Horse Show Association is an excellent source for dates and places. Call them at (540) 349-4600. Founded more than 50 years ago, this group also publishes *The Virginia Horse Journal* out of Warrenton. Below are just a few of the venues in the Blue Ridge.

Fox Chase Farm Inc.
23323 Fox Chase Farm Lane
Middleburg
(540) 687-5255
www.foxchasefarm.net
Head east on U.S. Highway 50 from Middleburg, and you'll spot the impressive rings, jumps, and barns of Fox Chase, a facility owned by Maureen Hanley. About two dozen weekend or Sunday shows are held here each year. Admission to the shows is free. This equestrian center also offers riding lessons and instructional clinics with Olympic riders several times a year.

Upperville Colt and Horse Show
US 50, Upperville
(540) 253-5760
www.upperville.com
This weeklong hunter/jumper show begins
the first Monday of June. Show events
start at 8:00 A.M. and continue until dark.
Several thousand spectators visit the
show each weekday, with nearly 1,500
horse-and-rider combinations competing
in hunter division, jumper classic, and
pony prix. Founded in 1853, the Upperville
show is billed as the "oldest horse show in
the United States" and draws riders ranging from young children to Olympic and
World Cup riders. Admission is $10 for
adults and free for children younger than
12 when accompanied by an adult.

The Roanoke Valley Horse Show
Salem Civic Center
1001 Roanoke Boulevard, Salem
(540) 389-7847
www.roanokevalleyhorseshow.com
Rated "A" by *USA Equestrian,* this June
event has been a national standout in
horse-lovers' country since 1971. The show
is sponsored by the Roanoke Valley Horse-
men's Association. It attracts more than
1,000 entries nationwide for prizes, including a grand prix purse of $50,000. It con-
tinues to be one of the top 10 shows in the
United States.

This is a truly special community effort
that brings in $13 million in new money
each year, with profits going to charity.
Tickets are $6.00 weekdays, $10.00 Friday,
and $12.00 Saturday and are available by
calling the Salem Civic Center at (540)
343-8100.

Warrenton Horse Show
U.S. Highway 29 Business, Warrenton
(540) 347-9442, (540) 788-4806
www.warrentonhorseshow.com
Founded in 1899, the Labor Day Warrenton
Horse Show is one of the few major horse
shows in which only one ring is utilized.
Find a seat, stay put, and let the action
unfold before you. The grounds are also
home to the annual Pony Show in late June

and the Labor Day Horse Show in September. Tickets are $5.00 plus $1.00 for the
shaded grandstand; the other show is free.

Commonwealth Park
13256 Commonwealth Parkway
Culpeper
(540) 825-7469, (845) 246-8833
www.hitsshows.com
Though it's off the beaten path on U.S.
Highway 522, this horse center has 900
stalls and eight competition rings that are
busy with hunter/jumper horse shows. Six
events are scheduled each year, attracting
the Olympic-class riders who live in the
area. Six horse shows are held here
throughout the year, including the U.S.
Grand Prix League Finals. Usually held in
late September or early October, this final
event of the season carries a $100,000
purse. The Winter National and Constitution Classic also are held here. Admission
to the events is free; call for a schedule.

Virginia Horse Center
487 Maury River Road, Lexington
(540) 464-2950
www.horsecenter.org
A showcase for the Virginia horse industry
and one of the top equine facilities in the
United States, the $12 million Virginia Horse
Center is home to several premier national
horse shows and three-day events.

The indoor Howard P. Anderson Coliseum is home to 4,000 spectator seats
and a 150-foot-by-300-foot show arena.
The facility can house 1,200 horses in permanent and temporary stalls. The Appomattox Mezzanine, which overlooks one of
the center's 14 show rings, can accommodate another 500 visitors. The center has
eight winterized barns, an enclosed
schooling area, an on-grounds restaurant,
and 90 camper hookups. Outdoor facilities
include the lighted Wiley Arena, four all-
weather dressage arenas, a speed events
ring, an announcer's pavilion, and a 5-mile
cross-country course, with steeplechase
and carriage-driving courses.

The East Complex, soon to be named
the Robert M. Reel Pavilion in honor of the

Over the Fences

Here are just some of the steeplechases and point-to-point races. Call to confirm starting times, locations, and dates. This was the lineup in 2004:

Casanova Hunt Point-to-Point:
February 21 at Buckland Farm in Gainsville, (540) 788-4806

Rappahannock Hunt Point-to-Point:
February 28, Bleu Rock Inn, Washington, (540) 547-2810

Blue Ridge Hunt Point-to-Point:
March 6 at Woodley Farm in Berryville, (540) 837-2262

Warrenton Hunt Point-to-Point:
March 13 at Arlie Race Course in Warrenton, (540) 347-1888 or (540) 347-5095

Piedmont Fox Hounds Point-to-Point:
March 20 at Salem Course in Upperville, (540) 684-3455

Farmington and Keswick Point-to-Point:
March 21 at Montpelier Race Course at Montpelier Station, (434) 980-9926

Orange County Hunt Point-to-Point:
March 27 at Locust Hill Farm in Middleburg, (540) 687-6528

Old Dominion Hounds Point-to-Point:
April 3 at Ben Venue Farm in Ben Venue, (540) 364-4573 or (540) 636-1507

Strawberry Hill Races:
April 10 at Colonial Downs in New Kent County, (804) 569-3238

Loudoun Hunt Point-to-Point:
April 11 at Oatlands in Leesburg, (703) 777-8480 or (540) 338-4031

Middleburg Spring Races:
April 17 at Glenwood Park in Middleburg, (540) 687-6545 or (540) 687-6595

Fairfax Hunt Point-to-Point:
April 18 at Belmont Country Club in Leesburg, (703) 787-6673

Foxfield Spring Races:
April 24 at Foxfield in Charlottesville, (434) 293-9501

Middleburg Hunt Point-to-Point:
April 25 at Glenwood Park in Middleburg, (540) 687-3100

Virginia Gold Cup:
May 1 at Great Meadow in the Plains, (540) 347-2612

Bull Run Hunt Point-to-Point:
May 2 at Brandywine Park in Culpeper, (703) 866-0507

Bedford County Point-to-Point:
May 8 at Wolf Branch Farm in Forest, (540) 297-3419

Glenwood Races:
September 11 at Glenwood Park in Middleburg, (540) 687-3455

Foxfield Fall Races:
September 26 at Foxfield in Charlottesville, (434) 293-9501

Virginia Fall Races:
October 2 and 3 at Glenwood Park in Middleburg, (540) 687-5662

Morven Park Races:
October 9 at Morven Park in Leesburg, (703) 777-2414

International Gold Cup:
October 16 at Great Meadow in the Plains, (540) 347-2612

Montpelier Hunt Races:
November 6 at Montpelier Race Course at Montpelier Station, (540) 672-2728

center's late executive director, was completed in 2002. The new complex includes two barns and another indoor show ring and a smaller warm-up ring. The new facility allows the center to host two indoor events at the same time.

The Center is also home to a gift shop and two museums. The Work Horse Museum in Anderson Coliseum contains farm equipment used by farmers before the advent of the tractor. It's open on most weekends or whenever there is an event. The other exhibition, the Sergeant Ed Henson Sr. VMI Cavalry Museum, is a memorial to the Cavalry Brigade at nearby Virginia Military Institute. Dedicated to Sgt. Edward L. Henson, the exhibition contains a collection of documents, photos, and memorabilia from 1920 to 1941. Tours are arranged by appointment, so call ahead.

With all these amenities, something is going on here almost all the time, from dressage competitions to draft-horse pulls. In addition to horse competitions, the center hosts rodeos, auctions, concerts, living-history Civil War encampments, Jack Russell terrier races, therapeutic riding demonstrations, and foxhound demonstrations. With 14 show rings, this 600-acre facility hosts more than 95 events each year.

COMBINED TRAINING

Combined training, also called three-day eventing or horse trials, is a discipline dating back to the training of war horses in Europe. It's also one of the most exciting horse sports to watch. Dressage, performed on the first day, is the ballet of horse sports, requiring great discipline. On the second day is an endurance phase involving long gallops and jumping through a challenging cross-country course. The third day, horses and riders are put through a structured course of fences to test the horses' agility, soundness, and willingness after the stress of the cross-country. The Blue Ridge area hosts several world-class events.

Morven Park Horse Trials
41793 Tutt Lane, Morven Park, Leesburg
(703) 777–2890
www.morvenpark.org
During the first week of October, you can catch the action over cross-country jumps designed by Tremaine Cooper. The backdrop for the event is a splendid white-columned mansion, once the home of Virginia governor Westmoreland Davis and his spunky, sidesaddle-riding wife. Treasures the couple collected during a lifetime of world travel are on display in the mansion. The mansion, gardens, the Museum of Foxhounds and Hunting, and the Carriage Museum are open during the event; admission to the mansion and both museums is $7.00. Admission to the trials is $10.00 and $20.00.

Morven Park also hosts a variety of events year-round, including hunter/jumpers and steeplechases. Admission to most events is free. Call or visit the Web site for schedules and information.

Middleburg Horse Trials
Highway 626, Glenwood Park
Middleburg
(540) 687–5449
www.middleburg.8k.com
Top riders in intermediate, preliminary, and novice trials participate in this event, which is held the final weekend in September. The Middleburg area is home to many Olympic riders, so the level of competition is high (though a new course has recently been added for novice riders). At Glenwood Park, which is also a steeplechase and horse show venue, spectators can see almost all of the course from the stands. Admission to the trials is free. Glenwood Park is 1 mile north of Middleburg on Highway 626, also called Foxcroft Road.

COMBINED DRIVING

One of the most colorful and elegant equestrian sports is competitive carriage driving. Competitions often are paired with three-day events because of their similarity. On the first day, drivers execute a series of dressage movements, much like a skater's compulsory figures. The second day is devoted to the marathon, a grueling cross-country dash through streams and around natural and man-made obstacles. In the third phase drivers dressed in formal attire wheel their teams through an intricate pattern of cones.

Local driving clubs also get together for pleasure rides or driving shows, such as the fall show at Middleburg's Foxcroft School (see our Annual Events and Festivals chapter). The Piedmont Driving Club in Boyce, (540) 955-2659, is your best source for information.

ENDURANCE RIDING

This is now an Olympic sport, but it's not the easiest competition for spectators to watch.

Old Dominion 100-mile Ride
4-H Center, Front Royal
(540) 933-6991, (540) 436-8367
www.olddominionrides.org
Held in early June, the Old Dominion is one of the most respected competitions in the country and often is a tune-up for the Olympics or World Championships. Riders camp overnight with their horses at the 4-H Center in Front Royal in preparation for a 5:00 A.M. start. Each rider has 24 hours to cover 100 miles of rugged terrain and is pulled from the competition if the horse fails to pass the frequent veterinary checks along the way. If you want to put out a little effort, you can hike to one of the veterinary checks or the river crossing to watch the horses come through. Call before you go, because they change the locations of the check stations each year. You probably won't want to hang around for the finish. Winners come in as darkness is falling, and the rest straggle in throughout the night. The Old Dominion endurance riders also plan 50- and 30-mile rides in April and October. The ride in late October is held in Fort Valley and

includes a two-day, 100-mile ride or limited 30- and 50-mile rides. The no frills event is always the second Sunday in April and features 30- and 50-mile rides.

JOUSTING

Maryland's state sport also has a loyal following in Virginia. Though it's patterned after the rivalry of knights of old, today's sport is done not in armor but in T-shirts and jeans. Despite the informal dress, you have to admire the skill of the riders who, at a full gallop, thread their lances through a series of three steel rings. The horse and rider usually cover the 90-yard course in less than eight seconds. We've listed the two major jousting events in Virginia.

Natural Chimneys Jousting Tournament
Highway 936, Mount Solon
(540) 350-2510
www.home.ricanet/uvrpa/jousting.htm
Listed as America's oldest continuously held sporting event, the Mount Solon tournament has been at the Natural Chimneys Regional Park every year since 1821. It started out as a contest to see which of two men would marry a local damsel, but today thousands visit the scenic park in mid-August to watch riders from Virginia, West Virginia, Maryland, and Pennsylvania test their marksmanship. Admission to the park is $6.00 per car. Bring along a blanket and picnic basket. If you want to stay longer, campsites are available, but call first, since they fill up fast. The seven towering rock formations at Natural Chimneys also serve as the backdrop for the National Hall of Fame Joust in mid-June.

National Jousting Championships
17501 Franklin Park, Purvellville
(434) 983-2989
www.nationaljousting.com
Virginia's jousting season, which runs from April through October, culminates with the national competition in Northern Virginia. The event began as the Day in the Park in Washington, D.C. and has been

held annually since the 1960s. Riders from all five Virginia clubs usually attend this big event. There is no cost to come watch.

DRESSAGE

Break out your top hat, white gloves, and tails! The elegant and ancient art of dressage can be found sprinkled throughout the Blue Ridge. Although the basic tenets of dressage date back to 400 B.C., most folks are probably more familiar with those famous white Lipizzan stallions from the Spanish Riding School in Vienna, Austria.

Dressage is the classic art of riding, where the rider uses subtle shifting of his weight, a squeeze of a leg, or a pull on the reins to lead his horse through a series of serpentine figures, sideways movements, and smooth transitions from a trot to a halt. But don't let the formal attire fool you; dressage is also a very competitive sport.

Although Virginia may be better known for its thoroughbreds and steeple-chase races, dressage shows, competitions, and workshops can be seen at Morven Park in Leesburg, (703) 777-2890, and the Virginia Horse Center in Lexington, (540) 464-2950.

To find out if an event corresponds with your visit, check with the Virginia Dressage Association at (540) 338-7810 or visit www.virginiadressage.org.

Fancy Hill Farm
100 Equus Loop, Natural Bridge
(540) 291-1000
www.fancyhillfarm.com
This equestrian center between Lexington and Natural Bridge off Interstate 81 boards, trains, and offers riding lessons as well as offers a variety of shows, clinics, and competition. Three large outdoor rings and an indoor arena allow for hunter/jumper competition and dressage schools year-round. Shows are usually held once a month, and there is no cost to come and watch. Fancy Hill has hosted International Dressage Clinics. Nicole Uphoff-Becker and Albrecht Hei-

demann were among participants for the April 1999 clinic. Uphoff-Becker, who has made four visits to Fancy Hill, was a record-setting rider for Germany in the Olympics. She and her horse, Rembrandt, won four gold medals in individual and team competition at the Games in Barcelona, Spain, and Seoul, Korea.

There are more than 285 horseback riding trails in Virginia. To find out what's in your area, contact the Virginia Horse Council at (804) 330-0345.

HUNT COUNTRY STABLE TOUR

Trinity Episcopal Church Annual Stable Tour
US 50, Upperville
(540) 592-3711
www.middleburgonline.com/stabletour
A dozen farms open their stables every year for this Memorial Day weekend event, which draws carloads of tourists. It's a rare opportunity to see places where horses live better than people, including philanthropist Paul Mellon's Rokeby Farm. Proceeds of the tour go into the church's outreach projects. Hours are 10:00 A.M. to 5:00 P.M. Saturday and Sunday. Tickets, good for both days, are $20 in advance and $25 after mid-May.

THOROUGHBRED RESCUE

Thoroughbred Retirement Farm
11407 Constitution Highway
Montpelier Station
(540) 672-3986
Montpelier, the home of President James Madison and his wife, Dolley, is once again home to thoroughbreds, temporarily. The retired racehorses are all waiting for good homes.

In November 2003, Montpelier partnered with the Thoroughbred Retirement

Foundation. While the foundation rescues former racehorses—some destined to be slaughtered—Montpelier offers the animals a safe haven on its 2,750-acre estate. When operating at full capacity, the farm can house between 60 and 80 horses, all waiting to be adopted.

The horses, some that at one time may have been valued at $50,000 or more, now can be adopted for anywhere between $500 and $2,500. Many have raced in big venues, including the Aqueduct Race Track in New York.

Visitors to Montpelier can see horses roam the pastures, much like they did when the Madisons lived here in the 1800s and the duPonts lived here in the 1900s. If you would like to take a horse home, the price is reasonable, but the rules are strict. You must prove that you have a good home for these thoroughbreds, and you must have a recommendation from a vet.

Also working along with the Thoroughbred Retirement Foundation are Historic Long Branch in Millwood and the Roanoke Valley Horse Rescue in Hardy.

POLO

Polo Great Meadow
Great Meadow, The Plains
(540) 253-5156
www.pologreatmeadow.org
Great Meadow is a 175-acre venue that hosts a variety of equine events, ranging from international three-day events to classic horse shows. But the polo ponies take center stage in the lighted stadium on Friday nights from June to September. Newspaperman Arthur W. "Nick" Arundel bought the abandoned farm in 1983 and gave it to the Meadow Outdoor Foundation, and now it is a premier showplace for horse and rider. The Friday Twilight Polo begins at 7:00 P.M. Each week there are different themes for tailgate parties. Admission to the stadium polo matches are $30 per car or $15 per person.

Virginia Polo Center
1082 Forest Lodge Lane, Charlottesville
(434) 979-0293, (434) 977–POLO
www.student.virginia.edu/~polo
The University of Virginia turns out some of the finest intercollegiate polo players in the country. Interest runs high among the student body when the UVA polo team plays arena polo at the Virginia Polo Center on Friday nights during the school year.

While the college students introduced polo to Charlottesville in 1954, the community wanted more than a spectator sport. Today, the local center also hosts two other community polo clubs, the Charlottesville Polo Club and Piedmont Women's Polo. The Charlottesville Polo Club, (434) 977-7656, plays two matches on Friday evenings beginning at 6:30 P.M. and a third on Sunday afternoons. The Friday matches are played in an arena, rain or shine. Sunday matches will be played on grass, weather permitting. The night games cost $4.00, but the noontime matches on Sunday are free. The women, who have been riding since 1989, play at 6:30 P.M. Saturday during the summer. The cost is $3.00, but those younger than 10 get in free. Both clubs welcome new members and are always willing to show you their ponies or help you learn about the game.

Roanoke Symphony Polo Cup
Green Hill Park, Diiguids Lane off Main Street, Salem
(540) 343-6221, (866) 277-9127
www.rso.com
Roanokers' opportunity to "Ponder the Ponies and Promote the Notes" has gone professional to include U.S. Polo Association-ranked teams in its match. Events feature a high-level 14–16-goal match. Crowds travel from throughout the mid-Atlantic and Northeast regions to attend this festive fund-raiser for the Roanoke Youth Symphony and its youth programs. Since 1996, the Polo Cup has featured works by a Virginia artist, including Marie Levine in 2003. The traditional divot-stomping is held at halftime. Not

Room and Boarding

Some people have difficulty finding hotels that will accept cats and dogs as overnight guests, but what happens when your best friend is a horse?

If you're vacationing in the Blue Ridge, you're in good hands. There are several nice bed-and-breakfasts that also have room at their inns for your four-legged companions, especially along our horse-country corridor. Here are just a couple of options:

Kelly's Ford Equestrian Center
16589 Edwards Shop Road, Remington
(540) 399-1779, (540) 399-1800
www.innatkellysford.com
Located on the grounds of the Inn at Kelly's Ford, this new stable offers box stalls, a heated wash rack, turnouts, and an adjacent bullpen for training. You may board your own horse or ride one of theirs. Boarding fee for inn guests is $20. Reservations must be made at least one week in advance to use the equestrian center. Kelly's Ford also hosts several horse shows from April through September.

The Bleu Rock Equestrian Center
12567 Lee Highway, Washington
(540) 987-3191, (540) 987-9522
www.bleurockinn.com

This facility shares the limelight with the Bleu Rock Inn and its nationally recognized restaurant. The equestrian center features full-service boarding, training, schooling, sales, and special events. You can board your pony or enjoy the other amenities, including a vineyard, orchard, ponds, polo ring, and steeplechase course. Polo matches are held here on weekends during the summer season. It will cost $30 for guests to board their horse.

Jordan Hollow Farm Inn
326 Hawksbill Park Road, Stanley
(540) 778-2285, (888) 418-7000
www.jordonhollow.com
This bed-and-breakfast caters to the equine travelers with accommodations for both horse and rider. While you can stay in one of the country inn's 15 cozy rooms, your horse can overnight at the Jordan Hollow Stables for $15. In the morning, riders are welcome to try out the open meadows or wooded trails on this 145-acre farm. Guided trail rides are available, but more experienced riders may go on their own.

only does the polo tournament provide a unique cultural experience, but it also allows patrons of the arts to enjoy good food and fun together.

General admission is reasonable (about $20 including parking) so that the revelry is accessible to all. For a hefty fee, however, you can rent tables for tailgate par-

ties and tents for private groups. These range in cost from approximately $200 to $1,500, depending on the size of tent or table you choose. Sodas and coffee are available during the activities. Tent and tailgate patrons have their names listed in the program as a gesture of appreciation, and corporate sponsors enjoy premium field position and recognition. The event is held in late September or early October.

POINT-TO-POINT AND STEEPLECHASE RACES

While both styles of competition feature races over fences, steeplechases generally offer big-money prizes and are sanctioned by the National Steeplechase Association. Point-to-points are sponsored by local hunts. While they often have top-notch steeplechase horses and riders in the field, point-to-points usually are attended by folks in mud boots and jeans. The fancy clothes and hats are saved for steeplechases. Either is good fun and a perfect excuse to prepare a sumptuous tailgate lunch.

Virginia has more steeplechases (about two dozen) than any other state and has as many point-to-points. Contact the Virginia Steeplechase Association in Middleburg for a complete schedule. If you're visiting the Blue Ridge between March and November, you can catch a race almost any Saturday. Here are just a few of the races (see our Annual Events and Festivals chapter for more).

The Virginia Gold Cup
Great Meadow, The Plains
(540) 347-2612, (800) 69-RACES
www.vagoldcup.com

For the past decade, this 77-year-old classic has been run at Great Meadow, an excellent facility once owned by newspaper magnate Arthur Arundel. It seems that all of Capitol Hill attends this see-and-be-seen event. Lavish tailgate parties are in full swing long before the first race at 1:30 P.M. All tickets are sold in advance, and you should arrive when the gates open at 10:00 A.M. to get a parking place, see the pre-race demonstrations, and cruise the booths. General admission parking, which admits a maximum of six per vehicle, costs about $60. The Gold Cup takes place the first Saturday in May. The 80th running coincides with Kentucky Derby

Day in 2005. Since 1922, more than 45,000 have attended the state's biggest steeplechase.

Great Meadow is also the venue for the International Gold Cup the third Saturday in October. This race attracts almost 25,000 folks each year. General admission parking, which admits six people per vehicle, costs about $50 in advance, $60 the week of the race. Admission price includes one car and six people.

Foxfield Races
Garth Road, Charlottesville
(434) 293-9501
www.foxfieldraces.com

Foxfield hosts two major steeplechase meets each year, events that draw top 'chasers and 20,000 spectators, some from as far away as New Jersey. Races are traditionally held the last Saturday in April and the last Sunday in September. The six-race card starts at 1:30 P.M. and features flat and steeplechase races. You'll want to get there early, though, to get a good parking spot and begin tailgating.

Sophisticated tailgate parties have become the norm. The scene is straight out of *Town and Country* magazine, with women in hats and smart outfits and men in natty tweeds. It's not unusual to see folks sipping champagne and nibbling caviar from silver plates on the back of a Rolls or BMW.

The fall races are more family friendly. Children will enjoy pony rides, Jack Russell terrier races, the parade of hounds, and a tent filled with all sorts of activities for young horse fans.

Tickets are $25, $35 within two weeks of the event, and must be purchased in advance. Depending upon location, you can also reserve a parking spot for anywhere from $100 to $600, which includes four admission tickets. Call to purchase advance tickets or to find out ticket office locations in Charlottesville.

The Foxfield Race Course is 5 miles west of the Barracks Road Shopping Center.

Middleburg Spring Races
Glenwood Park, Highway 626
Middleburg
(540) 687-6545
www.middleburgspringraces.com
Established in 1921, this is the oldest stee-plechase in the state. Usually held the third Saturday in April, the event attracts thousands of spectators to the 112-acre park. The purses are big, reaching up to $50,000, and the races feature top stee-plechase jockeys and horses.

You can buy food on the race grounds, but most folks usually bring their own pic-nics for tailgating. The gates open at 10:00 A.M. to allow for ample socializing before the races begin around 1:30 P.M. Admission is $15, $20, and $25. Glenwood Park is 1.25 miles north of Middleburg on Highway 626, also called Foxcroft Road.

Montpelier Hunt Races
Off Highway 20, Montpelier Station
(540) 672-2728
www.montpelier.org
This is the only public sporting event held at the home of a U.S. president. Set against the rolling hills of Orange County and the historic backdrop of James Madi-son's home, the Montpelier Hunt Races have become one of the key stops on the National Steeplechase Association circuit. Top horses and riders from across the country compete in this annual event held on the first Saturday in November.

The race has a long and rich history. The duPont family bought Montpelier in 1900, and in 1927 Marion duPont Scott (she married the actor Randolph Scott) and her brother, William, welcomed local folks and the well-to-do to their home for the first race. Sixty-eight years later, the Montpelier Hunt is still a favorite whether you come dressed in cutoffs or khakis.

A general admission ticket will get you in for $10.00 in advance or $15.00 at the gate, or you can pay from $1,200 to $20,000 for a reserved spot in the special hospitality area. Parking is $5.00 in advance, $10.00 on race day. An infield space is $35.00, $40.00 on race day.

Jack Russell terrier races usually begin around 10:30 A.M. for those who want to arrive early and set up their tailgate par-ties. Bring your fancy basket and partici-pate in the Dolley Madison tailgate competition. The first race begins at 1:00 P.M. The main house is open for tours, too (see our Attractions chapter).

RECREATION

Historically, visitors came to the Blue Ridge Mountains to partake of pristine waters and gaze upon lofty peaks, a tonic for body and soul. That's still true today—but mostly they come to play.

With so many leisure activities in the Blue Ridge, the wise visitor will plan an itinerary well in advance. However, getting sidetracked is also a regional pastime, hazardous only to a tight vacation schedule, certainly not to the spirit or health.

It is to the Blue Ridge that Virginia owes much of its international recognition in the realm of outdoor recreation. The big draw, of course, is the scenery. Mother Nature blessed Virginia's Blue Ridge with lush vegetation, sparkling streams, and mountain peaks that dress in dazzling colors for fall and pristine white in winter. Between the mountains are valleys patchworked with fields of grain and grassy meadows in which languid dairy cattle graze among wildflowers. Many small towns are postcard images, with covered bridges and steepled churches that withstood the Civil War.

In this spectacular setting are recreational opportunities for every budget, from the camper on a shoestring to the golfer luxuriating at the Homestead, one of our nation's most acclaimed resorts.

Among the region's greatest recreational treasures are its parks and forests. Two national forests with acres of precious wilderness have become one—the George Washington and Jefferson National Forests. The Shenandoah National Park, Virginia's mountain playground, is also here. State parks, including Claytor, Douthat, Sky Meadows, and Smith Mountain Lake, offer recreational opportunities galore, from cross-country skiing to horseback riding. And you never know who might be giving you lessons. Kim Severson from Plain Dealing Farm in Keene won a silver medal in the three-day event at the 2004 Olympics in Greece. John Williams of Middleburg also competed for the United States.

Two outdoor mega-attractions are here also—the Bikecentennial Trail that spans the country from Williamsburg to the West Coast, and the Appalachian Trail, stretching from Maine to Georgia. Natives in small towns take for granted a continuing stream of blaze orange-clad backpackers and bikers enjoying country byways.

Blue Ridge forest preserves offer some of the finest fishing and hunting in the Southeast.

Most visitors come to see rather than stalk, though, and they're never disappointed. The hills are home to black bear, deer, turkey, small game, and a variety of songbirds.

There's bountiful water in the region—fresh mountain streams, rivers, and lakes, including Smith Mountain Lake, the state's second-largest freshwater lake. These lakes and waterways offer the popular sports of boating, swimming, rafting, canoeing, and tubing—a pastime especially enjoyed by college students who tow a "refreshment" tube stocked with cold drinks and snacks. It's a great way to spend a hot summer afternoon.

If your idea of a hazard is a sand-filled bunker on the edge of a tiered green, you'll find a plethora of excellent public, semiprivate, and resort courses in the Blue Ridge.

As you're probably beginning to suspect, choosing an activity in the Blue Ridge Mountains is like trying to select a meal from a mile-long Virginia buffet. There are far too many recreational opportunities to list completely in these pages. We recommend that you send for brochures and guides offered by the Commonwealth of Virginia and tourism and recreation associations. This is especially important for many camping areas that require reservations. Look for information contacts listed within the various recreation categories in the following pages. Then go out there and have fun! You'll be in good company.

BOATING
Canoe Outfitters

The Blue Ridge region has many reputable canoe outfitters. Several are along the South Fork of the Shenandoah River, which meanders between the Massanutten and Blue Ridge mountain ranges before joining the Potomac River at Harpers Ferry, West Virginia. These outfitters also rent rubber rafts, kayaks, and tubes, the local's craft of choice for a lazy afternoon of drifting with the current.

Other outfitters are near the James River, the longest and largest river in Virginia.

Farther southwest is the New River, reputed to be second only to the Nile as the oldest river on Earth. (Atypical of most rivers, the New flows north.)

Most canoe outfitters will only allow you to travel down familiar waters, unless you're an expert and willing to assume the risks (financial and otherwise) of canoeing a less-traveled tributary. Generally speaking, a single fee includes the canoe rental, paddles, life jackets, maps, shuttle service, and an orientation.

Here are some good places to rent boats and equipment in the Blue Ridge region, from north to south.

Front Royal Canoe Company
8567 Stonewall Jackson Highway
Front Royal
(540) 635-5440, (800) 270-8808
www.frontroyalcanoe.com
This outfit, 3 miles south of the entrance to the Skyline Drive, rents canoes, kayaks, rafts, and tubes on the South Fork of the Shenandoah River from April 1 to October 31. Trips range from leisurely fishing to mild white-water adventures. Multiple-day

excursions also can be arranged. Canoe day trips cost between $35 and $50. Reservations are recommended but not required. Shuttle service for privately owned canoes and watercraft is available. They also offer guided horseback rides at Indian Hollow at Andy Guest Park, ranging from a half hour to 2 hours. (See our Kidstuff chapter for more information.)

Downriver Canoe Company
884 Indian Hollow, Bentonville
(540) 635-5526, (800) 338-1963
www.downriver.com
This company rents canoes, rafts, tubes, and kayaks for exploring the South Fork of the Shenandoah River, a good waterway for novices and moderately experienced canoeists. Detailed maps describing the river course and the best way to negotiate it are provided. The maps also point out the best camping areas, picnic sites, swimming holes, and fishing spots. Rentals run from $13 for a tube float to $120 for a two-day canoe trip. (See our Kidstuff chapter.)

Multiple-day trips can also be arranged. Reservations are recommended, but last-minute canoe trips are often possible. Open April 1 through October 31, this company also has a shuttle service for people with their own canoes.

Shenandoah River Trips
2047 Rocky Hollow Lane, Bentonville
(540) 635-5050, (800) 727-4371
www.shenandoahrivertrips.com
"Bring us your weekend . . . and we'll do the rest!" is this business's motto. It offers canoe, kayak, rafting, and tube rentals on the Shenandoah River and organizes fishing, camping, hiking, raft, and kayak trips. The outfitter will custom-design a weekend vacation for the entire family.

River Trips run daily from April 1 to November 1. Reservations are strongly recommended for any weekend or holiday. The business also rents fishing equipment and camping gear and sells fishing tackle and all kinds of supplies. Prices for river fun range from $12 for tubing to $20 a person, depending on the trip length and type of craft used.

Shenandoah River Outfitters
6502 South Page Valley Road, Luray
(540) 743-4159, (800) 6CANOE2
www.shenandoahriver.com
This outfit offers canoe, kayak, raft, and tube rentals and canoe sales. Situated on the Shenandoah River between the Massanutten Mountain Trails and the Appalachian Trail in the George Washington section of the national forest, this company is open year-round. Canoe rental averages $25 to $50 a day. Tubes rent for $15; kayaks cost $32 for a day. A six-person raft rents for $60 to $105, depending on the number of people. The company also provides a shuttle. They have river cabins, fully furnished, that you can canoe or drive to. Reservations are recommended for cabins.

ℹ️ *Two of the biggest tips for kayaking: 1) Don't go alone—paddle with a partner; and 2) wear a life preserver. A short-waisted personal flotation device is the most comfortable for kayaking.*

James River Reeling and Rafting
265 Ferry Street, Scottsville
(434) 286-4FUN
www.reelingandrafting.com
This business offers canoe, kayak, raft, and tubing trips for people at all levels of experience. It specializes in customizing overnight trips to suit the customer's fancy. Trips can be organized for convention groups, which get a 10 percent discount when 11 or more boats are rented. The company maintains a permanent campground on the river and offers two-day canoeing/rafting packages.

It will cost around $35 per boat for a 4-mile trip. The 12.5-mile float, which usually runs four to six hours, costs $47. For fishermen specializing in smallmouth bass, there is a $35 package for about two to three hours. Overnight excursions cost about $86. Tubing costs $15. The average kayak rental is $25 for a 7-mile trip, and the six-people raft rents for $20 a day.

The headquarters is on the corner of Main and Ferry Streets in downtown Scottsville. Here you'll find fishing and camping supplies and anything else you might have left behind. It's open April 1 through October 1.

James River Runners Inc.
10082 Hatton Ferry Road, Scottsville
(434) 286-2338
www.jamesriver.com
This outfitter, 35 minutes south of Charlottesville, specializes in family canoe, tubing, and rafting trips on the James River. Owners Christie and Jeff Schmick can arrange a variety of outings suitable for children 6 and older. They also arrange day and overnight trips for larger groups—even conventions. A special two-day package features canoeing for 9 miles the first day, camping overnight by the river, and tubing 3 miles the next day.

Canoe rentals cost $37 for a 3-mile trip, $51 for 9 miles, and $102 for an overnight excursion. Sit-on-top kayaks are less expensive: $23.50 for 3 miles; $33.50 for 9 miles. Four- and five-person rafts are available for $25.50 per person.

Group tubing trips can be arranged, and groups of 25 or more get a discount. Tubes rent for $15.00 each. Reservations are necessary for groups and recommended for everyone on the weekends. James River Runners is open March through October.

James River Basin Canoe Livery Ltd.
1870 East Midland Trail, Lexington
(540) 261-7334
www.canoevirginia.com
This outfit arranges day and overnight trips down both the Maury and James Rivers. You can take an adventurous run down Balcony Falls, the mighty rapids where the James breaks through the Blue Ridge Mountains. Or you can spend a cou-

ple of hours paddling down a slow stretch of the beautiful Maury. The staff gives a solid orientation, with instructions on safety and basic canoeing strokes. A video program also familiarizes canoeists with the stretch of river about to be boated.

James River Basin is open from 9:00 A.M. to 5:00 P.M. daily from May 1 to September 30 and by appointment anytime during the rest of the year. James River canoe trips range between $49.50 and $62.85. Canoe trips down the Maury are $29.50 to $60.00. Kayaks are less expensive, ranging from $37.00 to $49.00. Two-day overnight trips range from $76.00 to $80.00. Tack on two more days for $34.00 a day. One- to six-day trips are available.

New River Canoe Livery
Virginia Avenue, Pembroke
(540) 626-7189
Owner Dave Vicenzi rents canoes for trips along the New River in Giles County. The easiest trip is on the 7 miles of river between Eggleston to Pembroke, but the most popular outing is an 11-mile run from Pembroke to Pearisburg, which has several Class II (intermediate) white-water rapids. Eggleston to Pembroke costs $25, while Pembroke to Pearisburg is $30. When the water is high in the spring, Vicenzi allows customers to canoe down Walker and Wolf Creeks, tributaries of the New River. Multiple-day trips can also be arranged, but customers must supply their own camping gear. The Livery is open 10:00 A.M. to 6:00 P.M. Tuesday through Sunday from April through October.

Tangent Outfitters
1170 River Road, Radford
(540) 674-5202, (540) 626-4567
www.newrivertrail.com
You can canoe the New River or bike the New River Trail State Park with equipment from Tangent Outfitters. Not only does Tangent rent mountain bikes, but it also offers a wide assortment of river fun. You can rent your own canoe for $18 to $25, depending on the trip, or a kayak for $30 to $40. If you are more of a beginner, you

might want to sign up for a guided canoe or fishing trip. There are half-day and whole-day trips available as well as overnight trips, ranging from $50 to $65 a person. They have a shuttle service.

Other Boating Possibilities

Let's not forget boating on Virginia's beautiful lakes. Boats can be rented at several state parks in the heart of the mountains. Generally, boats are available on weekends beginning in mid-May and daily from Memorial Day through Labor Day weekend.

At **Douthat State Park,** (540) 862-8100, near Clifton Forge, you can rent rowboats, canoes, kayaks, hydrobikes, and paddleboats on a 50-acre lake stocked with trout. This park is listed on the National Register of Historic Places for the role its design played in the development of parks nationwide. Rowboats rent for $6.00 or $10.00 per hour if you want a motor. Hydrobikes are $5.00, paddleboats and kayaks are $6.00, and canoes are $8.00 an hour.

In Pulaski County, about an hour southwest of Roanoke, you can rent canoes, kayaks, fishing boats, and pontoon boats to take out on 4,500-acre **Claytor Lake.** Claytor Lake Marina, (540) 674-6000, provides fuel, a boat dock, a store, and food. The minimal rental for water craft is two hours. The cost ranges from $15 an hour to $250 a day, depending on the craft.

Fairy Stone State Park, (276) 930-2424, offers boating on its 168-acre lake adjoining Philpott Reservoir. Just minutes from the Blue Ridge Parkway, Fairy Stone is in Patrick County. Rowboats and canoes rent for $6.00 an hour, $22.00 a day, or $80.00 a week. Paddleboats cost $6.00 an hour, hydrobikes are $5.00 an hour, and kayaks for singles are $8.00 an hour or $10.00 for tandem. Motors with rowboats are also available at a higher charge.

Smith Mountain Lake has 500 miles of winding shoreline, and 20,600 acres of sparkling waters also offer countless possibilities for boating. About a dozen places rent various types of boats, from pontoons to motorboats and houseboats. For information and brochures, contact the Smith Mountain Lake Visitor Center at (800) 676-8203. The Bridgewater Marina, (540) 721-1639, handles rentals year-round. A 24-foot pontoon boat rents for $130 a day or $50 an hour, an inboard/outboard speedboat is $220 a day or $95 an hour, or you can rent the popular wave runner for $220 a day. Camper's Paradise (540-721-1175) and Parrot's Cove (800-488-4516) even rent out houseboats. Smith Mountain Lake State Park has rentals of smaller craft, including canoes and kayaks offered through Bridgewater Plaza at (540) 297-3642. The park also offers full-moon canoe trips from May through September. Experienced guides lead the trips, and no children younger than 5 are allowed. For details, call the park at (540) 297-6066.

You also will find ample boating opportunities in the George Washington and Jefferson National Forests, including the 43.5-mile **Gathright Dam** and **Lake Moomaw,** (540) 962-2214, 19 miles north of Covington. The largest lake in the National Forest, Lake Moomaw is popular for boaters. You can bring your own boat or rent one from Lake Moomaw Marina, (540) 279-4144, located at the north end of the lake. Pontoon boats rent for $150 to $200 a day, canoes for $30 a day or $20 for half a day, and bass boats for $80 a day or $50 for half a day. The half-day rentals are only for weekdays. It's the only marina on the lake, so be sure to stock up on food and supplies, fuel, and bait. There are also two boat ramps on the south side of the lake.

People can canoe or kayak on the Roanoke River from the Explore Park at no charge. There are two put-in points: inside the park proper (9:00 A.M. to 4:00 P.M. on the days the Blue Ridge Parkway Visitor Center is open); the other is at the end of Rut Rough Road, from dawn to dusk daily.

CAMPING

From primitive campsites to modern RV campgrounds with all the amenities, camping in the Blue Ridge Mountains is a four-season activity.

Forests cover two-thirds of Virginia, with most of it in the Blue Ridge Mountains. Camping here is a huge industry, offering an inexpensive, family-oriented recreational pastime whether you prefer KOA Kamping Kabins with all the comforts of home or a remote spot in the woods flat enough for your tent. At Blue Ridge campgrounds, you'll usually find swimming holes in cool mountain streams or lakes and copious hiking trails. Some places even have boat rentals and horseback riding.

National Forest Campgrounds

In the George Washington and Jefferson National Forests, most family camping is on a first-come, first-served basis. However, you can make reservations for Morris Hill at Lake Moomaw and for Trout Pond in the Lee Ranger District. Call (877) 444-6777 or go to www.reserveusa.com. Group camping is another exception for which reservations can be made, at least a week in advance. No rental cabins or other lodging is available in national forest campgrounds. If you want to bring along your pets for company, you can, but dogs must be leashed. Call (540) 265-5100 or visit www.southernregion.fs.fed.us/gwj for reservations or information. Among the nicest campgrounds in the national forest is Sherando Lake Recreation Area (540) 942-5965, which has three family campgrounds with 65 sites (30 with electrical hookups), flush toilets, and showers. The price to camp runs from $15 to $20 a night. The camping season in the national forest is generally early April through October.

State Park Campgrounds

Seven state parks in the Blue Ridge have campgrounds, and four also have cabins. Reservations for campsites and cabins must be made by calling the Virginia State Parks Reservation Center at (800) 933–PARK, or visit www.dcr.state.va.us. Depending upon availability, same-day reservations are accepted for just a few parks, or by Thursday for weekend arrival. Payment must be made within 14 days after the reservation is made and prior to arrival by credit card over the phone. Or you may mail a check, providing there is sufficient time to ensure arrival of payment. Reservations may be made up to 11 months in advance. The maximum camping period is 14 days in any 30-day period. Leashed pets are permitted. Overnight facilities open March 1 and close the first Monday in December.

Raymond "Andy" Guest Shenandoah River State Park
Highway 340, Warren County
(540) 622–6840

Opened in 1999, Andy Guest Park is one of Virginia's newest state parks and lies along the south fork of the Shenandoah River in Warren County. The park offers a large riverside picnic area with shelters, trails, river access, a scenic overlook, and a car-top launch area. You'll find 10 riverfront campsites, ranging from individual to group-size. To get to them you will have to travel by canoe or foot. (The farthest is 50 yards away.) A bathhouse with hot showers was added to the park in 2004.

Sky Meadows State Park
11012 Edmonds Lane, Delaplane
(540) 592–3556

Twelve primitive campsites are available by way of a 0.75-mile trail at this park in Fauquier and Clark Counties. The site, 2 miles from the Appalachian Trail, includes tent pads, fire rings, a lean-to shelter, pit toilets, and nonpotable water.

Smith Mountain Lake State Park
Highway 1, Huddleston
(540) 297–6066

Primitive camping is available, and there also are 24 sites with water and electrical hookups. The park also offers one three-bedroom cabin and 19 two-bedroom cabins.

James River State Park
Highway 1, Gladstone
(434) 933–4355

Not far from Appomattox Courthouse, this new park opened in June 1999 with two separate campgrounds. There are 22 primitive sites along the river at Canoe Landing and another seven at Branch Pond. There are also five primitive sites allotted for those camping with their horses. The campground is currently constructing developed sites, which will be ready in the spring of 2005, and cabins are planned for the future. The park has a concrete boat launch and a newly opened canoe livery where you can rent tubes, canoes, and kayaks for trips down the James. It also has six picnic shelters, an amphitheater, and trails for hiking, biking, and horseback riding.

No answer? If you're the type who likes to finalize your vacation plans in advance, remember that some of the sites, including many parks, boating facilities, and swimming areas, operate seasonally. If you can't get anyone on the phone, try again later.

Douthat State Park
Highway 1, Milboro
(540) 862–8100

One of six original campgrounds built by President Roosevelt's Civilian Conservation Corps, Douthat rents 25 log cabins and five concrete lodges. The cabins, lodges, and lakefront restaurant were all built by the CCC. Douthat also has 92 campsites on three campgrounds and 15 group campsites at this park that covers portions of Bath and Alleghany Counties. The park also features two completely furnished lodges, which accommodate 15 and 18 guests each.

Claytor Lake State Park
4400 State Park Road, Dublin
(540) 643-2500

There are 12 lakefront cabins available for rent on a weekly basis at this Pulaksi County park. Those who prefer to rough it can choose from 110 campsites in four campgrounds. Electrical and water hookups are available at 40 sites.

Fairy Stone State Park
967 Fairy Stone Lake Drive, Stuart
(276) 930-2424

This, too, was one of six original state parks opened by the CCC in 1936. Covering parts of Patrick and Henry Counties, Fairy Stone offers eight log cabins, 16 concrete block cabins, and a newly renovated lodge which sleeps 16. The log cabins were part of the original facilities. The park also includes 51 campsites with electric and water hookups.

DEVELOPED CAMPSITES

Developed campsites can accommodate one piece of camping equipment and/or one motor vehicle and a maximum of six people. Expect a grill, picnic table, and access to bathhouses on site. A standard site has no hookups, whereas those with hookups provide access to water and electricity for a few dollars more. Expect to pay the following nightly camping fees: primitive sites, $9.00 to $11.00; developed sites, $18.00 to $22.00; electric/water hookup sites, $23.00; pet fee, $3.00 per night per pet; cancellation fee, $10.00.

CABINS

Housekeeping cabins ranging from one room to two bedrooms are available in Claytor Lake, Douthat, Fairy Stone, and Smith Mountain Lake. During Memorial Day to Labor Day, a week's stay is required, unless there is availability within the month before the arrival date. A two-night minimum stay is required at all times. Reservations are required. Douthat and Fairy Stone State Parks have lodge facilities that accommodate up to 18 and 16 guests, respectively. Smith Mountain Lake has a new three-bedroom universally accessible cabin. It features a combination dining and living room, kitchen, and two bathrooms, including a universally accessible shower. The cabin can accommodate up to eight. The park also has several other partially accessible cabins.

Cabin rates are based on three seasons that vary by park and size of cabin. Rates per night during prime season range from $68.00 for an efficiency to $102.00 for a two-bedroom. During off-season, they are $51.00 a night for an efficiency to $76.00 for a two-bedroom. Weekly rates range from $409.00 to $699.00 during prime season. Extra beds cost $3.00 per night, and a pet fee is $5.00 per night per pet. The cancellation fee is $20.00 if more than 30 days in advance. Stays in the lodges cost much more, as they have multiple bedrooms.

GROUP CAMPING

Group camping is available with water/electric sites at Douthat and developed sites at Fairy Stone, with a minimum group of three sites required. Natural Tunnel has a large group camping area that accommodates up to 50 people for $61.00 per night. Sky Meadows State Park has primitive group camping for $9.00.

Organizations and Information Sources

For camping and visitor information and maps, we suggest the following sources:

The Blue Ridge Parkway Visitor Center at Explore Park, P.O. Box 8508, Roanoke, VA 24014-0508; (540) 427-1800 or (800) 842-9163

Virginia Hospitality and Travel Association (private campgrounds), 2101 Libby Avenue, Richmond 23230; (804) 288-3065; www.vhta.org

George Washington and Jefferson National Forests, 5162 Valleypointe Parkway, Roanoke 24019-3050; (540) 265-5100; www.southernregion.fs.fed.us/gwj

National Recreation group camping reservations; (877) 444-6777 or www.reserveusa.com

Shenandoah National Park, Route 4, Box 348, Luray 22835; (540) 999-3500, (800) 778-2851; www.nps.gov/shen

Virginia State Parks, Department of Conservation & Recreation, Division of State Parks, 203 Governor Street, Suite 213, Richmond 23219; general information, (804) 786-1712; brochures and reservations, (804) 225-3867, (800) 933-PARK, TDD number (804) 786-2121; www.dcr.state.va.us

Blue Ridge Parkway, 2551 Mountain View Road, Vinton 24179; (540) 767-2496

U.S. Army Corps of Engineers, operations manager, 1058 Philpott Dam Road, Bassett 24055; (276) 629-2703; www.saw.usace.army.mil/philpott/index.htm

Virginia Tourism Corp., 901 East Byrd Street, Richmond 23219; (804) 786-4484; www.virginia.org

Shenandoah Valley Travel Association, 277 West Old Cross Road, New Market 22844; (540) 740-3132; www.visit shenandoah.org

FISHING

Naturalist Henry David Thoreau once commented, "In the night, I dream of trout-fishing." In Virginia's Blue Ridge, anglers see their dreams become reality in clear, cold mountain streams, rivers, and lakes. Visitors can rest easy at night knowing that at any given moment, millions of fish are surging upstream or lying tantalizingly in wait in stone river recesses.

An aggressive conservation effort by the state is partly responsible for the plentiful fishing in the Blue Ridge. For example, the mountain streams found in Shenandoah National Park are one of the last completely protected strongholds of the native Eastern brook trout. Savvy Virginia tourism experts report that since Robert Redford's naturalistic film on fly-fishing, based on the book *A River Runs Through It,* the numbers of fly-fishing anglers in Virginia have been thicker than the black flies their artificial bait imitates. But don't worry—the out-of-the-way waters far outnumber those that aren't.

Here are a few tips about the best places to catch fish: brown trout—Lake Moomaw, Mossy Creek, and Smith River; largemouth bass—Smith Mountain Lake and James River; smallmouth bass—James River, Smith Mountain Lake, Claytor Lake, and Lake Philpott; striped bass—Claytor Lake and Smith Mountain Lake; and walleye—Philpott Lake and the Roanoke River.

And now for bragging rights! To name a few state records: smallmouth bass, 8 lbs., 1 oz., New River; Roanoke bass, 2 lbs., 6 oz., Smith Mountain Lake; striped bass, 53 lbs. 7 oz., Leesville Lake; walleye, 15 lbs., 15 oz., New River; and northern pike, 31 lbs., 4 oz., Motts Run Reservoir, a channel catfish, 31 lbs. from the Rappahannock River; a muskie, 45 lbs., New River. By the time you read this, some of these records might already be broken.

Figures for citation fish are equally impressive. In 1996 the James River set the record with 551 citations, followed by Smith Mountain Lake with 314 citations, the New River with 149, Claytor Lake and Philpott Reservoir with 108, and Lake Moomaw with 94.

The primary objective of this section is to direct you to some of the Blue Ridge's classic streams, rivers, and lakes—the ones where anglers aren't so close that they're crossing lines. After you get to your spot, you might want to rough it on your own. Or you can hire a guide.

The section of the Roanoke River that runs through Explore Park has very good fishing, and a fishing dock was recently added for easier river access. There's no charge to fish although a valid Virginia state license is required. One popular spot is inside the park (available from 9:00 A.M. to 4:30 P.M. the days the Blue Ridge Parkway Visitor Center is open), and the other is at the end of Rut Rough Road, which is available from dawn to dusk daily.

The Virginia Department of Game and Inland Fisheries—www.dgif.state.va.us—recommends literally hundreds of fishing places. You can find out about real gem day trips. An especially fun one for lovers of both fishing and horseback riding is the package offered by **Virginia Mountain Outfitters** in Buena Vista, near Lexington. Trips range from one to five days and include a clinic. Call Deborah Sensabaugh at Outfitters, (540) 261-1910, to find out more.

Farther north, in the charming tin-roofed town of Edinburg, **Murray's Fly Shop,** www.murraysflyshop.com, is a good place to find out where you can fish in the Shenandoah Valley for the really big ones. Proprietor Harry Murray is the author of several books, including *Trout Fishing in the Shenandoah National Park,* and promises to help you catch fish. Murray offers numerous clinics and can be reached at (540) 984-4212 for a complete list.

Wintergreen Resort, www.wintergreenresort.com, in Nelson County offers fly-fishing clinics and fly-fishing weekend retreats. Find out details for these at (434) 325-8180.

For details and the widest array of locations, the Department of Game and Inland Fisheries' *Virginia Fishing Guide* is a must. Traditionally, topographic maps published by the U.S. Geological Survey have been the most useful sources of information for anglers. These maps can tell you whether streams flow through open or forested land, how steep the land is, and where tributaries enter. Instructions on how to get both guides are listed at the end of this fishing section.

We hope you're now excited about all the fishing possibilities. But don't forget your license, which can be obtained from some county circuit court clerks, city corporation court clerks, and a variety of other authorized agents. You can also purchase a fishing license online at www.dgif.state.va.us/fishing. The first Saturday and Sunday in June have been designated as Free Fishing Days in Virginia. No fishing license of any kind is required for rod-and-reel fishing except in designated trout-stocked waters. A detailed booklet describing licensing requirements, game fish size and catch limits, special regulations (specific to certain areas), and other regulations can be obtained from the Virginia Department of Game and Inland Fisheries.

Fishing Licenses

Unless otherwise specified, resident license requirements apply annually to all persons who claim the Commonwealth of Virginia as their legal domicile. Nonresident fees apply annually as well, unless otherwise indicated. A 50 cent issuance fee, added to each of the following licenses, is not included in our listed fee.

RESIDENT

County or city resident to fish in county or city of residence, $5.00 per year

State resident to fish only, $12.00

To fish statewide for five consecutive days in private waters or public waters not stocked with trout, $5.00

State and county resident to trout fish in designated trout-stocked waters, $12.00 (in addition to regular fishing license)

Age 65 and older, $1.00

Virginia lifetime license, ranges from $10.00 to $250.00, depending on your age

NONRESIDENT

Nonresident to fish only, $30.00 per year

To fish for five consecutive days statewide in private waters or public waters not stocked with trout, $6.00

To fish in designated trout-stocked waters, $30.00 (in addition to regular fishing license)

Virginia lifetime license, $500.00

Safety Suggestions

Regardless of whether you're testing the waters of the Blue Ridge as an experienced angler or a novice, it doesn't hurt to remember safety at all times, especially cold-weather hazards. Although getting away from it all is most of the fun, don't forget to let somebody know where you are. Despite the best of precautions, you could fall in at some point. In hot weather, it's an inconvenience. In cold weather, which is most of the year, it can be fatal. Many anglers do not realize that hypothermia can strike when the temperature is in the 40s. Prevention is always best—wear waders with rough soles when fishing in streams and wear a life preserver when fishing in rivers and lakes. And don't forget to look out for snakes (timber rattlers and copperheads are the two poisonous species) and ticks, the latter of which are "fishing" for you!

Lakes

The following are some favorite fishing areas of the Blue Ridge. Source material for complete listings is included at the end of this Fishing section.

Rivanna Reservoir
Charlottesville area

Anglers consider this the best bet for fishing in the area surrounding this historic city. It supports good populations of bass, crappie, bluegill, and channel cats, with occasional walleye and muskie. There is a public boat ramp near the filtration plant of the Charlottesville water-supply reservoir, which may be reached from U.S. Highway 29 north of Charlottesville by taking Highway 631 (Rio Road) or Highway 743 west to Highway 659 or Highway 676. The ramp is at the end of Highway 659.

Lake Moomaw
Bath, Alleghany Counties

This flood-control reservoir was completed

Outdoor enthusiasts should be aware that hunters may use the same state and national forests during hunting season. It might be a good idea to check with the Department of Game and Inland Fisheries at (804) 367-1000 to find out the dates and locations of Virginia's various hunting seasons.

in 1981 with the closing of the Gathright Dam on the Jackson River. Ever since, its 43-mile shoreline has been a popular playground for residents of Alleghany, Bath, and Highland Counties. Much of the shoreline is adjacent to the Gathright Wildlife Management Area. Crappie fishing is outstanding, with 1.5-pounders common. There is an equal complement of largemouth and smallmouth bass. Thirty-seven citation rainbow trout have also been pulled from the lake. For more information, call the James River Ranger District in Covington, (540) 962-2214.

To reach the lake, get off Interstate 64 at exit 16 and follow U.S. Highway 220 to Highway 687, then to Highway 641 and Highway 666. The access point is 16 miles from the interstate.

Smith Mountain Lake
Bedford, Pittsylvania, Franklin Counties

Striped bass are prevalent at the 20,600-acre Smith Mountain Lake, which has been the source of numerous citation fish. More anglers appear to be converting to fishing live bait over artificial. A real pro, who has been fishing the lake since its beginnings with Appalachian Power Company in the '60s, says the secret to landing big stripers is live shad, which can be caught at dockside in casting nets.

The state's largest striper, 53 pounds 7 ounces, was caught in nearby Leesville Lake. At the rate these whoppers are growing, that record might soon be surpassed. If you're serious about getting one of the big ones, a professional guide is a great idea. Some good ones are Dave Sines, (540) 721-5007; or Spike Franceschini at Spike's Prime Time Fishing, (540) 297-5611. They'll try to ensure you don't go home with only tales about the one that got away.

The lake provides a lot of camping and recreational opportunities, including a swimming beach, through Smith Mountain Lake State Park, (540) 297-6066. To reach the lake from U.S. Highway 460, take Highway 43 to Highway 626 S.

Claytor Lake
4400 State Park Road, Dublin
This lake, also impounded by Appalachian Power, on the New River off Highway 660 in Pulaski County, is known for its fantastic white bass fishery, producing many citations annually. Claytor has traditionally been a good flathead catfish lake, too, with fish up to 25 pounds or more. Crappie also have shown good growth rates. Claytor Lake State Park, (540) 643-2500, provides camping, cottages, and a swimming beach. The lake is accessible by taking exit 101 from Interstate 81 to Highway 660. Follow this road for 3 miles to Claytor Lake.

Resources

STATE PUBLICATIONS

For the total scoop on fishing, the following titles are available from the Virginia Department of Games and Inland Fisheries, 4010 Broad Street, P.O. Box 11104, Richmond 23230-1104, (804) 367-1000: *Virginia Wildlife Calendar, Virginia Fishing Regulations,* and *Virginia Fishing Guide.* You can go online to www.dgif.state.va.us.

U.S. GEOLOGICAL SURVEY MAPS

Contact the Eastern Region USGS National Center, 12201 Sunrise Valley Drive, Reston, 20192; (703) 648-4000 or go to www.usgs.gov/ or call the store at (888) 275-8747.

VIRGINIA TOPOGRAPHIC MAPS

An outstanding collection of Virginia topographic maps is the *Virginia Atlas & Gazetteer,* published by DeLorme, 2 DeLorme Drive, Yarmouth, ME 04096; (800) 561-5105 or www.delorme.com.

BOOKS ON TROUT STREAMS

We recommend two great trout stream books: *Trout Streams of Virginia: An Angler's Guide to the Blue Ridge Watershed,* by Harry Slone, published by Backcountry Guides, and *A Fly Fisherman's Blue Ridge,* by Christopher Camuto, published by University of Georgia Press.

GOLF

Virginia is building a reputation for producing some of the finest players and courses in the country. Sam Snead, Lanny Watkins, Curtis Strange, and Vinny Giles are all homegrown talents. Arnold Palmer, Jack Nicklaus, and Gary Player also have come to the Commonwealth to design some of the most exciting places to play.

Virginia has more than 150 golf courses, many of which are in the mountains and valleys of the Blue Ridge, including two of the country's top golf resorts. The diverse topography of the region means that the courses vary widely, providing a never-ending challenge that draws visitors back year after year. The fact that Blue Ridge links are generally greener and 10 to 15 degrees cooler in the summer is another draw.

In this section we have listed a few of the best-known public, semiprivate, and military courses. Our list is by no means complete; we've simply tried to give you a sampling of what the state's top courses in the Blue Ridge have to offer. For more information on Virginia links, we recommend the following sources: Virginia State Golf Association, (804) 378-2300; Golf Promotions in Virginia, (800) GOLF-NVA; and Golf Virginia Resorts Association, (800) 93-BACK9.

Carper's Valley Golf Club
1401 Millwood Pike, Winchester
(540) 662-4319

Tree-lined fairways and gently rolling hills dominate this 150-acre course at the top of the Shenandoah Valley. Four lakes add to the scenic and competitive layout along the 6,125-yard par 70 course. Make sure your drive is accurate on the fourth hole. A severe dogleg left to right, this signature hole is heavily forested. From April to October the greens fee is $21.00 on the weekend and holidays and $18.00 during the week. Carts rent for $16.00 per rider for all 18 holes or $9.00 apiece for nine holes. Carts are required until 2:00 P.M. on weekends and holidays.

Meadows Farms Golf Course
4300 Flat Run Road, Locust Grove
(540) 854-9890
www.meadowsfarms.com

In 1993 nursery magnate Bill Meadows opened this Orange County course, a beautifully landscaped layout that boasts the country's longest hole. At nearly a half mile long, this 841-yard, par 6 has brought the course plenty of national attention. Two ponds come into play as you go up hills on this challenging dogleg right. Your best bet is to hit your tee shot short of the first pond, hit over the pond, then if you can carry the other pond on your third shot, you should be about 75 yards from the green. But don't forget to watch out for the clover-shaped bunker. Meadows recently added nine more holes, bringing the total to 27. The par 72 Island to Long is 6,312 yards, the par 72 Long to Waterfall is 6,320 yards, while par 70 Island to Waterfall is 5,560 yards. On the waterfall you actually drive your cart behind a 60-foot waterfall, then walk across a swinging bridge to get to the tee. On weekdays combined greens and cart fees run $32, $27 for seniors. On Friday the cost is $37 and $32. Greens and cart fees on Saturday and Sunday are $44.

Caverns Country Club
910 T. C. Northcott Boulevard, Luray
(540) 743-7111
www.luraycaverns.com

Near the famous Luray Caverns, this course offers the unique experience of golfing near cave openings, though it can be quite tricky getting your ball out of these hazards. The first hole sets the tempo on this hilly 6,499-yard, par 72 course. No. 1 is a long par 5 that measures about 500 yards. The greens fees are $26 Monday through Thursday, and $36 Friday through Sunday and holidays. Add an additional $14 per person if you want a cart.

Bryce Resort and Golf Course
1982 Fairway Drive, Bayse
(540) 856-2124, (800) 821-1444
www.bryceresort.com

Although this Shenandoah County resort is built right beside a mountain, golfers will enjoy a relatively flat course. It does takes a few challenging turns, starting right off the bat with a long par 5 dogleg on the first hole. On the back nine, No. 15 is one of the most picturesque holes on the course, a 140-yard par 3 with a pond off to the right. Stoney Creek also comes into play over the 6,277-yard, par 71 course.

There is also a miniature golf course nearby. Bryce, a golf and skiing resort, is near the West Virginia border (see our Resorts chapter). Cart and greens fees are $35 in the mornings and $30 after noon on the weekdays, and $50 for weekend mornings and $40 weekends after noon.

Shenandoah Valley Golf Club
134 Golf Club Circle, Front Royal
(540) 636-2641, (540) 636-4653

Some of the best golfers have tested their skills here at Shenandoah Valley. Once used as a qualifier for the Kemper Open, this Warren County club hosts the Mid-Atlantic PGA twice a year. This 27-hole par 72 course offers golfers three distinctively different looks over 6,399 yards, ranging from rolling hills to flat land in the valley. There's not much room for error on the Red nine. Also called the "old course," it is known for its narrow fairways and small greens. The White has two par 3s, both tight and tricky, while the Blue is the most difficult with a mixture of blind holes. The par 3 No. 2 on the Blue course is definitely a postcard hole. If you're looking for scenery, Shenandoah keeps a full-time flower gardener, and it shows with stunning flowerbeds throughout. Combined cart and greens fees range from $25 to $50.

Bowling Green Golf Club
838 Bowling Green Road, Front Royal
(540) 635-2024
Front Royal's premier golfing spot has two challenging 18-hole courses. The North is a 6,085-yard par 71, while the south course plays a par 70 over 5,587 yards. The older North course should offer more of a challenge. Greens fees during the week are $26 in the mornings, $20 in the afternoons. Weekend rates are $37 in the morning and $27 after 2:00 P.M. Walkers aren't allowed until 2:00 P.M. on weekends during the summer months.

Shenvalee
9660 Fairway Drive, New Market
(540) 740-9930, (540) 740-3181
www.shenvalee.com
This course opened its first nine holes in 1927. The second nine, added later, is more difficult, with a creek wandering in and out of the course. In 1993–94 a third nine was built, giving a somewhat open feel to the gently rolling course. Several holes are longer than 400 yards, adding considerable difficulty. Both the Old-to-Creek and Miller-to-Old are 5,600-yard par 72 courses. The Creek-to-Miller is a 5,636-yard par 71. Greens fees range from $34 to $38, while carts are an additional $13 to $26. Walking is not permitted on the Miller course.

The Homestead
US 220, Hot Springs
(540) 839-7739, (800) 838-1766
www.thehomestead.com
The nation's oldest first tee is still in use at the Homestead resort in Hot Springs, near the late golf legend Sam Snead's estate. After generations of ownership by the Ingalls family, the resort is now run by Club Resorts Inc., the same folks who resurrected North Carolina's Pinehurst.

Of the resort's three courses, the Cascades is acknowledged as one of the best mountain layouts in the country and has hosted six USGA championships. The par 70 6,256-yard course has three of the prettiest finishing holes to be found anywhere, with a stream, two ponds, and a small waterfall adding challenge as well as beauty. There is room for daring shots on the par 4 10th and par 5 17th holes, but the short par 3 18th over water is definitely one of the most memorable.

The Homestead Course, dating back to the 1890s, is one of the state's oldest. It's easier to score on the shorter par 72 5,816-yard course, so this has become a favorite with the resort's overnight guests. Add in the 6,295-yard par 72 Lower Cascades, and there are 54 excellent holes at the Homestead. In fact, the Cascades is the only course in the state to be rated in the nation's top 100 by both *Golf Digest* (39th) and *Golf Magazine* (43rd).

Cart and greens fees range from $110 to $205 for resort guests. Those who just come for a round on the links will pay between $140 and $240. It's one price whether you walk or ride. Caddies are available. The Homestead's Golf Advantage School specializes in instruction to adults and children.

Stoneleigh
35271 Prestwick Court, Round Hill
(540) 338-4653
www.stoneleighgolf.com
Some say a round at Stoneleigh is like a trip across the Atlantic, thanks in part to its designer, Lisa Maki. Maki, who studied in Scotland, structured out the par 72, 6,709-yard course with a series of stone walls and sloping angles. In fact, a stone wall fronts the green on the much-talked-about No. 2 hole. The hole plays uphill to a very small green, but once you're there it's

worth it. You can look out on a 20-mile view of the northern Virginia suburbs. If you feel you're a pretty fair shotmaker, don't wait too long to try this course. Play is limited on the weekend, but open to the public anytime during the week. Guest fees are $45 Monday through Thursday and $55 Friday through Sunday and holidays. There is a limit of three guests per member on weekends and holidays. Carts alone are $14 per person.

Algonkian
47001 Fairway Drive, Sterling
(703) 450-4655
www.nvrpa.org
This long 7,015-yard course bordering the edge of the Potomac River is operated by the Northern Virginia Regional Park Authority. Designed by Ed Ault, the Loudoun County course plays like two entirely different nines. The front is flat and open. Because of its long spacious fairways, Algonkian remains one of the Metro area's most popular courses. (It's only 30 miles from Washington, D.C., and 15 miles from Tyson Corner.) Adding to the challenge is the tight tree-lined back nine, which requires careful shot placement. Greens fees will run $18.25 for 9 holes and $23.75 on weekends. For 18 holes, it's $28.00 to $37.00. Carts rent for $15.25 for two people. Along with the golf course, Algonkian's 800-acre park includes something for the whole family, including an outdoor swimming pool; 18 holes of miniature golf; a nature trail; 12 riverside vacation cottages; boat launch access to the Potomac River; and picnic areas.

Lansdowne Golf Club
44050 Woodbridge Parkway, Leesburg
(703) 729-4071
www.lansdowneresort.com
Designed by Robert Trent Jones Jr., Lansdowne has been called one of the finest courses in the Washington, D.C., area. The back nine cuts through woods and runs adjacent to the Potomac River. The par 3 17th hole over water is a standout. The forgiving front nine, with its lush zoysia

fairways, is more open. Cart and greens fees are $92 on weekdays and $105 on weekends. All golfers are required to take a cart.

Raspberry Falls Golf and Hunt Club
Highway 15, Leesburg
(703) 779-2555
www.raspberryfalls.com
You can get an idea of what it's like to play the deep bunkers found on British Open courses at Gary Player's signature designed course in Leesburg. The 7,200-yard par 72 course was built on an old hunt club property in 1996. Water comes into play on only two holes at Raspberry Falls, but stacked sod bunkers can make things challenging on all but one hole. Watch out for No. 18—this par 5 is a long 550-yard dogleg. Greens and cart fees are $76 Monday through Thursday and $96 on the weekends. Walking is allowed.

Birdwood Golf Course
200 Ednam Drive, Charlottesville
(434) 296-2181, (800) 476-1988
www.boarsheadinn.com/activities/birdwood
The Boar's Head Inn's golf course has challenged young golfers for years. In fact, Birdwood has been ranked one of the top 10 collegiate courses in America by *Golf Digest*. A favorite of orange-and-blue-clad University of Virginia students, the 18-hole par 72 course has also hosted the NCAA East Regional Golf Tournament, the National Ladies Public Links Championship, and the Virginia State Amateur Golf Championship. Designed by Lindsay Evans, this tough course has a demanding finish, including the par 3 No. 14 hole. It may be short, but the plush green sits right on an island. Once private, this 6,821-yard championship course is now open to the public. Birdwood offers individual instruction, group clinics, video swing analysis, a pro shop, and the "19th Hole" for food and beverages. Carts, $9.00 for 9 holes and $18.00 for 18, are mandatory before noon on weekends. Greens fees are $50 weekdays, $60 weekends, and $28 after 4:30 P.M.

Wintergreen Resort
Highway 151, Wintergreen
(434) 325-8250
www.wintergreenresort.com

This Nelson County resort is consistently ranked among the nation's top golf destinations. Wintergreen's Stoney Creek course was rated the 34th best in the country by *Golf Digest,* while Devils Knob has been picked as one of Virginia's top 10 best courses. In 1990 designer Rees Jones cut the ribbon on the Stoney Creek course, a 7,005-yard par 72 valley layout. This roomy 18-hole course features bold mounding, similar to what is found on many British courses. You will want to watch out for the 410-yard 4th hole. The par 4 plays pretty straight, but there is a water hazard just right of the green.

Jones returned to unveil the Tuckahoe Nine at Stoney Creek. It has already been hailed as the most challenging and beautiful of the Wintergreen courses. The look is a little different than Stoney Creek's original 18, with more elevated tees, greens, and water. The ninth hole is the longest at 586 yards, but the 457-yard par 4 first hole is the most elevated tee on the course and is bordered on the right side by a lake.

Devils Knob, the highest course in the state at 4,000 feet, was designed in the 1970s along a challenging yet surprisingly level mountain ridge. Golfers were offered a new look after renovations were completed in 2003. Devils Knob added 10 new forward tees, rebuilt 44 bunkers, and reshaped three greens. Because of its elevation, Devils Knob offers a comfortable 70- to 85-degree temperature in the spring and summer. Tree-lined fairways can be found throughout the 6,500-yard course. If you are hoping to make the par 70 on this 18-hole course, good luck with the 600-yard double dogleg on No. 7.

Greens fees and cart fees for both courses are $90 from Monday through Thursday and $100 on Friday through Saturday. You can play nine holes for $57 on weekdays and $67 on three-day weekends.

Ivy Hill Golf Club
1327 Ivy Hill Drive, Forest
(434) 525-2680
www.ivyhillgc.com

This championship course is a 6,147-yard, par 72 challenge. With the mountains as a backdrop, it's a very scenic course, but it's also quite hilly. Because of the terrain, the staff tries to discourage golfers from walking—however, the adventurous may hike the course with bag in tow after 2:00 P.M. on the weekends. Although the front nine is open, there still isn't room to spray the ball too much. The back nine is a lot tighter and truly a challenge if you play from the tips. The par 4, 500-yard 7th hole is a standout. A 285-yard tee shot should put you in a landing area with little more than 200 yards to get to the green. Just bend the ball a little right to left to get there. Cart and greens fees are $33 weekdays and $38 on the weekends.

London Downs
1614 New London Road, Forest
(434) 525-4653
www.londondowns.com

Another championship course, London Downs, is a par 72 public course measuring 6,347 yards. The course was designed over gently rolling hills, but take extra care when approaching No. 7. You will have to carry a water hazard on the 150-yard hole to make par in three shots. Greens fees are $22 during the week and $27 on weekends. Carts are an additional $12, but you may walk if you're up to a little exercise.

Ole Monterey Club
1112 Tinkercreek Lane, Roanoke
(540) 563-0400

A public course built in 1926, Ole Monterey was designed by golfing legend Fred Findlay. The 6,623-yard par 71 layout is solid, and the holes are challenging. A long par 4 on No. 11 gives a view of what's in store. This uphill hole plays 410 yards from the white tees with a straightaway 425 from the blues. Greens and cart fees are $20 during the week and $35 on weekends. If your tee time is after 11:00

A.M. on Saturday and Sunday, the cost drops to $25. Nine holes will run $18 during the week and $20 on the weekend. During the summer months, walking is not allowed on weekends until after 3:00 P.M.

Countryside Club
1 Countryside Road, Roanoke
(540) 563-0391
www.countrysidegolfclub.com
A generally forgiving, open layout, this course features several difficult par 3s. One particularly difficult par 3 is the downhill No. 16 over water. Most of the generous land area over the gently rolling hills makes it an enjoyable 6,018-yard par 71 course. Weekend greens and cart fees are $40. It's $30 if you can go during the week. Before 11:00 A.M. on weekends and holidays, a cart is mandatory.

Blue Hills
2001 Blue Hills, Roanoke
(540) 344-7848
The price is right and the scenery is beautiful at this public Roanoke course. This par 71, 6,500-yard course is nestled in the mountains with gently rolling hills The 450-yard No. 12 is the signature hole here, with a sharp dogleg left with plenty of water to make things interesting. During the week, you can play a round for $35, $25 if you start after 2:00 P.M. On Friday through Sunday rates are slightly higher at $38 and $30, respectively. Blue Hills does offer twilight specials.

Hanging Rock
1500 Red Lane Extension, Salem
(540) 389-7275, (800) 277-7497
www.hangingrockgolf.com
With so many rolling hills, some have dubbed Hanging Rock a "roller coaster of elevation changes." No hole probably illustrates the moniker better than its signature par 4 No. 5. You start out with a tee shot from high above, follow up with a midrange second stroke, but then you have a decision to make. There are two greens. One is a straightaway shot, but it's straight uphill.

All you can see is the flag on this blind shot. Your other option is the green that is flanked by water on three sides. In fact the entire 18-hole par 72 course designed by Russell Breeden is surrounded by streams, boulders, and trees, not to mention a superb view of the mountains. Seventy-five different tees allow you to play Hanging Rock anywhere from 4,691 yards to 6,828. The course was named one of the top three courses in Virginia by *The Golfers Guide* readers survey. Fees are $42.50 on weekends, $25.50 if you play after 11:00 A.M. On weekdays the cost is $36.50 and $31.50, or any day of the week only $25.00 if you tee off after 3:00 P.M. Walkers are allowed on weekdays and late Saturday afternoons, but you probably won't want to try.

Draper Valley
2800 Big Valley Drive, Draper
(540) 980-4653
www.drapervalleygolf.com
Draper Valley is one of the golfing jewels in the southwestern portion of the state. Long hitters have been coming here in droves, with more than 35,000 rounds of golf played here each year. Tom McKnight, a 44-year-old golfer from nearby Galax, honed his talents here. In 1998 a national television audience watched the three-time Virginia State Amateur champion advance to the finals of the U.S. Amateur in upstate New York. He had plenty of opportunity to practice his big ball at Draper Valley. Stretching out to 7,046 yards, this par 72 course designed by Harold Louthern features wide fairways and large greens with picturesque mountain backdrops. Since it was built over farmland, there are not many trees, but there are a number of blind spots with holes playing downhill or back up on the mountainside. No. 9 is a gem with a scenic overlook of the lake and mountains, but the true test comes on all the par 3s with more than 190 yards from tee to green. Greens fees range from $19 to $30, with cart rental at $15.

Westlake
360 Chestnut Creek Drive, Hardy
(540) 721-4214
www.golfthewestlake.com
Golfers can test their skills at Westlake. Designed by Russell Breeden, Westlake is a par 72 course. Hilly and narrow, the 5,878-yard course is quite challenging, especially the last hole. No. 18 is a long par 4 dogleg right to left that ends with a water hazard right next to the green. Greens fees and carts are $36 from 8:00 A.M. to noon Monday through Thursday, $26 after noon, $21 after 4:00 P.M. Weekends are $41 to $46 before noon. Walking is allowed in the late afternoon.

HIKING

It almost goes without saying that Virginia is a hiker's paradise. *Walking* magazine named the Skyline Drive and Blue Ridge Parkway two of the country's most scenic routes leading to national park trails. And that is only the beginning.

It would be difficult to give a comprehensive list of hikes, but we can give you a small sampling. You might like the most popular and easily accessible, or perhaps you're drawn to the more remote in the rural parts of the state. We have thousands of trails crossing over diverse terrain, enough to fill several books. In fact, many good reference books have already been written on the subject. Among them, we recommend *Hiking Shenandoah National Park* by Bert and Jane Gildart, *Walking the Blue Ridge* by Leonard M. Adkins, *Hiking Virginia* by Bill and Mary Burnham, and *Hiking Virginia's National Forests* by Karin Wuertz-Schaefer.

---

i *When hiking, cycling, or taking on any outdoor activity, make sure to take plenty of water, even in cooler weather, as the rugged terrain can dehydrate you quickly. A good amount is two quarts per person per day.*

The folks at area camping and outdoor stores can be enormously helpful in trip planning. **Blue Ridge Mountain Sports** in Charlottesville, (434) 977-4400, not only carries a plethora of hiking and camping guides, but their hiking and camping experts organize trips every year. Other camping outfitters include **Rockfish Gap Outfitters** in Waynesboro, (540) 943-1461, **Blue Ridge Outdoors** in Roanoke, (540) 774-4311, and **Outdoor Trails Co.** in Lynchburg, (434) 386-4302.

Here's a selection of hiking opportunities in or near the Blue Ridge.

Appalachian Trail

Conservationist Benton MacKaye had a dream in 1921: to construct a hiking trail that would continuously connect the states along the Appalachian Mountain chain. His proposed "experiment in regional planning" was begun in 1922 and completed in 1937. This famous trail traverses 2,100 miles and 14 states from Georgia to Maine. In 1948 the first hiker walked the entire trail; today about 100 hikers every year complete the walk. The entire hike takes four to six months to finish.

Impressively, more than 500 miles of the Appalachian Trail (AT)—about a quarter of its total distance—wind through Virginia. The portion of the trail that runs through the Shenandoah National Park, starting in Front Royal and ending at Rockfish Gap at I-64, is considered by veteran hikers to be one of its most beautiful sections. The trail also passes through the Mount Rogers National Recreation Area, a spectacular stretch of land in southwest Virginia that includes the state's two highest peaks.

Hikers can find countless access points to the state's 500 miles of Appalachian Trail, and a variety of trips, daylong or much longer, can be planned around the trail. Perhaps the best guides to the AT are published by the Appalachian Trail Conference, the governing body of the trail. The organization puts out guidebooks to every section of the trail, complete with maps and access points. Four of these books are devoted to the Virginia-area trails: *Appalachian Trail Guide for the Shenandoah National Park, Appalachian Trail Guide for Southwest Virginia, Appalachian Trail Guide for Northern Virginia and Maryland,* and *Appalachian Trail Guide for Central Virginia.* Except for the Shenandoah National Park guide, the books do not cover side trails. These guides are available at many outdoor outfitters.

A large section of the AT in Virginia (from the Shenandoah National Park north) is maintained by the Potomac Appalachian Trail Club. For information about this section of the AT, contact the club at 118 Park Street SE, Vienna 22180, (703) 242-0315 or visit www.patc.net. The southern portions of the AT in Virginia are maintained and promoted by eight different trail clubs; for more information on these clubs and their coverage areas, contact the Appalachian Trail Conference headquarters at P.O. Box 807, Harpers Ferry, WV 25425-0807, (304) 535-6331. You can also visit www.appalachian trail.org.

Shenandoah National Park and the Skyline Drive

The Shenandoah National Park is a narrow park that follows along the Blue Ridge Mountains for almost 75 miles. Its 194,327 acres contain about 100 miles of the Appalachian Trail and 421 miles of other hiking paths. These range from rugged climbs up steep, rocky terrain to easy nature trails with interpretive guideposts. The Limberlost Trail was completed to give easy access to baby strollers and wheelchairs. (See the Blue Ridge Parkway and Skyline Drive chapter for more information.)

Excellent hiking maps and trail guides to the Shenandoah National Park are avail-

able at both visitor centers and entrance stations on the Skyline Drive and by mail from the Shenandoah National Park, 3655 U.S. Highway 211 E, Luray, (540) 999-3582, www.snpbooks.org.

The Shenandoah National Park and the Skyline Drive begin at Front Royal and end at Rockfish Gap just east of Waynesboro. A few of the unique day hikes in the park are described below.

Fox Hollow Nature Trail
Mile 4.6, Skyline Drive
Park in the Dickey Ridge Visitor Center to take this 1.2-mile circuit hike. This trail passes by the remnants of the Fox Family homesite—a walled cemetery, the family's house, a concrete-enclosed spring, and an old mill stone—a reminder of the displaced residents who once lived on this mountain before the government decided to build the drive. (The ruins of nearly 5,000 farm buildings can be found throughout the park.)

White Oak Canyon Falls
Mile 42.6, Skyline Drive
This is a popular and pleasant trail to the second-highest falls (86 feet) in the park. The 4.6-mile round-trip hike starts easily crossing the Limberlost Trail. The trail grows steeper as it enters the canyon. From a rock outcropping you will find a perfect view of the falls spilling over the canyon ledge. You may continue on to see five more falls, ranging from 35 to 62 feet, but the trail becomes steep and narrow and adds an additional 2.7 miles to your trip.

Big Meadows
Mile 51.3, Skyline Drive
Big Meadows, one of the few large treeless fields in the park, is great for hiking. Depending upon the season, you'll find wildflowers here that don't grow in the woods and strawberries and blueberries along the path. This is also an excellent place to see a diversity of wildlife, since many animals depend on this grassy area for sustenance. This is a 132-acre meadow,

the largest of its kind in the park, so you may wander until your heart's content.

Old Rag
Highway 600, near Nethers

To reach one of the park's most celebrated peaks, you have to leave the Skyline Drive and hike back in. There are two ways to get to the summit, but both start outside the park. A 7.2-mile circuit hike starts at the parking lot at Weakley Hollow Fire Road. Follow the blue blazes along the Ridge Trail. This is a steep and strenuous climb over, around, and between granite boulders, but it is also the most interesting because of these unique obstacles. These narrow rock-walled corridors are the remains of the dikes through which lava flowed 700 million years ago. If you don't mind a longer walk, you can avoid the boulders on your trip back to the car by taking the Saddle Trail to the Weakley Hollow Fire Road.

A second and easier climb to the summit is the 5.4-mile hike starting at Berry Hollow parking lot. Just follow the fire road to the Saddle Trail. This too is a steep climb, but you will bypass the boulders in the other hike. There are two shelters and a spring along this route. Please note, due to the popularity of this hike, there is a fee of $5.00 per person. The number of visitors per day is limited to 200 cars. No pets are allowed.

Blue Ridge Parkway

Rockfish Gap is the gateway to the Blue Ridge Parkway, the 469-mile-long scenic route that passes through the Cherokee Indian Reservation in North Carolina. The National Park Service maintains dozens of trails near the Parkway that are highly accessible, even for the laziest of walkers. But if you have the energy, you can hike through tunnels of rhododendron leading to rushing waterfalls or out to soaring peaks covered with mountain laurel and spruce.

Hiking in these mountains also provides a glimpse of what life was like for early settlers. It's not uncommon to stumble upon the crumbling rock foundation of an old cabin or a stone wall that used to keep in livestock. The ridges and valleys were inhabited by a few hardy souls when the Park Service began to obtain land for the Parkway decades ago.

Many trails lead to farms and communities that have been reconstructed by the Park Service. For instance, at the Mountain Farm Trail near Humpback Rocks (close to Charlottesville) you might see a ranger posing as a grandma and churning butter on the front porch of an old cabin, while brother John plucks a handmade dulcimer nearby.

Many interpretive programs are offered by the Park Service along Blue Ridge Parkway trails. Rangers conduct guided walks during the heaviest tourist months, talking about everything from endangered plants to old-time farming methods.

Most Blue Ridge Parkway trails are well marked and easy to find. However, Parkway maps are available at the visitor centers such as the one at Humpback Rocks. Write to the National Park Service, Blue Ridge Parkway, 199 Hemphill Knob. Asheville, NC 28803-8686, or call (828) 298–0398 or (828) 271–4779 or visit them at www.nps.gov/blri.

Here is a sample of some of the day hikes along or near the Blue Ridge Parkway. (See the Blue Ridge Parkway and Skyline Drive chapter for more hikes.)

Mountain Farm Trail
Mile 5.8

This quarter-mile-long trail along the Parkway is an easy, self-guiding route that begins at the Humpback Rocks Visitor Center, not too far from Charlottesville. It passes log cabins, chicken houses, and a mountaineer's garden, reminders of the everyday life of the Blue Ridge's former inhabitants.

Humpback Rocks Trail
Mile 6.1

This is a steep and rocky section of the Appalachian Trail that can be reached from the Mountain Farm Trail described previously. Then it's a strenuous 4-mile hike to the summit of Humpback Mountain, from which you can see Rockfish Gap and the Shenandoah National Park to the north, the Shenandoah Valley to the west, and the Rockfish River Valley to the east. In late spring, mountain laurel and azaleas make this a colorful, fragrant hike.

Peaks of Otter
Mile 87, Sharp Top
An ever-popular hike, you will find spectacular views from the top of this steep 1.5-mile climb in all directions (elevation is 3,875 feet). A shuttle bus provides service to the top of Sharp Top, for a fee. Sharp Top and its sister peak, Flat Top (elevation 4,001 feet), form the Peaks of Otter and the headwaters of Otter River.

Rock Castle Gorge Trail
Mile 168.8
This 10.8-mile strenuous loop in northern Patrick County is noted for its high meadows, sweeping views, waterfalls, and historical sites en route to the 3,572-foot summit of Rocky Knob. Along the way, you'll see a log shelter built by the CCC in the 1930s and old Rock Castle Pike, a pioneer road for wagons and carriages. Also keep an eye out for the 12-acre jumble of boulders called Bear Rocks, a haven for wildlife. Until the 1920s a mountain community thrived in this rugged area, where the rushing waters of Rock Castle Creek fueled sawmills and gristmills. This hike is one of several in the 4,200-acre Rocky Knob Recreation Area, which has a Park Service visitor center, campground, picnic areas, and rustic rental cabins.

George Washington and Jefferson National Forests

If you would like to hike any of the trails in the George Washington and Jefferson National Forests, you should have a map. These trails are used less than the Parkway trails and are not as well maintained.

All told there is a total of 2,000 miles of hiking trails on 1.8 million acres in Virginia's national forests. While many popular hikes are within easy reach, others are very difficult to get to. Your only access may be down dirt roads. Some trails may even require a little bushwhacking.

For a map of the George Washington or the Jefferson section write to Forest Headquarters, 5162 Valleypointe Parkway, Roanoke 24109-3050, or call (540) 265-5100, (888) 265-0019, or visit www.southernregion.fs.fed.us/gwj/.

Don't forget to yield. When hiking, give uphill hikers and horseback riders the right of way. On the water, nonpowered sailboats have the right of way in most circumstances. ℹ️

Massanutten Visitor Center
Highway 211, New Market Gap
(540) 740-8310
The Lee Ranger District has six paved, accessible trails that are half a mile or less in length, located between Front Royal and Harrisonburg. Another option is the 6.8 mile Massanutten Trail–Scothorn Gap Loop Hike, which starts a short distance up the road from the visitor center. The trail allows you to "scramble" to the top of a section of the very long ridge of Massanutten Mountain for an impressive view. The visitor center is open daily from April to October and weekends only until mid-November, when it closes for the winter.

Sherando Lake Recreation Area
96 Sherando Lake Road, Lyndhurst
(540) 942-5965
Most of the action at Sherando Lake takes place between the two lakes at this popular family campground in Augusta County. But for the landlubber, there are plenty of trails to choose from. The Blue Loop Trail to

Torry Ridge and the White Rock Falls trails are recommended for experienced hikers. Blue Loop and Torry Ridge combine for a steep 3-mile circuit hike. White Rock Gap is a little more moderate 2.5-mile climb that will lead you to the Blue Ridge Parkway and is good for family day hikes. The day use fee is $6.00 per car with two people, $8.00 per car with three or more.

Crabtree Falls Trail
Off Highway 56 near Montebello
Just off the Parkway, this 3-mile hike in Nelson County leads to the highest cascading falls in Virginia. Its trailhead is a parking lot on Highway 56, a few miles east of Montebello. Five major and several smaller waterfalls tumble down the mountain for a total of 1,200 feet. There are many overlooks along the way. You can see the Tye River Valley from the highest overlook at the upper falls. Hikers are advised to stay on the trails and off the slippery rocks. Fee is $3.00 per vehicle.

Cascades National Recreation Trail
Highway 623, near Pembroke
(540) 552-4641
West of Blacksburg you'll find wonderful hikes on the Appalachian Trail and in other recreation areas. One excellent 2-mile day hike follows Little Stoney Creek, which takes you to the 66-foot Cascades waterfall. Be aware, it will take you 4 miles, round-trip. The Civilian Conservation Corps constructed this beautiful trail in the 1930s. It's well maintained, with benches along the creek and pretty wooden bridges. During the summer the pathway is lush and heavily shaded, a perfect place to cool off. You can also take a dip in the clear mountain pool at the base of the falls. To get there, go to Pembroke, then take the road marked Cascades Recreation Area just east of the Dairy Queen on US 460.

Children's Forest Trail
In the National Children's Forest off
Highway 351, Covington
The Children's Forest Trail is a paved loop trail that begins and ends in the monument area of the National Children's forest. This is a universally accessible trail, good for strollers and wheelchairs. On April 27, 1971, an arsonist's fire blackened 1,176 acres in this part of the James River District of the National Forest. The area was planted on the 150th anniversary of Arbor Day in April of 1972 by children from all over the eastern United States. The names of the children who participated in the tree planting are stored in a time capsule scheduled to be opened in 2072. There is also a monument dedicated to the children at the trailhead near the time capsule.

The trail begins behind the monument and loops through a small portion of the forest. Many different plants such as grapevine, various oaks, and greenbrier grow here, as well as shortleaf pine planted by the children and a few scattered oaks. This walk should take 10 to 15 minutes to complete.

State Parks

The Blue Ridge's state parks offer great hiking opportunities. Some of our favorites are described here. For more information on state parks, call (800) 933-PARK, or go online to www.dcr.state.va.us.

Sky Meadows State Park
11012 Edmonds Lane, Delaplane
(540) 592-3556
The easily accessible Sky Meadows in Fauquier County, just outside Paris, was once a working Piedmont plantation. Its 1,863 acres along the eastern slope of the Blue Ridge entice weekend warriors with its maze of hiking trails, including a 3.6-mile stretch of the Appalachian Trail. The park has six hiking trails all together, from less than 1 mile to almost 2 miles long. There is a 1-mile nature trail. Pets are allowed but must be kept on a leash no longer than 6 feet. (See our Kidstuff chapter for more information.)

Douthat State Park
Highway 1, Millboro
(540) 862-8100
Douthat State Park, which spans Bath and Alleghany Counties, has 40 miles of wooded hiking trails from the long 4.5-mile Stony Run to the short one-quarter-mile Buck Lick Trail. Buck Lick was constructed by the Civilian Conservation Corps in the '30s and has 17 interpretive signs about geological features, trees, wild animals, lichens, and forest succession.

With 4,493 acres of scenic high ridges, Douthat has more miles of hiking trails than almost any other state park. The park's trails are color-coded and generally in good condition. A hiking map from the visitor center is recommended for long hikes. There is a $2.00 fee, $3.00 on weekends, for parking.

Smith Mountain Lake State Park and Visitor Center
Highway 626, Huddleston
(540) 297-6066
This 1,506-acre park is not just for water enthusiasts, although it's a great place for swimming at the beach area, paddleboating (rentals available), and boating. The park also offers camping, picnicking, a visitor center, interpretive programs, and 4.5 miles of hiking trails. Try out the three-bedroom cabin or one of the 19 two-bedroom cabins—some even have their own boat docks. An annual event held in May and gaining in popularity is the Smith Mountain Lake Triathlon. Parking is $3.00, $4.00 on the weekend.

New River Trail State Park & Shot Tower
176 Orphanage Drive, Foster Falls
(276) 699-6778
Following the course of the historic New River, this linear park is a 57-mile trail running from Galax to Pulaski, with more than 40 miles along the New River. The trail is now linked to other regional trails, creating a 132-mile network for hiking, biking, and horseback riding. There are several convenient parking areas and access points along its route. The southern terminus is on East Stuart Drive (Highway 58) in Galax. Parking fee is $3.00 on weekends, $2.00 on weekdays.

Others

Highland Wildlife Management Area
Off Highway 615, Highland County
(540) 468-2550
In Highland County, best known for its annual Maple Festival (see our Annual Events and Festivals chapter for details), you'll find endless possibilities for hiking in a 14,283-acre wilderness area that includes three tracks of land, Jack Mountain, Bull Pasture Mountain, and Little Doe Hill. One option is a strenuous 5-mile hike up an old fire road to 4,400-foot Sounding Knob, the best-known landmark in the county. The mountaintop has a grazed open area and splendid views. Sounding Knob Trail begins at the junction of Highway 615 and the Buck Hill Road, established by the Civilian Conservation Corps.

Goshen Pass Natural Area Preserve
Rockbridge County
(540) 265-5234
www.dcr.state.va.us.dnh
In 2002 the 936 acres of Goshen Pass in Rockbridge County was designated as a State Natural Area Preserve. There are several hikes here and along the larger Little North Mountain Wildlife Management Area that adjoins the preserve. The Wildlife Management area covers roughly 34,000 acres in both Rockbridge and Augusta Counties along Highway 39. The alluring hikes offer solitude and scenic views of the Maury River, a narrow steep-sided gorge, and forests of oak, pine, and hickory as well as an abundant array of flora and fauna of the adjacent Little North, Forge, and Hogback Mountains. Your best access is at a trailhead parking area at the swinging bridge near the northwest corner of the preserve. One of the most popular is a short hike that follows the river for about a half mile from

the bridge. There is also a 3-mile loop that follows Goshen Pass Trail up to Chambers Ridge, then heads northwest back to the bridge on Hunter's Trail. Guy's Run Trail (4.2 miles) and Little North Mountain Trail (12.8 miles) also should be easy to find.

Chessie Nature Trail
Off North Main Street, Lexington
(540) 463-3777

Linking historic Lexington with Buena Vista, this 7 miles of old Chesapeake and Ohio railroad grade is now owned and maintained by the Virginia Military Institute Foundation. The flat, easy path offers glimpses of the Maury River and is bordered by wildflowers in the spring. From U.S. Highway 11 in Lexington, turn on Old Buena Vista Road and go 1 mile. Informal parking is available along the side of the road, or stop by the visitor center in Lexington for directions daily from 9:00 A.M. to 6:00 P.M.

Ivy Creek Natural Area
Earlysville Road, Charlottesville
(434) 973-7772
www.avenue.org/icf

The 215-acre Ivy Creek Natural Area is an unspoiled stretch of forest, streams, and fields traversed only by footpaths. A network of 6 miles of trails includes self-guided ones. Ivy Creek is 2 miles north of the city. The area is open daily from 7:00 A.M. to dark. A one-story building was constructed in 1997 for indoor educational programs. There is a three-quarter-mile paved trail for those with special needs.

Ragged Mountain Natural Area
Reservoir Road, Charlottesville
(434) 973-7772
www.avenue.org/icf/RMNA

This 980-acre preserve opened in 1999, offering even more wilderness to the metropolitan city of Charlottesville. Managed by the city, Albemarle County, and the Ivy Creek Foundation, this land is filled with a forest of mature trees, two lakes, and 4 miles of shoreline. Outdoor enthusiasts will be challenged by 7 miles of rugged

trails, including the Main Trail, Peninsula Trail, and Upper Lake Trail. The preserve is open from 7:00 A.M. to dusk, but foundation members warn that hiking the often-steep trails may take between two and three hours. Make sure you allow enough time to make the trek before dark.

Rivanna Trails
Various locations, Charlottesville
(434) 923-9022
www.avenue.org/rivanna

In 1992 the Rivanna Trails Foundation started to create a trail system around the Rivanna River and its tributaries. The goal of the foundation is to build a trail encircling Charlottesville, and following the river and Meadow and Moore's Creeks. The 18 miles of the trail is almost complete and can provide a nice hiking experience close to town. While at times you're not but a few hundred feet from homes or roads, the trail provides a satisfying retreat into a natural setting. Along these community-wide trails, you will pass your neighbors out for a stroll with their dog, joggers, and bird-watchers. More than 90 species of birds have been identified along the trails, including warblers, herons, woodpeckers, owls, and hawks. The Greenbelt is one of the most popular sections for hikers, bikers, runners, and dog walkers. This paved 1.5-mile flat stretch also offers scenic views of the Rivanna River and is wheelchair accessible. It's located in Riverview Park, just off Riverside Avenue.

HORSEBACK RIDING

If you're unable—or unwilling—to explore these mountains on foot, by all means get on a horse, even if it's your very first time. You'll find that your mount is an amiable companion as well as a comfortable means to get to places you'd otherwise miss. If you squint your eyes just right, you can imagine you're an early frontiersman scouting the uncharted Blue Ridge wilderness. Experienced equestrians do it all the time—trailering their horses to state parks or national forests for a day or weekend of riding.

Several equestrian outfitters (particularly in the Shenandoah Valley) offer one- or two-hour rides for beginners, half- or full-day treks for the more experienced, and a variety of overnight trips, though steep insurance premiums are causing more outfitters to just focus on beginners.

You can rough it and camp beside a trout stream, grilling fresh trout over a campfire and listening to the whippoorwills at sunset. Or you can say good night to your horse at day's end and retire to a cozy country inn. Several inns specialize in guided trail riding, and most horse outfitters offer packages with nearby inns so that you can soak in a hot tub after a long day's ride (see our Bed-and-Breakfasts and Country Inns chapter). In this section, we list places that offer guided horseback trips to the public. The Blue Ridge also has many private liveries and horse clubs and a plethora of trails, both public and private.

Maintree Farm
4024 Thomas Mill, Leesburg
(703) 777-3279
www.hometown.aol.com/maintree
This boarding and training operation offers guests a rare opportunity to enjoy prime hunt country. The stable, across from the Loudoun Hunt kennels, takes out a mock hunt most Sunday mornings—a delightful two-hour ride. During fox-hunting season, the owners can arrange riding to the hounds with the Loudoun Hunt. If partner Beth Destanley rides out with you, ask her how she became one of the country's leading female steeplechase riders.

Group lessons are $30 per hour, and private lessons run $45 an hour. Though the stable caters to all levels, only experienced equestrians should expect to ride over fences. Reservations are required.

Marriott Ranch
5305 Marriott Lane, Hume
(540) 364-3741, (540) 364-2627
www.marriottranch.com
This 4,200-acre beef cattle ranch, owned and operated by Marriott International, is home to one of the largest Western trail-ride operations on the East Coast. Rides are usually 1.5 hours long and are available every day of the week except Monday. Rides go out at 10:00 A.M., noon, and 2:00 P.M. Tuesday through Sunday. Rates are $32.50 per person on weekdays and $35.00 on weekends; group rates are available. The minimum riding age is 10. The trails run through winding streams, open valleys, and wooded hills on the ranch.

Fort Valley Riding Stable
299 South Fort Valley Road, Fort Valley
(540) 933-6633, (888) 754-5771
www.fortvalleystable.com
Nestled in the middle of the Massanutten Mountains is scenic Fort Valley and the Fort Valley Stables and Horse and Mule Camp. Horseback riding is $33 per hour, $95 for a half-day guided trip, and $135 for an all-day trip that lasts about seven hours. The half- and full-day rides include lunch on the trail.

Shenandoah National Park
Skyland Stables, Milepost 42.5
(540) 999-2210, (800) 778-2851
www.nps.gov
There are 150 miles of trail open to horseback riders in the Shenandoah National Park. You may bring your own horse for a day ride or sign up for a guided trail ride at Skyland Stables. An hour-long ride costs $20 to $22, while you can take a longer 2.5-mile morning ride for $42. Pony rides also are available for youngsters. A 15-minute ride is $3.00, while a 30-minute ride costs $6.00. Tours go out from the park's Skyland Lodge daily from April through

Bring your binoculars! More than 200 species of birds have been identified in the Shenandoah National Park, including the common raven, barn owl, red-tailed hawk, turkey vulture, and scarlet tanager.

November, but the longer ride is held only on weekdays. If you want to saddle up, you must book a tour a day in advance. If you are bringing your own horse, the yellow blaze trails are open for riders.

Graves Mountain Lodge
Off Highway 670, Syria
(540) 923-4231
www.gravesmountain.com
This family-owned and -operated retreat has a heritage of hospitality dating back more than 135 years. Practice does make perfect, for the rustic mountain lodge has the right mix of life's simple pleasures (see our Bed-and-Breakfasts and Country Inns chapter). Porch-sitting ranks right up there with hiking, fishing, and swimming, especially after you've spent the day wildlife-watching from horseback.

The Lodge offers a variety of trips from one hour to overnight trail rides. You must be at least 8 years old and 4 feet tall to ride. Prices are $25 an hour, $65 for a half day, or $125 for a full day. There is also a working cattle package. Pony rides are offered for those too young to trail-ride, for $5.00.

Special times at the lodge are the April Spring Fling Festival, the June Festival of Music, and the October Apple Harvest Festival (see our Annual Events and Festivals chapter).

Jordan Hollow Farm Inn
326 Hawksbill Park Road, Stanley
(540) 778-2285, (888) 418-7000
www.jordanhollow.com
This is a wonderful vacation spot for horse lovers. The 145-acre farm is nestled in a secluded hollow between the Massanutten and Blue Ridge mountain ranges, 6 miles south of Luray. You can spend the night in one of the country inn's 15 rooms, dine on "American regional" cuisine, and ride horses through lovely meadows or woods. The Jordan Hollow Stables offer one-hour rides for $25 (at 10:30 A.M. and 2:30 P.M.) and one-and-a-half-hour rides for $35 (at 12:30 and 4:30 P.M.). Children must be 7 or older.

Horse owners are invited to stable their horses at Jordan Hollow Stables for $15

per night and enjoy the many miles of scenic trails on the farm. The innkeepers will guide these rides or lay out a trail course for experienced riders.

Mountaintop Ranch
1030 Mountaintop Ranch Road, Elkton
(540) 298-9542
www.mountaintopranch.com
The folks at this mountaintop ranch between Shenandoah and Elkton are surrounded on three sides by the Shenandoah National Park. Trails lace more than 3,000 acres of unspoiled meadows and forest land. Rides last anywhere from one hour to all day and cost $25 per person for the shortest trip, $50 for a two-hour ride. Other options include a half-day trip for $70. The full-day $125 rides include lunch and usually run about six hours. Groups of 10 or more receive a discount.

Woodstone Meadows Stable
2176 Saddle Trail, McGaheysville
(540) 289-6152
In the Shenandoah Valley across from Massanutten Resort, this outfit offers leisurely trail rides in the Massanutten Mountains. Everyone receives basic instructions before taking off on the trail. Five one-hour guided trail rides leave daily if weather permits. The 4:00 P.M. ride is dropped in the fall and winter. The cost is $30 per person, but you need to make reservations one to two days in advance. Riders must be at least 10 years old and be 4 feet 8 inches tall. The maximum weight is 240 pounds.

Wintergreen Resort-Rodes Farm Stables
Highway 613, Nellysford
(434) 325-8260
Guided trail rides in the mountains and Rockfish Valley are offered daily except Wednesday from mid-March through November. The activities include pony rides for kids, sunset trail rides through Rockfish Valley, riding lessons, horsemanship classes, and private rides for advanced riders.

Trail rides (English tack only) last an hour and 15 minutes. Pony rides (Western tack only) cost $14. Trail rides are $46, but you can arrange a private ride for $60. A riding lesson will run you about $37. Reservations are required. (For more information on Wintergreen, see our Resorts chapter.)

River Ridge Ranch
Highway 1, Box 119-1, Millboro
(540) 996-4148
www.ridetheridge.com

This 377-acre ranch about 10 miles from the Homestead in Bath County offers English or Western guided trail rides through unspoiled forests and fields. There's a spectacular view of the Cowpasture River Valley from one of the trails, and riders can count on seeing wildlife during any of the rides. Fees are $35 for an hour's ride or $100 for a half-day ride with lunch.

Highly popular are the Saturday night haywagon rides and cookouts atop River Ridge Mountain. We're not talking hot dogs on a clothes hanger, but New York strip steaks, barbecued chicken, or fresh mountain trout grilled over a campfire. Prices are $27.50 for adults, $12.00 for children.

River Ridge Ranch has one log cabin that sleeps eight with four safari-style tents. The ranch can accommodate 12 guests, who have access to fishing and swimming in the Cowpasture River as well as hiking. Cabins rent for $150 per night, double occupancy. Tents are $125 per night for double occupancy. All rates include a full country breakfast. River Ridge is open from April 1 to Thanksgiving.

The Homestead
US 220, Hot Springs
(540) 839-5500, (800) 838-1766
www.thehomestead.com

Guided trail rides are among the many activities offered at this highly acclaimed resort in Bath County. There are more than 100 miles of trails through beautiful mountain terrain and alongside the resort's golf courses. The riding master can accommodate either English- or Western-style riders. Guided rides are $95 an hour, $75 for groups. Rides depart the historic stables across from the hotel from 9:00 A.M. to 4:00 P.M. Reservations are necessary. Children who are at least 4 feet tall are welcome. (See our Resorts chapter for more on the Homestead.)

Virginia Mountain Outfitters
55 Lost Creek Lane, Buena Vista
(540) 261-1910

Outfitter Deborah Sensabaugh and her horses stay busy year-round on a variety of trips in the Blue Ridge and Allegheny Mountains. Half-day trail rides cover about 10 miles of mountain trails and include a noon lunch or afternoon tea.

The farm's main focus is offering guided one-, two-, and three-hour rides through mountain views, meadows, forests, and the meandering Sheep Creek. It's here by a lacy waterfall that you will stop for lunch.

Whether you prefer fox hunting or taking a mule on a long excursion, Lost Creek Farm can tailor an afternoon to suit your taste. There is even a summer horse camp for both young and old. If you are just beginning, lessons are available for $20 an hour.

The more advanced riders may want to saddle up when Sensabaugh heads out on two- to three-day camping adventures to explore new areas. Since Virginia Mountain Outfitters is not a licensed horseback provider with the National Forest, they are not allowed to charge fees for these longer trips. You are invited to ride along when the group is going out. Donations are accepted to go toward the expense of the trip.

HUNTING

A fellow once commented that he hunted to feed his body and his soul. In the Blue Ridge of Virginia, no hunter goes hungry.

As expected, wildlife is concentrated around farmland or other areas where there is food. With much of the Blue Ridge comprised of the 1.5 million acres of the George Washington and Jefferson National Forests and state lands, food for wildlife is abundant.

HUNTING LICENSES

Residents

    Age 16 and older, to hunt anywhere, statewide: $12.00

    To hunt in your city or county: $5.00

    Lifetime license: $10.00 to $250.00, depending upon age

Nonresidents

    To hunt anywhere, statewide: $80

    Three-day trip license: $40

    Lifetime license: $500

Other types of licenses or fees

    Annual permit for the National Forest: $3.00

    Stamps are required to hunt migratory birds: $5.00 to $15.00

Maps of the forests are sold through their regional offices listed at the end of this section. Ask about hunting regulations, license outlets, and seasons and bag limits for the particular county you plan to visit.

Hunting is allowed in designated areas of five Virginia state parks, including Fairy Stone, Grayson Highlands, and Hungry Mother. Special resource management hunts are held in James River and Smith Mountain Lake state parks. Also in Patrick County, **Primland Hunting Reserve** in Claudville, a half hour south of the Blue Ridge Parkway, is a well-known hunting preserve of 14,000 acres specializing in birds, deer, and even sporting clays. Call Rick Hill at (276) 251-8012 for details. Guides and dogs are available.

Managed hunts: One of the managed hunts in Virginia is the **C. F. Phelps WMA Deer Hunt for the Disabled.** Two permanently disabled hunters are chosen per day for this Fauquier County hunt during archery, muzzle-loading, and regular firearms seasons. Applications must be sent to the Virginia Department of Game and Inland Fisheries, attention Hogue Tract Hunt, 1320 Belman Road, Fredericksburg 22401. For details, call (804) 367-1000.

The Blue Ridge is home to most of the top counties for hunting in Virginia. Latest statistics from the Department of Game and Inland Fisheries show that Northern Virginia ranks at the top for deer harvests.

Fauquier County was first with 8,034 deer in 2003, while Loudoun was third with 7,522. A record 1,510 black bears were harvested in 2003, with Rockingham County leading the way with 133. Although the fall turkey season was down, Botetourt tied for first with 265 birds harvested. Bedford was No. 1 in the spring season with 532.

Whether you're going on your own or signing up with a hunting lodge, you're going to need a valid license, which can be obtained through clerks of circuit courts and other authorized agents (see listings in this section). Licenses and permits are good from July 1 through June 30. Hunting seasons and bag limits are set by the Virginia Department of Game and Inland Fisheries and vary according to county. Some counties are off-limits to hunters of certain species, while others have liberal hunting rules.

Take note that one outstanding hunting lodge is **Fort Lewis Lodge** in Millboro, Bath County. It's a mountain paradise. Call John Cowden at (540) 925-2314.

The best suggestion to assure you are hunting within the bounds of the rules and regulations is to send for the latest pamphlet from the Department of Game and Inland Fisheries, *Hunting and Trapping in Virginia Regulations.* The brochure lists everything you need to know about how and where to hunt in the Blue Ridge, or where to find specific game information. It also lists specific license requirements and fees. To obtain the brochure, write or call the **Department of Game and Inland Fisheries,** 4010 West Broad Street, Richmond 23230; (804) 367-1000; www.dgif.virginia.gov.

For other information about where to hunt in the Blue Ridge, write or call the following:

Virginia State Parks, 203 Governor Street, Suite 306, Richmond 23219; (804) 786-4377

George Washington and Jefferson National Forests, 5162 Valleypointe Parkway, Roanoke 24019; (540) 265-5100

ICE-SKATING

Charlottesville Ice Park
230 West Main Street, Charlottesville
(434) 817-1423, (434) 817-2400
www.icepark.com
Opened in 1996, the Charlottesville Ice
Park is getting plenty of local and regional
attention. Lessons and the Pro Shop cater
to both figure skaters and ice hockey
players. The rink even has its own hockey
team. Public skating times vary, so you will
want to call ahead. Admission is $6.00
with $1.50 for skate rental. Children 5 and
younger pay $2.75 and 25 cents for
skates. The ice park is on the west end of
the downtown pedestrian mall, close to
several theaters, movie houses, and a
plethora of restaurants and shops.

The Homestead
US 220, Hot Springs
(800) 838-1766, (540) 839-7740
The Homestead resort in Hot Springs
offers ice-skating action outdoors. The
Olympic-size rink is at the base of the ski
slopes and opens around Thanksgiving
weekend. Although it closes for Christmas,
skating usually runs from 9:00 A.M. to 5:00
P.M. daily through the second week in
March, weather permitting. The hours are
extended on the same evenings that the
resort holds night skiing. Skating costs
$10.00 for adults and $8.00 for children.
Ski-and-skate packages are available. (See
our Resorts chapter for more information
on this posh resort.)

MOUNTAIN BIKING

Virginia's Blue Ridge and neighboring
Allegheny Mountains are a mountain
biker's mecca. From technically and physically demanding single-track to gravel
roads and rider-friendly rail-trail conver-
sions, bikers have a wide range of terrain
to suit their abilities.

Randy Porter's book, *Mountain Bike!
Virginia,* provides specific descriptions for
mountain-biking destinations including

*If you are taking your bike out along
backcountry trails, remember that these
paths are not maintained for continuous
riding. You can expect to carry your
bicycle across obstacles.*

woods roads, trails, and rough roads west
of the Blue Ridge, primarily in the George
Washington and Jefferson National Forests.
Scott Adams' *Mountain Biking Virginia* provides details for some of Virginia's greatest
off-road bicycle rides as well as useful tips.

The majority of public land open to
mountain biking is in the George Washington and Jefferson National Forests, which
encompass more than 1.5 million acres of
mountain lands. The forests are divided
into a number of ranger districts, with individual maps available showing most of the
trails, forest roads, and other significant
features for two-wheel travel. The Washington and Jefferson National Forests contain several thousand miles of trails and
gravel roads, all of which are open to
mountain bikers, with the exception of the
Appalachian Trail and those trails within
designated wilderness areas.

If you are a beginning mountain-bike
rider, you should probably stick to forest
development roads until you get the hang
of using all the gears on sometimes long
climbs and steep descents. While single-
track riding—also called narrow trail riding—is often touted as the epitome of the
mountain-bike experience, ascents and
descents on rough, rocky, and sometimes
minimally maintained surfaces can be
pretty tricky.

For more information on Virginia bicycle clubs, maps, and rides, contact the Virginia Department of Transportation, State
Bicycle Coordinator, 1401 East Broad
Street, Richmond 23219; (800) 835-1203.

The Big Levels
Along Coal Road, near Sherando Lake
(540) 291-2188
The Big Levels area near Sherando Lake in

the Pedlar Ranger District of the Washington and Jefferson National Forests is a favorite for many mountain bikers. The Big Levels is a great place for pedaling along the relatively flat Reservoir Trail and Orebank Creek Road or any of the myriad unmarked former logging roads that meander through these 32,000 wooded acres.

Washington & Old Dominion Trail
21st Street, Purcellville
(703) 729-0596
www.wodfriends.org
Millions of riders in northern Virginia escape to this 45-mile asphalt route from the Purcellville Train Station trailhead in Loudoun County to Shirlington in Arlington County. It's a fairly flat route, and the asphalt paving makes it easier for the whole family to ride. Along the way, you'll pass several restored bridges and traverse a heavily wooded corridor. Closer to Arlington, the trail meets up with the 17-mile Mount Vernon Trail, giving bikers even more options.

Share the road and the trail. While bike riding the trails, anticipate meeting horse riders and hikers. Hold your riding speed down on narrow trails and when approaching blind curves.

Fenwick Mines
Off Highway 685, just past the Fenwick Mines picnic shelter
(540) 864-5195
This 19-mile loop begins and ends at Fenwick Mines Recreation Area. Hardier and more skillful riders will enjoy this trail as it ascends Bald Mountain via a number of tortuous switchbacks before arriving at the Bald Mountain Primitive Road.

Virginia's Explore Park
Milepost 115, Blue Ridge Parkway
(800) 842-9163, (540) 427-1800
www.explorepark.org

Explore Park is one of Virginia's premier educational and recreational facilities. The park offers a variety of experiences, from hiking, mountain biking, and fishing to outdoor historical and environmental education. Mountain biking at Explore Park is a wild ride with some of the best singletracks in the Roanoke Valley. There is a short beginner loop, a challenging 7-mile intermediate loop, and a technical advanced loop, if you're game. There is no charge to ride the well-maintained trails from dusk to dawn daily.

Walnut Creek Park
Old Lynchburg Road, Charlottesville
(434) 296-5844
There are 15 miles of twisting single-track trail in this Albemarle County park is designed with the intermediate rider in mind. There are plenty of challenging climbs and quick descents in the upper portion of the park. For the less experienced, an easier route follows along the lake's dam. There is a $4.50 entrance fee from Memorial Day to Labor Day; free the rest of the year.

Panorama Trails
750 Miller's Cottage Lane, Earlysville
(434) 974-7849
www.panoramatrails.com
If you love to ride outdoors, you must visit this private farm, which the owner, a mountain-biking aficionado himself, has opened up solely for mountain biking. Enjoy riding through the woods and over open meadows with a panoramic backdrop of the Blue Ridge Mountains, all right outside of Charlottesville. The farm provides more than 25 miles of single-track trails that travel over 850 acres. Some trails are for beginners, but primarily this is for the intermediate and advanced riders as riding involves hills, rocks, roots, creek, and log crossings. The $8.00 day permit can be purchased at several regional locations, including Extreme Sports, Blue Wheel Bikes, Downtown Athletic Store, and Blue Ridge Mountain Sports, all in Charlottesville, and Rockfish Gap Outfitters in Waynesboro. Be sure to

pick up a copy of the trail map. Riding is permitted daily from mid-January to October 1, and Sunday, Tuesday, Wednesday, and Thursday the rest of the year.

Wintergreen Resort
Highway 151, Wintergreen
(434) 325-8166
This Nelson County resort opened trails to mountain bikers. With more than 112 miles covering Wintergreen and the Big Levels area of the George Washington National Forest, there are plenty of routes to occupy hardy riders. The Outdoor Wilderness Leadership School at Wintergreen Resort can get you on your way. The Owls Center began guided bike tours with full-suspension bikes, trail maps, and shuttle service. A guided tour complete with equipment, transportation, and instruction is $75. You also can rent a BMX or mountain bike here.

North River Gorge Trail
Dry River District, off Highway 718 to
Forest Road 95
(540) 432-0187
This is one of the George Washington section's flatter trails. Beginning mountain bikers may find more comfort along this one. Use the parking lot for Wild Oak Trail.

Hidden Valley Trail
Warm Springs District, off Highway 621
on Forest Road 241
(540) 839-2521
Beginners may also enjoy this trail because of its flatness. An added bonus to riding on this route is the accessibility of a cool trout stream that runs adjacent to it, great for fishing or just cooling off.

New River Trail State Park & Shot Tower
176 Orphanage Drive, Foster Falls
(276) 699-6778
Heading into southwest Virginia, you'll find this splendid rail-trail conversion that offers fantastic mountain-biking opportunities. The 57-mile New River Trail is actually a state park that runs from Pulaski to Fries and Galax, 29 miles of it adjacent to

the New River, thought to be the second-oldest river in the world. Numerous access points are along the way, but your ride will be made easier by purchasing a $4.00 "Map and User's Guide." You can arrange a shuttle through Lanny Sparks at New River Bicycles, (540) 980-1741. His shop is in Draper, the 6-mile point along the trail.

Mountain Lake Resort
Mountain Lake
(800) 346-3334, (540) 552-4641
www.mountainlakehotel.com
Mountain Lake opened all 67 miles of its hiking trails for mountain bikers. The trails are wide, well marked, and feature a hard surface with low to no mud. Rated moderate to difficult, they offer a challenge for beginners and the more advanced riders. At 4,000 feet above sea level, Mountain Lake's trails offer spectacular views. Adult and children's mountain bikes—Trek 820s, 830s, and 220s—are available for rent along with helmets and child seats at the resort.

SWIMMING

Swimmers who enjoy the outdoors can count on the cool mountain streams, lakes, and even waterfalls of Virginia's Blue Ridge for the most refreshing dip they'll ever take.

Some of the best swimming can be found in the area's state parks and national forests. Picture yourself swimming at the bottom of a sparkling waterfall after a 2-mile hike at the Cascades in Pembroke in Giles County. Or how about lying on Claytor Lake's white sand beach in Pulaski County while horseback riders amble by! For the strong in spirit, there's icy-cold Cave Mountain Lake near Glasgow. All have sparse but clean and accommodating changing and shower facilities.

Families with small children will be interested in an abundance of private campgrounds with lovely swimming areas overseen by lifeguards. One of the best known is Shenandoah Acres Resort at Stuarts Draft, near the Waynesboro intersection of the Skyline Drive and the Blue Ridge Parkway.

Following is an Insiders' list of swimming sites definitely worth the drive from anywhere.

Municipal Pools

War Memorial Pool
Ridgeview Park, at end of Magnolia Avenue, Waynesboro
(540) 942-6767

War Memorial Pool, in the center of lovely Ridgeview Park, is surrounded by a playground, tennis courts, a baseball diamond, and an open field. The managers of this Olympic-size pool pride themselves on its cleanliness and pleasing view.

Open from Memorial Day to Labor Day, the pool's general admission hours are from 10:00 A.M. to 7:30 P.M. Monday through Saturday and 1:00 to 7:30 P.M. on Sunday. Fees were $1.00 for ages 15 and younger and $2.50 for folks 16 and older.

Gypsy Hill Park Pool
Constitution Drive, Staunton
(540) 886-6846

This L-shaped pool is Olympic-size and has a wading pool. The facility opens for the season around Memorial Day and closes Labor Day. It's open from 11:00 A.M. to 6:00 P.M. Monday through Saturday and from 1:00 to 6:00 P.M. on Sunday. Prices are $1.00 for ages 1 to 5, $1.50 for ages 6 to 12, and $2.50 for those 13 and older. Children younger than 1 get in free.

Roanoke City Pools
Fallon Park Pool, 2024 Dale Avenue
(540) 853-2206

Washington Park Pool, 1616 Burrell Avenue
(540) 853-2369

The City of Roanoke Parks and Recreation Department offers two outdoor municipal swimming pools. The pools are both L-shaped and 50 meters in length with a

diving well and an additional wading pool for youth younger than 6. The pools are open from Memorial Day to Labor Day. The pools follow the school calendar, opening in early June and closing in late August. The hours of operation are noon to 6:00 P.M. Sunday through Thursday and noon to 7:00 P.M. Friday and Saturday. Admission is $1.00 for ages 5 to 15, $2.00 for adults, and free for those 4 and younger. Both facilities offer swimming lessons through the Red Cross, as well as special events. Both facilities offer swimming lessons and special events and may be rented for special occasions during nonprogrammed hours.

Charlottesville Municipal Pools
Washington Park Pool
14th Street and Preston Avenue
(434) 970-3592

Charlottesville Onesty Pool, 300 Meade Avenue
(434) 295-7532

Charlottesville Crow Pool, Rosehill Drive
(434) 977-1362

Charlottesville Smith Pool, Cherry Avenue
(804) 977-1960

McIntire Pool, U.S. Highway 250 Bypass
(434) 295-9072

Forest Hills Pool, 1000 Forest Hills Avenue
(434) 296-1444

The city of Charlottesville boasts six municipal pools: two outdoor (Washington Park and Onesty), two indoor (Crow and Smith), and two wading pools (McIntire and Forest Hills). The outdoor and indoor pools are all 25 yards long, and the facilities feature showers, hair dryers, and lockers. The indoor pools are heated. The wading pools are small and shallow, designed for children 12 and younger.

The outdoor and wading pools are open from Memorial Day to Labor Day. The hours for the outdoor pools are noon to 6:00 P.M. Monday through Thursday and

noon to 8:00 P.M. Friday, Saturday, and
Sunday. The wading pools are open 10:30
A.M. to 5:30 P.M. Monday through Friday
and noon to 5:00 P.M. Saturday and Sunday. The indoor pools are open year-round,
but hours are widely varied, so call ahead
of time. Admission for nonresidents for the
outdoor and indoor facilities is $3.75 for
children and $4.50 for adults. There is no
charge for the wading pools.

Miller Park Pool
301 Grove Street, Lynchburg
(434) 847-1643, (434) 847-1759
Two play areas and a place for picnics surround this pool in Miller Park. The
Olympic-size pool features a high dive
and a kiddie area. Lessons are offered
each morning. Miller Park Pool is open
from Memorial Day through Labor Day.
Hours are noon to 6:00 P.M. Monday
through Saturday and 1:00 to 5:00 P.M.
Sunday. Admission is $1.50 for adults and
$1.00 for children.

Blacksburg Public Pools
Graves Avenue, Blacksburg

Patrick Henry Drive, Blacksburg
(540) 961-1135
www.blacksburg.gov/recreation
For indoor swimming, Blacksburg's 25-
yard indoor pool has six lanes, a sauna, a
spa, and a diving area. The Blacksburg
Aquatic Center is open Monday through
Friday from 6:00 A.M. to 9:00 P.M., Saturday from 9:00 A.M. to 9:00 P.M., and Sunday from 1:00 to 6:00 P.M. The fee until
7:00 P.M. is $2.50 for adults and $2.00 for
children and senior citizens. To swim after
7:00 P.M. it is $2.00 for adults and $1.50
for children and seniors. The pool is across
from Blacksburg High School.

Bisset Park Pool
Off Norwood Street, Radford
(540) 731-3633, (540) 731-3635
Radford's city pool is an Olympic-size
swimming pool in Bisset Park, just off Norwood Street, bordering nearly a mile of the
scenic New River. Its setting in a 58-acre

municipal park makes this pool unique. It is
surrounded by six lighted tennis courts,
lighted picnic shelters, playgrounds, a
gazebo, and fitness station. The facility is
open May 23 through Labor Day. Hours are
Monday through Friday 1:00 to 5:00 P.M.
and weekends 1:00 to 8:00 P.M. Admission
is $1.00 for ages 7 to 15 and $1.50 for ages
16 and older. Children younger than 5 are
admitted free with a paying adult.

State Park Swim Areas

Douthat State Park
Highway 1, Millboro
(540) 862-8100
Take a dip in the 50-acre lake at this state
park. There is a nice sandy beach with a
sunbathing area, bathhouse, and concession area. The facilities are generally open
from Memorial Day to Labor Day weekend.
A small fee is charged for day visitors, usually $3.00 for adults and $2.00 for kids.

*Never run a river, go hiking, mountain
biking, or camping without a good map
and without letting someone know
where you are going and when you
expect to get back.*

Fairy Stone State Park
Highway 346, Stuart
(276) 930-2424
This 168-acre lake adjoins the Philpott Reservoir. There is a beach for swimming, complete with its own bathhouse. Swimming
fees are $2.00 for ages 3 to 12 and $3.00 for
ages 13 and older. The facilities are open
from Memorial Day to Labor Day weekend.

Claytor Lake
4400 State Park Road, near Dublin
(540) 643-2500
At this beautiful park in Pulaski County,
you'll think you're on an ocean beach, with

the ample white sand surrounded by a full-service boat marina beside the sparkling water. Camping, horseback riding (rentals available), and sport fishing are also popular at this 4,500-acre lake and surrounding natural areas. The swimming season runs from Memorial Day to Labor Day. The parking fee (day-use fee) is $3.00 on weekdays and $4.00 on weekends. The cost to swim is $3.00 a person, free for those younger than 3.

Smith Mountain Lake State Park
Off Highway 626 S, Huddleston
(540) 297-6066

This lakefront beach nestled in the tall blue mountains of Bedford County offers a never-ending show of gliding sailboats in the distance. It's paradise for water enthusiasts and has a visitor center with especially good nature programs for the whole family during the summer. The swimming season runs from Memorial Day to Labor Day, and facilities include a bathhouse with hot showers and a concession stand.

National Forest Swim Areas

Sherando Lake
96 Sherando Lake Road, Lyndhurst
(540) 942-5965

Sherando Lake, in the George Washington and Jefferson National Forests, has two lakes. You can swim in the beautiful 24-acre main lake, which is set in a mountain hollow on the east flank of Torry Ridge. It has a sand beach and a bathhouse with warm showers. If you don't like so much sun, you can sit on the lawn beneath giant oak trees. There is also camping, boating, and fishing. Day-use rates are $6.00 for two people in a car, $8.00 for three or more, and $4.00 for individuals.

Cave Mountain Lake
Cave Mountain Lake Road, near Natural Bridge
(540) 291-2188, (540) 291-2745

This seemingly long trip to isolation is worth it. Cave Mountain Lake Campground, off Highway 781 in the Jefferson section of the national forest, is nearby with its unusual picnic tables and sites often surrounded by stone, set amidst large pines and hardwoods. There is a large open field with plenty of sunshine, and the lake is cool and refreshing. It's a real getaway. There is a bathhouse with warm showers. The cost for day use of the lake is $5.00 a carload. You can camp for $15.00 a night.

Cascades Recreation Area
Off Highway 623, near Pembroke
(540) 265-5100

Cascades in Giles County features a 2-mile hike to a 66-foot waterfall. Picture yourself hiking and then jumping into a cool, placid pool of water right under a thundering waterfall. This is one of the most photogenic sites in the New River Valley. Warning: Don't try jumping into the water from the cliffs of the waterfall. There have been at least three deaths in recent memory from those who did. This swimming area is not recommended for small children. For more information write George Washington and Jefferson National Forests, 5162 Valleypointe Parkway, Roanoke 24019.

ROCK CLIMBING

Climbing has grown in popularity in recent years in the Blue Ridge. Hitting the rocks isn't just for thrill-seeking daredevils. For fitness buffs, climbing offers a package deal: strength training, agility development, and an aerobic workout.

However, if you are new to climbing, you will want to "learn the ropes" before tackling anything too challenging.

There are many indoor climbing gyms in the Blue Ridge. Listed below are just some of the ones you can check out before heading to the mountains.

One word of caution. The sport has its own lingo and can be catching to those who climb regularly. "Dirt me" is a cool way to say "let me down" after either finishing or giving up on a top-rope climb. And there's "gumby," a climber—most often a novice—who is spread out on or below a climb.

Recreation Center
James Madison University, Harrisonburg
(540) 568-8700
www.jmu.edu/recreation/adventure
Here you will find a Nicros wall with 850 square feet of climbing surface. It measures 34 feet tall by 25 feet wide, with five top-rope stations and one lead climb.

Radford University Climbing Wall
East Main Street, Radford
(540) 831-5369
There is a 20-foot wall at this university facility. It includes more than eight area climbs and hundreds of holes.

Rocky Top Climbing Club
1279 Allied Street, Charlottesville
(434) 984-1626
This club offers 4,200 square feet of top-rope and lead climbs. The facility offers lockers, showers, and a climbing pro shop.

Wintergreen Resort
Highway 151, Wintergreen
(434) 325-8166
www.owlsadventure.com
The Outdoor Learning Center (OWLS) at Wintergreen has developed a climbing program to meet a variety of needs. The center offers both basic or comprehensive basic rock climbing and rappelling year-round. Skills taught include safety, technique, equipment identification, belaying, rappelling, and basic knots. Courses offered are for ages 12 and older on a limited basis. Reservations are required. A two-day clinic, which includes all equipment, transportation, and guide, costs $195. Three- and five-hour basic courses, which include all equipment, transportation, instruction, and guide, range from $65 a class to $50 an hour for a private lesson. There's also the 25-foot climbing wall in the Out of Bounds Adventure Center, (434) 325-8505, with three climbing routes that range from beginner to experienced. Cost is $15 for three climbs and includes equipment.

SKIING ❄

Skiing requires two things: mountains and snow. Virginia's Blue Ridge has both in abundance.

Throughout this book we've shown you that the Blue Ridge has more mountains than a redhead has freckles. Wintergreen and Massanutten, two of the region's four ski resorts, have vertical drops of 1,000 feet or better; they don't come any higher south of New York. Those mountains attract the white stuff and can keep it, with temperatures ranging 10 to 20 degrees lower than in the flatlands. Natural snowfall will vary from year to year, but the snow on the slopes stays surprisingly consistent because of aggressive snowmaking and the use of Snomax, a process that makes better snow at higher temperatures. Just because you're not driving in a blizzard doesn't mean they're not skiing up a storm at Wintergreen, Massanutten, Bryce, and the Homestead.

There is a catch, but you're going to like it. It's usually warmer skiing in the Blue Ridge than in New England or out West. At Wintergreen you can even ski and play golf the same day. Warm temperatures also account for the popularity of night skiing in the region. Three resorts described in this chapter have lighted slopes, which means more schuss for your buck on a ski trip. And night skiing rates are almost always cheaper than day rates.

You have to sleep sometime, but while you do, fleets of snowcats, highly sophisticated mechanical behemoths, are stalking the slopes, bulldozing moguls, pulverizing icy spots, and smoothing trails so that you're greeted with a brand-new surface come morning.

Getting all those skiers to the top of the mountain has led to more and faster lifts, including Virginia's first quad chair, at Massanutten, and the mid-Atlantic's first high-speed six-passenger lift, at Wintergreen.

Blue Ridge resorts also have kept pace with the shredders, those derring-do snowboard enthusiasts, by providing snowboard parks, rental boards, and lessons. All four resorts even offer the latest craze, snow tubing.

Since skiers have to rest, eat, and party, too, off-the-slope facilities at our four ski areas offer spas, après-ski activities, and good restaurants. These are year-round resorts (see our Resorts chapter), so they excel at everything, even keeping nonskiers happy.

More and more people are discovering that Virginia offers a terrific ski resort experience, with great skiing and activities for the whole family.

We've given you some rates that were in effect in winter 2004, but remember these may change according to many variables: whether you ski during the day or at night, bring your own equipment, stay at the ski resort or elsewhere, or take a private or group lesson. Generally, you can expect to pay $30 to $35 for a full-day midweek lift ticket and $40 to $50 for a weekend day pass. All the resorts have cost-saving packages. Look for some of the best prices on weekdays; you'll also find fewer lines and more room on the slopes Monday through Friday.

Of the four resorts listed here, only the Homestead rents cross-country skis and provides trails. But if you own your own equipment, you can make tracks alongside the Blue Ridge Parkway, the Skyline Drive, in Mount Rogers National Recreation Area in southwest Virginia, and almost anyplace with hiking trails or fire roads.

For free brochures and additional information on the four major ski resorts in Virginia, call Virginia Ski Line at (800) THE-SNOW, or write to the Virginia Department of Tourism, 901 East Byrd Street, Richmond 23219–4018.

PRICE CODE

This code reflects the price of an adult lift ticket for day skiing on a weekend. The price during the week is often reduced by at least $10.00. Youth, senior, and children's lift ticket prices are also usually reduced by $2.00 to $7.00.

$	$30–$42
$$	$43–$49
$$$	$50 and more

SHENANDOAH VALLEY

Bryce Resort $
1982 Fairway Drive, Basye
(540) 856–2121, (800) 821-1444
www.bryceresort.com
This intimate, family-oriented ski resort is not quite a two-hour drive from Washington, D.C., and three hours from Richmond. A few miles off Interstate 81, Bryce is tucked into the folds of the Shenandoah Mountains. It's owned by the approximately 350 families who own homes there. Many skiers drive to Bryce from the Washington, D.C., area, but the resort is also popular with the locals, particularly on weekday evenings, when they can ski under the lights and then warm up with a hot-buttered rum in the glass-walled Copper Kettle Lounge.

Manfred Locher, manager of the ski operations, and his brother, Horst, director of the ski school and an extensive racing program, have been at Bryce since the resort opened in 1965. Horst is a certified member of the Professional Ski Instructors of America and a certified ski coach of the United States Ski Coaches Association.

One of Bryce's notable features is its racing program. For more than 20 years, Bryce has sponsored NASTAR races, starting a trend among southern ski resorts. Every Saturday, Sunday, and holiday at 3:30 P.M., the NASTAR races begin, offering skiers the chance to test their abilities against the pros. The races are handicapped according to age and gender. Bryce also has a weekend ski program to train skiers for sanctioned U.S. Ski Association races.

The resort, whose summit elevation is 1,750 feet, covers approximately 25 acres. The longest run of the eight slopes is the Redeye at 3,500 feet. The slopes are serviced by two double-chairlifts and three surface lifts. The resort averages about 20 to 30 inches of natural snow annually but produces enough to blanket all trails.

If you're looking for a bargain, the resort offers the less expensive options of night skiing on Tuesday through Saturday, and Sunday if Monday is a holiday. It's $18.00 for an adult lift ticket, and the half-day lift ticket is not far behind. The full-day option on a weekend will cost you $40.00, and in many cases, the price for juniors and seniors is $5.00 less. Ski rentals range from $17.00 to $20.00, and snowboard rentals are $20.00 to $23.00. If you are younger than 5, you get a free lift ticket on all days, and those 70 and older get a free lift ticket on weekdays and non-holiday Mondays. Ski hours are 9:00 A.M. to 9:30 P.M., except for Monday, and on Sunday when Monday is not a holiday. It is advisable to call ahead during the nonpeak season or as the weather warms up, as hours may shorten and the resort may close some weekdays.

The Horst Locher Ski School is a PSIA member school and offers private and group lessons, including a SKIwee program for children ages 4 and a half to 8. The kids' half-day program spends one and a half hours on the snow, and the $46 cost includes a lift ticket, indoor activities, hot chocolate, and snack breaks, with a reduced price if your kids have their own equipment. There is a mini rider program for children ages 6 to 8 on weekends for beginners.

There are also first-time ski and snowboarding packages for those ages 8 to adult, and ski improvement lessons for boarders and skiers. The group lessons, which last just over an hour, are $22, while you can get a private lesson by appointment for $48. If you're a snow daredevil, you might want to check out the racing clinics, provided for adults and juniors (ages 6 to 12).

Bryce recently added a popular 800-foot tubing lane. It costs $15 for an hour-and-50-minute session. After a long day on the slopes, you can relax in the Ski Lodge, which houses the restaurant and the popular Copper Kettle Lounge. Here guests can grab a hearty breakfast or lunch, or enjoy fine dining—indoors and out under the stars, with mountain views from every table. Stick around for music and dancing afterward. Or participate in après-ski activities in the cozy lounge. Also in this building are the administrative and real estate offices. The second main building at Bryce is the Ski Lodge, which houses the ski shop. The third building has the ski school, the ski rental and repair facility, and the lift ticket sales.

In the summer, grass skiing and mountain boarding are popular sports at Bryce. Invented in Europe as a summer training method for skiers, grass skiing mimics snow skiing but substitutes short, treadlike skates for skis. Rentals and lessons in grass skiing are offered in the summer and fall.

Privately owned condos, chalets, and homes near the slopes are available for weekend rentals or long-term stays (see our Resort chapter for more information).

Bryce is 11 miles from I-81. Take exit 273 at Mount Jackson and then follow Highway 263 W to Bayse and Bryce Resort.

Massanutten Resort $
1822 Resort Drive
Massanutten
(540) 289-9441, (800) 207-MASS
www.massresort.com

An easy two-hour drive from Richmond, Washington, D.C., or Roanoke, Massanutten Resort sits in the heart of the Shenandoah Valley atop Massanutten Mountain, once a haven for moonshiners. The resort's 14 trails and 70 acres of skiing tower above an attractive, spacious lodge at the base. The lodge houses the ski patrol, the ski school, the cafeteria, a convenience store, and the Encounters Lounge, a glass-walled nightclub with a big dance floor. Another nice feature of the lodge is a large windowed room with tables and chairs where guests can bring their own food, "camp out" during the day, and watch the skiing without spending a dime. A rental shop and general store selling snacks, skis, snowboards, necessities, and souvenirs are close by.

The resort gets only about 34 inches of natural snowfall a year but has greatly expanded its snowmaking capability. Diamond Jim, a 3,300-foot run with a vertical drop of 1,110 feet (the most in all of Virginia, Pennsylvania, and Maryland) is Massanutten's most challenging slope, starting at the resort's highest point (2,860 feet) alongside ParaDice, the other expert trail (a 4,100-foot run). All slopes are lit for night skiing and are served by five lifts, including three doubles and one quad chairlift. Ski hours are 9:00 A.M. to 11:00 P.M. Your bargain option is again a night ski or a half-day ski (Monday to Friday only) for $23. The day or twilight lift ticket will cost an adult $35 during the week, and all options are reduced for juniors and seniors. Twilight session is 12:30 to 10:00 P.M. Day skiing is from 9:00 A.M. to 4:30 P.M. For the hearty individuals who don't feel this is enough skiing for one day, choose the extended day session from 9:00 A.M. to 10:00 P.M. Something to note is that active military pays the junior rates for lift tickets. Rentals will cost you $17 to $30, with a savings for juniors. Those younger than 5 and older than 70 get a free slope-use ticket. Also, for additional savings, season passes and multiday slope use and rental rates are available, as are group rates.

Snowboarding is allowed on all 14 slopes, but a big draw is the Massanutten Terrain Park. Opened in 1991, it has the reputation as one of the best in the mid-Atlantic region. It has bumps, and a quarterpipe is served by its own J-bar lift. A full-time crew grooms the park daily, shaping the transitions to keep the obstacles in good shape and changing the layout frequently to keep it fresh. Ski blades, snowboards, and twin-tip skis are permitted on the Terrain Park.

And don't forget the five-part competition MIROC Series, Massanutten's Intergalactic Race of Champions. Anyone who can strap on a snowboard can qualify for this race that competes for various prizes. Divisions include the men's beginner, men's expert, rock star, and the women's open. Register at the Terrain Park.

In 1997 Massanutten was the first Virginia resort to open a snow-tubing park. This activity is wildly popular, especially for families, because of the low cost, absence of tricky equipment to rent and operate, and because all ages can get in on the fun. The snow-tubing park has eight lanes, 900 feet long, and two tube lifts that pull the tube (with the rider in it) back up the slope. Tubing is from 9:00 A.M. to 9:00 P.M. daily and costs $16 for a two-hour session. There is no age limit, but those 37 to 44 inches tall should ride with an adult. A cautionary note: This activity is very popular and the resort sells tickets to owners and guests one day in advance (after 2:00 P.M.), so Saturday, Sunday, and holidays can be sold out the night before. There are advanced group reservations for groups of 15 or more for Monday through the late afternoon session on Thursday (nonholidays). All other sessions are sold first come, first served in person.

There are lots of lesson options for skiers and snowboarders. The ski and snowboard school is a member of the Professional Ski Instructors of America (PSIA) and the American Association of Snowboard Instructors (AASI). Lessons are provided for every level. Children ages 4 to 14 can begin their skiing and snowboarding experience in the Slope Sliders programs. Group lessons and rental packages are available for first-time skiers and snowboarders and for those who want to improve their skills. The Slope Sliders is for all levels, and skiing is for ages 4 to 12, snowboarding for ages 9 to 14. The $68 price for this activity includes a day slope-use ticket, rental equipment, lunch, and supervised instruction. Reservations are highly recommended.

The Massanutten Adaptive Ski School is another ski lesson option. The aim of the adaptive skiing instruction is to help individuals of all ages overcome a variety of challenges. This program follows the PSIA Adaptive Teaching Model and other progressions as defined by National Handicapped Sports. For those lucky enough to stay "on mountain," a sports complex called Le Club offers indoor swimming, a sauna, hot tubs, an exercise room, table tennis, and more.

To get there from I-81, exit onto Highway 33 E in Harrisonburg. Go 10 miles to Highway 644, where you will see signs to the resort.

EAST OF THE BLUE RIDGE

Wintergreen Resort $$
Highway 664, Wintergreen
(434) 325-2200, (800) 266-2444
www.wintergreenresort.com
Skiing magazine has called Wintergreen Resort "the South's single-best ski resort," and *Washingtonian* rated Wintergreen the "#1 fun ski getaway," and the resort continues to live up to its reputation in accommodations, restaurants, shops, and other amenities. The amenities definitely make it a fun place to hang out for those nonskiers in the family. In 1976, during the first full year of skiing, 30,000 made their way up Wintergreen's mountain. The mountain has 20 slopes over 90 skiable acres. The trails range from a vast beginners area to the Highlands, a three-slope complex with a drop of more than 1,000 feet, and runs up to 1.4 miles long for advanced skiers. In four years, $20 million in upgrades have resulted in the addition of the Blue Ridge Express, the mid-Atlantic's first high-speed six-passenger lift. The $1.8 million lift can transport 2,400 people an hour, at 1,000 feet a minute, taking a mere two and a half minutes to get back to the top. Other lifts include one quad, two triples, and a double chairlift, all able to move 9,000 skiers in an hour. The upgrades also brought in a tubing park and widened the Upper Wild Turkey advanced trail to allow for moguls

on one side and groomed snow on the other. The trail has been cited by *Skiing* magazine as the South's best. Night skiing on 12 lighted slopes is available every day.

The Alley is Wintergreeen's exciting terrain park, open to snowboarders and skiers alike. Virginia's first halfpipe features challenging spines, tabletops, and hips.

The best bargain is again night skiing Sunday through Thursday for $22. The half-day option (Monday through Friday only, nonholidays) is not far behind. Day-skiing hours are 9:00 A.M. to 4:30 P.M. and the cost ranges from $39 during the week to $52 on the weekends, with a couple dollars savings for youths on each option. There's also twilight skiing, which starts at 12:30 P.M., all for the same price as the day skiing. Call ahead for skiing conditions, (434) 325-2100. Ski rentals will cost you anywhere from $21 to $31, depending on which time slot you've selected. Again, children and those 70 and older can save some money on rentals. Snowboard rentals run from $31 up to $41 for adults, with a reduced price for youths.

There are reduced rates on lift tickets and rental equipment for groups of 15 or more, as well as winter lodging packages and a great value for those who ski often, found in the season passes.

Wintergreen's ski patrol is consistently ranked among the best in the nation by the National Ski Patrol Association. In addition, all skiers and snowboarders who rent equipment from Wintergreen are entitled to a free learn-to-ski lesson, an effort of the resort to promote safe skiing. There are also group intermediate and advanced lessons for children and adults, given daily, behind the Skyline Pavilion. If you really want to brush up on your skills, Wintergreen provides private lessons as well, from one hour

at a cost of $60 up to a three-hour lesson costing $150. Reservations are required.

Children have a variety of snow play and learning options through the Tree House camps. Those age 3 can participate in Snow Play, which is basic skiing instruction. Mogul Monkeys is a program for ages 4 to 12 and includes indoor and outdoor activities. Kids age 4 to 12 who want to do more outdoor activities can join Mountain Explorers, which focuses heavily on skiing. Kids in Action is a nonski camp for ages 2 and a half to 12.

In the 2002 the resort expanded the length and number of lanes to create the Plunge Tubing Park, providing fun for young and old alike. The eight lanes, 900 feet in length, feature a 100-foot vertical drop. All in all, the ride is equivalent to the height of a 10-story building! They are serviced by a lift that pulls tube and rider back to the top. The two-hour sessions cost $17 to $20 a person, and sessions are from noon to 8:00 P.M. Monday through Thursday, extended to 10:00 P.M. on Friday, and all day on Saturday and Sunday, starting at 10:00 A.M. While tickets go fast for this sport, Wintergreen does sell tickets a day in advance, but you must purchase them in person.

Wintergreen didn't forget the wee ones. Those younger than 2 can tube on the new Slide. The cost is $14. Another new attraction is the Out of Bounds Adventure Center. Kick off your skis and try the bungee trampoline, climb a 30-foot tower, or test out your wheels on the skate ramp. There's also a miniature golf, weather permitting, all next to the Lookout Restaurant.

You can ski in the morning and golf at the Stoney Creek course in the afternoon for the price of a ski ticket. The 3,000-foot difference in elevation between the mountaintop and the valley golf course translates into a 10- to 15-degree temperature change that makes it possible for you to golf and ski on the same day.

After a long day of skiing, or for those who want to do something other than the outdoorsy stuff, the Wintergreen Spa and Fitness Center offers a variety of activities as well as personal pampering options. The center features a state-of-the-art exercise room, personal fitness training, aerobics room, indoor and outdoor pools, hot tubs, boutique, and personal care facility. Enjoy a Swedish or deep-tissue massage, a facial, or one of several body treatments like a mountain mud wrap or an aromatherapy wrap. Advanced reservations are recommended.

A summit ski area, the resort's accommodations and facilities are at the top of the slopes. The restaurant and condominium complexes offer extraordinary views up the spine of the Blue Ridge and off to each side. To the west is the Shenandoah Valley and to the east, the Piedmont.

The resort's headquarters is the Mountain Inn, and guests can stop in the Gristmill Espresso/Cappuccino Bar for an Italian coffee or glass of wine by the fire in the lobby. Or browse the array of shops.

Wintergreen has seven eateries in all, plus a grocery store where you can get goods to stock the condo kitchen. The ever-popular Copper Mine features gourmet dining, and its unique open-pit copper fireplace adds to the cozy atmosphere. The Devils Grill Restaurant, located at the Devils Knob Golf Course and featuring a mountaintop view, serves dinner during the winter months. For something a little more casual, try the full-service Devils Grill Lounge for a hearty sandwich or burger.

Families and groups also like the casual dining at the Edge at Cooper's Vantage Restaurant.

Another nice option for dinner is the Stoney Creek Bar and Grill, set in the Wintergreen Valley with panoramic views of the Stoney Creek Golf Course. Reservations are required for dinner at the Copper Mine, Devils Grill, and Stoney Creek Bar and Grill. These three plus the Edge at Cooper's Vantage offer special menus for children ages 12 and younger. The Copper Mine and Devils Grill also provide vegetarian options.

For seasonal dining, check out the 4,000-square-foot Blue Ridge Terrace Grill, which offers outdoor barbecue and music on the slopes on weekends. This outdoor dining spot overlooks the ski slopes and is open weekdays and holidays during ski season, weather permitting. For those who can't tear themselves away from the slopes, Pryor's Porch Cafeteria is open in the Mountain Village during ski season and offers fast-food options.

Accommodations at Wintergreen consist of privately owned condominiums and single-family homes, which are rented. These furnished and carefully maintained accommodations range in size from a studio to five-bedroom condos and homes with two to seven bedrooms. Many have fully equipped kitchens, cozy fireplaces, and comfortable living areas. Rates vary from season to season, but the prices during the ski season can range from $177 a night for a studio for a weekend or holiday, to $402 a night for a two-bedroom villa or home, to $746 a night for a seven-bedroom home. Homes require a two-night minimum stay, three nights on a holiday. However, keep your eyes open for special deals, especially early and late in the season. For lodging and reservations, call (800) 266–2444.

From areas north or east of Wintergreen, follow Interstate 64 W to exit 107 (Crozet, U.S. Highway 250). Take US 250 W to Highway 151 S. and turn left. Follow Highway 151 S. for 14.2 miles to Highway 664 and turn right. Wintergreen is 4.5 miles ahead on Highway 664. You can also get to Wintergreen from the Blue Ridge Parkway via the Reeds Gap exit, between Mileposts 13 and 14. Look for the signs.

ALLEGHANY HIGHLANDS

The Homestead $$$
U.S. Highway 220, Main Street
Hot Springs
(540) 839–1766, (800) 838–1766
www.thehomestead.com
This elegant hotel became the South's first true ski resort when it opened its slopes in 1959. In the 1950s ski resorts in the north were experimenting with snowmaking. Under the direction of Austrian native Sepp Kober, known as the "Father of Southern

Skiing," investors spent nearly $1 million to develop a 3,000-foot slope on Warm Springs Mountain, along with side trails, a ski mobile, and a glass-walled lodge with a circular fire pit, ski equipment shops, and a rental service. Since then the slopes have grown 200 feet steeper, and a new multimillion-dollar snowmaking system provides more than 3 feet of snow. The four-wheeled ski mobile has been replaced with modern ski lifts. Nine runs are open for day skiing and slopes are open from 9:00 A.M. to 5:00 P.M. The Homestead does not offer night skiing, except on special weekends, such as the Saturday night of President's Day Weekend or during special events such as Winterfest. Guests of the resort receive complimentary lift tickets from January 2 to the end of the season—usually late February, depending on the weather. Adult lift tickets vary, depending on the day of the week, with a reduced price for children 12 and younger.

Snowboard aficionados can experience the snowboard park and a 260-foot-long halfpipe. The Playland Terrain Park was added in 2004, featuring rails, hits, and the halfpipe. Private snowboarding lessons also are available for $50 an hour.

At the base of the slopes is an Olympic-size ice-skating rink with instructors close at hand. Ski rentals will cost you $29 for adults, with a few dollars savings for children 12 and younger. Snowboards rent for $34 a day, all ages and days of the week.

The Homestead is renowned for its ski school and family atmosphere. There's the Bunny School for children ages 5 to 11, which can be either a half or a full day of ski instruction and other activities. Adults and children have the option of one-hour group lessons, costing $25, or a one-hour private lesson, starting at $50.

Not to be left out of the trend, the resort added snow tubing to the choices of outdoor activities during the 1998–99 season, and a two-hour session costs $20 a person. A tow rope pulls tube and rider back to the top.

For a real workout, the Homestead is the only Virginia resort that offers cross-country skiing. Take a two-hour guided cross-country skiing tour along the slopes and trails, or learn the basics of snowshoeing from one of the resort's experienced naturalists in a two-hour guided snowshoeing tour. The cost for these two activities starts at $35. For those who like a faster ride, try one of the most popular new winter activities—a guided snowmobile tour. Two can double up, and the half-hour ride costs $45 per snowmobile. Riders must be 16 or older and have a driver's permit. Hot cider is included in all four activities. Call ahead to check on the schedules, since they are at the mercy of natural snowfall and are held on different nights.

The resort offers various winter packages with special rates for families that include accommodations, breakfast and dinner daily, afternoon tea, lift tickets, ice skating, nightly movies, use of the fitness center and the spring-fed indoor pool, or spa treatments and complimentary green fees on the Old Course.

You'll want to take advantage of the Homestead's other sporting facilities, exquisite dining, and historic spa (see our Resorts chapter). By fall 2001, the resort had finished a multimillion-dollar restoration that included a complete refurbishment of 506 guest rooms, major restorations to the Great Hall and the Jefferson Parlor, establishment of the Washington Library, and the building and renovation of 20 specialty shops, as well as a multimillion-dollar renewal of the celebrated European-style spa. Previously called the Warm Springs Pools, they have been renamed the Jefferson Pools. A night's stay at the resort starts at $125 per person during ski season.

The Homestead is about 200 miles from Washington, D.C. Take exit 61 (Highway 257) off I-81, go south on Highway 42, then west on Highway 39. Follow US 220 into Hot Springs. For a lengthier but very scenic route, take I-64 W off I-81 near Lexington, then Highway 39 W to US 220 into Hot Springs.

RELOCATION

Virginia is a large and diverse state. Being natives, we've always considered the Blue Ridge area to be one of the best, being generally lower in people numbers and higher in natural resources. Of course, what with Charlottesville, Lynchburg, and Roanoke ranking so highly in the book *Cities Ranked and Rated* (by Sander and Sperling, 2004), the drive to relocate to the Blue Ridge area undoubtedly will increase those numbers a bit. And there are the visitors who discover what we who live here already know to be true: The scenic beauty, arts and cultural offerings, the amenities, the schools, and the warmth of the citizenry make it a place like no other.

Homes in the Blue Ridge can be found to fit every taste. You'll find modern homes perched atop mountain ridges in resorts such as Bryce, Wintergreen, and Massanutten or on the fairway at private communities such as Glenmore and Keswick near Charlottesville. If the classics are more your style, the region is rich in tin-roofed Victorians, such as those in Salem, Staunton, or Edinburg, and New York City–style brownstones in downtown Lexington and Lynchburg. If what you want is a primitive log cabin to fix up, check out the Alleghany Highlands or the southwestern part of the Blue Ridge. And if you're looking for a farm, consider the horse country of Loudoun and Albemarle Counties, the wine region of Warren County, gorgeous Catawba Valley near Roanoke, or isolated country estates in Loudoun, Fauquier, Alleghany, Highland, or Bath Counties. You will also find that you don't have to go to the ocean to live near the water. Smith Mountain Lake's Bernard Landing's condominiums and the town houses at Mallard Point along Claytor Lake's white sand beaches will convince you that you are already there.

Sales of existing homes in Virginia, including the Blue Ridge area, increased in 2003, with the average sales price hitting just over $200,000. Of course, there is a wide range in prices in this very diverse area, with the selling price of a home in the more rural, outlying counties being as low as $89,500, to the Northern Virginia area, including parts of Loudoun and Fauquier, costing as much as $399,500.

The occasional lucky visitor may stumble upon their dream homes, but your best bet is to let local real estate professionals know that you're looking. Homes in Middleburg, Warrenton, Charlottesville, South Roanoke, and Lexington are often sold by word of mouth before they ever see the marketplace. Realtors can also offer guidance on the best schools and shopping areas and the level of satisfaction in the neighborhood you're considering.

The following organizations can help you in making regional and statewide comparisons and can answer questions about purchasing or building a home in Virginia.

Home Builders Association of Virginia, 707 East Franklin Street, Richmond 23219–3534; (804) 643–2729; www.hbav.com

Virginia Association of Realtors, 10231 Telegraph Road, Glen Allen 23059; (804) 264–5033; www.varealtor.com

REAL ESTATE
Shenandoah Valley

FREDERICK COUNTY

The east end of the city of Winchester, a historic city in the northern Shenandoah Valley, and the southern part of Frederick County are growing rapidly. This is in part a result of the westward migration of Washington-based workers, people willing to commute an hour or so to their jobs in order to live in an area that's less crowded and less costly. But the Winchester area also has a good number of industries that keep the real estate market healthy.

Much of Winchester's beauty comes from the graceful old homes along tree-lined streets and row houses built before and during the Civil War. Many of these row houses, which are a short walk from the pedestrian-only downtown mall, are being restored and remodeled. You'll also see a lot of old homes that were built partially of stone. In the newer subdivisions, four- to five-bedroom modern homes are the norm, but you also find some developments of modestly priced homes on small lots in the county.

Frederick County has been averaging about 500 to 700 new homes since 1990. According to the 2000 census, the median value of homes in the county was $118,300. In the city of Winchester, the cost was slightly lower at $108,900.

For more information on real estate in Winchester and Frederick County, contact:

Blue Ridge Association of Realtors, 181 Garber Lane, Winchester 22602; (540) 667–2606; www. blueridgerealtors.com

Top of Virginia Building Association, P.O. Box 744, Winchester, VA 22604; (540) 665–0365

CLARKE COUNTY

Just to the east of Frederick County, in Clarke County, real estate prices are considerably higher. The 2000 census showed that the median cost of a home was $139,500, but by 2001 the average price of a three- to five-bedroom home in that beautiful, rural county ranged from $220,000 to $258,000. Also in Clarke, estates in the country sell for more than $1 million; however, these estates are usually handed down from one generation to the next, so they aren't often on the market.

Clarke County boasts quite a few 19th-century manor homes surrounded by rolling pastures, and these have attracted some of the county's wealthiest newcomers, Washingtonians willing to make the long commute to work or wanting a second home for the weekends.

For more information on real estate in Clarke County, contact:

Blue Ridge Association of Realtors, 181 Garber Lane, Winchester 22602; (540) 667–2606; www.blueridgerealtors.com

Top of Virginia Building Association, P.O. Box 744, Winchester, VA 22604; (540) 665–0365

WARREN COUNTY

Many federal employees and retirees have moved into Warren County, which includes the town of Front Royal, attracted by the beauty of the land, the relaxed pace, and lower real estate prices. The most prized properties here are those with a sense of privacy and clear views of the Shenandoah River or the mountains. While some vacation homes could be bought for as little as $90,000 in 2001, the median price reported in the 2000 census was $108,000. A historic estate in this county can cost in the millions, but it's rare that one comes on the market. Spacious new homes on the county's two golf courses, Shenandoah Valley Golf Club and Bowling Green, are nearing the half-million mark. These high-end prices are not reflective of the rest of Warren County. If you're looking for a more secluded spot, there are a few two-bedroom A-frames in Shenandoah Farms and other remote areas.

For more information on real estate in Warren County, contact:

Blue Ridge Association of Realtors, 181 Garber Lane, Winchester 22602; (540) 667–2606; www. blueridgerealtors.com

Top of Virginia Building Association, P.O. Box 744, Winchester, VA 22604; (540) 665–0365

SHENANDOAH COUNTY

Shenandoah County encompasses several quaint, historic towns, including Woodstock, Edinburg, and New Market, along with the Bryce Resort community in Basye. Retirees and young couples are always seeking weekend retreats here. Bryce Resort (see our Resorts chapter) in western Shenandoah County is an entirely different real estate market. The year-round resort community has chalets, condominiums, and town houses near the resort's ski slopes, lake, and other facilities. Prices vary depending upon the size of the property and its proximity to the slopes. (These range from efficiencies to houses that sleep 15 people.)

Overall in Shenandoah County the cost of a home, according to the 2000 U.S. Census, is $99,400.

For more information about real estate in Shenandoah County, contact:

Massanutten Association of Realtors, 106 West Spring Street, Woodstock 22664; (540) 459-2937; www.usamls.net/massanutten

Shenandoah County Home Builders Association, 225 Taylortown Road, Edinburg 22824, (540) 984-9218

PAGE COUNTY

Page County is more rural, with much of its land tucked between Massanutten Mountain and the Blue Ridge range farther east. Prices, too, are lower in Page County. With figures compiled by the 2000 census, Page was one of the more affordable places to live, with homes selling at a median range of $86,300.

Riverfront property is usually more expensive and hard to come by (the south fork of the Shenandoah River runs through Page County, and the north fork winds through Shenandoah County).

For the most part, architectural styles are simple—this is a rural, no-frills kind of region. The county has a few interesting old homes, but brick ramblers, Cape Cods, and modest, plainly built homes are more the norm.

For more information about real estate in Page County, contact:

Massanutten Association of Realtors, 106 West Spring Street, Woodstock 22664; (540) 459-2937; www.usamls.net/massanutten

ROCKINGHAM COUNTY

In the heart of the Shenandoah Valley, Harrisonburg is one of the fastest-growing cities in the state and the seat of Virginia's leading agricultural county, Rockingham.

Housing prices in this area accelerated during the 1980s but began leveling off in the '90s. By the time the census was taken in 2000, the median cost of homes in the county was $107,700. However, city dwellers paid considerably more: $122,700.

Just one year later, the average price of homes sold in Harrisonburg and Rockingham County ranged from $120,000 to $130,000.

It's increasingly difficult to find quality historic properties in many areas of the Blue Ridge but not in Harrisonburg and Rockingham County, where a good number of old homes, some needing renovation and others already restored, are often available. It is also fairly easy to find farm properties; dairy and poultry farming are the leading agricultural industries.

Massanutten Village, a year-round mountain resort community, is a 15-minute drive east of Harrisonburg. You'll find chalets, condominiums, and town houses near the resort's ski slopes, golf course, tennis courts, and swimming pools. A property owners' association maintains the roads, runs the police department, and manages the entire development. In 2001 the average price of homes here ranged from $90,000 to $200,000.

For more information contact:

Harrisonburg-Rockingham Association of Realtors, 633 East Market Street, Harrisonburg 22801; (540) 433-8855

Shenandoah Valley Builders Association, P.O. Box 1286, Harrisonburg, VA 22803; (540) 434-8005; www.valleybuilders.org

AUGUSTA COUNTY

Augusta County is growing by leaps and bounds, especially in the Stuarts Draft area. A number of industries have built plants there, including Hershey and Little Debbie Bakery, and this has led to a boom in housing. Farther west, more and more people from Washington, D.C., New York, and other northern states are retiring to the Staunton area, drawn to its rich history, pastoral beauty, and vibrant downtown.

According to the 2000 census, homes in the county sold for a median $110,900 price, while residents of the two incorporated cities paid less. Waynesboro homeowners, near the more industrial businesses, paid $89,300, while the median in Staunton was $87,500.

A great demand continues from newcomers to the area for big old homes and farmhouses, but both are in short supply. It isn't that they don't exist. These homes just rarely come on the market, and when they do, they go quickly.

Two major residential developments in Staunton are worth mentioning. Ironwood, a private community next to the Staunton Country Club, is characterized by spacious, red cedar homes with private gardens. Baldwin Place is a planned community in Staunton's north end, where the homes, streets, and even flora are reminiscent of early American villages. Numerous small, well-maintained developments throughout the county offer 5- to 20-acre parcels.

Staunton's downtown is being developed into a major tourist area worthy of repeat visits. Developers and families have grabbed up many of the charming, architecturally sound commercial buildings and homes, but a few may still be left.

For more information contact:

Staunton–Augusta Association of Realtors, 27 Stone Ridge Drive, Waynesboro 22980; (540) 946–4922; www.saarealtor.com

Augusta Homebuilders Association, P.O. Box 36, Waynesboro, VA 22980; (540) 942–4644; www.augustava.yourhba.com

ROCKBRIDGE COUNTY

Nearly half of Rockbridge County is rolling farmland, but its primary city, Lexington, has a historic downtown that demands a higher price tag.

A growing sentiment is that the influx of horse-loving "Yankees" attracted by the Virginia Horse Center (see our Horse Country chapter) has pushed the price of homes and real estate to nearly double over the past several years, while a wide disparity exists in the cost of farmland estates. While some estates have been listed in excess of $1 million, median cost of homes in the county was $92,400, according to the 2000 census. In the city, thanks to the historic homes that line the likes of Marshall Street, the cost rose dramatically to $131,900.

Lexington's historic downtown has long been popular for filming period movies. In 1938 Lexington's Virginia Military Institute was the setting for scenes in *Brother Rat;* more than 50 years later, in the summer of 1992, dirt was poured on the streets for the Civil War film *Sommersby.* More recently the historic school graced the screen in the 2003 movie *Gods and Generals.*

Lexington has numerous buildings and homes that represent most of the architectural styles prevalent in American communities during the 19th century. You will find Victorian cornices and stoops on Main Street, turreted Gothic buildings at Virginia Military Institute, Roman Revival, slender Tuscan columns, and bracketed pediments downtown. The town even has an Italianate villa on Tucker Street that dates to the late 1850s.

Lexington has average family developments with above-average prices, including homes in the suburban, family-oriented neighborhoods of Birdfield, Mount Vista, and Country Club Hills. The neighboring

---

ℹ️ *Just as in any area, price is determined by location, location, location! Charlottesville, Lexington, and Smith Mountain Lake are the priciest, driven up by a large influx of people attracted to horses and boating at the lake. Look for the cheapest land in the rural areas closer to far southwest Virginia.*

town of Buena Vista also offers some nice neighborhoods.

For more information contact:

Lexington–Buena Vista–Rockbridge Association of Realtors, 30 East Preston Street, Lexington 24450; (540) 464-4700

Augusta Homebuilders Association, P.O. Box 36, Waynesboro, VA 22980; (540) 942-4644; www.augustava.yourhba.com

Roanoke Valley

BOTETOURT AND CRAIG COUNTIES

If you looked at the entire Roanoke Valley—which ranged from expensive lakefront property around Smith Mountain Lake—the median price of homes in 2000 was $163,472.

The growing bedroom community of Botetourt County averages somewhat less—even recorded at $125,000—than the nearby Lake area, and finders' fees are often offered for farmland. Census figures from 2000 reported that the median range in Botetourt was $130,500.

Others choose to live farther out in rural Craig County and the Catawba Valley, where a wide variety of homes and large spreads are easier to find. Here the cost drops dramatically to $85,400.

For more information contact:

Roanoke Regional Home Builders Association, 1626 Apperson Drive, Salem 24153; (540) 389-7135; www.rrhba.com

ROANOKE COUNTY

The city of Roanoke's neighborhoods are well defined and often bound together by civic leagues and the Neighborhood Partnership, an energetic organization uniting neighborhoods for more than a decade by encouraging pride and fellowship. Popular areas range from pricey Hunting Hills in southwest Roanoke County to up-and-coming Wasena. The median cost for homes in the city was $80,300, according to the 2000 census.

Each year more and more Roanoke County land, including land next to the Blue Ridge Parkway, is being developed with high-end homes. For example, Strawberry Mountain homes averaged around $316,000 in early 2000. Genteel South Roanoke remains a favorite residential area, with a minuscule turnover in homes, some of which have sold for as much as $1 million. More affordable but equally nice are such family favorites as Raleigh Court and Penn Forest, where neighborhood block parties and nightly strolls are the norm. Taking all the county into account, census figures showed the median figure was $118,110.

Nearby Salem offers everything from downtown-area, tin-roofed, Victorian-style homes with stained glass to the more modest dwellings in Beverly Heights, where young families reside in ranch homes. Census figures listed the median cost of Salem homes at $104,200.

The adjoining town of Vinton offers pricey subdivisions such as Falling Creek and charming downtown wonders. Figures from 2002 show that the average price of a home sold in the Roanoke Valley area ranged from $133,000 to $167,000.

For more information contact:

Roanoke Valley Association of Realtors, 3130 Chaparral Drive SW, Roanoke 24018; (540) 772-0526; www.rvar.com

Roanoke Regional Home Builders Association, 1626 Apperson Drive, Salem 24153; (540) 389-7135; www.rrhba.com

East of the Blue Ridge

LOUDOUN COUNTY

If you are looking for property in Loudoun, start in Leesburg, the imaginary dividing line of real estate in the county.

As a rule of thumb, most of the area west of Leesburg is more rural, while the eastern portion is better suited to the D.C. business crowd. Generally, prices are lower in the west and increase as you get closer

Medical Needs

In case of emergency, you are in good hands. There are myriad facilities up and down both sides of the Blue Ridge that can assist your needs.

The University of Virginia Health System, still called the UVA Hospital by many locals, is perhaps the best known. When critical care is essential, other regional hospitals have transported patients here. UVA is one of the top 100 hospitals in the country for intensive care. In 2001, 42 of the hospital's doctors were listed in America's Top Doctors. That same year, *U.S. News and World Report* selected eight UVA specialties—endocrinology, cancer, urology, respiratory disease, geriatrics, kidney disease, neurology-neurosurgery, and ears, nose, and throat—in its *Best Hospitals 2001* issue.

Also listed in the Nation's Top 100 Hospitals were Carilion Roanoke Community and Carilion Roanoke Memorial hospitals for orthopedic and stroke care. Carilion also has a toll-free number, (800) 442-8482, which will link you up with one of 800 physicians in southwest Virginia.

Many facilities along the Blue Ridge cater to specific needs. Woodrow Wilson Rehabilitation Center in Fishersville offers therapy and training for those with disabilities to help them reenter the work force. A division of the Virginia Department of Rehabilitative Services, Woodrow Wilson was the first state-owned and -operated comprehensive rehabilitation center in the United States.

Western State Hospital in Staunton is a state-run psychiatric hospital, while Catawba Hospital near Salem is a part of the Department of Mental Health and Mental Retardation. Western State treats those between the ages of 17 and 64 who have been admitted through local community services. Catawba treats those older than 65. Catawba traces its history back to 1909, when it was the first tuberculosis sanatorium in Virginia.

Also near Salem is the Veterans Medical Center, which has offered care for thousands of veterans from across the state.

Listed below are just some of the facilities . . . in case of emergency.

Shenandoah Valley
Winchester Medical Center
1840 Amherst Street, Winchester
(540) 536-8000
www.valleyhealthlinc.com/frameset
_wmc.html

Shenandoah Memorial Hospital
759 South Main Street, Woodstock
(540) 459-1100
www.valleyhealthlinc.com

Warren Memorial Hospital
1000 North Shenandoah Avenue, Front Royal
(540) 636-0300
www.valleyhealthlinc.com

Page Memorial Hospital
200 Memorial Drive, Luray
(540) 743-4561
www.pagememorialhospital.org

Rockingham Memorial Hospital
235 Cantrell Avenue, Harrisonburg
(540) 433-4100
www.rmhonline.com

Augusta Medical Center
78 Medical Center Drive, Fishersville
(540) 932-4000, (800) 932-0262
www.augustamed.com

Woodrow Wilson Rehabilitation Center
Box W-1, Fishersville
(540) 332-7065, (800) 345-WWRC
www.wwrc.net

Western State Hospital
1301 Richmond Avenue, Staunton
(540) 332-8000
www.wsh.state.va.us

Stonewall Jackson Hospital
1 Health Circle, Lexington
(540) 458-3300
www.sjhospital.com

Roanoke Valley
Carilion Roanoke Memorial Hospital
1722 Jefferson Street, Roanoke
(540) 981-7000
www.carilion.com

Veterans Medical Center
1970 Roanoke Boulevard, Salem
(540) 982-2463
www.va.gov

Lewis-Gale Medical Center
1900 Electric Road, Salem
(540) 776-4000
www.lewis-gale.com

Catawba Hospital
5525 Catawba Hospital Drive, Catawba
(540) 375-4200
www.catawba.state.va.us

East of the Blue Ridge
Loudoun Hospital Center
44045 Riverside Parkway, Leesburg
(703) 858-6000, (888) 542-8477
www.loudounhealthcare.org

Fauquier Hospital
500 Hospital Drive, Warrenton
(540) 347-2550
www.fauquierhospital.org

Culpeper Regional Hospital
501 Sunset Lane, Culpeper
(540) 829-4100
www.culpeperhospital.com

Martha Jefferson Hospital
459 Locust Avenue, Charlottesville
(434) 982-7000
www.marthajefferson.org

University Health System
1215 Lee Street, Charlottesville
(434) 924-0000
www.hsc.virginia.edu

Children's Medical Center at University
of Virginia
1215 Lee Street, (434) 924-0000
www.med.edu.virginia/medical/clinic/
pediatrics/cmc/

Lynchburg General Hospital
1901 Tate Springs Road, Lynchburg
(434) 947-3000
www.centrahealth.com

Virginia Baptist Hospital
3300 Rivermont Avenue, Lynchburg
(434) 947-4000
www.centrahealth.com

Carilion Bedford Memorial Hospital
1613 Oakwood Street, Bedford
(540) 586-2441
www.carilion.com

Carilion Franklin Memorial Hospital
180 Floyd Avenue, Rocky Mount
(540) 483-5277
www.carilion.com

New River Valley Region
Montgomery Regional Hospital
3700 South Main Street, Blacksburg
(540) 951-1111
www.mrhospital.com

Carilion New River Valley Medical
Center
2900 Lamb Circle, Christiansburg
(540) 731-2000
www.carilion.com

Carilion Saint Albans Hospital
7516 Lee Highway, Radford
(540) 639-2481
www.carilion.com

Carilion Giles Memorial Hospital
1 Taylor Avenue, Pearisburg
(540) 921-6000
www.carilion.com

Pulaski Community Hospital
2400 Lee Highway, Pulaski
(540) 994-8100
www.pch-va.com

Alleghany Highlands
Alleghany Regional Hospital
1 ARH Lane, Low Moor
(540) 862-6011
www.alleghanyregional.com

Bath County Community Hospital
Rural Route 220, Hot Springs
(540) 839-7000
www.bcchospital.org

Martha Jefferson Hospital is one of two hospitals in Charlottesville. MARY ALICE BLACKWELL

to the new developments near Washington Dulles International Airport.

In fact, you can find a mixed bag of homes in Loudoun, ranging from Quaker and pre–Civil War homes to town houses and condominiums. In the east, Sterling and Sterling Park are two popular neighborhoods, while newer developments in Ashburn Village, Cascades, and Lansdowne create an ever-growing amount of new town houses and single-family homes.

You can find the older homes with more acreage in the western communities near Purcellville, Hillsboro, and Round Hill. Some of the largest—and most expensive—estates can be found near Middleburg.

In 2000 the census reported there were 74,235 housing units in the county, with a median price at $200,500, by far the highest in the Blue Ridge. However, prices climb rapidly. In one year's time, county-wide sales averaged $278,000.

For more information contact:

Dulles Area Association of Realtors, 803 Sycolin Road, Suite 222, Leesburg 20175; (703) 777-2468; www.dulles area.com

Northern Virginia Building Industry Association, 14160 Newbrook Drive, Chantilly 20151; (703) 817-0154; www.nvbia.com

FAUQUIER COUNTY

Location is everything in Fauquier County. The northern section is more upscale than some of the other surrounding counties because it lies in the heart of Virginia's hunt and wine country. Upperville and the Plains still play host to some of the oldest horse shows in the country. Many homes in the area also date back to the Civil War and have been meticulously restored to their early grandeur. In fact, North Wales, one of Fauquier's most distinguished homes, was listed on the market in 1997 for about $9 million. This estate, with eight cottages on 1,000 acres, is rich with history. Dating back to 1716, it survived both the Revolutionary and Civil Wars and was used as a safe haven for slaves as a

stop on the Underground Railroad.

If your tastes are a little more modest, southern Fauquier offers many single-family detached homes with much more affordable price tags. The median cost of homes in Fauquier was $162,700, according to the 2000 census. The areas around Bealeton on U.S. Highway 17 and Remington off U.S. Highway 29 have been strong growth areas.

For more information contact:

Greater Piedmont Area Association of Realtors, 47 Garrett Street, Warrenton 20186; (540) 347-4866; www.gpaar.com

Northern Virginia Building Industry Association, 14160 Newbrook Drive, Chantilly 20151; (703) 817-0154; www.nvbia.com

RAPPAHANNOCK COUNTY

In Rappahannock County you will find land-development rules are strict, ensuring that the quaintness and beauty of this county remain intact. With approximately 6,000 full-time residents (about the same number as lived here 100 years ago), Rappahannock has been able to keep out large-scale development. Only one town, Washington, is incorporated. No stoplights and no chain stores are to be found here, just markets and well-stocked country stores.

Thousands of visitors each year seek out the county's wonderful restaurants, bed-and-breakfasts, and antiques stores. As you might imagine, real estate is quite valuable in this area. The census figures were $129,300 for 2000.

For more information contact:

Greater Piedmont Area Association of Realtors, 47 Garrett Street, Warrenton 20186; (540) 347-4866; www.gpaar.com

Northern Virginia Building Industry Association, 14160 Newbrook Drive, Chantilly 20151; (703) 817-0154; www.nvbia.com

CULPEPER COUNTY

Since this scenic area is still within commuting distance to Washington, D.C., the strongest area of home sales is still in the northern section of Culpeper County. Those who don't mind the drive can often find larger homes with more land for the dollar than is available in the northern counties. While a few modestly priced town homes are sometimes listed, larger farms and semi-custom homes are on the market. The median cost of homes in 2000 was $123,300, according to census data.

For more information on Culpeper County, contact:

Greater Piedmont Area Association of Realtors, 47 Garrett Street, Warrenton 20186; (540) 347-4866; www.gpaar.com

Piedmont Virginia Building Industry Association, P.O. Box 897, Culpeper, VA 22761; (540) 825-7558; www.pvbia.org

MADISON COUNTY

A rural refuge, Madison County is home to part of the Shenandoah National Park and the scenic Graves Mountain Lodge (see our chapter on Bed-and-Breakfasts and Country Inns). The development rules are more relaxed here. The homes are mostly three bedrooms, although there are some two- and four-bedroom homes included. It is difficult to find historic Victorian or Colonial homes on the market; instead, the predominant styles are the brick rambler and simpler homes with vinyl siding. The median cost by census reports in 2000 was $100,600.

For more information contact:

Greater Piedmont Area Association of Realtors, 47 Garrett Street, Warrenton 20186; (540) 347-4866; www.gpaar.com

Piedmont Virginia Building Industry Association, P.O. Box 897, Culpeper, VA 22761; (540) 825-7558; www.pvbia.org

Blue Ridge Homebuilders Association, 2330 Commonwealth Drive, Charlottesville 22901; (434) 973-8652; www.brhba.org

GREENE COUNTY

One of Virginia's smallest counties in size, nearly one-fifth of Greene's 98,920 acres belong to the Shenandoah National Park.

While much of the land is covered by forest and farms, large parcels of property have been earmarked for subdivisions.

Cheaper land and affordable homes have turned Greene County into a popular bedroom community for young families willing to commute the short distance to nearby Charlottesville. In fact, Greene ranked ninth in the state for the highest net migration rate with a population of 15,200 in 2000.

While some older historic buildings line U.S. Highway 33 in Stanardsville, many of the homes for sale are newer constructions. The median home price in 2000 was $111,400, according to census figures. However, that figure has rocketed to $170,000 for the first half of 2004.

For more information on homes in Greene County, contact:

Charlottesville Area Association of Realtors, 550 Hillsdale Drive, Charlottesville 22901; (434) 817-2227; www.caar.com

Blue Ridge Homebuilders Association, 2330 Commonwealth Drive, Charlottesville 22901; (434) 973-8652; www.brhba.org

ORANGE COUNTY

The real estate market in Orange County, home of James Madison's Montpelier (see our Attractions chapter) and the Barboursville Winery (see our Wineries chapter), is more upscale. You will find a diversity of residential properties and prices that are generally lower than in Albemarle County, which includes Charlottesville. Median homes in Orange County cost $115,000 in the 2000 census report. Generally, the homes are scattered across the county because the local government has not allowed the growth of residential neighborhoods. In fact, only 3 percent of its 227,000 acres was developed in 2001.

Most of Orange County is zoned agricultural and used generally for farming and timber. Land cannot be subdivided into more than four parcels in any four-year period of time, making it extremely difficult to rezone agricultural land to residential. This is precisely what makes Orange such a desirable place to live for people who can afford the prices of some of the stately estates, antebellum homes, and spacious horse and cattle ranches.

For more information on homes in Orange County, contact:

Greater Piedmont Area Association of Realtors, 47 Garrett Street, Warrenton 20186; (540) 347–4866, www.gpaar.com

Piedmont Virginia Building Industry Association, P.O. Box 897, Culpeper, VA 22761; (540) 825–7558; www.pvbia.org

ALBEMARLE COUNTY

Albemarle County, which surrounds the city of Charlottesville, works hard to restrict growth and preserve its rural beauty. The local government has targeted Crozet and the Ivy area, a few miles west of Charlottesville, as growth areas and allows some higher-density development, such as the Highlands, a Crozet subdivision. But the Free Union area and many other parts of the county are slated to remain as rural as possible, with minimum requirements of one residence per 21 acres.

Charlottesville is one of the more expensive areas in Virginia in which to live, second only to Loudoun and Northern Virginia. People of great wealth are drawn to the area, captivated by the beauty of the land, its historic estates, and the city's cosmopolitan atmosphere. Two hospitals in the city attract doctors, and jokes abound about the number of lawyers—graduates of UVA who refuse to leave the area. In short, a lot of money floats around this area, and the real estate market has risen to the occasion.

This affluence is especially notable in the stretch of land west of the city along Barracks Road, toward Free Union and east of the city at the Keswick development. In the western area near Ivy, new homes can be found in the Rosemont subdivision. Near Farmington Country Club, also west of the city, stately homes run anywhere from $1 million to more than $2 million. Inglecress is another exclusive development along Barracks and Garth Roads.

Architectural styles of most of these new homes are similar—white columns and symmetrical porticos abound, though the Virginia farmhouse remains a staple in the county and in many subdivisions. Jefferson's Monticello and the University of Virginia are architectural models, at least on the exterior. But inside many new homes, you'll find contemporary features such as vaulted ceilings, skylights, and open spaces.

The Keswick community gives new meaning to the term "elegant," even by Charlottesville standards. This private, gated community has a maximum allowable density of about 100 home sites in two- to five-acre parcels. Amenities include an 18-hole Arnold Palmer signature golf course.

Also east of Charlottesville is Glenmore, a private, gated community off U.S. Highway 250. The 1,188-acre community is wrapped around an 18-hole, par 72 championship golf course, swimming facility, tennis complex, an on-site equestrian center with bridle trails, and miles of jogging and biking trails. The community will have only 750 homes at build-out, with home sites on the golf course, in deep woods, on grassy knolls, overlooking the 2.5-mile frontage on the Rivanna River, or with views of Thomas Jefferson's Monticello.

More than 100 homes in the Charlottesville area were built between the early 1700s and the Civil War era. Wealthy families, often using royal land grants, began migrating west from Richmond in the early 1700s. Such estates as Plain Dealing, Estouteville, and Edgemont are registered historic landmarks. Because so many historic homes are in the area, one or two may be on the market at any given time.

The city, which has no more room for development, has a few beautiful neighborhoods. Gracious old homes are concentrated in the Rugby Road area, but you'll find more modest, rambler-type homes and Cape Cods close to the university.

Census figures from 2000 showed that the median price for homes in Charlottesville was $119,000, while the county sticker was $161,100. Figures in 2004 climbed to $204,500 in the city and $261,200 in the county.

Some important phone numbers:
Charlottesville Area Association of Realtors, 550 Hillsdale Drive, Charlottesville 22901; (434) 817-2227; www.caar.com

Blue Ridge Homebuilders Association, 2330 Commonwealth Drive, Charlottesville 22901; (434) 973-8652; www.brhba.org

NELSON COUNTY

The character of Nelson County can be defined by its two major tourist attractions. Wintergreen, the state's largest resort, offers a taste of luxury associated with a weekend on the ski slopes (see our Resorts chapter), while the Waltons Museum houses a collection of memorabilia dedicated to a hard-working family that struggled to weather the Great Depression (see our Attractions chapter).

While hundreds of tourists are drawn to these Nelson destinations each year, more than 13,000 folks decided to call this diverse county their home.

Nelson, indeed, is an eclectic community. It's home to polo players, best-selling authors, farmers, retirees, and—with Charlottesville just a half hour's drive away—plenty of business commuters. Property can be found to accommodate just about any pocketbook. Look for higher prices as you get closer to Charlottesville and the mountains, but it is possible to find a few modest-priced homes in the southern reaches of the county.

Modest three- or four-bedroom homes can be found in Lovingston, Shipman, and parts of the county outside the Wintergreen Resort area. The median price from the 2000 census was $95,100. By the first half of 2004, that number had climbed to $232,000.

The Wintergreen Resort has luxury condominiums and single-family homes on the ridges overlooking the ski area, Devils Knob Golf Course, and the surrounding mountains.

In the valley is a growing community that has at its center the award-winning Stoney Creek Golf Course and the Rodes Farm Equestrian Center. About one hour from Charlottesville, Wintergreen is secluded from encroaching development by the Blue Ridge Parkway and Shenandoah National Park on the north and west and the George Washington and Jefferson National Forests to the south. More than half of Wintergreen's 11,000 acres have been set aside as permanent, undisturbed wilderness.

The 2002 price of condominiums ranged anywhere from $45,000 to $350,000, covering efficiencies to three-bedroom constructions. Homes listed from $125,000 to more than $600,000 and land from $25,000 to $250,000 per lot.

For more information contact:
Charlottesville Area Association of Realtors, 550 Hillsdale Drive, Charlottesville 22901; (434) 817-2227; www.caar.com

Blue Ridge Homebuilders Association, 2330 Commonwealth Drive, Charlottesville 22901; (434) 973-8652; www.brhba.org

LYNCHBURG, BEDFORD, AND FRANKLIN COUNTIES

Lynchburg and surrounding Bedford County comprise one of the most rapidly growing regions in the state. Among the areas of growth are Ivy Hill, a planned community around Ivy Lake, Ivy Hill Golf Course, and the popular Lake Vista; Poplar Forest, a neighborhood of fine homes on wooded lots carved out of Jefferson's land surrounding his home; Meadowwood, just outside the city on lots averaging two to three acres; and Meadowridge, homes on two- to three-acre lots close to the mountains.

In Lynchburg, you'll love the tree-bordered streets lined with two-story brick Colonials graced by manicured lawns.

Among the most prestigious and desirable are Peakland Place, Linkhorne Forest, Link Road, Rivermont Avenue, and Boonsboro Forest. New growth west of the city is due to land that is ripe for development. In addition, homeowners in several historic districts are turning formerly neglected turn-of-the-20th-century residences into glorious showcases. The most advanced renovation of these historic districts are

Diamond Hill and Garland Hill. Close behind are Federal Hill, College Hill, and Daniels Hill

South of Lynchburg, Smith Mountain Lake, which straddles the border between Bedford and Franklin Counties, attracts upscale buyers seeking waterfront golf communities, second homes, and retiree getaways. Some more popular communities are Chestnut Creek, Waters Edge, Waterfront, and Waverly. It's worth a boat trip around Smith Mountain Lake's 500 miles of shoreline just to see the architectural, custom-built splendor of some of the homes.

Rural farmsteads and homes in Bedford and Franklin Counties are more affordable and more available than in any of the other Roanoke bedroom communities.

Your best buys can be found within Lynchburg city limits. According to the 2000 census, the median cost of a home in the city was $85,300. Bedford County prices rose to $127,000, while Franklin was $105,000.

For more information, contact:

Lynchburg Association of Realtors, 3639 Old Forest Road, Lynchburg 24501; (434) 385-8760; www.Lynchburgmls.com

Builders & Associates of Central Virginia, P.O. Box 216, Forest, VA 24551; (434) 385-6018

Roanoke Regional Home Builders Association Inc., 1626 Apperson Drive, Salem 24153; (540) 389-7135; www.rrhba.com

New River Valley

MONTGOMERY, GILES, AND PULASKI COUNTIES

In Montgomery County, which surrounds the university towns of Blacksburg and Radford, the high salaries paid to professionals from Virginia Tech and Radford University have driven up the price of homes and land.

The price of premium farmland in neighboring Floyd and Giles Counties is

also affected by the high standard of living. Montgomery County is the highest priced area, according to the 2000 census. The median home costs $114,600 in Montgomery, while in Giles the number was $69,200, with Pulaski in at $80,000.

The New River area is considered one of the five major growth areas of Virginia, according to Realtor E.R Templeton of Raines Real Estate of Blacksburg.

Requests for finders are often posted on bulletin boards in little towns such as Newport.

Potential homeowners will most likely find Christiansburg and Pulaski the least expensive places to buy a home. The downtowns of Blacksburg and Radford offer true small-town atmospheres conducive to leisurely evening strolls, breathtaking parks (especially Radford's Bisset Park along the New River), and the likelihood of meeting others who enjoy an academically stimulating lifestyle. The towns are packed with apartment complexes and town houses for the thousands of students who live there.

Popular family developments near Blacksburg are Foxridge, Heathwood, Toms Creek Estates, and Westover Hills.

Some of Christiansburg's better-known developments are Craig Mountain, Diamond Point, Victory Heights, and Windmill Hills.

In Radford a family can buy a home in Sunset Village and in the newer developments of College Park and High Meadows. The median cost in Radford is $95,100, according to census statistics.

Many New River Valley residents opt to live in the environs of Giles, Floyd, and Pulaski Counties, where rural living is

If you would like to move to the area, check out the Virginia Chamber of Commerce Web site at www.vachamber.com. It offers relocation information including details on how to receive a free relocation package.

Media

Reading is big in the Blue Ridge, as evidenced by the large number of bookstores, authors, and newspapers that proliferate in the region. While the *Roanoke Times* is the largest paper in the Blue Ridge, two others from outside the area are also readily available at most stores. The *Richmond Times Dispatch* is headquartered in the state capital with bureaus throughout the commonwealth. The *Washington Post* is also widely read here. But if you want to find out what's happening in the town you're visiting—from local news and sporting events to grocery sales and movie listings—your best bet is to pick up a local paper. Several localities will even have free papers. Here is a list of just a few of the offerings:

Daily Newspapers
Charlottesville—*Daily Progress*
Covington—*Virginian Review*
Culpeper—*Star Exponent*
Harrisonburg—*News Record*
Lynchburg—*News and Advance*
Roanoke—*Roanoke Times and World News*
Staunton—*The Daily News Leader*
Waynesboro—*News Virginian*
Winchester—*The Winchester Star*

Nondaily Newspapers
Christiansburg—*Christiansburg News–Messenger*
Culpeper—*Culpeper News*
Floyd—*Floyd Press*
Leesburg—*Leesburg Today*
Leesburg—*Loudoun Times-Mirror*
Lexington—*News–Gazette*
Lexington—*Rockbridge Weekly*
Madison—*Madison County Eagle*
Orange—*Orange County Review*
Roanoke—*Blue Ridge Business Journal*
Stanardsville—*Greene County Record*
Sterling—*Loudoun Easterner*
Warrenton—*Fauquier Citizen*
Warrenton—*Fauquier Times-Democrat*
Washington—*Rappahannock News*

College Newspapers
Ferrum College—*Iron Blade*
James Madison University—*Breeze*
Radford University—*Tartan*
University of Virginia—*Cavalier Daily*
Virginia Tech—*Collegiate Times*
Washington and Lee University—*Trident*

Television
Not only does this medium give you a chance to be entertained while you rest your weary feet, television can bring you the latest developments in local news. Roanoke, the largest metropolitan city in the Blue Ridge, naturally has the most diversity, but there are several local stations in the larger cities. Some of them include:

Charlottesville—WHTJ-PBS, WVIR-NBC
Harrisonburg—WHSV-ABC, WVPT-PBS
Lynchburg—WSET-ABC
Roanoke—WDBJ-CBS, WSLS-NBC, WBRA-PBS, WDRL-UPN, WFXR-FOX
Woodstock—WAZT-IND

Newspapers keep you up to date on current events in the Blue Ridge. MARY ALICE BLACKWELL

Radio Stations

Along the Blue Ridge, there are a plethora of radio stations that will keep you tuned in to everything from the latest weather conditions to the popular hits of the day. As would be expected, the most stations seem to be clustered around the college towns. Harrisonburg had as many as 10 at one time. But even tiny Monterey, one of the least populated towns in the Blue Ridge, has its own FM station at WVLS 89.7. While there are way too many to list—nearly 130 at last count—we have tried to list some of the stations here that will also keep you informed with a mix of news, views, and sports.

Blacksburg—WUVT-FM 90.7, WFNR-AM 710
Charlottesville—WINA-FM 101.7, WTJU-FM 91.1, WVTU-FM 89.3, WCHV-AM 1260
Front Royal—WFTR-AM 1450
Harrisonburg—WSVA-AM 550, WMRA-FM 90.7, WXJM-FM 88.7
Leesburg—WAGE-AM 1200
Lexington—WREL-AM 1450, WMRL-FM 89.9
Lynchburg—WLNI-FM 105.9
Radford—WVRU-FM 89.9
Roanoke—WFIR-AM 960, WVTF-FM 89.1
Warrenton—WTOP-FM 107.7
Winchester—WNTW-AM 610

prevalent. Farms can be expensive, since a lot of professionals also like to live out in the country. The quality of farmland varies in each county, and it tends to be scarce, due to the area's beauty and proximity to the Blue Ridge Parkway. It probably is least expensive in Pulaski County. Numerous second homes have been built in Pulaski County's Claytor Lake area.

In downtown Pulaski professionals from Washington, D.C., and other metropolitan areas are renovating some of the Prospect Street mansions, notable for their witches' caps and winding front porches. An area short on bed-and-breakfast inns, downtown Pulaski probably has more old mansions that would lend themselves to this cause than any other place in the New River Valley.

If you're looking for a pleasant family development in Pulaski, consider Mountain View Acres or Newbern Heights, with houses priced from $120,000 to $250,000. Oak View is more expensive at $135,000 to $250,000 but considerably more affordable than a similar development in neighboring Montgomery County.

For more information, contact:

New River Valley Association of Realtors, 811 Triangle Street, Blacksburg 24060; (540) 953–0040; www.vrvar.com

New River Valley Home Builders Association, P.O. Box 2010, Christiansburg, VA 24068; (540) 381-0180; www.nrvhba.org

Alleghany Highlands

ALLEGHANY, BATH, AND HIGHLAND COUNTIES

This area, which includes the counties of Highland, Bath, and Alleghany, has no organized real estate board and no Multiple Listing Service. But local real estate agents say most homes typically sell for much less than a fourth of the price of their urban counterparts. Another rule of thumb, from Highland County's Building Permits Office, is that the cost of building a new home here is $100 per square foot compared to $200 in Northern Virginia.

The area also is unusual in that much of the rural, mountainous Highland County property is owned by people who don't live there. For example, half of the least-populated county in Virginia is owned by vacationers in the highest county east of the Mississippi. Real estate here is prized for its proximity to the Homestead (see our Resorts chapter), the Potomac and James Rivers, and hunting and fishing preserves.

Here you can buy farms with miles of split-rail fences on emerald-green pastures, maple sugar orchards, wooded tracts, trout farms, and cattle farms. It's obvious to visitors that the sheep outnumber the human population five to one. The census recorded only 1,826 dwellings in Highland in 2000. The cost of homes were $83,700 in Highland, $79,700 in Bath, and $77,500 in Alleghany, according to the census.

Many look to this area for retirement.

REAL ESTATE COMPANIES

A Realtor can be your best friend if you are contemplating a move. Not only will they have access to real estate listings, but they should also be your guide on taxes, schools, and local services. They should know which areas have good school districts, and they should be able to tell you where your houses of worship are located. There are literally hundreds of real estate companies up and down both sides of the Blue Ridge. Here's just a few to get you started:

Shenandoah Valley

ERA Jim Barb Realty Inc.
137 West Boscawen Street, Winchester
(800) 255–3171

Homeland Realty
9586 South Congress Street
New Market
(540) 740–3176

Mead Associates Inc.
21 North Main Street, Lexington
(540) 463-7168
www.meadproperties.com

Prudential Commonwealth Property
26 North Main Street, Lexington
(540) 463-4443
www.prucommonwealth.com

Real Estate III
105 Lee Jackson Highway, Suite 105
Staunton
(540) 885-3339, (800) 327-3433
www.realestateiii.com

Real Estate III
2542 Jefferson Highway, Suite 104
Waynesboro
(540) 943-3183, (800) 868-0023
www.realestateiii.com

RE/MAX Advantage
413 North Coalter Street, Staunton
(540) 886-3146

Sam Snead Realty Inc.
437 South Royal Avenue, Front Royal
(540) 635-9809

Weichert Realty Inc.
824 John Marshall Highway, Front Royal
(540) 635-8000

Roanoke Valley

Campbell Realty Inc.
3735 Plantation Road, Roanoke
(540) 977-1549, (800) 253-3569

Owens & Co. Realtors
38 Murray Farm Road, Roanoke
(540) 977-1777
www.roanokehomes.us

Stover Davis Realty and Associates
5049 Valley View Boulevard, Roanoke
(540) 777-3333, (800) 859-7261
www.stoverdavis.com

Waterfront Properties Realtors
Smith Mountain Lake
(540) 721-8659
www.smithmountainlake.com

East of the Blue Ridge

Century 21 Anchor Realtors
16475 Booker T. Washington Highway
Moneta
(540) 721-8881

Coldwell Banker Residential Brokerage
5306 Lee Highway, Suites 1 and 2
Warrenton
(800) 345-4849

Hunt Country Properties
108 West Washington Street
Middleburg
(540) 687-8807

Keller Williams Realty
703-B East Market Street, Leesburg
(703) 606-7277
www.mikewagner.com

Montague, Miller & Company Realtors
198 South Main Street, Suite 102
Amherst
(434) 946-5522
www.montaguemiller.com

Montague, Miller & Company Realtors
500 Westfield Road, Charlottesville
(434) 973-5393, (800) 793-5393
www.montaguemiller.com

Montague, Miller & Company Realtors
332 James Madison Highway, Culpeper
(540) 825-3300, (800) 825-6825
www.montaguemiller.com

Montague, Miller & Company Realtors
US 29 N, Madison
(540) 948-6655, (888) 948-2121
www.montaguemiller.com

Montague, Miller & Company Realtors
18 Pheasant Run, Nellysford
(434) 361-1512
www.montaguemiller.com

Montague, Miller & Company Realtors
132 East Main Street, Orange
(540) 672-7373, (866) 672-7373
www.montaguemiller.com

Real Estate III
Various locations in Charlottesville
P.O. Box 8186, Charlottesville, VA
(434) 817-9200, (800) 973-8338
www.realestateiii.com

Real Estate III
291 Gay Street, Washington
(540) 675-1373
www.realestateiii.com

Roy Wheeler Realty Co.
1100 Dryden Lane, Charlottesville
(434) 296-4170, (877) 560-2858
www.roywheeler.com

Roy Wheeler Realty Co.
617 Zachary Taylor Highway, Flint Hill
(540) 675-7171
www.roywheeler.com

Smith & Thurmond Inc.
5521 Fort Avenue, Lynchburg
(434) 237-6267
www.smiththurmond.com

Walsh & Associates, Inc.
142 East Main Street, Purcellville
(540) 338-5730
www.walshrealtors.com

Wintergreen Real Estate
P.O. Box 747, Wintergreen, VA
(434) 361-0500, (800) 325-2200
www.wintergreenrealestate.com

New River Valley

Owens & Co. Realtors
400 Roanoke Avenue, Christiansburg
(540) 382-5270
www.newrivervalley.owensandco.com

Raines Real Estate
318 North Main Street, Blacksburg
(540) 552-4201

RE/MAX All Stars
1645 Roanoke Road, Daleville
(540) 992-2525, (800) 507-9882
www.roanokehomesforsale.com

Alleghany Highlands

Clarkson & Wallace Inc.
P.O. Box 358, Warm Springs, VA
(540) 839-2609
www.clarksonandwallace.com

Shamrock & Stephenson Realty, Inc.
P.O. Box 398, Monterey, VA
(540) 468-3370
www.monterey-va-realestate.com

RETIREMENT

Determining the perfect place to retire takes planning, with careful consideration of individual tastes and personal needs. The Blue Ridge has numerous agencies and contacts to help you determine where you would be happiest. Here is a list, arranged by region, of helpful agencies or programs.

Shenandoah Valley

AGENCIES

Frederick County Parks and Recreation Department
107 North Kent Street, Winchester
(540) 665-5678
www.co.frederick.va.us

This recreation department offers an assortment of year-round activities for people 55 and older. Senior Clubs are active throughout the county. The cost to join is $6.00 per year, and members plan their own activities, such as bingo, potluck dinners, and regular trips. They also may participate in specially designed fitness classes, computer programs, and get homebound transportation.

Godfrey Miller Fellowship Center
28 South Loudoun Street, Winchester
(540) 667-5869

Built in 1785, this large stone and brick center is on Winchester's historic pedestrian mall. Activities include programs on arts and crafts, bingo, bridge, music, Bible study, and health care. There are lunches, picnics, trips, lectures, and weekly blood-pressure clinics. There is no charge to visit, but lunches and special trips have fees. Affiliated with the Grace Lutheran Church, the center is open from 10:00 A.M. to 3:00 P.M. Monday through Thursday.

Shenandoah Area Agency on Aging
207 Mosby Lane, Front Royal
(540) 635-7141, (800) 883-4122
www.shenandoahaaa.com

This agency provides elderly services to seniors in Clarke, Frederick, Page, Shenandoah, and Warren Counties as well as the city of Winchester. Programs include in-home service, case management, special activities, home-delivered meals, and meals in local senior centers. There is no charge for senior center meals, but donations are welcome.

Rockingham County Parks and
Recreation Department
20 East Gay Street, Harrisonburg
(540) 564-3160
www.rockinghamcounty.va.us

This department offers arts and crafts, cards, dominos, and other games to seniors at numerous locations throughout the county. There are even a Red Hat Society and a kayak club. There is no charge except for trips, such as the trip to the Wayside Theater ($25) or dinner-and-the-ater ($40) packages.

Augusta County Parks and Recreation
Department
P.O. Box 590, Verona, VA 24482-0590
(540) 245-5727
www.co.augusta.va.us

The seniors program at this recreation department focuses on classes and day trips. Fifty-Five Alive driving classes for senior citizens are also held here. There are fees for all classes and trips.

If you're in the market for a retirement community, start early. Allow yourself up to a year to compare and visit locations, especially if you need a large space. Many communities have waiting lists for two-bedroom units, which are tougher to come by.

The Valley Program for
Aging Services Inc.
325 Pine Avenue, Waynesboro
(540) 949-7141, (800) 868-VPAS

An enormous resource for area seniors, the Valley Program serves Rockingham, Augusta, Rockbridge, Bath, and Highland Counties. Services aimed at supporting independent living for seniors include case management, transportation, adult day care, personal care, and home-delivered meals. There is a day-care center in Waynesboro, and more facilities in the other counties. Each center plans activities to meet their individual needs.

AHC Hospice of the Shenandoah
64 Sports Medicine Drive, Fishersville
(540) 332-4909

Hospice provides a wide range of services from clinical care to emotional support for terminally ill patients and their families. This licensed chapter serves Staunton, Waynesboro, and Augusta County.

CLOSE-UP

Worship

If you are looking for a place to worship, the Blue Ridge houses everything from Anglican to Zen.

The range is vast. There's Monterey, with the Monterey Presbyterian and Highland Baptist Churches. Then there's Charlottesville, with more than 290 choices, including Baha'i Faith, Buddhist, Greek Orthodox, Jehovah's Witnesses, Mormon, Metropolitan, Quaker, Pentecostal, and Seventh Day Adventist, to name but a few.

The largest denomination, however, up and down both sides of the Blue Ridge is Baptist. Perhaps none has gotten more national recognition than Lynchburg's Thomas Road Baptist Church. With 35 members, Jerry Falwell founded this church in 1935—the same year he started ministering on TV and radio. Today Falwell is remembered far and wide for launching the Moral Majority and as a voice of the religious right in the political arena. A native of Lynch-

burg, Falwell also started the Lynchburg Christian Academy for students in preschool through 12th grade, and he founded and is still chancellor of Liberty University, an independent fundamental Baptist college of 10,000.

First Presbyterian Church of Staunton, founded in 1804, celebrated its 200th anniversary in 2004 as ministers who served over the past 35 years returned for a two-day celebration. With a strong emphasis on education, including educating women, the church along with other Presbyterian churches from surrounding counties helped launch a school under Presbyterian control. The Augusta Female Seminary was founded in 1842—we know it today as Mary Baldwin College. One of the church's ministers, the Rev. Joseph Ruggles Wilson, served as the school's principal. His son, Thomas Woodrow Wilson, was born in the church's manse.

But choice is still the key word in

RETIREMENT COMMUNITIES

Shenandoah Valley Westminster–Canterbury
300 Westminster–Canterbury Drive, Winchester
(540) 665-0156
www.svwc.org

This nonprofit life-care retirement community is affiliated with the Episcopal and Presbyterian Churches but is open to retirement-age people of all denominations. Services range from independent living and assisted living to complete on-site health care. Located 65 miles from Washington, D.C., this 65-acre campus includes 2.5 miles of walking trails, a 14-

acre restricted natural park, and vegetable and flower gardens.

Virginia Mennonite Retirement Community
1501 Virginia Avenue, Harrisonburg
(540) 564-3400
www.vmrc.org

The Mennonite Churches of Virginia offer a variety of cottages, apartments, townhomes, or condominiums at this 50-acre retirement community. If the need arises, there are also assisted-living private rooms and long-term nursing care available at Oak Lea with an Alzheimer's wing at Crestwood and garden. Open to all

Hebron Lutheran Church in Madison County dates back to 1717. MARY ALICE BLACKWELL

the Blue Ridge. Naturally, bigger cities, such as Roanoke, will have more places to worship, but even our small communities are grounded in faith. The village of Churchville, just outside of Staunton in Augusta County, got its name for the large number of churches along its main street.

When you arrive at your destination, check out the yellow pages. Often, local Saturday newspapers will carry announcements of upcoming services, too.

denominations, the campus adjoins Eastern Mennonite University.

Baldwin Park
21 Woodlee Road, Staunton
(540) 885-1122
www.sheltergrp.com
This retirement community close to downtown Staunton has studio and one- and two-bedroom apartments with window boxes and patios or balconies. All services, including meals, housekeeping, laundry, and activity programs, are provided. There is no entrance fee.

Roanoke Valley

AGENCIES

Family Service of Roanoke Valley
360 Campbell Street SW, Roanoke
(540) 563-5316
www.fsrv.com
Family Services offers information about home health care, insurance, Medicaid, and Medicare. Counseling and other mental-health-issue resources also are available. There is a sliding-scale fee for counseling.

League of Older Americans
706 Campbell Avenue SW, Roanoke
(540) 345-0451
www.loaa.org
The LOA publishes a newsletter six times a year, offers a full-time office and staff for concerns of seniors, and sponsors an annual picnic to raise funds for Meals on Wheels. This fund-raiser also allows seniors age 60 and older to mingle and discuss important legislation with local politicians. In addition to home-delivered meals, they offer case management and volunteer programs.

RETIREMENT COMMUNITIES

Brandon Oaks
3804 Brandon Avenue SW, Roanoke
(540) 776-2600
www.brandonoaks.net
Brandon Oaks offers several spacious floor plans plus dining, transportation, housekeeping, 24-hour security, an activities director, and on-site professional health care. The community has 148 units offered as one- and two-bedroom apartments, plus 12 single-family homes and 18 cottages. This is a three-tier community for residential living, assisted living, and a nursing home.

Elm Park Estates
4230 Elm View Road, Roanoke
(540) 989-2010
www.seniorhousing.net/ad/elmpark
Elm Park Estates is near hospitals, medical facilities, and shopping (Tanglewood Mall is across the street). Amenities include a craft room, library, beauty salon, and planned daily activities. Studios and one-bedroom and two-bedroom apartments are available. Pets are permitted.

The Park-Oak Grove
4920 Woodmar Drive SW, Roanoke
(540) 989-9501
www.parkoakgrove.com
This community offers seven spacious designs, varying in size from studios to one- and two-bedrooms units. A wellness staff is on-site. A first-floor art gallery has been the scene of numerous exhibits. A visit by Miss Virginia is an annual event. Inquiries are welcomed. Guided tours and complimentary lunches are easily arranged by calling during regular business hours.

Roanoke United Methodist Home
1009 Old Country Club Road NW
Roanoke
(540) 344-6248
www.roanokeunitedmethodisthome.com
Several types of living arrangements and levels of care are available to people of all faiths at this licensed continuing care retirement center with a social worker. The nationally accredited facility has social rooms, an activities staff, a chapel, and a large-print library with lots of books on tape. Guest rooms are available.

East of the Blue Ridge

AGENCIES

Loudoun County Area Agency on Aging
215 Depot Court SE, Leesburg
(703) 777-0257
The agency is a major contact for information and assistance for seniors and their family members. It oversees programs that provide meals, job placement, home care, and transportation.

The Retired Senior Volunteer Program lets seniors know where their skills may be needed in the community.

Rappahannock-Rapidan Community Service Board and Area Agency on Aging
15361 Bradford Road, Culpeper
(540) 825-3100
This agency serves five counties, and services include legal aid, health-insurance counseling, homebound meals, transportation, adult care, and a volunteer program that matches senior volunteers with activities in their communities. They also offer mental health and substance abuse pro-

grams. Centers are in Culpeper, Fauquier, Madison, Orange, and Rappahannock Counties.

Hospice of the Rapidan
1200 Sunset Lane, Culpeper
(434) 825-4840, (800) 676-2012
www.hotr.org
Regardless of their financial resources, residents in Fauquier, Rappahannock, Culpeper, Madison, and Orange Counties may benefit from the services of Hospice of the Rapidan. Hospice offers clinical care and emotional support for terminally ill patients and their loved ones.

Albemarle County Parks and Recreation
401 McIntire Road, Charlottesville
(434) 296-5844
www.albemarle.org
This large department oversees three recreation centers and eight parks over 2,000 acres. Included in its list of activities is a year-round exercise class for senior citizens at the Meadows Community Center in Crozet. This center, off Highway 240 in the western part of the county, has a kitchen and large meeting room. There is no charge for the exercise program.

Alzheimer's Chapter, Central & Western Virginia
1807 Seminole Trail, Suite 204
Charlottesville
(434) 973-6122
www.alzcwva.org
This association is a great source of education and information about Alzheimer's Disease for patients and their families. Call the toll-free number, (800) 272-3900, to obtain information about support groups, "SAFE RETURNS," educational programs, and the regional newsletter. Local services include caregiver support groups, a lending library of books and videos, and a caregiver resource file. Regional offices are located in Charlottesville, Harrisonburg, Lynchburg, and Roanoke.

Charlottesville Recreation and Leisure Services
Seventh and Market Streets
Charlottesville
(434) 970-3261, (434) 970-3592
www.charlottesville.org/recreation
The recreation department in Charlottesville offers activities for young and old at nine recreation centers and 25 parks. Since local residents have access to wonderful programs at the Senior Center and the Jefferson Area Board for Aging, the recreation department gears its services primarily to seniors who are more frail and elderly.

Activities range from ceramics and bingo to road trips to theatrical productions. The staff even takes programs and slide shows to local nursing homes.

Hospice of the Piedmont
2200 Old Ivy Road, Suite 2
Charlottesville
(434) 817-6900, (800) 975-5501
www.hopva.org
Hospice of the Piedmont includes teams of nurses, social workers, therapists, clergy, counselors, nutritionists, and trained volunteers who assist patients and their families in dealing with a limited life expectancy. The Piedmont area Hospice covers nine counties and the city of Charlottesville plus Albemarle, Greene, and Nelson Counties.

The Jefferson Area Board for Aging
674 Hillsdale Drive, Charlottesville
(434) 817-5222
www.jabacares.org
Senior services through JABA are many: case management, adult day care, home-delivered meals, home care, insurance counseling, and home safety and repair. The agency's goal is to support independent living for seniors. Through 10 senior centers and six outreach offices, JABA serves clients in Charlottesville and the counties of Albemarle, Nelson, Greene, Louisa, and Fluvanna. JABA provides adult day care and publishes *Silver Linings,* a free senior-oriented newspaper.

The Senior Center Inc.
1180 Pepsi Place, Charlottesville
(434) 974-7756
www.seniorcenterinc.com

This is an active center in a facility convenient to several Charlottesville retirement communities. Members can take part in classes, lectures, exercise groups, and entertainment programs. There are plenty of clubs for active seniors, including chess, math, drama, computer, dance, and racquetball clubs. There also is the innovative program JILL—Jefferson Institute for Life Long Learning—at the University of Virginia. Often taught by retired professors, these classes explore everything from American Indian art to relations between the United States and Iraq. The center is also home to Crafters' Corner, a consignment-style shop. All the handcrafted items are made by seniors and a portion of the sales goes to the senior center. Trips, both day trips and getaways, are scheduled regularly.

Central Virginia Area Agency on Aging
3024 Forest Hill Circle, Lynchburg
(434) 385-9070
www.cvaaa.com

This agency serves Bedford County as a clearinghouse for home health care referrals with all issues pertaining to seniors, such as transportation, meals, and prescription management. The agency serves Amherst, Appomattox, Bedford, and Campbell Counties, plus the cities of Lynchburg and Bedford. There are nutrition and diet centers and dining centers, too.

One of the first places to go when moving to Virginia is the Division of Motor Vehicles. Not only can you pick up your license and car tags, but you also can register to vote in your new locale. To find a location in your area, check out www.dmv.state.va.us. or call (800) 435-5137.

City of Lynchburg Department of Parks & Recreation
301 Grove Street, Lynchburg
(434) 847-1640
www.lynchburgva.gov

This department offers social stimulation to seniors through classes such as aerobics and day trips offered on an ongoing basis. Stop by and pick up a recreation guide and a monthly senior newsletter.

Southern Area Agency on Aging
433 Commonwealth Boulevard
Martinsville
(276) 632-6442
www.southernaaa.org

This agency acts as a clearinghouse in Franklin County for resource referral for health issues for seniors older than 60, home health care, legislation, and senior issues.

RETIREMENT COMMUNITIES

Branchlands Village
1300 Branchlands Drive, Charlottesville
(434) 973-9044

Conveniently located near the local senior center and shopping mall, this retirement community offers apartment living. There are 69 apartments ranging from studio to two-bedrooms. Residents have access to a variety of planned activities, such as bridge, poker, bingo, and sing-alongs, transportation services, housekeeping, and on-site dining. Exterior maintenance is included, and there is a party every month.

The Colonnades
2600 Barracks Road, Charlottesville
(434) 963-4198, (800) 443-8457
www.sunriseseniorliving.com

The Colonnades is on 59 acres, nearly half of which is a nature preserve with maintained walking trails. The community offers concierge and supplemental personal services, including transportation, housekeeping, and licensed nursing care. This independent and assisted-living community includes 40 cottages, 180 apartments with 44 assisted-living units, and 54 beds in the nursing facility. Other amenities include a cocktail lounge, dining room, library, heated pool, and craft center. There also is an associated health care center on grounds.

Martha Jefferson House
1600 Gordon Avenue, Charlottesville
(434) 293-6136
www.marthajeffersonhouse.org
Seniors live graciously in this beautiful 1920 Georgian mansion that's located in a wonderful neighborhood. Common living areas are tastefully decorated with antiques and fine furniture. Three meals are served daily. A nursing facility is attached.

Our Lady of Peace
751 Hillsdale Drive, Charlottesville
(434) 973-1155
www.our-lady-of-peace.com
This nondenominational, nonprofit facility offers four levels of care: independent living, assisted living, nursing care, and special dementia care. Operated by the Catholic Diocese, Our Lady of Peace is close to the senior center and shopping mall. Housekeeping, social activities, dining room, and transportation services are available.

University Village
2401 Old Ivy Road, Charlottesville
(434) 977-1800
www.universityvillage.biz
A beautiful facility with great views of the surrounding countryside, University Village offers 94 condos for independent seniors. An exercise room, dining room, and indoor pool are available to residents.

Valley View Retirement Community
1213 Long Meadows Drive, Lynchburg
(434) 237-3009
www.valleyviewretirement.com
Services at Valley View include meals, housekeeping, transportation, wellness

programs, and a community center with a hot tub and a visiting nurse, which are included in the monthly rental fee. The two-tier facility offers independent-living and assisted-living arrangements.

The facility has a country store, barber/beauty shop, a games and crafts area, and an exercise room.

Westminster Canterbury
501 VES Road, Lynchburg
(434) 386-3500, (800) 962-3520
www.wclynchburg.org
Residents at this community have a choice of eight apartment styles. This lifelong-term facility offers independent living, assisted living, and nursing home care. Services and amenities include a beauty/barber shop, housekeeping, and your choice of dining arrangements (either in your apartment or in the central area).

New River Valley

AGENCIES

New River Valley Agency on Aging
141 East Main Street, Suite 500, Pulaski
(540) 980-7720, (866) 260-4417
This agency provides resources for seniors, including referrals for home health care, legislative issues, part-time jobs, and retirement communities.

RETIREMENT COMMUNITIES

Warm Hearth Village Retirement Community
2607 Warm Hearth Drive, Blacksburg
(540) 961-1712, (540) 552-9176
www.retire.org
On a 220-acre wooded site, Warm Hearth has 103 one-level townhomes, apartments in three low-rise buildings, apartments for assisted living, and a long-term nursing facility, which includes specialized Alzheimer's and dementia care.

Alleghany Highlands

AGENCIES

Valley Program for Aging Services Inc.
325 Pine Avenue, Waynesboro
(800) 868-VPAS
This agency serves as a clearinghouse for health, legislative, and labor issues. It serves Bath, Highland, Rockbridge, Augusta, and Rockingham Counties. The agency provides the numerous services in order to help seniors stay independent and in-home as long as possible. You'll find adult day care, social activities, nutrition, homemaking, and transportation. Donations are solicited and some services are available on a sliding scale.

CHAMBERS OF COMMERCE

If you are thinking about moving to the area, local chambers of commerce are good places to start. They can provide you with information on hotels, real estate, apartments, insurance, schools, businesses, and the job market.

Shenandoah Valley

Berryville-Clarke County Chamber of Commerce
P.O. Box 365, Berryville, VA 22611
(540) 955-4200
www.clarkechamber.com

Broadway-Timberville Chamber of Commerce
103 Co Op Drive, Timberville
(540) 896-7413

Edinburg Area Chamber of Commerce
P.O. Box 511, Edinburg, VA 22824
(504) 984-8318

Front Royal-Warren County Chamber of Commerce
414 East Main Street, Front Royal
(540) 635-3185
www.frontroyalchamber.com

Greater Augusta Regional Chamber of Commerce
30 Ladd Road, Fishersville
(540) 324-1133
www.augustachamber.org

Harrisonburg-Rockingham Chamber of Commerce
800 Country Club Road, Harrisonburg
(540) 434-3862
www.hrchamber.org

Lexington-Rockbridge County Chamber of Commerce
100 East Washington Street, Lexington
(540) 463-5375
www.lexrockchamber.org

Luray Page County Chamber of Commerce
46 East Main Street, Luray
(540) 743-3915
www.luraypage.com

Mt. Jackson Chamber of Commerce
P.O. Box 111, Mount Jackson, VA 22842
(540) 477-3275

New Market Area Chamber of Commerce
P.O. Box 57, New Market, VA 22844
(540) 740-3212
www.shenandoah.com/newmarket

Strasburg Chamber of Commerce
132 West King Street, Strasburg
(540) 465-3187
www.strasburgva.com

Winchester-Frederick County Chamber
2 North Cameron Street, Winchester
(540) 662-4118
www.winchesterva.org

Woodstock Chamber of Commerce
P.O. Box 605, Woodstock, VA 22664
(540) 459-2542
www.woodstockva.com

Roanoke Valley

Botetourt County Chamber of Commerce
P.O. Box 81, Fincastle, VA 24090
(540) 473-8280
www.bot-co-chamber.com

Roanoke Regional Chamber of Commerce
212 South Jefferson Street, Roanoke
(540) 983-0770
www.roanokechamber.org

Salem-Roanoke County Chamber of Commerce
611 East Main Street, Salem
(540) 387-0267
www.s-rcchamber.org

East of the Blue Ridge

Amherst County Chamber of Commerce
154 South Main Street, Amherst
(434) 946-0990
www.amherstvachamber.com

Bedford Area Chamber of Commerce
305 East Main Street, Bedford
(540) 586-9401, (800) 933-9535
www.bedfordareachamber.com

Charlottesville Regional Chamber
P.O. Box 1564, Charlottesville, VA 22909
(434) 295-3141
www.cvillechamber.org

Culpeper County Chamber of Commerce
109 South Commerce Street, Culpeper
(540) 825-8628
www.culpepervachamber.com

Fauquier County Chamber of Commerce
P.O. Box 127, Warrenton, VA 20186
(540) 347-4414
www.fauquierchamber.org

Franklin County Chamber of Commerce and Tourism
261 Franklin Street, Rocky Mount
(540) 483-9542
www.franklincountyva.org

Loudoun County Chamber of Commerce
P.O. Box 1298, Leesburg, VA 20176
(703) 777-2176
www.loudounchamber.org

Lynchburg Regional Chamber
2015 Memorial Avenue, Lynchburg
(434) 845-5966
www.lynchburgchamber.org

Madison County Chamber of Commerce
110A North Main Street, Madison
(540) 948-4455
www.madison-va.com

Nelson County Chamber of Commerce
P.O. Box 182, Lovingston, VA 22949
(434) 263-5971
www.nelsoncounty.com

Orange County Chamber of Commerce
P.O. Box 146, Orange, VA 22960
(540) 672-5216
www.orangevachamber.com

Scottsville Chamber of Commerce
P.O. Box 11, Scottsville, VA 24590
(434) 286-9083
www.scottsvilleva.com

Smith Mountain Lake Chamber of Commerce
16430 Booker T. Washington Highway
Moneta
(540) 721-1203, (800) 676-8203
www.sml-chamber.com

New River Valley

Floyd County Chamber of Commerce
P.O. Box 510, Floyd, VA 24091
(703) 745-4407
www.community.floyd.va.us

Giles County Chamber of Commerce
101 South Main Street, Pearisburg
(540) 921-5000
www.home.i-plus.net/gcc

Montgomery County Chamber of
Commerce
612 New River Road, Christiansburg
(540) 382-4010
www.montgomery.org

Pulaski County Chamber of Commerce
4440 Cleburn Boulevard, Dublin
(540) 674-1991
www.pulaskichamber.info

Radford Chamber of Commerce
27 West Main Street, Radford
(540) 639-2202
www.radfordchamber.com

Alleghany Highlands

Alleghany Highlands Chamber of
Commerce
241 West Main Street, Covington
(540) 962-2178, (888) 430-5786
www.ahchamber.com

Bath County Chamber of Commerce
P.O. Box 718, Hot Springs, VA 24445
(540) 839-5409, (800) 628-8092
www.bathcountyva.org

Highland County Chamber of Commerce
P.O. Box 223, Monterey, VA 24465
(540) 468-2550
www.highlandcounty.org

EDUCATION

If natural beauty inspires learning, it is no wonder that the Blue Ridge is lined with some of the finest colleges and universities in Virginia. Shoot, why stop there? The University of Virginia and Virginia Tech have both been cited by national publications for their academic excellence. Tech, in the heart of the New River Valley, took a leading role in establishing one of the world's first electronic villages, while "Mr. Jefferson's University" in Charlottesville continues to turn out leaders in medicine, law, and business.

Every major city in the Shenandoah Valley has at least one college or university, and the area has several college preparatory, parochial, and military boarding schools. The Roanoke Valley is home to Roanoke College and Hollins. Excellent prep schools include North Cross and Roanoke Catholic.

Harrisonburg, the seat of Virginia's leading agricultural county of Rockingham, bustles with academic activity. James Madison University, Eastern Mennonite University, and Bridgewater College are within a few miles of each other. To the south, in historic Staunton, are Mary Baldwin College, a Presbyterian-affiliated school for women, and Stuart Hall, Virginia's oldest Episcopal preparatory school for girls.

Washington & Lee University and Virginia Military Institute sit in quaint, historic Lexington. VMI used to be the only public all-male college in the nation, but that ended with the class of 1997-98. In compliance with the Supreme Court's ruling to go coed or go private, the school now admits women cadets.

In addition to Mary Baldwin College, several esteemed private women's colleges are in the mountains and foothills of the Blue Ridge, including Hollins College in Roanoke, Randolph-Macon Woman's College in Lynchburg, and Sweet Briar College in Amherst.

South of Roanoke, the New River Valley is home to both Virginia Tech and Radford University, two of the most popular choices in Virginia higher education.

Charlottesville-area prep schools include St. Anne's–Belfield, Woodberry Forest in nearby Orange County, and the Miller School of Albemarle. Lynchburg is also home to five colleges and two business schools drawing more than 15,000 students each year.

Listed in this chapter in geographic order, north to south and east to west, are four-year colleges and some of the better-known preparatory schools in the Blue Ridge region. There are also 23 community colleges in Virginia, including the 114-acre Piedmont Virginia Community College near Monticello in Albemarle County.

Information on any of the two-year colleges is available from the State Council of Higher Education, (804) 225-2600.

COLLEGES AND UNIVERSITIES

Shenandoah Valley

Shenandoah University
1460 University Drive, Winchester
(540) 665-4581, (800) 432-2266
www.su.edu
Shenandoah University, affiliated with the United Methodist Church, was founded in 1875 in Dayton, Virginia, and moved to Winchester in 1960. Since then the university has developed into a comprehensive Level VI accredited institution of higher education. It offers more than 80 programs of study at the undergraduate, graduate, and professional levels in six schools: the College of Arts and Sciences, the Harry F. Byrd Jr. School of Business, the Shenandoah Conservatory, the School of Continuing Education, the Bernard J.

Dunn School of Pharmacy, and the School of Health Professions (nursing, respiratory care, occupational therapy, physician's assistant, sports medicine, and physical therapy).

In addition to the university's beautifully landscaped 75-acre campus, it maintains several state-of-the-art facilities in downtown Winchester and the former Winchester Hospital on the campus of the new Winchester Medical Center. It also operates a satellite campus in Leesburg.

Shenandoah University's student body of approximately 3,000 men and women represent 46 states and 42 countries.

Christendom College
Front Royal
(540) 636-2900, (800) 877-5456
www.christendom.edu

This small college was founded in 1977 to inspire and educate Catholic students for church lay leadership. The college emphasizes a close community life. The college is situated on a 100-acre campus of gently rolling land surrounded by the Blue Ridge Mountains. Bachelor of arts degrees are awarded in English, French, history, philosophy, political science and economics, classical studies, and theology. The college also offers master's degrees through the Notre Dame Graduate School in theological studies. The *U.S. News and World Report,* 2003, ranked Christendom first in the nation among all liberal arts colleges for "least debt incurred by its graduates." The school competes in the U.S. Collegiate Athletic Association in six varsity sports.

Eastern Mennonite University
1200 Park Road, Harrisonburg
(540) 432-4000
www.emu.edu

Christian values and global concerns are integrated with the learning process at this private college that was founded in 1917 to serve the educational needs of the Mennonite Church. The school has about 1,400 undergraduates, seminary students, graduate students, and students enrolled in the adult degree completion program.

This program is designed for working people who can complete their education without leaving their jobs.

In keeping with the church's heritage of peace and nonviolence, EMU has added a graduate-level conflict transformation program, in which people from all over the world can learn how to mediate conflict.

Students at Eastern Mennonite participate in a cross-cultural experience, from attending seminars in Africa and Europe to working with the Native American communities in Minnesota. The school ranks sixth nationally by the *U.S. News and World Report* in its study abroad rate with classes offered in Germany, Ghana, Japan, Russia, and the Middle East. EMU offers 45 majors, and in 1999 a distinctive MBA program was added. The most popular majors are business, education, biology, nursing, and social work. The 92-acre hillside campus is in the northern tip of the city of Harrisonburg. A state-of-the art athletic facility, University Commons, opened in the fall of 2000.

James Madison University
800 South Main Street, Harrisonburg
(540) 568-6211
www.jmu.edu

Flanked by the Blue Ridge Mountains to the east and the Alleghenies to the west, this beautiful 495-acre campus sits in the heart of the Shenandoah Valley. First called the State Normal and Industrial School for Women, the school opened in 1908 with 209 students and 15 faculty members. Today, with an average enrollment of 15,612, JMU is recognized as one of the top comprehensive coeducational public universities in the country. In the *U.S. News & World Report* annual publication, *America's Best Colleges, 2005,* JMU ranked third among all Southern master's universities, a position its held for 11 consecutive years.

The university offers a wide range of courses on the bachelor and master levels. The school also offers a doctorate in psychology. The strongest academic areas include the arts, education, communications, health and human services, business, and science and technology.

James Madison also offers an international internship program, with locations in the United Kingdom and France. Back on campus, the school's Service Learning Program is nationally known for giving students the opportunity to apply classroom learning to the real world. Students and parents alike will also be glad that internships are an integral part of the JMU curriculum.

More than 500 student athletes compete in 14 men's and 14 women's sports. The Convocation Center, a 7,600-seat arena, was added for sports and entertainment events. Other new construction in 2003–04 included the Biotechnology building for $25.5 million and the $9.5 million Plecker Academic Performance Center. The campus is within walking distance of downtown Harrisonburg.

Bridgewater College
402 East College Street, Bridgewater
(540) 828–8000
www.bridgewater.edu
This private, Church of the Brethren–affiliated college is 7 miles south of Harrisonburg. Bridgewater has been coed since it was founded in 1880. Its average enrollment is 1,563 students, and the most popular majors are business and biology. An excellent music program also attracts many students.

Bridgewater has been expanding athletic offices in light of its recent tradition of success on the gridiron. The Eagles finished fifth in the AFCA Division III College Football Poll in 2003. It was the third straight year Bridgewater finished in the top five in the nation and the fourth year in the top 15.

Mary Baldwin College
Corner of Frederick and New Streets
Staunton
(540) 887–7019, (800) 468–2262
www.mbc.edu
Founded in 1842, this private women's college enrolls about 2,116 undergraduates

and 126 graduates. Thirty-three major and 30 minor courses of study are offered, and the most popular are art, psychology, sociology, communications, and biology. Mary Baldwin also has taken advantage of the Shenandoah Shakespeare's move to Staunton to offer students an MFA in Shakespeare and Renaissance literature. The school is home to several innovative educational programs, including the Virginia Women's Institute for Leadership. VWIL is the only all-female corps of cadets in the world. A 1999 graduate of the first VWIL class, Army Capt. Sherri Sharpe, flew Chinook combat duty in Afghanistan and Iraq. Other successful programs include the Program for Exceptionally Gifted, the Adult Degree Program, and a Master of Arts and Teaching program. The college's premed majors maintain an exceptionally high acceptance rate at medical schools. In 2002 *U.S. News & World Report* ranked the college a top master's-level institution. The 54-acre historic campus is in downtown Staunton.

The cost for a Blue Ridge college education differs widely. Some admissions offices quote a combined cost for tuition and room and board, while others list them separately. When comparing costs, be sure to ask which cost-quoting formula they use.

Virginia Military Institute
Lecture Avenue, Lexington
(540) 464–7000
www.vmi.edu
Virginia Military Institute joins W & L in Lexington as a national treasure of tradition. Thomas J. Jackson, the immortal "Stonewall," taught here 10 years before heeding the call of the South in the Civil War. VMI has produced some of the most famous leaders in the world as graduates, including Gen. George C. Marshall, class of 1901, author of the Marshall Plan to recon-

struct Europe after World War II. A museum in his honor is next to the 12-acre parade ground, as is the VMI Museum that chronicles the history of the Institute. The VMI Post (campus) is a National Historic District, and the Cadet Barracks a National Historic Landmark.

This is the school that was portrayed in Ronald Reagan's film *Brother Rat,* about VMI's infamous Rat Line. Women joined the ranks for the first time in August 1997. Approximately 35 women were among the entering "Rat" class. The 1,300 cadets, now 5 percent female, pursue bachelor degrees in 14 disciplines in the general fields of engineering, science, and liberal arts. VMI participates in an international military academy exchange, with cadets spending semesters at institutions in England, Jordan, Australia, Germany, Thailand, and Taiwan. Undergirding all aspects of cadet life is the VMI Honor Code, to which all cadets subscribe. In 2002 *U.S. News & World Report* designated VMI a top public liberal arts college and ranked the engineering program one of the 20 best in the nation. VMI alumni have distinguished themselves in every American conflict since the Mexican War, including 500 alumni who served in Operation Desert Storm and the war in Afghanistan. The school has 15 intercollegiate athletic teams in the Big South Conference.

Washington and Lee University
116 North Main Street, Lexington
(540) 463-8400
www.wlu.edu

Washington and Lee University in historic Lexington was founded in 1749 and enrolls about 2,100 undergraduates and 360 law students. The university offers both bachelor and juris doctor (law) degrees, with the most popular majors being business administration, politics, economics, and English. The Williams School of Commerce, Economics, and Politics is the only nationally ranked business school at a liberal arts college. The *U.S. News and World Report,* 2004, ranked W & L 13th among liberal arts colleges. The university's inno-

vative writing center gives students tips on their personal, professional, and academic writing skills. The 1998–99 school year was a big one for Washington and Lee. It marked the 250th anniversary of the university and the 150th anniversary of its law school. The university is the ninth oldest in the country.

Its history is rich with historic names. In 1796 George Washington contributed 100 shares of canal stock in the James River Co. to Liberty Hall Academy, a Presbyterian seminary. The grateful trustees changed the school's name to Washington Academy in 1798 and to Washington College in 1813.

Gen. Robert E. Lee rode into town on his horse, Traveller, in 1865 and became the college's president until his death in 1870, at which time the name of the school was changed to Washington and Lee University. While there, Lee established the nation's first journalism program and its School of Law. Washington and Lee's gracious campus is designated a National Historic Landmark, with neoclassical brick buildings dating back to the generosity of Washington. Lee Chapel, on the tree-lined colonnade, is a focal point for students, who gather there for lectures, concerts, and special events. Lee designed the beautiful chapel and is buried there.

Washington and Lee is a charter member of the 14-college Old Dominion Athletic Conference and is a member of NCAA's Division III.

Washington and Lee has some fine athletic facilities and has undergone several construction projects in the last five years, including the W & L Turf Field, a multi-purpose field used for intramurals, club sports, and athletic contests. The 350-seat facility was completed fall 2000.

The W & L University Fitness Center is a 11,000-square-foot state-of-the-art complex, integrated in a 1900s Colonial refurbished building. Opened in August 2002, the structure is an architectural gem. The "T-shaped" layout allows users to work undisturbed. Originally built in 1914, the renovation enabled the complex to keep its colonial white pillars and columns, which give the fitness center a unique style.

Roanoke Valley

Hollins University
8060 Quadrangle Lane, Roanoke
(540) 362-6401
www.hollins.edu

Founded in 1842, Hollins College was the first chartered women's college in Virginia. Enrollment is more than 1,100, with 847 undergraduate women and 306 coed graduate students. Hollins awards a bachelor of arts degree with 29 majors and offers five graduate and preprofessional programs.

In 2004 *The Princeton Review* ranked this 475-acre campus number one in the nation for the "best quality of life."

Hollins enjoys a strong liberal arts focus, with nationally recognized programs in creative writing. Three Pulitzer Prize winners—Annie Dillard, Henry Taylor, and Mary Wells Ashworth—graduated from Hollins. Other notable alumni include *Time* publisher Lisa Valk Long, ABC News correspondent Ann Compton, and Elizabeth Forsythe Hailey, author of the best-seller *A Woman of Independent Means*. Hollins has the first graduate program for the writing and study of children's literature and is also noted for its international concentration. Hollins Repertory Dance Company has been selected to dance at the Kennedy Center in Washington, D.C., and Aaron Davis Hall in Harlem, New York.

More than half of the students study abroad, including participation in Hollins's Jamaica Service Program. This Peace Corps–like program combines immersion in the island's culture along with volunteer service projects. Hollins also offers its students internships at companies as diverse as CNN, Time, Nightline, the New York Stock Exchange, and the Metropolitan Museum of Art. Hollins's sports programs are also well known in the NCAA Division III and Old Dominion Athletic Conference.

Its riding center is popular for women who like to take their horses to college with them. No wonder, since its riding team has two national championships and has been in the top 10 five years in a row.

Roanoke College
221 College Lane, Salem
(540) 375-2500
www.roanoke.edu

Founded in 1842, Roanoke College moved to Salem in 1847 and was chartered as a four-year liberal arts college in 1853. Roanoke is the second-oldest Lutheran college in the nation and Virginia's only Lutheran college. Roanoke offers programs leading to the bachelor of arts, bachelor of science, and bachelor of business administration degrees. Within these programs, 33 majors, 28 minors, and 17 concentrations are offered, along with six preprofessional programs. Roanoke is consistently named as one of the region's best in *U.S. News & World Report's Annual Guide to America's Best Colleges. Money* magazine has recognized Roanoke as one of the top 10 colleges in the nation for giving "Dollars for Scholars," financial aid based on merit. Students with a taste for politics can take advantage of the college's Washington, D.C., internship program. Sixty percent of Roanoke's 1,900 students are from Virginia, with the remainder representing 38 states and 24 foreign countries.

Roanoke enjoys a long and distinguished history. Roanoke was one of the few Southern colleges to remain open during the Civil War. Roanoke also placed an emphasis on internationalization long before that idea came into vogue. In the 1870s through the 1890s, President Dreher recruited heavily among the Choctaw in Oklahoma Territory. Many of these students returned to leadership roles in the Choctaw Nation. The first Mexican student came in 1876, and the first Japanese student arrived in 1888. The first two Koreans ever to graduate from an American college or university received their degrees at Roanoke—Surh Kiu Beung in 1898 and

Kimm Kiusic in 1903. Roanoke's athletic history is a source of pride for alumni as well as for the Roanoke Valley. In 1938 Coach "Pap" White's Five Smart Boys won the state championship and went on to the national finals of the Metropolitan Basketball Writers Invitational tournament at Madison Square Garden, to which the NCAA and NIT tournaments were then secondary. In 1972 Coach Charles Moir led the Roanoke basketball team to the NCAA Division II championship. Roanoke fields 19 NCAA Division III teams.

East of the Blue Ridge

**University of Virginia
Emmet Street, Charlottesville
(434) 924-3601
www.virginia.edu**
"Mr. Jefferson's University" is the hub of the Charlottesville community. With its neoclassical buildings, white porticos, and graceful landscapes, the university's grounds are considered among the most beautiful in America.

UVA consistently heads lists of the country's best universities, and its system of 14 libraries is known for its excellence, recently garnering a top ranking from the American Association of Research Libraries. The university offers 48 bachelor's degrees in 46 fields, 94 master's degrees in 64 fields, six educational specialist degrees, two first-professional degrees (law and medicine), and 55 doctoral degrees in 54 fields.

The University of Virginia was named number two among public universities (tied with the University of Michigan), according to the 2005 *U.S. News & World Report*. Since *U.S. News* began ranking public colleges and universities in 1998, UVA has never been lower than second.

The university has succeeded in shaking its reputation of being a party school, notorious for its annual Easter parties and infamous mud slide near Fraternity Row. This is due in part to tougher entrance criteria—the number of applications far exceeds the space available for undergraduates. About 54 percent of all in-state applicants get in, and roughly 60 percent of undergraduates are Virginians. With the help of Dean M. Rick Turner and his outreach program for African-American students, the graduation rate is 87.2 percent, the highest African-American graduation rate among major public institutions in America.

The University of Virginia is especially noted for its schools of Law and Medicine and for the Colgate Darden Graduate School of Business Administration. The English department also ranks among the top in the country. UVA is known across the state for its Weldon Cooper Center for Public Service, which helps localities by collecting demographic and economic data for use in developing public policy. Total enrollment is about 19,643 graduate and undergraduate students.

UVA has 25 intercollegiate varsity sports (12 men's and 13 women's), more than 50 club sports, and intramural sports. The school plays in Division I-A in the Atlantic Coast Conference and has produced some nationally drafted football and basketball players. One of its best was Dawn Staley, who helped lead the U.S. women's Olympic team to its third gold medal in a row at the 2004 Olympics in Athens, Greece. She also carried the American flag during the opening ceremonies.

There are always construction projects under way on this campus. The Albert and Shirley Small Special Collections Library opened in August 2004, downstairs in the Harrison and Small building. The entire 72,000-square-foot building, including the Mary and David Harrison Institute for American History, Literature, and Culture, was completed in November 2004. A new basketball stadium is being built right next door to the old University Hall. The new facility, the John Paul Jones Arena, is scheduled to open for the 2006–2007 season.

Sweet Briar College
134 Chapel Road, Sweet Briar
(434) 381-6100
www.sbc.edu

Sweet Briar College is a nationally ranked, highly selective independent women's college of the liberal arts and sciences, offering the bachelor of arts and the bachelor of science degree. It is 12 miles north of Lynchburg in Amherst County, on 3,250 rolling acres in the foothills of the Virginia Blue Ridge. The college is known for its laboratory-based and equipment-intensive program in the sciences. Its program in international education, which includes study-abroad in France and Spain, attracts students from colleges across the country.

Sweet Briar's all-level riding program, which regularly snags national championships, boasts one of the best on-campus facilities in the country. The school's nationally recognized equestrian program offers an equine studies certificate program. Participants have been the champion or reserve champion 15 times and top rider in 2000. About 709 women from more than 40 states and 30 foreign countries choose from Sweet Briar's 37 majors, including interdepartmental and self-designed majors. The college also has an award-winning environmental studies program.

Liberty University
1971 University Boulevard, Lynchburg
(434) 582-2000
www.liberty.edu

Liberty University is a Christian, comprehensive, coeducational university committed to academic excellence. Liberty serves more than 10,000 students from 50 states and 80 nations at the undergraduate and graduate levels. The school was founded by Dr. Jerry Falwell, the TV evangelist who is also the founder of the Moral Majority. Liberty will celebrate its 35th anniversary in the autumn of 2005.

The school adheres to strict fundamental Christian principles. For example, no modern or classical music is permitted in dormitories, and a demerit system with fines is enforced for students caught listening to anything other than Christian music on campus. Liberty is accredited by the Southern Association of Colleges and Schools and offers 30 areas of study. Liberty offers an MBA degree, with working adults earning credits for real-world work experience. Liberty Baptist Theological Seminary offers master's degrees in religious education, divinity, religion, and theology. You can also obtain a master's degree in nursing and education and a doctorate in education. Liberty recently added a school of law.

Liberty's facilities include a 12,000-seat football stadium and the 9,000-seat Vines Convocation Center, which are used by the Flames athletic teams, who compete in the Big South Conference.

Lynchburg College
1501 Lakeside Drive, Lynchburg
(434) 544-8100, (800) 426-8101
www.lynchburg.edu

Nestled in the foothills of the Blue Ridge Mountains on 214 acres, Lynchburg College is known as one of the most beautiful campuses in the South. An independent, coeducational institution related to the Christian Church (Disciples of Christ). *U.S. News & World Report* in its *America's Best Colleges 2005* publication ranked Lynchburg College in the top tier of Southern universities that offer a full range of undergraduate programs and master's degrees. Lynchburg College is among 132 universities (59 private, 73 public) ranked in the Southeastern Universities–Master's category. The school serves approximately 2,000 undergraduate and graduate students from 38 states and 11 foreign countries.

Two teaching innovations at Lynchburg College that have received wide recognition are the Lynchburg College Symposium Readings (LCSR) program and the Senior Symposium. LCSR incorporates classical reading selections across the curriculum, while in the Senior Symposium, students read selections from the classics, prepare written analyses, and attend weekly lectures to discuss major themes addressed in the readings. Small classes and one-on-one interaction with professors are among the many benefits of an education at Lynchburg College.

Master's degrees are offered in business administration and education. The Corporate MBA program is designed for experienced employees and managers who wish to pursue an MBA with their peers at a level appropriate to their experience. The adult education program, Access, is for students older than 25 who want to earn an undergraduate degree. The Daura Gallery, named for the Catalan-American artist Pierre Daura, hosts several exhibitions featuring the work of many American and European artists throughout the year.

In keeping with its beauty and its stellar reputation, construction is under way on Centennial Hall, a state-of-the-art 67,000-square-foot classroom and laboratory facility that will house the School of Business and Economics, the Communication Studies program, foreign languages, and performing arts. The new building will provide areas for students to congregate and study and will include a 250-seat auditorium.

Randolph–Macon Woman's College
2500 Rivermont Avenue, Lynchburg
(434) 947-8000, (800) 745-7692
www.rmwc.edu
Randolph–Macon Woman's College, a four-year liberal arts college affiliated with the United Methodist Church, serves 737 women from 43 states and 47 countries. The school opened in 1893 with 36 boarding students and 12 professors. Main Hall is listed on the National Register of Historic Places. It sits on 100 acres near the Blue Ridge, with a 100-acre riding center nearby. For more than a century, women have come to the campus to prepare for a multifaceted life through rigorous academics, opportunities for cross-cultural experiences, and an emphasis on community service and involvement. Individual research and the unique sense of community that draw women to the campus are

enhanced further by the student-faculty ratio of 9 to 1.

Many students got to work behind the scenes on a major theatrical production in 1998. Valerie Harper, who played Rhoda on the *Mary Tyler Moore Show* and on her own sitcom, *Rhoda,* came to the college to work on her one-woman play, *All Under Heaven.* The production, based on one of Randolph–Macon's most celebrated graduates, Pearl S. Buck, played 15 sold-out performances before Harper took the production to Off-Broadway. Buck, the author of *The Good Earth,* was the first woman to win both a Pulitzer Prize and Nobel Prize.

All classes are taught by professors rather than teaching assistants, and the average class has 12 students. The college offers 40 programs of study and independent majors. The college's nationally recognized Maier Museum of Art features works by noted American artists including George Bellows, Thomas Hart Benton, Georgia O'Keeffe, and James McNeill Whistler. Also, many students choose to enhance their studies by going abroad. The Prime Time program is offered for women of nontraditional college age.

The value of asking questions and pursuing knowledge clearly is conveyed to Randolph–Macon students, many of whom further their studies. The college ranks high among private, four-year institutions nationwide in numbers of graduates going on to earn doctorates. The staff of the Career Development Center provides a one-on-one, four-year career preparation program, assisting students with graduate school and career decisions.

Ferrum College
40 Stratton Lane, Ferrum
(540) 365-2121, (800) 868-9797
www.ferrum.edu
Ferrum College's 700-acre campus is in the foothills of western Virginia's splendid Blue Ridge Mountains. The region's natural resources enhance the college's curriculum, which combines rigorous academics, a strong experiential learning component,

and a practical, "real life" emphasis. It's not unusual to find Ferrum students meeting class requirements by rappelling off rocky cliffs in Fairy Stone State Park, taking and analyzing water samples from nearby Smith Mountain Lake, leading schoolchildren on nature field trips, or spending a weekend backpacking through George Washington and Jefferson National Forests.

A private, coeducational, liberal arts United Methodist Church institution founded in 1913, Ferrum offers bachelor degrees in 33 majors as well as a distinctive teacher education program to its 1,000 students. Majors range from business administration to environmental science, from dramatic and theater arts to international studies, from criminal justice to recreation and leisure.

Ferrum College also makes valuable contributions to the economic, cultural, and community life in and around Franklin County. The college houses the Blue Ridge Institute and Museum, which is Virginia's official Center for Blue Ridge Folklore (see our Arts chapter); presents the popular Blue Ridge Dinner Theatre each summer (see our Arts chapter); offers leadership training and team-building opportunities to community groups through its high and low ropes courses; and presents a range of art exhibits, concerts, theatrical performances, lectures, and sporting events, nearly all of which are free and open to the public.

The college's impact in the community is perhaps communicated most strongly through the service activities undertaken by Ferrum students. Through the Bonner Scholars program, dozens of Ferrum students provide nearly 600 hours of volunteer service to the community each week, while other students and student groups also volunteer their time and talents to a range of service projects and agencies. Students in Ferrum's teacher education program also connect with the community as teacher aides and student teachers, spending thousands of hours annually in local classrooms.

New River Valley

Virginia Tech
**Southgate Drive, Blacksburg
(540) 231-6000, (540) 231-3548
www.vt.edu**
Virginia's largest and most diverse university, Virginia Tech has a pervasive presence in western Virginia as the largest employer in southwest Virginia. Virginia Tech enrolls more than 25,000 undergraduate and graduate students and has 60 undergraduate and 110 graduate degree programs. Virginia Tech consists of eight colleges: Agriculture and Life Sciences, Architecture and Urban Studies, Arts and Sciences, Business, Engineering, Natural Resources and Education, Veterinary Medicine, and Forestry. All 50 states and nearly 100 foreign countries are represented in the student body. *U.S. News & World Report* ranked Virginia Tech's undergraduate program as the 26th best among national public universities. Of all universities—public or private—*U.S. News* ranked Virginia Tech the 46th best value in the country, and they ranked the university's engineering program in the nation's top 25.

Tech's 2,600-acre main campus is in a town of 39,700 residents, in the scenic Blue Ridge Mountains. As you would expect, many students can't bear to leave Blacksburg after graduation, and legions of them stay to make it a top-notch, stimulating university town. Additional facilities include an 800-acre research farm (Kentland Farm), the Equine Center in Leesburg, and 12 statewide agricultural experiment stations. The Donaldson Brown Hotel and Conference Center is scheduled to open in summer 2005. This beautiful 193,000-square-foot facility will offer flexible and elegant space for meetings, conferences, and special events, as well as a campus home for alumni and friends. The hotel will offer 128 guest rooms and dining facilities. The Hotel Roanoke and Conference Center, 36 miles away, is also owned by Virginia Tech.

The Virginia Tech graduate centers in Roanoke, Abingdon, Hampton Roads, Richmond, and Northern Virginia provide working professionals graduate degree programs and classes from nationally ranked programs based at Virginia Tech's primary campus. Programs include business administration, education, engineering, public administration and policy, and information technology.

U.S. News & World Report has ranked Virginia Tech in its top 20 with National Merit Scholars and top 50 nationally in annually sponsored research. Its Corporate Research Center is home to more than 120 companies employing about 1,830 people. The Corporate Research Center is located adjacent to Virginia Tech, the largest research university in Virginia and among the top 50 in the nation. Virginia Tech conducts over $175 million per year in advanced research. The school ranks fourth in the nation in patents, 10th in licenses, and 13th in royalty income for universities without medical schools. Virginia Tech is a major source of research breakthroughs. As a land-grant university with a statewide mission, Tech is responsible for Virginia's Cooperative Extension Service, which is carried to 107 Virginia communities. Tech is also a leader among universities in the United States in the use of communications technology. The entire campus was connected with the town of Blacksburg and the world through the unique Blacksburg Electronic Village long before the invention of the Worldwide Web. The school has gained quite a bit of fame through this bold use of the electronic superhighway and produces 40 percent of Virginia's PhDs. It also is famous for its traditional Corps of Cadets.

Tech is a member of the Atlantic Coast Conference. It has a 65,115-seat stadium, offering some of the most popular spectator sports in the Blue Ridge. Be prepared for hourlong traffic jams when the Hokies play football at home.

Radford University
East Main Street, Radford
(540) 831-5000
www.radford.edu

The New River Valley's other major state-supported educational institution, Radford University enrolls more than 9,200 students in this residential community of 16,500. Radford is 36 miles southwest of Roanoke in the Blue Ridge Mountains. Founded in 1910, the former all-women college became coeducational in 1972. It averages 60 percent female and 40 percent male students. *U.S. News & World Report* has ranked Radford University in the top 25 master's level public universities in the South in its 2005 *Guide to America's Best Colleges*. In addition to the Graduate College, Radford has five colleges offering bachelor degrees: Arts and Sciences, Business and Economics, Education and Human Development, Waldron Health and Human Services, and Visual and Performing Arts. The graduate program offers master's degrees in various areas, including business administration, fine arts, music, communication sciences, education, criminal justice, psychology, English, and others. RU also extends its graduate and undergraduate programs to students in other areas through centers in Abingdon, Roanoke, and at Virginia Western Community College. Unique to Radford is its Business Assistance Center. It provides a wide range of services for small- and medium-size businesses in the area and offers opportunities for students to get real-life experience doing research and counseling. Seven RU professors have received Virginia's highest honor for faculty since inception of the state's Outstanding Faculty Award in 1986. The most recent RU honoree, music professor and composer Mark Camphouse, received the 2002 award.

As with Virginia Tech, many graduates elect to live and work in this beautiful college town beside the scenic New River. Radford belongs to the Big South Conference and NCAA Division I and offers 19 varsity sports.

Southwest Virginia

Emory & Henry College
P.O. Box 947, Emory, VA 24327
(276) 944-4121
www.ehc.edu
Founded in 1836, Emory & Henry is one of the few college campuses listed on the National Historic Register. The private liberal arts college enrolls more than 1,000 students on its 331 pristine acres in Emory. In 2002 it was listed among the top 10 most affordable liberal arts colleges.

Emory & Henry offers 28 programs of study, including international studies, premed, prelaw, and preengineering, as well as economics, business administration, art, theater, language, math, and computer science. It also ranks with the top 1 percent of U.S. colleges and universities in alumni giving. Students receive the full benefit of a high-quality faculty and a low student-faculty ratio of 13 to 1. It is ideal if you are interested in spectacular mountain views and easy access to the recreational opportunities they afford, including mountain climbing, hiking, and bicycling. The college is close to the historic town of Abingdon. As a member of the Old Dominion Athletic Conference, the college boasts 13 varsity sports for men and women in the NCAA Division III.

PREPARATORY SCHOOLS

Shenandoah Valley

Foxcroft School
22407 Foxhound Lane, Middleburg
(540) 687-5555
www.foxcroft.org
This prestigious boarding and day school for girls in grades 9 through 12 was founded in 1914 by Charlotte Noland, who served as the school's headmistress until she retired in 1955. Miss Charlotte valued such old-fashioned virtues as determination, courage, and character, but she wasn't above having a bit of fun. She said she wanted to establish a school that girls

"would hate to leave because they loved it." Alumni will attest to her success.

The school is set among 500 idyllic acres of orchards, fields, and streams near Middleburg. Local foxhunts meet frequently at the school, and many of the students participate in the hunt. The school has a definite equestrian tone—40 percent of the girls are involved in its excellent riding program, using one of the school's many horses or their own. The Foxcroft Stable, a gift from Jean duPont McConnel Shehan, provides 60 stalls where students can board their horses.

One hundred and eighty-three students represent 13 countries and 25 states; 30 percent of the students are international. The school is small, but the program is extensive. More than 70 courses, including advanced placement and opportunities for independent study, are available. Classes average 10 students to one teacher. The Currier Library is one of the largest independent school libraries in the country, offering approximately 50,000 print volumes as well as online sources, and serves as an active hub for the campus.

Notre Dame Academy
35321 Notre Dame Lane, Middleburg
(540) 687-5581
www.notredameva.org
A 100-acre campus surrounds this coed college preparatory school for day students in grades 9 through 12. The school, founded in 1965, has an affiliation with the Roman Catholic Church. Of the 285 students, 50 percent are Catholic. More than 92 percent of the 26 faculty have one or more advanced degrees and an average of eight years of teaching experience.

Notre Dame offers advanced-placement courses in 12 test areas, accelerated programs, independent study, and college credit through courses at local colleges. With 18 interscholastic sports available, intramural athletics are also an important part of a student's life here. Notre Dame had one of the first high school varsity Junior Olympic mountain biking teams in the United States, and both its boys' and girls' basketball teams were state ranked. Students are required to work 25 community service hours per year.

The school boasts a 100 percent college acceptance rate. The 70 graduates in the class of 2003 were accepted at more than 50 different colleges and universities, including William & Mary, Virginia Tech, Boston College, Columbia University, University of Virginia, VMI, Georgetown University, and Villanova, winning almost $1 million in scholarships. The campus is off U.S. Highway 50, west of Middleburg.

Randolph-Macon Academy
200 Academy Drive, Front Royal
(540) 636-5200, (800) 272-1172
www.rma.edu

This coed boarding school, affiliated with the United Methodist Church, is surrounded by a scenic 135-acre campus in the small town of Front Royal. The Upper School is an accredited prep school in grades 9 through 12, while the Middle School emphasizes a classical education in grades 6 through 8. The school also offers college credits for gifted seniors.

The school's structure is military, and RMA is the only coed boarding school in the country with an Air Force Junior ROTC program. All Upper School students are required to join the AFJROTC and take yearly aerospace science courses. The FAA-certified flight program trains students from ground school to their first solo flight, with the option to become licensed pilots.

Students excel in other areas as well. The speech and debate team rank number one in Virginia and Maryland. The school's marching band has performed at the St. Patrick's Day parade in New York City, at the Indianapolis 500, and at Walt Disney World.

RMA's small class size—10 students to one teacher in the Middle School and 15 to one in the Upper School—creates a good learning atmosphere, and faculty members emphasize the fundamentals and good study habits. In 2002 99 percent of its graduates went on to college.

The campus has an outdoor track, five tennis courts, and fields for baseball, field hockey, football, lacrosse, and soccer. Other sports facilities include a gymnasium and Nautilus room and indoor swimming pool. Renovations to the main building allowed for Internet and telephone access in each student's room. Total enrollment is about 381 students from 22 states and 11 countries.

Wakefield Country Day School
U.S. Highway 522, Flint Hill
(540) 635-8555
www.wakefieldcds.org

The late William E. Lynn and his wife, Pamela, were so concerned about the erosion of education standards in public schools that in 1972 they founded Wakefield. Initially, their goal was to provide a good, classical education for their own six children. Since then, scores of students from preschool through the 12th grade have benefited from the school's enriched curriculum. The school enrolls 200 day students from seven surrounding counties and a handful of international students who board with host families.

Studies include two required years of an ancient language as well as two required years of French or Spanish. The school has advanced-placement courses in English, science, math, foreign languages, history, and geopolitics. More than 90 percent of 2003 graduates were accepted into their college of choice, including Harvard, Brown, Bryn Mawr, Princeton, and Dartmouth. The school is 10 miles south of Front Royal.

Stuart Hall
235 West Frederick Street, Staunton
(540) 885-0356
www.stuart-hall.org

The oldest Episcopal girls' boarding school in Virginia, Stuart Hall was founded in 1844 as Virginia Female Institute. It was renamed in 1907 in honor of headmistress Mrs. Flora Cooke Stuart, the widow of Gen. J.E.B. Stuart.

The eight-acre campus has many ties to Civil War history. During the 1860s, Gen. Robert E. Lee served as the president of the school's board of visitors. When the nearby Virginia School for the Deaf and the Blind was turned into a Confederate hospital, Stuart Hall temporarily closed to make room for the VSDB students.

Today, the focal point of the campus is Old Main, a registered historic landmark that dates back to 1846 and houses offices, a $1.1 million library, art studios, and an auditorium. Stuart Hall has a rigorous college-preparatory program that includes 14 honors and nine advanced-placement courses. The school has an average class size of 10 and a 100 percent college acceptance rate. The school also stresses athletic as well as academic training with varsity competition in field hockey, basketball, tennis, soccer, softball, volleyball, and riding.

The faculty consists of 21 full-time members, including 13 with advanced degrees. Classes average seven students.

The school boards girls in grades 8 through 12 and recently added coed day classes in grades 5 through 12. The total enrollment is 142. The Upper School includes boarding students from the United States and abroad.

Roanoke Valley

North Cross School
4254 Colonial Avenue, Roanoke
(540) 989-6641, (888) 637-6641
www.northcross.org

North Cross is a coeducational college preparatory day school enrolling 535 students from prekindergarten through 12th grade. Its goal since its beginning in 1960 has been to prepare students "not just for college or a vocation, but for a full, rewarding life." The school offers a rigorous academic program with many offerings in the fine arts, outdoor education, community service, and athletics.

The school's 77-acre campus includes three academic buildings, including an art gallery, theater, library, and three computer labs. The Carter Athletic Center offers programs for the whole family, including an outstanding swim program, and the middle school offers a lateral climbing wall. The school teaches respect and responsibility through its honor code.

Roanoke Catholic School
621 North Jefferson Street, Roanoke
(540) 982-3532
www.roanokecatholic.com

Roanoke Catholic, founded in 1889, is a coeducational college preparatory school enrolling 594 students ages preschool to grade 12, 75 percent Roman Catholic. The school's stated mission is "to develop in students those characteristics and attitudes that will help them achieve full potential in all aspects of their lives." The school focuses on educating the whole child physically, intellectually, emotionally, and spiritually.

The school has a strong academic program in a Christian atmosphere. The inclusion of Christian morals and values is an integral part of the entire curriculum. Athletics is also important, with the school sponsoring and funding the Upper School sports program and sandlot soccer and basketball teams for the Lower School. In 2001 the preschool was relocated to the campus and is now housed in the Lower School building. The school in 2000 renovated the interior of the old Upper School, adding Internet-wired classrooms.

East of the Blue Ridge

Woodberry Forest
10 Woodberry Station, Woodberry Forest
(540) 672-3900, (888) 798-9371
www.woodberry.org
This Madison County boarding prep school for boys in grades 9 through 12 sits on 1,200 acres about 30 miles north of Charlottesville and 70 miles south of Washington, D.C. Independent and nondenominational, the school prepares students for successful performance at some of the best colleges and universities in the country.

Woodberry Forest offers a comprehensive Advanced Placement program and a curriculum that includes rigorous requirements in English, math, foreign language, history, science, art, music, and religion. About 391 boys from 23 states and 21 foreign countries attend the school, with about half coming from Virginia and North Carolina. The school was founded in 1889 by Robert S. Walker, a captain in the Confederate army who wanted a school to educate his six sons. Thomas Jefferson drew the floor plan for the headmaster's residence for his friend, William Madison, brother of James Madison.

The average class is 10 to 12 students. The 70 professors—more than two-thirds hold advanced degrees—also live on campus. The campus is beautiful, as one would expect of a school with a $153 million endowment. In 1997 a humanities center was dedicated, featuring a computer network that connects every dorm room, classroom, and office on the campus. Fine recreational facilities include an Olympic-size pool and a nine-hole golf course. The school has many teams in every sport, so each student has a chance to compete against other boys of similar athletic ability. Next to the Rapidian River, the Alpine Tower and climbing wall were added in 2001. One student in three receives tuition assistance.

The Blue Ridge School
Bacon Hollow Road, St. George
(434) 985-2811
www.blueridgeschool.com
The Blue Ridge School maintains an exceptional track record for boys whose grades do not reflect their academic potential. The school's success formula is based on a solid routine of class work, homework, and athletics—all done in a caring, supportive environment. Individual attention and encouragement are the cornerstone of the faculty's philosophy. But boys must keep up their end: Hard work in the classroom and outside community volunteer service is expected of them.

About 200 boys in grades 9 to 12 attend this scenic school, situated on nearly 1,000 beautiful acres just outside Charlottesville. All students board here, and the proximity to Charlottesville allows the school to take advantage of the town's offerings. Day trips, for example, to movies or to University of Virginia athletic events, are scheduled regularly.

The school's Outdoor Program makes use of the spectacular mountain setting with activities that include canoeing, mountain biking, rock climbing, and ropes courses. Athletics range from soccer and football to lacrosse and tennis. The arts programs includes music, drama, and studio art as well as a fine arts series that brings a variety of entertainment to the school. Improvements to the facilities in recent years include creating a student lounge, landscaping, and renovation of the weight room.

Many boys who enter this preparatory school are not sure if they will be able to attend college because of poor past performance in school. But the school boasts an almost 100 percent college acceptance rate. Graduates in 2002 were accepted at numerous colleges and universities, including University of Virginia, Auburn, Wake Forest, and James Madison University.

The Miller School of Albemarle
1000 Samuel Miller Loop, Charlottesville
(434) 823–4805
www.millerschool.org

The Miller School is an Albemarle County landmark in education and natural beauty. This college preparatory school sits on 1,600 beautiful acres 14 miles from Charlottesville. The campus covers farmland, orchards, forests, a pond, and a 12-acre lake for swimming, fishing, and canoeing.

The school's Victorian-style buildings, each a National Historic Landmark, are spectacular with redbrick, slate roofs, and a gorgeous clock tower. The school's unique architecture caught the eye of Hollywood film scouts, who used the campus as a setting for *Toy Soldiers* starring Louis Gossett Jr.

Opened in 1878, the Miller School combined a state-of-the-art industrial complex and vocational education with a classical academic program, producing graduates who went on to the Ivy League and others who became the artisans for the region and state.

Once known as a prestigious military academy for boys, Miller School began accepting girls in 1992. In 1995 the school returned to its historical roots and became an exploring member of the Coalition of Essential Schools, a group that emphasizes the mastery of information and skills. Many of the 30 faculty members have advanced degrees.

The Miller School is coeducational with an enrollment of 155, 75 percent of whom are boarding students in grades 6 through 12. Miller's program is composed of a quality academic college preparatory course of study, required afternoon activities featuring eight major sports and 16 teams, and a weekly service requirement. Service work is done in a three-hour block each week in either Civil Air Patrol (the school is still an official auxiliary of the U.S. Air Force), community action, environmental action, or campus initiatives.

St. Anne's–Belfield School
2132 Ivy Road, Charlottesville
(434) 296–5106
www.stab.org

Formed in 1970 by the merger of St. Anne's School, a girls' boarding school founded in 1910, with the Belfield School, a coed elementary school established in 1955, St. Anne's–Belfield is in its fourth decade of educating youngsters. The accredited school is near the University of Virginia on two campuses totaling more than 49 acres.

The school offers a day program for preschool through grade 12 and a five-day and a seven-day boarding program for grades 9 through 12. The school's philosophy stresses personal and educational growth.

The school has a student body of more than 843 and limits the boarding program to 15 percent of all students in order to maintain a family-like atmosphere. A full range of advanced-placement and honors courses are offered for upper-level students, while younger children study basic subjects as well as French, art, drama, computers, and physical education.

The school has fielded one of the top lacrosse teams in the region for several years, plus it also offers competition in a variety of sports, including squash, golf, and football.

Graduates advance to enroll in some of the nation's finest universities every year. Financial aid is available to families who demonstrate need. About 32 percent of the students receive financial assistance. Six buildings house 97 classrooms (including three computer labs and eight science labs), two libraries, and three gymnasiums. Recent additions to St. Anne's include a 32,000-square-foot Athletic and Convocation Center, a Student Activities Center, a baseball field, a softball field, and six tennis courts.

INDEX

A

Aberdeen Barn, 161
Abram's Delight Museum, 233
Academy of Fine Arts, 323
accommodations. *See* bed-and-breakfasts
  and country inns; hotels and motels;
  lodges and cabins; resorts
Acorn Inn, 111–12
Affair in the Square, 353
African-American History Month at
  Monticello, 330
Afton House Antiques, 220
Afton Mountain Bed & Breakfast, 112
Afton Mountain Vineyards, 389–90
AHC Hospice of the Shenandoah, 477
air travel, 45–50
Albemarle County
  attractions, 262–67
  bed-and-breakfasts and country inns,
    107–11
  hotels and motels, 68–71
  kidstuff, 295–98
  overview, 26–28
  real estate, 469–70, 475–76
Albemarle County Fair, 346–47
Albemarle County Parks and
  Recreation, 481
Aldie Harvest Festival, 352
Aldie Mill, 257, 382–83
Alexander's, 146
Algonkian, 431
Alleghany County
  arts, 327–28
  attractions, 277
  bed-and-breakfasts and country inns,
    118–19
  hotels and motels, 75
  overview, 40–41
  real estate, 474, 476
  restaurants, 175–76
  shopping, 229
Alleghany Highlands Arts Council, 327–28
Alleghany Highlands Arts & Crafts Center,
  229, 327
Alleghany Highlands Chamber of
  Commerce, 486
Alleghany Regional Hospital, 466
Alzheimer's Chapter, Central & Western
  Virginia, 481

Amerind Gallery, 202
AmeriSuites, 73
AmeriSuites Roanoke/Valley View Mall, 61
AMF Kegler's, 295
Amherst County
  arts, 323
  attractions, 268
  bed-and-breakfasts and country inns,
    114–15
  overview, 28–32
  shopping, 222–23
Amherst County Apple Harvest and Arts
  and Crafts Festival, 353
Amherst County Chamber of
  Commerce, 485
Amherst County Museum and Historical
  Society, 268
Amos Alonzo Stagg Bowl, 358
AmRhein Wine Cellar, 405–6
Andre Viette Farm and Nursery, 197
Andrew Minton Jewelers, 214
Angler's Lane, 222
Anne Spencer House and Garden, 268
Annual Charlottesville Antiques Show, 330
annual events, 329–58
Annual Orange Street Festival, 349
Annual Rockbridge Food and Wine
  Festival, 349
Annual Zoo Boo, 353
Another Dimension Inc., 210
Antiquers Mall, 213
Antiques by Braford, 200
Antiques Expo, 335
antiques stores, 190–94, 196–97, 200, 203–4,
  206–10, 212–14, 220, 222, 224–26, 230
Antiques to Envy, 222
Apple Barn II—Gifts and Collectibles, 202
Apple Barn Orchard and Apple Barn
  Store, 202
Apple Blossom Mall, 191
Apple Harvest and Butter-Making
  Festival, 349
Apple Harvest Arts & Crafts Festival, 348
Appleland Sports Center, 279
Applewood Inn & Llama Trekking, 88–89
Appomattox Court House National
  Historical Park, 386
Arborfest at the State Arboretum, 351
Archduke Music Holiday, 334

Armory Art Gallery, 324
Art Center in Orange, 315
Arthur's, 197
Art in the Park, 336
Artisans Center of Virginia, 306
Artists in Cahoots, 200, 309-10
Art Museum of Western Virginia, 289, 311
Art Museum of Western Virginia Sidewalk
   Art Show, 338
arts
      Alleghany Highlands, 327-28
      dance, 320
      East of the Blue Ridge, 314-24
      literary, 314, 321-23
      museums, 307, 318, 322-23
      music, 305, 309-10, 313-15, 320-21, 328
      New River Valley, 324-27
      Roanoke Valley, 311-14
      Shenandoah Valley, 304-10
      theater, 304, 306-10, 312-16, 318-20,
        324-26
      visual, 305-7, 309-12, 314-18, 322-26
Arts Council of the Blue Ridge, 311
Art Studio Pottery, 305
ArtVenture, 289
Ashby Inn & Restaurant, 97, 154
Ash Lawn-Highland, 262-63, 295
Ash Lawn-Highland Virginia Wine
   Festival, 334
Ash Lawn Opera Festival, 320, 341, 342-43
Atkins Lakeshore Gallery, 223
attractions
      Alleghany Highlands, 277-78
      caverns, 235-37, 239-41, 243, 245, 250
      covered bridges, 237, 275, 277
      East of the Blue Ridge, 257-73
      libraries, 233
      museums and historic attractions,
        233-47, 250-55, 257-73, 275-78
      New River Valley, 273-77
      other attractions, 234-35, 240,
        244-45, 248-50, 256, 271, 275
      Roanoke Valley, 250-56
      Shenandoah Valley, 233-50
      sporting events/spectator sports,
        242-43, 255, 266-67, 270, 273-74,
        276
      zoos, 247-48, 255-56
      See also kidstuff
Augusta County
      arts, 306-9
      attractions, 243-45
      bed-and-breakfasts and country inns,
        85-88
      hotels and motels, 58-60
      kidstuff, 285-86
      nightlife, 181-82
      overview, 11-13
      real estate, 461-62, 474-75
      restaurants, 142-45
      shopping, 196-200
Augusta County Parks and Recreation
   Department, 477
Augusta Medical Center, 465
August Court Days, 347
Autumn Hill Vineyards/Blue Ridge
   Winery, 390
Awful Arthur's Seafood Company, 146

B

Babcock House, 114-15
Back Street Cafe, 152
Bacova Guild Factory Outlet, 206
Baja Bean Co., 161-62, 185
Baldwin Park, 479
Balloon Adventures, 295
Balloons Unlimited, 292
Balls's Bluff Battlefield Regional Park, 382
Barboursville Vineyards, 390-91
Barnes & Noble Bookstore, 218
Barracks Road Shopping Center, 219-20
Bath County
      arts, 328
      attractions, 277
      bed-and-breakfasts and country inns,
        119-21
      hotels and motels, 75-76
      nightlife, 189
      overview, 41-42
      real estate, 474, 476
      restaurants, 177
      shopping, 230
Bath County Chamber of Commerce, 486
Bath County Community Hospital, 466
Bath County Historical Society Museum, 277
Battle of Cedar Creek Living History and
   Reenactment, 351
Bavarian Chef, The, 158
B & D Comics, 289
Beamers, 146-47
bed-and-breakfasts and country inns
      Alleghany Highlands, 118-22

East of the Blue Ridge, 95–116
New River Valley, 116–17
Roanoke Valley, 94–95
Shenandoah Valley, 78–94
See also hotels and motels; lodges and cabins; resorts
Bed & Breakfast Association of Virginia, 77
Bed & Breakfast at Llewellyn Lodge, A, 89
Bedford Area Chamber of Commerce, 485
Bedford City, 32–33
Bedford City/County Museum, 270, 300, 386
Bedford County
    arts, 324
    attractions, 270–71
    hotels and motels, 72
    kidstuff, 300
    overview, 32–33
    real estate, 470–71, 475–76
    restaurants, 173
    shopping, 224–25
Bedford Restaurant, The, 173
Bedford's Libertyfest, 345
Belle Boyd Cottage, 378
Belle Grae Inn, 85–86
Belle Grove Plantation, 233, 279–80, 377
Belle Meade Bed & Breakfast, 97–98
Bernard's Landing Resort and Conference Center, 130–32
Berryville–Clarke County Chamber of Commerce, 484
Bertines North, 158–59
Best Seller, The, 201
Best Value Inn, 71
Best Western Cavalier Inn, 68
Best Western Inn at Hunt Ridge, 60
Best Western Inn at Valley View, 62
Best Western Leesburg Hotel and Conference Center, 66–67
Best Western Mountain View, 75
Best Western Radford Inn, 74–75
Best Western Red Lion, 73
Best Western Staunton Inn, 58–59
Beverley, The, 142–43
Big Levels, The, 445–46
Big Meadows, 435–36
Big Meadows Campground, 364
Big Meadows Lodge, 362, 365
Big Meadows Wayside, 365
Billy's Ritz, 147
Biltmore Grill, 162, 180, 185
Binaba Shop, The, 204

Birdwood Golf Course, 431
Biscuit Run Studios, 316
Bisset Park Pool, 449
Blacksburg
    kidstuff, 301
    nightlife, 188
    overview, 35–36
    restaurants, 173
Blacksburg Aquatic Center, 301
Blacksburg Public Pools, 449
Blacksburg Transit, 52
Bleu Rock Equestrian Center, The, 415
Bleu Rock Inn, 98, 155
Blue Bird Cafe, 162
Blue Hills, 433
Bluemont Bed & Breakfast, 82
Bluemont Concert Series, 339
Blue Moon Restaurant, 173
Blue Ridge Antique Center, 225
Blue Ridge Arts Council Inc., 304–5
Blue Ridge Bed & Breakfast, 78
Blue Ridge Cafe, 160
Blue Ridge Dinner Theatre, 324
Blue Ridge Emporium, 210
Blue Ridge Folklife Festival, 300, 353–54
Blue Ridge Institute and Galleries, 272
Blue Ridge Institute Farm Museum, 272, 301
Blue Ridge Mountain Sports, 214–15, 221
Blue Ridge Music Center, 327
Blue Ridge Parkway
    accommodations, 370
    activities, 373
    backcountry camping, 372
    campgrounds, 370–72
    fishing, 372–73
    hikes, 369
    overlooks, 368–69
    picnic areas, 372
    places to eat, 372
    visitor centers, 368
Blue Ridge Parkway Visitor Center, 368
Blue Ridge Pig, The, 169
Blue Ridge Pottery, 212
Blue Ridge Restaurant Inc., 175
Blue Ridge School, The, 500
Blue Ridge Soap Box Derby Classic, 285, 336
Blue Stone Inn, 141
Blue Whale Books, 218
Blue Wheel Bicycles, 215
Boar's Head Inn, 126–27, 162

boating, 419–22

Bodo's Bagel Bakery and New York Sandwich Shop, 162–63

Bogen's Steakhouse, 173, 188

Bonnie Blue National Horse Show, 338

Book Cellar, The, 218

Booker T. Washington National Monument, 272–73, 300

Bookery, The, 201

Bookstack, The, 199

bookstores, 192, 193, 196, 199, 201, 205, 209, 218–19

Boone's Country Store, 225

Boones Mill Apple Festival, 350

Boot'ville, 212

Botetourt County
    attractions, 250–56
    overview, 16–17
    real estate, 463, 475
    shopping, 202–3

Botetourt County Chamber of Commerce, 485

Botetourt County Historical Museum, 250

Bottle and Pottery Show and Sale, 348

Boundary Rock Farm & Vineyard, 406

Bowling Green Golf Club, 430

Boxerwood Garden, 248

bozART Gallery, 316

Branchlands Village, 482

Brandon Oaks, 480

Breaux Vineyards, 391

Bren's, 193

Brick Oven, The, 163

Bridgewater Air Park, 49

Bridgewater College, 489

Bridgewater Plaza, 299–300

Brierley Hill, 89–90

Broadway-Timberville Chamber of Commerce, 484

Brookside Cabins, 56–57

Brookside Restaurant, The, 141

Brownstone Cottage, 78

Bryce Resort, 123–24, 282, 429, 453–54

Buckskin Manor Bed & Breakfast, 95

Budget Inn, 57

Buffalo Springs Herb Farm, 201–2, 248

Buffalo Wild Wings, 180

Bull Pen, 283

Burnley Vineyards and Daniel Cellars, 391–92

Burwell-Morgan Mill, The, 235

bus travel, 50–53

Byers Street Bistro, 181

C

Cackleberry Ridge, 203

Cafe Sofia, 138–39

Caledonia Farm–1812, 98–99

Calhoun's Restaurant and Brewing Company, 141–42, 180

Cambria Emporium, 226

Cameleer, The, 210

Campbell County attractions, 271–72

Campbell Realty Inc., 475

camping, 363–64, 370–72, 422–25

Camp Jeep, 342

Candlelight Christmas Tour, 356

Capt'n Sam's Landing, 143

Cardinal Point Vineyard and Winery, 392

Carilion Bedford Memorial Hospital, 465

Carilion Franklin Memorial Hospital, 466

Carilion Giles Memorial Hospital, 466

Carilion New River Valley Medical Center, 466

Carilion Roanoke Memorial Hospital, 465

Carilion Saint Albans Hospital, 466

Carlos Brazilian International Cuisine, 147

Carmello's, 163

Carolina Connection, 223

Carper's Valley Golf Club, 429

Carriage Tours of Historic Lexington, 248, 286–87

Cascades National Recreation Trail, 438

Cascades Recreation Area, 301, 450

Casey's Lounge, 180

Casino Club Restaurant, The, 177

Catawba Hospital, 465

Catawba restaurants, 151–52

Cat House, The, 215

Cat & Owl Steak and Seafood House, The, 175–76

Cattle Annie's, 187

Cave Mountain Lake, 450

caverns, 235–37, 239–41, 243, 245, 250

Caverns Country Club, 429

Cedar Creek Battlefield Foundation Reenactment, 377–78

Cedar Creek Battlefield Museum and Visitor Center, 280

Celebrating Patsy Cline Weekend, 348

Center in the Square, 256, 311

Central Virginia Area Agency on Aging, 482

Century 21 Anchor Realtors, 475

C.F. Phelps WMA Deer Hunt for the Disabled, 444

Cha Cha's, 214

Chalot's Antiques, 193–94

chambers of commerce, 484–86

Charity Home Tour Gala, 354

Charleys, 171

Charlottesville
  arts, 316–22
  nightlife, 185–87
  overview, 26–28
  restaurants, 161–69
  shopping, 213–20

Charlottesville–Albemarle Airport, 46

Charlottesville/Albemarle Visitors Center, 263

Charlottesville Crow Pool, 448–49

Charlottesville Fashion Square Mall, 220

Charlottesville Fun Park, 295

Charlottesville Historic Downtown Mall, 220

Charlottesville Ice Park, 295, 445

Charlottesville Municipal Pools, 448–49

Charlottesville Onesty Pool, 448–49

Charlottesville Recreation and Leisure Services, 481

Charlottesville Regional Chamber, 485

Charlottesville Smith Pool, 448–49

Charlottesville 10-Miler, 333

Charlottesville Transit Service (CTS), 51–52

Chateau Morrisette, 406

Chautauqua Festival in the Park, 340–41

Cheers, 183

Cheese Shop, The, 197

Chesapeake & Ohio Historical Society, 277

Chessie Nature Trail, 440

Chester Bed & Breakfast, 107–8

Chester House, 80

Chihamba of Dancescape, 320

children, activities for. See kidstuff

Children's Forest Trail, 438

Children's Medical Center at University of Virginia, 465

Christendom College, 488

Christensen Ridge Winery, 392

Christiansburg
  nightlife, 188
  overview, 36–37
  restaurants, 174

Christiansburg Microtel Inn & Suites, 73

Christmas at Oatlands Plantation, 354

Christmas at Point of Honor, 358

Christmas at the Market, 355

Christmas Candlelight Tour, 356

Christmas Gallery, 192

Christmas in Historic Old Town Warrenton, 357

Christmas Lights at Elks National Home, 358

Christmas Open House at Morven Park, 357

Christmas Store & Museum, The, 197

Chrysalis Vineyards, 392–93

Chuck E. Cheese's, 289

churches, 478–79

City of Lynchburg Department of Parks & Recreation, 482

Civil War
  Alleghany Highlands, 386
  East of the Blue Ridge, 382–86
  New River Valley, 386
  overview, 374–76
  reenactments, 379
  Roanoke Valley, 382
  Shenandoah Valley, 377–82
  tours, 384–85

Claiborne House Bed and Breakfast, The, 115–16

Clarion Hotel Roanoke Airport, 62

Clarke County
  attractions, 235
  bed-and-breakfasts and country inns, 79–80
  kidstuff, 281
  real estate, 460, 474–75
  restaurants, 140

Clarkson & Wallace Inc., 476

Classic Bath and the Homestead Collection, 230

Clayton's, 171

Claytor Lake State Park, 302, 421, 424, 428, 449–50

Claytor Lake State Park Arts and Crafts Show, 338

Cleo Driver Miller Art Gallery, 305

Clock Tower Tavern, 181–82

C.M. Crockett Park, 293

Coach Stop, The, 152

Cocoa Mill Chocolates, 200

Coffee Pot, The, 183

Coldwell Banker Residential Brokerage, 475

Collector's Showcase and Custom Framing, 227

College Inn, 164
colleges and universities
    East of the Blue Ridge, 492–95
    New River Valley, 495–96
    Roanoke Valley, 491–92
    Shenandoah Valley, 487–91
    Southwest Virginia, 497
Colonial Dining Room, The, 145
Colonial Mall, 199
Colonnades, The, 482–83
Colony House Motor Lodge, 62
Comfort Inn, 57, 60, 67, 71, 73, 75
Comfort Inn Charlottesville, 68
Comfort Inn–Roanoke/Troutville, 62
Comfort Inn Staunton, 59
Comfort Suites at Ridgewood Farm, 62
Comic, Game, and Hobby Place,
    The, 295–96
Commonwealth Park, 409
Community Children's Theatre, 296, 318
Community School Strawberry
    Festival, 289, 338
Confederate Memorial Service, 340
Consignment House Unlimited, 213
Consolidated Shoe Store, 223
Constitution Day Celebrations, 349
Copper Mine Restaurant & Lounge, The, 170
C & O Restaurant, 163
Cork Street Tavern, 139
Corned Beef & Co., 147, 183
Cottage Farm Bed & Breakfast, 90
Count Pulaski Festival, 354
Country Gardens, 210
country inns. See bed-and-breakfasts and
    country inns
Country Morning Antiques, 212
Countryside Club, 433
Country Store Antique Mall, 212
County Sales, 228–29
Coupe deVille's, 164
Court Square Tavern, 164
Court Square Theater, 306
Courtyard by Marriott, 57
Courtyard by Marriott–North, 68
Courtyard by Marriott–UVA/Medical
    Center, 68
covered bridges, 15, 237, 275, 277
Crabtree Falls Trail, 438
Crafts Shop of Covington, Inc., The, 229
Craig County
    overview, 17–18

real estate, 463, 475
    shopping, 203
Crawford Saddlery, 213
Crossroads Mall, 205–6
Crozet Arts and Crafts Festival, 337, 351
Crystal Caverns at Hupp's Hill, 236
Culpeper Antique & Marketplace, 209
Culpeper Christmas Open House, 355
Culpeper County
    arts, 315
    attractions, 260–61
    bed-and-breakfasts and countryinns, 102
    hotels and motels, 67–68
    nightlife, 184–85
    real estate, 467–68, 475–76
    restaurants, 157–58
    shopping, 209–10
Culpeper County Chamber of
    Commerce, 485
Culpeper Day, 336
Culpeper Regional Airport, 50
Culpeper Regional Hospital, 465
Curiosity Shop Antiques, 194

D

Daedalus Bookstore, 218
Daily Grind, The, 179
dance, 320
Dancing Fire Gallery, 190
Daniel Harrison House, The, 241
Daniel Monument, 383
Dark Hollow Falls Trail, 361
Dave's Downtown Taverna, 180
Days Inn, 67
Days Inn Charlottesville–University, 68
Days Inn Luray, 57
Days Inn Lynchburg, 71
Dayton Autumn Celebration, 353
Dayton Farmers' Market, 194
Deanville Fallow Deer Farm, 192–93
Deck the Halls Open House, 358
Deer Meadow Vineyard, 388
Delaplane Strawberry Festival, 336
De Loach Antiques, 213
Department of Game and Inland
    Fisheries, 444
Depot Grille, The, 143
Depot Restaurant, The, 154
Designer Goldsmiths, 207
Devils Grill at Devils Knob Golf
    Clubhouse, 170

Diamond Hill General Store and Garden Center, 223
Dickens of a Christmas, 358
Dickey Ridge Visitor Center, 360
Dinosaur Land, 281
Dixie Caverns, 250
Dodona Manor, Gen. George C. Marshall Home, 257
Doe Run High Country Property Management, 137
Doe Run Lodge Resort and Conference Center, 370
Dogwood Festival, 333
Dolley Madison's Birthday, 336-37
Dominion Skating Center, 294
Doo Dah Day, 333
Doubletree, 69
Douthat State Park, 421, 423-24, 439, 449
Down Home Bed & Breakfast, 94
Downriver Canoe Company, 282, 419
Drama of Creation, The, 182
Draper Valley, 433
Dudley Mart & Restaurant, 172
Dulaney's Lounge, 187
Dulles Town Center, 208
Dulwich Manor Bed and Breakfast, 115
Dundo Campground, 364
Durty Nelly's, 185
Dusty's Antique Market, 196

E

E.A. Clore Sons, Inc., 210
Eagle Nest Restaurant, 176
Eagles Nest, 49
Easter Egg Hunt, 331
Eastern Mennonite University, 488
Eastern Mennonite University Planetarium, 283
Econo Lodge, 62-63
Edelweiss German Restaurant, 143
Edge, The, 170, 187
Edinburg, 9
Edinburg Area Chamber of Commerce, 484
Edinburg Mill, 379
Edinburg Ole Time Festival, 349
Edith Carrier Arboretum, 241
Ed Jaffe Gallery, 315
education
    colleges and universities, 487-97
    preparatory schools, 497-501
El Charro, 142

Elder's Antique and Classic Automobiles, 197
Eleanor D. Wilson Museum, 312
Eljo's, 215
Elks National Home, 271, 300
Elkton Autumn Days Festival, 352
Elkwallow Wayside, 364
Elm Park Estates, 480
El Rodeo Mexican Restaurant, 147-48
Emerson Creek Pottery, 225
Emory & Henry College, 497
Emporium, The, 197-98
Encore! Artful Gifts, 227
Encounters Lounge, 181
Endless Caverns, 240-41
English Inn, The, 69
ERA Jim Barb Realty Inc., 474
Ernest "Pig" Robertson Trout Fishing Rodeo, 335
Escafe, 164
Evening of Elegance, An, 338
Exchange, The, 179
Exchange Hotel and Civil War Museum, 383
Executive Motel, 75
Explore Park, 373

F

Fairy Stone State Park, 421, 424, 449
falconry, 134
Fall Fiber Festival & Sheep Dog Trails, 352
Fall Fly-In, 350-51
Fall Foliage Festival, 354
Fall Hunt Country Antiques Fair, 351
Falling Water Cascades National Scenic Trail, 369
Fallon Park Pool, 448
Falwell Aviation Inc., 50
Family Drive-In Theatre, 280
Family Services of Roanoke Valley, 479
Family Wintertide Weekend, 357-58
Fancy Hill Farm, 413
Fantastico-Ristorante Italiano Inn/Lounge-Piano Bar, 154-55
Farfelu Vineyard, 393
Farm Basket, The, 171
Farm Basket Shop, 222
farmers' markets, 194
Farmhouse, The, 174
Fauquier County
    attractions, 260
    bed-and-breakfasts and country inns, 97

hotels and motels, 67
kidstuff, 293–94
overview, 23–24
real estate, 467, 475–76
restaurants, 154–55
shopping, 208–9
Fauquier County Chamber of
 Commerce, 485
Fauquier County Fall Farm Tour, 349
Fauquier Hospital, 465
Fayerweather Gallery, 316–17
Fenwick Mines, 446
Ferrum College, 494–95
Festival Around Town, 340
Festival in the Park, 290
Festival of the Book, 331
festivals, 329–58
Fifth Avenue Presbyterian Church
 Window, 256
Fincastle Festival, 350
Fine Arts Center for the New River Valley,
 The, 227, 326
Finicky Filly, The, 207
Firmstone Manor, 118
First Colony Winery, 393
First Lady, The, 230
First Night Harrisonburg, 356
First Night Leesburg, 357
First Night Virginia, 357
First Night Waynesboro, 356
First Night Winchester, 356
Fisherville, 12–13
fishing, 365, 372–73, 425–28
Flat Top Trail, 369
Flea Market, 192
Fletcher Collins Theatre, 307
Flossie Martin Gallery, 325
Floyd Country Store, 188–89, 327
Floyd County
 arts, 326–27
 attractions, 276–77
 nightlife, 188–89
 overview, 39–40
 restaurants, 175
 shopping, 228–29
Floyd County Chamber of Commerce, 485
Flying Circus Aerodome, 294, 336
Folk Arts and Crafts Festival, 335
Forest Hills Pool, 448–49
Fort Harrison, 380
For the Birds, 226

Fort Lewis Lodge, 119–20, 444
Fort Valley Riding Stable, 441
Foster–Harris House, 99
Founder's Day, 330
Fountain Hall Bed & Breakfast, 102
Four Brothers Packing House, 220
Four County Players, 316
401 South Nightclub, 184–85
Four Points by Sheraton, 57
Fourth of July Celebration, 341, 344
Fourth of July Firemen's Carnival, 343
Fourth of July Hot Air Balloon Rally, 344
Four & Twenty Blackbirds, 155–56
Fox Chase Farm Inc., 408
Foxcroft School, 497
Fox Den Antique Mall, 208–9
Foxfield Races, 416
Fox Hollow Nature Trail, 435
fox hunting, 408
Franklin Cliffs Overlook, 361
Franklin County
 arts, 324
 attractions, 272–73
 bed-and-breakfasts and country
  inns, 115–16
 kidstuff, 300–301
 overview, 33–34
 real estate, 470–71, 475–76
 restaurants, 173
 shopping, 225–26
Franklin County Chamber of Commerce
 and Tourism, 485
Franklin County Fall Arts and Crafts
 Festival, 355
Frederick County
 arts, 304
 attractions, 233–34
 bed-and-breakfasts and country inns,
  78–79
 hotels and motels, 54–55
 kidstuff, 279–81
 nightlife, 179–80
 overview, 6–7
 real estate, 459–60
 restaurants, 138–40
 shopping, 190–91
Frederick County Fair, 341
Frederick County Parks and Recreation
 Department, 476–77
Frederick House, 86
Frederick Nichols Gallery and Studio, 316

Freeman-Victorious Framing, 215
Fret Mill Music, 204–5
Fridays After Five, 334
From the Heart, 225–26
Frontier Culture Museum, 243–44, 285
Front Royal, 7–8
Front Royal Antique and Flea Market, 191
Front Royal Canoe Company, 281, 419
Front Royal–Warren County Airport, 48
Front Royal–Warren County Chamber of
    Commerce, 484
Fun-N-Games Family, 300
Fun Shop, The, 207
Funzone, 283

G

Gallery of Mountain Secrets, 230–31
Gallery 108, LLC, 204
Garth Newel Music Center, 328
Gathright Dam, 422
Gay Street Inn, The, 99
Gazebo, The, 223–24
Gemstone Collection, The, 215
Gen. Stonewall Jackson's Headquarters
    Museum, 377
general stores, 223–25, 229, 231
George C. Marshall Museum and
    Library, 245, 287
George Washington National Forest, 283
George Washington's Office Museum, 233–34
Gift and Thrift, 195
Gift Niche, The, 205
Gifts Ahoy, 224
Giles County
    attractions, 275
    kidstuff, 301
    overview, 37–38
    real estate, 471, 474, 476
    restaurants, 174–75
Giles County Chamber of Commerce, 486
Giles County Historical Society
    Museums, 275
Ginseng Mountain Store, 231
Glen Burnie Historic House, Gardens, 234
Godfrey Miller Fellowship Center, 477
Golden Tub Bath Shop, 198
golf, 428–34
Gone Coco, 205
Good Things On the Market, 290
Goshen Pass Natural Area Preserve, 439–40
Grand Caverns, 243, 285

Grand Caverns Bluegrass Festival, 348
Grandma's Bait, 198
Grandma's Memories, 227
Graves Mountain Apple Harvest
    Festival, 352
Graves Mountain Festival of Music, 336
Graves Mountain Fourth of July, 343
Graves Mountain Lodge, 102–3, 159,
    294, 442
Graves Mountain Spring Fling, 333
Gravity Lounge, The, 185–86
Gray Ghost Vineyards, 393–94
Greater Augusta Regional Chamber of
    Commerce, 484
Greater Lynchburg Transit Company, 52
Greater Roanoke Valley Metro Transit
    Company, 51
Greater Shenandoah Valley Fair, 340
Greene County
    bed-and-breakfasts and country
        inns, 104–5
    overview, 25
    real estate, 468, 475–76
    restaurants, 160
    shopping, 212–13
Greene County Fair, 347
Greene House Shops, 212
Greenock House Inn, 105
Green Tree, The, 152
Green Valley Book Fair, 196
Grille at Prince Michel, The, 159–60
Guilford Ridge Vineyard, 388
Gypsy Hill Park, 285–86
Gypsy Hill Park Pool, 448

H

Hales Ford Store, 224
Hall of Fame Joust, 339–40
Hamiltons, 224
Hamiltons', 164
Hampton Inn, 54, 57–58, 59, 60, 69
Hampton Inn Airport, 63
Hampton Inn and Suites, 69
Hampton Inn New River Valley, 73–74
Hampton Inn Salem, 63
Hampton Inn Tanglewood, 63
Handcraft House, 211
handcrafts stores, 195, 202–4, 214, 220–22,
    225–31
Handley Regional Library, 233
Handworks Gallery, 190–91

Hanging Rock, 433

Hanging Rock Battlefield, 382

Hardware Store Restaurant, The, 165

Harmony Hill, 112–13

Harper's Lawn Ornaments, Water Gardens, Paths, and Ponds, 195

Harrisonburg, 10–11

Harrisonburg Children's Museum, 284

Harrisonburg Public Transportation, 52

Harrisonburg–Rockingham Chamber of Commerce, 484

Harrisonburg–Rockingham Historical Society Heritage Center, 241, 380

Harrison Museum of African-American Culture, 250–51, 290

Harry F. Byrd Sr. Visitor Center, 360

Hatton Ferry, 263

Haunting Tales, 249, 337–38

Hawksbill Trail, 361

Hazel River Inn Restaurant, 157

health care, 464–66

Hearth N' Holly Inn, 85

Heartwood Bookshops, 218–19

Heirloom Originals, 226

Henry Street Heritage Festival, 350

Herbert Barbee Confederate Monument, 379–80

Heritage House, 100

Heritage Repertory Theatre, 318–19

Hickory Hill Vineyard, 394

Hidden Brook Winery, 394

Hidden Valley Bed & Breakfast, 120

Hidden Valley Trail, 447

High Country Restaurant at Doe Run Lodge, 372

Highland County

    arts, 327–28

    attractions, 278

    bed-and-breakfasts and country inns, 121–22

    hotels and motels, 76

    overview, 42–43

    real estate, 474, 476

    restaurants, 178

    shopping, 230–31

Highland County Chamber of Commerce, 486

Highland County Crafts, 231

Highland County Maple Festival, 331

Highland Inn, 76, 178

Highland Maple Museum, 278

Highland Wildlife Management Area, 439

High Meadows Vineyard Inn, 108–9

High Valley Antiques and Collectibles, 230

hiking, 361, 369, 434–40

Hillandale Park, 284

Hill High's Country Store, 207

Hill Top Berry Farm and Winery, 394–95

Historical Community Market, 171

Historic Garden Week, 249, 331, 332

Historic Long Branch, 235

Historic Millwald Theatre, 302

Historic Staunton Foundation Christmas House Tour, 356

Historic Stonewall Theatre, 328

History Museum and Historical Society of Western Virginia, 251, 290

Hobby Horse, 230

Hokie House Restaurant, 188

Holiday House Tour, 355–56

Holiday Inn, 54, 67, 74

Holiday Inn Airport, 63

Holiday Inn Culpeper, 67

Holiday Inn Express, 54–55, 58, 60, 63

Holiday Inn Express Lynchburg, 71–72

Holiday Inn Express Roanoke, 63–64

Holiday Inn Hotel Tanglewood, 64

Holiday Inn–Monticello, 70

Holiday Inn Staunton, 59

Holiday Inn University Area Conference Center, 69–70

Hollins University, 491

Holt's For the Home, 198

Holy Land USA Nature Sanctuary, 271

Homeland Realty, 474

Homeplace, The, 151–52

Homestead, The, 133–37, 302, 430, 443, 445, 457–58

Homestead Dining Room, The, 177

Homestead Inn on Claytor Lake, 117

Honeysuckle Hill, 198

Hopkins Planetarium, 252, 291

horseback riding, 366–67, 440–43

horses

    combined driving, 411–12

    combined training, 411

    dressage, 413

    endurance riding, 412

    fox hunting, 408

    jousting, 412–13

    point-to-point and steeplechase races, 410, 416–17

polo, 414–16
shows, 408–11
stable tours, 413
thoroughbred rescue, 413–14
Horton Cellars Winery/Montdomaine Cellars, 395
Hospice of the Piedmont, 481
Hospice of the Rapidan, 481
hospitals, 464–66
Hot Air Balloon Festival and Airshow, 346
HotCakes, 165
Hotel Roanoke & Conference Center, 64
hotels and motels
Alleghany Highlands, 75–76
East of the Blue Ridge, 66–73
New River Valley, 73–75
Roanoke Valley, 61–66
Shenandoah Valley, 54–61
See also bed-and-breakfasts and country inns; lodges and cabins; resorts
Hotel Strasburg, 55–56, 140–41
Howard Johnson Inn, 67
Howard Johnson Inn and Restaurant, 60–61
Howard Johnsons, 64
Huckleberry's Restaurant, 174, 188
Hull's Drive-In Theatre, 249, 287
Hummingbird Inn, The, 90–91
Humpback Bridge, 277
Humpback Rocks, 286
Humpback Rocks Trail, 436–37
Humpback Rock Visitor Center, 368
Hunt Country Properties, 475
Hunt Country Winter Antiques Show, 329–30
hunting, 443–44

I

Ice Cream Cottage, 224
ice-skating, 445
Ikenberry, 203
Imperial Wok, 176
Independence Celebration, 345
Ingalls Field, 50
Inn at Afton, The, 59
Inn at Burwell Place, The, 94–95
Inn at Court Square, 109
Inn at Keezletown Road, The, 86
Inn at Kelly's Ford, 102, 157
Inn at Little Washington, The, 100–101, 156
Inn at Meander Plantation, The, 103–4
Inn at Monticello, 109–10

Inn at Narrow Passage, The, 81
Inn at Sugar Hollow Farm, The, 110
Inn at the Crossroads, 110
Inn at Vaucluse Spring, The, 78–79
inns. See bed-and-breakfasts and country inns
International Bass Bonanza, 340
Irish Crystal Co., The, 207
Iris Inn, The, 87
It's About Thyme, 158
Ivy Creek Natural Area, 440
Ivy Hill Golf Club, 432
Ivy Inn, The, 165

J

Jackson Statue, 383
James Burke House Eatery, 176
James Madison Museum, 261
James Madison University, 242–43, 488–89
James Madison University Masterpiece Season Series, 306
James McHone Antique Jewelry, 194
Jameson Inn, 58
James River Basin Canoe Livery Ltd., 420–21
James River Reeling and Rafting, 296, 420
James River Runners Inc., 296, 420
James River State Park, 423
James River Visitor Center, 368
Jazz in the Park, 309
Jazz Street Grill, 187
Jeane Dixon Museum and Library, 237–38
Jefferson Area Board for Aging, The, 481
Jefferson Center, 256, 313
Jefferson Lodge, The, 64–65
Jefferson National Forest, 283
Jefferson Vineyards, 395–96
Jimmy's Steak and Seafood Grill, 179–80
Joan Palmer Antiques, 212
Johnson's Charcoal Beef House, 152–53
Jolly Roger Haggle Shop, 196
Jones Memorial Library, 268
Jordan Hollow Farm Inn, 82, 415, 442
Joshua Wilton House, Inn, and Restaurant, 85, 142
jousting, 412–13
J's Gourmet, 191
July Celebration, 345

K

Kaleidoscope, 350
Keep Bed and Breakfast, The, 91

Keller & George, 215
Keller Williams Realty, 475
Kelly's Ford Equestrian Center, 415
Kelly's Korner Racing Kollectibles, 213
Keswick Hall at Monticello and Keswick
    Club, 127–28
kidstuff
    Alleghany Highlands, 302
    East of the Blue Ridge, 292–301
    New River Valley, 301–2
    Roanoke Valley, 289–92
    Shenandoah Valley, 279–89
Killahevlin, 80–81
Kimberly's, 191
King Family Vineyards, 396
King's Victorian Inn, 120–21
Kirstens, 157–58
Ki Theatre, 314
Kluge Estate Winery and Vineyard, 396–97
Kluge-Ruhe Aboriginal Art Collection of the
    University of Virginia, The, 318
Krazy May, 173

L
La De Da, 205
Lafayette Hotel, The, 104, 160
Lake Inn at Westlake Corner, 72
Lakeview Restaurant at Douthat State
    Park, 176
Landing Restaurant at Bernard's Landing
    Resort, The, 172
Landwirt Vineyards, 388
Lansdowne Golf Club, 431
Lansdowne Grill at Lansdowne Resort, 153
Lansdowne Resort, 125–26
L'Arche Bed and Breakfast, 116
Latimer-Shaeffer Theatre, 306
L'Auberge Provencale, 79–80, 140
Lavender Hill Farm, 91–92
L'Aventura, 165
League of Older Americans, 480
Lee Chapel and Museum, 245–46
Leesburg Animal Park, 292
Leesburg Colonial Inn, 95–96
Leesburg Corner Premium Outlets, 208
Leesburg Emporium and Smoke Shop, 207
Leesburg Flower and Garden Festival, 333
Lee Statue, 383
Lenfest Center for the Performing Arts, 310
Les Fabriques, 215
Les Yeux du Monde at dot 2 dot, 317

Levy's, 216
Lewis-Gale Medical Center, 465
Lewis Mountain Cabins, 363
Lewis Mountain Campground, 364
Lexington
    attractions, 245–50
    bed-and-breakfasts and country
        inns, 88–94
    hotels and motels, 60–61
    kidstuff, 286–89
    nightlife, 182–83
    overview, 13–15
    restaurants, 145–46
    shopping, 200–202
Lexington-Rockbridge County Chamber of
    Commerce, 484
Liberty University, 493
Library, The, 148
Lightfoot Restaurant, 153
Lily's, 148
Limberlost Trail, 361
Lime Kiln Theater, 182–83, 287, 310
Lincoln Day Ceremony, 330
Lincoln Homestead and Cemetery, 241
Linden Vineyards, 397
L'Italia Restaurant, 142
literary arts, 314, 321–23
Literary Festival, 314
Little Gallery, The, 224
Little John's, 165–66
Little Shop of Madison, The, 211
Live Arts, 319
Livestock Auction, 329
Living Christmas Tree, 358
Living History Days, 355
Local Colors, 334
lodges and cabins
    Blue Ridge Parkway, 370
    Skyline Drive, 361–63
Loft Mountain Campground, 364
Loft Mountain Wayside, 365
London Downs, 432
Longwood Cemetery, 386
Lost Creek Vineyard and Winery, 397
Loudoun County
    attractions, 257–60
    bed-and-breakfasts and country
        inns, 95–96
    hotels and motels, 66–67
    kidstuff, 292–93
    overview, 23

real estate, 463, 467, 475–76
restaurants, 152–54
shopping, 206–8
Loudoun County Area Agency on Aging, 480
Loudoun County Chamber of Commerce, 485
Loudoun County Civil War Roundtable, 330
Loudoun Heritage Farm Museum, 257
Loudoun Hospital Center, 465
Loudoun Museum, The, 257, 382
Loudoun Transit Service, 51
Loudoun Valley Vineyard, 397–98
Lovingston Cafe, 170
Lucketts Fair, 346
Luigi's, 148, 182
Luray, 10
Luray Car and Carriage Caravan, 240
Luray Caverns, 239–40, 282
Luray Caverns Airport, 48
Luray Page County Chamber of Commerce, 484
Luray Singing Tower, 240
Luray Zoo, 282–83
Lynchburg
    arts, 323–24
    attractions, 268–70
    bed-and-breakfasts and country inns, 114–15
    hotels and motels, 71–72
    kidstuff, 298–99
    nightlife, 187–88
    overview, 28–31
    real estate, 470–71, 475–76
    restaurants, 171–72
Lynchburg College, 493–94
Lynchburg Community Market, 222
Lynchburg General Hospital, 465
Lynchburg Hillcats, 270
Lynchburg Museum at Old Court House, 268–69, 384
Lynchburg Regional Airport, 46–47
Lynchburg Regional Chamber, 485

M
Mabry Mill Coffee Shop, 276–77, 372
Mabry Mill Trail, 369
Macado's, 148–49, 174
Mac and Bob's, 151, 183
Madison County
    bed-and-breakfasts and country inns, 102–4

kidstuff, 294
overview, 24–25
real estate, 468, 475–76
restaurants, 158–60
shopping, 210–11
Madison County Chamber of Commerce, 485
Madison County Fair, 345
Magic Valley, 280
Magnolia House Inn, 92
Maier Museum of Art, 323
Main Street Bar and Grill, 181
Main Street Mill, 140
Main Street Shops, 203
Maintree Farm, 441
malls, 191, 196, 199, 205–6, 208, 219–20, 223, 227
Mama's Treasures, 193
Mansion House Restaurant, 153
Maple Hall, 145
Mark Addy, The, 113
Market Street Wineshop, 216
Marriott Ranch, 294, 441
Martha Jefferson Hospital, 465
Martha Jefferson House, 483
Martha's Cafe, 166
Mary Baldwin College, 489
Massanutten Resort, 284, 454–55
Massanutten Visitor Center, 437
Mathews Arm Campground, 363–64
Mayfest, 335
Mayhurst Inn, 105–6
McCormick Farm, 246
McDowell Presbyterian Church, 386
McGuffey Art Center, 317
McIntire Pool, 448–49
MDA Car Show, 331
Mead Associates Inc., 475
Meadows Farms Golf Course, 429
Meander Inn, The, 113–14
media, 472–73
medical care, 464–66
Mediterranean Italian & Continental Cuisine, 149
Meems Bottom Bridge, 237
MegaDome Theater, 252
Memorial Day Horse Fair and Auction, 335
Meriwether's, 171–72
Michael's Bistro and Taphouse, 186
Michie Tavern, 166, 263–64
Middleburg, 23

Middleburg Horse Trials, 411
Middleburg Spring Races, 417
Middle Street Gallery, 314
Middleton Inn, 101
Middletown, 7
Miki Liszt Dance Company, The, 320
Miller Park Pool, 449
Miller's, 186
Miller School of Albemarle, The, 501
Mill Mountain Coffee & Tea, 149, 184
Mill Mountain Theatre, 290, 312
Mill Mountain Zoo, 255-56, 290-91
Mill Street Grill, 182
Millwood Crossing, 190
Milton Hall Bed & Breakfast Inn, 118-19
Milton House Bed & Breakfast, 82-83
Mincer's, 216
Minda's Distinctive Clothing &
   Accessories, 216
MingQuing Antiques, 213
MinuteMan MiniMall, 209
Mish Mish, 226-27
Miss Virginia Pageant, 340
Monsoon, 166
Montague, Miller & Company
   Realtors, 475, 476
Montgomery County
   arts, 324-26
   attractions, 273-75
   bed-and-breakfasts and country
      inns, 116-17
   hotels and motels, 73-74
   overview, 35-37
   real estate, 471, 474, 476
   shopping, 226-27
Montgomery County Chamber of
   Commerce, 486
Montgomery Museum and Lewis Miller
   Regional Art Center, The, 326
Montgomery Regional Hospital, 466
Monticello, 264, 296
Monticello Independence Day and Natural-
   ization Ceremony, 341
Montpelier, 261-62
Montpelier Hunt Races, 355, 417
Moomaw, Lake, 422, 427
Morven Park, 257-58, 292-93
Morven Park Horse Trials, 411
motels. See hotels and motels
Motel 6, 65
Motormile Speedway, 273

mountain biking, 445-47
Mountain Cove Vineyards and
   Winegarden, 398
Mountain Farm Trail, 436
Mountain Lake Resort, 132-33, 447
Mountain Lake Resort Restaurant, 174-75
Mountain Laurel Inn, 121-22
Mountaintop Ranch, 442
Mount Jackson, 9
Mount Zion Old School Baptist Church, 383
Mt. Jackson Chamber of Commerce, 484
Mulligan's Golf Center, 284
Mulligan's Pub & Eatery, 182
Murray's Fly Shop, 426
Museum of American Presidents, 238
Museum of Culpeper History, 260-61
Museum of Geological Science, 273
museums, art, 307, 318, 322-23
museums and historic attractions, 233-47,
   250-55, 257-73, 275-78
music, 305, 309-10, 313-15, 320-21, 328
Music for Americans, 344
My Friends and Me, 207, 293

N
Naked Mountain Vineyard, 398
Napoleon's, 155
National Air and Space Museum Steven F.
   Udvar-Hazy Center, 258-59
National D-Day Memorial, 270
National Jousting Championships, 412-13
Natural Bridge, 61, 246
Natural Bridge Caverns, 245
Natural Bridge of Virginia, 287-88
Natural Bridge Resort, 124-25
Natural Bridge Wax Museum, 246
Natural Bridge Zoo, 247, 288
Natural Chimneys, 244-45
Natural Chimneys Jousting Tournament,
   346, 412
Naturalist Center, The, 259-60, 293
Nawab Indian Cuisine, 149-50
Neighborhood Art Show, 337
Nelson County
   arts, 322-23
   attractions, 267-68
   bed-and-breakfasts and country
      inns, 111-14
   kidstuff, 298
   nightlife, 187
   overview, 28

real estate, 470, 475–76
restaurants, 169–71
shopping, 220–21
Nelson County Chamber of Commerce, 485
Nelson County Summer Festival, 340
Nelson Fine Arts Gallery, 310
Newbern Fall Festival of Arts and Crafts, 354
New Dominion Bookshop, 219
New London Airport, 50
New Market, 9–10
New Market Airport, 48–49
New Market Area Chamber of
    Commerce, 484
New Market Battlefield Days Inn, 56
New Market Battlefield State Historical
    Park and Hall of Valor Civil War
    Museum, 238, 380
New Market Heritage Days, 351
New Mountain Mercantile, 228
Newport Agricultural Fair, 347
New River Canoe Livery, 421
New River Mall, 227
New River Trail State Park & Shot
    Tower, 439, 447
New River Valley Agency on Aging, 483
New River Valley Airport, 50
New River Valley Horse Show, 338
news media, 472–73
newspapers, 472
Newtown Heritage Festival, 341
nightlife
    Alleghany Highlands, 189
    East of the Blue Ridge, 184–88
    New River Valley, 188–89
    Roanoke Valley, 183–84
    Shenandoah Valley, 179–83
Norris House Inn, The, 96
North Cross School, 499
Northern Exposure, 166–67
North Mountain Vineyard & Winery, 388–89
North River Gorge Trail, 447
North-South Skirmish Association National
    Skirmish, 351
North-South Skirmish Association Spring
    Nationals, 337
Notre Dame Academy, 497–98
Nuts & Sweet Things, 291

O

O. Winston Link Museum, 251–52, 253
Oakencroft Vineyard and Winery, 398

Oak Grove Folk Music Festival, 346
Oak Grove Players, 307–8
Oak Ridge Estate, 267
Oaks Victorian Inn, The, 116–17
Oasis Winery, 398–99
Oatlands Plantation, 260, 293
Oddfella's Cantina, 189
Of Ale and History Beer Festival, 337
Old Cabell Hall, 321
Old Church Gallery, 326
Old City Cemetery Museums and
    Arboretum, 269
Old Country Store, 203
Old Court House Civil War Museum, 377
Old Dominion 100-mile Ride, 412
Olde Salem Days, 350
Olde Virginia Barbecue, 173
Old Fiddler's Convention, 347–48
Old House Vineyards, 399
Old Jail Museum, The, 260
Old Lucketts Store Antiques, The, 206–7
Old Michie Theatre, The, 296, 319
Old Rag, 436
Old South Antiques Ltd., 200
Old Sperryville Bookshop & Coffee
    House, 209
Old Town Spring Festival, 337
Ole Monterey Club, 432–33
Omni Charlottesville Hotel, 70
Once Upon a Time, 196
Opera Roanoke, 313
Orange County
    arts, 315–16
    attractions, 261–62
    bed-and-breakfasts and country
        inns, 105–7
    overview, 25–26
    real estate, 468–69, 475–76
    restaurants, 160–61
Orange County Airport, 49
Orange County Chamber of Commerce, 485
Orange County Fair, 343–44
Orbit Billiards & Cafe, 186
orchards, 203
Orvis Factory Outlet, 206
Orvis Retail Store, 206
O'Suzannah, 214
Otter Creek Campground, 371
Otter Creek Restaurant and Craft Shop, 372
Our Lady of Peace, 483
Outback Lodge, 186

outlet stores, 199–200, 206, 208, 223, 225, 226
Owens & Co. Realtors, 475, 476
Oyster House Antiques, 213–14

P

P. Buckley Moss Museum, 307
Page County
    arts, 305
    attractions, 239–40
    bed-and-breakfasts and country
      inns, 82–84
    hotels and motels, 56–57
    kidstuff, 282–83
    overview, 10
    real estate, 461, 474–75
    restaurants, 141
    shopping, 193
Page County Heritage Festival, 351–52
Page Memorial Hospital, 464
Page Valley Agricultural Fair, 347
Palais Royal Inc./Yves Delorme, 216
Palladio Restaurant, 160–61
Palms, The, 183
Pampered Palate Cafe, 143
Panorama Trails, 296–97, 446–47
Pano's, 142
Paper Treasures, 193
Pappagallo, 200–201
Park, The, 184
Park-Oak Grove, The, 480
Patchwork Plus, 195
Patrick Henry Hotel, The, 65
Patrick Henry Women's Auxiliary Christmas
    Tea, 358
Patsy Cline Gravesite, 234
Peaks of Otter, 437
Peaks of Otter Campground, 371
Peaks of Otter Lodge, 72, 370, 372
Peaks of Otter Visitor Center, 368
Peaks of Otter Winery, 399
Peanut Butter and Jelly, 201
Peddler Antiques, The, 224–25
Perspective Art Gallery, 325
Pest House Medical Museum and
    Confederate Cemetery, 299, 384–85
Peter Kramer Cabinetmaker, 209
Piedmont Vineyards and Winery, 400
Pine Knoll Gift Shop, 193
Pine Room at Hotel Roanoke, The, 184
PJ's Carousel Collection, 228

Plantation Days at Highland, 342–43
Plow & Hearth, 211, 216
PMD Screen Printing, 205
Point of Honor, 269–70, 299
point-to-point and steeplechase races, 410, 416–17
polo, 414–16
Polo Great Meadow, 414
Poor Farmers Market, 229
Potomac Appalachian Trail Club Cabins, 363
preparatory schools
    East of the Blue Ridge, 500–501
    Roanoke Valley, 499
    Shenandoah Valley, 497–99
President James Madison's Birthday, 330
Presidents Lounge, The, 189
Priest Overlook, The, 369
Primland Hunting Reserve, 444
Prince Michel of Virginia Vineyards, 400–401
Printer's Ink, 205
Prism, The, 186–87, 321
Prospect Hill Cemetery, 378
Prudential Commonwealth Property, 475
Pub, The, 181
public transit, 50–52
Pulaski Blue Jays, 276
Pulaski City, 38–39
Pulaski Community Hospital, 466
Pulaski County
    arts, 326
    attractions, 276
    bed-and-breakfasts and country
      inns, 117
    hotels and motels, 75
    kidstuff, 302
    overview, 38–39
    real estate, 471, 474, 476
    shopping, 227–28
Pulaski County Chamber of Commerce, 486
Pulaski County Courthouse, 276
Pulaski Railway Station, 276
Pullman Restaurant, The, 143–44
Purcell Company Ltd., The, 216–17
Purcell Park, 284

Q

Quail at the Woods Antiques, 209–10
Quality Inn at Christiansburg, 74
Quality Inn-Roanoke/Salem, 65
Quality Inn Shenandoah Valley, 56
Quality Inn Skyline Drive, 55

Quality Inn–University, 70
Quality Inn Waynesboro, 59–60
Quest Bookshop Inc., 219
Quilts Unlimited, 230

R

Radford
    hotels and motels, 74–75
    kidstuff, 301
    overview, 38
    shopping, 227
Radford Bisset Park Pool, 301
Radford Chamber of Commerce, 486
Radford Highlanders Festival, 354
Radford University, 496
Radford University Art Museum, 325
Radford University Climbing Wall, 451
Radford University College of Visual and
    Performing Arts, 326
radio stations, 473
Radisson–Lynchburg, 72
Ragged Mountain Natural Area, 440
Ragged Mountain Running Shop, 217
Rainbow Hill Eatery, 141
Raines Real Estate, 476
Ramada Inn, 56
Ramada Inn and Conference Center
    Salem, 65
Ramada Inn & Conference Center, 72
Ramada Limited, 74
Ramada Limited–Monticello, 70
Ram's Head Bookshop, 205
Randolph–Macon Academy, 498
Randolph–Macon Woman's College, 494
Rappahannock Cellars, 401
Rappahannock County
    arts, 314–15
    bed-and-breakfasts and country
        inns, 97–102
    overview, 24
    real estate, 467, 475–76
    restaurants, 155–57
    shopping, 209
Rappahannock–Rapidan Community
    Service Board and Area Agency on
    Aging, 480–81
Rapture, 167
Raspberry Falls Golf and Hunt Club, 431
Raymond "Andy" Guest Shenandoah River
    State Park, 423
Read It Again, Sam, 219

real estate
    Alleghany Highlands, 474, 476
    East of the Blue Ridge, 463, 467–71,
        475–76
    New River Valley, 471, 474, 476
    Roanoke Valley, 463, 475
    Shenandoah Valley, 459–63, 474–75
Real Estate III, 475, 476
Rebec Vineyards, Inc., 401
recreation
    boating, 419–22
    camping, 363–64, 370–72, 422–25
    fishing, 365, 372–73, 425–28
    golf, 428–34
    hiking, 361, 369, 434–40
    horseback riding, 366–67, 440–43
    hunting, 443–44
    ice-skating, 445
    mountain biking, 445–47
    rock climbing, 450–51
    skiing, 452–58
    swimming, 447–50
Recreation Center, 451
Red Carpet Inn, 70
Red Fox Fine Art, 208
Red Fox Inn, The, 96
Red Fox Tavern, 153–54
Red Hill: The Patrick Henry National
    Memorial, 271–72, 299
Red Roof Inn, 70–71
Reenactment of the Battle of New
    Market, 335
Relax Inn, 61
RE/MAX Advantage, 475
RE/MAX All Stars, 476
Residence Inn by Marriott, 71
resorts
    Alleghany Highlands, 133–37
    East of the Blue Ridge, 125–32
    New River Valley, 132–33
    Shenandoah Valley, 123–25
    Southwest Virginia, 137
    See also bed-and-breakfasts and
        country inns; hotels and motels;
        lodges and cabins
Restaurant at Chateau Morrisette, The, 175
restaurants
    Alleghany Highlands, 175–78
    Blue Ridge Parkway, 372
    East of the Blue Ridge, 152–73
    New River Valley, 173–75

Roanoke Valley, 146–52
Shenandoah Valley, 138–46
Skyline Drive, 364–65
retirement and senior services
Alleghany Highlands, 484
East of the Blue Ridge, 480–83
New River Valley, 483
Roanoke Valley, 479–80
Shenandoah Valley, 476–79
Reuel B. Pritchett Museum, 241–42
Rex's Sports Bar, 185
Richard's Antiques, 192
Rivanna Reservoir, 427
Rivanna Trails, 440
River'd Inn, 81–82
River Ridge Mall, 223
River Ridge Ranch, 443
Riverside Park, 385–86
Roanoke
arts, 311–14
attractions, 250–56
bed-and-breakfasts and country
inns, 94–95
hotels and motels, 61–66
kidstuff, 289–92
overview, 19–20
restaurants, 146–51
Roanoke Antique Mall, 203
Roanoke Catholic School, 499
Roanoke City Pools, 448
Roanoke Civic Center, 313
Roanoke College, 491–92
Roanoke County
overview, 18–22
real estate, 463, 475
shopping, 203–6
Roanoke Festival in the Park, 338
Roanoke Mountain Campground, 371
Roanoke Regional Airport, 47–48
Roanoke Regional Chamber of
Commerce, 485
Roanoker Restaurant, The, 150
Roanoke Star, 184
Roanoke Symphony Orchestra, 313–14
Roanoke Symphony Polo Cup, 350, 414–16
Roanoke United Methodist Home, 480
Roanoke Valley Horse Show, 340, 409
Roanoke Weiner Stand, 150
Rockbridge Community Festival, 347
Rockbridge County
arts, 309–10

attractions, 245–50
bed-and-breakfasts and country
inns, 88–94
kidstuff, 286–89
nightlife, 182–83
overview, 13–15
real estate, 462–63, 474–75
restaurants, 145–46
shopping, 200–202
Rockbridge Mountain Music and Dance
Festival, 350
Rockbridge Regional Fair, 344
Rockbridge Vineyard, 389
Rock Castle Gorge Trail, 437
rock climbing, 450–51
Rockfish Gap Outfitters, 198
Rockingham County
arts, 305–6
attractions, 240–43
bed-and-breakfasts and country
inns, 85
hotels and motels, 57–58
kidstuff, 283–85
nightlife, 180–81
overview, 10–11
real estate, 461, 474–75
restaurants, 141–42
shopping, 193–96
Rockingham County Fair, 345–46
Rockingham County Parks and Recreation
Department, 477
Rockingham Memorial Hospital, 465
Rocky and Brenda's Gold and Silver, 198
Rocky Knob Cabins, 370
Rocky Knob Campground, 371–72
Rocky Knob Visitor Center, 368
Rocky Mount hotels and motels, 73
Rocky Top Climbing Club, 451
Rococo's, 167
Rodeway Inn, 65–66
Rolling Hills Antique Mall, 194
Rotunda, 264–65
Rowe's Family Restaurant and Bakery, 144
Royal Oak Bookshop, The, 192
Roy Wheeler Realty Co., 476
Ruffner House Inn, The, 83
Rush River Antiques, 209
Ryan's Fruit Market, 195

S
Saigon Cafe, 167

Salem
    attractions, 250–56
    bed-and-breakfasts and country
        inns, 94–95
    hotels and motels, 61–66
    overview, 20–21
    restaurants, 151
Salem Avalanche, 255
Salem Fair, 344
Salem Museum and Historical Society,
    The, 252
Salem-Roanoke County Chamber of
    Commerce, 485
Sampson Eagon Inn, The, 87
Sam Snead Realty Inc., 475
Sam Snead's Tavern, 177
Sam's on the Market, 205
Sara Schneidman Gallery, 315
Sawhill Gallery, 305–6
Scarpa, 217
School House Fabrics, 229
schools
    colleges and universities, 487–97
    preparatory schools, 497–501
Science Museum of Western Virginia,
    252, 291
Scotto's Italian Restaurant and Pizzeria, 144
Scottsville Chamber of Commerce, 485
Scottsville Museum, 265
Second Story Book Shop, 201
Second Street Gallery, 317
Sedalia Center, 324
Selu Conservancy and Retreat Center, 275
Senior Center Inc., The, 482
senior services. See retirement and senior
    services
1776, 230
1776 Grille, 177
1763 Inn and Restaurant, 97, 155
Shadows, The, 106
Shakespeare at the Ruins, 346
Shakin' at the Station, 309
Shamrock & Stephenson Realty, Inc., 476
Sharkey's Grill, 188
Sharp Rock Vineyards, 401–2
Sharp Top Trail, 369
ShenanArts Inc., 308
Shenandoah Acres Resort, 286
Shenandoah Apple Blossom Festival,
    280, 334
Shenandoah Area Agency on Aging, 477

Shenandoah Caverns, 236–37
Shenandoah County
    arts, 305
    attractions, 236–39
    bed-and-breakfasts and country inns,
        81–82
    hotels and motels, 55–56
    kidstuff, 282
    overview, 8–10
    real estate, 460–61, 474–75
    restaurants, 140–41
    shopping, 192–93
Shenandoah County Fair, 345
Shenandoah Heritage Farmers' Market, 194
Shenandoah Memorial Hospital, 464
Shenandoah National Park, 441–42
Shenandoah River Outfitters, 283, 420
Shenandoah River Trips, 419–20
Shenandoah Shakespeare, 308
Shenandoah Summer Music Theatre, 304
Shenandoah University, 487–88
Shenandoah University's Ohrstrom-Bryant
    Theatre, 304
Shenandoah Valley Art Center, 306–7
Shenandoah Valley Bach Festival, 339
Shenandoah Valley Balloon Fest, 351
Shenandoah Valley Crafts and Gifts, 193
Shenandoah Valley Discovery Museum, 280
Shenandoah Valley Golf Club, 429–30
Shenandoah Valley Music Festival, 282,
    305, 341
Shenandoah Valley Regional Airport, 49
Shenandoah Valley Westminster-
    Canterbury, 478
Shenandoah Vineyards Inc., 389
Shenanigans, 217
Shenvalee Golf Resort, The, 56, 430
Shen-Valley Flea Market, 191
Sherando Lake Recreation Area, 286,
    437–38, 450
Sheridan Livery Inn, 61
Shoney's Inn, 55
Shoppes at Mauzy, The, 194
shopping
    Alleghany Highlands, 229–31
    antiques, 190–94, 196–97, 200,
        203–4, 206–10, 212–14, 220, 222,
        224–26, 230
    bookstores, 192, 193, 196, 199, 201, 205,
        209, 218–19
    East of the Blue Ridge, 206–26

farmers' markets, 194

general stores, 223–25, 229, 231

handcrafts, 195, 202–4, 214, 220–22, 225–31

malls, 191, 196, 199, 205–6, 208, 219–20, 223, 227

New River Valley, 226–29

orchards, 203

outlet stores, 199–200, 206, 208, 223, 225, 226

Roanoke Valley, 202–6

Shenandoah Valley, 190–202

specialty shops, 190–93, 195–201, 204–18, 221–24, 226–31

Showalter's Orchard and Greenhouse, 195

Shrine Circus, 330

Signet Gallery, 214

Silver Linings, 199

Silver Thatch Inn, 111, 167–68

Simonpietri's Gift and Pawn Shop, 192

Sinking Creek Bridge, 275

skiing

Alleghany Highlands, 457–58

East of the Blue Ridge, 455–57

Shenandoah Valley, 453–55

Sky Bryce Airport, 48

Skyland Lodge, 361–62, 364–65

Skyline Caverns, 235–36, 281

Skyline Drive

backcountry camping, 364

cabins, 363

campgrounds, 363–64

fishing, 365

hikes, 361

horseback riding, 366–67

lodges, 361–62

overlooks, 361

overview, 281–82

picnic areas, 365

places to eat, 364–65

visitor centers, 360

Sky Meadows State Park, 294, 423, 438

Sleep Inn Tanglewood, 66

Sleepy Hollow Farm, 106–7

Smithfield Plantation, 273

Smith Mountain Flowers, 224

Smith Mountain Lake

boating, 422

fishing, 427–28

hotels and motels, 72

kidstuff, 299–300

overview, 31–32

restaurants, 172–73

shopping, 223–24

Smith Mountain Lake Airport, 50

Smith Mountain Lake Chamber of Commerce, 485

Smith Mountain Lake Fall Festival, 354

Smith Mountain Lake State Park, 300, 423, 439, 450

Smith & Thurmond Inc., 476

Smokehouse Winery, 402

Soda Fountain at Timberlake's Drugstore, 297

Sorghum Festival, 353

South Court Inn, 83–84

Southern Area Agency on Aging, 482

Southern Culture, 168

Southern Inn, 145

Southern Kitchen, 141

Southern Lamp & Shade Showroom, 226

Southern Soldier Statue, 386

Southern Star, 220

Southern Taste, 230

South River Country Inn, 104–5

South River Grill, 144

Sperryville Emporium, 209

Splathouse, 297

sporting events/spectator sports, 242–43, 255, 266–67, 270, 273–74, 276

Sporting Gallery, The, 208

sports. See recreation

Spring Garden Show, 334

Spring Hill Cemetery, 386

Spring House Tavern, The, 141

Spring Wildflower Symposium, 336

Spruce Creek Gallery, 220–21, 322

Spudnut Coffee Shop, 168

St. Anne's–Belfield School, 501

St. Maarten Cafe, 167

St. Patrick's Day Parade, 331

Starr Hill Restaurant, Brewery, & Music Hall, 168, 187

State Arboretum of Virginia, The, 235

Staunton–Augusta Art Center, 307

Staunton, 11–12

Stedman House, 221

Steeles Tavern Manor, 92–93

steeplechase and point-to-point races, 410, 416–17

Stephens City, 6–7

Steppin' Out, 347

Stocked Market Holiday Bazaar, 355
Stoneleigh, 430–31
Stone Mountain Vineyards, 402
Stoneridge Bed & Breakfast, 93–94
Stone's Cafeteria, 174
Stonewall Brigade Band, 309
Stonewall Jackson Hospital, 465
Stonewall Jackson House, 246–47, 288, 381
Stonewall Jackson Memorial Cemetery and
  National Cemetery, 377, 381
Stonewall Jackson Museum at Hupp's Hill,
  238–39, 282, 378
Stonewall Jackson's Headquarters, 234
Stonewall Vineyards and Winery, 402
Stoney Creek Bar & Grill, 170–71
Stony Man Overlook, 361
Stover Davis Realty and Associates, 475
Strasburg, 8
Strasburg Chamber of Commerce, 484
Strasburg Emporium, 192
Strasburg Museum/Train Station, 239, 378
Strawberry Festival and Mountain Heritage
  Day, 339
Stuart Hall, 499
Stuarts Draft, 12–13
Studios on the Square, 204
Sugar Tree Country Store and Sugar
  House, 231
Sugar Tree Inn, 94
Sun Bow Trading Company, 214
Sunday's Child, 201
Sunset Hills Bed & Breakfast, 101–2
Super 8 Motel, 68, 75
Suter's Handcrafted Furniture, 195–96
Swedenburg Estate Vineyard, 403
Sweeney's Curious Goods, 222
Sweet Briar College, 493
Sweet Things, 288
swimming, 447–50

T
Tack Box, The, 208
Talbot's, 217
Tangent Outfitters, 421
Tanglewood Mall, 206
Tap Tap, 217
Tarara Vineyard & Winery, 403
Taste of the Mountains Main Street
  Festival, 348
Tastings, 168–69
T.C. Trotters, 187–88

television, 472
Texas Tavern, 150, 184
theater, 304, 306–10, 312–16, 318–20, 324–26
Theater at Lime Kiln, 337
Theatre Arts Department, 325–26
Theatre at Washington, The, 315
Theda's Studio, 227
Thistle Tree Forge, 315
Thomas Jefferson Birthday
  Commemoration, 333
Thomas Jefferson's Poplar Forest, 270–71, 299
Thornrose House at Gypsy Hill, 88
Thoroughbred Retirement Farm, 413–14
Three Hills Inn, 121
309 Market Street Grille, 151
Timberlake Drugstore, 217–18
To the Rescue National Museum, 252–54,
  291
Towers Shopping Center, 206
Toy Museum at Natural Bridge, The, 288
train travel, 53
transportation
  air travel, 45–50
  highways and byways, 44–45
  metro bus lines, 50–52
  public transit, 50–52
  train travel, 53
  trans-city bus lines, 52–53
Travelodge–Roanoke North, 66
Trinity Episcopal Church Annual Stable
  Tour, 413
Troutville hotels and motels, 61–66
T.S. Eways, 218
Tucano's Restaurant, 139
Tuckahoe Antique Mall, 220
Tuesday Evening Concert Series, 321
Tuscarora Mill Restaurant, 154
TV, 472
200 South Street Inn, 111

U
Unicorn Winery, 403
universities. See colleges and universities
University Cemetery, 383
University Health System, 465
University Libraries, 275
University of Virginia, 297, 492
University of Virginia Art Museum, 318
University of Virginia Bookstore, 219
University of Virginia Charlottesville, 266–67
University of Virginia Department of

Drama, 320
University of Virginia Library, 265–66
University of Virginia Rotunda, 264–65
University Village, 483
Upperville Colt and Horse Show, 339, 409
Upstairs, Downstairs, 228

V

V. Earl Dickinson Building for the Humanities and Social Sciences, 317–18
Valhalla Vineyards, 406–7
Valley Framing Studio and Gallery, 199
Valley Green Art Gallery, 221
Valley League Baseball, The, 243
Valley Mall, 196
Valley Program for Aging Services Inc., The, 477, 484
Valley View Mall, 206
Valley View Retirement Community, 483
Veramar Vineyard, 403–4
Veritas Winery, 404
Verona Antique Mall, 196–97
Veterans Medical Center, 465
Victorian Festival, 331, 333
Villa Appalaccia Winery, 407
Village Inn, The, 58, 142
vineyards. See wineries
Vinny's New York Pizza & Pasta, 160
Vintage Virginia Wine Festival, 339
Vinton, 21–22
Vinton Antique Mall, 203–4
Vinton Dogwood Festival, 333
Vinton July Fourth Celebration, 344
Vinton Old-Time Bluegrass Festival Competition, 347
Violino Ristorante Italiano, 139
Virginia Baptist Hospital, 465
Virginia Born and Bred, 201
Virginia Center for the Creative Arts, 323
Virginia Commonwealth Games, 344
Virginia Company, The, 218
Virginia Dare Cruises and Marina, 172
Virginia Department of Tourism, 77–78
Virginia Discovery Museum, 266, 297–98
Virginia Fall Foliage Festival, 352
Virginia Festival of the Book, 321–22
Virginia Film Festival, 322, 352–53
Virginia Garlic Festival, 353
Virginia Gold Cup Races, The, 416
Virginia Handcrafts, Inc., 222
Virginia Horse Center, 288, 409, 411

Virginia Made Shop, The, 199
Virginia Mennonite Retirement Community, 478–79
Virginia Metalcrafters, The, 199–200, 286
Virginia Military Institute, 489–90
Virginia Military Institute Museum, 247, 289, 381
Virginia Mountain Outfitters, 426, 443
Virginia Museum of Transportation, 254–55, 291
Virginia Mushroom and Wine Festival, 334
Virginian, The, 169
Virginia Polo Center, 414
Virginia Quilt Museum, 242
Virginia Regional Transit Association, 52
Virginia Safari Park, 247–48, 288–89
Virginia School of the Arts, 323–24
Virginia's Explore Park, 254, 292, 446
Virginia's Natural History Retreat, 349
Virginia Special Olympics, 329
Virginia State Championship Chili Cook-off, The, 338
Virginia Tech, 273–74, 301, 495–96
Virginia Tech Montgomery Executive Airport, 49–50
Virginia Wine Festival, 346
visual arts, 305–7, 309–12, 314–18, 322–26
vital statistics, 4–5
Vivace, 169

W

Wade's Mill, 202, 249–50
Wakefield Country Day School, 498
Walnut Creek Park, 446
Walsh & Associates, Inc., 476
Walton's Mountain Country Store, 221
Walton's Mountain Museum, 267–68, 298
War Memorial Pool, 448
Warm Hearth Village Retirement Community, 483
Warren County
    arts, 304–5
    attractions, 235–36
    bed-and-breakfasts and country inns, 80–81
    hotels and motels, 55
    kidstuff, 281–82
    overview, 7–8
    real estate, 460, 474–75
    restaurants, 140
    shopping, 191–92

Warren County Fair, 345
Warren County Fairgrounds, 191
Warren Memorial Hospital, 464
Warren Rifles Confederate Museum,
    236, 379
Warrenton, 23-24
Warrenton Horse Show, 409
Warrenton Pony Show, 294
Washington and Lee University, 381-82,
    490-91
Washington and Old Dominion Railroad
    Regional Park, 293
Washington Dulles International
    Airport, 45-46
Washington & Old Dominion Trail, 446
Washington Park Pool, 448
waterfalls, 366-67, 371
Waterfront Properties Realtors, 475
Waterwheel Restaurant, The, 177
Waynesboro, 12-13
Waynesboro Heritage Museum, 244
Waynesboro Players, 309
Waynesboro Village Outlet Mall, 200
Wayside Inn, 79, 139-40
Wayside Theatre, 280-81, 304
Weasie's Kitchen, 144
Weichert Realty Inc., 475
Western State Hospital, 465
Westlake, 434
Westminister Canterbury, 483
Westminister Organ Concert Series, The, 321
Whimsies, 218
White Elephant, 208
White Fence Bed & Breakfast, 84
White Hall Vineyards, 404
White House Restaurant, 172-73
White Oak Canyon Falls, 435
White Swan Gallery, 199
Wilderness Ranch in Bluegrass
    Hollow, 75-76
Wilderness Road Regional Museum, 276, 386
Wildflour Cafe and Catering, 151
Wildflour II Market and Bakery, 151
Willowcroft Farm Vineyards, 404-5
Willow Grove Inn, 107, 161
Willson-Walker House, 145-46
Wilson School of Dance, 320
Winchester
    overview, 6
    shopping, 190-91

Winchester Book Gallery, 281
Winchester-Frederick County Chamber, 484
Winchester Medical Center, 464
Winchester Regional Airport, 48
Windham Winery, 405
Wine Festival, 350
wineries
    East of the Blue Ridge, 389-405
    Shenandoah Valley, 388-89
    Southwest Virginia, 405-7
Wingate Inn, 55, 61
Wintergreen Performing Arts, 322-23
Wintergreen Real Estate, 476
Wintergreen Resort, 128-30, 298, 426, 432,
    447, 451, 455-57
Wintergreen Resort-Rodes Farm
    Stables, 442-43
Wintergreen Summer Music Festival, 344
Wintergreen Winery, Ltd., 405
W & L Mock Convention, 249
Women's Four-Miler, 348-49
Woodberry Forest, 500
Woodrow Wilson Museum and
    Birthplace, 244
Woodrow Wilson Open House, 356
Woodrow Wilson Rehabilitation
    Center, 465
Woodruff House Inns, 84
Woodstock, 8-9
Woodstock Chamber of Commerce, 484
Woodstone Meadows Stable, 442
Woody's Baha Bar and Grill, 188
Wool Days, 335
Wright Place Antique Mall, 204
Wright's Dairy Rite, 144-45
Wyndham Roanoke Airport Hotel, 66
Wythe County kidstuff, 302

Y

Yankee Horse Ridge Overlook, 369
Ye Olde Salem Christmas, 358
Yoder's Country Market, 211
You Made It!, 284-85
Yuletide Traditions at Ash Lawn-
    Highland, 357
Yuletide Traditions at Michie Tavern, 357
Yuletide Traditions Monticello, 357

Z

zoos, 247-48, 255-56

ABOUT THE AUTHORS

MARY ALICE BLACKWELL

Except for a couple of years in Canada, Mary Alice Blackwell has spent most of her life in the Blue Ridge. Born in Staunton, educated in Blacksburg, Mary Alice is now the features editor for the *Daily Progress* in Charlottesville.

Although she had planned on teaching history, journalism picked her instead. The underground newspaper she printed in high school should have been an early warning sign, but Mary Alice never considered putting fingers to the keyboard until the summer of 1973. That was when the sports editor for the *Staunton Leader* stopped by her softball game and asked the young catcher if she would like to be a stringer for the local paper. She had never met Hubert Grim Jr. before, but she has remained his grateful pupil since.

In less than two years, Mary Alice went from a part-time writer to assistant sports editor. During her 13-year stint in sports, she covered everything from college football to high school wrestling. Along the way she had the privilege of interviewing the likes of Lee Trevino, Ralph Sampson, and a young athlete who came back from open-heart surgery to play tennis for his high school.

When Mary Alice went off to finish her communications degree at Virginia Tech, she continued to be a full-time writer, first as the sports editor of the *News Messenger* and later as the managing editor of the *Fayette Tribune* in West Virginia.

After backpacking across Europe, Mary Alice came back to the Blue Ridge. Hiking the scenic trails of the Skyline Drive proved more relaxing than toting a backpack through the streets of Paris. Her job at the *Progress* has given Mary Alice the added opportunity to encounter many more exciting people and places in the heart of Virginia's Blue Ridge. She hopes others will get the same opportunity after reading *Insiders' Guide® to Virginia's Blue Ridge*.

ANNE PATTERSON CAUSEY

Anne Causey grew up in the Tidewater area, specifically the busy city of Virginia Beach. While most people will tell you they've never met an actual native of Virginia Beach, she proudly reports that she is one, as is her father, grandmother, and great-grandparents (having traveled here in their teens from Denmark and Sweden). Anne is a true descendant of the watermen who made their living in the Chesapeake Bay. Her grandfather wandered down the eastern shore to settle at Virginia Beach.

But Anne felt a different calling. After high school, she headed west toward the mountains of Virginia for a college degree at Radford University and, later, work as a reporter at a small newspaper in Christiansburg. While she enjoyed a brief stint in West Virginia, as editor of the *Meadow River Post,* once there she realized she had ventured too far west. The ocean called her back, and she settled on a compromise, putting down roots near the city of Charlottesville.

After returning to school for her master's at James Madison University and teaching reluctant freshmen basic writing, she decided that contrary to her previous expectations, teaching was not her calling. Anne took a public relations and event-management position, setting up author signings, lectures, and workshops at the local Barnes and Noble bookstore. Becoming restless once again, Anne took a job in the Science and Engineering Library of the University of Virginia. In the spring of 2004, she migrated to the Special Collections Library at UVA, where she assists patrons in accessing the rare books and manuscripts and teaches classes that use the materials. This premier collection and the new Harrison/ Small building that houses it (doors opened in August 2004) are themselves priceless Virginia treasures.

Anne always has enjoyed any work involving writing and reading; one of her proudest accomplishments was founding the literary magazine at her alma mater, Radford University.

She has written fiction (unpublished), and for 10 years she wrote a regular biweekly column for Charlottesville's *Daily Progress.* Anne is the coauthor of the 11th edition of *Insider's Guide®: Williamsburg and Virginia's Historic Triangle.* Besides writing and reading, Anne also loves to travel and explore the countryside of this beautiful state through hiking, biking, and camping.

HELP US KEEP THIS GUIDE UP TO DATE

Every effort has been made by the authors and editors to make this guide as accurate and useful as possible. However, many things can change after a guide is published—phone numbers change, facilities come under new management, etc.

We would love to hear from you concerning your experiences with this guide and how you feel it could be improved and be kept up to date. While we may not be able to respond to all comments and suggestions, we'll take them to heart and we'll also make certain to share them with the authors. Please send your comments and suggestions to the following address:

The Globe Pequot Press
Reader Response/Editorial Department
P. O. Box 480
Guilford, CT 06437

Or you may e-mail us at:

editorial@GlobePequot.com

Thanks for your input, and happy travels!

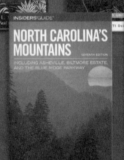